CRITICAL SURVEY
OF
LONG FICTION

CRITICAL SURVEY
OF
LONG FICTION

English Language Series

REVISED EDITION

A-Bur

1

Edited by
FRANK N. MAGILL

SALEM PRESS
Pasadena, California   Englewood Cliffs, New Jersey

SECOND PRINTING

Library of Congress Cataloging-in-Publication Data
Critical survey of long fiction. English language series/
   edited by Frank N. Magill. — Rev. ed.
      p.   cm.   .
   Includes bibliographical references and index.
   1. English fiction—Dictionaries. 2. American
fiction—Dictionaries. 3. English fiction—
Bio-bibliography. 4. American fiction—
Bio-bibliography. 5. Novelists, English—
Biography—Dictionaries. 6. Novelists, American—
Biography—Dictionaries.
I. Magill, Frank Northen, 1907-   .
PR821.C7   1991
823.009'03—dc20   91-19694
ISBN 0-89356-825-2 (set)   CIP
ISBN 0-89356-826-0 (volume 1)

PRINTED IN THE UNITED STATES OF AMERICA

PUBLISHER'S NOTE

Magill's *Critical Survey of Long Fiction, English Language Series: Revised Edition*, updates and expands, in eight volumes, the original edition of 1983. This major revision of the original set contains a total of 347 articles: 332 on individual novelists, plus 14 comprehensive "overview" essays and a glossary of terms and techniques. A one-volume *Supplement* to the *Critical Survey*, published in 1987, contained 41 articles on new novelists in all languages; English-language novelists from this volume have been incorporated into the *Revised Edition*; 32 of these were revised to bring them up to date.

Of the 347 articles in the current edition, 25 (7 percent) are completely new, never-before-published entries on novelists who have come to be regarded as established figures of the mainstream. Included in this group are Julian Barnes, T. Coraghessan Boyle, Louise Erdrich, Charles Johnson, and Gloria Naylor. Other novelists were added because their significance has now extended beyond a particular genre or otherwise narrower appeal: from Ray Bradbury, Elmore Leonard, and Joseph Wambaugh to such diverse figures as David Lodge and Salman Rushdie.

Fully 46 percent (159) of the articles have been substantially revised to reflect the current status of the author's development and opus, in terms of both life events and literary career. In most of these cases, especially where still-living authors are concerned, new publications, new biographies and critical studies, new honors and awards, and new biographical events necessitated careful scrutiny of all sections of these articles. The reader will also find many of these articles to contain one or more pages of additional "Analysis," updating the critical interpretation of these authors' works in the light of their recent production. Another group among the revised articles constitutes authors who have died in the past decade. These articles underwent similar revision; in cases where little had changed in the author's literary career, the essential facts of death were added and small alterations were made in the text.

Fewer than half the articles (145, or 42 percent) were deemed sufficient to stand as they were originally published. Nevertheless, these entries, too, were re-read for any previous errors or possible emendations. In any event, all articles—whether substantially revised, new, or basically the same—were updated in one substantial respect: In place of the original secondary bibliographies which appeared at the ends of these articles, new, updated, and annotated bibliographies appear. These bibliographies provide the interested reader with possibilities for further reading about the author and his or her works, up to the time of publication of the *Revised Edition*.

In the final volume, those interested in obtaining an overview of the development and subgenres of the novel will find fourteen essays which appeared in the original edition. Of these, nine have been revised and updated, and one has been completely rewritten. Four of the essays detail the development of the novel from its origins through its manifestations in England and America; eight examine the major subgenres of the novel, from picaresque through science fiction. Finally, a comprehensive glossary, entitled "Terms and Techniques," will prove useful to beginning students of fiction.

The comprehensive subject index, listing names of literary personages, titles of works receiving substantial discussion, and literary terms and concepts, has, of course, been revised to cite new material.

An updated list of contributors of articles, as well as those who contributed updated bibliographies and text, appears in the front matter to the first volume. The expertise and efforts of these individuals are gratefully acknowledged.

CONTRIBUTORS

Michael Adams

Timothy Dow Adams

Patrick Adcock

S. Krishnamoorthy Aithal

Terry L. Andrews

Andrew J. Angyal

Stanley Archer

Edwin T. Arnold III

Marilyn Arnold

Bryan Aubrey

Linda C. Badley

Peter Baker

Dean R. Baldwin

Jane L. Ball

Thomas Banks

Dan Barnett

Carl Brucker

Carol M. Barnum

David Barratt

Joseph F. Battaglia

Robert Becker

Kirk H. Beetz

Kate Begnal

Todd K. Bender

Frank Bergmann

Randi Birn

Frederick Bowers

Harold Branam

Anne Kelsch Breznau

J. R. Broadus

Domenic Bruni

Mitzi M. Brunsdale

Hallman B. Bryant

Paul Budra

C. F. Burgess

Karen Carmean

Leonard Casper

Edgar L. Chapman

Allan Chavkin

John R. Clark

Samuel Coale

John L. Cobbs

John J. Conlon

Deborah Core

David Cowart

Carol I. Croxton

Diane D'Amico

Reed Way Dasenbrock

J. Madison Davis

Frank Day

Paul J. deGategno

Bill Delaney

Joan DelFattore

Lloyd N. Dendinger

A. A. DeVitis

Richard H. Dillman

Henry J. Donaghy

David C. Dougherty

Virginia A. Duck

David B. Eakin

Grace Eckley

Wilton Eckley

Bruce L. Edwards, Jr.

Robert P. Ellis

Ann Willardson Engar

Thomas L. Erskine

Howard Faulkner

John H. Ferres

Richard A. Fine

Bruce E. Fleming

Robert J. Forman
June M. Frazer
Kenneth Friedenreich
Miriam Fuchs
Robert L. Gale
Kristine Ottesen Garrigan
James R. Giles
L. H. Goldman
Dennis Goldsberry
Peter W. Graham
John R. Griffin
James Grove
Stephen I. Gurney
Angela Hague
Jay L. Halio
David Mike Hamilton
Robert D. Hamner
Terry L. Hansen
John P. Harrington
Robert Hauptman
Melanie Hawthorne
William J. Heim
Terry Heller
Greig E. Henderson
Erwin Hester
Jane Hill
James Hodge
Watson Holloway
Linda Howe
Edward W. Huffstetler
Mary Anne Hutchinson
Archibald E. Irwin
Charles M. Israel
Abdul R. JanMohamed
Clarence O. Johnson
D. Barton Johnson
Judith L. Johnston

Betty H. Jones
Jane Anderson Jones
Feroza Jussawalla
Deborah Kaplan
Anna B. Katona
Richard Keenan
Catherine Kenney
Sue L. Kimball
Anne Mills King
James Reynolds Kinzey
John V. Knapp
Paula Kopacz
Sarah B. Kovel
Lawrence F. Laban
Brooks Landon
Eugene S. Larson
Donald F. Larsson
Paul LaValley
Norman Lavers
Penelope A. LeFew
Henry J. Lindborg
Robert Emmet Long
Michael Lowenstein
Philip A. Luther
Reinhart Lutz
James J. Lynch
Tim Lyons
Barbara A. McCaskill
Andrew Macdonald
Gina Macdonald
James C. MacDonald
Fred B. McEwen
Richard D. McGhee
Dennis Q. McInerny
David W. Madden
Bryant Mangum
Lois A. Marchino

CONTRIBUTORS

Patricia Marks
Bruce K. Martin
Paul Marx
Anne Laura Mattrella
Charles E. May
Laurence W. Mazzeno
Jean-Pierre Metereau
Vasa D. Mihailovich
Joseph R. Millichap
Kathleen Mills
Sally Mitchell
Robert A. Morace
Carole Moses
Lynn C. Munro
Earl Paulus Murphy
Brian Murray
John M. Muste
William Nelles
William F. Nelson
Stella A. Nesanovich
Martha Nochimson
George O'Brien
Robert M. Otten
Cóilín Owens
Donald Palumbo
Robert J. Paradowski
Makarand Paranjape
John G. Parks
David B. Parsell
William Peden
William E. Pemberton
Robert C. Peterson
Alice Hall Petry
Janet Polansky
Karen Priest
Charles H. Pullen
Victor J. Ramraj

Honora Rankine-Galloway
K. Bhaskara Rao
Edward C. Reilly
Rosemary M. Canfield Reisman
Samuel J. Rogal
Deborah D. Rogers
Carl Rollyson
Joseph Rosenblum
David Sadkin
Arthur M. Saltzman
Dale Salwak
John K. Saunders
June H. Schlessinger
Thomas C. Schunk
Kenneth Seib
Joan Corey Semonella
Lynne P. Shackelford
Vasant A. Shahane
Millicent Sharma
Walter Shear
Frank W. Shelton
John C. Shields
T. A. Shippey
Jack Shreve
R. Baird Shuman
Anne Waterman Sienkewicz
Charles L. P. Silet
Linda Simon
Katherine Snipes
Sherry G. Southard
Sharon Spencer
Brian Stableford
William B. Stone
W. J. Stuckey
Mary Ellen Stumpf
Stan Sulkes
James Sullivan

Eileen Tarcay

Thomas J. Taylor

Christopher J. Thaiss

Lou Thompson

Gary Topping

Charles Trainor

Linda F. Tunick

Nancy Walker

Ronald G. Walker

John Michael Walsh

Bernice Larson Webb

Judith Weise

Steven Weisenburger

John P. Welle

Craig Werner

Dexter Westrum

Bruce Wiebe

Roger E. Wiehe

Chester L. Wolford

Philip Woodard

Jennifer L. Wyatt

Michele Wender Zak

New Editorial Provided by

Jo-Ellen Lipman Boon
Edward Huffstetler
John M. Muste
James Weigel

Steven Weisenberger
John Wilson
Donna Winchell
Mark R. Winchell

New Bibliographies Provided by

Michael Adams
James Baird
Dan Barnett
David Barratt
Irene Brandenburg
J. R. Broadus
David L. Bullock
Leonard Casper
Thomas Cassidy
Bill Delaney
James E. Devlin
Thomas L. Erskine
Ann Davison Garbett
Sharon M. Harris
John R. Holmes
Kimberly L. Jacobs
Shakuntala Jayaswal
Leon Lewis
Janet Lorenz
Reinhart Lutz
Richard D. McGhee

Kathleen Mills
George O'Brien
Robert M. Otten
David B. Parsell
Mary Ellen Pitts
Victoria Price
Rosemary M. Canfield Reisman
James W. Robinson, Jr.
Jill Rollin
Joseph Rosenblum
Robert Ross
Dale Salwak
Judith Schnee
Thomas Schunk
R. Baird Shuman
James Sullivan
Binah Taylor
Terry Theodore
Paul R. Waibel
Jennifer L. Wyatt
Robert E. Yahnke

LIST OF AUTHORS IN VOLUME 1

CRITICAL SURVEY
OF
LONG FICTION

CHINUA ACHEBE

Born: Ogidi, Nigeria; November 16, 1930

Principal long fiction
Things Fall Apart, 1958; *No Longer at Ease*, 1960; *Arrow of God*, 1964; *A Man of the People*, 1966; *Anthills of the Savannah*, 1987.

Other literary forms
The twelve short stories of Chinua Achebe, written over a period of twenty years, were first published together in England by Heinemann under the title *Girls at War* (1972), though most of them had already appeared in various periodicals and in a Nigerian publication, *The Sacrificial Egg and Other Short Stories* (1962). Achebe's poems, most of them written during the Biafran crisis (1967-1970), came out soon after the war as *Beware, Soul Brother and Other Poems* (1971), and a year later in an enlarged edition. Doubleday then published this Heinemann collection in America as *Christmas in Biafra and Other Poems* (1973). Achebe has gathered together various autobiographical, political, literary, and cultural essays under the intriguingly optimistic title, *Morning Yet on Creation Day* (1975), published by both Doubleday and Heinemann. In 1983, Heinemann published his short book, *The Trouble with Nigeria*, challenging his contemporaries to overcome their growing resignation. *Hopes and Impediments* (Doubleday, 1987) brings together some fifteen essays, mainly on literature and the writer's role and covering a twenty-three-year period, some of them previously published, including five from *Morning Yet on Creation Day*. Achebe has also written the children's stories, *Chike and the River* (1966) and, jointly with John Iroaganachi, *How the Leopard Got His Claws* (1972). Finally, Achebe has helped edit two collections of short stories, *Winds of Change: Modern Short Stories from Black Africa* (1977), and *African Short Stories* (1985).

Achievements
From the beginning of his literary career, with the publication of *Things Fall Apart*, Achebe recognized and accepted his role as that of spokesman for black Africa. The primary function of that role was to reinterpret the African past from an African's point of view. This he successfully does in *Things Fall Apart* and *Arrow of God*, which correct the imperialist myth of African primitivism and savagery by re-creating the Igbo culture of the Eastern Region of Nigeria, its daily routines, its rituals, its customs, and especially its people dealing with one another in a highly civilized fashion within a complex society. The reinterpretation necessitated, as well, a look at the invading culture; Achebe tilted the balance in the Africans' favor by

depicting individuals in the British administration as prejudiced, imperceptive, unnecessarily bureaucratic, and emotionally impotent. Since his main subject was the African crisis, he did not go to great pains to explore the private lives of the British or to mollify the British public. He needed to show that white civilization and white people were not intrinsically superior, and to restore to the African a respect for his own culture and his own person. Achebe did not conceive his role as that of a mere propagandist, however, as any reader of the novels would acknowledge. His interpretation paid due respect to Western civilization and seriously criticized aspects of his own. In spite of certain fictional shortcuts—which some critics regard as crucial flaws—Achebe's attempt was to arrive at an objective appraisal of the conflict between Africa and the West. In fact, the central focus of his three other novels—*No Longer at Ease, A Man of the People*, and *Anthills of the Savannah*—set in contemporary times, is on the failure of Africans to meet challenges in the modern world. Of these, the first two are satirical attacks, the third a subtle blend of irony, compassion, and traditional wisdom, and a sane perspective on the chaotic Nigerian scene.

Achebe's importance as a spokesman for and to his own people has drawn criticism from some Western readers who are more interested in the quality of a novel than in its social function. Achebe has had several angry words to say to such aesthetically minded critics. His defense is that literature is a human and humane endeavor, not primarily a formal one. Still, one can easily defend his novels on aesthetic grounds, even arguing, as Charles Larson has done, that Achebe is actually an innovative writer who has transformed the novel to suit the African setting. Certainly, the most remarkable thing that Achebe has done, especially in *Things Fall Apart* and *Arrow of God*, is to transform the English language itself into an African idiom. Bernth Lindfors and others have demonstrated the skill with which Achebe uses imagery, allusions, figures of speech, proverbs, sentence patterns, standard English, and various forms of substandard English to capture a particular historical moment as well as the African mentality, but just as important to unify the novels around major motifs and themes. Achebe has not written mere social documents or social manifestos, but creditable works of literature that can stand the test of critical analysis. Achebe's contribution to the African world goes far beyond his five novels, but they are his major literary achievement.

Biography

Chinua Achebe was born on November 16, 1930, in Ogidi, in the Eastern Region of Nigeria. He gives some details about his family and his early life in an essay, "Named for Victoria, Queen of England" (1973, in *Morning Yet on Creation Day*). His parents, Isaiah and Janet Achebe, were both Christian, his father an evangelist and church teacher. His maternal grandfather, like Okonkwo in *Things Fall Apart*, was a wealthy and distinguished community leader. He was not Christian but exercised tolerance when Achebe was converted. Achebe was baptized Albert Chinualumogu after Queen Victoria's consort, but dropped the Albert while at his university, evidently as a reaction against the British and his Christian heritage. He explains, however, that he was never really torn between the two cultures. There was no agony such as one finds in African writers such as Cheikh Hamidou Kane. Achebe enjoyed the ritual of both religions. He did come to wonder if the apostates were not the Christians rather than the pagans, but he cites advantages brought in by Christianity: education, certain humane reforms, paid jobs. There seems to have been a pragmatic and tolerant strain in Achebe from the beginning.

For his secondary education, Achebe attended Government College, Umuahia (1944-1947), and he received his B.A. degree from University College, Ibadan, in 1953. During the next twelve years he worked for the Nigerian Broadcasting Corporation, first as producer in Lagos (1954-1958), then as controller in Enugu (1959-1961), and finally as Director of External Broadcasting in Lagos (1961-1966). In 1961, he married Christiana Chinwe Okoli. They have two sons and two daughters. Also during these years Achebe wrote his first four novels, beginning with his most famous, *Things Fall Apart* in 1958, and ending with *A Man of the People* in 1966. Achebe explains his novelistic career as the result of a revolution in his thinking during the nationalist movement after World War II. He decided that foreigners really could not tell the Nigerian story adequately. Joyce Cary's *Mister Johnson* (1939) was a prime example of this failure. Achebe regarded *Things Fall Apart* as an atonement for his apostasy, a ritual return to his homeland. As a consequence of his eight-year achievement as a novelist, Achebe was named chairman of the Society of Nigerian Authors and became a Member of Council at the University of Lagos. He also received the New Statesman Award for his third novel, *Arrow of God*. Among other honors were a Rockefeller Travel Fellowship to East and Central Africa (1960) and a UNESCO Travel Fellowship to the United States and Brazil (1963). It is clear that by 1966 Achebe was a distinguished member of the international literary community.

In 1967, however, his career was interrupted by the outbreak of the war in Biafra, Achebe's Igbo homeland in the Eastern Region of Nigeria. It came to be essentially a civil war. Achebe joined the Biafran Ministry of Information and played a diplomatic role in raising money for the Biafran cause. Bound as he was by emotional ties and personal commitment to his country's fate, Achebe had no time to write novels. All he could manage were short poems, which were published a year after the war was over (1971).

Achebe's career since the war has been taken up primarily by the academic world. In 1972, he was a Senior Research Fellow at the Institute of African Studies at the University of Nigeria in Nsukka. From 1972 to 1975, he was Professor at the University of Massachusetts at Amherst, and in 1975-1976

4

Critical Survey of Long Fiction

at the University of Connecticut. He then became Professor at the University of Nigeria, Nsukka, and ten years later was again at the University of Massachusetts (1987-1988). Three of his publications during that time were a collection of short stories, *Girls at War*, written over a period of years going back to his university days; a collection of essays, *Morning Yet on Creation Day*, which give his views on a number of issues from the Biafran War to the problems of African literature in the Western world; and a book-length essay on the Nigerian situation, *The Trouble with Nigeria* (1983). When it seemed that Achebe had left his career as a novelist behind him, twenty-one years after *A Man of the People*, he produced the carefully crafted *Anthills of the Savannah* (1987), bringing up-to-date the apparently futile attempts to end the vicious cycles of corruption and coups in Nigeria.

Achebe's standing in the intellectual and literary world is deservedly high. Numerous institutions, such as Dartmouth College and the Universities of Massachusetts, Sterling, and Southampton, have granted him honorary doctorates. He holds the impressive and influential position of Founding Editor of the African Writers Series, which, more than any other publisher, is responsible for the worldwide recognition of literary talent from the African continent and the propagation of African points of view.

Analysis

Chinua Achebe is probably the best-known and, at the same time, the most representative African novelist. He may very well have written the first African novel of real literary merit—such at least is the opinion of Charles Larson—and he deals with what one can call the classic issue that preoccupies his fellow novelists, the clash between the indigenous cultures of black Africa and a white, European civilization. He avoids the emotionally charged subject of slavery and concentrates his attention on the political and cultural confrontation. His five novels offer, in a sense, a paradigm of it. He begins in *Things Fall Apart* with the first incursion of the British into the Igbo region of what became the Eastern Region of Nigeria, and his subsequent novels trace (with some gaps) the spread of British influence into the 1950's, and beyond that into the post-independence period of the 1960's. The one period he slights, as he himself admits, is the generation in transition from traditional village life to the new Westernized Africa. He had difficulty imagining the psychological conflict of the man caught between two cultures. There is no example in Achebe of Cheikh Hamidou Kane's "ambiguous adventure." He does, however, share with Kane and with most other African novelists the idea that his function as a writer is a social one.

Achebe insists repeatedly on this social function in response to Western critics who tend to give priority to aesthetic values. He seems to suggest, in fact, that the communal responsibility and the communal tie are more fundamental than artistic merit for any writer, but certainly for the African writer and for himself personally at the present stage in African affairs. He describes himself specifically as a teacher. His purpose is to dispel the colonial myth of the primitive African and to establish a true image of the people and their culture. This message is intended, to some extent, for a Western audience, but especially for the Africans themselves, since they have come to believe the myth and have internalized the feeling of inferiority: Achebe's aim is to help them regain their self-respect, recognize the beauty of their own cultural past, and deal capably with the dilemmas of contemporary society. It is important, however, that Achebe is not fulfilling this role as an outsider. He returns to the traditional Igbo concept of the master craftsman and to the *Mbare* ceremony to explain the functional role of art in traditional society. He insists that creativity itself derives from a spiritual bond, the inspiration of a shared past and a shared destiny with a particular people: the alienated writer such as Ayi Kwei Armah cannot be in tune with himself and is therefore likely to be imitative rather than truly creative. It would appear, then, that Achebe values originality and freshness in the management of literary form, but considers them dependent on the sensitivity of the writer to his native setting.

Whereas Achebe's motivation in writing may be the restoration of pride in the African world, his theme, or rather the specific advice that he offers, albeit indirectly, is much more pragmatic. He does not advocate a return to the past or a rejection of Western culture. Like other African writers he decries the destructive consequences of colonial rule: alienation, frustration, and a loss of cohesiveness and a clear code of behavior. He recognizes as well, however, certain undesirable customs and superstitions that the foreign challenge exposed. His practical advice is to learn to cope with a changing world. He teaches the necessity of compromise: a loyalty to traditional wisdom and values, if not to tribal politics and outmoded customs, along with a suspicion of Western materialism but an openness to Western thought. He notes that in some cases the two cultures are not so far apart: Igbo republicanism goes even beyond the British-American concept of democracy, a view that the Ghanaian novelist, Armah, has developed as well. Unlike the Negritude writers of francophone Africa, Achebe, in his attempt to reinterpret the African past, does not paint an idyllic picture. He regrets the loss of mystery surrounding that past, but chooses knowledge, because he considers judgment, clarity of vision, and tolerance—virtues that he locates in his traditional society—to be the way out of the present confusion and corruption.

This key idea of tolerance pervades Achebe's work. One of his favorite stories (Yoruba, not Igbo) illustrates the danger in dogmatism. The god Echu, who represents fate or confusion, mischievously decides to provoke a quarrel between two farmers who live on either side of a road. He paints himself black on one side and white on the other, then walks up the road between the two farmers. The ensuing argument is whether the stranger is black or white. When he walks back down the road, each farmer tries to outdo the other in apologizing for his mistake. Achebe's most pervasive vehicle for this idea of tolerance, however, is in the concept of the *chi*, which is central to Igbo cosmology. Achebe interprets it as the ultimate expression of individualism, the basic worth and independence of every man. Politically it means the rejection of any authoritarian rule. Morally it means the responsibility of every man for his own fate. The *chi* is his other self, his spiritual identity responsible for his birth and his future. Thus, while one's *chi* defines his uniqueness, it also defines his limitations. As Achebe frequently notes in his novels, no one can defeat his own *chi*, and the acceptance of one's limitations is the beginning of tolerance.

It is the social purpose, this "message" of tolerance in Achebe's novels, that dictates the form. His plots tend to be analytic, static, or "situational," as Larson argues, rather than dynamic. Instead of narrative movement, there is juxtaposition of past and present, of the traditional and the modern. Achebe achieves balance through comparison and contrast. He uses exposition more than drama. His main characters tend to be representational. Their conflicts are the crucial ones of the society. The protagonists of the two novels set in the past, *Things Fall Apart* and *Arrow of God*, are strong men who lack wisdom, practical sense, an ability to accept change, and a tolerance for opposing views. The protagonists of *No Longer at Ease* and *A Man of the People* are weak and vacillating. They accept change but are blinded by vanity and have no satisfactory code of conduct to resist the unreasonable pressures of traditional ties or the corruption and attractions of the new age. The two male protagonists of *Anthills of the Savannah*, also hindered by vanity, prove inadequate idealists in a power-hungry environment and wake up too late to their lack of control over events. An even more predominant feature of the five novels is their style. Achebe makes the necessary compromise and writes in English, a foreign tongue, but manipulates it to capture the flavor of the native Igbo expression. He does this through dialect, idiom, and figurative language, and through proverbs that reflect traditional Igbo wisdom, comment ironically on the inadequacies of the characters, and state the central theme.

Thus Achebe manages, through the authorial voice, to establish a steady control over every novel. To some extent one senses the voice in the proverbs. They represent the assessment of the elders in the clan, yet the wisdom of the proverb is itself sometimes called into question, and the reader is invited to make the judgment. In general, it is Achebe's juxtaposing of character, incident, proverb, and tone that creates the total assessment. Against this background voice one measures the pride, vanity, or prejudice of the individuals who, caught in the stressful times of colonial or postcolonial Nigeria, fail to respond adequately. The voice does not judge or condemn; it describes. It reminds the Nigerian of the danger of self-deception. It also recognizes the danger of failing to communicate with others. Achebe keeps ever in mind the tale (found in numerous versions all over Africa) of mankind whose message to Chukwa (the Supreme Deity) requesting immortality is distorted by the messenger and thus fails in its purpose. The voice he adopts to avoid the distortion is one of self-knowledge, practical sense, pragmatism, and detachment, but also of faith, conviction, and humor. The voice is, in a sense, the message itself, moderating the confrontation between Africa and the West.

Significantly, Achebe takes the title of his first novel, *Things Fall Apart*, from W. B. Yeats's apocalyptic poem "The Second Coming," which prophesies the end of the present era and the entrance on the world's stage of another that is radically different. *Things Fall Apart* treats the early moments of that transition in an Igbo village. For those people the intrusion of the British is as revolutionary as the coming of a second Messiah, Yeats's terrible "rough beast." To some extent, Achebe creates a mythic village whose history stretches back to a legendary past. Chapters are devoted to the daily routines of the people, their family life, their customs, games, and rituals, their ancient wisdom, their social order, and legal practices. Achebe remains a realist, however, as he identifies also certain flaws in the customs and in the people. Superstition leads them to unnecessary cruelties. The protagonist, Okonkwo, reflects a basic conflict within the society. He is, on the one hand, a respected member of the society who has risen through hard work to a position of wealth and authority. He conscientiously accepts the responsibilities that the elders lay on him. At the same time, he is such an individualist that his behavior runs counter to the spirit of traditional wisdom. His shame over his father's weak character provokes him to be excessive in proving his own manhood. There is a defensiveness and uncertainty behind his outward assertiveness. It is true that the clan has its mechanisms to reprimand and punish the Okonkwos for their errant behavior. Nevertheless, even before the British influence begins to disturb the region, the cohesiveness of the clan is already in question.

One particular chink in Okonkwo's armor, which identifies a weakness also in the clan as it faces the foreign threat, is his inflexibility, his inability to adapt or to accept human limitations. Since he, in his youth, overcame adversity (familial disadvantages, natural forces such as drought and excessive rains, challenges of strength as a wrestler) he comes to believe that he has the individual strength to resist all challenges to his personal ambition. He cannot accept the presence of forces beyond his control, including the forces of his own personal destiny. It is this and the other aspects of Okonkwo's character that Achebe develops in the first section of the novel against the background of the tribe to which he belongs. Part I ends with the symbolic act of Okonkwo's accidentally killing a young man during a funeral ceremony. Like death, the act is beyond his control and unexplainable, yet it is punishable. The elders exile him for seven years to the village of his mother's family. This separation from his village is itself symbolic, since in a way Okonkwo has never belonged to it. While he is away, the village changes. With the coming of the missionaries, traditional religious practices begin to lose their sanction, their absoluteness. In Part III, Okonkwo returns from exile but finds that his exile continues. Nothing is as it was. Open hostility exists between the new religion and the traditional one. The British government has begun to take over authority from the elders. The novel ends with Okonkwo's irrational killing of a messenger from the British District Officer and with his subsequent suicide. Okonkwo rightly assumes, it would seem, that no authority now exists to judge him: the old sanctions are dead, and he refuses to accept the new ones. He must be his own judge.

There is, however, if not a judge, a voice of reason and compassion, detached from the action but controlling its effects, that assures Okonkwo of a fair hearing. The voice is heard in the proverbs, warning Okonkwo not to challenge his own *chi* (his own spiritual identity and destiny), even though another proverb insists that if he says yes his *chi* will say yes too. It is heard in the decisions of the elders, the complaints of the wives, and the rebellion of Okonkwo's own son, Noye, who turns to Christianity in defiance against his father's unreasonableness. It is found in the tragic sense of life of Okonkwo's uncle, Uchendu, who advises this man in exile to bear his punishment stoically, for his sufferings are mild in comparison to those of many others. Achebe locates his voice in one particular character, Obierika, Okonkwo's closest friend and a man of thought rather than, like his friend, a man of action. In the important eighth chapter, Achebe measures his protagonist against this man of moderation, reflection, and humor, who can observe the white invader with tolerance, his own society's laws with skepticism, and, at the end of the novel, his dead friend with respect and compassion, Achebe's voice can even be seen in the ironically insensitive judgment of the District Commissioner as the novel closes. As superficial and uninformed as that voice might be in itself, Achebe recognizes that the voice nevertheless exists, is therefore real, and must be acknowledged. The final view of Okonkwo and of the village that he both reflects and rejects is a composite of all these voices. It is the composite also of Okonkwo's own complex and unpredictable behavior, and of his fate which is the result of his own reckless acts and of forces that he does not comprehend. Amid the growing chaos one senses still the stable influence of the calm authorial voice, controlling and balancing everything.

From the early 1900's of *Things Fall Apart*, Achebe turns in his second novel, *No Longer at Ease*, to the mid-1950's just before independence. The protagonist, Obi Okonkwo, grandson of the tragic victim who lashed out against British insolence, resembles to some extent his grandfather in his inadequacy to deal with the pressures of his society, but has far different loyalties. The novel begins after things have already fallen apart; Nigeria is between societies. Obi no longer belongs to the old society. His father is the rebellious son of Okonkwo who left home for the Christian church and was educated in mission schools. Obi received a similar education and was selected by his community to study in England. This financial and personal obligation to Umuoria plagues Obi throughout the novel, for after his Western education he no longer shares the old customs and the old sense of loyalty. He considers himself an independent young man of the city, with a Western concept of government and administration. After his return from England he receives a civil service job and has visions of reforming the bureaucracy. The story is thus about the practical difficulties (it is not really a psychological study) of an ordinary individual separating himself cleanly from the past while adapting to the glitter and temptations of the new. Obi faces two particular problems. He has chosen to marry a woman, Clara, who belongs to a family considered taboo by the traditional community. He attempts to resist family and community pressure, but eventually succumbs. Meanwhile, Clara has become pregnant and must go through a costly and embarrassing abortion. Obi essentially abandons his responsibility toward her in his weak, halfhearted respect for his family's wishes. He likewise fails at his job, as he resists self-righteously various bribes until his financial situation and morals finally collapse. Unfortunately, he is as clumsy here as in his personal relations. He is arrested and sentenced to prison.

As in his first novel, Achebe's subject is the individual (and the society) inadequate to the changing times. His main concern is again a balanced appraisal of Nigerian society at a crucial stage in its recent history, because the greatest danger, as Achebe himself observes, is self-deception. He presents a careful selection of characters whose vanity, prejudice, or misplaced values allow them only a partial view of reality. Obi is, of course, the main example. He leaves his home village as a hero, is one of the few Nigerians to receive a foreign education, and, as a civil servant and proud possessor of a car, is a member of the elite. His vanity blinds him to such an extent that he cannot assess his proper relationship to his family, to Clara, or to his social role. His father, caught between his Christian faith and tribal customs, cannot allow Obi his independence. Mr. Green, Obi's British superior at the office, is trapped by stereotypical prejudices against Africans. There is no one individual such as Obierika within the novel to provide a reasonable interpretation of events.

One nevertheless feels the constant presence of Achebe as he balances these various voices against one another. Achebe also assures perspective by maintaining a detached tone through irony, wit, and humor. The narrator possesses the maturity and the wisdom that the characters lack. This novel also shows Achebe experimenting with structure as a means of expressing the authorial voice. The novel opens (like Leo Tolstoy's *The Death of Ivan Ilych*, 1886) with the final act, the trial and judgment of Obi for accepting a bribe. Achebe thus invites the reader to take a critical view of Obi from the very beginning. There is no question of getting romantically involved in his young life and career. This distancing continues in the first three chapters as Achebe juxtaposes present and past, scenes of reality and scenes of expectation. The real Lagos is juxtaposed directly against the idyllic one in Obi's mind. A picture of the later, strained relationship between Obi and Clara precedes the romantic scenes after they meet on board ship returning from England. Through this kind of plotting by juxtaposition, Achebe turns what might have been a melodramatic story of young love, abortion, betrayal, and corruption into a realistic commentary on Nigerian society in transition. In *Things Fall Apart* he rejects a paradisal view of the African past; in *No Longer at Ease* he warns against selfish, irresponsible, and naïve expectations in the present.

In his third novel, *Arrow of God*, Achebe returns to the past, taking up the era of British colonization a few years after the events of *Things Fall Apart*. The old society is still intact, but the Christian religion and the British administration are more firmly entrenched than before. Achebe again tries to re-create the former Igbo environment, with an even more elaborate account of the daily life, the customs and rituals, and with the scattering throughout of traditional idioms and proverbs. The foreigners, too, receive more detailed attention, though even the two main personalities, Winterbottom and Clarke, hardly achieve more than stereotyped status. Rather than work them late into the story, this time Achebe runs the two opposing forces alongside each other almost from the very beginning, in order to emphasize the British presence. Now it is the political, not the religious, power that is in the foreground, suggesting historically the second stage of foreign conquest, but the Church also takes full advantage of local political and religious controversy to increase its control over the people. Achebe continues to be realistic in his treatment of traditional society. It is not an idyllic Eden corrupted by satanic foreign power. In spite of the attractive pictures of local customs, the six villages of Umuaro are divided and belligerent, and, in two instances at least, it is ironically the British government or the Christian church that ensures peace and continuity in the communal life. By this stage in the colonization, of course, it is difficult (and Achebe does not try) to untangle the causes of internal disorder among the Igbo.

Like Okonkwo, the protagonist in *Arrow of God* is representative of the social disorder. In him Achebe represents the confidence in traditional roles and beliefs challenged not only by the new British world view, but also by forces within. Personal pride, egotism, and intolerance sometimes obscure his obligation to the welfare of the community. Whereas Okonkwo is one among several wealthy members of the clan, Ezeulu occupies a key position as the priest of Ulu, chief god of the six villages. Thus the central cohesive force in the society is localized in this one man. In another way, too, Ezeulu differs from Okonkwo. Whereas Okonkwo stubbornly resists the new Western culture, Ezeulu makes such gestures of accommodation that his clan actually accuses him of being the white man's friend. Instead of disowning his son for adopting Christianity, he sends Oduche to the mission school to be his spy in the Western camp. Ezeulu's personality, however, is complex, as are his motives, Accommodation is his pragmatic way of preserving the clan and his own power. When the opportunity arises for him to become the political representative of his people to the British government, he refuses out of a sense of loyalty to his local god. This complexity is, however, contradictory and confusing, thus reflecting again the transitional state of affairs during the early colonial period. Ezeulu does not always seem to know what his motives are as he jockeys for power with Winterbottom and with the priest Idemili. In trying to save the community he sets up himself and his god as the sole sources of wisdom. As priest—and thus considered half man and half spirit—he may, as Achebe seems to suggest, confuse his sacred role with his human vanity.

It is in the midst of this confusion that Achebe again questions the existence of absolutes and advises tolerance. The central concept of the *chi* reappears. Does it say yes if man says yes? If so, man controls his own destiny. If not, he is severely limited. In any case, the concept itself suggests duality rather than absoluteness. Even Ezeulu, while challenging the new power, advises his son, Oduche, that one "must dance the dance prevalent in his time." Chapter 16, in which this statement appears, contains the key thematic passages. In it one of Ezeulu's wives tells her children a traditional tale about a people's relation with the spirit world. It turns upon the importance of character—the proper attitude one must have toward oneself and toward the gods. A boy accidentally leaves his flute in the field where he and his family had been farming. He persuades his parents to let him return to fetch it. An encounter with the spirits, during which he demonstrates his good manners, temperance, and reverence, leads to material reward. The envious senior wife in the family sends her son on a similar mission, but his rudeness and greed lead only to the visitation of evils on human society. The intended message is obvious, but the implied one, in the context of this novel, is that traditional values appear to be childhood fancies in the face of contemporary realities.

At the end of the chapter, Ezeulu puts those realities into focus. He describes himself as an arrow of god, whose very defense of religious forms threatens the survival of his religion, but he goes on to suggest the (for him) terrifying speculation that Oduche, his Christian son, and also Christianity and the white man himself, are arrows of god. At the end of his career, Ezeulu is opening his mind to a wide range of possibilities. This tolerance, however, is double-edged, for as Achebe seems to suggest, man must be not only receptive to unfamiliar conceptions, but also tough enough to "tolerate" the pain of ambiguity and alienation. Ezeulu is too old and too exhausted to endure that pain. The final blow is his son's death while performing a ritual dance. Ezeulu interprets it as a sign that Ulu has deserted him.

Indeed, the voice in *Arrow of God* is even more ambiguous than that in the first two novels. There is no Obierika to correct Ezeulu's aberrations. Akueke, his friend and adviser, is not a sure guide to the truth. Achebe works through dialogue even more than in *Things Fall Apart*, and the debates between these two men do not lead to a clear answer. Akueke cannot decipher the priest's motives or anticipate his actions. Ezeulu, as a strange compound of spirit and man, is to him "unknowable." Nor does Achebe make the task any easier for the reader. Ezeulu does not seem to understand his own motives. He considers himself under the spiritual influence of his god. His sudden, final decision not to seek a reconciliation with his people he imagines as the voice of Ulu. He thus sacrifices himself and his people (as well as the god himself) to the will of the god. Achebe remains silent on the issue of whether the voice is the god's or Ezeulu's. One can only speculate that since the society created the god in the first place (or so the legend went), it could also destroy him.

Like *No Longer at Ease*, Achebe's fourth novel, *A Man of the People*, seems rather lightweight in comparison with the two historical novels. It takes place not in Nigeria but in an imaginary African country, a few years after independence. Achebe seems to be playing with some of the popular situations in contemporary African literature, as though he were parodying them. The main character, Odili, has relationships with three different women: Elsie, a friend from the university who functions as a sort of mistress, but who remains a shadowy figure in the background; Jean, a white American with whom he has a brief sexual relationship; and Edna, a beautiful and innocent young woman with whom he "falls in love" in a rather conventional Western sense. There is also the typical estrangement of the university-educated son from his traditionally oriented father. Achebe contrives a somewhat romantic reconciliation during the last third of the novel. Finally, while all of Achebe's novels are essentially political, this one pits two candidates for public office against each other, with all the paraphernalia of personal grudges, dirty tricks, campaign rhetoric, and even a military coup at the end that ironically makes the election meaningless. (In fact, it was already meaningless because the incumbent, Nanga, had arranged that Odili's name not be officially registered.) Furthermore, the contest is a stock romantic confrontation between the idealism of youth and the corrupt opportunism of an older generation. While the story might at first glance appear to be a melodramatic rendering of the romantic world of love and politics, it so exaggerates situations that one must assume Achebe is writing rather in the comic mode.

Along with this choice of mode, Achebe also creates a more conventional plot line. The rising action deals with the first meeting after sixteen years between Odili, a grammar school teacher, and Nanga, the "man of the people," Odili's former teacher, local representative to Parliament, and Minister of Culture. In spite of his skepticism toward national politics, Odili succumbs to Nanga's charm and accepts an invitation to stay at his home in the city. The turning point comes when Odili's girl friend, Elsie, shamelessly spends the night with Nanga. Odili sees this as a betrayal by Elsie, even though he himself feels no special commitment to her. More important, Odili feels betrayed and humiliated by Nanga, who does not take such incidents with women at all seriously. His vanity touched by this rather trivial incident, Odili suddenly reactivates his conscience over political corruption and vows to seek revenge. The attack is twofold: to steal Edna, Nanga's young fiancée, who is to be his second wife, and to defeat Nanga in the next elections. Odili's motives are obviously suspect. The rest of the novel recounts his gradual initiation into love and politics. The revenge motive drops as the relationship with Edna becomes serious. The political campaign fails, and Odili ends up in the hospital after a pointless attempt to spy on one of Nanga's campaign rallies. Again, it is tempting to treat this as a conventional initiation story, except that Odili's experiences do not really cure him of his romantic notions of love and politics.

For the first time, Achebe elects to use the first-person point of view: Odili tells his own story. This may be the reason that the balancing of effects through juxtaposition of scenes and characters does not operate as in the earlier works. The tone is obviously affected as well: Odili is vain and pompous, blind to his own flaws while critical of others. Hence, Achebe has to manipulate a subjective narrative to express the objective authorial voice, as Mark Twain does in *The Adventures of Huckleberry Finn* (1884) or (to use an African example) Mongo Beti in *Le Pauvre Christ de Bomba* (1956, *The Poor Christ of Bomba*). The primary means is through Odili's own partial vision. Odili frequently makes criticisms of contemporary politics that appear to be just, and therefore do represent the judgment of Achebe as well. At the same time, Odili's affected tone invites criticism and provides Achebe with an occasion to satirize the self-deception of the young intellectuals whom Odili represents. Achebe also expresses himself through the plot, in which he parodies romantic perceptions of the contemporary world. In addition, he continues to include proverbs in the mouths of provincial characters as guides to moral evaluation.

Achebe emphasizes one proverb in particular to describe the political corruption in which Nanga participates. After a local merchant, Josiah, steals a blind beggar's stick to make his customers (according to a figurative twist of reasoning) blindly purchase whatever he sells, the public reacts indignantly with the proverb: "He has taken away enough for the owner to notice." Unlike Achebe's narrator in the first three novels, Odili cannot allow the proverb to do its own work. He must, as an academic, analyze it and proudly expand on its meaning. He had done this before when he became the "hero" of Jean's party as the resident expert on African behavior and African art. He may very well be correct about the political implications of the proverb, that the people (the owners of the country) are now being blatantly robbed by the politicians, but he fails to identify emotionally with the local situation. Nor is he objective enough to admit fully to himself his own immoral, hypocritical behavior, which he has maintained throughout the novel. He is an egotist, more enchanted with his own cleverness than concerned about the society he has pretended to serve. In like manner, at the close of the story Odili turns the real death of his political colleague, Max, into a romantic fantasy of the ideal sacrifice. Totally pessimistic about the reliability of the people, he returns once again to the proverb to illustrate their fickle behavior as the melodramatic villains: they always return the Josiahs to power. Achebe may to some extent share Odili's view of the public and the national leadership it chooses, but he is skeptical of the Odilis as well; and hence he positions the reader outside both the political structure and Odili as an observer of the society. Achebe, then, even in this first-person narrative did not abandon his authorial voice, nor the role of social spokesman that he had maintained in all his other novels.

Achebe's fifth novel, *Anthills of the Savannah* (1987), written twenty-one years after his fourth, shares some of its interests. Achebe once again makes the situation political and the setting contemporary. As in *A Man of the People*, the country, Kangan, is fictitious (though the resemblance to Nigeria is again hardly disguised), but somewhat later in the independence period, perhaps in the 1970's or the early 1980's. Also, once again, the main actors in the drama knew one another under different circumstances in the past. Whereas the former relationship between Nanga and Odili was teacher and student, the three male protagonists of *Anthills of the Savannah* are of the same generation and first knew one another as fellow students at Lord Lugard College when they were thirteen years old. The novel deals with their lives during twenty-seven years, including their experiences in England at the University of London, their adventures in love, and their choice of careers. These years are shown only through flashbacks, however, for the focus is on a two-week period in the present, on the edge of a political crisis, when they are forty years old.

Achebe does not present his narrative in a straight chronological line; not only are there flashbacks, but even during the two-week present he recounts, or has his characters recount, events are out of chronological order—a technique Achebe used in his other novels as well to control reader response. The events of this two-week period begin, as the novel does, on a Thursday morning as Sam, now His Excellency, President of Kangan, presides over his weekly cabinet meeting. Sam had decided long before, following the advice of his headmaster at Lord Luggard, to choose the army over a medical career because it would turn him into a "gentleman." His choice proved to be a good one when, after a military coup two years earlier, he was named president of the new government. A fellow student at Lord Luggard, Christopher

Oriko, became his minister of information. Chris used his influence over Sam to name five of the twelve cabinet members and to appoint another old school friend, Ikem Osodi, editor of the *National Gazette*. The political conflict in the novel focuses on these three men, though Sam as a character remains largely in the background. The relationship between Chris and Sam has become increasingly strained over the two-year period, as Sam has expanded his drive for status into an ambition to be president for life with total authority. He is now highly suspicious of Chris and has appointed the tough, ruthless Major Johnson Ossai as his chief of staff and head of intelligence. Chris, meanwhile, as he himself admits in the opening chapter, has become an amused spectator and recorder of events, almost indifferent to the official drama before him. Such an attitude has also driven a wedge between him and Ikem, who, as a crusading journalist, has continued to attack government incompetence and to represent and fight for the hapless public, while Chris has counseled patience and diplomacy in dealing with Sam.

The inciting force on this Thursday is a delegation from Abazon—the northern province of Kangan devastated, like Nigeria's own northern regions, by drought—that has come to the capital city of Bassa to seek relief. Ikem has only recently written an editorial, his allegorical Hymn to the Sun that dries up the savannah, accusing the president (the sun) of responsibility and promoting the delegation's cause. Sam at first feels threatened by the loud demonstrations outside his office, but when he learns that the delegation consists of only six elders and that the rest of the demonstrators are Bassa locals, he decides to use the situation to rid himself of his old school buddies and to entrench himself in power surrounded by loyal henchmen such as Ossai. Chris and Ikem do not realize what is going on behind the scenes— nor does the reader—until events get beyond their control. Within hours, Sam has Ikem arrested and murdered (though the official version is shot while resisting arrest for plotting "regicide"), the Abazon delegation put in prison, and Chris declared an accomplice of both. Chris himself has managed to escape, hiding out with friends and sympathizers and eventually in disguise traveling by bus past roadblocks to the Abazon province. There he learns that a military coup has toppled Sam from his throne and that Sam has mysteriously disappeared. Ironically, at this very moment, in the midst of riotous celebration at a roadblock, Chris is shot by a police sergeant while trying to prevent him from abducting and raping a girl. The novel leaves no hope that the next regime will offer Kangan any better leadership.

The men in this modern African state consistently fail to bring the persistent political incompetence under control. Sam is a variation on the Nanga type, the amoral, self-serving servant of power who does not foresee the consequences of his ruthless treatment of others. This naïveté of the tyrant is matched by the naïve idealism of the moral crusader, Ikem, and the naïve detachment of the philosophical observer, Chris. While most of the novel is an omniscient third-person narrative, with Achebe providing a clear, balanced perspective, five of the first seven chapters are told in first person, with Chris and Ikem being two of the three narrators. Inside their minds, the reader sees a false self-confidence that Achebe eventually parleys into a chauvinism, apparently characteristic of the African male. For the first time in his novels, Achebe takes up the feminist theme, stating flatly that women need to be a major part of the solution to Africa's woes. Sam, as perceived by the third character-narrator, Beatrice, Chris's fiancée, treats women as sex objects, as he invites Beatrice to a dinner party at his lake retreat, assuming that she will be honored to serve her president. The two male protagonists, Ikem and Chris, innocent carriers of long-held assumptions, treat the women they love too lightly, and neither understands until only days before their deaths the wisdom and spiritual power of Beatrice, the central female character in the novel.

In fact, Beatrice herself seems only half aware of her strength until the crisis in Kangan puts it to the test. In chapters 6 and 7, which she narrates, she reveals the change that takes place in her. Chapter 6 is her account of the visit to Sam's retreat, where her defensiveness and vanity obscure her actual superiority over the other guests, including a young American female reporter who uses her sexuality to gain access to Sam. Beatrice sees herself, rather vaingloriously at this point, as a sacrificial shield to protect Sam—a symbol for her of the African leader—from the white temptress. Still, she rebuffs Sam's sexual advances, and he, insulted and humiliated, sends her home in ignominy. Beatrice sees dimly, however, the role that she must play. In chapter 7, she receives help from Ikem, who visits her for the last time before his death. With her help he has made a great discovery, for she had long accused him of male chauvinism, and he reads to her the "love letter" that she has inspired. It is a feminist recantation of his chauvinism, a rejection of the two traditional images of women, both found in biblical and in African sources: the woman as scapegoat, the cause of evil and man's suffering, and the woman idealized as the mother of the male god, called upon to save the world when man fails. His final word on the insight she had given him, however, is that the women themselves must decide their role; men cannot know. Beatrice tells this story of Ikem's last visit in her journal, written months after Ikem has died. Only then is she able to put the pieces of the tragedy together in her mind.

Chris, too, begins to see a special power in Beatrice during the weeks of crisis. She becomes for him a priestess of sexual and spiritual resources who could, as a prophetess, tell the future. Indeed, it is Beatrice (a literary allusion to Dante's Beatrice which is only one of several whimsical allusions in the novel) who warns Chris and Ikem that they must mend their relationship, that tragedy is in store not only for them but also for Sam. They do not take her seriously enough, however, as they soon discover. Yet Achebe does not allow the elevation of Beatrice into the traditional Igbo role of half-woman, half-spirit (the Chielo of *Things Fall Apart*, as Beatrice herself notes), to be the work of the characters alone. In chapter 8, Achebe himself, as omniscient narrator, recounts the Igbo legend of the sun-god who sent his daughter to earth as a harbinger of peace. This legend suggests that henceforth woman must stand as mediator between man and his desires, but this too is not Achebe's final word on the subject. As Ikem says in his confession to Beatrice in chapter 7, "all certitude must now be suspect."

In the last chapter, Achebe tries to bring together his thoughts on women and numerous other themes throughout the novel. The scene is Beatrice's flat and the time is nine months after the tragedy. Those present are a family of friends, including among others Elewa, Ikem's fiancée; Agatha, Beatrice's housekeeper; and Abdul Medani, the army captain who secretly helped Chris escape from Bassa. The occasion is the naming ceremony for Elewa and Ikem's twenty-eight-day-old daughter. The women, along with the men present, are trying to put their lives and, symbolically, the lives of their countrymen in order. Beatrice fears, however, that they are all fated pawns of "an alienated history." They acknowledge the value of people and the living ideas that they leave behind, the importance of humor and the need to laugh at oneself, the "unbearable beauty" even of death, and the community of all religions that can dance the same dance. They learn that women can perform tasks usually reserved for men; since Ikem is not present, Beatrice, the priestess, names the child: Amaechina, the path of Ikem, a boy's name for a baby girl. Elewa's uncle, a male representative of traditional thinking, arrives to preside over the naming but instead pays homage to the young people in the room. "That is how to handle this world," he says, "give the girl a boy's name," make her "the daughter of all of us."

It is important not to take oneself too seriously. Sam, Ikem, and Chris forgot, as Beatrice had to remind them, that their story is not "the story of this country," that "our story is only one of twenty million stories." That reminder may be the main message in *Anthills of the Savannah*, that the other millions of people are not ants caught in a drought, retreating from the sun into their holes, but people with their own stories. As the elder in the Abazon delegation reminds Ikem, the story is the nation's most valued treasure, the storyteller possessed by Agwu, the god of healers and the source of truth. Beatrice, like Ikem and Chris, is a writer, a teller of stories. Uchendu, in *Things Fall Apart*, warns that all stories are true; this fifth novel, itself full of proverbs, stories, legends, and political allegory of the sun shining on the anthills of the savannah, is an ambitious exposé and a compassionate vision of the future.

Thomas Banks

Other major works

SHORT FICTION: *The Sacrificial Egg and Other Short Stories*, 1962; *Girls at War*, 1972.

POETRY: *Beware, Soul Brother and Other Poems*, 1971, 1972; *Christmas in Biafra and Other Poems*, 1973.

NONFICTION: *Morning Yet on Creation Day*, 1975; *The Trouble with Nigeria*, 1983; *Hopes and Impediments*, 1987; *Nigerian Topics*, 1987.

CHILDREN'S LITERATURE: *Chike and the River*, 1966; *How the Leopard Got His Claws*, 1972 (with John Iroaganachi); *The Flute*, 1977; *The Drum*, 1977.

Bibliography

Dathorne, O. R. *African Literature in the Twentieth Century.* Minneapolis: University of Minnesota Press, 1975. Dathorne's general thesis is that the African writer and his characters respond consciously to their cultural environment—the historic split between tradition and contemporary life. The nine-page segment "Chinua Achebe: Ancestor Worshipper" identifies Achebe's response as a tribute to the past in his two historical novels and an indictment of the present in his first two contemporary novels.

Gunner, Elizabeth. *A Handbook for Teaching African Literature.* London: Heinemann, 1987. Addressed to British secondary school teachers, this useful text contains chapters on *Things Fall Apart* and *No Longer at Ease*. Each chapter specifies the appropriate grade level of the novel and provides an overview of the content and setting, a brief (one-paragraph) biography, various suggestions for classroom use, and a bibliography of teaching aids, both audiovisual and textual.

Innes, C. L., and Bernth Lindfors, eds. *Critical Perspectives on Chinua Achebe.* Washington, D.C.: Three Continents Press, 1978. This collection of essays by twenty different critics offers the most comprehensive overview of Achebe's work. Contains a brief introduction to Achebe's life and background, five general assessments of his fiction, commentaries on his first four novels and his poetry, and an extensive bibliography.

Killam, G. D. *The Novels of Chinua Achebe.* London: Heinemann, 1969. This introductory explication of the first four novels, with one chapter devoted to each, quotes from them extensively and touches on Achebe's principal themes and objectives. Killam argues that Achebe, in his self-designated role as educator, places characters of universal appeal in a particular cultural and political context to clarify the African situation for an audience that extends beyond Africa.

Larson, Charles R. *The Emergence of African Fiction.* Bloomington: Indiana University Press, 1972. Larson's general thesis is that the form of the novel changes and that traditional Western criteria may not apply to African fiction. In the chapter, "Chinua Achebe's *Things Fall Apart*: The Archetypal African Novel," Larson tries to isolate the typically African manner of telling a story, a structure based on situation rather than on character.

Moore, Gerald. *Twelve African Writers*. Bloomington: Indiana University Press, 1980. An extensive reworking of Moore's earlier book, *Seven African Writers* (London: Oxford University Press, 1962). The chapter on Achebe examines his first four novels. Moore prefers *Arrow of God* for its denseness and complexity and praises Achebe for his fair-mindedness, but suggests that his next novel (yet to be written at the time) should offer what the first four do not: a vision for the future.

Nkosi, Lewis. *Tasks and Masks: Themes and Styles of African Literature*. Essex, England: Longman, 1981. Nkosi has scattered comments on Achebe in the first third of the book and provides a largely sympathetic assessment of his two historical novels as reliable accounts of precolonial and colonial Igbo society.

Palmer, Eustace. *The Growth of the African Novel*. London: Heinemann, 1979. A lengthy chapter on the first four novels examines Achebe's success in merging theme, character, structure, and setting in *Things Fall Apart*, the failure of the more ambitious *Arrow of God* to repeat this performance, and the masterful control of language in his otherwise less substantial contemporary novels.

Wren, Robert M. *Achebe's World: The Historical and Cultural Context of the Novels*. Washington, D.C.: Three Continents Press, 1980. The purpose of this seemingly authoritative and well-documented presentation is to clarify what might be confusing to a reader not familiar with the Nigerian context. Offers comforting evidence that Achebe's fiction (his first four novels) is an essentially truthful and reliable guide to the historical Nigeria. Includes an extensive glossary of terms and a helpful bibliography.

JAMES AGEE

Born: Knoxville, Tennessee; November 27, 1909
Died: New York, New York; May 16, 1955

Principal long fiction

The Morning Watch, 1951; *A Death in the Family*, 1957.

Other literary forms

James Agee's earliest published book, *Permit Me Voyage* (1934), was a collection of poems, his second a nonfiction account of Alabama sharecroppers in the Depression. He and photographer Walker Evans lived with their subjects for eight weeks in 1936 on a *Fortune* magazine assignment, with a number of critics hailing the resulting book, *Let Us Now Praise Famous Men* (1941), as Agee's masterpiece. From 1941 through 1948, Agee wrote film reviews and feature articles for *Time* and *The Nation*; thereafter, he worked on film scripts in Hollywood, his most notable screenplay being his 1952 adaptation of C. S. Forester's novel *The African Queen* (1935). He also wrote an esteemed television script on Abraham Lincoln for the *Omnibus* series in 1952. *Letters of James Agee to Father Flye* (1962) contains his thirty-year correspondence with an Episcopalian priest who had been his teacher.

Achievements

The prestigious Yale Series of Younger Poets sponsored Agee's first book, Archibald MacLeish contributing its introduction. Agee went on to gain an unusual degree of literary fame for a man who published only three books, two of them slim ones, in his lifetime. Sometimes accused of wasting his talent on magazine and film hack work, Agee lavished the same painstaking attention on film reviews as on his carefully crafted books. His film work was highly prized by director John Huston, and their collaboration on *The African Queen* (1952) resulted in a film classic. His greatest fame developed posthumously, however, when his novel *A Death in the Family* won a 1958 Pulitzer Prize. Three years later, Tad Mosel's dramatization of the novel, *All the Way Home* (1960), earned another Pulitzer. The continued popularity of Agee's work attests his vast human sympathy, his unusual lyrical gift, and his ability to evoke the tension and tenderness of family life in both fiction and nonfiction.

Biography

Born in Knoxville, Tennessee, on November 27, 1909, James Rufus Agee was the son of Hugh James Agee, from a Tennessee mountain family, and Laura Whitman Tyler, the well-educated and highly religious daughter of a businessman. His father sang mountain ballads to him, while his mother passed on to him her love of drama and music. Hugh Agee's death in an automobile accident in the spring of 1916 profoundly influenced young Rufus, as he was called in the family.

Agee received a first-rate education at St. Andrew's School, near Sewanee, Tennessee, where he developed a lifelong friendship with Father James Harold Flye; at Phillips Exeter Academy, Exeter, New Hampshire; and at Harvard College, where in his senior year he edited the *Harvard Advocate*. Upon his graduation in 1932, he went immediately to work for *Fortune* and later its sister publication, *Time*. Over a sixteen-year period, he did a variety of staff work, reviewing, and feature stories while living in the New York metropolitan area.

From 1950 on, Agee spent considerable time in California working mostly with John Huston, but his health deteriorated. Highly disciplined as a writer, Agee exerted less successful control over his living habits, with chronic insomnia and alcohol contributing to a succession of heart attacks beginning early in 1951. Agee was married three times and had a son by his second wife and three more children by his third, Mia Fritsch, who survived him. He succumbed to a fatal heart attack in a New York taxicab on May 16, 1955, at the age of forty-five.

Analysis

Neither James Agee's novella *The Morning Watch* nor his novel *A Death in the Family* offers much in the way of plot. The former covers a few hours of a boy's Good Friday morning at an Episcopalian boys' school, the latter a few days encompassing the death and funeral of a young husband and father. His fiction develops a remarkable lyric intensity, however, and dramatizes with sensitivity the consciousness of children. He presents the minutiae of life as experienced by his characters at times of maximum awareness and thereby lifts them out of the category of mere realistic detail into the realm of spiritual discovery.

Even a cursory glance at the facts of Agee's life reveals how autobiographically based his fiction is. There is no reason to doubt that St. Andrew's, where he spent the years from ten to sixteen, supplies the framework for *The Morning Watch*, or that Agee's own family, seen at the time of Hugh Agee's fatal accident, furnishes the building blocks of the more ambitious *A Death in the Family*. At the same time, Agee permitted himself artistic freedom in selecting, altering, and arranging the facts of raw experience. It is clear that his literary appropriation of his childhood owes much to reflection and interpretation in the light of maturity.

Agee was a writer who stayed close to home in his work. His fiction displays no trace of the two-thirds of his life spent mainly in New England, New York, and California. As is so often the case with Southern writers, Agee's work is imbued with a sense of his origins, of folk traditions viewed in their own right and in competition with the emerging urban culture. The South, with its insistence on the primacy of personal and familial relationships, was in his bones. In keeping to his earliest and most vividly felt years, Agee created a convincing context in which experiences of universal significance can unfold.

At the beginning of *The Morning Watch*, a preadolescent boy and several of his classmates are awakened in the wee hours of Good Friday morning to spend their assigned time in an overnight vigil in the school chapel as part of the Maundy Thursday–Good Friday devotions. Anyone who has experienced a period of religious scrupulosity in childhood will respond to Agee's presentation of Richard. While his friends fumble and curse in the darkness, Richard prepares for adoration. Once in the chapel before the veiled monstrance, he strives to pray worthily despite the inevitable distractions of potentially sinful thoughts, the dangers of spiritual pride, and the torture of the hard kneeling board. Richard wonders whether he can make a virtue of his discomfort: To what extent is it proper for him to suffer along with the crucified Savior? Agee brings Richard intensely alive and conveys the power and the puzzlement of mighty spiritual claims at this stage of life.

The narrative also develops from the start Richard's sense of his relationships with the other boys, most of whom, he realizes, lack his delicate spiritual antennae. After the stint in the chapel is over, he and two classmates do not return to the dormitory as expected but decide on an early morning swim. Their adventure is presented in a heavily symbolic way. Richard dives into deep water at their swimming hole, stays down so long that his friends begin to worry, and emerges before his lungs give out. The boys torture and kill a snake, with Richard (who, like Agee himself, cannot bear to kill) finishing off the job. He debates in his mind whether the snake is poisonous and whether to wash the slime from his hand, deciding finally in the negative. He carries back to the school a locust shell he has found on the way. The snake, which seemingly cannot be killed, suggests both ineradicable evil and, in its victimization, Christ; the locust shell, which he holds next to his heart, seems to represent suffering in a purer form. Richard's dive into the water and subsequent resurfacing obviously symbolize his own "death" and "resurrection" in this Christian Holy Week.

Some critics have noted the influence of James Joyce on this novella. Certainly Richard resembles in certain ways the young protagonists of some of Joyce's *Dubliners* (1914) stories as well as Stephen Dedalus in *A Portrait of the Artist as a Young Man* (1916). Attracted by religious mysteries and artifacts, Richard wishes to appropriate them for his own purposes. He senses the conflict of religion with the world, evinces distaste for the practices of the latter, and hopes to fashion a life that blends the best of both. While Richard's appropriation of religious rite and doctrine is less consciously the artist's than is that of Stephen Dedalus, the reader senses that his individualistic spirituality will inevitably bring him into a Joycean conflict with conservative religious practice.

Since *The Morning Watch*, despite its provocatively ambiguous conflict between the world and the spirit, is somewhat labored and precious, and since Agee's short stories were few and insignificant, his reputation as an important American novelist rests primarily on one book which he did not quite complete before his early death, *A Death in the Family*. As he left it, the story begins at the supper table of the Follet household in Knoxville, Tennessee, in about 1915, and ends just after Jay Follet's funeral on the third day following. Agee had written a short descriptive essay, "Knoxville: Summer 1915" (which makes an appropriate preface to the novel), and six additional sections, which together make up about one-fifth the length of the narrative.

Although all the six scenes (as they will be termed here) pertain to times prior to that of the main story, it remains unclear where Agee intended to place them, or whether he would have used stream-of-consciousness flashbacks, a story-within-a-story technique, or perhaps another method suggested by his cinematic experience to incorporate them. Surely he intended to use them, for they illuminate and enrich the death story despite the absence of any formal linkage among them or collectively to the narrative. The editorial decision to print three of them after each of the first two parts of the three-part narrative seems as logical as any other way under the circumstances.

The novel has no single protagonist. Jay Follet, strong, tall, and taciturn, is described most specifically, at one point being compared to Abraham Lincoln, though apparently more handsome. Last seen alive a third of the way through the narrative, he appears in five of the six scenes and remains the main object of the other characters' thoughts in the last two parts of the narrative. At various stages, each important family member reflects on him: his wife, Mary, son Rufus, brother Ralph, Mary's parents, Joel and Catherine, Mary's aunt Hannah and her brother Andrew, and even Jay's and Mary's three-year-old daughter, also named Catherine. Agee employs Rufus and Mary as a focus most frequently. No point of view outside the family circle intrudes, and, except on two occasions when the six-year-old Rufus interacts with neighborhood children outside, attention is focused on family members exclusively. Throughout the novel, Agee juxtaposes the tensions and tendernesses of domestic life. The reader is constantly made to feel not only how much the family members love one another but also how abrasive they can be. Recognizing that a family does not succeed automatically, Agee portrays a continual struggle against external divisive pressures and selfishness within.

Jay and Mary's marriage has withstood a number of strains. First of all, their origins differ greatly. Mary's people are the citified, well-educated Lynches; the Follets are Tennessee mountain folk. The couple's ability to harmonize their differences is exemplified in the second of the six scenes.

Rufus notes that when singing together, his father interprets music flexibly, "like a darky," while his mother sings true and clear but according to the book. Rufus particularly admires his father's sense of rhythm. Sometimes, the boy observes, his mother tries to sing Jay's way and he hers, but they soon give up and return to what is natural.

Jay's father, who indirectly causes Jay's death, is one point of difference. Mary's antipathy to him is known to all the Follets, but even Jay realizes that his likable father is weak of character. When Jay's brother calls and informs him that their father is very ill, Jay wastes no time in preparing to go to him, despite his suspicion that the unreliable Ralph has greatly exaggerated the danger. It is on his return trip, after learning that his father is all right, that a mechanical defect in Jay's car causes the crash that kills him instantly.

Jay's drinking problem, a Follet weakness, has also distressed his wife, and Jay has vowed to kill himself if he ever gets drunk again. In one of the scenes, Rufus, aware that whiskey is a sore point between his parents, accompanies his father when he stops at a tavern, and it appears that he has overcome his habit of excess, but his reputation has spread. Both the man who finds Jay's body and the children who later taunt Rufus on the street corner attribute his accident to drunken driving, and Mary has to fight off the temptation to consider the possibility.

Religion is another divisive issue. Jay does not appear to be a denominational Christian, while Mary is, like Agee's own mother, a fervent Episcopalian. The men on both sides of the family are either skeptics or thoroughgoing unbelievers. A devotee of Thomas Hardy's fiction, Mary's father, Joel, has little use for piety or what he calls "churchiness." Although he originally disapproved of Mary's marriage to Jay, he has come to terms with Jay, whom he views as a counterweight to Mary's religiosity. Mary's brother Andrew carries on open warfare with the Christian God. When he first hears of Jay's accident, Mary senses that he is mentally rehearsing a speech about the folly of belief in a benevolent deity. Even young Rufus is a budding skeptic. Told that God has let his father "go to sleep," he ferrets out the details and concludes that the concussion he has heard about, "not God," has put his father to sleep. When he hears that his father will wake up at the Final Judgment, he wonders what good that is. The women accept the inscrutable as God's will, but the men take an agnostic stance and fear the influence of the church. Father Jackson, the most unpleasant person in the novel, ministers to Mary in her bereavement. Rufus quickly decides that the priest's power is malevolent and that, were his real father present, the false father would not be allowed into his home.

Some hours after the confirmation of Jay's death, Mary feels his presence in the room, and though Andrew and Joel will not concede any kind of spiritual visitation, they acknowledge that they too felt "something." Later, Andrew tells Rufus of an event he considers "miraculous": the settling of a butterfly on Jay's coffin in the grave and the creature's subsequent flight, high into the sunlight. The men's unbelief, then, is not positivistic; they recognize the possibility of a realm beyond the natural order, but they bitterly oppose the certified spiritual agent, Father Jackson, as too self-assured and quick to condemn.

To counter the estrangements brought on by cultural and religious conflicts in the family, reconciliations dot the narrative. Rufus senses periodic estrangements from his father and then joyful feelings of unity. Jay frequently feels lonely, even homesick. Crossing the river between Knoxville and his old home, he feels restored. To go home is impracticable, bound up with a vanished childhood. In one of the scenes, the family visits Rufus' great-great-grandmother. It is a long, winding journey into the hills and into the past. It is apparent that none of the younger generations of Follets has gone to see the old woman in a long time. Rufus, who has never been there, comes home in a way impossible to his father. The old woman, more than a hundred years old, barely acknowledges any of her numerous offspring, but she clasps Rufus, the fifth-generation descendant, who is joyful to her. On other occasions, Jay, by imaginative identification with Rufus, can feel as if he is his "own self" again.

Mary also feels alternate waves of friendship with, and estrangement from, her father. He, in turn, has a wife with whom communication is difficult because of her deafness. When Catherine cannot hear her husband, she seldom asks him to repeat himself, as if fearful of exasperating him. In this way, she is insulated from his unbelief. Although they talk little, they communicate by gestures and physical closeness. Agee shows him taking her elbow to help her over a curb and carefully steering her up the street toward their home. Rufus and his father are usually silent on their walks; they communicate by sitting together on a favorite rock and watching passersby.

Much of the talk following Jay's death is irritable and nerve-shattering. Andrew dwells thoughtlessly on the one-chance-in-a-million nature of Jay's accident, for which his father rebukes him. Mary begs Andrew to have mercy and then hysterically begs his forgiveness, upon which her aunt censures her for unwarranted humility. Both Mary and Andrew are enduring crises, however, and are hardly responsible for what they say. She is resisting the temptation to despair of God's mercy; he is trying to come to terms with a possibly meaningless universe. Andrew communicates best with services; throughout the hours of distress, he is unfailingly helpful.

The truest communication exists between Jay and Mary. When he is not silent, he can be sullen or wrathful. As he prepares to set forth on his journey to his father's, Mary dreads the "fury and profanity" she can expect if, for example, the car will not start, but this sometimes harsh husband stops in the bedroom to recompose their bed so it will look comfortable and inviting when she returns to it. She disapproves of his drinking strong coffee, but she makes it very strong on this occasion because she knows he will appreciate it. By dozens of such unobtrusive deeds, Jay and Mary express their love, which prevails over the numerous adverse circumstances and personal weaknesses that threaten it.

Long before he began work on *A Death in the Family*, Agee expressed his intention to base a literary work on his father's death. The eventual novel is thus deeply meditated and very personal. At the same time, it attains universality by means of its painstaking precision. In the Follets can be seen any family that has striven to harmonize potentially divisive differences or has answered courageously a sudden tragedy. As in loving families generally, the tensions do not disappear. At the end, Andrew, for the first time in his life, invites Rufus to walk with him. Sensing the negative feelings in his uncle, Rufus nevertheless is afraid to ask him about them. Walking home with this man who can never replicate his father but who will fill as much of the void as possible, Rufus comes to terms with his father's death in the silence that in Agee's fiction communicates beyond the power of words. In this reconstruction of his own most momentous childhood experience, Agee portrays the most difficult reconciliation of all.

Robert P. Ellis

Other major works
SHORT FICTION: "A Mother's Tale," 1952; *Four Early Stories by James Agee*, 1964; *The Collected Short Prose of James Agee*, 1968.

SCREENPLAYS: *The Red Badge of Courage*, 1951 (based on Stephen Crane's novel); *The African Queen*, 1952 (based on the novel by C. S. Forester); *The Bride Comes to Yellow Sky*, 1952 (based on Crane's short story); *Noa Noa*, 1953; *White Mane*, 1953; *Green Magic*, 1955; *The Night of the Hunter*, 1955; *Agee on Film: Five Film Scripts*, 1960.

POETRY: *Permit Me Voyage*, 1934; *The Collected Poems of James Agee*, 1968.

NONFICTION: *Let Us Now Praise Famous Men*, 1941; *Agee on Film: Reviews and Comments*, 1958; *Letters of James Agee to Father Flye*, 1962.

Bibliography
Barson, Alfred. *A Way of Seeing: A Critical Study of James Agee*. Amherst: University of Massachusetts Press, 1972. A revisionist view of Agee, whose earliest critics thought that the writer's talents were dissipated by his diverse interests, causing him not to produce enough quality material, but who judged him to have been improving and focusing his skills at the time of his death. Barson inverts this thesis, stating that Agee's finished work should not be so slighted, and that his powers were declining when he died. Contains notes and an index. Should not be confused with *A Way of*

Seeing: Photographs of New York (New York: Viking Press, 1965), a collection of photographs by Helen Levitt with an essay by Agee.

Bergeen, Laurence. *James Agee: A Life*. New York: E. P. Dutton, 1984. The definitive biography of Agee, based on interviews with those who knew him and examinations of his papers. Also contains illustrations, notes, a bibliography of Agee's writings, a bibliography of works about him, and an index.

Kramer, Victor A. *James Agee*. Boston: Twayne, 1975. This short introduction to the life and works of Agee is a good book for the beginning researcher. Besides providing a biography of the writer and a careful discussion of all of his major works, Kramer also includes a chronology of Agee's life, an annotated bibliography, and an index.

Madden, David, ed. *Remembering James Agee*. Baton Rouge: Louisiana State University Press, 1974. An excellent collection of memories about and assessments of Agee by his friends and co-workers, including Walker Evans, Dwight Macdonald, Father James Harold Flye, John Huston, and Agee's wife, Mia Agee. Also includes illustrations and a detailed chronology of Agee's life.

Moreau, Geneviève. *The Restless Journey of James Agee*. Translated by Miriam Kleiger. New York: William Morrow, 1977. Although Moreau states that her study of Agee is not a formal biography but an attempt to relate his work to his life, it is detailed enough to serve the purposes of both biography and criticism. Provides notes, an index, and a critical bibliography, and an extensive bibliography of Agee's own writings.

Ohlin, Peter H. *Agee*. New York: I. Obolensky, 1966. The first book-length analysis of Agee's works, with particular emphasis on his prose. Contains an index, a bibliography of Agee's writings, and a critical bibliography.

Seib, Kenneth. *James Agee: Promise and Fulfillment*. Pittsburgh, Pa.: University of Pittsburgh Press, 1968. As the subtitle indicates, Seib's study rescues Agee from the critical judgment that his work was more potential than performance. Maintains that Agee's contemporaries could not recognize his greatness because they judged him by traditional standards, when the writer was actually striking out in new directions that they did not understand. Agee is a link between the traditional man of letters and the new media of film and television. Contains notes, an index, a bibliography of works about Agee, and a bibliography of Agee's writings. Includes a list of his film and book reviews, which are often hard to track down.

CONRAD AIKEN

Born: Savannah, Georgia; August 5, 1889
Died: Savannah, Georgia; August 17, 1973

Principal long fiction

Blue Voyage, 1927; *Great Circle*, 1933; *King Coffin*, 1935; *A Heart for the Gods of Mexico*, 1939; *Conversation: Or, Pilgrim's Progress*, 1940; *The Collected Novels of Conrad Aiken*, 1964.

Other literary forms

Conrad Aiken was one of the most prolific of modern American writers, publishing more than forty separate volumes of poetry, novels, plays, short stories, and criticism. Aiken published five collections of stories, culminating in the *Collected Short Stories of Conrad Aiken* (1966). He is the author of *Mr. Arcularis* (1957), a play based on an adaptation by Diana Hamilton of his short story of the same title. His nonfictional writing includes introductions to *Two Wessex Tales by Thomas Hardy* (1919) and *Selected Poems of Emily Dickinson* (1924), as well as a lifetime of reviews, originally published in such leading journals as *The New Republic, Poetry, The Dial, The Nation,* and *The New Yorker*, and collected in *A Reviewer's ABC: Collected Criticism of Conrad Aiken from 1916 to the Present* (1958). An earlier critical work was *Skepticisms: Notes on Contemporary Poetry* (1919). His most famous nonfictional work, and one of his most lasting contributions to American literature, is his third-person autobiography *Ushant: An Essay* (1952). He published twenty-nine collections of poetry; the best of his early poems were collected in *Selected Poems* (1929), while the best of his total poetic output can be found in *Collected Poems* (1953, 1970). In addition, Aiken served as editor for numerous anthologies of poetry, including *A Comprehensive Anthology of American Poetry* (1929), and was a contributing editor of *The Dial* from 1917 to 1918. Finally, under the pseudonym Samuel Jeake, Jr., Aiken was a London correspondent for *The New Yorker* from 1934 to 1936.

Achievements

Aiken's literary reputation is based on his poetry, for which he received the Pulitzer Prize in 1930, the National Book Award in 1954, and the Bollingen Prize in 1956. Despite these major awards, his reputation seems fixed among the most major of minor poets, a position that virtually all of his critics agree is too low. Of his fiction, the short stories "Silent Snow, Secret Snow" and "Mr. Arcularis" are often anthologized and discussed, though few of his others are ever mentioned. His reputation as a novelist is even more tenuous; none of his novels is now in print, and few critical articles about them have been published. When his first novel, *Blue Voyage*, appeared, its initial reputation as an experimental novel and its personal revelations about Aiken's interior life brought the book some notoriety. Subsequent critical opinion, however, has treated *Blue Voyage* as an inferior version of James Joyce's *A Portrait of the Artist as a Young Man* (1916) or *Ulysses* (1922). *Great Circle*, Aiken's second novel, was praised by literary critics as a psychological case study and was admired by Sigmund Freud himself for its Freudian overtones. Aiken's last three novels received little praise or attention. *A Heart for the Gods of Mexico* was not even published in America until the collected edition of his novels appeared. Aiken himself considered *King Coffin* a failure; he admits in *Ushant* that his last novels were unsuccessful, and says that he does not mind his relative obscurity, but in a letter to his friend Malcolm Cowley, he wrote "Might I also suggest for your list of Neglected Books a novel by c. aiken called *Great Circle*, of which the royalty report, to hand this morning, chronicles a sale of 26 copies in its second half year?" Current critics, like Aiken's contemporaries, see the major value of his novels in their experimental nature, their Freudian images, and their amplification of the themes of Aiken's poetry.

Biography

Conrad Potter Aiken was born in Savannah, Georgia, on August 5, 1889. Both of his parents were New Englanders. His mother, Anna Potter Aiken, was the daughter of William James Potter, minister of the Unitarian First Congregational Society of New Bedford, Massachusetts, and a friend of Ralph Waldo Emerson. His father, William Ford Aiken, was a physician educated at Harvard. The central event of his childhood—and in fact of his whole life—took place in 1900 when, as an eleven-and-a-half year old boy, he discovered the dead bodies of his parents. Aiken's father had killed his mother with a revolver and then shot himself. This event remained forever embedded in his psyche. As Aiken writes in *Ushant*, "He had tiptoed into the dark room, where the two bodies lay motionless, and apart, and, finding them dead, found himself possessed of them forever."

Following this crucial event, Aiken's two brothers were separated from him, and he spent the remainder of his childhood living with a great-great aunt in New Bedford. He attended the Middlesex School in Concord and, in 1907, entered Harvard University during the same period as T. S. Eliot, John Reed, Walter Lippmann, E. E. Cummings, and Robert Benchley. At college, Aiken was president of the Harvard *Advocate*, a frequent contributor to the Harvard *Monthly*, and a leader among his classmates in literary discussions, but he also established a pattern which was to hold true throughout his life—he was always a loner, following neither particular schools of criticism nor prevailing literary styles. Placed on probation for poor class attendance as a senior, Aiken left Harvard in protest and spent half a year in Europe, thus establishing another constant pattern: for the remainder of his life he made frequent trips to Europe, living as often abroad as at home until World

War II, after which he lived in New England, primarily in Brewster, Massachusetts.

Following his return to Harvard, Aiken was graduated in 1912 and immediately began writing poems for his first collection, *Earth Triumphant and Other Tales in Verse* (1914). For the rest of his life, Aiken supported himself solely by his writing, except for a brief stint as an English tutor at Harvard in 1927. He married three times, divorcing his first wife, Jessie McDonald, after eighteen years of marriage and the rearing of three children; his second wife, Clarice Lorenz, he divorced after seven years. He remained married to his third wife, Mary Hoover, from 1937 until his death from a heart attack on August 17, 1973, in Savannah, Georgia, the city of his birth, to which he had returned to complete the great circle of his life.

For most of his career, Aiken simultaneously worked on his poetry, fiction, and criticism. From 1925 to 1935, he alternated short-story collections with novels. In 1939 and 1940, he published his last two novels, *A Heart for the Gods of Mexico* and *Conversation*, thereafter concentrating on poetry and criticism. During the 1920's and 1930's, Aiken was involved with such American expatriates as T. S. Eliot, Ezra Pound, and Malcolm Lowry, yet he was always deliberately apart from the center of artistic circles, choosing, for example, to live in London and Brewster rather than Paris and New York. The best source of information about Aiken's relation with other writers is *Ushant*, in which Eliot, Pound, and Lowry appear as the Tsetse, Rabbi Ben Ezra, and Hambo.

Analysis

The central event in Conrad Aiken's personal life—the murder-suicide of his parents—was also the central event of his artistic life, for all of his literary work is in some way aimed at coming to terms with the childhood tragedy. In *Ushant*, Aiken says of his parents that "he was irrevocably dedicated to a lifelong—if need be—search for an equivalent to it all, in terms of his own life, or work; and an equivalent that those two angelic people would have thought acceptable." The search for understanding of his personal tragedy motivated Aiken to try to understand the universal tragedy of modern man, what Joseph Warren Beach called "moral terror," the basic question of good and evil in the human heart that American writers have been struggling with since the advent of American letters. Aiken's search for a way to maintain equilibrium in the face of his contradictory love for his parents and his revulsion for their deaths lies outside of theological or conventional ethical questions; his search centered on his own consciousness, on himself. The major subject of each of his five novels is a search for self, an interior exploration—often expressed metaphorically as a circular journey. *Blue Voyage* and *Great Circle* focus on psychological understanding in which the protagonist attempts to get back to himself by a circular analysis of his past. *King Coffin* is a psychological horror story of a madman's decision to murder a complete stranger, a decision that eventually leads the protagonist around full circle until he kills himself. *A Heart for the Gods of Mexico* presents a literal journey—a train trip from Boston to Mexico—in which the narrator attempts to reconcile the beauty and strangeness of the changing landscape with the impending death of his woman companion. Finally, *Conversation* describes the circular arguments in a lover's quarrel which eventually runs its course, returning to its starting place.

In each novel, Aiken's chief character is trying to complete what in plane geometry is called a great circle of a sphere, a circle whose plane passes through the center of the sphere. For Aiken's protagonists, the circle is a descent into their pasts and the sphere is the shape of their lives. Because of this self-analysis, each novel is introspective and confessional. Taken together, the novels chart a series of points on Aiken's great circle, a graphic display of his search for understanding his own life. Each novel is based, in varying degrees, on autobiographical details from his life, and each is discussed in *Ushant*, where Aiken says "the artificer, in the very act of displaying himself in the new shape of the artifact, must remain wholly neutral to that part of himself which is his subject—which is to say, his all."

Aiken's attempt to get to the bottom of or to the other side of his parents' deaths led him on a series of physical voyages between America and Europe and on a series of literary voyages between poetry and fiction, which he called in his 1958 poem "The Crystal," "The westward pour of the worlds and the westward pour of the mind." In both his life and his art he speaks of a constant tension between two opposing forces: a desire for artistic expression, for bringing art to bear on the chaos of human existence which was in constant confrontation with what Frederick Hoffman calls "the shock of reality, which continually challenges the creative spirit and, in moments of terror or violence, may even severely dislocate it." Although the shortest distance between two points may be a straight line, when those points are located within these opposing spheres, then the shortest arc between the comfort of art and the moral terror of reality becomes the great circle that Aiken so thoroughly and so gracefully traced in his novels.

Writing in 1952 about his first novel *Blue Voyage* (which in *Ushant* he calls, half ironically, *Purple Passage*), Aiken said it was "a compromise in which the voice of Joyce had been too audible." This Joycean comparison refers to the hero of the novel, William Demarest, who has booked a second-class passage aboard a steamship enroute to England, ostensibly to search for his lost love Cynthia, but actually to search within himself for an explanation of his feelings about Cynthia and about himself as a writer. Demarest clearly resembles Aiken, both in autobiographical detail (when Demarest's parents die he is sent as a boy to live in New Bedford) and in critical reputation (Demarest names as his literary weakness the inability to present a "theme energetically and simply" instead of dressing it "in tissue upon tissue of proviso and aspect . . . from a hundred angles"). The novel is also Joycean in style, for when Demarest discovers that Cynthia is actually on board the ship, he returns to his stateroom and launches himself into a lengthy regression which Jay Martin in his *Conrad Aiken: A Life of His Art* (1962) calls a "preconscious monologue." This regression is filled with allusions to self-crucifixion, bizarre sexual dreams, fragments of popular songs, bits of English poetry, extended lists of numbers, noises, and a constant repetition of the capitalized word MISERY, all accompanied by the incessant throbbing of the ship's engines.

Jay Martin sees *Blue Voyage* as an attempt at combining the confessional and the aesthetic novel, and like *A Portrait of the Artist as a Young Man*, Aiken's first novel includes discussions of its hero's theories about art and literature with Aiken's Cranley/Lynch figure, a man named Silverstein, who acts as Demarest's psychoanalyst. *Blue Voyage* tries to go beyond Joyce's early work in terms of experimentation, for in the sixth chapter, Aiken presents a lyrical out-of-the-body experience in which the main characters of the novel perform a hallucinatory ritualistic parody of the Crucifixion which results in Cynthia's being metamorphosized into a Gothic stained-glass window. The book ends with a series of undelivered letters from Demarest to Cynthia which alternate between intense self-loathing and a passionate attempt to explain the letter writer to his lost love, to himself, and, by extension, to explain Aiken to his readers. As Demarest says in his second letter, "It is precisely the sort of thing I am always trying to do in my writing—to present my unhappy reader with a wide-ranged chaos—of actions and reactions, thoughts, memories and feelings—in the vain hope that at the end he will see that the whole thing represents only *one moment, one feeling, one person.*"

In his autobiography, Aiken's second novel, *Great Circle*, appears as *Dead Reckoning*, a punning title that encompasses the major themes of the novel: navigation along the great circle as a metaphor for exploration of the psyche of a man whose world, like the author's, turns over with the horrifying discovery of his parents' betrayal by sudden death. *Great Circle* opens with its protagonist, Andrew Cather, on board a train to Cambridge, where he will surprise his wife in the act of adultery, an act that was forewarned both by a friend and by signs the protagonist has refused to see. Andrew Cather, who is often called "One-eye Cather" because of an ambiguously explained injury to one eye, is not able to stop the marital infidelity he knows is coming, any more than the Cyclops in Homer's epic can avoid Odysseus' prophesied appearance.

Cather's discovery leads him to Aiken's familiar dilemma: how to maintain balance in the face of moral terror. Cather's initial response is to avoid the terror by avoiding consciousness of it, at first by maintaining a false air of melodrama about the situation and then by repeatedly drinking himself into a stupor. The combination of drunkenness and estrangement from his wife, whose adultery was consummated with Cather's best friend, causes him to fall into the lengthy reverie about his childhood which constitutes all of Chapter II, the most successfully sustained section in all of Aiken's prose fiction. This section is a sensually lyrical evocation of the summer in Cather's childhood in Duxbury, Massachusetts, during which he first felt the strangeness of his father's absence and his mother's attachment to his Uncle David. The chapter is Joycean in style and Faulknerian in content, full of lyrical passages that call up ocean and shore. Like Maisie from Henry James's *What Maisie Knew* (1897) or William Faulkner's Quentin Compson from *The Sound and the Fury* (1929), the young Andy Cather slowly comes to awareness about the sexuality of the adults who move around him. Reading a letter from his father to his mother, Andy Cather realizes imperfectly that his mother is having an affair with his uncle. The chapter ends with Andy's terrible discovery of the bodies of his mother and her lover, drowned during a storm. Speaking of this chapter, Jay Martin says, "Aiken intends it to be real, an exact and complete account of his experience insofar as it entered the consciousness of the boy."

The third chapter of *Great Circle* consists of a night-long amateur psychoanalysis session in which Cather speaks an exhaustive monologue in an attempt at talking through his marital problems in the present, the horror of his childhood discovery, and the interconnection between the two events. Realizing that he unconsciously associates the physical intimacies of marriage with the discovery of his mother, dead in his uncle's embrace, Cather makes an actual trip to Duxbury, thus confronting and completing the great circle voyage through his past and his psyche. Aiken's novel reflects Henry David Thoreau's argument at the conclusion of *Walden* (1854) that "Our voyaging is only great-circle sailing," for the horrible scene from his protagonist's childhood is, of course, suggestive of Aiken's own childhood tragedy. The image of circularity echoes throughout the novel, from the title to the description of Cather "hurrying from point to point on the earth's surface, describing his swift little arc" to the later statement that he is running "round in mad circles, like a beheaded hen." Later, Cather says to himself about the origin of his problems, "It is your own little worm-curve; the twist that is your own life; the small spiral of light that answers to the name of Andrew Cather." The entire second chapter is enclosed within outsized parentheses, suggestive of the great-circle, and in one of his childhood revelations, Cather remembers an old riddle—"Rats live on no evil star," a palindrome that "spells the same thing backward"—which reminds the reader that Andrew Cather's initials backward are Conrad Aiken's, and that Cather's attempt at rescuing his marriage through a series of therapeutic returns to his childhood is also Aiken's attempt at resolving his own problems by writing about them in novels.

Aiken's third novel, *King Coffin*, is the only one he leaves out of *Ushant*, probably because he considered it to be a major failure, unredeemable by subsequent analysis. Although most critics refer to *King Coffin* as a major failure, if they mention it at all, Aiken's best critic, Jay Martin, argues that the author meant *King Coffin* as a parody of a psychological novel, playing "lightly with a serious psychological subject while still retaining a real sense of its dignity and importance." The subject of the novel is an insane plan conceived half in jest by Jasper Ammen (a name suggestive of E. A. Robinson's *King Jasper*, 1936) to demonstrate his innate superiority by murdering an ordinary person chosen at random—a person Ammen comes to call "a specimen man" or "the anonymous one." The motive for the murder is the achievement of a perfectly pure relationship, in Ammen's simplification of Nietzschian/Emersonian ideas, between the superior man and the ordinary one. Initially, Ammen claims he has chosen his victim and is studying the dailiness of his life as background for a novel about "pure" murder, a novel he plans to call *King Coffin*.

As the actual novel progresses, Ammen begins to think of Jones, his intended victim, as "one-who-wants-to-be-killed." This short novel ends with Ammen's too-close identification with his victim; seeing that Jones's wife's newly born baby has died, Ammen decides that the perfect ending to his plan would be his own murder, thereby bringing the novel full circle: the random victim has unconsciously caused Ammen to kill himself. Although Jay Martin sees *King Coffin* as its protagonist's "attempt to recognize and resolve his own strangeness, to realize his ego completely by fully understanding its complexity," most critics have seen the book as a competent murder-mystery at best, clearly the least successful of Aiken's novels. Because Jasper Ammen is labeled a psychotic at the start of the novel, the rationalizations he uses for his bizarre plan never become compelling; they are neither the ravings of a madman nor the thoughts of a superior human. Instead they fall somewhere in between. *King Coffin* is considerably shorter than Aiken's previous novels and interesting mainly for its conception: Aiken creates a psychopathic killer who pretends to write the book that Aiken actually writes, just as the narrator of *Ushant*, a character Aiken calls only D., discusses his attempt at writing the very autobiography in which one reads his discussion.

Aiken's penultimate novel, *A Heart for the Gods of Mexico*, returns to the author's now-familiar themes. The story tells of a lengthy train trip from Boston to Mexico by day coach, taken by a woman who knows she is soon to die of heart failure; her fiancé, who is unaware of her condition; and her friend, who is half in love with her. Noni, the young woman who is soon to die, puzzles over her upcoming death in a manner that recalls *King Coffin*: "It seems so ridiculously random . . . it's *that* that's so puzzling." Unlike the psychopathic protaganist of that novel, however, the young woman is a sympathetic character. She and her friend are constantly struggling with such questions as whether the subterfuge is ethical, whether the trip is hastening her inevitable death, and whether the startling tropical beauty of Mexico should make them forget the impending death or revel in it.

Both critics and its author have described *A Heart for the Gods of Mexico* as a curious failure; the novel contains brilliant landscape scenes, strong and affecting portrayals of character, particular Noni's, and a passionate depiction of the traveler's meeting in Cuernavaca with Hambo, Aiken's name for Malcolm Lowry, the author of *Under the Volcano* (1947). Unlike *Blue Voyage* and *Great Circle*, however, this book lacks form. The trip is too long in getting started, and too much local color is presented along the way. *A Heart for the Gods of Mexico* is the shortest of Aiken's novels. The book offers no flashbacks, no self-analysis, no sense of any concentric structure except for the shape imposed on the novel by the narrative of the trip itself, Noni's "greatcircle to Mexico" upon which she takes her "heart as an offering to the bloodstained altar of the plumed serpent."

Aiken's last novel, *Conversation*, records the bitterly circular quarrel of Timothy and Enid Kane, whose marital argument, like the one in *Great Circle*, is (on the surface, at least) about infidelity, this time on the part of the male. In some ways, the novel deals with feminism; Enid Kane wants to live in an urban environment while her husband, a painter, wants to live in the country on Cape Cod rather than remain in the city painting commissioned portraits. Timothy sees the journey to the country as a chance to get back in touch with his natural artistic creativity; his wife sees the move as "all that nonsense of yours about plain living and high thinking, about living the natural and honest life of our Pilgrim ancestors, and being independent—but it's no good for a woman." While Enid is wrong in thus belittling her husband's desire to paint freely, Timothy is also wrong in hiding the fact that the move is partly to get away from his in-town affair. The bucolic escape turns into a series of get-togethers with bohemian Greenwich Village artists and poets, such as Karl Roth, who represents the poet Maxwell Bodenheim. Enid Kane's reference to the Pilgrims suggests one of the connections between this portrait of the artist as a young married man, the novel's subtitle, and the excerpts from *A Journal of the Pilgrims at Plymouth* (1962) that head each chapter of the novel. Like the early visitors to Massachusetts, Timothy Kane wants to recapture a spirit of freedom so that he can overcome the sterility he has felt, both in his art and in his life, since the birth of his daughter. Although his daughter's birth represents the highest womanly creative act in his wife's mind, and although his daughter's freshly imaginative outlook on nature is exactly the kind of artistic rebirth Timothy is looking for, he comes to see during the course of the long, circuitous argument that his repressed anxieties about the physical details of his daughter's birth are the cause of his inability to hold a conversation with his wife. Like Andrew Cather, who is disgusted by the "filthy intimacies" of marriage, Timothy Kane finds the effect of childbirth, what his friend calls "that butcher-shop and meaty reality," to be "something for which love's young dream hadn't at all been prepared. A loss of belief."

The argument in *Conversation* continues along Aiken's familiar circular path, until, like a snake with its tail in its mouth, it comes back to where it began and resolves itself with the reunion of the Kanes and a decision to have a son; however, since no one can predict the sex of an unborn child before conception, it is clear that this resolution will likely lead the couple back onto another loop of their argument. In the middle of his last novel, Aiken presents a scene in which Kane is comparing his idea of marriage while still engaged with his vision after his child's birth. Using the metaphors of poetry and prose, Kane gives Conrad Aiken's final critical assessment of the relationship between his own work in the two genres: "The poetry had been too pure a poetry, its further implications (of all that the body, and passion, could exact, or time and diurnal intimacy dishevel and destroy) had been too little understood; and when the prose followed, it had inevitably seemed only too ingrainedly prosaic."

This assessment is accurate. Despite their relative merits, Aiken's five novels would probably not be read today were it not for the poetic reputation of their author. In his autobiography, Aiken says of his parents' deaths that "he was to discover, while at Harvard, that the staining sense of guilt and shame had been mysteriously exorcised, as no longer there," but clearly some degree of both guilt and shame must have remained throughout the author's life, despite the therapy gained from writing these five novels.

Timothy Dow Adams

Other major works

SHORT FICTION: *Bring! Bring! and Other Stories*, 1925; *Costumes by Eros*, 1928; *Among the Lost People*, 1934; *Short Stories*, 1950; *Collected Short Stories*, 1960; *Collected Short Stories of Conrad Aiken*, 1966.

PLAYS: *Fear No More*, 1946; *Mr. Arcularis: A Play*, 1957.

POETRY: *Earth Triumphant and Other Tales in Verse*, 1914; *Turns and Movies and Other Tales in Verse*, 1916; *The Jig of Forslin*, 1916; *Nocturne of Remembered Spring and Other Poems*, 1917; *The Charnel Rose*, 1918; *Senlin: A Biography and Other Poems*, 1918; *The House of Dust*, 1920; *Punch: The Immortal Liar*, 1921; *Priapus and the Pool*, 1922; *The Pilgrimage of Festus*, 1923; *Prelude*, 1929; *Priapus and the Pool and Other Poems*, 1925; *Selected Poems*, 1929; *John Deth: A Metaphysical Legend, and Other Poems*, 1930; *Gehenna*, 1930; *The Coming Forth by Day of Osiris Jones*, 1931; *Preludes for Memnon*, 1931; *And in the Hanging Gardens*, 1933; *Landscape West of Eden*, 1934; *Time in the Rock: Preludes to Definition*, 1936; *And in the Human Heart*, 1940; *Brownstone Eclogues and Other Poems*, 1942; *The Soldier: A Poem by Conrad Aiken*, 1944; *The Kid*, 1947; *Skylight One: Fifteen Poems*, 1949; *The Divine Pilgrim*, 1949; *Collected Poems*, 1953, 1970; *A Letter from Li Po and*

Other Poems, 1955; *The Fluteplayer*, 1956; *Sheepfold Hill: Fifteen Poems*, 1958; *Selected Poems*, 1961; *The Morning Song of Lord Zero*, 1963; *A Seizure of Limericks*, 1964; *Cats and Bats and Things with Wings: Poems*, 1965; *The Clerk's Journal*, 1971; *A Little Who's Zoo of Mild Animals*, 1977.

NONFICTION: *Skepticisms: Notes on Contemporary Poetry*, 1919; "Introduction," in *Two Wessex Tales by Thomas Hardy*, 1919; "Introduction," in *Selected Poems of Emily Dickinson*, 1924; *Ushant: An Essay*, 1952; *A Reviewer's ABC: Collected Criticism of Conrad Aiken from 1916 to the Present*, 1958; *Selected Letters of Conrad Aiken*, 1978.

ANTHOLOGIES: *A Comprehensive Anthology of American Poetry*, 1929; *Twentieth Century American Poetry*, 1944.

Bibliography

Butscher, Edward. *Conrad Aiken: Poet of White Horse Vale*. Athens: University of Georgia Press, 1988. A definitive biography, this lengthy, well-illustrated book relies heavily on psychological theory, mostly Freudian, and primary sources to trace Aiken's life. The bibliography is extremely helpful, including not only the standard items but also Aiken's edited anthologies and his critical essays, and a list of relevant psychological texts and studies.

Denney, Reuel. *Conrad Aiken*. Minneapolis: University of Minnesota Press, 1964. An early, short volume, which covers both Aiken's prose and his poetry, though the latter, especially in the case of *Senlin: A Biography and Other Poems*, receives more attention. Looks briefly at the novels and the short story "Silent Snow, Secret Snow," but is more interested in Aiken's experimental prose narrative, *Ushant: An Essay*. Includes a selected bibliography.

Hoffman, Frederick. *Conrad Aiken*. New York: Twayne, 1962. A useful volume on Aiken, offering a succinct reading, through a Freudian approach, of Aiken's prose and poetry, which Hoffman believes is Aiken's most significant literary contribution. Includes a chronology of Aiken's life, a bibliography of his work, and an annotated bibliography of the books and articles written about him.

Marten, Harry. *The Art of Knowing: The Poetry and Prose of Conrad Aiken*. Columbia: University of Missouri Press, 1988. Marten applies his knowledge of Aiken's life to his poetry and prose, which receive equal treatment in this critical study. *Senlin: A Biography and Other Poems* is at the center of Aiken's life and work, and the focus is on the narrative voice in the poems. The explications of poems are short because many are discussed. Includes a bibliography.

Martin, Jay. *Conrad Aiken: The Life of His Art*. Princeton, N.J.: Princeton University Press, 1962. After a general review of Aiken's reputation as a poet, traces the evolution of consciousness and self-awareness in Aiken's poetry. The approach is appropriately Freudian (Aiken was himself a Freudian); one chapter is entitled "Word, World, Wound." Stresses the experimental nature of Aiken's poetry, Martin seeing Aiken, partly because of the notion of poet as sage, as remarkably similar to W. B. Yeats.

WILLIAM HARRISON AINSWORTH

Born: Manchester, England; February 4, 1805
Died: Reigate, England; January 3, 1882

Principal long fiction

Sir John Chiverton, 1826 (with John Partington Aston); *Rookwood*, 1834; *Crichton*, 1837; *Jack Sheppard*, 1839; *The Tower of London*, 1840; *Guy Fawkes*, 1841; *Old Saint Paul's*, 1841; *The Miser's Daughter*, 1842; *Windsor Castle*, 1843; *Saint James's*, 1844; *James the Second*, 1848; *The Lancashire Witches*, 1849; *The Star-Chamber*, 1854; *The Flitch of Bacon*, 1854; *The Spendthrift*, 1856; *Mervyn Clitheroe*, 1858; *Ovingdean Grange*, 1860; *The Constable of the Tower*, 1861; *The Lord Mayor of London*, 1862; *Cardinal Pole*, 1863; *John Law*, 1864; *The Spanish Match*, 1865; *Auriol*, 1865; *The Constable de Bourbon*, 1866; *Old Court*, 1867; *Myddleton Pomfret*, 1868; *The South-Sea Bubble*, 1868; *Hilary St. Ives*, 1869; *Tower Hill*, 1871; *Talbot Harland*, 1871; *Boscobel*, 1872; *The Manchester Rebels of the Fatal '45*, 1872 (originally published as *The Good Old Times*); *Merry England*, 1874; *The Goldsmith's Wife*, 1875; *Preston Fight*, 1875; *The Leaguer of Latham*, 1876; *Chetwynd Calverley*, 1876; *The Fall of Somerset*, 1877; *Beatrice Tyldesley*, 1878; *Beau Nash*, 1879; *Stanley Brereton*, 1881.

Other literary forms

Most of William Harrison Ainsworth's work in forms other than the novel was limited to juvenilia. Before reaching nineteen, he had published dramas, poems, essays, tales, and translations in local Manchester periodicals. He also wrote several short books of verse and a brief political pamphlet before he became known as a novelist. Later, he contributed some reviews and verse to annuals and magazines. The songs and ballads scattered throughout his novels were collected for separate publication in 1855 and reprinted in 1872. Ainsworth's association with periodicals was long and significant. Most of his novels were first published as magazine serials. He edited *Bentley's Miscellany* (1839-1841 and 1854-1868), *Ainsworth's Magazine* (1842-1854), and the *New Monthly Magazine* (1846-1870).

Achievements

Ainsworth has often been considered the heir of Sir Walter Scott. After writing two books that were criticized for glamorizing criminals, he produced dozens of solid historical novels that were entertaining, moral, and educational. Some featured real historical figures; others used invented characters who took part in significant events. Ainsworth's books had vivid scenes and exciting conflicts. They were filled with accurate detail about costume, food, ceremony, and architecture. Although *Windsor Castle* and *The Tower of Lon-*

don were novels, generations of tourists used them for guidebooks. Ainsworth covered the significant monarchs that were too recent to be in William Shakespeare's plays. Most ordinary people in the nineteenth century had their sense of English history largely from Scott, Shakespeare, and Ainsworth.

Ainsworth, however, contributed virtually nothing to the development of the novel; he merely did—and not nearly so well—what Scott had done before him. The literary novel was turning to realistic social and psychological examinations of contemporary life. Ainsworth's significance is as an author and editor of popular literature. His books refined and preserved elements of popular theater and Gothic fiction, adapting them to mid-century modes of publication. His novels are characterized by heightened confrontations and recurring climaxes; the techniques of suspended narration and the resources of serial construction; supernatural excitements, vivid tableaux, and memorable spectacles; a preference for romantic underdogs; and moral simplicity. Ainsworth made these touchstones of popular writing briefly respectable and then handed them down to the authors who catered to the much broader mass reading public of the late nineteenth century.

Biography

William Harrison Ainsworth was born February 4, 1805, to a prosperous family in Manchester. His father was a solicitor who had a substantial house on a good street, a suburban summer residence, and a fondness for collecting information about crime and criminals. Even before he could read, Ainsworth adored his father's stories of highwaymen and ghosts. Although he was brought up in a strict atmosphere of Whiggism and Nonconformity, Ainsworth also grew to love lost causes. From early youth he adopted Jacobite and Tory ideals.

When he was twelve, Ainsworth was sent to the Manchester Free Grammar School. He became passionately fond of the stage, and from the age of fifteen wrote and acted plays with schoolboy friends. One of them, *Giotto: Or, The Fatal Revenge*, included a dreadful storm, terrible and mysterious events, signs of the supernatural, and minute descriptions of scenery, buildings, and costumes.

In the next few years, Ainsworth published anonymous or pseudonymous pieces in a number of magazines, briefly edited a periodical of his own, and wrote to Charles Lamb for advice about two metrical tales and three short songs that he published in 1822 as *Poems* by Cheviot Ticheburn. Leaving school at seventeen, Ainsworth became an articled clerk; in 1824, when his father died, he went to London for further legal education. At the age of twenty-one he qualified as a solicitor. In 1826, however—almost as soon as he had finished preparing to practice law—he published the historical romance he had written with a fellow clerk in Manchester, married Anne Frances ("Fanny") Ebers, and took over the publishing and bookselling branches of his father-in-law's business.

Ainsworth hoped to conduct a gentlemanly trade that would publish good books which were not popular enough for other publishing houses, but he soon found the prospects were not what he had imagined; although he met many authors and produced some good works, his firm's biggest success was a cookbook. In 1829, after returning briefly to law, he became part of the circle formed by William Maginn to contribute to *Fraser's Magazine for Town and Country*—a circle that included Theodore Hook, Samuel Taylor Coleridge, Thomas Carlyle, and William Makepeace Thackeray and was therefore intimately linked to literary fashion. Ainsworth started begging friends for plots. Finally, inspired by Ann Radcliffe's Gothic fiction, he published *Rookwood* in April, 1834, a work that was an immediate success with both critics and public.

The next ten or twelve years were Ainsworth's best. His novels sold phenomenally. For much of the time he was producing two at once: *Guy Fawkes* ran in *Bentley's Miscellany* between January, 1840, and November, 1841, while at the same time *The Tower of London* came out in monthly parts in 1840, and *Old Saint Paul's* was serialized in the *Sunday Times* during 1841. Even while writing two novels at once, Ainsworth was a successful and conscientious editor. He succeeded Charles Dickens at the helm of *Bentley's Miscellany* in 1839 and then, in 1842, began *Ainsworth's Magazine*. He was also a social celebrity who gave elaborate dinners for friends, including virtually everyone active in literature during the 1840's.

By the decade's end, Ainsworth was rerunning his early novels in *Ainsworth's Magazine* and repeating scenes and characters in the new books he wrote. In 1853 he moved to Brighton. Although he continued to write constantly for almost thirty more years and although, as an editor, he still influenced the course of popular fiction, he was no longer—physically, creatively, or socially—at the heart of nineteenth century literature.

Almost nothing is known of Ainsworth as a private person. Neither of his wives shared his public life. Fanny, who bore him three daughters, separated from him three years before she died in 1838. Sarah Wells, who gave him another daughter in 1867, was married to Ainsworth secretly some time before they moved to Reigate in 1878. There he continued to write for whatever he could earn. His last novel was being serialized in a provincial newspaper when he died on January 3, 1882.

Analysis

Popular fiction requires, above all else, a work that holds the reader's interest. The best popular authors, furthermore, are generally those who believe and delight in the books they write. William Harrison Ainsworth began to publish just after Sir Walter Scott's death. There was as yet no clearly discernible indication of the direction fiction would take, but there was a vogue for stories about history and crime. These topics suited Ainsworth's personal taste—his early interest in his father's tales, his love of acting exciting roles, his fondness for Scott, Lord Byron, Christopher Marlowe, and for Gothic novelists such as M. G. Lewis and Ann Radcliffe. Before long, the vogue for such stories had passed. Its other practitioners, including Charles Dickens, moved on to different styles and themes, but Ainsworth remained in the groove he had carved. His method of composition bred a narrative technique that secured the reader's involvement but did not encourage analytical thought. His mind was attracted by snatches of legend, by the mood surrounding a place, by the intensely realized scenes without antecedents or consequences that often feature in daydreams. His books have very complicated stories but often lack a plot in the sense of shape, point, or consequence. His most successful works gain apparent unity because they are linked to a single place or use a well-known historical event as a frame. Ainsworth was not creative in the broad sense; he depended on research because it supplied a mass of details which helped disguise the fact that he lacked Scott's ability to create the texture and spirit of the past. The accurate details also gave Ainsworth's books respectability for a mass public that was becoming increasingly self-conscious; historical distance permitted both Ainsworth and his readers to be emotionally involved in scenes of horror, conflict, and danger.

Ainsworth's stories are far too complicated to summarize. At least three or four series of events move simultaneously; typically, one is historical, one uses fictional characters acting in historical events, and a third involves comic figures. Each individual story line is itself intricate. In any plot, at any moment, present action may be suspended by the entrance of a stranger who proceeds to recount the course of his life to date, and the stranger's narrative may itself be suspended for its own internal interruptions. The method is not, strictly speaking, dramatic, because the reader is likely to forget just what question is driving the story onward. The individual scenes, however, are vividly realized. Inevitably, at the end of an installment, one set of characters is left dangling, and a new set is taken up in the next. Ainsworth's creative use of the breaks imposed by the medium (in this case serialization) and his control of lighting effects and angles of vision anticipate the techniques of popular film and television.

Especially useful for creating effects, the topics of history and the supernatural were used by Ainsworth because they supplied cruelty, torture, flight, combat, and chills down the spine, tools for the *manipulation of emotions*. The supernatural elements that appear in almost all of Ainsworth's novels are used primarily for effect; Ainsworth neither explains the uncanny events nor does he (as serious Gothic novelists would) explore the mystery of evil. The supernatural, such as murders, storms, and riots, arouses emotional response; and the unreality of the supernatural may, like the distance of history, help rationalist readers from an industrialized world to release emotions that are no longer acceptable in daily life.

Ainsworth virtually always has at least one character who is disguised, who is using a false name, or who has mysterious, confused, obscure parentage. After two or three of Ainsworth's books, the reader learns that one can never be certain who people really are. The stories of concealed parentage and shifting identity allow readers in the most humdrum circumstances to step imaginatively into the shoes of a countess, a knight, or even royal offspring, secure in the expectation that anyone might turn out to be royalty in disguise. The device is a psychological strategy for Ainsworth, the bourgeois son of a Nonconformist family from a bleak industrial town who chose to become a Royalist, a Tory, and a Jacobite. It is also a paradigm for the escapism beloved by readers who found themselves increasingly interchangeable cogs in the nineteenth century's bureaucratic and commercial machines.

An immediate best-seller, *Rookwood* not only is typical Ainsworth but also might serve as a model to teach generations of adventure writers about constructing narrative books. The opening sentence reveals two people seated in a burial vault at midnight. The rest of the long first paragraph holds the reader's curiosity about these people in abeyance while it describes the architecture and effigies of the mausoleum in order to create an air of foreboding. The first chapter alternates passages of partial exposition with scenes of strong emotion; the second chapter is a chase built from a series of captures, struggles, and escapes. At the chapter's climax, Luke Rookwood—the protagonist—dives into a pool and does not emerge; the chapter ends, leaving him underwater. The next several chapters introduce other characters, new lines of action, and a great deal more historical exposition before telling the reader what happened to Luke.

Rookwood virtually catalogs the devices made popular by Gothic novelists thirty years earlier. In the opening chapter, Ainsworth introduces the inheritance theme and Luke's confused parentage, a death omen, croaking ravens, a Gypsy Queen, a preserved corpse with a significant ring on its finger, an evil Jesuit, a moving statue, a dead hand, and writing on the wall. The rest of the book supplies duels between relatives, a deathbed curse, a runaway bride, a portrait that changes expression, underground caverns, a supernatural summons, a miniature with an inscription that gives a clue to the past, a rediscovered marriage certificate, secret passageways, stormy nights, an interrupted burial, a purely incidental death by thunderbolt, corpses swaying from the gibbet, talismans, a deserted priory where gypsies dwell, a character who masquerades as a ghost, infallible prophecies in verse, love potions, a marriage in a subterranean shrine (formerly an anchorite's cell) with a corpse on the altar, disguises, a bride substituted for another in the dark, a heroine drugged into passivity, a battle between gypsies and highwaymen, and a faithless lover who dies from kissing a poisoned lock of hair. In the final scene, the villainess is shoved by a statue into a sarcophagus, where she perishes.

Like the typical Gothic romance, *Rookwood* has a Byronic hero of mixed good and evil (Luke), a persecuted maiden (Eleanor), and a romantic hero who gets the girl (Ranulph). Ranulph and Eleanor are uninteresting, and even Luke is not very successful; he arouses some sympathy at the outset because he is an underdog, but his transformation to villain is not explored fully enough to be convincing. To berate Ainsworth for lack of originality, however, is to miss the point. He used the traditional Gothic devices for the very reason that they were conventional; they had become a code, an emotional shorthand that triggered known responses. Ainsworth was thus able to control the reader's mood, orchestrate the emotional response, and build to repeated transports of excitement.

The most interesting character in *Rookwood* is Dick Turpin, the highwayman. He appears in an outstanding sequence that has little to do with the book's plot: after accidentally killing one of his friends, Turpin rides with a pistol in each hand and the reins between his teeth, barely ahead of pursuers, the entire distance from London to York. The action peaks every twenty miles or so when Turpin encounters characters from the main plot or exerts a superhuman effort to outfight or outrun the law.

Rookwood was almost totally unplanned; Ainsworth's visit to a gloomy mansion inspired him to attempt a deliberate imitation of Ann Radcliffe. He researched thieves' cant so he could include English highwaymen in place of Italian bandits; he interspersed dramatic songs, comic ballads, and gypsy dances as if he were writing a melodrama for the stage; and he decided how to solve the mysteries as he went along. The most telling indication of Ainsworth's relationship to his work is that he wrote the twenty-five thousand words of Turpin's ride to York in a day and a night of continuous work. He was so fully absorbed by the scene and its emotion that he continuously wrote until it was finished.

Setting remained an essential stimulus to Ainsworth's imagination. The architectural-historical books, of which *The Tower of London* is a good example, were largely responsible for his reputation as a novelist who supplied education along with the excitement. The single setting and the historical events should have helped Ainsworth focus the novel. The story that he chose, however, illuminates the artistic difficulties that grew from his ability to become wholly absorbed in his characters' emotions.

The Tower of London covers the struggle for the throne between the Protestant Lady Jane Grey and the Catholic Queen Mary. The book opens with a magnificent processional, described in exhaustive detail from contemporary sources. Within the frame of this processional, Ainsworth dangles passages of historical exposition, scenes from an assassination conspiracy, confrontations between as-yet-unidentified characters, a thunderstorm, a warning from an old crone, a moment of love at first sight, and other elements that establish emotional tone and provide the narrative hook. The handling of the historical plot line, however, shows how little the story element mattered to Ainsworth; he frequently reminds readers of the outcome already determined by history so that curiosity about the ending is not a prime motive for reading on.

The book is a good example of Ainsworth's visual imagination and the reciprocal influence of novel and stage. Ainsworth worked closely with his illustrator, George Cruikshank. After their previous collaboration on *Jack Sheppard*, they had seen that Cruikshank's illustrations were almost immediately turned into living tableaux for stage versions of the book. Before beginning each monthly part of *The Tower of London*, Ainsworth and Cruikshank visited the Tower together and decided on the exact setting. They examined the architectural detail, explored the possibilities for light and shadow and composing human forms, and decided what events would take place. Ainsworth apparently learned from the stage how to control the source of light. He conceals the identity of characters by showing them in profile against backlight; he blinds onlookers with sudden brightness; and, inevitably, he extinguishes candles or torches at crucial moments.

Ainsworth continued to manipulate feelings by using dungeons, secret passageways, and torture chambers; he describes—with full detail—a martyr burned at the stake and a prisoner gnawed by rats. The humor supplied in a running subplot about three giants and a dwarf is also largely visual. Ainsworth has trouble linking the characters from history with the fictional people acting out his typical story of concealed birth, attempted seduction, and true love. The historical scenes are sometimes well realized, in particular the scenes between Lady Jane and Lord Dudley that dramatize the conflict of patriotism and faith. Nevertheless, Ainsworth's emotional connection to the characters—which makes the scenes so powerful—virtually prevents him from shaping any opinion on the moral conflict. Although the book depicts a struggle in which Queen Mary is generally seen as the villain, he cannot despise her. At any given moment, his sympathy is entirely engaged by the character at the center of the scene he is writing. Thus, even with the Tower imposing unity, the book remains a collection of vivid fragments.

By the time of *Old Saint Paul's*, serious literary critics were beginning to dismiss Ainsworth and his novels. The best they could say was that his books were educational, but Richard H. Horne, in *A New Spirit of the Age* (1844), objected that even the history was nothing but "old dates, old names, old houses, and old clothes" and called *Old Saint Paul's* "generally dull, except when it is revolting." Part of the problem, for critics, was the simple fact that Ainsworth had become so popular. *Old Saint Paul's* was apparently the first novel serialized in an English newspaper. The *Sunday Times* paid Ainsworth one thousand pounds for first rights alone; after the book had run in weekly installments through 1841, he was able to sell it again in monthly parts, in three volumes, and in a steady stream of cheap, illustrated, and popular editions. It is still available in inexpensive form.

Artistically, the book is one of Ainsworth's most competent; a coherent invention integrates the history, the melodrama, and even the comedy. The story follows London grocer Stephen Bloundel and his family through the plague of 1665 and the fire of 1666. Most of the characters are fictional, although one historical person, the libertine Earl of Rochester, provides a unifying strand by pursuing the grocer's blue-eyed daughter Amabel from one end of the tale to the other. The story lines are adroitly interwoven (perhaps because Ainsworth was not tied to actual historical confrontations); the comic subplot involving a hypochondriac servant advances and comments on the main action while it supplies laughs. Memorable minor characters include the plundering nurse Judith Malmayns and the religious fanatic Solomon Eagle.

As always, Ainsworth is best at painting scenes. There are unforgettable pictures of London with green grass in the streets, of live burials and mass graves, of Saint Paul's filled with victims of plague, of King Charles II in a mad masque of death. In *Rookwood* (as in Gothic novels) the past simply provides distance and strangeness; it gives readers an excuse to enjoy vicariously passion, cruelty, and sheer excitement. *Old Saint Paul's* allows the same indulgence of feelings, but the novel's scenes of death and sexual passion have a legitimate relationship to the heightened sense of life and death implicit in the historical events.

The moral outlook of *Old Saint Paul's* suggests one reason why Ainsworth remained popular with middle-class and lower-middle-class readers long after the literary mainstream had left him behind. The grocer Stephen Bloundel is a rock of individualism and self-sufficiency; as a husband and a father he knows what is best for his family, rules with an iron hand, and preserves not only their lives but also (even in the face of fire) most of their goods. The protagonist—Bloundel's apprentice Leonard Holt—is intelligent, industrious, ambitious, loyal, and as successful as any Horatio Alger hero. His master makes him a partner; his suggestions about fighting the fire are so practical that King Charles gives him a title. Furthermore, his girl friend turns out to be an heiress in disguise and somehow, during the week of unrelieved fire-fighting, he manages to acquire new clothes suited to his improved station in life. Although Rochester and his crowd are seen as evil libertines through most of the book, Leonard has no ill-feeling toward them at the end. This paradoxical moral attitude—which despises the upper classes for idleness and sexuality yet rewards the industrious hero by giving him wealth and a title—is virtually universal in the cheap literature of mid-century.

The historical vein supplied boundaries and permissable exaggerations that gave free play to what Ainsworth could do well. He was much less successful when he attempted a partly autobiographical book in the manner of Dickens' *David Copperfield* (1849), his was entitled *Mervyn Clitheroe*; or, when he wrote sensation novels (including *Old Court*, *Myddleton Pomfret*, and *Hilary St. Ives*). The most popular form of the 1860's (and the direct ancestor of thrillers and detective stories), the sensation novel required tight plotting and a convincing contemporary milieu; Ainsworth's modern tales used his typical devices of misplaced inheritance, concealed identity, and inexplicable supernatural events, but the gaps tended to show when the actors wore modern dress.

If he was not particularly adept at writing sensation novels, however, Ainsworth was good at finding people who could. His middlebrow popular magazines effectively encouraged tight serial construction, the accumulation of incidents, and the interweaving of plots so that each installment could end in suspense. He discovered and encouraged two of the bestselling authors of the 1860's and 1870's, Ouida (Marie Louise de la Ramée) and Mrs. Henry Wood, whose famous *East Lynne* was written for *New Monthly Magazine* between 1859 and 1861 when Ainsworth was its editor. He reputedly read all submissions and wrote letters of advice to young authors. He also knew how to promote himself and was not above giving dinners to cultivate the influential librarian Charles Edward Mudie.

After the success of *Rookwood* in 1834, Ainsworth was a novelist everyone read. His first books were reviewed by leading journals; Ainsworth's *Jack Sheppard* sold more copies on first appearance than did Dickens' *Oliver Twist*, which came out at the same time. By the late 1860's, though, some of Ainsworth's novels were published only in penny magazines and sixpenny paperback editions. By the end of the century, he was generally considered boys' reading, a novelist to be classed with such writers as Frederick Marryat and G. A. Henty.

Ainsworth had not changed; the novel and the reading public had. The division between mass literature and serious literature grew wider as the number of literate consumers for popular fiction burgeoned. Eight of Ainsworth's novels ran as serials in *Bow Bells*, a penny-weekly magazine that featured household advice and needlework patterns; the romantic-historical-Gothic mode continued popular in *Bow Bells* and persisted as a women's escapist form into the twentieth century. At a Manchester testimonial in 1881, it was said that the Free Library had 250 volumes of Ainsworth's works in order to meet the demand by readers from the artisan class. The influence of his technique can be traced, finally, through the Jack Harkaway serials at the end of the century and on into the Hardy Boys books—which share with Ainsworth's best novels the spooky buildings, caves and underground passages, the effective use of lighting, the suspended narration, and the exclamation marks at the end of chapters.

Sally Mitchell

Other major work

POETRY: *Ballads*, 1855.

Bibliography

Abbey, Cherie D. ed. *Nineteenth-Century Literature Criticism*. Detroit: Gale
  Research, 1986. Cites Ainsworth as a "minor but celebrated Victorian
  novelist." Presents his writing in its two forms, the Newgate novels and the
  historical romances, and includes some biographical details. Also includes
  extracts from reviews and essays from the 1830's through 1979, which are
  helpful in assessing critical responses to Ainsworth.

Hollingsworth, Keith. *The Newgate Novel, 1830-1847: Bulwer, Ainsworth,
  Dickens, and Thackeray*. Detroit: Wayne State University Press, 1963. Discusses the Newgate theme in nineteenth century literature, including critical commentary on Ainsworth's Newgate fiction and his association with
  Charles Dickens and E. M. Forster. Valuable for placing Ainsworth in this
  genre. Also covers his later writings and his work as editor of *New Monthly
  Magazine*.

Kelly, Patrick. "William Ainsworth." In *Victorian Novelists After 1885*. Vol. 1
  in *Dictionary of Literary Biography*, edited by Ira B. Nadel and William E.
  Fredeman. Detroit: Gale Research, 1983. Provides some helpful background
  information on Ainsworth's early years, the influences on his writing, and
  his later years as an editor. Cites *Rookwood* and *Jack Sheppard* as novels
  worthy of attention, and also discusses his third novel, *Crichton*. Notes the
  influence of Sir Walter Scott on Ainsworth's historical novels. Considers
  Ainsworth an important figure of literary culture in the 1830's and 1840's,
  despite his inability to adapt to changing times and new readers.

Maxwell, Richard. "City Life and the Novel: Hugo, Ainsworth, Dickens."
  Comparative Literature 30 (Spring, 1978): 157-171. Maxwell notes that
  Ainsworth's unfinished *Revelations of London* (1845-1846) and *Old Saint
  Paul's* reflect Ainsworth's fascination with French literature. Concedes that
  there are strengths in *Revelations*, but faults it for the lack of plot development. A partially favorable commentary; however, portrays Ainsworth in
  his later years as an "aimless eccentric without a place in the modern
  world."

Worth, George J. *William Harrison Ainsworth*. New York: Twayne, 1972.
  Worth's full-length study of Ainsworth cites him as an "intriguing novelist . . . who deserves to be read." Discusses the major aspects of his
  writing, along with some background information on his long life, but does
  not deal with his short stories, poems, and plays. A sympathetic study of
  Ainsworth, valuable in part because there is so little current secondary
  material available.

RICHARD ALDINGTON

Born: Portsmouth, England; July 8, 1892
Died: Sury-en-Vaux, France; July 27, 1962

Principal long fiction
Death of a Hero, 1929; *The Colonel's Daughter*, 1931; *All Men Are Enemies*, 1933; *Women Must Work*, 1934; *Very Heaven*, 1937; *Seven Against Reeves*, 1938; *Rejected Guest*, 1939; *The Romance of Casanova*, 1946.

Other literary forms
Richard Aldington was one of the principal imagist poets. His imagist poems each render one impression of a scene, and most of them are short. "Whitechapel," which is frequently anthologized, evokes the sounds and sights of a particular section of London. His poems were collected in small volumes, including *Images* (1915) and *Images of War* (1919), among many others. The full range of his poetic skills can be seen in *The Complete Poems of Richard Aldington* (1948).

Aldington conceived masterfully ironic short stories. Set in England in the modern period, these stories frequently pit an individual idealist against a hypocritical society. *Roads to Glory* (1930) and *Soft Answers* (1932) contain the best of these contemporary sketches.

Aldington's translations of French, Italian, Greek, and Latin poems, fiction, and prose number more than twenty-eight volumes, including among others, poems by Folgore Da San Gemignano which Aldington entitled *The Garland of Months* (1917), Voltaire's *Candide and Other Romances* (1927), Julien Benda's *The Great Betrayal* (1928), and *The Decameron of Giovanni Boccaccio* (1930).

Aldington's literary reviews and critical studies demonstrate his scholarship, his genial wit, and his delight in the critical evaluation of contemporary and classical literature. His astounding capacity for work enabled him to produce hundreds of entertaining and informative essays of literary history and criticism. His introductions to the 1953 Penguin editions of D. H. Lawrence are valuable for their personal and critical insight. Aldington's collected short essays, most of them originally published as review essays in periodicals, include: *Literary Studies and Reviews* (1924), *French Studies and Reviews* (1926), and *Artifex: Sketches and Ideas* (1935).

His biographical and critical studies delighted and infuriated readers. Aldington wrote his first biography, *Voltaire* (1925), about the satirist who shared Aldington's skepticism. The next two biographies championed the work of a contemporary novelist, then under attack: *D. H. Lawrence: An Indiscretion* (1927) and *D. H. Lawrence: A Complete List of His Works, Together with a Critical Appreciation* (1935). *The Duke, Being an Account of the Life & Achievements of Arthur Wellesley, 1st Duke of Wellington* (1943) was Aldington's most popular historical biography; for this rollicking life story, Aldington won the James Tait Black Memorial Prize in 1947. The great majority of his critical biographies were published after Aldington ceased to write satirical fiction. Of interest to literary historians are his later studies of contemporary writers: *D. H. Lawrence: Portrait of a Genius But . . .* (1950), *Ezra Pound and T. S. Eliot, A Lecture* (1954), *A. E. Housman and W. B. Yeats, Two Lectures* (1955), and *Lawrence L'Imposteur: T. E. Lawrence, the Legend and the Man* (1954). The Prix de Gratitute Mistralienne was awarded to Aldington's *Introduction to Mistral* (1956).

Achievements

Aldington, judged on the basis of his contemporary influence as a poet, reviewer, and novelist, should be regarded as one of the major modernists; that his current reputation fails to match his achievements evidences the uncertainties of literary fame. His best-selling novel, *Death of a Hero*, despite its enormous popularity in the decade after its publication in English and its many translations, is out of print and will probably remain unavailable. Sparked by the publication of various collections of his letters, there has been a revival of interest in Aldington as a literary figure who knew other writers, but there has not been a comparable resurgence of scholarly interest in his work. His biographical studies of D. H. and T. E. Lawrence were widely read and almost as widely denounced when first published, because they presented brutally honest portraits of their subjects; in the context of current literary biographies, their critical attitude toward lionized literary greats seems measured, and perhaps even mild. Aldington's literary essays are models of clear, evaluative prose. His imagist poems, which were lauded by other poets and critics of poetry when first published, still seem fresh, though the Imagist movement ended more than fifty years ago. Aldington's long fiction appealed to a large reading public, who delighted in his satire, his wit, and his richly detailed portraits of contemporary culture.

Biography

Richard Aldington was born Edward Godfree Aldington in Portsmouth, England, on July 8, 1892. *Life for Life's Sake: A Book of Reminiscences* (1941), his genial autobiography, presents an amusing, cordial, and meticulously honest persona to his readers. That version of Aldington's personality is also celebrated in *Richard Aldington: An Intimate Portrait* (1965), sketches written by twenty-two people who knew him (including Roy Campbell, Lawrence Durrell, T. S. Eliot, Herbert Read, Alec Waugh, and Henry Williamson), and lovingly collected by Alister Kershaw and Frédéric-Jacques Temple. Those letters which have been published—*A Passionate Prodigality*, Aldington's letters to Alan Bird, 1949-1962 (1975) and *Literary Lifelines*, correspondence between Richard Aldington and Lawrence Durrell (1981)—reveal a witty, considerate, and self-deprecating egotist, who could, when angered by incompetence, hypocrisy, or prejudice, portray his target in a pitiless satire; he could also ridicule weaknesses in friends and in writers he greatly admired. The subjects were not always able to see the humor in his satirical sketches.

Contradicting the more generous interpretations of Aldington's character and behavior, there is the unflattering fictionalized portrait of Rafe in *Bid Me to Live* (1960), a novel by H. D. (Hilda Doolittle, Aldington's wife from 1913 to 1938, though their marriage dissolved during World War I). Until the forthcoming biography of Aldington by Charles Doyle is published, a completely accurate and detailed account of his life will be impossible; it is possible, however, to divide his long literary career into four broad phases: imagist poet from 1912 to 1919; literary essayist and translator from 1919 to 1928; novelist from 1928 to 1938; and critical biographer from 1939 to 1957.

From his childhood, Aldington recalled with pleasure long walks through the English country unspoiled by automobile traffic, his observations as an amateur naturalist and astronomer, and freely reading romances and British poetry in his father's large, general library. He also remembered, and satirized in his novels, the sentimentality, patriotic chauvinism, and narrow philistine manners of middle-class, Victorian citizens in the city of Dover. Like the hero of his novel, *Rejected Guest*, Aldington attended University College, London, and, like the hero of *Very Heaven*, he was forced to leave college by his father's financial failure. In 1911, Aldington began his professional career by reporting sporting events for a London newspaper and, in his spare time, writing poetry for publication. He was introduced to Ezra Pound and H. D. by Brigit Patmore, and he soon met Harold Monro, William Butler Yeats, May Sinclair, and Ford Madox Ford.

Aldington's first literary life, which ended in World War I, was given focus by his relationship with H. D. (they were married in October, 1913) and his involvement in the Imagist movement in poetry. Aldington credits H. D. with writing the first imagist poems, influenced by Greek forms, written in the free verse of the French symbolists. The imagists avoided the florid language of Georgian poetry by paring images to concrete, exact details and revising for concise, clear diction. In Aldington's view, H. D.'s aesthetic sense influenced his poetry, and also that of D. H. Lawrence and Amy Lowell. The point of Aldington's exaggeration, surely, is to remove Pound from the leadership of the imagists, and he insists that Pound merely named the group, arranged for the first publications in the Chicago magazine, *Poetry*, in 1912, and organized the first anthology, entitled *Des Imagistes*, in 1914. Critical of Pound's despotic editorship, Aldington clearly preferred the democratic efficiency of Lowell, who organized and published three volumes entitled *Some Imagist Poets*, in 1915, 1916, and 1917. These three volumes included the work of Aldington, H. D., John Gould Fletcher, F. S. Flint, D. H. Lawrence, and Lowell. Aldington himself organized one more collection, *Imagist Anthology* (1930), but his imagist poetry, which was written simultaneously with that of H. D., belongs to his prewar world. The English periodical that became home for imagist poetry was *The Egoist*, formerly *The New Freewoman*, managed by Dora Marsden and Harriet Shaw Weaver, with Aldington as its literary editor from 1914 to 1916, sharing the post with H. D. once he entered the army.

Aldington's attitude toward fiction-writing and some of his style as a novelist were certainly influenced by Ford, whom Aldington served as a private secretary while Ford was composing *The Good Soldier* (1915), his novel about the collapse of an era, and *When Blood Is Their Argument* (1915), a propagandist attack on German culture. The psychologically unbalanced narrator, the convoluted time of the narrative, and the ranting tone of Aldington's *Death of a Hero* owe much to Ford's writing during the first year of the war. Aldington singles out Ford's war tetralogy, *Parade's End* (1924-1928), for praise, and it is useful to remember that Aldington wrote his own war book after Ford's had been published. Ford assumes an almost mythic place in Aldington's literary history, as one of the last Englishmen to believe in and support a republic of letters. For Aldington, the war destroyed that idealistic world, and the war itself forced a painful break in his life.

Feeling his duty but denying all moral aims of war, Aldington volunteered in 1916 and served until February of 1919, concluding his service as a captain in the army, and returning to England with lingering shell shock. His wartime experiences appear in deliberately phantasmagoric descriptions in *Death of a Hero*, and his postwar nightmares are described in *All Men Are Enemies*. During the war, he had begun an affair with Dorothy Yorke (their relationship continued until 1928) and separated from his wife. A fictionalized account of Aldington's choice between wife and lover may be found in George Winterbourne's complicated relations with Elizabeth and Fanny in *Death of a Hero*, but the physical appearance of the two women has been interchanged. Aldington's version of H. D.'s wartime life, her refusal of sexual relations with him, the birth of her daughter, Perdita (whose father's identity she concealed), her subsequent pneumonia, and her recovery under the care of Bryher (Winifred Ellerman), may be found fictionalized in *Women Must Work*.

The second phase in Aldington's literary career began when Ellerman persuaded her father, Sir John Ellerman, to use his influence to arrange a job for Aldington as a critic of French literature with *The Times Literary Supplement*. With that steady income, and the royalties from his poems and translations, Aldington and Yorke settled in a cottage in Berkshire formerly occupied by D. H. Lawrence. Aldington satirizes the stultifying social hierarchy and the narrow cultural life of provincial England after the war in *The Colonel's Daughter*. During this period, Aldington developed his new friendships with Herbert Read, who shared his experience in the war, and T. S.

Eliot, whom he portrayed satirically in *Stepping Heavenward* (1931). In 1926, during the general strike, Aldington, like the hero of *All Men Are Enemies*, worked to bring out *The Times*, and he witnessed the violence between workers and police. He also strengthened his old friendship with D. H. Lawrence, as they discussed their growing alienation from their native land.

The beginning of the third phase in his literary life was in 1928: he began writing his first novel, he decided to leave England, and he broke off his affair with Dorothy Yorke to begin one with Brigit (Ethel Elizabeth) Patmore (their relationship lasted until 1938). By 1928, Aldington was receiving an adequate income in royalties from his accumulated publications, and he was able to move to Paris. There he met Hart Crane, Ernest Hemingway, James Joyce, and Thomas Wolfe, and became close friends with Jean Paulhan. He began writing *Death of a Hero* in Paulhan's resort house on Isle de Port-Cros. *Death of a Hero* was an enormously popular success, was published in numerous translations, and increased Aldington's financial security. During the decade of 1928 to 1938, he wrote seven novels satirizing British culture. His travels through Italy, Spain, and Portugal made him acutely aware of the changing political scene, and, in 1935, he relocated in the New World, as Lawrence had done earlier. After a short period in New York, he moved to a farm in Connecticut, where he remained during World War II.

In 1938, Aldington broke his relationship with Patmore, divorced H. D., and married Netta McCulloch, the ex-wife of Patmore's son. His new marriage produced a much beloved daughter, Catherine, who remained with her father after the marriage dissolved in 1950. From July, 1944, through April, 1946, Aldington worked in Los Angeles, writing movie scripts and completing *The Romance of Casanova*. At the end of that period, disenchanted with American culture, Aldington returned to France.

Aldington wrote no more novels, concentrating on critical biographies, including *Lawrence L'Imposteur* (1954), demythologizing Lawrence of Arabia, with disastrous consequences to his own reputation and sales. Aldington's carefully researched book demolished the heroic myth that T. E. Lawrence had created in *Seven Pillars of Wisdom* (1926), but the reading public chose to remain loyal to the romantic Lawrence of Arabia. That critical biography so damaged Aldington's credibility that his own novels declined in popularity and in critical acclaim. Aldington's satirical fiction became associated with his attack on Lawrence, and a myth of Aldington as the bitter, unbalanced, even envious writer overshadowed most subsequent evaluations of his work.

Financial difficulties resulting from the hostile response to his *Lawrence L'Imposteur* required Aldington to live a quiet life, in a cottage near Sury-en-Vaux. In his seventieth year, he accepted an invitation to visit the Soviet Union, where he was lionized for his sharp critiques of British culture (his equally biting satires of Communist fanatics were quietly ignored). Shortly after his return to France in 1962, Aldington died.

Analysis

Richard Aldington, one of the generation who were young adults in 1914, felt compelled to chronicle the impact of World War I on English culture and society, and all seven of his novels published between the wars explore some aspect of that obsession. Only the first of these novels describes the war itself, but all of them portray the social degeneration which Aldington connected with World War I. This fiction satirizes English class snobbery, moral hypocrisy, selfish commercialism, insensitivity to art, faddish adherence to publicized avant-garde figures, and a culpable ignorance of sexual feelings, which the Victorian generation repressed and the generation of 1914 indulged without restraint, with disastrous consequences.

Aldington's great war novel, *Death of a Hero*, though a popular success, was sharply criticized as a ranting, inartistic piece of writing. D. H. Lawrence, having read the manuscript, warned his friend, "if you publish this, you'll lose what reputation you have—you're plainly on your way to an insane asylum." Early reviewers found the novel's style "uncontrolled," "exasperatingly diffuse," and "puerile." Aldington let himself in for a flood of misguided critical response, because he disregarded the modernist preference for authorial impassivity. Eschewing the example of Gustave Flaubert and Joyce, Aldington found his models in Laurence Sterne and Ford Madox Ford. In *Death of a Hero*, as in Sterne's *The Life and Opinion of Tristram Shandy*, (1759-1767) and Ford's *The Good Soldier* (1915), readers find discursive narration, defense of feeling, confusion of author and narrator, temporal dislocation, polemical intrusion, and a tone shifting unexpectedly from angry indignation to ironic self-mockery.

Working through a monomaniacal narrator, Aldington nevertheless orders his madman's chaotic discourse by suggesting three formal analogies for the novel: a threnody, a tragedy, and a symphony. A threnody is a funeral lamentation which may be written as a choral ode or as a monody; Aldington chose the single-voiced monody, and the narrator's personality, disturbed by his war experience, distorts the story significantly, as a detailed analysis of Aldington's novel reveals. For example, the narrator begins speculating, "I sometimes think that George committed suicide in that last battle of the war," but by the time he narrates the death, the suicide is not a speculation, but a fact. By revealing the death of his hero at the beginning, the narrator rejects suspense; as in the performance of a Greek tragedy, the emotive and intellectual response of the audience is manipulated not by the facts of the case, but by the rendition. Although the narrator specifically mentions Aeschylus' *Oresteia* (458 B.C.), the analogy to his tragic tale is by contrast. Both heroes are tormented by Furies, but Athena, goddess of war and wisdom, intervenes at Orestes' trial to give Apollo's logic triumph over the Furies' passion; in George's war, there is no logical resolution, and the desire for revenge creates a war of attrition—significantly George dies in the final year of World War I.

The symphonic form of the novel is emphasized in the tempo markings given to the four sections. The Prologue, dealing with the postwar world, is marked "allegretto," suggesting the spasmodic grasping for pleasures as a response to the suppressed guilt of the survivors in the 1920's. In Part II, "vivace" sets the pace of England's economic growth in the 1890's, which is connected with the fanatical patriotism of the Boer War, with an affected enthusiasm for culture, and with hypocritical attitudes toward sexuality. In Part III, "andante cantabile" marks the self-satisfied ease of the Georgian era, just before the war. The war itself is treated in Part IV, "adagio," a funeral march commemorating the death of George's generation. As in a symphony, there are several repeated and counterpointed motifs. "Bread and babies" is one of these motifs, linking economic growth and demands with increased population and ignorance about contraception. The "bread and babies" motif is heard in the narration of George's marriage and early career, in the sordid story of his parents' courtship and marriage, and, during the war, as one analysis of the forces making war inevitable. This motif is interwoven with others throughout the narrative, creating a complex pattern unlike the linear structure of a polemical speech. Neither an unedited memoir of a shell-shocked veteran nor a propagandistic tract, this novel is distinguished by its formal composition.

Aldington's deliberate use of sentiment, of repetition, of discontinuities in narrative time, of digressions, and of sudden shifts in mood reflect not only his narrator's postwar hysteria, but also his decision to address his readers' affective responses. Working in the tradition of Sterne and Ford, Aldington wrote a satiric novel that attempted to chronicle the transitional years from 1890 to 1918 in English cultural history.

Aldington's second novel, *The Colonel's Daughter*, demonstrates his control of a satiric narrative and his mastery of psychological and realistic detail, but the subject, Georgie Smithers, while sympathetically analyzed, is a caricature. A plain girl, Georgie fully shares the narrow cultural and moral perspective of her parents, unquestioning servants to the British Empire. Despite her service as a volunteer nurse, she has been untouched by the revolution in manners and morals introduced by war. She still wears her hair long, unbobbed, and her dress resembles a girl guide's uniform. A knowledgeable narrator presents Georgie's actions and some of her thoughts, offering occasional judgments; supplementing the narrator is a skeptical character, Purfleet, whose attitude toward Georgie shifts from amusement, to pity, to infatuation, to calculating irony. Naïvely, she reveals her desire to be married in her declaration, "I adore babies," and she would make any sincere man of her class a docile, faithful wife; unfortunately, there are few such relics left in her world. The one candidate who fortuitously appears, having been isolated from change by his position as civil servant in the colonies, treats her as a sister, and is easily seduced by a more fashionably amoral girl. Georgie reveals her compassionate nature and essential human goodness as she defends a working-class girl who becomes pregnant before she is married. Once Georgie overcomes her shock, she acts generously and intelligently to arrange a marriage, a job, and a home for the girl. As the reader contrasts her character with the mean-spirited people around her, Aldington's critique of English morality emerges. Under Purfleet's guidance, Georgie awakens to her own sexual desires, but she attracts no acceptable mate. After her father's death, Georgie finds herself fully conscious of being trapped in her poverty, in her duty to her mother, and in her solitude.

Appended to the novel is a short satiric and farcical epilogue, in which Bim and Bom, two Russians, attack the economic and social bases of English culture. In style and mood, this epilogue differs radically from the body of this sentimental, psychologically realistic novel, but Aldington's attack on hypocrisy, materialistic values, social injustice, and prudery remains the same.

All Men Are Enemies, Aldington's third novel, presents the odyssey of Anthony Clarendon from 1900 to 1927. Like Homer, Aldington begins his modern odyssey with a council of gods determining the fate of his hero. Athena, goddess of wisdom, gives the hero the gift of loving truth—clearly not the gift of devious Odysseus. Aphrodite places him under her erotic influence. Artemis, goddess of pain in childbirth, promises to stir up hatred for Clarendon. Ares promises him strength. The exiled goddess Isis, whom Aldington introduces to Zeus's council, dooms the hero to seek a lost beauty and an impossible perfection. Until the last pages of this novel, the curse of Isis prevails.

The first part of Clarendon's life includes his intellectual and emotional education, his first loves, and ends in 1914, as he parts from his perfect mate, Katha, an Austrian with whom he has enjoyed an ideal affair. The literary source of Katha's primal eroticism may be glimpsed in the D. H. Lawrentian name of her English aunt, Gudrun. The war separates these lovers, and the remaining three-fourths of the novel chronicles Clarendon's long, painful journey back to Katha.

Aldington skillfully describes the vivid nightmares and suicidal apathy of the war veteran, Clarendon, who condemns the meaningless frivolity and opportunism of postwar society. Clarendon's roots in prewar English culture have been destroyed, not only by his wartime experience of the blind hatred, nor by the deaths, but also by the pressures to conform: he observes, with profound regret, a friend encased by "a facetious social personality so long and carefully played up to that it had ended by destroying the real personality." He avoids that fate by leaving England, separating from his wife, and aimlessly traveling in Europe. By chance, a mutual acquaintance helps him relocate Katha, and they are reunited after a speedy automobile pursuit, a rough boat ride, and a tenderly hesitant courtship. As Odysseus is reconciled with Penelope, so Clarendon and Katha resume their idyllic love. The novel's conclusion celebrates the future happiness of these two battered survivors, their passion freely expressed. However improbable, the romantic denouement seems to fulfill Clarendon's wish that the postwar world not be as superficial as he had believed. Aldington's subsequent novels are less optimistic.

Women Must Work addresses the tragedy, as Aldington sees it, of the liberated career woman, who, despite her idealistic dreams, becomes selfish, unconsciously repeats the mistakes of her parents' generation, and, consequently, fails to enjoy her financial and social success. Etta Morison's culturally narrow childhood in a bourgeois family instills in her a desire to escape from restraint. Introduced to the woman suffrage movement by a friend named Vera, Etta plans her escape, learning the clerical skills by which she hopes to earn an independent living. Her strategy, advancement through education, has been a successful formula for heroes of the *Bildungsroman*, but, for a young woman, education opens fewer doors. Without her family's approval, Etta flees to London, finds a cheap room in a nearly respectable boardinghouse, and takes an underpaid job she hopes will lead to advancement; instead, it leads to near starvation and an improper proposal from her boss.

Unlike the unfortunate, fallen heroines of the naturalistic novel, Etta escapes the corrupting forces of her environment and moves into a better situation. She throws herself onto the mercy of a kind, wealthy woman devoted to woman suffrage and is hired as her personal secretary. As in a traditional romance, Etta falls in love with an attractive young nephew, but she scruples to take advantage of her position within her benefactor's house. The war separates the confessed lovers and then almost unites them, but Etta, after preparing for and promising her lover all the sexual joy she had previously denied him, again refuses, because her brother has been declared missing at the front. The young man, frustrated and uncomprehending, does not communicate with her again until the war's end, but then returns to attempt a reconciliation, only to find Etta pregnant by a wartime lover who has abandoned her. Unable to trust a man's fidelity, Etta rejects her soldier and turns to Vera, and the two women retreat into a pastoral cottage, where Etta's daughter is born. Their futile attempts to manage a farm reflect Aldington's own postwar experience and also demonstrates the impracticality of a pastoral retreat from the problems of the modern world. Casting off the faithful Vera, Etta rises again with the assistance of yet another woman, who launches her on a successful career in advertising—an occupation selected to symbolize the postwar commercial society. There is no moral triumph in her success once she returns to the city. Etta succeeds in advertising because she has learned to use people and to manipulate their desires to meet her own.

Etta's story resolves into a series of renunciations and frustrations which transform her personality, so that the idealistic young woman who longed to be independent becomes a hard, competitive, selfish, and tyrannical success in the business world. She has survived but at a cost that seems too great. Aldington's judgment is clear in his portrayal of Etta's unintentional alienation of her own rebellious, independent daughter. Despite herself, Etta repeats her parents' mistake by determining the life she wishes for her daughter, rather than allowing her daughter the liberty to choose for herself.

In its narrative, *Women Must Work* records the successive failure of several traditional fictional forms. The *Bildungsroman*, the naturalistic novel, the romance, the novel of the soil, and the urban success story all collapse as models for Etta's life. In Aldington's nightmare, the postwar degeneration of cultural and moral norms abandons both the novelist and the hero in a wilderness.

Aldington's fifth novel, *Very Heaven*, a nostalgic return to the outmoded *Künstlerroman*, portrays a sensitive, intelligent, individualist, Chris Heylin, as he encounters his society's hypocritical ethical codes, dullness, and huddling homogeneity. Forced to leave college by his incompetent father's financial failure, Chris confronts his mother's calculating plans for advancement through marriage. Although unable to prevent his sister's unwise union with a rich older man (who later infects her with venereal disease), he denounces her exchange of sex for money. Refusing a similarly advantageous marriage with an older, richer woman with whom he has enjoyed an affair, Chris makes his way alone in the city of London, living in a small, dirty apartment, toiling as an underpaid librarian and flunky to a condescending and conceited man with great wealth and a desire to flaunt it. His life brightens with the addition of a lover who has no sexual inhibitions, and who perfectly understands his problems. (Given the implicit determinism of Aldington's fictional world, the reader wonders what parents and upbringing produced this idyllic modern woman.)

After the hero has apparently attained happiness, in the prospect of a teaching job in a private school, a continuing love affair, and an extended European tour, he suffers a double disappointment, losing his promised job through rumors of his immoral affair and losing the sponsor of his European tour through arguments over religious and intellectual independence. The novel expires in Chris's lengthy meditation on his future, as he faces the sea and contemplates suicide. His meditation concludes with his refusal of despair, his renunciation of all formal codes, and his determination to try once more. The hero's final act, turning to walk toward the light of the town, deliberately recalls the end of D. H. Lawrence's *Sons and Lovers* (1913). This ending, inappropriate to the social reality depicted in Aldington's novel, seems unsuited to the practical character of Chris, whose idealism has been tempered by his contact with postwar materialism. Chris has been portrayed as a survivor, not a dreamer. This odd conclusion belongs to a novel written before World War I.

Seven Against Reeves offers a sympathetic, though comical portrait of a retired businessman beseiged by his ungrateful, socially ambitious family and by a series of leeches—gentry and artists—who want some of his earned money. Despite the punning allusion of its title, this novel does not resemble Aeschylus' tragedy *Seven Against Thebes* (467 B.C.). The picaresque adventures of Reeves, at home, in Venice, and on the Riviera, pit English generosity, shrewdness, and misplaced self-confidence against various exploiters, domestic and foreign. Reeves's gullibility and good intentions dimly reflect England's political history in the period between the wars, though Aldington's aim is less political than moral. The denouement, which is probably farcical, celebrates the authoritarian in Reeves as he asserts his own will over his wayward family; the parallel with the dictatorships briefly mentioned throughout this 1938 novel is unfortunate, for Aldington seems to be echoing or mocking a popularly sentimental conclusion. The father's strict authority over his family cannot be expected to solve their various, complicated problems, nor will his return to business restore moral order to English society.

Rejected Guest, which vividly portrays the life of the idle rich in the late 1930's, originates in the social disruption of World War I. Aldington consciously takes up one of the stereotyped stories, that of the illegitimate war baby, and uses it as a vehicle for exploring the postwar dislocation of values. Exposing the hypocrisy of assertions that, in this modern age, illegitimacy arouses no shameful prejudice, Aldington presents society's repeated rejection of David Norris. David's father was killed in the war; his mother abandoned him to his maternal grandparents to make a respectable marriage. Hurt by the ostracism of his home town and seeking to escape the poverty of his maternal family, David enrolled in University College, London, but lacked sufficient funds to complete his degree. Desperate, he applied to his wealthy paternal grandfather, who, moved by sentiment and remorse, and checked by shame, supplied a stipend large enough for David to live luxuriously, on the conditions that David live abroad and never claim kinship. Suddenly, with the values imposed by years of poverty, David finds himself living with a playboy guardian among the wealthy elite on the Riviera. He adapts, but, through his outsider's observations on the customs and morals of the international set, Aldington continues his satirical attack on postwar society.

Aldington's indictment of hypocrisy and selfishness seems, once again, to be mitigated by eros, as David falls helplessly in love with Diana, an independent and passionate young woman. Swimming, sailing, and making love in the blue Mediterranean, they plan a year-long sail through the tropics. When the Munich crisis threatens war, however, Diana's selfish instincts reassert their control, and she abandons him. David's wealthy grandfather dies without having provided for him in his will, and David is forced to accept a job as an office boy in London. The war baby finds no home among the people who produced him, for, as a living reminder of their failure in World War I, David disrupts their comfortable illusions. The political parallel in Aldington's ironic moral fable may be heard when David's playboy guardian advises him, "Kindly remember that I am only acting in your own interests," and David interrupts: "as the Nazi said when he robbed the Jew." The social elite of England and Europe, playing on the Riviera, choose to ignore their world's political affairs until war threatens to spoil their idleness. Aldington's critique of their selfish indifference is unambiguous.

Aldington's eighth and final novel, the historical fantasy, *The Romance of Casanova*, abandons the social and psychological problems of the twentieth century. A purely entertaining novel, *The Romance of Casanova* presents Giacomo Casanova as an elderly man wondering if he was ever loved for himself rather than for his reputation or his skill as a lover. Answering that doubt, Casanova narrates his affair with Henriette, the romance of his youth. He was captivated with her beauty even before learning her name, and he describes their lovemaking in passionate detail. Their affair was destroyed by his own infidelity and by his ambitious involvement in political intrigues. The novel was perhaps influenced by Aldington's measure of Hollywood's standards, clearly lower than his own as a novelist of the 1930's.

In her *Composition as Explanation* (1926), Gertrude Stein wrote that the most significant effect which World War I had had on literature was to force a contemporary self-consciousness. Her suggestion helps explain not only the themes but also the experimental forms of Aldington's long fiction. His contemporary self-consciousness demanded affective response to the war and its aftermath. He rejected Joyce's method in *Ulysses* (1922), which he found vulgar and incoherent, and embraced D. H. Lawrence's eroticism and cult of the personality. Though he denied that he was an interpreter of his age, he believed that an author's composition was shaped by the spirit of his time. Like Stein, he believed the attitude of the writer had changed as a result of the war; writers of his own age, he felt, were reacting against stagnation. His own fiction, reacting against the stagnation of old forms and the formlessness of modernist prose, provoked much hostile literary criticism yet won a following of appreciative readers. The uneven reputation of Aldington as a novelist validates Stein's paradoxical 1926 dictum: "The creator of a new composition in the arts is an outlaw until he is a classic."

Judith L. Johnston

Other major works

SHORT FICTION: *At All Costs*, 1930; *Last Straws*, 1930; *Roads to Glory*, 1930; *Two Stories: Deserter and The Lads of the Village*, 1930; *A War Story*, 1930; *Stepping Heavenward*, 1931; *Soft Answers*, 1932.

PLAYS: *A Life of a Lady*, 1936 (with Derek Patmore).

POETRY: *Images (1910-1915)*, 1915; *Latin Poems of the Renaissance*, 1915 (translation); *Reverie: A Little Book of Poems for H. D.*, 1917; *The Love of Myrrhine and Konallis, and Other Prose Poems*, 1917; *Images of War*, 1919;

Images of Desire, 1919; *Images*, 1919; *War and Love (1915-1918)*, 1919; *The Berkshire Kennet*, 1923; *Exile and Other Poems*, 1923; *A Fool i' the Forest*, 1924; *Hark the Herald*, 1928; *Collected Poems*, 1929; *A Dream in the Luxembourg*, 1930; *The Eaten Heart*, 1929; *Movietones*, 1932; *The Poems of Richard Aldington*, 1934; *Life Quest*, 1935; *The Crystal World*, 1937; *The Complete Poems of Richard Aldington*, 1948.

NONFICTION: *Literary Studies and Reviews*, 1924; *Voltaire*, 1925; *French Studies and Reviews*, 1926; *D. H. Lawrence: An Indiscretion*, 1927; *Artifex: Sketches and Ideas*, 1935; *D. H. Lawrence: A Complete List of His Works, Together with a Critical Association*, 1935; *W. Somerset Maugham: An Appreciation*, 1939; *Life for Life's Sake: A Book of Reminiscences*, 1941; *The Duke, Being an Account of the Life & Achievements of Arthur Wellesley, 1st Duke of Wellington*, 1943; *Jane Austen*, 1948; *Four English Portraits, 1801-1851*, 1948; *The Strange Life of Charles Waterton, 1782-1865*, 1949; *D. H. Lawrence: An Appreciation*, 1950; *D. H. Lawrence: Portrait of a Genius But . . .* , 1950; *Ezra Pound and T. S. Eliot, A Lecture*, 1954; *Lawrence L'Imposteur: T. E. Lawrence, the Legend and the Man*, 1954; *Pinorman: Personal Recollections of Norman Douglas, Pino Orioli, and Charles Prentice*, 1954; *A. E. Housman and W. B. Yeats, Two Lectures*, 1955; *Lawrence of Arabia: A Biographical Inquiry*, 1955; *Introduction to Mistral*, 1956; *Frauds*, 1957; *Portrait of a Rebel: The Life and Work of Robert Louis Stevenson*, 1957; *Richard Aldington: Selected Critical Writings, 1928-1960*, 1970 (Alister Kershaw, editor); *A Passionate Prodigality*, 1975 (Alan Bird, editor); *Literary Lifelines*, 1981 (Lawrence Durrell, editor).

TRANSLATIONS: *The Poems of Anyte of Tegea*, 1915; *The Garland of Months*, 1917; *Greek Songs in the Manner of Anacreon*, 1919; *The Poems of Mealeager of Gadara*, 1920; *The Good-Humoured Ladies*, 1922; *French Comedies of the XVIIIth Century*, 1923; *Voyages to the Moon and the Sun*, 1923; *A Book of "Characters" from Theophrastus*, 1924; *Dangerous Acquaintances*, 1924; *Candide and Other Romances*, 1927; *Fifty Romance Lyric Poems*, 1928; *The Great Betrayal*, 1928; *Remy de Gourmont, Selections from All His Works*, 1929; *Alcestis*, 1930; *The Decameron of Giovanni Boccaccio*, 1930; *Great French Romances*, 1946.

Bibliography

Doyle, Charles. *Richard Aldington: A Biography*. Carbondale: Southern Illinois University Press, 1989. This most comprehensive and up-to-date biography of Aldington does ample justice to his many-faceted gifts as a writer. The chapter on "The T. E. Lawrence Affair, 1950-55," concerning Aldington's biography of Lawrence, makes fascinating reading not only for Aldington's debunking of the Lawrence myth but also for all the intricacies and legalities involved in publishing controversial material. Includes a valuable contribution to secondary material on Aldington.

Gates, Norman T. *The Poetry of Richard Aldington: A Critical Evaluation and an Anthology of Uncollected Poems*. University Park: Pennsylvania State University Press, 1974. A thorough study that reviews the criticism of Aldington's poetry from 1910 to the early 1970's and assesses his position as a poet and speaker of his time. This scholarly and appreciative work has located 129 uncollected poems in newspapers, periodicals, and unpublished manuscripts, as well as early books of his poetry omitted from *The Complete Poems*. Includes a valuable bibliography of primary and secondary sources.

Kershaw, Alister, and Frederic-Jacques Temple, eds. *Richard Aldington: An Intimate Portrait*. Carbondale: Southern Illinois University Press, 1965. A compilation of essays and reminiscences on Aldington and his literary contribution, presented by the editors as a tribute. Contributors include such notable authors as Samuel Beckett, C. P. Snow, and Arthur Miller, as well as critics from the Soviet Union, where Aldington's work has a strong following.

McGreevy, Thomas. *Richard Aldington: An Englishman*. London: Chatto & Windus, 1931. Reprint. New York: Haskell House, 1974. An earlier, full-length study of Aldington, with critical commentary of his works only up to 1931. An appreciative study, it covers Aldington's novels and poems, with emphasis on *Death of a Hero*.

Smith, Richard Eugene. *Richard Aldington*. Boston: Twayne, 1977. A comprehensive survey of Aldington's work, noting that his leadership in the imagist movement during the 1920's was but a small part of his varied and productive literary career. Includes criticism of Aldington's major novels as well as his work as a biographer, translator, and critic. A selected bibliography is provided.

THOMAS BAILEY ALDRICH

Born: Portsmouth, New Hampshire; November 11, 1836
Died: Boston, Massachusetts; March 19, 1907

Principal long fiction

Daisy's Necklace and What Came of It, 1857; *The Story of a Bad Boy*, 1870; *Prudence Palfrey*, 1874; *The Queen of Sheba*, 1877; *The Stillwater Tragedy*, 1880; *The Second Son*, 1888.

Other literary forms

During his prolific literary career, Thomas Bailey Aldrich published short stories, poems, essays, and verse plays. Many of his letters are included in Ferris Greenslet's *The Life of Thomas Bailey Aldrich* (1908).

Achievements

Aldrich was one of America's best-known literary figures during the latter half of the nineteenth century. As a poet, he was already a popular success in 1855—at age nineteen. Ten years later, after having his more mature and less sentimental poetry praised by Henry Wadsworth Longfellow, Ralph Waldo Emerson, James Russell Lowell, and Oliver Wendell Holmes, he was considered worthy enough to be included in Ticknor & Fields's prestigious "Blue and Gold Series" of verse. He further enhanced his reputation when he turned to fiction in the late 1860's. *The Story of a Bad Boy* was enormously popular, and Aldrich's short stories soon were a consistent feature of *The Atlantic*. For the rest of his career, this magazine was his favorite place of publication, for its predominately genteel audience enjoyed his serialized novels and his clever, well-crafted short stories with surprise endings.

His stature as a major writer, strengthened during his successful tenure as editor of *The Atlantic*, was certainly apparent in 1884 when *The Critic*, a New York literary magazine, asked its readers to name the forty most important American writers. Aldrich finished seventh, outpolling Henry James, Mark Twain, Walt Whitman, and Bret Harte. Twenty years later his importance was again strikingly affirmed when he was one the first fifteen artists named to the National Academy of Arts and Sciences.

Aldrich's reputation, however, plummeted after his death. Critics such as H. L. Mencken, C. Hartley Grattan, and Vernon Louis Parrington denigrated his accomplishments, dismissing him as shallowly optimistic, blindly conservative, and uninteresting. They believed that he had nothing to say to the modern, post-World War I reader. Aldrich's stock has never recovered, and now he is primarily interesting to those who study the relationship between the genteel tradition and the growth of realism, particularly how his poetry possibly foreshadows the imagists; how his *The Story of a Bad Boy* breaks ground for Twain's "boys' books"; how his female characters reflect his age's literary treatment of women; and how *The Stillwater Tragedy* fits into the history of the American economic novel.

Biography

Thomas Bailey Aldrich was born in Portsmouth, New Hampshire, the sleepy seaport town he nostalgically re-created in much of his fiction—most notably in *The Story of a Bad Boy*, his autobiographical homage to adolescence. An only child, his early years were a bit unsettled because his father, in a restless search for business success, first moved the family to New York City in 1841 and then to New Orleans in 1846. In 1849, Aldrich's parents sent him back to Portsmouth for a better education, but his plans for entering Harvard suddenly ended when his father died of cholera. In 1852, because of his family's uncertain financial state, he had to accept a job as a clerk in his uncle's New York City counting house.

In 1855, after publishing his first book of poems (filled with echoes of John Keats, Alfred Tennyson, and Longfellow) and after having become well known with his sentimental and extremely popular "The Ballad of Baby Bell," Aldrich left his uncle's business. Having decided to be a man of letters, he spent the rest of the 1850's publishing more poetry, beginning his career as an editor by working for the *Home Journal* (1855-1859) and the *Saturday Press* (1859-1860), and writing his first novel, *Daisy's Necklace and What Became of It*—a confused, uninteresting attempt to burlesque the saccharine fiction of "the Feminine Fifties." At the same time, he was moving back and forth between two New York social-literary crowds: the genteel circle which included Bayard Taylor, E. C. Stedman, and Richard Stoddard, and the radical, bohemian circle which included Whitman.

Temperamentally uncomfortable with the rebellious, flamboyant bohemians, Aldrich in the 1860's inevitably found his intellectual home in the more conservative group. He felt, in fact, that the luckiest day of his life was when he moved to Boston in 1866 to be the editor of the periodical *Every Saturday*. Married by then, he settled into the fashionable life of Beacon Hill and became, as he once proudly noted, "Boston-plated." Deeply committed to this genteel society, Aldrich, unlike his friend William Dean Howells, never seriously questioned its values, and his art reflects this acceptance.

From 1868 to 1873, Aldrich turned from poetry and devoted himself to fiction, publishing *The Story of a Bad Boy* and his most famous short story, "Marjorie Daw." In 1874, after *Every Saturday* failed, he moved to Ponkapog (a village twelve miles from Boston) and spent six quiet, happy, and productive years writing poems, novels, and sketches. This idyll ended in 1881 when he replaced Howells as the editor of *The Atlantic*, a position Aldrich held until 1890. After this, he spent his remaining years writing, traveling overseas, and supervising the collecting of his works.

Analysis

Alexander Cowie, in *The Rise of the American Novel* (1948), called Thomas Bailey Aldrich an "Indian Summer writer." By this he meant that Aldrich's art represents a late and pleasantly light blooming of the genteel New England literary tradition. It is an easygoing, entertaining, and edifying art which attempts to break no new ground and usually does not disturb its readers.

Cowie's description is apt because it points to the conservatism and optimism resting at the heart of Aldrich's novels. Always ready to defend the traditional way, Aldrich reacts against the forces which threaten the established, secure order. Thus he nostalgically celebrates the idyllic, old-fashioned New England village while looking with disgust on the modern, industrialized towns and cities; he promotes the beauties of American capitalism while warning against the dangers of labor unions; he trusts the security of orthodox religious beliefs while shying away from the uncertainties of modern thought; and he affirms the ideal of the prudent, measured life while suspecting all types of erratic, impulsive behavior. In his fiction, then, tradition continually collides with the disruptive energy of change; and Aldrich usually depicts the triumph of orthodox values in such a struggle.

To make sure that his readers understand this conservative position, Aldirch clarifies and stresses it through his use of the narrative voice. Continually entering the novels, this voice always belongs to a cultured man who is a mirror image of Aldrich himself. In *Daisy's Necklace and What Came of It*, he is a well-read young writer grappling with a first novel filled with pastoral reveries, literary criticism (including an offhand attack of Walt Whitman), and editorials espousing various traditional beliefs. In *The Story of a Bad Boy*, he is this same young man grown a bit older. He now meditates on his lost youth and lingers over his birthplace, the ancient town of Rivermouth. Like Twain's St. Petersburg in *The Adventures of Tom Sawyer* (1876), this setting is enveloped in a romantic mist: its gigantic elms, its old houses, its crumbling wharves, and its memories of past glories evoke a time of past innocence for the narrator. This persona in Aldrich's next two novels, *Prudence Palfrey* and *The Queen of Sheba*, becomes an anonymous Victorian gentleman who is distanced from the Rivermouth setting, imperiously commenting on the struggles of young love, on the town's foibles, and on the dangers of rash behavior. Finally, in *The Stillwater Tragedy*, Aldrich uses this same gentleman to defend ardently the American businessman against the demands of the radical working man.

Aldrich's faith in the superiority of the genteel value system, a faith embodied in these narrators, helped him to maintain his conviction that art should be optimistic and instructive. He believed that art should never be morbid because it then had a subversive, unhealthy, and depressing effect on the audience. Also, it should avoid the low and vulgar areas of life, for such material inevitably undercuts the beauties of literature. Instead, the artist should work to maintain a hopeful, buoyant, noble tone as he creates wholesome, affirmative, radiant works. Then he will succeed in uplifting the reader.

This view of art, which centers on his not upsetting or challenging his audience's existing value system, helps explain Aldrich's reservations about Whitman's and Emily Dickinson's poetry, as well as his antipathy toward the naturalism of Émile Zola. It also accounts for his urge to create happy endings within his novels and his usual unwillingness to stare too long at the darker sides of life. For example, *Prudence Palfrey*, *The Queen of Sheba*, and *The Stillwater Tragedy* end with the young lovers realizing their marriage plans after melodramatically overcoming various tensions and hardships. In each case, the narrative voice makes certain to assure the reader that the couples will live happily.

This is not to say that Aldrich never treats the more somber aspects of human existence. Most notably, in every novel, Aldrich creates orphaned, vulnerable protagonists who experience loneliness and alienation while missing the guidance of strong parental figures. Through them, Aldrich, who shared his culture's devotion to the family, tries to objectify the emotional trauma he felt when his father died. This darker side of his vision also appears when he examines—sometimes in a truncated way—the more irrational sides of human behavior: jealousy in *Prudence Palfrey*, madness in *The Queen of Sheba*, and uncontrollable rage in *The Stillwater Tragedy*. In the end, though, Aldrich usually avoids fully confronting this intriguing part of his fictional world. As a result, he is able to maintain the sunny climate of his novels—although the reader finds it difficult to forget or ignore the moments of danger and sadness haunting Aldrich's Indian Summer writing.

Early in 1869, *The Story of a Bad Boy* first appeared as a serial in the juvenile magazine *Our Young Folks*. Apparently Aldrich felt that it would primarily appeal to an adolescent audience; however, the novel's widespread popularity during the remainder of the nineteenth century indicates that it attracted the older reader, too. To a great extent, its general success stemmed from Aldrich's realistic treatment of his hero, Tom Bailey. He wanted the boy to be different from the saintly and unbelievable little "grown-ups" moralizing their way through the popular fiction of his time. This is why Aldrich calls Tom a "bad boy": it is his striking way of stressing that he will not create a pious stick figure. Rather his boy will be an amiable, impulsive flesh-and-blood human being who, like most healthy children, gets into a bit of trouble. Tom's badness, then, is not that of a subversive, delinquent child. Usually he respects adult authority, whether it emanates from his father, grandfather, or schoolteacher. He also frequently agrees with their criticisms of his occasionally wayward behavior. Thus Tom is Aldrich's realistic version of the genteel adolescent, and the boy's respectability explains why the novel has only the illusion of a conflict between Tom and his community.

This conception of Tom seems quite conventional now, but the boy's "badness" was a refreshing change for Aldrich's audience, who had grown tired of reading about perfect children. William Dean Howells, for example, in his review of the novel praised its resolution to show a boy's life as it is, not as it ought to be. In addition, As Walter Blair notes in *Mark Twain and Huck Finn* (1960), *The Story of a Bad Boy* might have spurred Twain's conception of *The Adventures of Tom Sawyer*. Although Twain was not much impressed when he first read Aldrich's novel in 1869, it probably helped him see the potential in writing a more realistic "boy's book." It also provided Twain with an example of the narrative strategy he would eventually employ, with variations, in his own novel: he saw how Aldrich generated a type of double perspective by having an adult narrator re-create an adolescent's vision of the world. This structure enables Aldrich to create a sense of tension as he moves the reader back and forth between the viewpoints of Tom Bailey the boy, who is spontaneous and sometimes adventurously foolish, and Tom Bailey the man, who is prudent and nostalgic.

When Aldrich locates the reader within the boy's perspective, he concentrates on dramatizing, rather than explaining, Tom's experiences. There are many of these moments, and they accumulate to give a strong sense of the everyday reality of childhood. They include Tom's boring Sundays in his grandfather's religious household, his trips to the woods and cliffs, his scuffles with other boys, his playacting, his winter exploits, and his elaborate pranks designed to upset temporarily the staid life of Rivermouth. These moments also include the novel's darker times. For example, in one of the most haunting scenes in Aldrich's fiction, Tom witnesses the death of his playmate Binny Wallace. The horrified Tom watches as the helpless boy, trapped on a runaway boat, drifts out to sea toward certain destruction. The boat gets ever smaller, the sea grows choppier, and then Binny disappears into the night which suddenly seems to sob with the cries of ghosts. Here, Aldrich lets Tom's consciousness tell the story and consequently the incident is alive in all its terror. Moreover, at other times, Aldrich objectifies his own sense of familial loss through Tom's perception (when the lonely boy yearns to be reunited with his parents and when he grieves over the death of his father); these episodes represent Aldrich's most personal examination of his bittersweet childhood.

Yet in all these episodes, no matter how deeply Aldrich immerses the reader within the boy's consciousness, one rarely forgets the adult point of view always hovering over Tom's story. Employed for many purposes, this voice speaks directly to both the adolescents and the adults in Aldrich's audience.

When the narrator speaks to the young, he becomes the friendly Victorian moralist drawing lessons from his own childhood and instructing them about the evils of smoking, the advantages of a boy learning how to box, the value of working hard, and the dangers in being impulsive. He is the voice of mature wisdom; and his prudence is often set in polite opposition to the values of

Tom Bailey the boy. This strategy, which allows Aldrich to critique as well as appreciate Tom's adventures, thus protects the novel from becoming a hymn to the anarchy of adolescence.

The narrator, however, becomes much more appealing (because he is not so smug or patronizing) when he speaks to adults. Intensely nostalgic, he luxuriates in remembering, with great detail, the Rivermouth of his youth. At the same time, his awareness of being caught in time occasionally makes him brood about death. He thinks about the fates of his boyhood chums who have already died. He also thinks about his dead father—confessing that he has never completely recovered from losing this sacred companion (here Aldrich directly states his feelings through the narrator). With these recollections and musings, Aldrich succeeds in creating a sharp, often poignant juxtaposition of childhood and adulthood. He touches upon the adult reader's desire to freeze time, so that cherished moments and people can be rescued from the always withering past. Most important, in catching this desire, he makes *The Story of a Bad Boy* more than a book only for boys.

Like *The Story of a Bad Boy*, Aldrich's *Prudence Palfrey* is a readable, episodic work set in Rivermouth and narrated by a persona closely aligned to Aldrich's conservative values. Yet it is not nearly as autobiographical as its predecessor, and Aldrich's decreasing reliance upon his personal experiences results in a weak plot. Having to create most of the story out of his imagination or from materials outside the realm of his immediate experience, Aldrich too often falls back on melodramatic strategies to further the plot. The hero John Dent loves Prudence Palfrey, a young woman having the qualities found in the stereotypical heroine of the popular genteel novel: she is earnest, pale, attractive, and, as her name indicates, prudent. The lovers are separated when Dent travels West to make his fortune, for without money, he cannot marry her. In a long section not well integrated into the novel, Aldrich describes John's Western experiences, as the young man makes a fortune, loses it to a villain, and then wanders in despair. In the meantime, the villain—who has an unnatural hatred for John—goes East, enters Rivermouth under the guise of being its new minister, and begins courting Prudence. Finally, in a thoroughly contrived denouement, complete with a secret will, striking coincidences, treacherous schemes, and sudden revelations, John returns home, unmasks the villain, suddenly becomes rich, and marries Prudence.

Such a plot hardly makes for great fiction. Still, in two ways, the work is important to an understanding of how Aldrich's aesthetic vision developed. First, it points to his changing conception of his genteel narrative voice, setting the direction for the magisterial persona of his next two novels, *The Queen of Sheba* and *The Stillwater Tragedy*. Less personal, less nostalgic, and less vulnerable than Tom Bailey in *The Story of a Bad Boy*, the anonymous narrator of *Prudence Palfrey* does not describe and relive his own childhood experiences. He is much more removed from the action which he oversees, and this distance allows him to assume a more objective stance toward Rivermouth. Thus while he obviously respects the town's backwoods tranquility and its preservation of traditional moral values, the narrator also can be quite critical of it. This tougher side of his perspective leads him to comment sarcastically on the pretensions of its wealthy inhabitants, to chide its gossiping, to laugh at its taste in architecture, and to note that it desperately needs new blood because it is in danger of becoming a sterile place.

Besides its employment of the narrative voice, *Prudence Palfrey* is interesting because, more than any of his other novels, it reflects Aldrich's devotion to the ideals of work, duty, discipline, and prudence. At times, it almost seems to be a casebook espousing the Victorian values affirmed by Thomas Carlyle in *Sartor Resartus* (1835); the major tensions in *Prudence Palfrey* invariably arise because its two most interesting characters, John Dent and his uncle Ralph Dent, fail to follow the model of the one-dimensional Prudence, who always behaves with restraint.

John Dent, for example, must curb his immoderate, often self-indulgent behavior before he can be worthy enough to marry Prudence. At the beginning of the novel, the narrator (who repeatedly celebrates the disciplined life) warns that John, whose father has just died, is in a perilous position. Because he is orphaned, he lacks the necessary guidance, and the narrator suggests that this loss of a loving but restraining hand makes John more susceptible to the specious attraction of the romantic quest. For John, this quest is linked to his desire to become suddenly rich in the gold fields: he dreams of a big nugget waiting for him and therefore rejects the Victorian ethic of working hard for long-term, more enduring rewards. Further, he rashly declares that he *will* come back rich or not come back at all.

Like all of Aldrich's undisciplined characters, John suffers. He becomes immersed in the outlaw society of the Western mining towns and yearns for the ordered Rivermouth. He becomes the victim of his dishonest partner. Finally, because of his lack of inner strength, he loses faith in himself after his reversals and sinks into self-pity. All this suffering, however, eventually purges him of his arrogance, light-mindedness, and impetuosity. The chastened John returns to Rivermouth—which he now values for its old-fashioned peace and integrity—and behaves like a conscientious young gentleman worthy of inheriting the money left to him by Parson Hawkins. (Even the Parson's will upholds the Victorian belief in work because it stipulates that John must try to become self-reliant before he can receive the money).

For the first half of *Prudence Palfrey*, Ralph Dent struggles, like his nephew, to control his emotions. Caught between his strong sense of duty as Prudence's surrogate father (the orphaned young woman is his ward) and his increasing sexual attraction toward her, the elder Dent frequently lets jealousy rule him. It leads him to instigate the dismissal of Parson Hawkins, whose friendship with Prudence seems to be standing between Dent and his ward. This action, along with his equally rash championing the new liberal minister without examining his background, causes Rivermouth to lose its conservative, safe old minister and to become victimized by the impostor. In addition, Dent's jealousy makes him react too violently to his nephew's desire to marry Prudence. As a result, instead of helping the confused young man, he spurs John's wild decision to go West.

At times, Dent is almost reminiscent of the evil stepfathers of melodrama, yet one finally sees him as a much more intriguing and sympathetic figure than these cardboard characters. As he confronts, with horror, the true nature of his attraction to Prudence and as he tries to overcome his passion, Dent becomes a complex portrait of a man frightening in his inability to control his feelings, pathetic in his love for the unsuspecting Prudence, and honorable in his efforts not to violate her trust in him. Thus he is potentially Aldrich's most tragic character. Aldrich abruptly defuses Dent's inner conflict before the halfway point of the novel, however, by having him suddenly conquer his passion. In the name of duty, Dent buries it for the rest of the novel—and the reader feels short-changed. It is not unbelievable that the uncle would eventually stifle his passion; but it *is* inconceivable, after the way he has struggled, that the decision should suddenly be so easy. Aldrich appears to have shied away from the full implications of this character, perhaps because he was afraid that Dent's dilemma was about to upset the comic intent of the novel.

The Stillwater Tragedy, Aldrich's contribution to the plethora of economic novels written in America during the last quarter of the nineteenth century, is his most ambitious attempt at long fiction. In his previous novels, he had not openly confronted social issues, although the pressures of the Gilded Age, the Industrial Revolution, and urban life are in the backgrounds of *The Story of a Bad Boy*, *Prudence Palfrey*, and *The Queen of Sheba*. Such issues, however, come to the forefront in *The Stillwater Tragedy*, as Aldrich leaves his usual Rivermouth setting to concentrate on the conflict between business and the rising labor unions in a small New England factory town. Most important, in depicting this struggle, Aldrich uses his fiction to express, as Walter Fuller Taylor explains in *The Economic Novel in America* (1942), a Right-Center, moderately conservative, middle-class economic vision. He attacks labor unions as disruptive forces endangering the American Dream while sympathizing with and often idealizing businessmen.

Aldrich tries to appear open-minded about the labor question, so he creates some "good" workers who are honest, simple, hard-working men. He also has his hero Richard Shackford acknowledge that workers, if unjustly treated, have a right to strike. Yet Aldrich finally fails in his attempt to be objective because he spends most of the novel depicting what he sees as the usual strike: an absurd, destructive act in which radical labor organizers, whom he calls ghouls, mislead the confused workers into betraying their fair-minded employers.

In building his conservative case, Aldrich overtly ties the passions motivating the labor union to one of the primary themes in his fiction: the dangers of any type of excessive human behavior. Therefore he argues, often through his narrator, who is an apologist for American business, that the labor unions' stubborn, irrational demands (especially their not permitting owners to hire apprentices to fill out the work force) ultimately hurt the workers by keeping the economic market unnaturally depressed. Aldrich also argues that most of the labor troubles are caused by foreign anarchists who enter America still nurturing their wild Old World angers. Finally, he explicitly portrays the "good" worker as the man who respects law and order, reasons out his position, and consequently obeys the commonsense policies of his farseeing employer. In contrast, the "bad" worker permits his emotions to rule him; this behavior is evidenced in the actions of the novel's two most important agitators—Torrini, a self-destructive, ungrateful drunkard who uses his eloquence to inflame the workers, and Durgin, a spiteful parasite who eventually commits murder.

To reinforce this theme, Aldrich goes so far as to show that Shackford's weakest moment in the novel is when the young man lowers himself to Torrini's level of behavior. Having always been cursed with a terrible temper, Aldrich's hero becomes outraged by the Italian's insubordination and gets involved in a physical confrontation with the worker. The workers, in response to this incident, admire Shackford for his use of force. Yet Aldrich makes sure that the reader takes a wider perspective, for he has Shackford's fiancée Margaret Slocum—another of Aldrich's perfectly prudent genteel heroines— rebuke her young man for not showing "the beauty of self control." Here, Margaret is certainly speaking for Aldrich, who has pitted two different value systems against each other in this episode to stress the moral superiority of the more sophisticated, affluent one. It is this superiority which makes Margaret's father so magnanimous toward his prodigal workers, causes Margaret to become an administering angel during the strike as she brings food to the workers' suffering families, and leads Shackford to forget Torrini's past abuses as he nurses the mortally injured worker. Obviously, Aldrich does everything he can to make the upper-class characters above criticism.

This obvious bias is one of the three major reasons the novel fails. In devoting so much of his energy to elevating the Slocums and Shackford, Aldrich never treats with any complexity the other side of the conflict. He rarely examines with sympathy or understanding the reasons why workers in the late 1870's felt the need to strike; and he never makes any of the workers more than one-dimensional—probably because he was too divorced from their lives to create a complex characterization.

The novel also fails because Aldrich cannot seem to decide whether he is writing a murder mystery, an antiunion polemic, or a conventional love story. As a result, the three story lines do not cohere into a whole, although they sometimes merge temporarily. Finally, *The Stillwater Tragedy* suffers because Aldrich's intrusive narrator tends to explain away the work's conflicts. After listening to his dogmatic and sometimes strident comments, the reader better understands why Howells frequently lamented Aldrich's reliance on this type of authorial voice. Howells felt that it undercut the fictional illusion and made his friend too often appear more like an essayist than a novelist. Even Aldrich at times felt that such intrusions could be a liability; for example, he criticized Henry James's *The American* (1877) for not being dramatic enough because of its omnipresent narrative voice. This criticism is strikingly ironic in the light of the fact that James eventually made the dramatic method the cornerstone of his fiction, while Aldrich never escaped his tendency to disrupt the dramatic flow of his narratives through editorializing.

James Grove

Other major works
SHORT FICTION: *Out of His Head: A Romance*, 1862; *Marjorie Daw and Other People*, 1873; *Miss Mehetabel's Son*, 1877; *A Rivermouth Romance*, 1877; *A Midnight Fantasy, and the Little Violinist*, 1877; *Two Bites at a Cherry*, 1894; *A Sea Turn and Other Matters*, 1902.
PLAY: *Judith of Bethulia*, 1904.
POETRY: *The Bells: A Collection of Chimes*, 1855; *The Course of True Love Never Did Run Smooth*, 1858; *The Ballad of Babie Bell and Other Poems*, 1859; *Pampinea*, 1861; *Poems*, 1863; *The Poems of Thomas Bailey Aldrich*, 1865; *Cloth of Gold*, 1874; *Flower and Thorn*, 1877; *Baby Bell*, 1878; *Friar Jerome's Beautiful Book*, 1881; *XXXVI Lyrics and XII Sonnets*, 1881; *The Poems of Thomas Bailey Alrich*, 1882; *Mercedes and Later Lyrics*, 1884; *The Poems of Thomas Bailey Aldrich*, 1885; *Wyndham Towers*, 1890; *The Sisters' Tragedy, with Other Poems Lyrical and Dramatic*, 1891; *Unguarded Gates and Other Poems*, 1895; *Later Lyrics*, 1896; *Judith and Holofernes*, 1896; *The Poems of Thomas Bailey Aldrich*, 1897; *A Book of Songs and Sonnets Selected from the Poems of Thomas Bailey Aldrich*, 1906.
NONFICTION: *From Ponkapog to Pesth*, 1883; *An Old Town by the Sea*, 1893; *Ponkapog Papers*, 1903.
MISCELLANEOUS: *Poems of Robert Herrick: A Selection from "Hesperides" and the "Noble Numbers,"* 1900 (edited).

Bibliography
Aldrich, Mrs. Thomas Bailey. *Crowding Memories*. Boston: Houghton Mifflin, 1920. Written after Aldrich's death, this biography by his wife presents

a noncritical view of the author. The text's greatest value is its anecdotal stories about Aldrich and illustrations of the author, his residences, and his friends.

Cowie, Alexander. *The Rise of the American Novel*. New York: American Book, 1948. Analyzes Aldrich's works in the context of regional fiction, comparing his work to that of Edward Eggleston, George Washington Cable, Constance Fenimore Woolson, and Mary Noailles Murfree. Asserts that what Aldrich lacks in depth as a writer is compensated for by his wit and ease of reading.

Greenslet, Ferris. *The Life of Thomas Bailey Aldrich*. 1908. Reprint. Port Washington, N.Y.: Kennikat, 1965. A comprehensive biography of Aldrich. Several chapters detail his youth and apprenticeship, with significant attention given to Aldrich's editorship of *The Atlantic Monthly* during the 1880's and to his novels and poetry. An excellent bibliography and illustrations are included.

Samuels, Charles E. *Thomas Bailey Aldrich*. New York: Twayne, 1965. Presents a brief biography of Aldrich, followed by chapters that analyze his poetry, short stories and sketches, major novels, and theoretical commentaries. Concludes with a discussion of Aldrich's literary reputation and a selected bibliography.

Sattelmeyer, Robert, and J. Donald Crowley, eds. *One Hundred Years of Huckleberry Finn: The Boy, His Book, and American Culture*. Columbia: University of Missouri Press, 1985. An extensive collection of essays including comparative analyses of Aldrich's and Twain's works, especially in terms of Aldrich's *The Story of a Bad Boy* (1870). Alan Gribben briefly but astutely argues that Aldrich's novel has not received due analysis in terms of its influence on *The Adventures of Tom Sawyer*.

NELSON ALGREN
Nelson Ahlgren Abraham

Born: Detroit, Michigan; March 28, 1909
Died: Sag Harbor, New York; May 9, 1981

Principal long fiction

Somebody in Boots, 1935; *Never Come Morning*, 1942; *The Man with the Golden Arm*, 1949; *A Walk on the Wild Side*, 1956; *The Devil's Stocking*, 1983.

Other literary forms

Although Nelson Algren is known primarily as a novelist, some critics believe that the short story, because it does not make the structural demands the novel does, is a more appropriate genre for him, and his *The Neon Wilderness* (1947) has been acclaimed one of the best collections of short stories published in the 1940's. *Chicago: City on the Make* (1951) is a prose poem which has been variously described as a social document and a love poem to the city that serves as the center of Algren's fictional world. Similar non-fiction writings include *Who Lost an American?* (1963), a self-described "guide to the seamier sides" of several cities, including Chicago, and *Notes from a Sea Diary: Hemingway All the Way* (1965); both books combine travel writing and personal essays. What little poetry Algren wrote that is not included in his novels (*The Man with the Golden Arm*, for example, concludes with a poem of the same name which Algren terms an "epitaph") is included in *The Last Carousel* (1973), along with some unpublished stories and sketches. He also collaborated with H. E. F. Donohue on the book *Conversations with Nelson Algren* (1964), a series of interviews. *Nelson Algren's Own Book of Lonesome Monsters* (1962), an anthology to which he contributed a preface and the concluding story, sounds Algren's recurring theme: Man is always alone.

Achievements

While Algren's first novel, *Somebody in Boots*, failed commercially, it drew the attention of serious literary critics, who were even more impressed by his second novel, *Never Come Morning*, which won for Algren in 1947 one thousand dollars from the American Academy of Arts and Letters. Also in 1947, he received a grant from the Newberry Library to assist him in the writing of *The Man with the Golden Arm*, which subsequently received the National Book Award in 1950. Since many of the stories in *The Neon Wilderness* had previously appeared in the O. Henry Memorial collections or in *Best American Stories*, Algren's stature as a first-class writer of fiction was assured by 1950. Because his fictional world, for the most part, was Chicago, Algren is frequently linked with James T. Farrell and Richard Wright, who belong to what some critics have termed the "Chicago School." While he denied any literary indebtedness to Farrell and Wright, Algren admitted that his work was influenced by Carl Sandburg, partly because Algren's prose tends to the poetic, so much so that he has been termed by Malcolm Cowley "the poet of the Chicago slums."

Maxwell Geismar has termed Algren a "neo-naturalist" with roots in the American realistic tradition of Stephen Crane, Theodore Dreiser, and Ernest Hemingway (Algren acknowledged his debt to Hemingway, who in return hailed Algren as, after William Faulkner, among America's first writers). Unfortunately, critics, including Geismar, have also found many of the excesses of naturalism—melodrama, romanticism, oversimplification of characters and motives, and "over-writing"—in Algren's work, which has also been assailed for its formlessness. What Algren lacks in style and form, however, he more than compensates for in rich detail and insightful observations about what George Bluestone has called the "world's derelicts," those unfortunates who had largely been ignored, even by those writers who were ostensibly concerned with the "lumpen proletariat." In fact, so preoccupied is he with the victims of the American Dream, those losers customarily associated with the Depression, that one seldom encounters the other America in his fiction. Consequently, some readers have found his work dated, and while *The Man with the Golden Arm* and *A Walk on the Wild Side* were both filmed (in 1955 and 1962, respectively), thereby testifying to Algren's popularity, his critical standing declined. Yet from 1945 to 1960, he was among America's most acclaimed writers because of his focus and his vision, both of which were compatible with post–World War II America.

Biography

Nelson Ahlgren Abraham was born in Detroit, Michigan, on March 28, 1909, to second-generation Chicagoans, who moved back to Chicago when Algren was three years old. From 1912 until 1928, Algren absorbed the Chicago environment that was to become the center of his fictional world. After receiving his journalism degree from the University of Illinois in 1931, he began traveling across the Southwest, working at odd jobs (door-to-door coffee salesman in New Orleans, migrant worker, co-operator of a gasoline station in Texas, and carnival worker) and gathering the raw material that he later transformed into his fiction, particularly *A Walk on the Wild Side*. After serving time for stealing a typewriter (an oddly appropriate theft for a writer), he returned to Chicago, where he continued his "research" on the Division Street milieu and began to write short stories, poems, and his first novel, *Somebody in Boots*, a Depression tale about the Southwest that became, after extensive revision, *A Walk on the Wild Side*.

After World War II—he served three years in the army—Algren legally shortened his name, returned again to Chicago, and within five years enjoyed a reputation as one of America's finest fiction writers. *The Man with the Golden Arm* received the National Book Award, and several stories were also recognized for their excellence. *A Walk on the Wild Side* and its subsequent filming, as well as the cinematic adaptation of *The Man with the Golden Arm*, brought Algren to the height of his popularity during the 1950's and 1960's, but aside from some travel books and his last novel, his writing career essentially ended in 1956. In his later years, he taught creative writing, before spending his last years on *The Devil's Stocking*, a thinly veiled fictional treatment of the trial and imprisonment of Reuben "Hurricane" Carter, a middleweight boxer. The "novel" did little to restore Algren's literary reputation.

Analysis

Whether the setting is Chicago or New Orleans, Nelson Algren's characters live, dream, and die in an environment alien to most Americans, many of whom have achieved the financial success and spiritual failure endemic to the American Dream. His characters are, at their best, losers in the quest for success; at their worst, they are spectators, not even participants, in that competitive battle. While his protagonists do aspire to escape from their environments, to assume new identities, and to attain that American Dream, they are so stunted by their backgrounds and so crippled with their own guilt that their efforts are doomed from the start and their inevitable fate often involves the punishment that their guilt-ridden souls have unconsciously sought. In *Never Come Morning*, Bruno cannot escape his guilt for allowing Steffi to be raped by his gang and almost welcomes his punishment for the murder of another man; in *The Man with the Golden Arm*, Frankie Machine cannot escape his guilt for the accident that incapacitates his wife and so can end his drug addiction only by hanging himself; in *A Walk on the Wild Side*, Dove cannot escape his guilt for having raped Terasina, to whom he returns after having been blinded in a fight. In all three novels, the guilt that the man experiences from having abused a woman leads to a self-destructive impulse that negates his attempt to escape from his environment and produces the punishment he seeks.

Although it is not his first published novel (*Somebody in Boots*, a commercial failure that Algren revised and reissued as *A Walk on the Wild Side*, was his first published novel), *Never Come Morning* is Algren's first major novel. As the chronicle of a young man's passage from boyhood to manhood, *Never Come Morning* is another, albeit more cynical, American initiation novel, in which Bruno Bicek's initiation leads to his death. Like many young men, Bruno dreams of escaping from the ghetto through professional sports, either boxing or baseball ("Lefty" Bicek is a pitcher), but Algren quickly indicates, through similar chapter headings, that Bruno shares a "problem" with Casey Benkowski, his idol, whose defeat in the ring foreshadows Bruno's eventual defeat in life. Bruno's dreams are illusory, the product of the media: He reads *Kayo* magazine, sees pictures of boxers on matchbook covers, and watches Jimmy Cagney movies. His dream of becoming a "modern Kitchel," a former Polish-American boxing champion, reflects his desire to become someone else, to define his success in terms of other people, not himself. To become a successful man, he seeks status as the president and treasurer of the Warriors, his street gang, but his allegiance to the gang reflects his childish dependence on the group, not his adult leadership of it. His "other-directedness" also affects his relationship with Steffi, whom he seduces partly in order to gain status from the Warriors, who subsequently assert their own sexual rights to her. Rather than defend her and reveal the very "softness" that wins the readers' respect, he yields to the Warriors, thereby forsaking independence and manhood and incurring the guilt that eventually destroys him.

Like most of Algren's women, Steffi has a supporting role and exists primarily in terms of the male protagonist. She is the agent by which he comes of age sexually, acquires his spiritual guilt, eventually becomes an independent man, and finally, since she has alienated the informant Bonifacy, is doomed. Despite being the victim of a gang rape, Steffi retains her capacity for love and forgiveness, limited as that is, and becomes the stereotyped "whore with the heart of gold" whose love enables the "hero," antiheroic as he is, to overcome the odds. Her passivity is reflected symbolically through Algren's description of the fly without wings in Steffi's room: After he "seduces" her, Bruno destroys the fly. Later, when Bruno wins a Kewpie doll and subsequently and unthinkingly destroys it, Algren ties the fate of the doll, an appropriate symbol, to Steffi, who is won and destroyed by Bruno. Steffi's fate seems even crueler than Bruno's, since he will "escape" in death but Steffi will remain trapped with the other prostitutes who endure at "Mama" Tomek's brothel.

Before he is incarcerated, Bruno does mature through a series of tests that prove his manhood. Although he cannot articulate his love and desire for forgiveness, he does come to understand that love is compatible with manhood. When he arranges a fight for himself with Honeyboy Tucker, he acts independently; when he overcomes Fireball Kodadek and Tiger Pultoric, Bonifacy's thugs, he overcomes his fear of physical mutilation (Fireball's knife) and of his idol and father figure (Pultoric is the former champion). Before he can "be his own man," Bruno must overcome his childish dependence and hero worship. Bruno's subsequent victory over Tucker makes his earlier symbolic victory official and gives him the identity he seeks as a promising "contender," but that identity is destroyed when he is arrested only minutes later and sent to jail.

Images of imprisonment pervade the novel, which is concerned with the institutions that house inmates. When Bruno first serves time, Algren digresses to describe prison life, just as he does when he recounts Steffi's life at the brothel, where she is no less a prisoner. While she is there, she dreams of a "great stone penitentiary" and of the "vault" that is the barber's room. The prison and the brothel are appropriate institutions for a city which Algren compares to a madhouse. (Algren also sees the prostitutes as inmates of an insane asylum.) There is no escape for Steffi or Bruno, just as there is no real morning in this somber tale of darkness and night. Algren's Chicago is America in microcosm: As madhouse, prison, and brothel, it is an insane, entrapped world where people "sell out," thereby prostituting themselves.

In *The Man with the Golden Arm*, also set in Polish-American Chicago, Algren reiterates many of the themes, images, and character types that exist in *Never Come Morning*. Although the novel's controversial theme of drug addiction has received much attention, Algren is not concerned with drug addiction per se, but with the forces, external and internal, that lead to the addictive, dependent personalities that render people unable to cope with their environments or escape from them. Once again, Algren's characters are life's losers, "the luckless living soon to become the luckless dead," the "wary and the seeking, the strayed, the frayed, the happy and the hapless, the lost, the luckless, the lucky and the doomed" who become the "disinherited," those who emerge "from the wrong side of its [America's] billboards." The "hunted who also hope" in *Never Come Morning* become the "pursued" in *The Man with the Golden Arm*, which also relies on naturalistic metaphors comparing people and animals.

Since the characters are themselves victims of a system that excludes them, it seems ironic that they should experience guilt, but Algren's protagonist, Frankie Machine, is trapped by the guilt he feels at having been responsible for the car accident that has paralyzed Sophie, his wife. (Since Sophie has induced the paralysis—there is nothing physically wrong with her—his guilt is even more ironic.) Sophie uses Frankie's guilt to "hook" (a word suggesting addiction) him, punish him, and contribute to their self-destructive mutual dependence. Algren describes Frankie's guilt as "slow and cancerous" and even has Louie, the pusher, attribute drug addiction to the desire for self-punishment. Frankie, the "pursued," is not alone in his guilt, for Algren portrays Record Head Bednar, the "pursuer," as also afflicted by a consuming guilt. As the agent of "justice," he feels "of all men most alone, of all men most guilty of all the lusts he had ever condemned in others." Bednar, who is hardly without sin, must nevertheless "cast the first stone."

Sin and guilt permeate this novel, which belabors religious imagery, particularly that concerning the crucifixion. The controlling metaphor in the novel is Sophie's "luminous crucifix," which she uses to enslave Frankie. Sophie states, "My cross is this chair. I'm settin' on *my* cross. . . . I'm *nailed* to mine." When her friend Violet suggests that she is driving in her own "nails,"

Sophie evades the issue because her "crucifixion," while voluntary, is not selfless but selfish. Algren observes the parallels between Sophie and Christ—both have been betrayed and bleed for the sins of others—but Sophie lacks love. In another parody of the crucifixion, Sparrow protests to Bednar, "You're nailin' me to the cross, Captain"; Bednar responds, "What the hell you think they're [the politicians] doin' to me?" Although they have enough religious teaching to mouth biblical allusions, Algren's characters use Christianity only as popular culture, as a source, like advertising and the movies, of reference to their own ego-centered worlds. Although Algren suggests that "God had forgotten His own," at least in Frankie's case, it is at least equally true that, as Sophie confesses, she and Frankie have forgotten God. Sophie's pathetic, self-centered musing about God having gone somewhere and keeping His distance indicate that He has no place in the world of Division Street. Surely Algren's allusion to the gamblers' God, who watches Sparrow's "fall," reflects the post-Christian modern world.

In Algren's naturalistic world, the characters are seen as caged animals waiting to be slaughtered. At the beginning of the novel, Frankie, who waits for justice from Bednar, watches a roach drowning in a bucket and is tempted to help it, but the roach dies before he intercedes, just as Frankie dies without anyone interceding for him. Algren's metaphor for the trapped Sophie is equally flattering. When she hears the mousetrap in the closet snap shut, "she felt it close as if it had shut within herself, hard and fast forever." Even Molly Novotny, who resembles Steffi in being a "fallen woman" and agent of redemption, is depicted as living in a "nest." In fact, Algren uses the animal imagery to suggest Frankie's impending fate. When Frankie is apprehended for stealing irons, Algren uses "over-fed hens" and "bosomy biddies" to describe the saleswomen and then has Frankie glimpse "a butcher holding a broken-necked rooster." Since Frankie finally hangs himself, the glimpse is ironically prophetic. Frankie's addiction is also expressed in animal terms: Frankie has a "monkey on his back," and while he temporarily rids himself of the monkey, permanent escape is impossible. The two caged monkeys at the Kitten Klub shriek insults at the patrons and serve as the metaphor incarnate for Frankie's addiction.

Frankie's addiction is also expressed in terms of an army buddy also addicted to morphine, Private McGantic, whose "presence" is akin to the monkey's. By the end of the novel Frankie has "become" Private McGantic: Frankie calls himself "Private Nowhere," suggesting both the identification and the lack of direction. "Private McGantic" is, however, only one of Frankie's identities; the novel recounts his futile attempt to become someone other than Frankie Machine (the assumed name reflects his lost humanity), the Dealer. He wants Molly to call him the "Drummer," not the "Dealer," but he never becomes a professional musician, and part of his tragedy is that he does not know who he is: "Who am I anyway, Solly?" The answer Solly

(Sparrow) gives, "Be yourself," is a meaningless cliché, an example of circular reasoning because Frankie does not know what his "self" is. The official inquest into the death of Francis Majcinek (Frankie's "real" name) establishes nothing of consequence (his addiction is not even alluded to) except that he is the "deceased," one of the "luckless dead" Algren mentions earlier in the novel. Even his fictional life is not "real": It is a "comic strip" from birth to death.

A Walk on the Wild Side, Algren's fourth novel, is a reworking of *Somebody in Boots*, published some twenty years earlier. As a result, although it resembles the other two in its characters, loose structure, and imagery, it also looks back to an earlier time, the Depression, and its setting is New Orleans rather than Chicago. Once again, Algren focuses on prison inmates, whose "kangaroo court" justice is superior to the justice they receive "outside," and on prostitutes, who also "serve their time" and are compared to caged birds (the brothel is an "aviary"). Despite their situation and their pasts, they are "innocent children" in their naïveté and illusions, and one of them is the means by which the hero is redeemed. Other notable characters include the freaks and the cripples who frequent Dockerty's "Dollhouse" and who are the physical counterparts of the emotional cripples in the novel. Achilles Schmidt, legless former circus strongman, is the exception, for he has found psychological strength through the accident that should have "crippled" him. It is only when Dove Linkhorn, the protagonist, is blinded and therefore "crippled" by Schmidt that he rids himself of the illusions that have weakened him.

A parody of the Horatio Alger myth of the American Dream, *A Walk on the Wild Side* concerns an ambitious young man who "wants to make something of himself" and leaves the farm to find fame and fortune in the city. Dove's journey is "educational," in terms of the reading instruction he receives and the culture he acquires, as well as the "lessons" he learns about capitalism and life in general. At the beginning of the novel, Dove is an "innocent," as his name suggests, but that "innocence" is not sexual—he rapes Terasina, the Earth Mother who is also his first "mentor"—but experiential, in that he believes in the "Ladder of Success" with "unlimited opportunities" for "ambitious young men." Algren offers Dove a naturalistic parable of capitalism, particularly on the tenuous nature of life at the top. The headless terrapin in the fish market struggles to the top by using its superior strength in "wading contentedly over mothers and orphans," but its reign as King of the Turtles is short-lived, and it has literally and symbolically "lost its head." Algren adds that Dove does not know that "there was also room for one more on the bottom." Before he reaches the bottom, Dove becomes a salesman, the epitome of the enterprising capitalist; the coffee scam and the phony beauty-parlor certificate racket, while illegal, are also seen as integral parts of capitalism.

Before he achieves his greatest success as a "salesman" of sex, Dove works, appropriately, in a condom manufacturing plant, which also sells sex. In his role as "Big Stingaree" in Finnerty's brothel, he is paid to perform an art which involves the "deflowering" of "virgins," who are played by prostitutes. In effect, the brothel, the primary setting in the novel, also serves as the symbolic center since Algren presents a society that has sold itself, has "prostituted" itself to survive. Ironically, the real prostitutes in the brothel are morally superior to the "prostitutes" in mainstream American society, the "Do-Right Daddies," the powerful people who crusade against sin but also sin within the laws they create.

Hallie Breedlove, a prostitute, "sins," but she is capable of love and compassion, first with Schmidt and then with Dove, with whom she leaves the brothel. The "escape" is futile, however, for her subsequent pregnancy, in the light of her black "blood," threatens their future, and she believes that she can have her child only if she returns to her past, the mulatto village where she was born. Dove lacks her insight and in his attempt to find her is jailed, released, and then loses his sight in a battle with Schmidt. Metaphorically, however, in searching for her, he finds himself, and in losing his vision, he gains insight. Having learned that the "loser's side of the street" is superior to the "winners'," Dove abandons his quest for success and returns to his Texas hometown to be reconciled to Terasina. Unlike Bruno and Frankie, Dove not only survives but also resolves to deal constructively with the guilt caused by his sin against his woman.

Algren's last novel, *The Devil's Stocking*, is not so much a "novel" as a fictional treatment of Reuben Carter's trial and imprisonment. What began as an *Esquire* assignment, covering a boxer's murder trial, grew to "novel" proportions, probably because of the boxing and the trial, both of which appear in his other novels. The Algren characters—prostitutes, gamblers, police officers, and petty crooks—reappear in the novel about Carter, renamed Ruby Calhoun for fictive purposes. Because of its geographical and chronological distance from his earlier novels, as well as its blending of fact and fiction, it is not among the works for which Algren will be remembered.

Despite the qualified optimism of *A Walk on the Wild Side*, Algren's novels tend to paint a negative image of capitalistic American society with its nightmarish American Dream. Chicago and New Orleans become microcosms of America, a country marked by images of madness, imprisonment, and prostitution. In that world, virtue, such as it is, resides on the "loser's side of the street," in the prisons and the brothels. Constricted by their backgrounds, Algren's male protagonists typically strive to escape and assume a new identity, sin against a woman (thereby incurring guilt that compounds their problems), serve time in prison (presented as a place of refuge), and pursue a self-destructive course that leads inevitably to death or mutilation.

Thomas L. Erskine

Other major works

SHORT FICTION: *The Neon Wilderness*, 1947; *The Last Carousel*, 1973 (also includes sketches and poems).

NONFICTION: *Chicago: City on the Make*, 1951; *Who Lost an American?*, 1963; *Conversations with Nelson Algren*, 1964; *Notes from a Sea Diary: Hemingway All the Way*, 1965.

ANTHOLOGY: *Nelson Algren's Own Book of Lonesome Monsters*, 1962.

Bibliography

Corrington, John William. "Nelson Algren Talks with NOR's Editor-at-Large." *New Orleans Review* 1 (Winter, 1969): 130-132. Describes Algren as an important force in contemporary American literature. In the interviews, Algren discusses his early fiction and his more recent writings and comments on his sense of the artist's social responsibility.

Cox, Martha Heasley, and Wayne Chatterton. *Nelson Algren*. Boston: Twayne, 1975. This well-executed critical biography traces the development of Algren's major works, with a section on symbolism and an overall assessment for each. The concluding chapter refers to Algren as both poet—he continued to write poetry that echoed his fictional themes—and prophet—in his fictional approach to social consciousness. A chronology, notes, and a bibliography are included.

Donohue, H. E. F., with Nelson Algren. *Conversations with Nelson Algren*. New York: Hill & Wang, 1964. A book of interviews (from 1962 and 1963). Effectively covers Algren's family background, experiences as a wanderer during the Depression, and notions of the writer's role in relation to society.

Karl, Frederick R. *American Fictions: 1940-1980*. New York: Harper & Row, 1983. A brief but insightful analysis which links *The Man with the Golden Arm* to Stephen Crane's *Maggie: A Girl of the Streets* and to James T. Farrell's *Studs Lonigan* books. Calls Algren a forerunner of the "Beat" literature of the 1950's, in which the characters chose their lives of drugs and poverty, but notes that Algren's characters are caught in an existence they did not choose.

Pitts, Mary Ellen. "Algren's El: Internalized Machine and Displaced Nature." *South Atlantic Review* 52 (November, 1987): 61-74. Focuses on Chicago's elevated railway as a symbol of entrapment in the inner city in Algren's major works; the prisonlike bars of the El's framework symbolize the circumscription of the characters' lives and echo the "danger" of technology—the enclosing of the human mind that occurs when technology is unquestioned. Details from Algren's fiction are thoroughly explored.

KINGSLEY AMIS

Born: London, England; April 16, 1922

Principal long fiction

Lucky Jim, 1954; *That Uncertain Feeling*, 1955; *I Like It Here*, 1958; *Take a Girl Like You*, 1960; *One Fat Englishman*, 1963; *The Egyptologists*, 1965 (with Robert Conquest); *The Anti-Death League*, 1966; *Colonel Sun: A James Bond Adventure*, 1968 (as Robert Markham); *I Want It Now*, 1968; *The Green Man*, 1969; *Girl, 20*, 1971; *The Riverside Villas Murder*, 1973; *Ending Up*, 1974; *The Alteration*, 1976; *Jake's Thing*, 1978; *Russian Hide-and-Seek*, 1980; *Stanley and the Women*, 1984; *The Old Devils*, 1986; *Difficulties with Girls*, 1988; *The Folks that Live on the Hill*, 1990.

Other literary forms

Kingsley Amis is best known as a novelist, but readers have turned often to his other writings for the insight they give into the man and his fiction. Many of the themes which are explored in depth in his novels are expressed indirectly in the peripheral works. He has published two collections of short stories, entitled *My Enemy's Enemy* (1962) and *Collected Stories* (1981). *Dear Illusion*, a novella, was published in 1972 in a limited edition of five hundred copies. His collections of poetry include: *Bright November* (1947), *A Frame of Mind* (1953), *A Case of Samples: Poems, 1946-1956* (1956), *The Evans Country* (1962), *A Look Round the Estate: Poems, 1957-1967* (1967), and *Collected Poems: 1944-1979* (1979). He edited *The New Oxford Book of Light Verse* (1978). Amis' criticism covers an extremely wide range; in addition to studies of figures as diverse as Jane Austen and Rudyard Kipling, he published one of the first significant critical books on science fiction, *New Maps of Hell: A Survey of Science Fiction* (1960), a work that has done much to encourage academic study of the genre and to win recognition for many gifted science-fiction writers. *Socialism and the Intellectuals* (1957), *The James Bond Dossier* (1965), *Lucky Jim's Politics* (1968), *On Drink* (1972), and four volumes of collected science fiction, edited with Robert Conquest and entitled *Spectrum: A Science Fiction Anthology* (1961, 1962, 1963, 1965) offer further evidence of the extraordinary range of his work.

Achievements

Almost from the beginning of his career, Amis has enjoyed the attention of numerous and influential commentators. Because his works have been filled with innovations, surprises, and variations in techniques and themes, it is not surprising that until recently critics and reviewers alike have found it difficult to make a definitive statement about his achievements. The range of his work is extraordinary: fiction, poetry, reviews, criticism, humor, science fiction, and biography. Of all of his writings, however, his achievement depends most upon his novels.

Amis' early novels are considered by many critics to be "angry" novels of protest against the contemporary social, political, and economic scene in Britain. The themes include: resentment of a rigid class stratification; rejection of formal institutional ties and relationships; discouragement with the economic insecurity and low status of those without money; loathing of pretentiousness in any form; and disenchantment with the past. Because many of Amis' contemporaries, including John Wain, John Osborne, John Braine, and Alan Sillitoe, seemed to express similar concerns, and because many came from working or lower-middle-class backgrounds, went to Oxford or Cambridge, and taught for a time at a provincial university, journalists soon spoke of them as belonging to a literary movement. The "Angry Young Men," as their fictional heroes were called, were educated men who did not want to be gentlemen. Kenneth Allsop called them "a new, rootless, faithless, classless class" lacking in manners and morals; W. Somerset Maugham called them "mean, malicious and envious . . . scum," and warned that these men would some day rule England. Some critics even confused the characters with the writers themselves. Amis' Jim Dixon (in *Lucky Jim*) was appalled by the tediousness and falseness of academic life; therefore, Dixon was interpreted as a symbol of antiintellectualism. Dixon taught at a provincial university; therefore, he became a symbol of contempt for Cambridge and Oxford. Amis himself taught at a provincial university (Swansea); therefore, he and Dixon became one and the same in the minds of many critics. Like all literary generalizations, however, this one was soon inadequate. The most that can be said is that through Amis' early heroes there seemed to sound clearly those notes of disillusionment that were to become dominant in much of the literature of the 1950's.

Because it seems so artless, critics have also found Amis' fiction difficult to discuss. His straightforward plotting, gift for characterization, and ability to tell a good story, they say, are resistant to the modern techniques of literary criticism. Because Amis lacks the obscurity, complexity, and technical virtuosity of James Joyce or William Faulkner, these critics suggest that he is not to be valued as highly. In many of the early reviews, Amis is described as essentially a comic novelist, an entertainer, or an amiable satirist not unlike P. G. Wodehouse, the Marx Brothers, or Henry Fielding. Furthermore, his interest in mysteries, ghost stories, James Bond thrillers, and science fiction confirms for these critics the view that Amis is a writer lacking depth and serious intent.

Looking beyond the social commentary and entertainment found in Amis' work, other critics find a distinct relationship between Amis' novels and the "new sincerity" of the so-called Movement poets of the 1950's and later. These poets (including Amis himself, Philip Larkin, John Wain, and D. J. Enright, all of whom also wrote fiction) saw their work as an alternative to the symbolic and allusive poetry of T. S. Eliot and his followers. In a movement away from allusion, obscurity, and excesses of style, the Movement poets encouraged precision, lucidity, and craftsmanship. They concentrated on honesty of thought and feeling to emphasize what A. L. Rowse calls a "businesslike intention to communicate with the reader." Amis' deceptively simple novels have been written with the same criteria he imposed on his poetry; one cannot read Amis with a measure suitable only to Joyce or Faulkner. Rather, his intellectual and literary ancestors antedate the great modernist writers, and the resultant shape is that of a nineteenth century man of letters. His novels may be appreciated for their commonsense approach. He writes clearly. He avoids extremes or excessive stylistic experimentation. He is witty, satirical, and often didactic.

Amis' novels since 1980 have added a new phase to his career. One of the universal themes which has most engaged Amis and about which he has a rich variety of things to say and show is the relation between men and women, both in and out of marriage. Since 1980, he has moved away from the broad scope of a society plagued by trouble to examine instead the troubles plaguing one of that society's most fundamental institutions—relationships—and the conflicts, misunderstandings, and drastically different responses of men and women to the world. Most of his characters suffer anxiety-ridden, blighted marriages. Often they seem intelligent but dazed, as if there were something they had lost but they cannot quite remember what it was. Something has indeed been lost, and loss is at the heart of all of Amis' novels, so that he is, as novelist Malcolm Bradbury calls him, "one of our most disturbing contemporary novelists, an explorer of historical pain." From the beginning of the canon, Amis has focused upon the absence of something significant in modern life: a basis, a framework, a structure for living, such as the old institutions like religion or marriage once provided. Having pushed that loss in societal terms to its absolute extreme in the previous novels, Amis now studies it in personal terms, within the fundamental social unit. In *The Old Devils*, for example (for which he won the 1986 Booker Fiction Prize), his characters are not going to regain the old, secure sense of meaning that their lives once held, and Amis does not pretend that they will. What success they manage to attain is always partial. What, in the absence of an informing faith or an all-consuming family life, could provide purpose for living? More simply, how is one to be useful? This is the problem that haunts Amis' characters, and it is a question, underlying all of his novels, that comes to the forefront now.

In looking back over Amis' career, critics have found a consistent moral judgment quite visible beneath the social commentary, entertainment, and traditional techniques that Amis employs. Beginning in a world filled with verbal jokes, masquerades, and incidents, Amis' view of life grew increasingly pessimistic until he arrived at a fearfully grim vision of a nightmare world filled with hostility, violence, sexual abuse, and self-destruction. Critics, therefore, view Amis most significantly as a moralist, concerned with the ethical life in difficult times. Amis' response to such conditions has been to use his great powers of observation and mimicry both to illuminate the changes in postwar British society and to suggest various ways of understanding and possibly coping with those changes. For all these reasons, one can assert that Amis has achieved a major reputation in contemporary English fiction, and, as is so often the case today, his is an achievement that does not depend upon any single work. It is rather the totality of his work with which readers should reckon.

Biography

Kingsley William Amis was born in London on April 16, 1922. His father, William Robert, was an office clerk with Coleman's Mustard and fully expected his only child to enter commerce. His son's intention, however, was to be a writer—a poet, really—though it was not until the publication of his rollicking and irreverent first novel, *Lucky Jim*, in 1954, that Amis achieved his goal.

By Amis' own account, he had been writing since he was a child. Writing became for him a means of coming to terms with certain fears. As a boy he suffered from the routine terrors of childhood—fear of the dark, fear of the future, fear of other children, fear of his parents' disapproval—but as he grew older the subjects of his fears changed. He was a complicated individual; depression alternated with laughter, and an inner loneliness counterbalanced his social charm. Typically, one fear involves his health. Like many of his characters, one of his strongest fears was and continues to be the fear of loneliness. "Being the only person in the house is something I wouldn't like at all," he said, years later. "I would develop anxiety. By this I mean more than just a rational dislike of being alone and wanting company but something which means, for me, becoming very depressed and tense. I've always been terribly subject to tension. I worry a lot."

Kingsley Amis as an author and his characters themselves often seem to be running scared, playing out their lives while always looking over their shoulders, afraid that the truth of life's meaninglessness will catch up to them. Amis admits that writing fiction encourages the illusion that there is some sense in life. "There isn't," he says, "but if that's all you thought, you'd go mad." In his fiction, if not in life, he can pretend that there is a pattern in events and that the suffering of his characters can be justified, or explained, or atoned for, or made all right. Such power to conjure up meaning where it otherwise may not exist brings with it the "wonderful feeling of being Lord of Creation."

Long before Amis was to experience this power, he was merely a schoolboy at St. Hilda's local fee-paying school. At St. Hilda's he learned French from Miss Crampton and he also developed a crush on his English teacher, Miss Barr, "a tall, Eton-crowned figure of improbable eloquence." It is in these inauspicious surroundings, he says, humorously, that perhaps "we can date my first education into the glories of our literature." Perhaps because of Miss Barr but more probably because of his temperament and interests, he developed a fascination for anything to do with writing—pens, paper, erasers.

His interest may have been piqued at St. Hilda's but his first literary efforts occurred at Norbury College. There he was exposed to the vast entertainment that the days held for a British public school boy in the 1930's: under the tutelage of his teachers, he began to write stories and poems. His first published work of fiction, a three-hundred-word adventure story called "The Sacred Rhino of Uganda," appeared in the school magazine. In the fall of 1934, he entered the "really splendid" City of London School—a day school of seven hundred boys, overlooking the Thames by Blackfriars Bridge. Amis read much during this period. He specialized in the classics until he was sixteen, then switched to English, but later would wish that he had been more interested in scripture and divinity at the time and had been touched by the wings of faith, a wish that his fiction would ultimately demonstrate. He also read French. Early artistic delights included watercolors, Dadaism, and architecture. He especially loved to read poetry, and with his keen mind and quick sensibilities he could take in a considerable amount of material quickly.

In the prewar year of 1939, while he was in the sixth form, Amis and many of his school chums were suddenly surprised to find themselves being sent to Marlborough College in Wiltshire as evacuees; there he spent the next five terms. He found himself in the small country town of Marlborough, one of the most undisturbed countrysides remaining in the southwest of England. There, in vivid contrast to the suburbia he knew in Clapham, Amis was initiated into the beauties and mysteries of nature, and for the rest of his life he would carry images of Marlborough with him and re-create them in his fictional country scenes.

Amis' first novel, *The Legacy*, written while he attended St. John's College at the University of Oxford (1941-1942, 1945-1947), was rejected by fourteen publishers. Eventually Amis abandoned it altogether, having come to regard it as boring, unfunny, and derivative. Although his studies at Oxford were interrupted by the war, Amis persisted, earning his B.A. (with honors) and M.A. degrees in English.

Several factors influenced Amis' development into a writer whose stories and style are unique and universally recognized. His comic proclivities were encouraged by his father—a man with "a talent for physical clowning and mimicry." Amis describes himself as "undersized, law-abiding, timid," a child able to make himself popular by charm or clowning, who found that at school he could achieve much by exploiting his inherited powers of mimicry. His school friends have testified to Amis' capacity for making people laugh. Philip Larkin's description of their first meeting (1941), in the 1963 introduction to his own novel, *Jill*, suggests that it was Amis' "genius for imaginative mimicry" which attracted him: "For the first time I felt myself in the presence of a talent greater than my own." John Wain has also recalled how, in the "literary group" to which both of them belonged, Amis was a "superb mimic" who relished differences of character and idiom.

This period of "intensive joke swapping," as Larkin called it, continued when Amis entered the army in 1942. He became an officer, served in the Royal Signals, and landed in Normandy in June, 1944. After service in France, Belgium, and West Germany, he was demobilized in October, 1945. He recalls how he and a friend wrote part of a novel based on "malicious caricatures" of fellow officers. This period also was to provide material for such stories as "My Enemy's Enemy," "Court of Inquiry" (based on a personal experience), and "I Spy Strangers," but its immediate effect was to open his eyes to the world, to all sorts of strange people and strange ways of behaving.

Amis' status as an only child also contributed to his development as a writer, for he found himself looking at an early age for "self-entertainment." He satisfied this need by reading adventure stories, science fiction, and boys' comics. During these years, too, Amis became interested in horror tales. He recalls seeing the Boris Karloff version of *Frankenstein* and *The Mummy* and the Fredric March version of *Dr. Jekyll and Mr. Hyde*. Since that time, Amis has been interested in what might be called the minor genres on grounds of wonder, excitement, and "a liking for the strange, the possibly horrific." Amis became aware that the detective story, various tales of horror or terror, and the science-fiction story provided vehicles for both social satire and investigation of human nature in a way not accessible to the mainstream novelist.

Along with his natural comic gifts, his interest in genre fiction, and his war experiences, Amis' development was influenced by his early exposure to an English tradition which has resisted the modernist innovations so influential in America and on the Continent today. His dislike for experimental prose, for mystification, may be traced in part to the influence of one of his tutors at Oxford, the Anglo-Saxon scholar Gavin Bone, and to his readings of certain eighteenth century novelists whose ability to bring immense variety and plenitude to their work without reverting to obscurity or stylistic excess appealed to the young Amis.

Amis attributes his personal standards of morality both to his readings in Charles Dickens, Henry Fielding, and Samuel Richardson and to the training in standard Protestant virtues he received while growing up at home. Both of his parents were Baptists, but in protest against their own forceful religious indoctrination, their visits to church became less and less frequent as they grew older, Any reader of Amis' works soon becomes aware that there is in his writings a clear repudiation of traditional Christian belief. Nevertheless, from his parents he received certain central moral convictions which crystallized a personal philosophy of life and art. Hard work, conscientiousness, obedience, loyalty, frugality, patience—these lessons and others were put forward and later found their way into his novels, all of which emphasize the necessity of good works and of trying to live a moral life in the natural—as opposed to the supernatural—world.

Analysis

Kingsley Amis' fiction is characterized by a recurring preoccupation with certain themes and concepts, with certain basic human experiences, attitudes, and perceptions. These persistent themes are treated with enormous variety, however, particularly in Amis' novels which draw on the conventions of genre fiction—the mystery, the spy thriller, the ghost story, and so on. Of the twenty novels Amis has published, his development as a seriocomic novelist is especially apparent in *Lucky Jim, Take a Girl Like You, The Anti-Death League, The Green Man*, and *The Old Devils*, his most substantial and complex works, each of which is representative of a specific stage in his career. All five of these novels are set in contemporary England. Drawing upon a variety of traditional techniques of good storytelling—good and bad characters, simple irony, straightforward plot structure, clear point of view—they restate, in a variety of ways, the traditional pattern of tragedy: a man, divided and complex, vulnerable both to the world and to himself, is forced to make choices that will determine his destiny. Built into this situation is the probability that he will bring down suffering on his head and injure others in the process.

In *Lucky Jim*, for example, Amis establishes a comic acceptance of many of life's injustices in the academic world. The novel is distinguished by clear-cut cases of right and wrong, a simple irony, and knockabout farce. Because he has neither the courage nor the economic security to protest openly, the hero lives a highly comic secret life of protest consisting of practical jokes and rude faces, all directed against the hypocrisy and pseudointellectualism of certain members of the British Establishment. While only hinted at in *Lucky Jim*, Amis' moral seriousness becomes increasingly evident beginning with *Take a Girl Like You*. Whereas in *Lucky Jim* the values are "hidden" beneath a comic narrative, gradually the comedy is submerged beneath a more serious treatment. Thus, *Take a Girl Like You* is a turning point for Amis in a number of ways: the characterization is more complex, the moral problems are more intense, and the point of view is not limited to one central character. Distinguished also by a better balance between the comic and the serious, the novel is more pessimistic than its predecessors, less given to horseplay and high spirits.

In later novels such as *The Anti-Death League* and *The Green Man*, Amis continues to see life more darkly, shifting to an increasingly metaphysical, even theological concern. Contemporary England is viewed as a wasteland of the spirit, and his characters try vainly to cope with a precarious world filled with madness and hysteria, a world in which love and religion have become distorted and vulgarized. Threatened with death and ugly accidents by a malicious God, Amis' characters feel powerless to change, and in an attempt to regain control of their lives, act immorally. Amis' ultimate vision is one in which all of the traditional certainties—faith, love, loyalty, responsibility, decency—have lost their power to comfort and sustain. Man is left groping in the dark of a nightmare world. In the later *The Old Devils*, Amis' study of a Wales and a Welshness that have slipped out of reach forever clearly shows a culmination of his increasing damnation of Western society, portrayed through the microcosm of human relationships. The final picture is one of the aimlessness of old age, the meaninglessness of much of life itself.

In *Lucky Jim*, a bumbling, somewhat conscientious hero stumbles across the social and cultural landscape of contemporary British academic life, faces a number of crises of conscience, makes fun of the world and of himself, and eventually returns to the love of a sensible, realistic girl. This is the traditional comic course followed by Amis' first three novels, of which *Lucky Jim* is the outstanding example. Beneath the horseplay and high spirits, however, Amis rhetorically manipulates the reader's moral judgment so that he leaves the novel sympathetic to the hero's point of view. By triumphing over an unrewarding job, a pretentious family, and a predatory female colleague, Dixon becomes the first in a long line of Amis' heroes who stand for common sense and decency; for the belief that life is to be made happy now; for the notion that "nice things are nicer than nasty things."

To develop his moral concern, Amis divides his characters into two archetypal groups reminiscent of the fantasy tale: the generally praiseworthy figures, the ones who gain the greatest share of the reader's sympathy; and the "evil" characters, those who obstruct the good characters. Jim Dixon (the put-upon young man), Gore-Urquhart (his benefactor or savior), and Christine Callaghan (the decent girl to whom Dixon turns) are among the former, distinguished by genuineness, sincerity, and a lack of pretense. Among the latter are Professor Welch (Dixon's principal tormentor), his son, Bertrand (the defeated boaster), and the neurotic Margaret Peele (the thwarted "witch"), all of whom disguise their motives and present a false appearance.

One example should be enough to demonstrate Amis' technique—the introduction to the seedy, absentminded historian, Professor Welch. In the opening chapter, Amis establishes an ironic discrepancy between what Welch seems to be (a scholar discussing history) and what he is in reality (a "vaudeville character" lecturing on the differences between flute and recorder). Although he tries to appear a cultured, sensitive intellecutal, all of the images point to a charlatan leading a boring, selfish life. His desk is "misleadingly littered." Once he is found standing, "surprisingly enough," in front of the college library's new-books shelf. Succeeding physical description undercuts his role-playing: he resembles "an old boxer," "an African savage," "a broken robot." What is more, his speech and gestures are mechanized by cliché and affectation. Professing to worship "integrated village-type community life" and to oppose anything mechanical, he is himself a virtual automaton, and becomes more completely so as the novel progresses. Although Amis does not term Welch a ridiculous phony, the inference is inescapable.

Central to the novel's theme is Dixon's secret life of protest. Although he hates the Welch family, for economic reasons he dares not rebel openly. Therefore, he resorts to a comic fantasy world to express rage or loathing toward certain imbecilities of the Welch set. His rude faces and clever pranks serve a therapeutic function—a means by which Dixon can safely release his exasperations. At other times, however, Dixon becomes more aggressive: he fantasizes stuffing Welch down the lavatory or beating him about the head and shoulders with a bottle until he reveals why he gave a French name to his son.

In Amis' later novels, when the heroes' moral problems become more intense, even life-threatening, such aggressive acts become more frequent and less controlled. In this early novel, however, what the reader remembers best are the comic moments. Dixon is less an angry young man than a funny, bumbling, confused individual for whom a joke makes life bearable. There are, of course, other ways in which to react to an unjust world. One can flail at it, as does John Osborne's Jimmy Porter (*Look Back in Anger*, 1957). One can try to escape from it, as will Patrick Standish in *Take a Girl Like You*, or, one can try to adapt to it. Like Charles Lumley's rebellion against middle-class values in John Wain's *Hurry On Down* (1953), Dixon's rebellion against the affectations of academia ends with an adjustment to the society and with a partial acceptance of its values. By remaining in the system, he can at least try to effect change.

Ostensibly another example of the familiar story of initiation, Amis' fourth novel, *Take a Girl Like You*, contains subtleties and ironies which set it apart from *Lucky Jim*. The characterization, the balance between the comic and the serious, and the emphasis on sexual behavior and the pursuit of pleasure blend to make this novel a significant step forward in Amis' development as a novelist.

The plot of this disturbing moral comedy is built around a variety of motifs: the travelogue and the innocent-abroad story, the theme of love-in-conflict-with-love, and the country-mouse story of an innocent girl visiting the big city for the first time. Jenny Bunn, from whose point of view more than half of the novel is narrated, is the conventional, innocent young woman who has not been touched by deep experience in worldly matters. Like Jim Dixon, she finds herself in an unfamiliar setting, confronting people who treat her as a stranger with strange ideas. Out of a simpleminded zeal for the virtues of love and marriage, she becomes the victim of a plausible, nasty man.

Jenny carries out several artistic functions in the story. She is chiefly prominent as the perceptive observer of events close to her. Again like Dixon, she is able to detect fraud and incongruities from a considerable distance. When Patrick Standish first appears, for example, she understands that his look at her means he is "getting ideas about her." Amis draws a considerable fund of humor from Jenny's assumed naïveté. His chief device is the old but appropriate one of naïve comment, innocently uttered but tipped with truth. Jenny, a young girl living in a restrictive environment and ostensibly deferential toward the attitudes and opinions of the adults who compose that environment, yet also guided by her own instinctive reactions, may be expected to misinterpret a great deal of what she observes and feels. The reader follows her as she is excited, puzzled, and disturbed by Patrick's money-mad and pleasure-mad world—a world without fixed rules of conduct. Many of the "sex scenes" between them are built upon verbal jokes, comic maneuvers, digressions and irrelevancies, all of which give life to the conventional narrative with which Amis is working.

Patrick Standish, from whose point of view a little less than half of the novel is narrated, is the antithesis of the good, moral, somewhat passive Jenny. Like the masterful, selfish Bertrand Welch, he is a womanizer and a conscious hypocrite who condemns himself with every word he utters. In spite of Patrick's intolerable behavior and almost crippling faults, Amis maintains some degree of sympathy for him by granting him more than a surface treatment. In the earlier novels, the villains are seen from a distance through the heroes' eyes. In *Take a Girl Like You*, however, an interior view of the villain's thoughts, frustrations, and fears allows the reader some measure of understanding. Many scenes are rhetorically designed to emphasize Patrick's isolation and helplessness. Fears of impotence, cancer, and death haunt him. He seeks escape from these fears by turning to sex, drink, and practical jokes, but this behavior leads only to further boredom, unsatisfied longing, and ill-health.

Also contributing to the somber tone of the novel are secondary characters such as Dick Thompson, Seaman Jackson, and Graham MacClintoch. Jackson equates marriage with "'legalised bloody prostitution.'" MacClintoch complains that, for the unattractive, there is no charity in sex. Jenny's ideals are further diminished when she attends a party with these men. The conversation anticipates the emotional barrenness of later novels, in which love is dead and in its place are found endless games. Characters speak of love, marriage, and virtue in the same tone as they would speak of a cricket game or a new set of teeth.

With *Take a Girl Like You*, Amis leaves behind the hilarity and high spirits on which his reputation was founded, in order to give expression to the note of hostility and cruelty hinted at in *Lucky Jim*. Drifting steadily from bewilderment to disillusionment, Jenny and Patrick signal the beginning of a new phase in Amis' moral vision. Life is more complex, more precarious, less jovial. The simple romantic fantasy solution at the end of *Lucky Jim* is not possible here.

The Anti-Death League represents for Amis yet another extension in philosophy and technique. The conventions of the spy-thriller provide the necessary framework for a story within which Amis presents, from multiple viewpoints, a world view that is more pessimistic than that of any of his previous novels. A preoccupation with fear and evil, an explicit religious frame of reference, and a juxtaposition of pain and laughter, cruelty and tenderness all go to create a sense of imminent calamity reminiscent of George Orwell's *Nineteen Eighty-Four* (1949). No longer does Amis' world allow carefree, uncomplicated figures of fun to move about, relying upon good luck and practical jokes to see them through their difficulties. Life has become an absurd game, and the players are suffering, often lonely and tragic individuals, caught in hopeless situations with little chance for winning the good life, free from anxieties, guilts, and doubts.

As the controlling image, the threat of death is introduced early in the novel in the form of an airplane shadow covering the principal characters. Related to this scene is an elaborate metaphor drawn from the language of pathology, astronomy, botany, and thermonuclear war. Part I of the three-part structure is entitled "The Edge of a Node"—referring to Operation Apollo, an elaborate project designed to destroy the Red Chinese with a horrible plague. As the narrative progresses, the characters are brought to the edge or dead center of the node.

Related to this preoccupation with death is the sexual unhappiness of the characters. Jim Dixon's romps with Margaret are farcical and at times rather sad. Patrick Standish's pursuit and conquest of Jenny Bunn are disgusting and somewhat tragic. In *The Anti-Death League*, the characters' pursuit of love and sex leads only to unhappiness and even danger. Two disastrous marriages and several unhappy affairs have brought Catherine Casement to the brink of madness. An unfaithful husband and a possessive lover have caused Luzy Hazell to avoid any emotional involvement whatsoever. A desire to get away from love impels Max Hunter, an alcoholic and unabashed homosexual, to join the army.

Along with the inversion of love, Amis dramatizes an inversion of religion. In place of a benevolent, supreme being, Amis has substituted a malevolent God whose malicious jokes lead to death and tragic accidents. In protest, Will Ayscue, the army chaplain, declares war on Christianity as the embodiment of the most vicious lies ever told. Max Hunter writes a poem against God ("To a Baby Born Without Limbs"), organizes the Anti-Death League, and demolishes the local priory. James Churchill cites Max Hunter's alcoholism, the death of a courier, and Catherine's cancer as reasons for retreating from a world gone bad. While, in the preceding novels, laughter helps the heroes cope with specific injustices, in *The Anti-Death League*, laughter only intensifies the horror, the pain. Sometimes Amis shifts abruptly from laughter to pain to intensify the pain. A lighthearted moment with Hunter in the hospital is followed by a depressing scene between Catherine and Dr. Best. News of Catherine's cancer is juxtaposed with Dr. Best's highly comic hide-and-seek game.

Hysteria, depression, boredom: these are some of the moods in the army camp, bespeaking a malaise and a loss of hope from which neither sex nor religion nor drink offers any escape. Although the reader both condemns and laughs at the characters' foibles, he feels a personal involvement with them because he sees the suffering through the sufferers' eyes. Alone, trying to regain control of their lives, they act irresponsibly and immorally. Only Moti Naidu—like Gore-Urquhart, a moral voice in the novel—speaks truth in spite of the other characters' tragic mistakes. His recommendations that they aspire to common sense, fidelity, prudence, and rationality, however, go unheeded.

Although *The Green Man* offers the same preoccupation with God, death, and evil as *The Anti-Death League*, the novel is different from its predecessor in both feeling and technique. The work is, to begin with, a mixture of social satire, moral fable, comic tale, and ghost story. Evil appears in the figure of Dr. Thomas Underhill—a seventeenth century "wizard" who has raped young girls, created obscene visions, murdered his enemies, and now invades the twentieth century in pursuit of the narrator's thirteen-year-old daughter. God also enters in the person of "a young, well-dressed, sort of after shave lotion kind of man," neither omnipotent nor benevolent. For him, life is like a chess game whose rules he is tempted to break. A seduction, an orgy, an exorcism, and a monster are other features of this profoundly serious examination of dreaded death and all of its meaningless horror.

The novel is narrated retrospectively from the point of view of Maurice Allington. Like Patrick Standish and James Churchill, he spends most of his time escaping, or trying to escape, from himself—and for good reason. Death for him is a fearful mystery. Questions of ultimate justice and human destiny have been jarred loose of any religious or philosophical certainties. He suffers from "jactitations" (twitching of the limbs) as well as unpleasant and lengthy "hypnagogic hallucinations." What is more, problems with self extend to problems with his family and friends: he is unable to get along well with his wife or daughter, and his friends express doubts about his sanity. In fact, the only certainty Maurice has is that as he gets older, consciousness becomes more painful.

To dramatize Maurice's troubled mind, Amis also employs supernatural machinery as an integral part of the narrative. The windowpane through which Maurice sees Underhill becomes a metaphor for the great divide between the known, seen world of reality and the unknown, hence fearful world of the supernatural. Dr. Underhill, a doppelgänger, reflects Maurice's own true nature in his selfish, insensitive manipulation of women for sexual ends. Also, Underhill's appearances provide Maurice with an opportunity to ennoble himself. In his pursuit and eventual destruction of both Underhill and the green monster, Maurice gains self-knowledge—something few of Amis' characters ever experience. He realizes his own potential for wickedness, accepts the limitations of life, and comes to an appreciation of what death has to offer as an escape from earthbound existence. For the first time in his life, Maurice recognizes and responds to the loving competence of his daughter, who looks after him when his wife leaves.

On one level, this elaborately created story is a superbly entertaining, fantastic tale. On another level, it is a powerful and moving parable of the limitations and disappointments of the human condition. Unlike *Lucky Jim* and *Take a Girl Like You*, both of which are rooted in the real world and are guided by the laws of nature, *The Green Man*—and to some extent *The Anti-Death League*—employs fantastic and surreal elements. Ravens, specters, vague midnight terrors, all associated with guilt and despair, provide fitting emblems for Maurice's self-absorbed condition.

The Old Devils is not an easy book to read, but it is an almost irresistibly easy book to reread. It is one of Amis' densest novels, its many different characters and their stories diverging, interweaving, and dovetailing with a striking precision that requires the utmost concentration of the reader. The novel has no central hero-narrator, no Jamesian *disponible*; each of the major characters claims his (or her) own share of reader attention. Though their talks and thoughts wander from topic to topic casually, appearing aimless and undirected, actually the inner workings of the characters are carefully regulated, as are the descriptive comments by the omniscient narrator, to support, define, develop, and ultimately embody the novel's themes.

In terms of narrative, the story itself is painted in muted tones. Alun Weaver has chosen to retire from his successful television career in London as a kind of "professional Welshman" and third-rate poet and return after thirty years with his beautiful wife, Rhiannon, to South Wales. The novel explores, over a span of a few months, the effect of this return on their circle of old friends from university days. The old devils—a group of Welsh married couples all in their sixties and seventies—include Malcolm Cellan-Davies, an unsung local writer, and his wife, Gwen; Peter Thomas, a chemical engineer, and his wife, Muriel; Charlie Norris, the proprietor of a restaurant, and his wife, Sophie; Percy and Dorothy Morgan; and Garth Pumphrey, a former veterinarian who with his wife, Angharad, now attends to business at a local pub. Of the five couples, the first three have never left their home town or accomplished anything very remarkable; their lives have passed them by. They are old now, retired from their professions, and do little else but drink heavily, a device Amis has often used to lower his characters' defenses and reveal their true emotional states. As Sophie says of her husband, "I never realised how much he drank till the night he came home sober. A revelation, it was."

The physical ill health the cronies worry about extends to the spiritual health of their marriages. With the exception of Rhiannon, her daughter Rosemary, and a few minor characters, the women in this novel not only are plain, hard, sharp, critical, or cross but also lack any reasonable relation with their husbands that would make significant communication possible. Only Alun and Rhiannon, married for thirty-four years, seem still to have an appetite for life and love as well as drink, and most of their misunderstandings lead only to teasing, not to disaster. Their arrival, however, arouses conflict among their old friends. "You know," says Muriel early in the novel, "I don't think that news about the Weavers is good news for anyone." The conflict comes in part because their return revives memories of various youthful liaisons and indiscretions, and also because the egotistical Alun immediately sets out to re-woo the three women with whom he had affairs in the old days.

Yet *The Old Devils* is about more than an aging present; it is also very much about the past and its impingements upon everyone. Many of the characters in *The Old Devils* are carrying scars from bitterness and regret because of something that happened in their lives long ago, something they hide carefully from the world, but on which their conscious attention is fixed. Past choices weigh heavily on all of them. These memories, like the memories of the aging characters in earlier novels, touch various notes, some sweet, some sour, some true and others a bit off pitch. Indeed, these old devils are bedeviled by worries and fears of all kinds that deepen their uncertainty about life and increase their preoccupation with the past. Amis points out that one of the reasons old people make so many journeys into the past is to satisfy themselves that it is still there. When that, too, is gone, what is left? In this novel, what remains is only the sense of lost happiness not to be regained, only the awareness of the failure of love, only the present and its temporary consolations of drink, companionship, music, and any other diversions they might create, only a blind groping toward some insubstantial future. Neither human nor spiritual comfort bolsters their sagging lives and flagging souls; Malcolm speaks for all the characters, and probably for Amis himself, when he responds to a question about believing in God: "It's very hard to answer that. In a way I suppose I do. I certainly hate to see it all disappearing."

As in earlier novels, Amis finds in the everyday concerns of his ordinary folk a larger symbolic meaning, which carries beyond the characters to indict a whole country. By the end of the novel, one character after another has uncompromisingly attacked television, the media, abstract art, trendy pub decor, rude teenagers, children, shoppers, rock music, Arab ownership of shops and pubs, and anything that smacks of arty or folksy Welshness. The point, says Malcolm, sadly, is that Wales is following the trends from England and has found a way of destroying the country, "not by poverty but by prosperity." The decline and the decay, he says, are not the real problem. "We've faced that before and we've always come through." What he abominates is the specious affluence. "It's not the rubble I deplore," he says, "it's the vile crop that has sprung from it." Both extremes—decay and affluence— are suggested by the homes the characters occupy, and unhappiness characterizes either extreme. Amis' awareness of rooms, of houses, and of what they reveal about their inhabitants is a critical commonplace. Here, in each instance, the description of a character's personal environment is a means of rendering his or her appalled and irritated perception of the world.

Amis' characterization in *The Old Devils*, however, goes beyond a study of that final form of human deterioration. Rather, the novel examines an often debilitating process of moral and spiritual decay, a lessening of these people as human beings as life goes on and their hopes have dimmed along with their physical and mental powers. Perhaps Rhiannon, the most well-rounded of Amis' female characters in the novel, has kept her spiritual core more intact than any of the old devils. Without a doubt she holds a certain moral superiority over her husband in a way that is reminiscent of Jenny Bunn (in *Take a Girl Like You*), and the differences in man and wife are played against each other. Rhiannon emerges as the voice of common sense in the novel, serene and utterly down-to-earth; Alun is condemned, by his actions and words, as a shallow, worldly, selfish man. In the end, he meets death, while Rhiannon survives and, in fact, looks ahead to future happiness. The two are unreconciled at Alun's death, no mention is made of her mourning, no homage is paid to his memory, and at the end of the novel she turns to Peter, her lover of forty years before. She finally forgives him for his long-ago abandonment, and the two begin to look forward to spending their last years together.

That event is one of two at the end of the novel that vitiate its undertone of pain, despair, and anxiety. The other positive event is the wedding of Rosemary, the Weavers' daughter, to William, the son of Peter and Muriel, suggesting the replacing of the older generation by the new, which in one sense is heralded by the author as a sign of progress and fulfillment. The reader feels that they will go on to live somewhat happy, placid lives. Despite the overriding negativism in the novel, there is some possibility of redemption. In *The Old Devils*, Amis pictures two relatively attractive people who show promise of living and working together peacefully, using their energy to make a new world instead of destroying an existing one.

In retrospect, it is clear that Kinglsey Amis is a moralist as well as a humorist. The early novels exhibit a richly comic sense and a considerable penetration into character, particularly in its eccentric forms. With *Take a*

Girl Like You, Amis begins to produce work of more serious design. He gives much deeper and more complex pictures of disturbing and distorted people, and a more sympathetic insight into the lot of his wasted or burnt-out characters. In all of his novels, he fulfills most effectively the novelist's basic task of telling a good story. In his best novels—*Lucky Jim, Take a Girl Like You, The Anti-Death League, The Green Man*, and *The Old Devils*—Amis tries to understand the truth about different kinds of human suffering, and then passes it on to the reader without distortion, without sentimentality, without evasion, and without oversimplification. His work is based on a steadying common sense.

Dale Salwak

Other major works

SHORT FICTION: *My Enemy's Enemy*, 1962; *Dear Illusion*, 1972; *Collected Short Stories*, 1980.

POETRY: *Bright November*, 1947; *A Frame of Mind*, 1953; *A Case of Samples: Poems, 1946-1956*, 1956; *The Evans Country*, 1962; *A Look Round the Estate: Poems, 1957-1967*, 1967; *Collected Poems: 1944-1979*, 1979.

NONFICTION: *Socialism and the Intellectuals*, 1957; *New Maps of Hell: A Survey of Science Fiction*, 1960; *What Became of Jane Austen? and Other Questions*, 1970; *Tennyson*, 1973; *Kipling and His World*, 1975.

ANTHOLOGIES: *Spectrum: A Science Fiction Anthology*, 1961, 1962, 1963, 1965 (edited with Robert Conquest); *The New Oxford Book of Light Verse*, 1978 (edited); *The Golden Age of Science Fiction*, 1981.

MISCELLANEOUS: *The James Bond Dossier*, 1965; *Lucky Jim's Politics*, 1968; *On Drink*, 1972; *An Arts Policy?*, 1979; *Everyday Drinking*, 1983; *How's Your Glass?*, 1984.

Bibliography

Bradbury, Malcolm. *No, Not Bloomsbury*. London: A. Deutsch, 1987. In a major critical study of Amis, Bradbury devotes a chapter to consider the comic fiction through *The Old Devils* as Amis moves from being angry to bitter. It notes his moral seriousness, his honesty, and his humor. Includes a chronology and an index.

Bradford, Richard. *Kingsley Amis*. London: Edward Arnold, 1989. This key study shows how Amis can disrupt the complacent distinctions between the popular novelist and the literary technician. The author argues that it is time to readjust the critical criteria for the recognition of a major contemporary author. Includes secondary bibliography and index.

Gardner, Philip. *Kingsley Amis*. Boston: Twayne, 1981. This first full-length study of Amis' life and career treats his novels (through *Jake's Thing*), poetry, and nonfiction, paying particular attention to the recurrence of certain themes and character types, to his modes of comedy, and to the relationship between his life and fiction. The text is supplemented by a chronology, notes, a good selected bibliography (including a list of secondary sources with brief annotations), and an index.

Lodge, David. *Language of Fiction*. New York: Columbia University Press, 1966. This important essay considers Amis in the light of poet Stephen Spender's distinction between modern and contemporary. Although Amis rejects the modern mode, he is important because of his use of language, his awareness of his limits, and his "sardonic" sense of literature.

McDermott, John. *Kingsley Amis: An English Moralist*. Basingstoke, England: Macmillan, 1989. This first British book-length study of Amis' work and attitudes seeks to show that the novels are serious as well as funny, that they are distinctively English, and that they offer a wide range of approaches to significant questions of human motives and human behavior. It finds that Amis is more artful than he pretends or gives himself credit for. Includes an excellent primary and secondary bibliography and an index.

Morrison, Blake. *The Movement: English Poetry and Fiction of the 1950s*. New York: Oxford University Press, 1980. This book offers the first full-length treatment of the English writers who became known as the Movement. It covers Amis' friendships at Oxford, his social background, and his political and religious beliefs (or nonbeliefs). Includes an index.

Rabinovitz, Rubin. *The Reaction Against Experiment in the English Novel, 1950-1960*. New York: Columbia University Press, 1966. The first extended examination of Amis' literary judgments in his fiction, poetry, reviews, and nonfiction. It finds that Amis dislikes experimentation for its own sake. He prefers a more direct, conventional style, appealing to common sense, and thus is similar to both eighteenth century and early nineteenth century novelists. Includes an excellent bibliography listing Amis' essays, reviews, and secondary sources.

Ritchie, Harry. *Success Stories: Literature and the Media in England, 1950-1959*. London: Faber, 1988. This important study explores the early years of Amis' career, including the reasons behind the development of the so-called "Angry Young Man" label. Includes an index.

Salwak, Dale. *Kingsley Amis: A Reference Guide*. Boston: G. K. Hall, 1978. This indispensable bibliography covers secondary materials through 1977. Each entry is annotated and indexed. The introduction offers a comprehensive overview of the development of Amis' literary reputation.

_____, ed. *Kingsley Amis: In Life and Letters*. New York: St. Martin's Press, 1990. In this revealing volume, the editor brings together the impressions, reminiscences, and judgments of twenty of Amis' friends and avid readers. The essays cover Amis' novels and poetry as well as his interest in science fiction; his tenures at Swansea, Princeton, and Vanderbilt; his style; his changing social and moral attitudes; and his personality. Includes a primary and secondary bibliography, an index, and eight pages of photographs.

MARTIN AMIS

Born: Oxford, England; August 25, 1949

Principal long fiction

The Rachel Papers, 1973; *Dead Babies*, 1975 (also known as *Dark Secrets*, 1977); *Success*, 1978; *Other People: A Mystery Story*, 1981; *Money: A Suicide Note*, 1984; *London Fields*, 1989.

Other literary forms

Invasion of the Space Invaders (1982), a history of video games; *The Moronic Inferno: And Other Visits to America* (1986), a collection of journalistic pieces on America; and *Einstein's Monsters* (1987), a collection of short stories reflecting life in the shadow of nuclear weapons, are among Amis' other works.

Achievements

Martin Amis has been a force on the modern literary scene since his first novel, *The Rachel Papers*, won the Somerset Maugham Award for 1974. Critical and popular acclaim accompanied his sixth novel, *London Fields*, which was a best-seller on both sides of the Atlantic. Amis has a powerfully comic and satiric vision of the ills of contemporary society, which he caricatures in a way that has reminded many reviewers of Charles Dickens. Amis spares his reader little in his depiction of low-life characters in all their physical grossness and emotional aridity. The emptiness and corruption inherent in a materialistic culture are recurring themes of his work. Yet in spite of the often-sordid subject matter, Amis' novels are illuminated by their stylistic exuberance and ingenuity. More than one critic has remarked on the American flavor of his work, and he is regularly compared to Tom Wolfe and Saul Bellow.

Biography

The son of the novelist Kingsley Amis, Martin Amis spent his early years in Swansea, in south Wales, where his father held a teaching position at Swansea University. The family spent a year in Princeton, New Jersey, in 1959, and then moved to Cambridge, England. Amis' parents were divorced when Amis was twelve, and this had a disruptive effect on his schooling: he attended a total of fourteen different schools in six years. In 1968 he entered Exeter College, Oxford, and was graduated in 1971 with first-class honors in English. He immediately became editorial assistant for *The Times Literary Supplement* and began writing his first novel, *The Rachel Papers*. In 1975 Amis became assistant literary editor of the *New Statesman*, and his second novel, *Dead Babies*, was published in the same year.

In 1980, when Amis was a writer and reviewer for the London newspaper

The Observer, he reported his discovery that the American writer Jacob Epstein had plagiarized as many as fifty passages from *The Rachel Papers* for his own novel *Wild Oats* (1979). The accusation created a storm in the literary world. Epstein quickly conceded that he had indeed copied passages from Amis' novel and others into a notebook which he had then inadvertently used for his own novel. Thirteen deletions were made for the second American edition of Epstein's book, but Amis was infuriated because he thought that the revisions were not sufficiently extensive.

Martin Amis was married to an American professor of aesthetics, Antonia Phillips, in 1984. They have two sons, Louis and Jacob, and make their home in London.

Analysis

Martin Amis remarked in an interview that he wrote about "low events in a high style," and this comment gives a clue to the paradox his work embodies. Although the content of his novels is frequently sordid and nihilistic—dictated by the depressing absence in his characters of traditional cultural values—Amis' rich, ornate, and continually inventive style lifts the novels to a level from which they give delight. "I would certainly sacrifice any psychological or realistic truth for a phrase, for a paragraph that has a spin on it," Amis has commented. The result is that Amis' novels, in spite of the fact that they are often uproariously hilarious, do not make easy or quick reading. Indeed, Kingsley Amis has remarked that he is unable to get through his son's novels because of their ornate style, which he attributes to the influence of Vladimir Nabokov.

Amis' first novel, *The Rachel Papers*, set the tone for most of his subsequent work, although his later novels, beginning with *Money*, have exhibited greater depth and range, as the force of his satire—his immense comic hyperbole—has steadily increased. Furthermore, one senses a sharp moral awareness in *Money* and *London Fields*, although Amis chooses not to offer any solutions to the individual and social ills he identifies so acutely.

The Rachel Papers is a lively but fairly innocuous satire about the turbulent adolescence of Charles Highway, the first-person narrator. Highway is a rather obnoxious young man, a self-absorbed intellectual studying for his Oxford examinations and aspiring to become a literary critic. The action takes place the evening before Highway's twentieth birthday and is filled out by extensive flashbacks. A substantial portion of Highway's intellectual and physical energy is devoted to getting his girlfriend Rachel into bed and to writing in his diary detailed descriptions of everything that happens when he succeeds. Amis' hilarious and seemingly infinitely inventive wordplay is never more effectively displayed than when Highway is describing his sexual adventures.

Dead Babies, which chronicles the weekend debaucheries of a group of nine privileged young people, is considerably less successful than Amis' first novel, and Amis has since declared his own dislike for it. The theme seems to be a warning about what happens when traditional values (the dead babies of the title) are discarded. For the most part, however, the characters are too repulsive, and their indulgence in drugs, sex, alcohol, and violence too excessive, for the reader to care much about their fate.

In *Success*, Amis chronicles a year in the lives of two contrasting characters. The handsome and conceited Gregory comes from an aristocratic family and appears to have all the worldly success anyone could want. He shares a flat in London with his foster brother Terry, who from every perspective is Gregory's opposite. Terry comes from the slums, he is physically unattractive and has low self-esteem, and he is stuck in a boring job which he is afraid of losing. The two characters take turns narrating the same events, which they naturally interpret very differently. As the year progresses, there is a change. Gregory is gradually forced to admit that his success is little more than an illusion. He has been fooling himself most of the time, and realization of his true ineptitude and childlike vulnerability causes him to go to pieces. Meanwhile, Terry's grim persistence finally pays off: he makes money, loses his self-hatred, and finally acquires a respectable girlfriend. For all of his crudity and loutishness, he is more in tune with the tough spirit of the times, in which traditional values are no longer seen to be of any value, and those who in theory represent them (like Gregory) have become effete.

Success is a clear indication of Amis' pessimism about life in London in the 1970's. Frequently employing extremely coarse language, the novel depicts some of the least attractive sides of human nature, and although this grimness is relieved (as in almost all Amis' books) by some ribald humor, on the whole *Success* is a depressing and superficial book. Indeed, it had to wait nine years after publication in Great Britain before an American publisher would take it on.

In Amis' fourth novel, *Other People: A Mystery Story*, he appears to have been trying to write something with more philosophical and existential depth than the satires that came before. This time the protagonist is a young woman, who suffers from total amnesia. Released from hospital, she wanders alone through alien city streets, viewing other people as a separate species and virtually unable to distinguish between animate and inanimate things. Taking the name Mary Lamb, she experiences life in complete innocence, having to relearn everything that being alive involves: not only who she is but also the purpose of everyday things such as shoes and money. She mixes with a range of people from drunks and down-and-outs to upper-class degenerates, at the same time edging closer to a discovery of her real identity. It transpires that her real name is Amy Hide and that everyone thinks that she was killed after being brutally attacked by a man. Adding to the surreal atmosphere of the novel is a mysterious character called Prince, whom Mary/Amy keeps encountering. Prince seems to fulfill many roles: he is a policeman, perhaps also the man who attacked her, and a kind of tutelary spirit, an awakener, under whose guidance she discovers her own identity.

Other People was written according to what is known in Great Britain as the Martian school of poetry, a point of view in which no knowledge about human life and society is assumed. This technique is intended to allow the most mundane things to be examined in a fresh light. Although Amis achieves some success in this area, the novel is spoiled by excessive obscurity. The novelist has simply not left enough clues to his intention, and the reader is left to grasp at bits of a puzzle without being able to construct an intelligible whole. Realizing that few people had grasped his meaning, Amis explained in an interview what his intention had been:

> Why should we expect death to be any less complicated than life? Nothing about
> life suggests that death will just be a silence. Life is very witty and cruel and
> pointed, and let us suppose that death is like that too. The novel is the girl's death,
> and her death is a sort of witty parody of her life.

This may not be of much help to readers who are especially puzzled by the novel's concluding pages. Perhaps the most rewarding parts of the novel are Amis' depictions of the characters Mary encounters; their physical and mental deformities are captured with merciless wit.

In *Money: A Suicide Note*, Amis continued to devote attention to what he undoubtedly depicts best: people who have been deformed, who have failed to reach their full human growth, by the shallow materialism of the age. Yet the scope of *Money* is far wider and more impressive than anything Amis had produced before: not only is it much longer, but it also fairly rocks with vulgar energy. Clearly, Amis has finished his writing apprenticeship and is moving into top gear.

The protagonist is John Self, a wealthy, early-middle-aged maker of television commercials who is visiting New York to direct what he hopes will be his first big motion picture. Yet the project runs into every difficulty imaginable, and after a series of humiliating experiences Self ends up back in London with nothing. The problem with Self is that although he is wealthy, he is uneducated and lacks all culture. He lives at a fast pace but spends his money and his time entirely on worthless things—junk food, alcohol, pornography, television. Satisfying pleasures continually elude him. Amis himself has commented on Self: "The world of culture is there as a sort of taunting presence in his life, and he wants it but he doesn't know how to get it, and all his responses are being blunted by living in the money world."

Amis' attack on the "money world" continues in *London Fields*, although Amis' finest novel is far more than that. It is at once a comic murder-mystery and a wonderfully rich and varied evocation of the decline of civilization at the end of the millennium. Many of the comic scenes are worthy of Charles Dickens, and the plot is acted out against a cosmic, apocalyptic background, as the planet itself seems to be on the brink of disintegration.

Set in post-Thatcherite London in 1999, the plot centers on three main characters. The first is the antiheroine Nicola Six. Nicola has a gift for seeing the future, and she has a premonition that on her next birthday, which happens to be her thirty-fifth, she will be murdered by one of two men she meets at a London pub called the Black Cross. She sets out to avenge herself in advance by using her sexual power to entice them and draw them to ruin. Nicola is a temptress of the first magnitude, and Amis employs comic hyperbole (as he does throughout the novel) to describe her: "Family men abandoned sick children to wait in the rain outside her flat. Semi-literate builders and bankers sent her sonnet sequences."

The second character, the possible murderer, is Keith Talent. Talent is probably Amis' finest creation, a larger-than-life character who might have stepped out of the pages of Dickens. He is a petty criminal, compulsive adulterer, wife-beater, and darts fanatic. He makes a living by cheating people, whether it be by selling fake perfume, running an outrageously expensive taxi service, or doing botched household repair jobs. He earns more money than the prime minister but never has any, because he loses it each day at the betting shop. Keith is not totally bad but wishes that he were: he regards his redeeming qualities as his tragic flaw. Obsessed with darts and television (which for him is the real world), his driving ambition is to reach the televised finals of an inter-pub darts competition. The miracle of the novel is that Amis has succeeded, as with John Self in *Money*, in making such a pathetic character almost likable.

The second possible murderer is Guy Clinch. Clinch is quite different from Keith Talent. He is a rich, upper-class innocent "who wanted for nothing and lacked everything." One of the things he lacks is a peaceful home life, after his wife, Hope, gives birth to Marmaduke, a ferocious infant who almost from birth is capable of acts of quite stunning malice and violence. (The only nurses who can cope with him are those who have been fired from lunatic asylums.) Once more the comedy is irresistible.

The convoluted plot, with its surprise ending, is narrated by a terminally ill American writer named Samson Young, who is in London on a house swap with the famous writer Mark Asprey. That the absent Asprey's initials are the same as those of Martin Amis is perhaps no coincidence. Young is in a sense the author's proxy, since he is himself gathering the material and writing the story of *London Fields* for an American publisher. To make matters even more subtle, a character named Martin Amis also makes an appearance in the novel, just as there had been a Martin Amis character in *Money*. Deconstructing his own fictions in this manner, Amis reminds the reader that in the manipulative world he depicts, he himself is the chief manipulator, but his own novel is only one fiction in a world of fictions.

The setting of *London Fields* is integral to the plot. The London of the near future possesses an oppressive, almost Blakean apocalyptic atmosphere. Not only has urban prosperity evaporated—parts of the city have sunk back into squalor—but the natural environment is in rapid decay also. Everyone is talking about the weather, but it is no longer simply small talk. Weather patterns are violently unstable; the sun seems to hang perpetually low in the sky, and rumors of impending cosmic catastrophe abound. The threat of a nuclear holocaust remains. When Nicola Six was a child, she invented two imaginary companions and called them Enola Gay and Little Boy. Enola Gay is the name of the airplane that dropped the first atom bomb, nicknamed Little Boy, on Hiroshima in 1945. Yet Samson Young, the narrator, calls nuclear weapons "dinosaurs" when compared to the environmental disasters that now threaten the earth. Eventually Young refers to the situation simply as "The Crisis," a term that also well describes the human world that Amis ruthlessly exposes, in which love, decency, and genuine feeling have been superseded by violence, greed, and lust. Microcosm and macrocosm are joined in a kind of horrible, frenzied dance of death. The world of *London Fields*, in which people and planet hurtle helplessly toward disaster, is where all Amis' fiction has been leading.

Although some feminists have reservations about Amis' work (and it is true that most of his male characters treat their women with contempt), he is a formidable and critically acclaimed writer, certainly one of the most accomplished of the generation of English writers who came of age in the 1970's. Few others could have attempted a work on the scale of *London Fields*. Together with Salman Rushdie, Julian Barnes, and Peter Ackroyd—in their different ways—Amis has broken through the neat, middle-class boundaries of much contemporary English fiction and reached out toward a fiction that is more challenging and comprehensive in its scope.

Bryan Aubrey

Other major works

NONFICTION: *Invasion of the Space Invaders*, 1982; *The Moronic Inferno: And Other Visits to America*, 1986.

SHORT FICTION: *Einstein's Monsters*, 1987.

Bibliography

Haffenden, John. *Novelists in Interview*. New York: Methuen, 1985. The most extensive published interview that Amis has given. He talks candidly about his work, giving valuable insight into *The Rachel Papers*, *Other People*, and *Money*. He discusses, among other things, the style and language of his novels, his moral concerns, the purpose of art, and what he owes to his novelist father.

Marowski, Daniel G., ed. *Contemporary Literary Criticism*. Vol. 38. Detroit,

Mich.: Gale Research, 1986. Includes a summary of Amis' work and achievements up to *Money*, as well as extensive extracts from reviews of *Dead Babies*, *Success*, *Other People*, and *Money*, from both Great Britain and the United States. Volume 4 (1975) and volume 9 (1978) in the same series also have sections on Amis.

Stout, Mira. "Martin Amis: Down London's Mean Streets." *The New York Times Magazine*, February 4, 1990, 32. A lively feature article, in which Amis, prodded by Stout, discusses a range of topics, including *London Fields*, his interest in the environment, his early life and career, his relationship with his father, the state of the novel as a form, the Thatcher government, middle age, and his daily work routine.

SHERWOOD ANDERSON

Born: Camden, Ohio; September 13, 1876
Died: Colón, Panama Canal Zone; March 8, 1941

Principal long fiction

Windy McPherson's Son, 1916; *Marching Men*, 1917; *Winesburg, Ohio*, 1919; *Poor White*, 1920; *Many Marriages*, 1923; *Dark Laughter*, 1925; *Beyond Desire*, 1932; *Kit Brandon*, 1936.

Other literary forms

In addition to *Winesburg, Ohio*, which some critics regard as a collection of loosely related short stories, Sherwood Anderson produced three volumes of short stories: *The Triumph of the Egg* (1921); *Horses and Men* (1923); and *Death in the Woods and Other Stories* (1933). He published two books of prose-poems, *Mid-American Chants* (1918) and *A New Testament* (1927). *Plays: Winesburg and Others* was published in 1937. Anderson's autobiographical writings, among his most interesting prose works, include *A Story Teller's Story* (1924); *Tar: A Midwest Childhood* (1926), and the posthumously published *Sherwood Anderson's Memoirs* (1942). All three are such a mixture of fact and fiction that they are sometimes listed as fiction rather than autobiography. Anderson also brought out in book form several volumes of journalistic pieces, many of which had appeared originally in his newspapers: *Sherwood Anderson's Notebook* (1926); *Perhaps Women* (1931); *No Swank* (1934); *Puzzled America* (1935); and *Home Town* (1940). *The Modern Writer* (1925) is a collection of lectures.

Achievements

Anderson was not a greatly gifted novelist; in fact, it might be argued that he was not by nature a novelist at all. He was a brilliant and original writer of tales. His early reputation, which brought him the homage of writers such as James Joyce, Ford Madox Ford, Gertrude Stein, Ernest Hemingway, and F. Scott Fitzgerald, were the stories published in *Winesburg, Ohio*, *The Triumph of the Egg*, and *Horses and Men*. Anderson had published two novels before *Winesburg, Ohio* and was to publish five more afterward, but none of these achieved the critical success of his short pieces.

Anderson's difficulties with the novel are understandable when one sees that his great gift was for rendering moments of intense consciousness—"epiphanies," as James Joyce called them—for which the short story or the tale is the perfect vehicle. The novel form requires a more objective sense of a world outside the individual consciousness as well as the ability to move characters through change and development, and to deal to some extent with the effect of character on character. The best parts of Anderson's novels are those scenes in which he deals, as in the short stories, with a minor character trapped by his own eccentric nature in a hostile world.

Another serious limitation to Anderson's talent as a novelist was his inclination to preach, to see himself as a prophet and reformer and to make sweeping generalizations that are as embarrassing as they are inartistic. Even in *Poor White*, probably his best novel, his characters run to types and become, finally, representative figures in a social allegory. In his worst novels, the characters are caricatures whose absurdity is not perceived by their author. Anderson's style, which could at times work brilliantly, became excessively mannered, a kind of self-parody, which was a sure sign that he had lost his grip on the talent that had produced his best and earlier work.

Winesburg, Ohio is without doubt Anderson's great achievement. It is a collection of tales striving to become a novel; indeed, most critics regard it as a novel, a new form of the novel, which, though perhaps first suggested by Edgar Lee Master's *Spoon River Anthology* (1915), took on its own expressive form and became the model for later works such as Hemingway's *In Our Time* (1924) and William Faulkner's *The Unvanquished* (1938). A few of the Winesburg stories, such as "Godliness," are marred by a tendency to generalization, but on the whole they assume the coherence and solidity of such masterpieces as Mark Twain's *The Adventures of Huckleberry Finn* (1884) and Stephen Crane's *The Red Badge of Courage* (1895), which bristle with implications not only about the life of their times but also about the present. If Anderson had published only *Winesburg, Ohio*, he would be remembered and ranked as an important minor American novelist.

Biography

Sherwood Anderson was born September 13, 1876, in Camden, Ohio, to Irwin and Emma Anderson. When he was eight years old, his family moved to Clyde, Ohio, where Anderson spent his most impressionable years. In later life, Anderson remembered Clyde as an ideal place for a boy to grow up; it became a symbol of the lost innocence of an earlier America. Many of his best stories have a fictionalized Clyde as their setting, and his memory of it shaped his vision of the American past and became a measure of the inadequacies of the industrialized, increasingly mechanized America of city apartments and bloodless sophistication.

Anderson's family was poor. Irwin Anderson, a harness maker, was thrown out of work by industrialization and periods of economic instability. Thus he was forced to work at various odd jobs, such as house painter and paper hanger. Anderson's mother took in washing, while Sherwood and his brother did odd jobs to help support the family. In his autobiographical accounts of growing up, *A Story Teller's Story*, *Tar*, and *Memoirs*, Anderson expresses his humiliation at his impoverished childhood and his resentment toward his father for the inability to support his family. Anderson was particularly bitter about the hardship inflicted on his mother, to whom he was deeply attached. He held his father accountable for his mother's early death, and in *Windy McPherson's Son* one may see in the portrait of the father Anderson's view of his own father as a braggart and a fool whose drunkenness and irresponsibility caused the death of his wife. In time, Anderson's attitude toward his father softened; he came to see that his own gifts as a storyteller were derived from his father, who was a gifted yarn-spinner. Even more important in Anderson's development as a writer was the sympathy awakened in him by his father's failures. A braggart and a liar, Irwin Anderson nevertheless had romantic aspirations to shine in the eyes of the world; his pathetic attempts to amount to something made him grotesque by the standards of the world. An underlying tenderness for his father grew stronger as Sherwood Anderson grew older, enabling him to sympathize with those people in life who become the victim of the wrong kinds of dreams and aspirations. The portrayal of the narrator's father in "The Egg" is one example of Anderson's eventual compassion for such individuals.

Anderson's young manhood, however, was marked by a rejection of his father and a worship of progress and business success. He eagerly embraced the current version of the American dream as exemplified in the Horatio Alger stories: The poor boy who becomes rich. Anderson's own career followed that pattern with remarkable fidelity. He took on any odd job that would pay, whether it was selling papers or running errands, and earned himself the nickname "Jobby." After a brief stint in the army during the Spanish-American War and a year at the Wittenburg Academy completing his high school education, Anderson started in advertising in Chicago and moved up the financial ladder from one position to the next until he became the owner of a paint factory in Elyria, Ohio, the success of which depended upon his skill in writing advertising letters about his barn paint.

Anderson's personal life also developed in a traditional way. In 1904 he married a young woman from a middle-class family, had three children, and associated with the "best" people in Elyria. Around 1911, however, contradictory impulses at work in Anderson precipitated a breakdown. He worked hard at the paint factory and at night spent increasing amounts of time in an attic room writing fiction. The strain eventually took its toll, aided by the pressures of conflicting values: Anderson wanted business and financial success, yet, deep down, he believed in something very different. One day, without warning, he walked out of his paint factory and was later found wandering about the streets in Cleveland, dazed and unable to give his name and address. After a short stay in the hospital, Anderson returned to Elyria, closed out his affairs, and moved to Chicago.

Anderson later told the story of his departure from the paint factory and each time he told it, the details were different. Whatever the exact truth, the important fact appears to be that his breakdown was the result of serious strain between the kind of life he was leading and the kind of life something in him was urging him to live. Rex Burbank in *Sherwood Anderson* (1964) remarks that the breakdown was moral as well as psychological; it might also be called spiritual as well, for it had to do with feelings too vague to be attached to questions of right and wrong. Anderson, in his best work, was something of a mystic, a "Corn Belt mystic" one detractor called him, and his mystical sense was to be the principal source of his gift as a fiction-writer, as well as his chief liability as a novelist.

Anderson's life after he left the paint factory in Elyria was a mixture of successes and failures, wanderings from Chicago to New York, to New Orleans, and finally to Marion, Virginia, in 1927, where he built a house and became the publisher of two local newspapers. His first marriage had ended in divorce shortly after he moved to Chicago; he married three more times, his last to Eleanor Copenhaver, a Virginian. Anderson's financial status was always somewhat precarious. His reputation had been established early among Eastern intellectuals who were attracted to what they saw as Anderson's primitivism, a quality he learned to cultivate. Except for *Dark Laughter*, however, which was something of a best-seller, none of his books was very successful financially, and he was forced to lecture and to do journalistic writing. His most serious problem, though, was the waning of his creative powers and his inability after 1923 to equal any of his earlier successes. During his later years, before his final and happiest marriage. Anderson often was close to a breakdown, a state brought on by artistic and financial difficulties.

During his years in Virginia and under the influence of his fourth wife, Anderson increasingly became interested in social problems. He visited factories, wrote about labor strife, and lent his name to liberal causes. His deepest commitment, however, was not to politics but to his own somewhat vague ideal of brotherhood, which he continued to espouse. In 1941, while on a goodwill tour to South America for the State Department, he died of peritonitis.

Analysis

All novelists are to some extent autobiographical, but Sherwood Anderson is more so than most; indeed, all of Anderson's novels seem to arise out of the one great moment of his life, when he walked out of the paint factory and left behind the prosperous middle-class life of Elyria. In his imagination, his defection from material success took on great significance and became not only the common paradigm for his protagonists, but also the basis for his message to the modern world. Industrialization and mechanization, money-making, advertising, rising in the world, respectability—all of which Anderson himself had hankered after or had sought to encourage in others—became in his fiction the target of criticism. This is not to accuse him of insincerity, but only to point out the extent of his revulsion and the way in which he made his own personal experience into a mythological history of his region and even of the modern world. Anderson's heroes invariably renounce materialism and economic individualism and their attendant social and moral conventions and seek a more spiritual, more vital existence.

Anderson's first published novel, *Windy McPherson's Son*, though set in Caxton, Iowa, is clearly based on Anderson's boyhood in Clyde, Ohio, and his later years in Elyria and Chicago. Sam McPherson is a fictionalized version of "Jobby" Anderson, with his talent for money-making schemes; his father, like Anderson's own, is a braggart and liar who frequently disgraces his hardworking wife and ambitious son in front of the townspeople of Caxton. After his mother's death, Sam leaves Caxton and takes his talent for money-making to Chicago, where in effect he takes over management of an arms manufacturing plant. Sam becomes rich and marries the boss's daughter, but, instead of finding satisfaction in his wealth and position, he discovers that he is dissatisfied with business success and his childless marriage. He walks out of the business, abandons his wife, and wanders through the country attempting to find meaning in existence. After discovering that "American men and women have not learned to be clean and noble and natural, like their forests and their wide, clean plains," Sam returns to his wife Sue, bringing with him three children he has adopted. Out of some sense of responsibility, he allows himself to be led back into the darkened house from which he had fled, a curious and unsatisfactory "happy" ending.

Marching Men, Anderson's second novel, repeats the same basic pattern: success, revolt, search, revelation, elevation—but in a less convincing way. The setting is Coal Creek, a Pennsylvania mining town. The hero is Beaut McGregor, who rebels against the miners' passive acceptance of their squalid existence and escapes to Chicago, where he becomes rich. McGregor continues to despise the miners of Coal Creek until he returns for his mother's funeral; then, he has an awakening, a sudden illumination that gives him a spiritual insight that alters his existence. He sees the miners as men marching "up out of the smoke," and that insight and the marching metaphor become the inspiration for McGregor's transformation. Back in Chicago, he becomes the leader of a new movement called the "marching men," an organization as vague and diffuse as its aim: to find "the secret of order in the midst of disorder," in order that "the thresh of feet should come finally to sing a great song, carrying the message of a powerful brotherhood into the ears and brains of the marchers." A great march takes place in Chicago on Labor Day, and though the marching of the men makes its power felt when the day is over, it is clear that the movement, whatever its temporary success, has no future. The marchers disperse in roving gangs, and an "aristocratic" opponent of the movement muses on its success and failure, wondering whether in deliberately turning away from the success of business and embracing the ultimate failure of the marching men, Beaut McGregor did not achieve a higher form of success.

Though a failure as a novel, *Marching Men* is interesting as Anderson's attempt to give expression to his own kind of achievement and as a place to experiment with concepts successfully handled later in *Winesburg, Ohio*. Anderson had given up success in the business world for a precarious career as a writer; he saw himself as a prophet preaching ideals of brotherhood that had nothing to do with political movements or social programs, but that expressed a mystical yearning for order and unity. The metaphor of the marching men was intended to express this vague ideal. The quest for order and brotherhood was a theme to which Anderson was to return in his next novel, *Winesburg, Ohio*, where he found the form best suited to its expression. The format of *Marching Men*, with its lack of convincing motivation and realistic development, exposed the inadequacy of Anderson's marching metaphor for sustaining a full-length realistic novel.

Winesburg, Ohio is Anderson's masterpiece, a collection of interrelated stories which are less like chapters than like the sections of a long poem; within these pieces, however, there is what might be called a submerged novel, the story of George Willard's growth and maturation. Willard appears in many of the stories, sometimes as a main character, but often as an observer or listener to the tales of other characters. There is the story of Alice Hindeman, who refuses to elope with Ned Curry because she does not want to burden him and eventually runs naked out into the rain. There is also Wing Biddlebaum in "Hands" and Elmer Cowley of "Queer," who desperately try to be normal but only succeed in being queerer than ever. There is the Reverend Curtis Hartman, who spies through a chink in his study window the naked figure of Kate Swift and ends by having a spiritual insight: Christ manifest in the body of a naked woman. These minor characters raise an important critical question: What bearing have they on the submerged *Bildungsroman*?

In five stories, beginning with "Nobody Knows" and ending with "Sophistication" and including "The Thinker," "An Awakening," and "The Teacher," George Willard moves from a lustful relationship with Louise Trunion to a feeling of respectful communion with Helen White, discovering the ultimate reverence for life which Anderson describes as the only thing that makes life possible in the modern world. The discovery was one he himself had made in the early years of his newfound freedom in Chicago, following his escape from the paint factory. In "An Awakening," the pivotal story in the submerged novel, George is made to undergo a mystical experience in which he feels himself in tune with a powerful force swinging through the universe; at the same time, he feels that all of the men and women of his town are his brothers and sisters and wishes to call them out and take them by the hand, including, presumably, the so-called grotesques of the other stories.

The precise relationship of these other stories to those that constitute the growth and maturation of George Willard is a matter of continual critical conjecture, for *Winesburg, Ohio* is the kind of book that does not give up its meanings easily, partly because the kind of meaning the book has can only be suggested, but also because Anderson's way of suggesting is so indirect, at times even vatic. Anderson was possibly influenced by the French post-Impressionist painters such as Paul Cézanne and Paul Gauguin, whose works he had seen in Chicago; and his interest in rendering subjective states indirectly might well parallel theirs. Whether such influences were in fact exerted is arguable. What is clear, however, is that Anderson was by temperament an oral storyteller and that he depended upon tone, colloquial language, and folk psychology rather than the more formal structures of the novelist. In *Winesburg, Ohio* he was also a poet, working by suggestion and indirection, a method that produces intellectual and narrative gaps which the reader is obliged to cross under his own power.

One of the chief critical issues of *Winesburg, Ohio* is the nature of Anderson's characters. In an introductory story, "The Book of the Grotesque" (an early title for the novel), Anderson supplied a definition of a grotesque as one who took a single idea and attempted to live by it, but such a definition, while it can be applied to some characters such as Doctor Parcival of "The Philosopher," hardly fits others at all. In an introduction to the Viking edition of *Winesburg, Ohio* (1960), Malcolm Cowley suggested that the problem of the Winesburg characters was an inability to communicate with one another. Jarvis Thurston's article in *Accent* (1956), "Anderson and 'Winesburg': Mysticism and Craft," offers a more compelling view; the Winesburg characters, Thurston says, are all spiritual questers, and their often violent behavior is symptomatic, not of their inability to communicate, but of a blockage of the spiritual quest. Only George Willard succeeds in that quest, when he undergoes, in "An Awakening," a transcendent experience. Burbank, however, in *Sherwood Anderson*, emphasizes the difference between Willard and the other characters of *Winesburg, Ohio* in this way: they are all "arrested" in a state of loneliness and social isolation. George, on the other hand, because he has heard the stories of the grotesques and has absorbed their lives, has managed to break out of a meaningless existence into a meaningful one. Burbank calls George "an artist of life."

Whatever view one takes of Anderson's characters, it is clear that no simple explanation will suffice, especially not the old writer's, though some critics think of him as Anderson's spokesman. Indeed, the prospect of a single idea summarizing and explaining all of the characters seems ironic in the light of the old writer's assertion that such simplemindedness produces grotesques. *Winesburg, Ohio* has its own kind of unity, but it has its own kind of complexity as well. It is a book of contradictory impulses that stands conventional judgment on its head; at times it is funny and often at the same time profoundly sad. It is a book in praise of the emotions, but, at the same time, it is aware of the dangers of emotional excess.

Winesburg, Ohio was well received by reviewers and even had a moderate financial success. It also confirmed, in the minds of Eastern critics such as Van Wyck Brooks and Waldo Frank, Anderson's authentic American genius. He was seen as part of that native American tradition that came down through Abraham Lincoln, Walt Whitman, and Mark Twain, expressing the essential nature of American life, its strengths, its weaknesses, and its conflicts.

Winesburg, Ohio has not been without its detractors. From a certain point of view, the antics of a character such as Alice Hindeman dashing naked into the rain are ridiculous, and Anderson's style at times slips into the mode of the fancy writer of slick fiction; even his mysticism can be ridiculed if one sees it as Lionel Trilling does in *The Liberal Imagination* (1950) as a form picking a quarrel with respectable society. Despite its faults, however, *Winesburg, Ohio* still lives—vital, intriguing, moving. It remains a modern American classic, expressing in its eccentric way a certain quality of American life that is all but inexpressible.

Anderson's next novel was to be a more traditional sort of work with a hero and a heroine and a "happy" ending that included the requisite embrace, though the hero and the embrace were anything but popularly traditional. Hugh McVey, the protagonist of *Poor White*, is the son of a tramp, born on the muddy banks of the Mississippi and content to live there in a dreamy, sensual existence until taken up by a New England woman who does her best to civilize him. Hugh is tall and lanky, rather like Lincoln in appearance if more like Huck Finn in temperament. When Sarah Shepard, the New England woman, leaves Missouri, Hugh goes East to the town of Bidwell, Ohio, where he becomes the town's telegrapher, and then, out of boredom, begins inventing laborsaving machinery. Being naïve and something of a social outcast, Hugh is unaware of the changes his inventions make in Bidwell. He thinks he is making life easier for the laborers, but opportunists in the town get hold of Hugh's inventions; the factories they bring into being exploit both Hugh and the farm laborers, who, without work in the fields, have swarmed into the new factories, slaving long hours for low pay. Inadvertently, Hugh has succeeded in corrupting the lives of the very people he had set out to help.

Clearly, the story of McVey's "rise" from a dreamy loafer into a rich inventor and the changes that take place in Bidwell from a sleepy farm community into a bustling factory town are meant to tell the story of mid-America's transformation from a primitive, frontier society of hardworking, God-fearing people to an urban society that differentiates between the rich and the poor, the exploiters and the exploited, the slick new city types and the country-bred factory hands. It is meant to be a pathetic story. In welcoming industry and mechanization—and for the best of reasons—America has managed to stamp out and stifle the older, more primitive but vital life of the frontier. McVey's "love" affair is less clearly and convincingly done. He marries, is separated, and then reunited with the daughter of the rich farmer who exploits him. This part of the novel attempts to make a statement, presumably, about emotional life in the new industrial period, but it seems contrived and mechanical compared with the chapters dealing with McVey's rise.

Poor White, then, is not an entirely successful novel. There are too many flat statements and not enough scenes; the character of McVey—part Lincoln, part Huck Finn, part Henry Ford—seems at times too mechanical. Still, *Poor White* has its moments; it is an ambitious attempt to deal fictionally with the changes in American life which Anderson himself had experienced in his journey from poor boy to businessman to writer. It is by common assent his best novel after *Winesburg, Ohio*.

After *Poor White*, Anderson's career as a novelist seriously declined. He continued to write and to publish novels: *Many Marriages* in 1923, and in 1925, *Dark Laughter*, which became a best-seller. Both novels, however, betray what Anderson himself condemned in other writers: the tendency to oversimplify the psychological complexities of human nature. Both novels are anti-Puritan tracts, attacking sexual repression, which writers and popular critics of the day singled out as the source of so much modern unhappiness. In *Many Marriages*, John Webster, a washing-machine manufacturer who has found true sexual fulfillment with his secretary, decides to liberate his militantly virginal daughter by appearing naked before her and lecturing her and her mother on the need to free their sexual impulses. *Dark Laughter* retells the story of Anderson's escape from the paint factory by inventing an improbable hero who gives up his career as a journalist and goes back to the town in which he grew up. There he becomes the gardener and then the lover of the factory owner's wife, an experience meant to suggest the interrelation of physical and spiritual love.

Both *Many Marriages* and *Dark Laughter* suffer from Anderson's inability to think through the implications of his theme and to dramatize it effectively with developed characters and situations. The same limitations are reflected in his last two published novels, *Beyond Desire*, a novel about labor unions and strikes, which is badly confused and poorly written, and *Kit Brandon*, the story of a young woman who is the daughter-in-law of a bootlegger. The weaknesses of these last four novels show that Anderson's talent was not essentially novelistic. His real strengths lay in rendering an insight or an illumination and in bodying forth, often in a sudden and shocking way, an unexplained and unexplainable revelation: Wash Williams smashing his respectable mother-in-law with a chair, or the Reverend Curtis Hartman rushing out into the night to tell George Willard that he had seen Christ manifest in the body of a naked woman. Both of these scenes are from *Winesburg, Ohio*, a book that by its structure did not oblige Anderson to develop or explain his grotesque characters and their sudden and violent gestures. In *Many Marriages* and *Dark Laughter*, scenes of nakedness and sexual awakening are made ridiculous by Anderson's attempt to explain and develop what is better left evocative.

After his death in 1941, Anderson was praised by writers such as Thomas Wolfe and William Faulkner for the contribution he had made to their development and to the development of modern American fiction. Though he was limited and deeply flawed as a novelist, he ranks with Mark Twain, Stephen Crane, and Ernest Hemingway as an important influence in the development of American prose style, and he deserves to be remembered as the author of *Winesburg, Ohio* and a number of hauntingly evocative short stories.

W. J. Stuckey

Other major works

SHORT FICTION: *The Triumph of the Egg*, 1921; *Horses and Men*, 1923; *Death in the Woods and Other Stories*, 1933.

PLAY: *Plays: Winesburg and Others*, 1937.

POETRY: *Mid-American Chants*, 1918; *A New Testament*, 1927.

NONFICTION: *A Story Teller's Story*, 1924; *The Modern Writer*, 1925; *Tar: A Midwest Childhood*, 1926; *Sherwood Anderson's Notebook*, 1926; *Hello Towns!*, 1929; *Perhaps Women*, 1931; *No Swank*, 1934; *Puzzled America*, 1935; *Home Town*, 1940; *Sherwood Anderson's Memoirs*, 1942.

Bibliography

Anderson, David D., ed. *Sherwood Anderson: Dimensions of His Literary Art*. East Lansing: Michigan State University Press, 1976. A 141-page collection of critical essays treating Anderson's fiction from several perspectives, including his theories of fiction, his approach to desire, and the isolation of his characters.

Matthew, George C. "Ohio's *Beulah Land*: Or, Plantation Blacks in the Fiction of Sherwood Anderson." *College Language Association Journal* 25 (June, 1982): 405-413. Studies Anderson's treatment of African Americans, particularly the influence of stereotypes from plantations in the Southern states.

Rideout, Walter B., ed. *Sherwood Anderson: A Collection of Critical Essays*. Englewood Cliffs, N.J.: Prentice-Hall, 1974. Treats Anderson from a variety of perspectives: as prophet, storyteller, and maker of American myths (177 pages).

Stouk, David. "Sherwood Anderson and the Postmodern Novel." *Contemporary Literature* 26, no. 3 (1985): 302-316. Considers Anderson's innovations in plot and characterization in relation to postmodernist fiction.

Townsend, Kim. *Sherwood Anderson*. Boston: Houghton Mifflin, 1987. This critical biography traces Anderson's life and the development of his fiction (370 pages).

White, Ray Lewis, ed. *The Achievement of Sherwood Anderson: Essays in Criticism*. Chapel Hill: University of North Carolina Press, 1966. This collection of essays treats an important variety of subjects, including isolation, Freudianism, and socialism in Anderson's texts, as well as his development as an artist (270 pages).

AYI KWEI ARMAH

Born: Sekondi-Takoradi, Ghana; 1939

Principal long fiction
The Beautyful Ones Are Not Yet Born, 1968; *Fragments*, 1969; *Why Are We So Blest?*, 1972; *Two Thousand Seasons*, 1973; *The Healers*, 1978.

Other literary forms
Although Ayi Kwei Armah is primarily a novelist, he has written and published in other forms as well. Among his short stories, "Yaw Manu's Charm" has appeared in *The Atlantic* (1968) and "The Offal Kind" in *Harper's* (1969). His poem "Aftermath" is included in *Messages: Poems from Ghana* (1970). Armah has also worked as a translator for *Jeune Afrique* and the Algerian-based *Révolution Africaine*. His polemical essay, "African Socialism: Utopian or Scientific," appeared in *Présence Africaine* (1967).

Achievements
Though Armah has become Ghana's best-known writer on the international scene, he would probably prefer to measure his achievement by the reception of his African audience. He is vulnerable to suspicion and resentment both in Africa and abroad. Not only has he remained in exile from his own nation, choosing to live in other African countries, in Paris, and in the United States, but he has also attacked virulently the corruption and materialism of his country's elite and has absolutely condemned the white race (whether European or Arab) for its perverted mentality and for its past and present role in the destruction of African culture. There is an abrasive quality about Armah's early novels—their oppressive naturalism, their sadomasochistic sexuality, their melodramatic casting of blame—that demands more than mere tolerance on the part of his audience. These novels require the reader to go beyond the vehicle to the attitude and the argument that it reveals. A reasonably careful reading will get beyond this abrasiveness and may even dispel the suspicion and resentment, because Armah's real achievement lies in his making the novel not a simple outlet for his venom, but a functional instrument in the African cause. Armah is one of the few truly experimental African novelists. He takes a Western literary form and shapes it into a voice for the African in the modern world.

In his first novel, *The Beautyful Ones Are Not Yet Born*, he turns naturalism and romantic irony into a symbolic, existential statement. In the next two novels, he experiments with narration through multiple points of view. In all three cases, his purpose is to explore the isolation of the individual African in his transformed society. It is evident that Armah is searching for a voice. In the last two novels the voice is that of the traditional historian and storyteller of the tribe. The Western concept of point of view merges with the oral tradition, and fictional realism merges with history, legend, and myth. Armah does not engage in experimentation for its own sake: technique and form are in the service of the larger human concern, the preservation of a culture and the fulfillment of his role within it.

Biography

Ayi Kwei Armah was born in 1939, in the seaport town of Sekondi-Takoradi in western Ghana. Unlike the unnamed protagonist of his first novel, Armah was able to attend mission schools and Achimota College, near the capital city of Accra, and he then received scholarships to continue his education in America. Like the "man" in *The Beautyful Ones Are Not Yet Born*, however, his early life was dramatically influenced by the effects of colonial rule. During World War II, the British sent Ghanaians to fight in Burma and on other battlefields; the postwar period was marked by economic crises, social unrest and strikes, the rise of political parties, and the achieving of independence.

Armah did not experience directly the events after independence. In 1959, he received a scholarship to attend Groton School in Massachusetts. He went on to Harvard, where he was graduated *summa cum laude* in Sociology. In 1963, he visited Algeria and worked as translator for the *Révolution Africaine*. He saw at firsthand what was happening in African countries after independence: a continuation of the old policies, of African subservience, and of poverty. The novel *Why Are We So Blest?* appears to be a distillation of Armah's experiences during these years.

During his brief return to Ghana in 1966, Armah attempted to apply his American education and his talents as a writer in various ways. He was a research fellow at the University, a journalist, a teacher of English, and a television scriptwriter. His second novel, *Fragments*, appears to be a spiritual biography of this frustrated attempt to adapt himself again to his society. In 1967, Armah was again in the United States, attending Columbia University on a writing fellowship, and then in Paris as editor-translator for the news magazine *Jeune Afrique*. In 1968, he taught at the University of Massachusetts and published his first novel, *The Beautyful Ones Are Not Yet Born*, which traces the Ghanaian experience from World War II to the overthrow of Kwame Nkrumah in 1966 but concentrates on the corruption in Ghanaian society around the time of the coup.

Armah has continued to teach at universities in diverse locales, both in Africa and abroad. He has held academic appointments at the Teachers' College in Dar es Salaam, Tanzania; the University of Lesotho; the University of Wisconsin at Madison; and in Nigeria.

Analysis

Ayi Kwei Armah's novels have provoked conflicting reactions. On the one hand, one can argue that Armah is essentially Western, not African. He is certainly not African in the manner of the Nigerian novelist Chinua Achebe. While Achebe's works are to some degree "social documents," Armah moves rapidly from social realism to a symbolic level, even within his first novel. His succeeding novels move away from external detail toward the inner life and the idealism of legend and myth. Achebe is a realist, Armah a romantic. Achebe maintains an objective stance in his analysis of the colonial and postcolonial eras in Nigeria. Armah's voice is strident and polemical. Whereas Achebe is likely to make the society itself as important a "character" as the individual protagonist, Armah, in his early works at least, focuses on the individual consciousness.

Armah's novels thus bear the obvious marks of contemporary European and American fiction. His protagonists are alienated anti-heroes who deserve sympathy and who are essentially correct in their moral attitudes, but who are ineffectual misfits. The society itself is clearly wrong but defeats the individual moral man through sheer force of numbers, viewing such protagonists as madmen or criminals. In fact, this society is the typical twentieth century wasteland, whether it is in Ghana, northern Africa, or the United States. Armah's Ghanaians resemble black Americans trying to be white in order to participate fully in the technological age. Finally, the protagonist within this society resembles, and often in fact is, the isolated artist—a typical Western figure, not at all African.

One can easily argue that if these are not incidental features, they are at least sketched into a larger picture that identifies Armah with an essentially African sensibility. Judging from his first five novels and not emphasizing simply the early works, one could conclude that Armah is an African writing for Africans. For him, the identity of the African artist is inseparable from the society that he serves. He would not want to be judged according to the Western criterion of art for its own sake, or by Western standards of what makes a satisfactory novel. He tries to make his novels functional within an African context. His primary stress is on the individual African sensibility isolated from his society. His novels are a search not so much for private redemption as for communal salvation, and in this respect he reflects an essentially African rather than Western mentality. He is a philosophical novelist: realism is in the service of, or sacrificed to, an idea. He is a social critic searching for a philosophical and historical framework. His protagonists are social failures but heroes in the cause of the greater Africa. His ultimate purpose is pan-African in scope, and his experimentation with technique and form, even though the source may be Western, is a search for the appropriate voice to further the end of common understanding.

Though the novels individually could not be called *Bildungsromans*, together they appear, in retrospect, to trace the individual protagonist from confusion and frustration to a sense of wholeness and communal belonging.

The "man" in *The Beautyful Ones Are Not Yet Born* cannot be sure of his own identity or his moral values because he receives no reinforcement from his society, while Densu in the fifth novel, *The Healers*, rejects his immediate society and joins a small outcast community that understands the larger African tradition.

Armah has some interesting things to say sociologically as well. Like most contemporary African novelists, he deals with the traumatic experience of colonialism, the rapid change from traditional to modern society, the effects of the slave trade and of Western influence in general, the difficulties of adapting to the technological age, the political corruption immediately after independence, and the cultural vacuum. His novels move from the narrow confines of one Ghanaian city in *The Beautyful Ones Are Not Yet Born* to the larger international scene of America, Europe, and North Africa, in order to show at firsthand those forces that helped create the filth and artificiality surrounding his protagonist. In *Two Thousand Seasons* and *The Healers*, Armah leaves the 1960's to give a picture of African society in the distant and recent past. In general, he argues that foreign exploitation has perverted the traditional communal values, which are, if anything, superior to the ones that have replaced them. What seems to concern Armah particularly, however, are the psychological implications of this displacement. The protagonists of the second two novels are mentally disturbed and require professional therapy or convalescence. Juana of *Fragments* is a psychologist, and the outcast priests of *Two Thousand Seasons* and *The Healers* are practitioners of traditional therapies. The essential problem that Armah identifies is the impotence and extreme depression of the sensitive individual rejected by the westernized African society. In addition, Armah explores the nightmares and dreams of his frustrated protagonists, and in the last two novels seeks an answer to frustration through the revival of racial consciousness in myth and legend. The ultimate purpose of his novels is therapeutic.

If the central issue in Armah's novels is the relationship between the individual and his community, then *The Beautyful Ones Are Not Yet Born* is a depressing omen. The main character, the center of consciousness, has no name—not so much because he represents all men or even because he represents the man of integrity, though these are possible readings, but because he is anonymous. Society does not recognize his existence. He is an outcast because he attempts to hold on to moral values while the rest of society has succumbed to bribery, corruption, and materialism. This isolation is total. Even his own family urges him to advance himself for their benefit within the corrupt system. The isolation, however, extends beyond family and community. Even in this first novel, Armah introduces the historical context. The "man" is trapped within the present. He has no sense of belonging to a Ghanaian or to an African tradition. He cannot identify the source of his integrity or of his moral judgment. Hence, he resides in a historical void which makes him question the very values that give him sustenance. Honesty seems unnatural, cruel, obstinate, even criminal and insane.

The story evolves at a specific time in the contemporary history of Ghana. Though Armah does not give dates, it is clear that the early episodes (Chapters 1-12) take place late in Kwame Nkrumah's reign, in the mid-1960's. The final three chapters deal with the hours just after Nkrumah's fall in February, 1966. The "man" is a controller for the railroad, a husband, and the father of two children. Armah describes in naturalistic detail a day in the man's life, his journey to and from work, the oppressiveness of the physical surroundings, the boring, insignificant responsibilities of his job, and the return home to an unsympathetic and accusing wife. The only dramatic event in these first chapters is the man's rejection of a bribe. To seek relief and reassurance, he pays a visit to his former teacher, who shares his moral awareness and can explain to some extent the origin of the present malaise, but who has withdrawn from society. The teacher has no family and hence no compelling responsibility. He refuses to participate in the corruption but also declines to fight it. All he can do for the man is understand his situation. He is, nevertheless, the first of a series of figures in the five novels who represent the wisdom of a way of life that Ghana no longer knows. Within this realistic and cynical first novel it is not surprising that the teacher lacks the confidence and the vision necessary to save the man or his society. In spite of this, Armah leaves no doubt as to the importance of the teacher and his philosophical appraisal of contemporary Ghana. He places the visit at the very center of the novel. From this point, the man must accept total isolation. He cannot lean on his elder and former guide: he must find his own solution.

The problem that faces the man in the final third of the novel involves him in the corruption of an old classmate who is a minister under Nkrumah. His wife and mother-in-law agree to participate in the illegal purchase of a fishing boat, which is primarily for the benefit of Minister Koomsan. When the man refuses complicity, he becomes even more of an outcast within the family. His wife constantly measures him against the successful Koomsan, who has surrounded himself with the things of modern civilization. The last three chapters, however, reverse the situation. Nkrumah falls. Koomsan, a pitifully frightened victim of the coup, comes to the man for aid. The two escape from the house just as the authorities arrive, and the man leads him to the fishing boat and to exile. The man himself swims back to shore and to his family. Though he has involved himself in the corruption he despises, the act of saving Koomsan must be seen as a heroic and humane gesture. The man's wife, at least, now recognizes his courage and his worth. The novel thus moves from almost total submergence in the repulsive details of daily life to a romantic but ironic act of heroism, whose ultimate significance is nevertheless left ambiguous.

Armah is already suggesting the larger movement from realism to myth in the figurative and even symbolic dimension of the narrative. What first strikes the reader's attention, in fact overwhelms him, is the vivid and disgusting insistence on the filth, the excrement, and the vomit that one touches and breathes in the city. Yet this physical reality is at the same time the political and moral corruption that the society discharges as it continues to pursue and consume the "things" of Western technology. Koomsan's escape through the latrine is symbolically a wallowing in his own excrement. A second symbol special to this novel is the chichidodo bird, which despises excrement but subsists on the worms that the excrement nourishes: the man, as much as he may try to remain free of taint, is implicated in the social guilt. Finally, Armah uses a third image, the stream, that recurs in all four of the other novels. He seems to identify water in a traditional way as a purifying agent. During one of his walks, the man notices, in an otherwise muddy stream, a perfectly clear current which seems to have no source. He associates it with a gleam of light—his own moral awareness—a clarity of vision that he cannot trace to any source. He sets this clarity against the brightness of new things imported from the West, but it is not strong enough or permanent enough to give him hope. In spite of his heroism, his baptismal dip in the ocean, and his "rebirth," he still must recognize at the end that "the beautyful ones are not yet born."

In *Fragments*, Armah continues the exploration of the individual and his obligation to both family and community. The scene again takes place in the later 1960's, but the situations are considerably changed. Baako Onipa (the hero now has a name, which means "Only Person") is a "been-to," a member of the educated elite who has spent five years studying in the United States. In this respect, he resembles Armah himself, an American-educated intellectual who must have had similar difficulties readjusting to Ghanaian society. Like Armah, Baako is a writer searching for a role within his newly independent nation. No longer is the protagonist buried in lower-class poverty. His education gives him access to prominent men in the community and to the "things" of modern technology. He thus has the means to satisfy the expectations of his family, especially his mother. He resembles the man, however, in his inability to sacrifice his personal integrity in order to take advantage of his opportunities. In a sense, his situation is even more critical than that of the man. He is a highly sensitive artist. Whereas the man has perceived the "madness" of his obstinacy, Baako has already experienced insanity in America and is on the edge of it again throughout this novel, the title of which, *Fragments*, is thus particularly appropriate.

The story does not follow a clear chronological path, because Armah has chosen to present it through three centers of consciousness. The emphasis is thus not on the exterior world but, much more obviously than in *The Beautyful Ones Are Not Yet Born*, on the psychological responses to the world of the two main characters, Baako and Juana, a Puerto Rican psychologist who becomes Baako's confidante, and of Baako's grandmother, Naana, who represents the traditional wisdom of the people. The novel opens with Naana recalling Baako's ritual departure five years before and her anticipation of his cyclical return. Baako does return, unannounced however, to avoid the inevitable ritual ceremony. He dreads to face his family because he brings no gifts and because he knows that he will be unable to fulfill his mother's expectations. His mother expects what the man's wife expected in *The Beautyful Ones Are Not Yet Born*, money and the comforts of the modern age. Baako, in his rebellion against this imitation of Western values, goes to his former teacher, Ocran, for advice. Ocran has himself chosen to pursue his profession as an artist in solitude, because he sees no possibility for useful work within the contemporary Ghanaian society. Against Ocran's advice, the less experienced Baako has decided to make the attempt by turning his talents as novelist to a more public role as a television scriptwriter. He hopes to transform popular Ghanaian myths into scripts for television, and in general to raise the consciousness of the people by introducing them to the true traditions of Ghana. The authorities, preferring to use the television screen as an instrument of propaganda, reject this proposal as dangerous. Baako goes back to the privacy of the writing table and, thus isolated, gradually loses his mind. His family places him in an asylum, from which he is about to be rescued by Juana as the novel closes.

The threat of insanity, in fact, has plagued Baako from the very beginning. He goes to Juana for help early in the novel. She becomes his lover and, along with Ocran, his spiritual guide. The novel thus ends as does *The Beautyful Ones Are Not Yet Born*, ambiguously—but with a note of hope, and with the nucleus of a new community, two Ghanaians and the outsider, Juana, who represents not the evils of white society, but the sensitivities of a minority. Furthermore, Ocran seems to offer a temporary compromise between the two extremes that have driven Baako to insanity, a compromise that Armah develops in the later novels. Whereas society and family demand that Baako yield to their values, and Baako, while recognizing his inherent need for identity within the community, must maintain his integrity, Ocran proposes a kind of synthesis: Baako cannot expect to achieve his goal immediately. He must submit to a temporary isolation from the present society and work for the larger community of the future. Naana reinforces this view as her commentary closes the novel with a picture of contemporary Ghana in fragments. This novel thus has raised the argument to a more philosophical level than that of *The Beautyful Ones Are Not Yet Born* by using four different characters who reflect on the problem of the perceptive individual within a materialistic society.

In other ways, too, Armah moves away from the naturalism of his first novel. Even the naturalistic scenes, such as the killing of the "mad" dog, are obviously symbolic of something beyond themselves. Just as Juana observes a crowd of soldiers who close in on a dog that they only suspect to be mad, so she watches the community and the family judge and incarcerate Baako for his "insane" ideas. The novel also incorporates ritualistic and religious elements. Naana contrasts the unifying role of traditional ritual with the fragmentation of the present. The mother appeals to an itinerant, spiritualist preacher to aid her in praying for Baako's return. Baako and Juana discuss the similarities between Catholicism and animism, as opposed to the isolating force of Protestantism. Baako is concerned in particular with myth: he contrasts his overseas experience with the traditional hero's departure and triumphal return to save the community. He and Juana repeat the myth of Mame Water, who rises from the sea periodically to meet her lover and give him special powers, but at the same time leaves him with an excruciating sense of isolation. The water itself, like the stream from *The Beautyful Ones Are Not Yet Born*, flows into *Fragments*. Baako pictures himself swimming upstream against a cataract; water still seems to be a purifying force and the stream itself the natural flow of history.

In retrospect, *Why Are We So Blest?* appears to be a transition between Armah's first two novels and the mythical ones to follow. It continues the trend away from realistic description toward a study of multiple consciousness, a philosophical reflection, a larger international context, and an emphasis on personal relationships. The time of the novel, however, remains the same, the mid-to-late 1960's, as does the central premise: the individual isolated from his community and hence from his own identity. Again, Armah seems to be drawing from his own experience, this time as a student in an American university, and from the guilt feelings that inevitably arise in one who is given special treatment while his country suffers from the very hands that feed him. In a sense, the Ghanaian character, Modin, is Baako receiving the education that is so useless to him upon his return, though Armah has a far different fate for this avatar. The other major African character, Solo, shares with Modin a situation that Armah has not created in the first two novels. They both remain abroad, completely detached from their societies, Modin as a student and would-be revolutionary, Solo as a disillusioned revolutionary in exile. Solo, the dispassionate observer, finds in Modin a reincarnation (with variations) of his own past fascination with revolution and with a Western woman. This third major character is Aimée Reitsch, a white American coed of German ancestry, whose perverted fascination with Africa and with Modin precipitates his destruction.

The narrative in *Why Are We So Blest?* resembles that of *Fragments* in that it, too, has three centers of consciousness. The two principal actors in the drama, Modin and Aimée, have kept journals about their experiences, which Aimée leaves with Solo after Modin's death. Solo thus functions as editor, providing personal information and commentary and arranging the journal entries to reconstruct the story of their lives and his encounter with them in northern Africa. He opens the novel with an account of his own life before he met them and fills out this autobiography at intervals throughout the book. He is a reviewer of books eking out an existence in the fictional town of Laccryville (Algiers) and making occasional visits to the headquarters of a revolutionary organization which he once wished to join.

The story of Modin and Aimée, as Solo reconstructs it, goes back to Modin's days as a scholarship student in African Studies at Harvard. Immediately after arriving, he receives a warning from Naita, the black secretary of his sponsor, that he must not trust those who have brought him to America. They actually consider him their property. Modin eventually realizes that she is right about the white race in general being the black man's destroyer, but makes the mistake of considering Aimée an exception. He leaves for Africa with her to join the revolutionary organization in Laccryville. Its leaders are suspicious of Aimée and hence reject them both. Solo meets them and would like to do something to save Modin, but realizes that he is doomed. Modin and Aimée take off on a futile hitchhiking journey across the Sahara, only to be picked up by white male racists who sexually abuse them and leave Modin to die. Aimée returns to her middle-class life in America and Solo is left frustrated in his isolation. It would seem, however, that Solo as author has finally found his voice, and is fulfilling a useful function after all in this "book" that he is offering to the public. That is, Solo has discovered the role that Armah himself has chosen.

In this respect, *Why Are We So Blest?* looks forward to the positive and hopeful tone of the next two novels. What the "man" and Baako lacked, Solo has discovered. In other ways, too, this novel looks forward. The stream as a motif reappears, but it is no longer muddy as in *The Beautyful Ones Are Not Yet Born*, and the swimmer is no longer fighting against the current. Instead, Solo is observing its continuous flow and waiting for a place to enter and become a part of it. Madness, obsession, and psychological tension continue to be significant motifs, but while *Fragments* ends with Baako in an asylum, this novel opens with Solo's overcoming a bout of mental depression by committing himself to a month's convalescence in a hospital. His return to health accompanies a transformation in his view of society, the nature of revolution, and the role of militants. By this third novel, also, Armah has transformed the African female figure into a kind of soulmate. Naita possesses sexual purity, a natural grace, and a wisdom that could have been Modin's salvation. She attains an almost mythical dimension. The most significant symbol in the novel, in fact, is sexuality. Through it, Armah exposes the selfish aggressiveness of the white female and the cruel Fascism of the white male. The novel announces with violent acerbity a thesis that appears for the first time in Armah's fiction, the essential animosity between black and white. It bears the sure stamp of the Black Muslim movement that must have deeply affected him in America. The white race becomes identified as the destroyer, the enemy. The African has lost his identity because the white race has taken away the tradition and the community that gave him meaning.

In *Two Thousand Seasons*, Armah prophesies a more fruitful course. He makes a leap of faith in his narrative style and, more important, in his promise of an answer to the frustrated heroes of the first three novels. This novel has no hero, unless it be the community itself. No isolated personality is trapped within his own consciousness. The narrator, as character, is the ubiquitous member of every generation who knows the true history of the tribe. He is the "griot," the tribal historian, the wise man, the poet. He is a member of the select few whose task it is to maintain the spiritual coherence of the group. The story he tells is the group's chronicle. Thus Armah, as author, effaces himself by adopting the traditional and anonymous role of historian—a significantly symbolic act since Armah must recognize that he too finds his identity only if he merges with the community.

The chronicle begins a thousand years (two thousand seasons) ago, when the Akan tribe, probably intended to represent the black race, living in peace, harmony, and "reciprocity" on the edge of the desert, succumbs to the "predators" of the north, the Arab/Muslim civilization of North Africa. The narrator describes the destruction of the social order and the enslavement of the people. It is here that the community first loses its cohesiveness. A small nucleus of people, particularly women of the tribe, initiate and lead a revolt, and then a migration away from the desert toward the south. The eventual destination is present-day Ghana, but the people arrive only to find another threat from the sea. The Europeans have begun their exploitation of the continent. The last half of the novel concentrates on the disintegration of the tribe as the forces from without create division within. The narrator focuses on one particular period, when one generation of youths undergoing initiation escapes into the forest and organizes a resistance movement. A seer named Isanusi leads them and trains them in the "Way," the traditional values of the tribe. Their king, Koranche, subsequently persuades them to return, deceives them, and sells them into slavery. They are able to escape from the slave ship and make their way back to the forest retreat, bringing with them new recruits. These guerrilla warriors, the "beautyful ones," operate against the oppressive authorities who have betrayed the tribal traditions.

Armah has thus solved the essential problem facing the protagonists of the early novels. He has achieved the synthesis adumbrated by Ocran in *Fragments*. Though it may be impossible to join and serve the particular society in Ghana today, it is possible to participate spiritually in the larger society and in the genuine traditions of the people. This solution certainly explains the mythical and romantic mode of this novel in contrast to the naturalism or realism at the base of the first three. No longer caught within the contemporary world of the 1960's, the initiates of *Two Thousand Seasons* belong to an ancient tradition. A mythical pattern controls the novel. The tribe begins in Eden, falls from grace, and moves toward the cyclical return. It is this confidence in the future and in the total pattern of life that separates this novel from its predecessors. The racism of *Why Are We So Blest?* becomes a struggle for cultural identity on a panoramic scale. The whites, whether Muslim or Christian, are the enemy. Their culture is oppressive and destructive to blacks. They represent class divisions and hierarchical structures. The African "way" is reciprocity, equality, and a sharing of responsibility and power. Armah is obviously dealing in romantic terms. He is also trying to find his own *modus vivendi*: a justification of his "exile" and a role within the larger pattern of his nation's fate.

Armah calls *The Healers* a historical novel. It is, to be sure, based on particular events in the 1870's during the Second Asante War, and Armah's purpose—as in the previous novels, especially *Two Thousand Seasons*—is to offer an interpretation of Ghanaian (African) society and to reevaluate African history. His method, however, is not so much historical as romantic and mythical. The story is a mixture of fact and fiction, and the characters and events conform to an idea of the essential African mentality and the future of the African continent. It thus continues the optimistic chronicle of the previous novel. The storyteller is again the "anonymous" griot. The tale begins as an epic, *in medias res*. It proceeds immediately to narrate the initiation of nine Asante boys into manhood. Densu is obviously a young man of heroic proportions. He refuses to engage in the wrestling contest because the competition required violates the spirit of cooperation that he values. He nevertheless demonstrates his superior strength and grace in this and other games, while finally refusing to win to avoid being named the next chief in the tribe. He resists this temptation held out by Ababio, the evil adviser who remains Densu's nemesis throughout the novel. Densu's ambition is to join the spiritual ones, the "priests" or "healers" who live as outcasts in the forest and who preserve the values of the community which are being perverted by ambitious men such as Ababio. Before he can realize this goal, however, he must not only convince Damfo, the chief healer, and his spiritual guide, that he can truly sacrifice the things of common life, but also overcome Ababio's scheme to condemn him falsely for murder, and to engage in the war against the British as General Nkwanta's aid. The novel ends melodramatically with the betrayal and defeat of the Asante army, the last-minute acquittal of Densu at the murder trial, and the various African tribes dancing on the beach, ironically brought together by the invading British.

Armah thus suggests a future Pan-African unity. For the present, however—if the events of the 1870's offer a paradigm for the contemporary situation—the solution to the sociological and psychological problems facing Ghanaians is much the same as that proposed in *Two Thousand Seasons*. The perceptive individual who works for a solution must not expect an immediate communal identity. Again, Armah clarifies the choices available through romantic simplification. In *Two Thousand Seasons*, the proponents of the Way face a challenge from the white predators and destroyers and from the zombies among their own people. In *The Healers*, the choice is between competition and manipulation on the one hand, and cooperation and inspiration on the other. Densu chooses to leave his tribe because he knows that the leaders and the people are not ready for the essential virtues of the true community. Instead, he is initiated by Damfo into the community of healers. Damfo, in his dealings with other people, never resorts to manipulation or even persuasion, but rather relies on spiritual understanding and respect. This is presented as the only way to establish a genuine community.

In this fifth novel, Armah seems to be consciously drawing in all the threads from his early works. The "beautyful ones," it would seem, are born, but they reside outside the society itself, preparing for the future. Unlike the "man," they fully accept the pain of nonconformity. The healer, Damfo, fulfills the tasks that frustrate the teacher, Ocran, Juana, Naana, and Solo. In his conversations with Densu, he employs a method of instruction that is both Socratic and therapeutic. The philosophical and psychological conflicts that plague the early heroes thus find their resolutions in the spiritual communication and intimate friendship between priest and initiate. Nightmares become dreams of self-discovery. Body, mind, and spirit achieve harmony in Densu. He sees the chaos of the present within the perspectives of history. He is also at home in the natural world. The stream that flows as a minor motif through the other novels is a significant part of the setting in *The Healers*. Densu wins the swimming contest not by competing but by becoming at one with the natural element. He later escapes arrest by holding on to roots at the bottom of the stream and breathing through a hollowed-out cane. Even later, he and Damfo master the stream in a long journey against the current. Finally, in this river of life Densu contemplates his own image and purpose. Clearly, Armah creates a hero in *The Healers* who has found his place in the stream of history, a hero who gives meaning to Armah's own chosen role in his community.

Thomas Banks

Other major works

SHORT FICTION: "Yaw Manu's Charm," in *The Atlantic*, 1968; "The Offal Kind," in *Harper's*, 1969.

POETRY: "Aftermath," in *Messages: Poems from Ghana*, 1970.

NONFICTION: "African Socialism: Utopian or Scientific," in *Présence Africaine*, 1967.

Bibliography

Fraser, Robert. *The Novels of Ayi Kwei Armah: A Study in Polemical Fiction*. London: Heinemann, 1980. An excellent place for the general reader to start. The first chapter provides the context of liberation and resistance informing Armah's work and is followed by five chapters on individual novels. Conclusion, bibliography, and index.

Palmer, Eustace. "Negritude Rediscovered: A Reading of the Recent Novels of Armah, Ngugi, and Soyinka." *The International Fiction Review* 8 (1981): 1-11. This discussion of the concept of negritude pays particular attention to three works: Wole Soyinka's *Season of Anomy*, James Ngugi's *Petals of Blood*, and Armah's *Two Thousand Seasons*. Notes.

Research in African Literatures 18 (Summer, 1987). A special issue on Ayi Kwei Armah including three articles, a bibliography of studies in African literature at a Nigerian university, and seventeen book reviews. Notes on contributors.

Shyam, Jai. "Plights of Contemporary Life in Recent African Fiction." *The Arizona Quarterly* 4 (Autumn, 1986): 248-260. A scholarly article discussing the alienating results of Western individualism in African society as depicted in novels by four writers. Armah's *The Beautyful Ones Are Not Yet Born* and *Fragments* are discussed.

Wright, Derek. *Ayi Kwei Armah's Africa: The Sources of His Fiction*. London: Hans Zell, 1989. Traces the African background of Armah's fiction, particularly the early novels, and provides a broad cultural and anthropological context. Useful for the student and reader already familiar with Armah's work and seeking more specialized analysis. Chapter notes, bibliography, and index.

_____. "Ritual Modes and Social Modes in African Fiction: The Case of Ayi Kwei Armah." *World Literature Written in English* 27 (1987): 195-207. A more specialized discussion focusing on Armah's *The Beautyful Ones Are Not Yet Born* from the perspective of a structural model. Notes.

MARGARET ATWOOD

Born: Ottawa, Canada; November 18, 1939

Principal long fiction

The Edible Woman, 1969; *Surfacing*, 1972; *Lady Oracle*, 1976; *Life Before Man*, 1979; *Bodily Harm*, 1981; *The Handmaid's Tale*, 1986; *Cat's Eye*, 1989.

Other literary forms

A skillful and prolific writer, Margaret Atwood has published many volumes of poetry. *Double Persephone* (1961), *The Animals in That Country* (1968), *The Journals of Susanna Moodie* (1970), *Procedures for Underground* (1970), *Power Politics* (1971), *You Are Happy* (1974), *Selected Poems* (1976), *Two-Headed Poems* (1978), *True Stories* (1981), *Interlunar* (1984), and *Selected Poems II* (1987) have enjoyed a wide and enthusiastic readership, especially in Canada. During the 1960's, Atwood published in limited editions poems and broadsides illustrated by Charles Pachter: *The Circle Game* (1964), *Kaleidoscopes Baroque: A Poem* (1965), *Speeches for Dr. Frankenstein* (1966), *Expeditions* (1966), and *What Was in the Garden* (1969). Atwood has also written and illustrated books for children, including *Up in the Tree* (1978) and *Anna's Pet* (1980). Her volumes of short stories, a collection of short fiction and prose poems (*Murder in the Dark*, 1983), a volume of criticism (*Survival: A Thematic Guide to Canadian Literature*, 1972), and a collection of literary essays (*Second Words*, 1982) further demonstrate Atwood's wide-ranging talent. In 1982, Atwood coedited the revised *Oxford Book of Canadian Poetry*. She has also written articles and critical reviews too numerous to list. She has contributed prose and poetry to literary journals such as *Acta Victoriana* and *Canadian Forum*, and her teleplays have been aired by the Canadian Broadcasting Corporation.

Achievements

Early in her career, Atwood's work was recognized for its distinction. This is particularly true of her poetry, which has earned her numerous awards, including the E. J. Pratt Medal in 1961; the President's Medal from the University of Western Ontario in 1965; and the Governor-General's Award, Canada's highest literary honor, for *The Circle Game* in 1966. Twenty years later, Atwood again won this prize for *The Handmaid's Tale*. Atwood won first prize from the Canadian Centennial Commission Poetry Competition in 1967, and won a prize for poetry from the Union League Civic and Arts Foundation in 1969. Honorary doctorates have been conferred by Trent University and

Queen's University. Additional prizes include the Bess Hokins Prize for poetry (1974); the City of Toronto Award (1977); the Canadian Bookseller's Association Award (1977); the St. Lawrence Award for Fiction (1978); the Canada Council Molson Prize (1980); and the Radcliffe Medal (1980).

Biography

Margaret Atwood was born in Ottawa, Ontario, Canada, on November 18, 1939, the second of Carl Edmund and Margaret Killam Atwood's three children. At the age of six months, she was backpacked into the Quebec wilderness, where her father, an entomologist, pursued his special interests in bees, spruce budworms, and forest tent caterpillars. Throughout her childhood, Atwood's family spent several months of the year in the bush of Quebec and northern Ontario. She did not attend school full time until she was twelve.

Though often interrupted, Atwood's education seems to have been more than adequate. She was encouraged by her parents to read and write at an early age, and her creative efforts started at five, when she wrote stories, poems, and plays. Her serious composition, however, did not begin until she was sixteen.

In 1961, Atwood earned her B.A. in the English honors program from the University of Toronto, where she studied with poets Jay Macpherson and Margaret Avison. Her M.A. from Radcliffe followed in 1962. Continuing graduate work at Harvard in 1963, Atwood interrupted her studies before reentering the program for two more years in 1965. While she found graduate studies interesting, Atwood's energies were largely directed toward her creative efforts. To her, the Ph.D. program was chiefly a means of support while she wrote. Before writing her doctoral thesis, Atwood left Harvard.

Returning to Canada in 1967, Atwood accepted a position at Sir George Williams University in Montreal. By this time, her poetry was gaining recognition. With the publication of *The Edible Woman* and the sale of its film rights, Atwood was able to concentrate more fully on writing, though she taught at York University and was writer-in-residence at the University of Toronto. In 1973, Atwood divorced her American husband of five years, James Polk. After the publication of *Surfacing*, she was able to support herself through her creative efforts. Atwood moved to a farm near Alliston, Ontario, with Canadian novelist Graeme Gibson. Their daughter, Eleanor Jess Atwood Gibson, was born in 1979. In 1980, Atwood's family returned to Toronto, where Atwood and Gibson became active in the Canadian Writers' Union, Amnesty International, and the International Association of Poets, Playwrights, Editors, Essayists, and Novelists (PEN).

Analysis

For Margaret Atwood, an unabashed Canadian, literature is a means to cultural and personal self-awareness. "To know ourselves," she writes in *Survival*, "we must know our own literature; to know ourselves accurately, we need to know it as part of literature as a whole." Thus, when she defines Canadian literary concerns, she relates her own as well, for Atwood's fiction grows out of this tradition. In her opinion, Canada's central reality is the act of survival: Canadian life and culture are decisively shaped by the demands of a harsh environment. Closely related, in Atwood's view, to this defining act of survival is the Canadian search for territorial identity—or, as Northrop Frye has put it, "Where is here?"

Atwood's heroines invariably discover themselves to be emotional refugees, strangers in a territory they can accurately label but one in which they are unable to feel at home. Not only are they alienated from their environment, but also they are alienated from language itself; for them, communication becomes a decoding process. To a great degree, their feelings of estrangement extend from a culture that, having reduced everything to products, threatens to consume them. Women are particularly singled out as products, items to be decorated and sold as commodities, though men are threatened as well. Indeed, Canadian identity as a whole is in danger of being engulfed by an acquisitive American culture, though Atwood's "Americans" symbolize exploitation and often turn out to be Canadian nationals.

Reflective of their time and place, Atwood's characters are appropriately ambivalent. Dead or dying traditions prevent their return to a past, a past most have rejected. Their present is ephemeral at best, and their future inconceivable. Emotionally maimed, her heroines plumb their conscious and unconscious impressions, searching for a return to feeling, a means of iden- tification with the present.

Atwood often couches their struggle in terms of a journey, which serves as a controlling metaphor for inner explorations: the unnamed heroine of *Surfacing* returns to the wilderness of Quebec, Lesje Green of *Life Before Man* wanders through imagined Mesozoic jungles, Rennie Wilford of *Bodily Harm* flies to the insurgent islands of Ste. Agathe and St. Antoine. By setting contemporary culture in relief, these primitive sites define the difference between nature and culture and allow Atwood's heroines to gain new per- spectives on their own realities. They can see people and places in relation to each other, not as isolated entities. Ultimately, however, this resolves little, for Atwood's novels end on a tenuous note. Although her heroines come to terms with themselves, they remain estranged.

Supporting her characters' ambivalence is Atwood's versatile narrative tech- nique. Her astringent prose reflects their emotional numbness; its ironic restraint reveals their wariness. Frequent contradictions suggest not only the complexity of her characters but also the antagonistic times they must survive. By skillful juxtaposition of past and present through the use of flashbacks, Atwood evokes compelling fictional landscapes which ironically comment on the untenable state of modern men and women. Still, there remains some hope, for her characters survive with increased understanding of their world.

Despite everything, life does go on.

The first of Atwood's novels to arouse critical praise and commentary, *Surfacing* explores new facets of the *Bildungsroman*. What might have been a conventional novel of self-discovery develops into a resonant search for self-recovery imbued with mythic overtones and made accessible through Atwood's skillful use of symbol and ritual. At the same time, Atwood undercuts the romantic literary conventions on which *Surfacing* is built by exposing the myth of ultimate self-realization as a plausible conclusion. To accept the heroine's final emergence as an end in itself is to misread this suggestively ironic novel.

The unnamed heroine of *Surfacing*, accompanied by her lover Joe and a married couple named David and Anna, returns to the Canadian wilderness where she was reared in hopes of locating her missing father. His sudden disappearance has recalled her from a city life marked by personal and professional failures which have left her emotionally anesthetized. While her external search goes forward, the heroine conducts a more important internal investigation to locate missing "gifts" from both parents. Through these, she hopes to rediscover her lost ability to feel. In order to succeed, however, she will need to expose the fiction of her life.

At the outset of her narrative, the heroine warns her readers that she has led a double life when she recalls Anna's question, "Do you have a twin?" She denies having one, for she apparently believes the elaborate fiction she has created, a story involving a spurious marriage, divorce, and abandonment of her child. As additional protection, the heroine has distanced herself from everyone. She refers to her family as "they," "as if they were somebody else's family." Her relationship with Joe is notable for its coolness, and she has only known Anna, described as her best friend, for two months.

By surrounding herself with friends whose occupation of making a film significantly entitled *Random Samples* reveals their rootlessness, the heroine seeks to escape the consequences of her actions. Indeed, she describes herself both as a commercial artist, indicating her sense of having sold out, and as an escape artist. Reluctantly approaching the past she sought to escape, the heroine feels as if she is in foreign territory.

That she feels alienated by the location of her past is not surprising, for she is an outsider in a number of telling ways: of English descent in French territory; a non-Catholic, indeed nonreligious person among the devout; a woman in a man's world. Her French is so halting that she could be mistaken for an American, representing yet another form of alienation, displacement by foreigners. Most of all, she is a stranger to herself. Rather than focusing on her self-alienation, she is consumed by the American usurpation of Canada, its wanton rape of virgin wilderness, in order to avoid a more personal loss of innocence.

Canada's victimization by Americans reflects the heroine's victimization by men. Having been subjected to the concept that "with a paper bag over their head they're all the same," the protagonist is perceived as either contemptible or threatening. Her artistic skills are denigrated by a culture in which no "important" artists have been women. Even her modest commercial success is treated as a personal assault by Joe, who has an "unvoiced claim to superior artistic skills." By telling herself that the wilderness can never recover from abuse, the protagonist denies her own recovery. Although she feels helpless at the beginning of the novel, she soon rediscovers her own capabilities, and as these are increasingly tested, she proves to be a powerful survivor. Thus, the wilderness, a self-reflection, provides the key to self-discovery.

Perhaps the most important lesson the heroine learns is that the wilderness is not innocent. Her encounter and response to a senselessly slaughtered heron evoke a sense of complicity, leading her to reflect on similar collusion in her brother's animal experiments when they were children. Finding her refuge in childhood innocence blocked, the heroine goes forward with her search. Once again, nature provides information, for in discovering her father's body trapped underwater, she finally recognizes her aborted child, her complicity in its death by yielding to her lover's demands. On a broader scale, she acknowledges death as a part of life and reclaims her participation in the life-process by conceiving a child by Joe.

In a ceremony evocative of primitive fertility rites, she seduces her lover. Then, assured of her pregnancy, she undergoes a systematic purgation in order to penetrate to the very core of reality. During this process, the protagonist discovers her parents' gifts—her father's sense of sight and her mother's gift of life. With body and mind reunited, she takes an oath in which she refuses to be a victim. Whole, she feels free to reenter her own time, no longer either victim or stranger.

Atwood's procedure for bringing her heroine to this state of consciousness is remarkable for its intricacy. Though she distrusts language, the protagonist proceeds to tell her story by describing what she sees. Since she has lost her ability to feel, much of this description seems to be objective—until the reader realizes just how unreliable her impressions can be. Contradictions abound, creating enormous uncertainty as intentional and unintentional irony collide, lies converge, and opinion stated as fact proves to be false. Given this burden of complexity, any simple conclusion to *Surfacing* is out of the question. Clearly, Atwood hints at a temporary union with Joe, but this is far from resolving the heroine's dilemma. Outer reality, after all, has not altered. Thus, Atwood's open-ended conclusion is both appropriate and plausible, for to resolve all difficulties would be to give in to the very romantic conventions which her fiction subverts.

Coming after the Gothic comedy of *Lady Oracle*, *Life Before Man* seems especially stark. Nevertheless, its similarity with all of Atwood's novels is apparent. A penetrating examination of contemporary relationships, it peels away protective layers of deceptions, stripping the main characters until their fallible selves are presented with relentless accuracy. Lesje Green and Elizabeth and Nate Schoenhof are adrift in a collapsing culture in which they struggle to survive. As she focuses on each character, Atwood reveals unrecognized facets of the others.

In this novel, wilderness and culture converge in the Royal Ontario Museum, where Lesje works as a paleontologist and Elizabeth works in public relations. There is little need for the bush country of Quebec, since culture is something of a jungle itself. Unlike the Mesozoic, however, the present anticipates its own extinction because of abundant evidence: pollution, separatist movements, political upheaval, lost traditions, disintegrating families. Man is in danger of drowning in his own waste. Whatever predictability life held in the past seems completely absent; even holidays are meaningless. Still, the novel is fascinated with the past, with the behavior of animals, both human and prehistoric, and with the perpetuation of memory, particularly as it records the history of families.

As in *Surfacing*, a violent death precipitates emotional withdrawal. Most affected is Elizabeth Schoenhof, whose lover Chris has blown off his head as a final gesture of defiance, the ultimate form of escape. His act destroys Elizabeth's sense of security, which resides both in her home and in her ability to manipulate or predict the actions of others. A supreme manipulator, Elizabeth attempts to make everyone act as reasonably as she. Not surprisingly, Elizabeth has at least two selves speaking different languages, genteel chic and street argot, and what passes for "civilized" behavior is merely an escape from honest confrontation with such basic human emotions as love, grief, rejection, and anger. In fact, all of the novel's characters prefer escape to self-realization, and while they pay lip service to social decorum, they quietly rebel.

Their rebellious emotions are reflected in the larger world, a political world aflame with separatist zeal. Rene Levesque, with whom Nate identifies, is gaining momentum for the separation of Quebec and the reestablishment of French as the major language, threatening to displace the English. Indeed, the world seems to be coming apart as international, national, and personal moves toward separation define this novel's movement. As a solution, however, separation fails to satisfy the characters' need to escape, for no matter how far they run, all carry the baggage of their past.

Elizabeth in particular has survived a loveless past, including abandonment by both parents, the painful death of her alcoholic mother, her sister's mental breakdown and drowning, and her Auntie Muriel's puritanical upbringing. All of this has turned Elizabeth into a determined survivor. Beneath her polished exterior is a street fighter from the slums, a primitive. Indeed, Elizabeth recognizes an important part of herself in Chris. Nate and Lesje share a different kind of past, where love created as much tension as affection.

Lesje's Jewish and Ukrainian grandmothers treated her as disputed territory, speaking to her in languages she could not understand and driving her to seek refuge in her fantasy world of Lesjeland.

Feeling like a refugee in treacherous territory, each character attempts to build a new, stable world, notwithstanding the continual impingement of the old, messy one. Nate, having forsaken his mother's futile idealistic causes to save the world, falls in love with Lesje, whom he envisions as an exotic subtropical island free from rules. For a time, Elizabeth inhabits a clean expanse of space somewhere between her bed and the ceiling, and Lesje explores prehistoric terrain, wishing for a return to innocence. When these fantasies diminish in power, the characters find substitutes, challenging the reader to reexamine the novel's possibilities.

Despite its bleak tone, its grimy picture of a deteriorating culture, its feeling of estrangement and futility, its rejection of simplistic resolutions, *Life Before Man* is not without hope. Each character emerges at the end of this novel with something he or she has desired. Nate has Lesje, now pregnant with his child—a child who, in turn confirms Lesje's commitment to life by displacing her preoccupation with death. Having exorcised the evil spirits of her past, Elizabeth experiences a return of direct emotion.

There is, however, a distinct possibility that the apparent resolution is as ambivalent as that of *Surfacing*. What appears to be a completely objective third-person point of view, presiding over chapters neatly cataloged by name and date, sometimes shifts to first-person, an unreliable first-person at that. Through her revolving characters, their identification with one another, and their multiple role-reversals, Atwood creates contradictory, problematic, and deceptive human characters who defy neat categorization. Taken separately, Nate, Elizabeth, and Lesje can easily be misinterpreted; taken as a whole, they assume an even more complex meaning, reflecting not only their own biased viewpoints but also the reader's. Atwood's ability to capture such shifting realities of character and place is one of her chief artistic distinctions.

Rather like the narrator of *Surfacing*, Rennie Wilford in *Bodily Harm* has abandoned her past, the stifling world of Griswold, Ontario, to achieve modest success as a free-lance journalist. To Rennie, Griswold represents values of duty, self-sacrifice, and decency found comic by contemporary standards. It is a place where women are narrowly confined to assigned roles which make them little better than servants. Rennie much prefers city life, with its emphasis on mobility and trends such as slave-girl bracelets and pornographic art. In fact, Rennie has become an expert on just such trends, so adept that she can either describe or fabricate one with equal facility. Having learned to look only at surfaces, Rennie has difficulty accepting the reality of her cancerous breast, which *looks* so healthy.

Her cancer serves as the controlling metaphor in the novel, spreading from diseased personal relationships to a political eruption on St. Antoine. Indeed, the world seems shot through with moral cancer. The symptoms are manifest: honesty is a liability, friends are "contacts," lovers are rapists, pharmacists are drug pushers, and no one wants to hear about issues. What should be healthy forms of human commerce have gone out of control, mirroring the rioting cells in Rennie's breast. When confronted by yet another manifestation of this malaise, a would-be murderer who leaves a coil of rope on her bed, Rennie finds a fast escape route by landing a magazine assignment on St. Antoine.

Her hopes of being a tourist, exempt from participation and responsibility, are short-lived as she is drawn into a political intrigue more life-threatening than her cancer. Before reaching St. Antoine, she learns of its coming election, ignoring Dr. Minnow's allusions to political corruption and makeshift operations. What puzzles her most about their conversation is his reference to the "sweet Canadians." Is he being ironic or not, she wonders. Her superficial observations of island life reveal little, though plenty of evidence points to a violent eruption. Rennie seems more concerned about avoiding sunburn and arrest for drug possession than she is about the abundant poverty and casual violence. Her blindness allows her to become a gun-runner, duped by Lora Lucas, a resilient survivor of many injurious experiences, and Paul, the local connection for drugs and guns, who initiates Rennie into genuine, albeit unwilling, massive involvement.

As a physical link to life, Paul's sexual attention is important to Rennie, who appreciates the value of his touch. His hands call forth the "missing" hands of her grandmother, her doctor's hands, and Lora's bitten hands, hands which deny or offer help. Paul's "aid" to the warring political factions, like Canada's donation of canned hams and Rennie's assistance, is highly questionable, and the results are the reverse of what was planned. Trying to escape from his botched plan, Rennie is brought to confront her own guilt.

Again, Atwood uses flight as a route to self-discovery and deprivation as a source of spiritual nourishment. In Rennie's case, however, these are externally imposed. In her underground cell, with only Lora as company, Rennie ultimately sees and understands the violent disease consuming the world, a disease growing out of a human need to express superiority in a variety of ways and at great spiritual expense. Rennie becomes "afraid of men because men are frightening." Equally important, she understands that there is no difference between *here* and *there*. Finally, she knows that she is not exempt: "Nobody is exempt from anything."

If she survives this ordeal, Rennie plans to change her life, becoming a reporter who will tell what truly happened. Once again, though, Atwood leaves this resolution open to questions. Rennie is often mistaken about what she sees and frequently misinterprets events. Her entire story may well be a prison journal, an account of how she arrived there. When projecting her emergence from prison, she uses the future tense. For Atwood's purposes, this is of relative unimportance, since Rennie has been restored in a way she never anticipated. In the end, stroking Lora's battered hand, Rennie finally embodies the best of Griswold with a clear vision of what lies beneath the surface of human reality.

In *The Handmaid's Tale*, Atwood's fiction turns from the realistic to the speculative, though she merely takes the political bent of the 1980's to its logical—and chilling—conclusion. Awash in a swill of pollution, promiscuity, pornography, and venereal disease, late twentieth century America erupts into political and religious battles. Rising from the ashes is the Republic of Gilead, a theocracy so conservative in its reactionary bent that women are channeled into roles as Daughters, Wives, Marthas (maids), Econowives, and Handmaids (mistresses).

The narrator, Offred (referring to her status as a possession of her master), is among the first group of Handmaids, fertile women assigned to high-ranking government officials. Weaving between her past and present in flat, almost emotionless prose, Offred draws a terrifyingly real picture of a culture retreating to fundamentalist values in the name of stability. At first, her prose seems to be accurate, a report from an observer. Deeper in the story, readers come to understand that Offred is numb from all that has changed in her life. Besides, she does not trust anyone, least of all herself. Still, as a survivor, she determines to stay alive, even if that means taking risks.

Her loss of freedom and identity create new hungers in Offred: curiosity about the world, a subversive desire for power, a longing for feeling, a need to take risks. In many ways, *The Handmaid's Tale* is a novel about what loss creates. Gilead, in fact, is created partially in response to men's loss of feeling, according to Fred, Offred's Commander. Yet Offred takes little comfort in his assurance that feeling has returned.

As she knows, feeling is ephemeral, often unstable, impossible to gauge. Perhaps this is why her characterization of others in the novel seems remote. While Offred observes gestures, facial movements, and voice tone, she can only guess at intent. Implicit in the simplest statement may be an important message. Thus, Offred decodes all kinds of communication, beginning with the Latin inscription she finds scratched in her wardrobe: "Nolite te bastardes carborundorum." Even this injunction, however, which becomes her motto, is a corruption. Though desperate for communication, Offred cautiously obscures her own message. Her struggle to understand reflects Atwood's familiar theme of the inability to truly understand another person, another situation.

By having Offred acknowledge the impossibility of accurately decoding messages, Atwood calls attention to the narrative itself. Another interesting fictional element is the narrative's remove in time. Offred tells her story in the present, except when she refers to her life before becoming a Handmaid. Ironically, readers learn that not only is she telling her story after events, but her narrative has been reconstructed and presented to an audience at a still greater temporal remove. All of this increases the equivocal quality of the novel and its rich ambiguity.

While Atwood demands attention, she provides direction in prefatory quotations. Most revealing is her quotation from Jonathan Swift's "A Modest Proposal." Like Swift's satire, Atwood's skates on the surface of reality, often snagging on familiar actions and only slightly exaggerating some attitudes, especially those commonly held about women. Perennial issues of a woman's place, the value of her work, and her true role in society, are at the center of this novel.

These concerns appear again in *Cat's Eye*, but in a more subdued form. In subject and theme, *Cat's Eye* is an artistic retrospective. Elaine Risley, a middle-aged painter, is called to Toronto to prepare for her first artistic retrospective. Risley takes the occasion to come to terms with the dimensions of self in time, which she perceives as a "series of transparencies, one laid on top of another." Her return to Toronto, where she grew up, gives her an opportunity to look through the layers of people and events from her present position on the curve of time. This perspective, often ironic and tenuous, allows Risley to accept herself, including her foibles.

Cat's Eye takes full advantage of Atwood's visual style as it reiterates the importance of perspective in relation to change. The novel's art theme emphasizes interpretation while simultaneously satirizing the kind of inflated yet highly subjective criticism published for public consumption. Atwood's most personal novel to date, *Cat's Eye* tackles the physics of life and art and arrives at Atwood's least ambiguous conclusion. Returning to her family in Vancouver, Risley notes that the starlight she sees is only a reflection. Still, she concludes, "it's enough to see by."

Atwood's own vision is as informed and humane as that of any contemporary novelist. Challenging her readers to form their own judgments, she combines the complexity of the best modern fiction into the moral rigor of the great nineteenth century novelists. Atwood's resonant symbols, her ironic reversals, and her example challenges readers and writers alike to confront the most difficult and important issues of the contemporary world.

Karen Carmean

Other major works

SHORT FICTION: *Dancing Girls*, 1977; *True Stories*, 1982; *Murder in the Dark*, 1983; *Bluebeard's Egg*, 1983.

POETRY: *Double Persephone*, 1961; *The Circle Game*, 1964; *Talismans for Children*, 1965; *Kaleidoscopes Baroque: A Poem*, 1965; *Speeches for Dr. Frankenstein*, 1966; *Expeditions*, 1966: *The Animals in That Country*, 1968; *What Was in the Garden*, 1969; *The Journals of Susanna Moodie*, 1970; *Procedures for Underground*, 1970; *Power Politics*, 1971; *You Are Happy*,

1974; *Selected Poems*, 1976; *Two-Headed Poems*, 1978; *True Stories*, 1981; *Snake Poems*, 1983, *Interlunar*, 1984; *Selected Poems II*, 1987.

NONFICTION: *Survival: A Thematic Guide to Canadian Literature*, 1972; *Second Words: Selected Critical Prose*, 1982; *Margaret Atwood: Conversations*, 1990.

CHILDREN'S LITERATURE: *Up in the Tree*, 1978; *Anna's Pet*, 1980 (with Joyce Barkhouse).

EDITED TEXT: *The Oxford Book of Canadian Poetry*, 1982.

Bibliography

Davey, Frank. *Margaret Atwood: A Feminist Poetics*. Vancouver: Talonbooks, 1984. A critical study on Atwood's poetry and short stories, including a chapter on her controversial book *Survival*. Examines Atwood's writing with regard to her use of language, images, and symbols to reveal the hidden.

Davidson, Arnold E., and Cathy N. Davidson, eds. *The Art of Margaret Atwood: Essays in Criticism*. Toronto, Canada: Anansi, 1981. A collection of thirteen essays on Atwood that address her multiplicity and illuminate different aspects of her work. All the contributors have written extensively on Canadian literature.

Grace, Sherrill E., and Lorraine Weir. *Margaret Atwood: Language, Text, and System*. Vancouver: University of British Columbia Press, 1983. A collection of essays, scholarly in emphasis, on Atwood's novels and poetry. The nine readings examine different aspects and focal points within her work. A discussion of individual texts and a continuous reading of Atwood's larger themes. Not for the beginning reader of Atwood.

Hite, Molly. *The Other Side of the Story: Structures and Strategies of Contemporary Feminist Narrative*. Ithaca, N.Y.: Cornell University Press, 1989. Feminist criticism on the writing of Atwood, Alice Walker, and Jean Rhys. The chapter on Atwood presents an insightful commentary on her novel *Lady Oracle* with reference to other criticism available on this novel. Discusses the novel's Gothic elements, the use of satire, and its political implications.

Mendez-Egle, Beatrice, ed. *Margaret Atwood: Reflection and Reality*. Edinburg, Tex.: Pan American University Press, 1987. A compilation of critical essays on Atwood, including an interview with the author during her visit to Pan American University in November, 1983. These essays trace in Atwood's works the journey from insecurity to self-discovery. Also examines her novels *Surfacing*, *The Edible Woman*, *Bodily Harm*, and *Lady Oracle*, with references to the place of magic and fairy tales in her work.

Rosenberg, Jerome H. *Margaret Atwood*. Boston: Twayne, 1984. A full-length study on Atwood with emphasis on critical commentary, although Rosenberg presents a capsule biography of Atwood's earlier years. In addition to an analysis of Atwood's five novels up until 1983, also discusses her nonfiction and critical studies, such as *Survival*, and her poetry. Includes a chronology and a useful selected bibliography.

St. Andrews, Bonnie. *Forbidden Fruit: On the Relationship Between Women and Knowledge in Doris Lessing, Selma Lagerlöf, Kate Chopin, Margaret Atwood*. Troy, N.Y.: Whitston, 1986. Discusses Atwood's psychological novel *Surfacing*, which won the coveted Governor-General's Award, in the light of women's quest for knowledge in order to attain unity and identity. An appreciative essay on Atwood with much valuable commentary on this novel.

LOUIS AUCHINCLOSS

Born: Lawrence, New York; September 27, 1917

Principal long fiction

The Indifferent Children, 1947; *Sybil*, 1951; *A Law for the Lion*, 1953; *The Great World and Timothy Colt*, 1956; *Venus in Sparta*, 1958; *Pursuit of the Prodigal*, 1959; *The House of Five Talents*, 1960; *Portrait in Brownstone*, 1962; *The Rector of Justin*, 1964; *The Embezzler*, 1966; *A World of Profit*, 1968; *I Come as a Thief*, 1972; *The Partners*, 1974; *The Winthrop Covenant*, 1976; *The Dark Lady*, 1977; *The Country Cousin*, 1978; *The House of the Prophet*, 1980; *The Cat and the King*, 1981; *Watchfires*, 1982; *Exit Lady Masham*, 1983; *The Book Class*, 1984; *Honorable Men*, 1985; *Diary of a Yuppie*, 1986; *The Golden Calves*, 1988; *Fellow Passengers*, 1989; *The Lady of Situations*, 1990.

Other literary forms

While best known as a novelist, Louis Auchincloss has been a prolific and successful writer in a variety of other literary forms. Among his strongest collections of short fiction are *The Romantic Egoists* (1954), *Powers of Attorney* (1963), and *Tales of Manhattan* (1967), each of which presents stories linked by narration, characters, or theme in such a way as to resemble a novel. An accomplished critic, Auchincloss has published studies of a wide range of writers, from William Shakespeare to Edith Wharton; among his best-known critical works are *Reflections of a Jacobite* (1961) and *Reading Henry James* (1975). *Life, Law, and Letters: Essays and Sketches* (1978) consists chiefly of essays on literary subjects, while the autobiographical memoir *A Writer's Capital* (1974) provides valuable insight into the formation of Auchincloss' outlook. Finally, Auchincloss has published several heavily illustrated biographies or group biographies intended for a general readership; among these works are *Richelieu* (1972), *Persons of Consequence: Queen Victoria and Her Circle* (1979), *False Dawn: Women in the Age of the Sun King* (1984), and *The Vanderbilt Era: Profiles of a Gilded Age* (1989).

Achievements

During the 1950's, Auchincloss emerged as a strong social satirist and novelist of manners, rivaling in his best work the accomplishments of John Phillips Marquand and John O'Hara. Unlike those writers, however, Auchincloss was clearly an "insider" by birth and breeding, belonging without reservation to the social class and power structure that he so convincingly portrayed. With the waning of the tradition represented by figures such as Marquand and

O'Hara, Auchincloss stands nearly alone as an American novelist of manners, unrivaled in his analysis of social and political power.

Freely acknowledging his debt to Henry James and Edith Wharton as well as to Marcel Proust and the Duc de Saint-Simon, Auchincloss continues to transform the stuff of success into high art, providing his readers with convincing glimpses behind the scenes of society and politics where top-level decisions are often made for the most personal and trivial of reasons. As a rule, his featured characters are credible and well developed, if often unsympathetic; Auchincloss' apparent aim is to describe what he has seen, even at the risk of alienating readers who care so little about his characters as not to wonder what will become of them. At the same time, Auchincloss' characteristic mode of expression leaves him open to accusations that he is an "elitist" writer, featuring characters who are almost without exception white, Anglo-Saxon, and Protestant. Such accusations, however, do little to undermine the basic premise that emerges from the body of Auchincloss' work: for good or for ill, the people of whom he writes are those whose decisions and behavior have determined the shape of the American body politic.

Biography

Louis Stanton Auchincloss was born September 27, 1917, in Lawrence, New York, where he spent his entire life except for his years of education and military service. A graduate of the prestigious Groton School, he entered Yale University in 1935 with plans to become a writer, only to withdraw several months short of graduation in 1939 after his initial efforts at publication had been rejected. Deciding instead to pursue a career in law, he received his LL.B. degree from the University of Virginia in 1941 and worked briefly for the firm of Sullivan and Cromwell in New York City before joining the Navy, from which he emerged in 1945 with the rank of lieutenant.

Returning to Sullivan and Cromwell after World War II, Auchincloss again tried his hand at creative writing, this time with demonstrable success. In 1951, he withdrew from the practice of law and devoted himself to writing full time, only to decide after some three years that law and literature were indeed compatible, even symbiotic, and that the writer's life excluding all other pursuits was a bore. In 1954, he returned to the practice of law with the Manhattan firm of Hawkins, Delafield, and Wood, of which he has been a partner since 1958. The previous year, he had married the former Adele Lawrence, to whom he has since dedicated several of his publications. Three children were born to them: John Winthrop Auchincloss in 1958, Blake Leay Auchincloss in 1960, and Andrew Sloane Auchincloss in 1963. Auchincloss retired from Hawkins, Delafield, and Wood in 1986.

Analysis

For a writer with a full-time professional career, Louis Auchincloss has been astoundingly prolific, producing nearly one book of fiction or nonfiction each year since the age of thirty. Like that of many highly prolific writers, the quality of his work is decidedly uneven. At his best, however, Auchincloss meets and surpasses the standard set by J. P. Marquand and John O'Hara for twentieth century American social satire, displaying a resonant erudition that somehow eluded the two older writers even in their brightest moments. Even in the best of his novels, the results of Auchincloss' erudition are sometimes too conspicuous for the reader's comfort, but they can easily be overlooked in favor of the authenticity displayed by characters portrayed in convincing situations.

To date, Auchincloss' reputation as a major writer rests primarily on novels written during the 1960's, a time somewhat past the vogue of social satire in the United States but coinciding neatly with the author's full maturity: the worst of his mistakes were behind him, and he had not yet experienced the temptation to repeat himself. *Pursuit of the Prodigal*, published in 1959, shows Auchincloss approaching the height of his powers, yet not quite free of his earlier mode as he portrays the tribulations of a "maverick" lawyer who is uncomfortable with the conventions into which he was born. Set in the immediate postwar years, *Pursuit of a Prodigal*, despite the distinct insider's voice, shows a clear indebtedness to Marquand's *Point of No Return*, published a decade earlier. The following year, however, Auchincloss broke new and enviable ground with *The House of Five Talents*, ostensibly the memoirs, composed in 1948, of the septuagenarian Miss Gussie Millinder, heiress and survivor of an impressive nineteenth century New York fortune. The author's demonstrated skill at characterization and narration served clear notice of his new, mature promise, soon to be fulfilled with *Portrait in Brownstone*, *The Rector of Justin*, and *The Embezzler*, any one of which would suffice to confirm Auchincloss' reputation as the successor to O'Hara and Marquand as a master observer of American society and a superior stylist.

It is hardly surprising that Auchincloss has achieved his greatest success with books narrated by the characters themselves, frequently by two or more characters in successive sections of one novel. Although his early novels and certain of his short stories bear witness to his control of third-person narration, Auchincloss is doubtless at his best when assuming the voice and persona of a featured character, striking a thoroughly convincing tone of vocabulary, style, and reflection. At times, his narrators are authentically unreliable without, however, approaching the virtuoso performances sought and achieved by Marquand in such works as *The Late George Apley* (1937) or *H. M. Pulham, Esq.* (1941). Unlike Marquand, Auchincloss seeks less to ridicule his characters than to represent them true to life, allowing the reader to draw his or her own conclusions. It is to Auchincloss' credit that he can credibly assume such diverse personae as those of Miss Gussie Millinder and the three main characters of *The Embezzler*, as well as the slightly fussy schoolmaster who narrates *The Rector of Justin*.

Given the fact that Auchincloss has chosen to serve as a chronicler of his generation and those immediately preceding, it stands to reason that a number of his featured characters are drawn rather closely upon recognizable models—perhaps too closely in *The House of the Prophet*, rather less so in *The Embezzler* and *The Rector of Justin*. Such a practice has both its benefits and its pitfalls. At his best, Auchincloss meets and surpasses the aims of the finest historical fiction, showing rounded characters where the record presents only flatness. On other occasions, however, his presentation is so sparse as to require the reader's knowledge of the facts behind the fiction. This is not to say, however, that any of Auchincloss' novels are simple *romans à clef*; in each case, Auchincloss is careful to discover and point a message that goes far deeper than a simple recitation of documented facts.

Together with the highest-minded of his characters, Auchincloss exhibits and values a strong sense of moral and ethical responsibility; unlike certain of his predecessors and erstwhile competitors in the genre, he never indulges in sensationalism or exposé for its own sake. Even when scandal invades the lives of his characters, as often it must, there is no perceptible intent to scandalize or titillate the reader. Indeed, given the Proustian atmosphere that reigns in many of Auchincloss' novels, the reader often waits in vain for the comic catharsis, however slow to build, with which Marcel Proust frequently rewards his readers' patience. Still, it must be noted that Auchincloss presents all but the meanest of his characters with considerable indulgence, providing a human warmth that is totally lacking in the work of such satirists as Sinclair Lewis and often absent in the more bitter works of O'Hara and Marquand.

A New Yorker by proclivity as well as by birth, Auchincloss remains, above all, a New York novelist; his characters, like their author, spend most of their time in the metropolis, leaving it only for such traditional watering-places as Newport and Bar Harbor, or for higher civic duty in Washington, D.C. The author's sense of place serves to illustrate and to explain the dominant role traditionally played by New Yorkers in the shaping of American society.

In the first work of his "mature" period, *The House of Five Talents*, Auchincloss undertakes a personal record of upper-level Manhattan society through the still-perceptive eyes of one Augusta Millinder, age seventy-five, whose immigrant grandfather, Julius Millinder, founded one of the less conspicuous but more durable of the major New York fortunes. The Millinders had, by the time of Augusta's birth in 1873, established a position of quiet dominance, based upon diversified investments. The world in which Augusta and her more attractive elder sister Cora grew to maturity was thus one of easy movement and understated privilege, pursued frequently aboard yachts and in private railroad cars. As a memoirist, Augusta remains securely inside the closed world that she describes, yet she is privileged to have a gift for shrewd observation.

As the second and less attractive of two daughters, "Gussie" Millinder learned at an early age to view male admiration with a jaundiced eye. Indeed, the only man to whom she ever became engaged had proposed several years earlier to her vacuous sister Cora, who subsequently married a French prince. Although it seems likely that Lancey Bell, a rising young architect, has proposed to Gussie in good faith, she remains so skeptical that she breaks the engagement, having developed such inner resources that she no longer believes marriage to be necessary or desirable. In fact, the marriages in and around Gussie's family do little to encourage her faith in that institution. Soon after ending her engagement, Gussie becomes a reluctant participant in the dismantling of her own parents' marriage and household. Her father, aged sixty, has become enamored of a former actress half his age and wishes to marry her, supported in his folly by Gussie's older brother Willie and sister-in-law Julia.

Although the divorce and remarriage eventually take place as planned, Gussie has discovered in the meantime her own increasingly formidable talent for high-minded meddling. She has also begun to explore the extent of a freedom uniquely available to rich and well-read spinsters. Although dissuaded from attending college in her youth, she has taken enough courses at Columbia during her early adulthood to qualify her for part-time teaching in a private school. Later, around the age of forty, she becomes deeply involved in volunteer work. By 1948, when she at last addresses herself to her memoirs, she has led a life both independent and fulfilling, but not without its disappointments.

Appropriately, Gussie's greatest disappointments have less to do with spinsterhood than with her various relatives, many of whom seem to have a singular talent for ruining their lives, at least when measured by Gussie's demanding but forgiving standards. Gussie's personal favorite appears to have been her nephew Lydig, a versatile and talented former army flight instructor who tries his hand at various pursuits successfully but without commitment, only to seek fulfillment in a life of adventure. Having taken up mountain-climbing, he dies in an avalanche around the age of thirty, a year before the stock market crash of 1929.

The changes wrought by the Depression and its consequences upon the Millinders are recorded with a sympathetic but dispassionate eye by Gussie, whose own personal fortune is sufficiently great to sustain major loss without requiring more than minimal changes in her privileged life-style. Among the few things she is obliged to forfeit is her private railroad car, while the chauffeured limousine remains. To the others, Gussie remains a rock of stability in a river of change, able to avert disaster with a well-placed loan (or gift) and a bit of timely meddling. At seventy-five, however, she admits that her interventions have not always been the right ones, much as they may have seemed so at the time. Several marriages remain broken beyond all possible repair and certain of her cousins face congressional investigation for their leftist sympathies.

Self-aware, yet not too much so for credibility, Gussie Millinder remains one of Auchincloss' most engaging narrators and one of his most satisfying creations, combining in her large and slightly outrageous person the best qualities of observer and participant in the action that she records.

Auchincloss' next novel, *Portrait in Brownstone*, attempts a broader picture of New York society. While fulfilling much of the promise held forth by *The House of Five Talents*, it falls short of its predecessor in tightness of construction, in part because of a multiplicity of narrative voices and viewpoints. Each chapter is presented from the viewpoint of a particular character, and while certain characters speak for themselves, others do not, presumably because their self-awareness is so limited as to require the author's third-person intervention.

The principal character of *Portrait in Brownstone*, although never a viewpoint character, is one Derrick Hartley, a minister's son from New England whose Harvard education and contacts facilitate his rapid rise within the presumably closed world of New York high finance. In the hands of O'Hara or Marquand, such a character as Derrick would emerge as a perceptive outsider with just a hint of the romantic hero; Auchincloss, however, presents Derrick as a thoroughgoing professional and opportunist, quick to impose his own stamp upon the closed world that almost did not allow him within its confines. He is also quick to enjoy and exploit the attentions of two female cousins, nieces of the employer whom he will eventually replace.

Set principally in the period during and surrounding World War I, *Portrait in Brownstone* underlines the contrast between "old money" and well-bred industry. Derrick, although polished and considerably less of an arriviste than certain of Auchincloss' later protagonists, has a talent for making money that renders him conspicuous among the Denison descendants, for whom the presence of money has obviated the need for making it.

After a brief and disastrous infatuation with the treacherous and ultimately unhappy Geraldine, Derrick returns his attentions to the younger, somewhat plainer cousin, Ida Trask, who had been his first love. Although disabused of her earlier illusions, Ida agrees to marry Derrick and soon bears him two children, a daughter and then a son. Ida, as a main viewpoint character, narrates much of the novel's action, developing considerably as a character in proportion to a growing awareness of her own innate strengths; for Ida is a survivor, a resourceful, intelligent woman who, born in a later time, might well have rivaled her own husband's success. In any case, she is the only woman in the novel who could possibly handle the strains of marriage to a hard-driving businessman such as Derrick, whose strongest attentions and affections are reserved for his work. Like Gussie Millinder, Ida has developed character and intelligence in the absence of great beauty. Unlike Gussie, however, she is willing and able to function competently within the demands of marriage and parenthood. Because of her intelligence and understanding, her marriage to Derrick survives a number of shocks, including their daughter's marital problems and a late-blooming affair between Derrick and Geraldine.

Minor character that she may be, it is Ida's cousin Geraldine whose life and eventual suicide polarize the action of the novel. Although it is Ida who should resent Geraldine and not the other way around, Geraldine continues to envy Ida's relatively stable marriage and often genuine happiness. As Ida observes, "She remained to the end the little girl who had come down with a bright face and bright flowing hair to find in her Christmas stocking a switch and a book of sermons while mine was crammed with packages that I dared not open." Childless despite several marriages, resentful of Derrick's mechanical approach to lovemaking during their brief affair, Geraldine begins drinking heavily to dull the pain of bright promise unfulfilled.

Among the other characters portrayed in some detail are the Hartleys' two children, born shortly before World War I. Dorcas, who has inherited her father's temperament but little of his discipline, seeks a career of her own in publishing that is cut short by her marriage to a rebellious young editor who accepts the Hartleys' largesse while professing to scorn its source. Eventually, Dorcas enters into a second marriage with one Mark Jesmond, an associate of Derrick who, during an earlier career as a lawyer, had handled the details of her divorce from the editor. Dorcas at last finds fulfillment of sorts in assisting Mark in efforts to "depose" her father from headship of his firm, much as Derrick himself had done years earlier to Ida's uncle Linnaeus Tremain. Dorcas' brother Hugo, meanwhile, is beginning to enter adulthood at the age of thirty-five, thanks mainly to his mother's direct intervention in the choice of his wife and career: Ida, it seems, has begun to assert herself as a matriarch.

Although marred by loose construction and a multiplicity of viewpoints, *Portrait in Brownstone* is notable for the keenness of its observation and the presentation of several memorable scenes. In any case, Auchincloss' readers did not have long to wait before the publication of *The Rector of Justin*, considered by several critics to be the finest of his novels.

Despite the fact that it shares with *Portrait in Brownstone* the potential pitfalls of loose construction and multiple viewpoints, *The Rector of Justin* is considerably more successful both as novel and as document. Auchincloss manages to broaden the appeal of the novel through his choice of subject matter, focusing upon the concept and execution of the American preparatory school. In analyzing the life and career of one Francis Prescott, founder of "Justin Martyr, an Episcopal boys' boarding school thirty miles west of Boston," Auchincloss provides through various viewpoint characters a thoughtful examination of a powerful American institution.

The main narrator of *The Rector of Justin* is Brian Aspinwall, whose arrival at Justin coincides with the outbreak of World War II in Europe. Brian has recently returned to the United States after several years of study at Oxford, where doctors have diagnosed a heart murmur that renders him unfit for service in the British Army. Unsure as yet of his vocation to become an Episcopal priest, Brian welcomes the prospect of teaching at Justin as an opportunity to test his suitability for the priesthood as well as for teaching, another possibility. Drawn gradually deeper into the affairs of the school and its founder-headmaster, Brian records his observations and experiences in a journal that forms the backbone of the book. Later, as the idea of recording the school's history begins to take form in his mind, he includes the testimony—both oral and written—of Dr. Prescott's family, friends, and former students. The result is thus more unified and better organized than *Portrait in Brownstone*, despite the old-maidish Brian's obvious limitations both as narrator and as observer.

By the time of Brian's arrival, Francis Prescott is nearly eighty years of age and long overdue for retirement; as both founder and headmaster, however, he is such an institution that no one has given serious thought to replacing him. Brian vacillates between admiration and harsh criticism for the old man and his "muscular Christianity." To Brian's incredulity, the aging Prescott remains unfailingly democratic in pronouncements both public and private, seemingly unaware of the fact that he and his school have helped to perpetuate an American class system that Prescott personally deplores. This basic irony continues to animate the novel, providing as it does the subject matter for Brian's continuing research.

Early in the novel, Brian learns that Prescott, as a young man, took pains to examine at close range the British public-school system preparatory to founding a boarding school of his own; at no point does Prescott or anyone near him appear to have considered the difference between British aristocracy and American democracy. In fact, many of the questions raised in Brian's mind are left hanging, at least for the reader, calling attention to the anomalous role of private education in America. Prescott, for his part, continues to deny the existence of an American ruling class even when faced with evidence to the contrary from his own alumni rolls.

Brian's continuing research gradually uncovers a wealth of conflicting evidence concerning Prescott's accomplishment. It is clear in any case that the realization of Prescott's lifelong dream has been achieved only at great personal cost. Brian finds the darker side of Justin's history in both a document penned by the long-dead son of the school's charter trustee, on whose behalf Prescott's efforts failed miserably, and in the spoken recollections of Prescott's youngest daughter, ironically named Cordelia. When Brian meets her, Cordelia is in her middle forties, an unreconstructed Greenwich Village bohemian with nymphomaniacal tendencies that, on one occasion, send Brian fleeing for his life. Prescott, it seems, did much to ruin not only her early first marriage but also a later liaison with a mortally wounded veteran of World War I. Cordelia ascribes much of her unhappiness to the fact that both men, as "old boys" of Justin Martyr, perceived a higher obligation to her father than to herself.

Ending with Prescott's death in retirement at age eighty-six, *The Rector of Justin* concludes much as it began, undecided as to the ultimate value of Prescott's achievement. Brian, however, has made a decision; now a fully ordained priest, he continues as a member of the faculty at Justin Martyr.

Together with *The House of Five Talents*, *The Rector of Justin* stands as one of Auchincloss' more impressive accomplishments; in few of his other novels are the interdependent questions of privilege and responsibility discussed with such thoughtfulness or candor. If the book has a major weakness it is that the characters, especially Prescott himself, are often stretched so flat as to strain the reader's belief; even then, it is possible to accept flatness in the case of a character who adamantly refuses to admit life's ambiguities.

Published some two years after *The Rector of Justin*, *The Embezzler* builds on the author's known strengths to provide a strong social satire in the tradition of O'Hara and Marquand, yet transcends the accomplishments of both authors with its spareness and authority. Recalling in its essentials one of the subplots in *The House of Five Talents*, wherein Gussie Millinder reluctantly covers the defalcations of a distant relative threatened with exposure, *The Embezzler* credibly re-creates the heyday of high finance in America before, during, and after the crash of 1929.

The title character and initial narrator of *The Embezzler* is Guy Prime, writing in 1960 to set straight the record of his notoriety some twenty-five years earlier. His antagonist and eventual successor as narrator is Reginald (Rex) Geer, an erstwhile friend and associate since college days. The gathering tension between the two men, reflected in the conflict between their recollections of the same events, provides the novel with its major human interest. "Yes," reflects Guy Prime in the early pages of the novel,

> . . . they would all cut me dead in the street today, my old friends. Rex Geer, who might be a haberdasher in Vermont but for our Harvard friendship, would turn away his stony countenance and splash me with the wheels of his Rolls-Royce. Alphonse de Grasse, his partner, and one of my old golf foursome, might furtively nod as he hurried by, but only if he was sure that Rex's glassy eye was not upon him.

Throughout the novel, it is up to the reader to weigh conflicting testimony and to form his or her own considered judgments.

Grandson of a former Episcopal bishop of New York, Guy Prime has grown up less rich than other of Auchincloss' main characters. His breeding and Harvard education, however, qualify him to function competently at the upper reaches of Manhattan's financial establishment. His classmate Rex Geer, like

Derrick Hartley the son of a rural New England parson, is perhaps even better suited than Guy to the "art" of making money. Rex is not, however, a social climber; to interpret him as such, as a number of the characters do, is to oversimplify a personality of multiple and often conflicting motivations. Guy, for his part, is hardly less complex, an essentially humane man whose interactions with his fellow mortals are inevitably compounded by a flair for the dramatic and a tendency toward hero-worship.

From the start, the friendship of Guy Prime and Rex Geer is complicated by their interlocking relationships with women whom neither man quite understands. The first of these is Guy's wealthy cousin Alix Prime, a doll-like heiress with whom Rex falls suddenly and disastrously in love, quite to his own consternation. Although ambitious and industrious, Rex is immune to the blandishments of inherited wealth and quite undone by the common opinion that he covets Alix for her money. The second woman is Guy's wife Angelica, reared mainly in Europe by her expatriate mother. An affair in middle life between Rex and Angelica permanently alters the lives of all three characters, serving at least in part as Guy's justification for his ventures into thievery. To Guy's way of thinking, the affair between his wife and his best friend suffices to suspend his belief in permanent values; the fact remains, however, that Guy has already begun to borrow large sums of money from Rex to cover high-risk stock market activities. With the increase of risk, Guy "simply" begins to pledge the value of securities that have been left in trust with his firm.

Later testimony supplied by Rex (and by Angelica herself in a short con-cluding chapter) casts serious doubt upon some of the assertions made by Guy in the brief memoir that has been discovered following his death in 1962. Even so, there are few hard-and-fast answers to the questions that remain in the reader's mind. Auchincloss does not make any serious attempt to justify the plainly unethical conduct of his principal character; what he seeks, rather, is a credible re-creation of a significant moment in recent American history, leading immediately to the extensive financial reforms implemented by the administration of Franklin D. Roosevelt. To a far greater degree than in his earlier novels, Auchincloss presents characters caught and portrayed in all their understandably human ambiguity. Despite its limited scope and relative brevity, *The Embezzler* may well be the tightest and finest of Auchincloss' novels to date.

A prophet, according to Scripture, is not without honor save in his own house. In *The House of the Prophet*, Auchincloss, drawing from that proverb, has fashioned a novel based loosely on the life of the prominent political journalist Walter Lippmann. The novel's protagonist, Felix Leitner, a re-spected attorney, widely read pundit, and adviser to presidents, emerges diminished from the examination of his life undertaken by Roger Cutter, an erstwhile assistant and aspiring biographer. A variety of lesser narrative voices, including those of Leitner's two former wives, do their best to show the private truth behind the public image.

As in many of his later efforts, Auchincloss in *The House of the Prophet* returns with diminished success to a number of conventions and devices that have served him well in the past: the basic format of the novel, including the fussy, would-be "historian," owes much to *The Rector of Justin*, while Leitner, speaking occasionally in his own voice, recalls both Rex Geer and Guy Prime of *The Embezzler*. Although the action and characters are both credible and engrossing, *The House of the Prophet* gives the disturbing impression of a novel that one has already read, in which only the names and certain of the circumstances have been changed.

In its weakest moments, *The House of the Prophet* borders upon self-parody. Roger Cutter, the "main" narrator whose memories and intentions form the backbone of the novel, often comes across as Brian Aspinwall in caricature: rendered impotent for life by a diabetic crisis sustained in early adulthood, Roger is (even more obviously than the old-maidish Brian) cast in the role of house eunuch, free to observe and record the master's movements while remaining immune to any possible entanglement with the numerous female characters. Only in its documentary interest and its plausible interpretations of recent American history does *The House of the Prophet* bear serious comparison with the strongest of the author's earlier novels.

Viewed purely as a "political" novel, *The House of the Prophet* is a creditable example of the genre, showing that Auchincloss, when he chooses, can examine politics with the same shrewd powers of observation that he customarily applies to business and the law. As Leitner the pundit grows increasingly conservative with the onset of old age, his changing opinions are attributed less to the ossification of his mind than to the necessary tension between the "prophet" and his changing times. Toward the end of his life, for example, Leitner prepares a brilliant but outrageous column suggesting that America, through the forced resignation of Richard Nixon, "is engaging in one of the most ancient of tribal rituals: the burial of the fisher king." Roger Cutter, appalled by the likely consequences should such opinions be allowed to appear in print under Leitner's respected byline, acts quickly and effectively to have the column suppressed. Leitner's intelligence, however touched by senility, remains as keen and sensitive as ever; he has simply outlived his own time.

In *The House of the Prophet* and subsequent works, Auchincloss has continued to explore the exercise of power and responsibility in American society. His reputation, however, rests primarily on his masterworks of the 1960's—*The House of Five Talents*, *The Rector of Justin*, *The Embezzler*—in which he achieved the fullest and most deftly nuanced expression of his characteristic themes.

David B. Parsell

Other major works

SHORT FICTION: *The Injustice Collectors*, 1950; *The Romantic Egoists*, 1954; *Powers of Attorney*, 1963; *Tales of Manhattan*, 1967; *Second Chance*, 1970; *Narcissa and Other Fables*, 1983; *Skinny Island: More Tales of Manhattan*, 1987.

NONFICTION: *Reflections of a Jacobite*, 1961; *Pioneers and Caretakers: A Study of Nine American Women Novelists*, 1965; *Motiveless Malignity*, 1969; *Edith Wharton: A Woman in Her Time*, 1971; *Richelieu*, 1972; *A Writer's Capital*, 1974; *Reading Henry James*, 1975; *Life, Law and Letters: Essays and Sketches*, 1979; *Persons of Consequence: Queen Victoria and Her Circle*, 1979; *False Dawn: Women in the Age of the Sun King*, 1984; *The Vanderbilt Era: Profiles of a Gilded Age*, 1989.

Bibliography

Bryer, Jackson R. *Louis Auchincloss and His Critics*. Boston: G. K. Hall, 1977. A comprehensive, annotated bibliography of works by and about Auchincloss from 1931 to 1976. The first secondary sourcebook dealing exclusively with Auchincloss and his work, it remains authoritative in its record of his developing reputation as a writer.

Dahl, Christopher C. *Louis Auchincloss*. New York: Frederick Ungar, 1986. The first book-length study of Auchincloss' work, examining his novels and stories in chronological order and offering a balanced view of his accomplishments. Of special interest is the investigation of the boundaries between fiction and fact, which explores possible historical antecedents for characters and plot in *The Embezzler*, *The House of the Prophet*, and *The Rector of Justin*.

Kane, Patricia. "Lawyers at the Top: The Fiction of Louis Auchincloss" *Critique: Studies in Modern Fiction* 7 (Winter, 1964-1965): 36-46. Kane describes Auchincloss as a "facile writer" who speaks with authority on the twentieth century climate of finance in legal practice. Gives particular attention to this collection of short stories *Powers of Attorney* and his novel *A Law for the Lion*, and compares his fictional characters to those of William Faulkner, James Baldwin, Nathaniel Hawthorne, and Mark Twain. The footnotes make reference to other novels by Auchincloss and reviews on his works.

Milne, Gordon. *The Sense of Society*. Rutherford, N.J.: Fairleigh Dickinson University Press, 1977. This overview of the American novel of manners devotes a chapter to Auchincloss, stressing his characterizations and prose style.

Parsell, David B. *Louis Auchincloss*. Boston: Twayne, 1988. Begins with a summary of Auchincloss' own views on the novels of J. P. Marquand and John O'Hara and proceeds to locate Auchincloss within the "novel of manners" tradition, with particular attention paid to recurrent themes. In his "thesis" chapter, Parsell attempts to reconstruct Auchincloss' fictional universe, showing its relation to recent American political and social history.

Tuttleton, James W. *The Novel of Manners in America*. Chapel Hill: University of North Carolina Press, 1972. The first academic critic to discuss Auchincloss, Tuttleton deals with his work at length in his penultimate chapter, focusing primarily on *The House of Five Talents* and *Portrait in Brownstone*, concluding that, in the main, Auchincloss' other novels deal less with manners than with "character."

JANE AUSTEN

Born: Steventon, England; December 16, 1775
Died: Winchester, England; July 18, 1817

Principal long fiction
Sense and Sensibility, 1811; *Pride and Prejudice*, 1813; *Mansfield Park*, 1814; *Emma*, 1815; *Northanger Abbey*, 1818; *Persuasion*, 1818; *Sanditon*, 1975.

Other literary forms
In addition to her six novels, Jane Austen was the author of various short juvenile pieces, most of them literary burlesques mocking the conventions of the eighteenth century novel. Her other works are *Lady Susan*, a story told in letters and written c. 1805; *The Watsons*, a fragment of a novel written about the same time (both appended by J. E. Austen-Leigh to his 1871 *Memoir of Jane Austen*); and *Sanditon*, another fragmentary novel begun in 1817 and first published in 1925. All these pieces appear in *Minor Works* (Vol. VI of the *Oxford Illustrated Jane Austen*, 1954, R. W. Chapman, editor). Jane Austen's surviving letters have also been edited and published by Chapman.

Achievements
Austen, who published her novels anonymously, was not a writer famous in her time, nor did she wish to be. From the first, though, her novels written in and largely for her own family circle, gained the notice and esteem of a wider audience. Among her early admirers were the Prince Regent and the foremost novelist of the day, Sir Walter Scott, who deprecated his own aptitude for the "big Bow-Wow" and praised her as possessing a "talent for describing the involvements and feelings and characters of ordinary life which is to me the most wonderful I ever met with." Since the days of Scott's somewhat prescient praise, her reputation has steadily grown. The critical consensus now places Jane Austen in what F. R. Leavis has termed the "Great Tradition" of the English novel. Her talent was the first to forge, from the eighteenth century novel of external incident and internal sensibility, an art form that fully and faithfully presented a vision of real life in a particular segment of the real world. Austen's particular excellences—the elegant economy of her prose, the strength and delicacy of her judgment and moral discrimination, the subtlety of her wit, the imaginative vividness of her character drawing—have been emulated but not surpassed by subsequent writers.

Biography
Jane Austen's life contained little in the way of outward event. Born in 1775, she was the seventh of eight children. Her father, the Reverend George Austen, was a scholarly clergyman, the rector of Steventon in rural Hamp-

shire. Mrs. Austen shared her husband's intelligence and intellectual interests, and the home they provided for their children was a happy and comfortable one, replete with the pleasures of country life, genteel society, perpetual reading, and lively discussion of ideas serious and frivolous. Jane Austen, who never married, was devoted throughout her life to her brothers and their families, but her closest relationship was with her older sister Cassandra, who likewise remained unmarried and whom Austen relied upon as her chief critic, cherished as a confidante, and admired as the ideal of feminine virtue.

On the rector's retirement in 1801, Austen moved with her parents and Cassandra to Bath. After the Reverend George Austen's death in 1804, the women continued to live for some time in that city. In 1806, the Austens moved to Southampton, where they shared a house with Captain Francis Austen, Jane's older brother, and his wife. In 1808, Edward Austen (who subsequently adopted the surname Knight from the relations whose two estates he inherited) provided his mother and sisters with a permanent residence, Chawton Cottage, in the Hampshire village of the same name. At this house, Austen was to revise her manuscripts that became *Sense and Sensibility*, *Pride and Prejudice*, and *Northanger Abbey* and to write *Mansfield Park*, *Emma*, and *Persuasion*. In 1817, it became evident that she was ill with a serious complaint whose symptoms seem to have been those of Addison's disease. To be near medical help, she and Cassandra moved to lodgings in Winchester in May, 1817. Austen died there less than two months later.

Analysis

Jane Austen's novels—her "bits of ivory," as she modestly and perhaps half playfully termed them—are unrivaled for their success in combining two sorts of excellence that all too seldom coexist. Meticulously conscious of her artistry (as, for example, is Henry James) Austen is also unremittingly attentive to the realities of ordinary human existence (as is, among others, Anthony Trollope). From the first, her works unite subtlety and common sense, good humor and acute moral judgment, charm and conciseness, deftly marshaled incident and carefully rounded character.

Austen's detractors have spoken of her as a "limited" novelist, one who, writing in an age of great men and important events, portrays small towns and petty concerns, who knows (or reveals) nothing of masculine occupations and ideas, and who reduces the range of feminine thought and deed to matrimonial scheming and social pleasantry. Though one merit of the first-rate novelist is the way his or her talent transmutes all it touches and thereby creates a distinctive and consistent world, it is true that the settings, characters, events, and ideas of Austen's novels are more than usually homogeneous. Her tales, like her own life, are set in country villages and at rural seats, from which the denizens venture forth to watering places or travel to London. True, her characters tend to be members of her own order, that prosperous and courteous segment of the middle class called the gentry. Unlike her novel-writing peers, Austen introduced few aristocrats into the pages of her novels, and the lower ranks, though glimpsed from time to time, are never brought forward. The happenings of her novels would not have been newsworthy in her day. She depicts society at leisure rather than on the march, and in portraying pleasures her literary preference is modest: architectural improvement involves the remodeling of a parsonage rather than the construction of Carlton House Terrace and Regent's Park; a ball is a gathering of country neighbors dancing to a harpsichord, not a crush at Almack's or the Duchess of Richmond's glittering fête on the eve of Waterloo.

These limitations are the self-drawn boundaries of a strong mind rather than the innate restrictions of a weak or parochial one. Austen was in a position to know a broad band of social classes, from the local lord of the manor to the retired laborer subsisting on the charity of the parish. Some aspects of life that she did not herself experience she could learn about firsthand without leaving the family circle. Her brothers could tell her of the university, the navy in the age of Nelson, or the world of finance and fashion in Regency London. Her cousin (and later sister-in-law) Eliza, who had lost her first husband, the Comte de Feuillide, to the guillotine, could tell her of Paris during the last days of the old regime. In focusing on the manners and morals of rural middle-class English life, particularly on the ordering dance of matrimony that gives shape to society and situation to young ladies, Austen emphasizes rather than evades reality. The microcosm she depicts is convincing because she understands, though seldom explicitly assesses, its connections to the larger order. Her characters have clear social positions but are not just social types; the genius of such comic creations as Mrs. Bennet, Mr. Woodhouse, and Miss Bates is that each is a sparkling refinement on a quality or set of qualities existing at all times and on all levels. A proof of Austen's power (no one questions her polish) is that she succeeds in making whole communities live in the reader's imagination with little recourse to the stock device of the mere novelist of manners: descriptive detail. If a sparely drawn likeness is to convince, every line must count. The artist must understand what is omitted as well as what is supplied.

The six novels that constitute the Austen canon did not evolve in a straightforward way. Austen was, memoirs relate, as mistrustful of her judgment as she was rapid in her composition. In the case of *Pride and Prejudice*, for example, readers can be grateful that when the Reverend George Austen's letter offering the book's first incarnation, *First Impressions* (1797), to a publisher met with a negative reply, she was content to put the book aside for more than a decade. *Sense and Sensibility* was likewise a revision of a much earlier work. If Austen was notably nonchalant about the process of getting her literary progeny into print, one publisher with whom she had dealings was yet more dilatory. In 1803, Austen had completed *Northanger Abbey* (then entitled *Susan*) and through her brother Henry's agency had sold it to Crosby and Sons for ten pounds. Having acquired the manuscript, the publisher did not think fit to make use of it, and in December, 1816, Henry Austen repurchased the novel. He made known the author's identity, so family tradition has it, only after closing the deal. For these various reasons the chronology of Austen's novels can be set in different ways. Here, they will be discussed in order of their dates of publication.

Sense and Sensibility, Austen's first published novel, evolved from *Elinor and Marianne*, an epistolary work completed between 1795 and 1797. The novel is generally considered her weakest, largely because, as Walton Litz convincingly argues, it strives but fails to resolve "that struggle between inherited form and fresh experience which so often marks the transitional works of a great artist." The "inherited form" of which Litz speaks is the eighteenth century antithetical pattern suggested in the novel's title. According to this formula, opposing qualities of temperament or mind are presented in characters (generally female, often sisters) who despite their great differences are sincerely attached to one another.

In *Sense and Sensibility*, the antithetical characters are Elinor and Marianne Dashwood, the respective embodiments of cool, collected sense and prodigal, exquisite sensibility. In the company of their mother and younger sister, these lovely young ladies have, on the death of their father and the succession to his estate of their half-brother, retired in very modest circumstances to a small house in Devonshire. There the imprudent Marianne meets and melts for Willoughby, a fashionable gentleman as charming as he is unscrupulous. Having engaged the rash girl's affections, Willoughby proceeds to trifle with them by bolting for London. When chance once again brings the Dashwood sisters into Willoughby's circle, his manner toward Marianne is greatly altered. On hearing of his engagement to an heiress, the representative of sensibility swoons, weeps, and exhibits her grief to the utmost.

Meanwhile, the reasonable Elinor has been equally unlucky in love, though she bears her disappointment quite differently. Before the family's move to Devonshire, Elinor had met and come to cherish fond feelings for her sister-in-law's brother Edward Ferrars, a rather tame fellow (at least in comparison with Willoughby) who returns her regard—but with a measure of unease. It soon becomes known that Ferrars' reluctance to press his suit with Elinor stems from an early and injudicious secret engagement he had contracted with shrewd, base Lucy Steele. Elinor high-mindedly conceals her knowledge of the engagement and her feelings on the matter. Mrs. Ferrars, however, is a lady of less impressive self-control; she furiously disinherits her elder son in favor of his younger brother, whom Lucy then proceeds to ensnare. Thus Edward, free and provided with a small church living that will suffice to support a sensible sort of wife, can marry Elinor. Marianne—perhaps because she has finally exhausted her fancies and discovered her latent reason, perhaps because her creator is determined to punish the sensibility that throughout the novel has been so much more attractive than Elinor's prudence—is also provided with a husband: the rich Colonel Brandon, who has long loved her but whom, on account of his flannel waistcoats and his advanced age of five-and-thirty, she has heretofore reckoned beyond the pale.

The great flaw of *Sense and Sensibility* is that the polarities presented in the persons of Elinor and Marianne are too genuinely antithetical to be plausible or dynamic portraits of human beings. Elinor has strong feelings, securely managed though they may be, and Marianne has some rational powers to supplement her overactive imagination and emotions, but the young ladies do not often show themselves to be more than mere embodiments of sense and sensibility. In her second published novel, *Pride and Prejudice*, Austen makes defter use of two sisters whose values are the same but whose minds and hearts function differently. This book, a complete revision of *First Impressions*, the youthful effort that had, in 1797, been offered to and summarily rejected by the publisher Cadell, is, as numerous critics have observed, a paragon of "classic" literature in which the conventions and traditions of the eighteenth century novel come to full flowering yet are freshened and transformed by Austen's distinctive genius.

The title *Pride and Prejudice*, with its balanced alliterative abstractions, might suggest a second experiment in schematic psychology, and indeed the book does show some resemblances to *Sense and Sensibility*. Here again, as has been suggested, the reader encounters a pair of sisters, the elder (Jane Bennet) serene, the younger (Elizabeth) volatile. Unlike the Dashwoods, however, these ladies both demonstrate deep feelings and perceptive minds. The qualities alluded to in the title refer not to a contrast between sisters but to double defects shared by Elizabeth and Fitzwilliam Darcy, a wealthy and well-born young man she meets when his easygoing friend Charles Bingley leases Netherfield, the estate next to the Bennets' Longbourn. If so rich and vital a comic masterpiece could be reduced to a formula, it might be appropriate to say that the main thread of *Pride and Prejudice* involves the twin correction of these faults. As Darcy learns to moderate his tradition-based view of society and to recognize individual excellence (such as Elizabeth's, Jane's, and their Aunt and Uncle Gardiners') in ranks below his own, Elizabeth becomes less dogmatic in her judgments, and in particular more aware of the real merits of Darcy, whom she initially dismisses as a haughty, unfeeling aristocrat.

The growing accord of Elizabeth and Darcy is one of the most perfectly satisfying courtships in English literature. Their persons, minds, tastes, and even phrases convince the reader that they are two people truly made for each other; their union confers fitness on the world around them. Lionel Trilling has observed that, because of this principal match, *Pride and Prejudice* "permits us to conceive of morality as style." Elizabeth and Darcy's slow-growing love may be *Pride and Prejudice*'s ideal alliance, but it is far from being the only one, and a host of finely drawn characters surround the heroine and hero. In Jane Bennet and Charles Bingley, whose early mutual attraction is temporarily suspended by Darcy and the Bingley sisters (who deplore, not without some cause, the vulgarity of the amiable Jane's family), Austen presents a less sparkling but eminently pleasing and well-matched pair. William Collins, the half pompous, half obsequious, totally asinine cousin who, because of an entail, will inherit Longbourn and displace the Bennet females after Mr. Bennet's demise, aspires to marry Elizabeth, but, when rejected, gains the hand of her plain and practical friend Charlotte Lucas. Aware of her suitor's absurdities, Charlotte is nevertheless alive to the advantages of the situation he can offer. Her calculated decision to marry gives a graver ring to the irony of the novel's famous opening sentence: "It is a truth universally acknowledged, that a single man in possession of a good fortune, must be in want of a wife." The last of the matches made in *Pride and Prejudice* is yet more precariously based. A lively, charming, and amoral young officer, George Wickham, son of the former steward of Pemberley, Darcy's estate, and source of many of Elizabeth's prejudices against that scrupulous gentleman, first fascinates Elizabeth, then elopes with her youngest sister, mindless, frivolous Lydia. Only through Darcy's personal and financial intervention is Wickham persuaded to marry the ill-bred girl, who never properly understands her disgrace—a folly she shares with her mother. Mrs. Bennet, a woman deficient in good humor and good sense, is—along with her cynical, capricious husband, the ponderous Collins, and the tyrannical Lady Catherine De Bourgh—one of the great comic creations of literature. Most of these characters could have seemed odious if sketched by another pen, but so brilliant is the sunny intelligence playing over the world of *Pride and Prejudice* that even fools are golden.

Mansfield Park, begun in 1811 and finished in 1813, is the first of Austen's novels to be a complete product of her maturity. The longest, most didactic, least ironic of her books, it is the one critics generally have most trouble reconciling with their prevailing ideas of the author. Although *Mansfield Park* was composed more or less at one stretch, its conception coincided with the final revisions of *Pride and Prejudice*. Indeed, the critics who offer the most satisfying studies of *Mansfield Park* tend to see it not as a piece of authorial bad faith or self-suppression, a temporary anomaly, but as what Walton Litz calls a "counter-truth" to its immediate predecessor.

Pleased with and proud of *Pride and Prejudice*, Austen nevertheless recorded her impression of its being "rather too light, and bright, and sparkling"—in need of shade. That darkness she found wanting is supplied in *Mansfield Park*, which offers, as Trilling observes in his well-known essay on the novel, the antithesis to *Pride and Prejudice*'s generous, humorous, spirited social vision. *Mansfield Park*, Trilling argues, condemns rather than forgives:

"its praise is not for social freedom but for social stasis. It takes full notice of spiritedness, vivacity, celerity, and lightness, only to reject them as having nothing to do with virtue and happiness, as being, indeed, deterrents to the good life."

Most of the action of *Mansfield Park* is set within the little world comprising the estate of that name, a country place resembling in large measure Godmersham, Edward Austen Knight's estate in Kent; but for her heroine and some interludes in which she figures, Austen dips into a milieu she has not previously frequented in her novels—the socially and financially precarious lower fringe of the middle class. Fanny Price, a frail, serious, modest girl, is one of nine children belonging to and inadequately supported by a feckless officer of marines and his lazy, self-centered wife. Mrs. Price's meddling sister, the widowed Mrs. Norris, arranges for Fanny to be reared in "poor relation" status at Mansfield Park, the seat of kindly but crusty Sir Thomas Bertram and his languid lady, the third of the sisters. At first awed by the splendor of her surroundings, the gruffness of the baronet, and the elegance, vigor, and high spirits of the young Bertrams—Tom, Edmund, Maria, and Julia—Fanny eventually wins a valued place in the household. During Sir Thomas' absence to visit his property in Antigua, evidence of Fanny's moral fineness, and the various degrees in which her cousins fall short of her excellence, is presented through a device that proves to be one of Austen's most brilliant triumphs of plotting. Visiting the rectory at Mansfield are the younger brother and sister of the rector's wife, Henry and Mary Crawford, witty, worldly, and wealthy. At Mary's proposal, amateur theatricals are introduced to Mansfield Park, and in the process of this diversion the moral pollution of London's Great World begins to corrupt the bracing country air.

Just how the staging of a play—even though it be *Lovers' Vows*, a sloppy piece of romantic bathos, adultery rendered sympathetic—can be morally reprehensible is a bit unclear for most twentieth century readers, especially those who realize that the Austens themselves reveled in theatricals at home. The problem as Austen here presents it lies in the possible consequences of role-playing: coming to feel the emotions and attitudes one presents on the stage or, worse yet, expressing rather than suppressing genuine but socially unacceptable feelings in the guise of mere acting. In the course of the theatricals, where Fanny, who will not act, is relegated to the role of spectator and moral chorus, Maria Bertram, engaged to a bovine local heir, vies with her sister in striving to fascinate Henry Crawford, who in turn is all too ready to charm them. Mary Crawford, though it is "her way" to find eldest sons most agreeable, has the good taste to be attracted to Edmund, the second son, who plans to enter the Church. Mary's vivacity, as evidenced by the theatricals, easily wins his heart.

Time passes and poor Fanny, who since childhood has adored her cousin Edmund, unintentionally interests Henry Crawford. Determined to gain the affections of this rare young woman who is indifferent to his charms, Crawford ends by succumbing to hers. He proposes. Fanny's unworldly refusal provokes the anger of her uncle. Then, while Fanny, still in disgrace with the baronet, is away from Mansfield Park and visiting her family at Portsmouth, the debacle of which *Lovers' Vows* was a harbinger comes about. The *homme fatal* Henry, at a loss for a woman to make love to, trains his charms on his old flirt Maria, now Mrs. Rushworth. She runs away with him; her sister, not to be outdone in bad behavior, elopes with an unsatisfactory suitor. Mary Crawford's moral coarseness becomes evident in her casual dismissal of these catastrophes. Edmund, now a clergyman, finds solace, then love, with the cousin whose sterling character shines brightly for him now that Mary's glitter has tarnished. Fanny gains all she could hope for in at last attaining the heart and hand of her clerical kinsman.

Austen's next novel, *Emma*, might be thought of as harmonizing the two voices heard in *Pride and Prejudice* and *Mansfield Park*. For this book, Austen claimed to be creating "a heroine whom no one but myself will much like," an "imaginist" whose circumstances and qualities of mind make her the self-crowned queen of her country neighborhood. Austen was not entirely serious or accurate: Emma certainly has her partisans. Even those readers who do not like her tend to find her fascinating, for she is a spirited, imaginative, healthy young woman who, like Mary Crawford, has potential to do considerable harm to the fabric of society but on whom, like Elizabeth Bennet, her creator generously bestows life's greatest blessing: union with a man whose virtues, talents, and assets are the best complement for her own.

Emma's eventual marriage to Mr. Knightley of Donwell Abbey is the ultimate expression of one of Austen's key assumptions, that marriage is a young woman's supreme act of self-definition. Unlike any other Austen heroine, Emma has no pressing need to marry. As the opening sentence of the book implies, Emma's situation makes her acceptance or rejection of a suitor an act of unencumbered will: "Emma Woodhouse, handsome, clever, and rich, with a comfortable home and happy disposition, seemed to unite some of the best blessings of existence; and had lived nearly twenty-one years in the world with very little to distress or vex her."

Free though circumstance allows her to be, Emma has not been encouraged by her lot in life to acquire the discipline and self-knowledge that, augmenting her innate intelligence and taste, would help her to choose wisely. Brought up by a doting valetudinarian of a father and a perceptive but permissive governess, Emma has been encouraged to think too highly of herself. Far from vain about her beauty, Emma has—as Mr. Knightley, the only person who ventures to criticize her, observes—complete yet unfounded faith in her ability to judge people's characters and arrange their lives. The course of *Emma* is Miss Woodhouse's education in judgment, a process achieved through repeated mistakes and humiliations.

As the novel opens, the young mistress of Hartfield is at loose ends. Her beloved governess has just married Mr. Weston, of the neighboring property, Randalls. To fill the newly made gap in her life, Emma takes notice of Harriet Smith, a pretty, dim "natural daughter of somebody," and a parlor-boarder at the local school. Determined to settle her protégée into the sort of life she deems suitable, Emma detaches Harriet from Robert Martin, a young farmer who has proposed to her, and embarks upon a campaign to conquer for Harriet the heart of Mr. Elton, Highbury's unmarried clergyman. Elton's attentiveness and excessive flattery convince Emma of her plan's success but at the same time show the reader what Emma is aghast to learn at the end of Book I: that Elton scorns the nobody and has designs upon the heiress herself.

With the arrival of three new personages in Highbury, Book II widens Emma's opportunities for misconception. The first newcomer is Jane Fairfax, an elegant and accomplished connection of the Bates family and a girl whose prospective fate, the "governess trade," shows how unreliable the situations of well-bred young ladies without fortunes or husbands tend to be. Next to arrive is the suave Mr. Frank Churchill, Mr. Weston's grown son, who has been adopted by wealthy relations of his mother and who has been long remiss in paying a visit to Highbury. Finally, Mr. Elton brings home a bride, the former Augusta Hawkins of Bristol, a pretentious and impertinent creature possessed of an independent fortune, a well-married sister, and a boundless fund of self-congratulation. Emma mistakenly flatters herself that the dashing Frank Churchill is in love with her, and then settles on him as a husband for Harriet; she suspects the reserved Miss Fairfax, whose cultivation she rightly perceives as a reproach to her own untrained talents, of a clandestine relationship with a married man. She despises Mrs. Elton, as would any person of sense, but fails to see that the vulgar woman's offensiveness is an exaggerated version of her own officiousness and snobbery.

Thus, the potential consequences of Emma's misplaced faith in her judgment intensify, and the evidence of her fallibility mounts. Thoroughly embarrassed to learn that Frank Churchill, to whom she has retailed all her hypotheses regarding Jane Fairfax, has long been secretly engaged to that woman, Emma suffers the death-blow to her smug self-esteem when Harriet announces that the gentleman whose feelings she hopes to have aroused is not, as Emma supposes, Churchill but the squire of Donwell. Emma's moment of truth is devastating and complete, its importance marked by one of Jane Austen's rare uses of figurative language: "It darted through her, with the speed of an arrow, that Mr. Knightley must marry no one but herself!" Perhaps the greatest evidence of Emma's being a favorite of fortune is that Mr. Knightley feels the same as she does on this matter. Chastened by her series of bad judgments, paired with a gentleman who for years has loved and respected her enough to correct her and whom she can love and respect in turn, Emma participates in the minuet of marriage with which Austen concludes the book, the other couples so united being Miss Fairfax and Mr. Churchill and Harriet Smith (ductile enough to form four attachments in a year) and Robert Martin (stalwart enough to persist in his original feeling).

Emma Woodhouse's gradual education, which parallels the reader's growing awareness of what a menace to the social order her circumstances, abilities, and weaknesses combine to make her, is one of Austen's finest pieces of plotting. The depiction of character is likewise superb. Among a gallery of memorable and distinctive characters are Mr. Woodhouse; Miss Bates, the stream-of-consciousness talker who inadvertently provokes Emma's famous rudeness on Box Hill; and the wonderfully detestable Mrs. Elton, with her self-contradictions and her fractured Italian, her endless allusions to Selina, Mr. Suckling, Maple Grove, and the *barouche landau*. Life at Hartfield, Donwell, and Highbury is portrayed with complexity and economy. Every word, expression, opinion, and activity—whether sketching a portrait, selecting a dancing partner, or planning a strawberry-picking party—becomes a gesture of self-revelation. *Emma* demonstrates how, in Austen's hands, the novel of manners can become a statement of moral philosophy.

Northanger Abbey was published in a four-volume unit with *Persuasion* in 1818, after Austen's death, but the manuscript had been completed much earlier, in 1803. Austen wrote a preface for *Northanger Abbey* but did not do the sort of revising that had transformed *Elinor and Marianne* and *First Impressions* into *Sense and Sensibility* and *Pride and Prejudice*. The published form of *Northanger Abbey* can therefore be seen as the earliest of the six novels. It is also, with the possible exception of *Sense and Sensibility*, the most "literary." *Northanger Abbey*, like some of Austen's juvenile burlesques, confronts the conventions of the Gothic novel or tale of terror. The incidents of her novel have been shown to parallel, with ironic difference, the principal lines of Gothic romance, particularly as practiced by Ann Radcliffe, whose most famous works, *The Romance of the Forest* (1791) and *The Mysteries of Udolpho* (1794), had appeared several years before Jane Austen had begun work on her burlesque.

Like *Emma*, *Northanger Abbey* is centrally concerned with tracing the growth of a young woman's mind and the cultivation of her judgment. In this less sophisticated work, however, the author accomplishes her goal through a rather schematic contrast. As an enthusiastic reader of tales of terror, Catherine Morland has Gothic expectations of life despite a background most unsuitable for a heroine. Like the Gothic heroines she admires, Catherine commences adventuring early in the novel. She is not, however, shipped to Venice or Dalmatia, but taken to Bath for a six-week stay. Her hosts are serenely amiable English folk, her pastimes the ordinary round of spa pleasures; the young man whose acquaintance she makes, Henry Tilney, is a witty clergyman rather than a misanthropic monk or dissolute rake. Toward this delightful, if far from Gothic, young man, Catherine's feelings are early inclined. In turn, he, his sister, and even his father, the haughty, imperious General Tilney, are favorably disposed toward her. With the highest expectations, Catherine sets out to accompany them to their seat, the Abbey of the novel's title (which, like that of *Persuasion*, was selected not by the author but by Henry Austen, who handled the posthumous publication).

At Northanger, Catherine's education in the difference between literature and life continues. Despite its monastic origins, the Abbey proves a comfortable and well-maintained dwelling. When Catherine, like one of Radcliffe's protagonists, finds a mysterious document in a chest and spends a restless night wondering what lurid tale it might chronicle, she is again disappointed: "If the evidence of her sight might be trusted she held a washing-bill in her hand." Although Catherine's experience does not confirm the truth of Radcliffe's sensational horrors, it does not prove the world a straightforward, safe, cozy place. Catherine has already seen something of falseness and selfish vulgarity in the persons of Isabella Thorpe and her brother John, acquaintances formed at Bath. At Northanger, she learns that, though the General may not be the wife-murderer she has fancied him, he is quite as cruel as she could imagine. On learning that Catherine is not the great heiress he has mistakenly supposed her to be, the furious general packs her off in disgrace and discomfort in a public coach.

With this proof that the world of fact can prove as treacherous as that of fiction, Catherine returns sadder and wiser to the bosom of her family. She has not long to droop, though, for Henry Tilney, on hearing of his father's bad behavior, hurries after her and makes Catherine the proposal which he has long felt inclined to offer and which his father has until recently promoted. The approval of Catherine's parents is immediate, and the General is not overlong in coming to countenance the match. "To begin perfect happiness at the respective ages of twenty-six and eighteen is to do pretty well," observes the facetious narrator, striking a literary pose even in the novel's last sentence, "and . . . I leave it to be settled by whomsoever it may concern, whether the tendency of this work be altogether to recommend parental tyranny, or reward filial disobedience."

Persuasion, many readers believe, signals Austen's literary move out of the eighteenth century and into the nineteenth. This novel, quite different from those that preceded it, draws not upon the tradition of the novelists of the 1790's but on that of the lionized poets of the new century's second decade, Sir Walter Scott and Lord Byron. For the first time, Austen clearly seems the child of her time, susceptible to the charms of natural rather than improved landscapes, fields and sea cliffs rather than gardens and shrubberies. The wistful, melancholy beauty of autumn that pervades the book is likewise romantic. The gaiety, vitality, and sparkling wit of *Pride and Prejudice* and *Emma* are muted. The stable social order represented by the great estate in

Mansfield Park has become fluid in *Persuasion*: here the principal country house, Kellynch Hall, must be let because the indigenous family cannot afford to inhabit it.

Most important, *Persuasion*'s heroine is unique in Jane Austen's gallery. Anne Elliott, uprooted from her ancestral home, spiritually isolated from her selfish and small-minded father and sisters, separated from the man she loves by a long-standing estrangement, is every bit as "alienated" as such later nineteenth century heroines as Esther Summerson, Jane Eyre, and Becky Sharp. Anne's story is very much the product of Austen's middle age. At twenty-seven, she is the only Austen heroine to be past her first youth. Furthermore, she is in no need of education. Her one great mistake—overriding the impulse of her heart and yielding to the persuasion of her friend Lady Russell in rejecting the proposal of Frederick Wentworth, a sanguine young naval officer with his fortune still to make and his character to prove—is some eight years in the past, and she clearly recognizes it for the error it was.

Persuasion is the story of how Anne and Frederick (now the eminent Captain) Wentworth rekindle the embers of their love. Chance throws them together when the vain, foolish Sir Walter Elliott, obliged to economize or rent his estate, resolves to move his household to Bath, where he can cut a fine figure at less cost, and leases Kellynch to Admiral and Mrs. Croft, who turn out to be the brother-in-law and sister of Captain Wentworth. Initially cool to his former love—or rather, able to see the diminution of her beauty because he is unable to forgive her rejection—the Captain flirts with the Musgrove girls; they are sisters to the husband of Anne's younger sister Mary and blooming belles with the youth and vigor Anne lacks. The old appreciation of Anne's merits, her clear insight, kindness, highmindedness, and modesty, soon reasserts itself, but not before fate and the Captain's impetuosity have all but forced another engagement upon him. Being "jumped down" from the Cobb at Lyme Regis, Louisa Musgrove misses his arms and falls unconscious on the pavement. Obliged by honor to declare himself hers if she should wish it, Wentworth is finally spared this self-sacrifice when the susceptible young lady and the sensitive Captain Benwick fall in love. Having discovered the intensity of his devotion to Anne by being on the point of having to abjure it, Wentworth hurries to Bath, there to declare his attachment in what is surely the most powerful engagement scene in the Austen canon.

Though the story of *Persuasion* belongs to Anne Elliott and Frederick Wentworth, Austen's skill at evoking characters is everywhere noticeable. As Elizabeth Jenkins observes, all of the supporting characters present different facets of the love theme. The heartless marital calculations of Mr. Elliott, Elizabeth Elliott, and Mrs. Clay, the domestic comforts of the senior Musgroves and the Crofts, and the half fractious, half amiable ménage of Charles and Mary Musgrove all permit the reader more clearly to discern how rare and true is the love Anne Elliott and her captain have come so close to losing. The mature, deeply grateful commitment they are able to make to each other is, if not the most charming, surely the most profound in the Austen world.

Peter W. Graham

Other major works

SHORT FICTION: *Minor Works*, 1954 (Vol. VI of the *Oxford Illustrated Jane Austen*, R. W. Chapman, editor).

NONFICTION: *Jane Austen's Letters*, 1952 (R. W. Chapman, editor).

Bibliography

Bush, Douglas. *Jane Austen*. New York: Macmillan, 1975. Addressed to students and general readers, this survey by an eminent scholar provides a straightforward introduction to Austen's work. Overviews of Austen's England, her life, and her early writings set the stage for chapter-length discussions of her six novels; two unfinished works, *The Watsons* and *Sanditon*, also receive a chapter each.

Grey, J. David, ed. *The Jane Austen Companion*. New York: Macmillan, 1986. An encyclopedic guide to Austen's life and works. Among the topics covered are "Characterization in Jane Austen," "Chronology of Composition," and "Editions and Publishing History." There are brief essays on "Dancing, Balls, and Assemblies," "Dress and Fashion," "Post/Mail," and many other aspects of everyday life in Austen's time. Each essay includes a bibliography. An indispensable resource.

Halperin, John, ed. *Jane Austen: Bicentenary Essays*. New York: Cambridge University Press, 1975. Written especially for this volume, the nineteen essays collected here represent a diversity of critical approaches. Among several background essays, Jane Aiken Hodge's "Jane Austen and Her Publishers" is particularly interesting. Each of the novels is the subject of at least one essay; there are three essays on *Mansfield Park* and two each on *Pride and Prejudice* and *Emma*. Includes a select bibliography.

Hardy, Barbara. *A Reading of Jane Austen*. New York: New York University Press, 1976. A thematic approach to Austen's fiction (Hardy does not discuss Austen's juvenilia or her fragmentary works). In the first chapter, "The Flexible Medium," Hardy argues that while Austen was not, on the surface, a radical innovator, she nevertheless transformed the genre in which she worked: "Indeed she may be said to have created the modern novel." Two later chapters provide a valuable study of Austen's handling of narrative point of view and of "telling and listening" in her novels. Lacks an index.

Honan, Park. *Jane Austen: Her Life*. New York: St. Martin's Press, 1987. One of numerous biographies of Austen. Uses new sources which provide more detailed information about Austen's life. While based on facts gleaned from letters and other family documents, the aim is for more of a narrative than a sourcebook, attempting to provide insight into Austen's thought and personality. It is an interesting approach but speculative, as it is hard to be certain what Austen was thinking, even with the use of private correspondence. Should be helpful to anyone who needs to know more about Austen's life. Also includes a family tree, illustrations of the Austen family and their homes and friends, and an appendix of studies relating to Austen.

Lane, Maggie. *Jane Austen's England*. New York: St. Martin's Press, 1986. This fascinating book is full of illustrations which give Austen's readers a look at the world of her novels. Arranged chronologically, taking the reader to the places Austen would have gone, usually through contemporary paintings. The text is useful; the first chapter, "The England of Jane Austen's Time," gives a good basic summary of social conditions around the beginning of the nineteenth century. Includes references to the novels; for example, Lane quotes the Box Hill episode from *Emma* and provides a painting of Box Hill. Also includes a map, a short bibliography, and an index.

Mooneyham, Laura G. *Romance, Language, and Education in Jane Austen's Novels*. New York: St. Martin's Press, 1986. Covers all six of Austen's complete novels, theorizing that a relationship exists among language, education, and romance. Asserts that the romance between heroine and hero is in itself educational for the heroine because romance offers the opportunity for open communication. This approach is provocative and useful, especially because it emphasizes Austen's own preoccupations. Each chapter discusses a separate novel, which may be useful for the study of one of Austen's works.

Sulloway, Alison. *Jane Austen and the Province of Womanhood*. Philadelphia: University of Pennsylvania Press, 1989. Attempts to place Austen into a framework of "women-centered" authors from the tract-writers Mary Astell, Mary Wollstonecraft Godwin, and Catharine Macaulay, to novelists Fanny Burney, Maria Edgeworth, and Charlotte Smith. Counters early views of Austen as a conservative woman upholding the status quo in her novels. Suggests that Austen was a moderate feminist who sought reforms for women rather than outright revolution. Instead of reading Austen's novels separately, Sulloway focuses on themes which she calls "provinces": the ballroom (dancing and marriage), the drawing room (debate), the garden (reconciliation). A valuable book which is thought-provoking and not overly theoretical.

Thompson, James. *Between Self and World: The Novels of Jane Austen*. University Park: Pennsylvania State University, 1988. Takes a Marxist, historicist approach to Austen, reading her work as a comment on the changing attitudes toward the eighteenth century from publicly oriented to more individualistic. Considers Austen the first novelist to place love and affection at the center of an ideal marriage, suggesting a movement away from the historical, political "outside" world toward a private intimate domestic ideal. While overly limiting his arguments by making such claims for Austen, Thompson's comments are nevertheless worthwhile and illuminating. Arranged by topics rather than by novel; one interesting chapter is on marriage proposals.

Williams, Michael. *Jane Austen: Six Novels and Their Methods*. New York: St. Martin's Press, 1986. Emphasizes text over interpretation, focusing on the artistic strategies Austen employs to produce a desired effect. Attempts to move beyond the older style of novel criticism which only categorized the stylistic elements of a novel. Brings Austen's activity as a writer to the forefront, demonstrating her emphases and concerns, in the end seeing Austen as a writer who deals deliberately with ambiguities. This approach is promising, but most of Williams' assertions about the specific novels seem simplistic. Focuses on one novel in each chapter. The index and bibliography are concise but useful.

JAMES BALDWIN

Born: New York, New York; August 2, 1924
Died: St. Paul de Vence, France; November 30, 1987

Principal long fiction

Go Tell It on the Mountain, 1953; *Giovanni's Room*, 1956; *Another Country*, 1962; *Tell Me How Long the Train's Been Gone*, 1968; *If Beale Street Could Talk*, 1974; *Just Above My Head*, 1979.

Other literary forms

Before he published his first novel, James Baldwin had established a reputation as a talented essayist and reviewer. Many of his early pieces, later collected in *Notes of a Native Son* (1955) and *Nobody Knows My Name: More Notes of a Native Son* (1961), have become classics; his essays on Richard Wright, especially "Everybody's Protest Novel" (1949) and "Many Thousands Gone" (1951), occupy a central position in the development of "universalist" Afro-American thought during the 1950's. Culminating in *The Fire Next Time* (1963), an extended meditation on the relationship of race, religion, and the individual experience in America, Baldwin's early prose demands a reexamination and redefinition of received social and cultural premises. His collections of essays *No Name in the Street* (1971) and *The Devil Finds Work* (1976) reflected a more militant stance and were received less favorably than Baldwin's universalist statements. *The Evidence of Things Not Seen* (1985) is a book-length essay on the Atlanta child-murders, while *The Price of the Ticket: Collected Nonfiction 1948-1985* (1985) includes all of Baldwin's essay collections as well as a number of previously uncollected pieces. Less formal and intricate, though in some cases more explicit, reflections of Baldwin's beliefs can be found in *A Rap on Race* (1971), an extended discussion with Margaret Mead, and *A Dialogue* (1975), a conversation with Nikki Giovanni.

Baldwin also wrote children's fiction (*Little Man, Little Man*, 1975), the text for a photographic essay (*Nothing Personal*, 1964, with Richard Avedon), an unfilmed scenario (*One Day, When I Was Lost: A Scenario Based on The Autobiography of Malcolm X*, 1972), drama, and short stories. Most critics prefer Baldwin's first play, *The Amen Corner* (written mid-1950's, published 1965), to *Blues for Mister Charlie* (1964) despite the latter's four-month Broadway run. Although he published little short fiction after the collection *Going to Meet the Man* (1965), Baldwin was an acknowledged master of the novella form. "Sonny's Blues" (1957), the story of the relationship of a jazz musician to his "respectable" narrator-brother, anticipates many of the themes of Baldwin's later novels and is widely recognized as one of the great American novellas.

Achievements

Baldwin's public role as a major Afro-American racial spokesman of the 1950's and 1960's, guarantees his place in American cultural history. Though not undeserved, this reputation more frequently obscures than clarifies the nature of his literary achievement, which involves his relationship to Afro-American culture, existential philosophy, and the moral tradition of the world novel. To be sure, Baldwin's progression from an individualistic, universalist stance through active involvement with the integrationist Civil Rights movement to an increasing sympathy with militant Pan-Africanist thought parallels the general development of Afro-American thought between the early 1950's and the mid-1970's. Indeed, his novels frequently mirror both Baldwin's personal philosophy and its social context. Some, most notably *Another Country*, attained a high degree of public visibility when published, leading to a widely accepted vision of Baldwin as a topical writer. To consider Baldwin primarily as a racial spokesman, however, imposes a stereotype which distorts many of his most penetrating insights and underestimates his status as a literary craftsman.

More accurate, though ultimately as limited, is the view of Baldwin primarily as an exemplar of the Afro-American presence in the "mainstream" of the American tradition. Grouped with Ralph Ellison as a major "post-Wright" black novelist, Baldwin represents, in this view, the generation which rejected "protest literature" in favor of "universal" themes. Strangely at odds with the view of Baldwin as racial spokesman, this view emphasizes the craftsmanship of Baldwin's early novels and his treatment of "mainstream" themes such as religious hypocrisy, father-son tensions, and sexual identity. Ironically, many younger Afro-American novelists accept this general view of Baldwin's accomplishment, viewing his mastery of Jamesian techniques and his involvement with Continental literary culture as an indication of alienation from his racial identity. Recasting Eldridge Cleaver's political attack on Baldwin in aesthetic terms, the Afro-American writer Ishmael Reed dismisses Baldwin as a great "white" novelist. A grain of truth lies in Reed's assertion; Baldwin rarely created new forms. Rather, he infused a variety of Euro-American forms, derived from Wright and William Faulkner as well as from Henry James, with the rhythms and imagery of the Afro-American oral tradition.

Like the folk preacher whose voice he frequently assumed in secular contexts, Baldwin combined moral insight with an uncompromising sense of the concrete realities of his community, whether defined in terms of family, lovers, race, or nation. This indicates the deepest level of Baldwin's literary achievement; whatever his immediate political focus or fictional form, he possessed an insight into moral psychology shared by only a handful of novelists. Inasmuch as the specific circumstances of this psychology involve American racial relations, this insight aligns Baldwin with Wright, Faulkner,

Mark Twain, and Harriet Beecher Stowe. Inasmuch as his insight involves the symbolic alienation of the individual, it places him with American romantics such as Nathaniel Hawthorne and European existentialists such as Albert Camus. Since his insight recognizes the complex pressure exerted by social mechanisms on individual consciousness, it reveals affinities with James Joyce, George Eliot, and Ellison. As a writer who combined elements of all of these traditions with the voice of the anonymous Afro-American preacher, Baldwin cannot be reduced to accommodate the terms of any one of them. Refusing to lie about the reality of pain, he provided realistic images of the moral life possible in the inhospitable world that encompasses the streets of Harlem and the submerged recesses of the mind.

Biography

James Baldwin once dismissed his childhood as "the usual bleak fantasy." Nevertheless, the major concerns of his fiction consistently reflect the social context of his family life in Harlem during the Depression. The dominant figure of Baldwin's childhood was clearly that of his stepfather, David Baldwin, who worked as a manual laborer and preached in a storefront church. Clearly the model for Gabriel Grimes in *Go Tell It on the Mountain*, David Baldwin had moved from New Orleans to New York City, where he married Baldwin's mother, Emma Berdis. The oldest of what was to be a group of nine children in the household, James assumed a great deal of the responsibility for the care of his half-brothers and sisters. Insulated somewhat from the brutality of Harlem street life by his domestic duties, Baldwin, as he describes in *The Fire Next Time*, sought refuge in the Church. Undergoing a conversion experience, similar to that of John in *Go Tell It on the Mountain*, at age fourteen in 1938, Baldwin preached as a youth minister for the next several years. At the same time, he began to read, immersing himself in works such as *Uncle Tom's Cabin* (1852) and the novels of Charles Dickens. Both at his Harlem junior high school, where the Afro-American poet Countée Cullen was one of his teachers, and at his predominantly white Bronx high school, Baldwin contributed to student literary publications. The combination of family tension, economic hardship, and religious vocation provides the focus of much of Baldwin's greatest writing, most notably *Go Tell It on the Mountain*, *The Fire Next Time*, and *Just Above My Head*.

If Baldwin's experience during the 1930's provided his material, his life from 1942 to 1948 shaped his characteristic approach to that material. After he was graduated from high school in 1942, Baldwin worked for a year as a manual laborer in New Jersey, an experience which increased both his understanding of his stepfather and his insight into America's economic and racial systems. Moving to Greenwich Village in 1943, Baldwin worked during the day and wrote at night for the next five years; his first national reviews and essays appeared in 1946. The major event of the Village years, however, was

Baldwin's meeting with Richard Wright in the winter between 1944 and 1945. Wright's interest helped Baldwin secure first a Eugene F. Saxton Memorial Award and then a Rosenwald Fellowship, enabling him to move to Paris in 1948.

After his arrival in France, Baldwin experienced more of the poverty which had shaped his childhood. Simultaneously, he developed a larger perspective on the psychocultural context conditioning his experience, feeling at once a greater sense of freedom and a larger sense of the global structure of racism, particularly as reflected in the French treatment of North Africans. In addition, he formed many of the personal and literary friendships which contributed to his later public prominence. Baldwin's well-publicized literary feud with Wright, who viewed the younger writer's criticism of *Native Son* (1940) as a form of personal betrayal, helped establish Baldwin as a major presence in Afro-American letters. Although Baldwin's first novel, *Go Tell It on the Mountain*, was well-received critically, it was not so financially successful that he could devote his full time to creative writing. As a result, Baldwin continued to travel widely, frequently on journalistic assignments, while writing *Giovanni's Room*, which is set in France and involves no black characters.

Returning to the United States as a journalist covering the Civil Rights movement, Baldwin made his first trip to the American South in 1957. The essays and reports describing that physical and psychological journey propelled Baldwin to the position of public prominence which he maintained for more than a decade. During the height of the movement, Baldwin lectured widely and was present at major events such as the March on Washington and the voter registration drive in Selma, Alabama. In addition, he met with most of the major Afro-American activists of the period, including Martin Luther King, Elijah Muhammad, James Meredith, and Medgar Evers. Attorney General Robert Kennedy requested that Baldwin bring together the most influential voices in the black community, and, even though the resulting meeting accomplished little, the request testifies to Baldwin's image as a focal point of Afro-American opinion. In addition to this political activity, Baldwin formed personal and literary relationships—frequently tempestuous ones—with numerous white writers, including William Styron and Norman Mailer. A surge in literary popularity, reflected in the presence of *Another Country* and *The Fire Next Time* on the best-seller lists throughout most of 1962 and 1963, accompanied Baldwin's political success and freed him from financial insecurity for the first time. He traveled extensively throughout the decade, and his visits to Puerto Rico and Africa were to have a major influence on his subsequent political thought.

Partly because of Baldwin's involvement with prominent whites and partly because of the sympathy for homosexuals evinced in his writing, several black militants, most notably Eldridge Cleaver, attacked Baldwin's position as "black spokesman" beginning in the late 1960's. As a result, nationalist spokesmen such as Amiri Baraka and Bobby Seale gradually eclipsed Baldwin in the public literary and political spotlights. Nevertheless, Baldwin, himself sympathetic to many of the militant positions, continued his involvement with public issues, such as the fate of the Wilmington, North Carolina, prisoners which he addressed in an open letter to Jimmy Carter shortly after Carter's election to the presidency. In his later years, though he returned periodically to the South, Baldwin lived for much of the time in France and Turkey. It was in St. Paul de Vence, France, that he died, on November 30, 1987.

Analysis

Uncompromising in his demand for personal and social integrity, James Baldwin from the beginning of his career charged the individual with full responsibility for his or her moral identity. Both in his early individualistic novels and his later political fiction, he insisted on the inadequacy of received definitions as the basis for self-knowledge or social action. Echoing the existentialist principle "existence precedes essence," he intimated the underlying consistency of his vision in the introductory essay in *Notes of a Native Son:* "I think all theories are suspect, that the finest principles may have to be modified, or may even be pulverized by the demands of life, and that one must find, therefore, one's own moral center and move through the world hoping that this center will guide one aright." This insistence on the moral center and movement in the world cautions against associating Baldwin with the atheistic or solipsistic currents of existential thought. Never denying the possibility of transcendent moral power—which he frequently imaged as the power of love—he simply insisted that human conceptions must remain flexible enough to allow for the honest perception of experience. Fully recognizing the reality of existential pain and despair, Baldwin invoked honesty and self-acceptance as the necessary supports for the love capable of generating individual communication and at least the groundwork for political action.

Baldwin's social vision, reflecting his experience in a racist culture, acknowledges the forces militating against self-knowledge and moral responsibility. Each of his novels portrays a series of evasive and simplifying definitions built into religious, economic, and educational institutions. These definitions, which emphasize the separation of self and other, control the immediate contexts of individual experience. As a result, they frequently seem to constitute "human nature," to embody the inevitable limits of experience. While sympathizing with the difficulty of separating the self from context without simultaneously denying experience, Baldwin insists that acquiescing to the definitions inevitably results in self-hatred and social immorality. The individual incapable of accepting his or her existential complexity flees to the illusion of certainty provided by the institutions which assume responsibility for directing moral decisions. This cycle of institutional pressure encouraging existential evasion insuring further institutional corruption recurs in each of Baldwin's novels. On both personal and social levels, the drive to deny the reality of the other—racial, sexual, or economic—generates nothing save destruction. Derived from the streets of Harlem rather than from Scripture, Baldwin's response echoes Christ's admonition to "love thy neighbor as thyself." The derivation is vital; in Baldwin's novels, those who extract the message from the Bible rather than from their lives frequently aggravate the pain which makes evading reality seem attractive.

The immediate focus of Baldwin's attention gradually shifted from consciousness to context, creating the illusion of a change in his basic concerns. While he always worked in the realistic tradition of the novel, his choice of specific forms paralleled this shift in thematic focus, though again his later work indicates an underlying unity in his fiction. His first novel, *Go Tell It on the Mountain*, employs a tightly focused Jamesian form to explore the developing awareness of the adolescent protagonist John Grimes, who is not yet aware of the evasive definitions conditioning his experience. After a second Jamesian novel, *Giovanni's Room*, Baldwin adapted the relatively unstructured Dreiserian mode in *Another Country* and *Tell Me How Long the Train's Been Gone*. Characters such as Rufus Scott and Vivaldo Moore in *Another Country* continue to struggle for individual awareness, but Baldwin's new narrative stance emphasizes the impact of the limiting definitions on a wide range of particular social circumstances. Attempting to balance the presentation of consciousness and context, Baldwin's last two novels, *If Beale Street Could Talk* and *Just Above My Head*, synthesize the earlier technical approaches. Returning to the immediate focus on the individual consciousness in these first-person narratives, Baldwin creates protagonists capable of articulating their own social perceptions. Consciousness and context merge as Baldwin's narrators share their insights and, more important, their processes with their fellow sufferers.

These insights implicitly endorse William Blake's vision of morality as a movement from innocence through experience to a higher innocence. Beginning with an unaware innocence, individuals inevitably enter the deadening and murderous world of experience, the world of the limiting definitions. Those who attempt to deny the world and remain children perish alongside those who cynically submit to the cruelty of the context for imagined personal benefit. Only those who plunge into experience, recognize its cruelty, and resolve to forge an aware innocence can hope to survive morally. Specifically, Baldwin urges families to pass on a sense of the higher innocence to their children by refusing to simplify the truth of experience. This painful honesty makes possible the commitment to love despite the inevitability of pain and isolation. It provides the only hope, however desperate, for individual or social rejuvenation. To a large extent, Baldwin's career developed in accord with the Blakean pattern. John Grimes begins his passage from innocence to experience in *Go Tell It on the Mountain*; Rufus Scott and Vivaldo Moore, among others, struggle to survive experience in *Another Country*, which intimates the need for the higher innocence. Baldwin's last two novels portray the entire process, focusing on the attempt first to find and then to pass on the higher innocence. *Just Above My Head*, with its middle-aged narrator and his teenaged children, clearly represents a more highly developed and realistic stage of the vision than *If Beale Street Could Talk*, with its teenaged mother-narrator and her newborn infant.

Go Tell It on the Mountain centers on the religious conversion and family relationships of John Grimes, whose experience parallels that of Baldwin during his youth. Although he believes himself to be the natural son of Gabriel Grimes, a preacher who, like Baldwin's stepfather, moved to New York after growing up in the South, John is actually the son of Gabriel's wife Elizabeth and her lover, Richard, who committed suicide prior to John's birth. Growing up under the influence of his hypocritical and tyrannical stepfather, John alternately attempts to please and transcend him. Gabriel expends most of his emotional energy on his openly rebellious son Roy, whose immersion in the violent life of the Harlem streets contrasts sharply with John's involvement with the "Temple of the Fire Baptized," the storefront church where his conversion takes place. To the extent that Baldwin organizes *Go Tell It on the Mountain* around John's attempt to come to terms with these pressures, the novel appears to have a highly individualistic focus.

The overall structure of the novel, however, dictates that John's experience be viewed in a larger context. Of the three major sections of *Go Tell It on the Mountain*, the first, "The Seventh Day," and the third, "The Threshing Floor," focus directly on John. The long middle section, "The Prayers of the Saints," a Faulknerian exploration of history, traces the origins of John's struggle to the experience of his elders, devoting individual chapters to Elizabeth, Gabriel, and Gabriel's sister Florence. Together the prayers portray the Great Migration of blacks from South to North, from rural to urban settings. Far from bringing true freedom, the movement results in a new indirect type of oppression. As Elizabeth recognizes: "There was not, after all, a great difference between the world of the North and that of the South which she had fled; there was only this difference: the North promised more. And this similarity: what it promised it did not give, and what it gave, at length and grudgingly with one hand, it took back with the other." Even in his most individualistic phase, then, Baldwin is aware of the power of institutional pressures. The origins of John's particular struggle against the limiting definitions go back to their impact on both Elizabeth and Gabriel.

Elizabeth's relationship with John's true father, at least in its early stages, appears to offer hope for at least a limited freedom from external definition. Highly intelligent and self-aware, Richard struggles to transcend the limitations imposed on black aspiration through a rigorous program of self-education, which he shares with Elizabeth. Despite his intelligence and determination, however, Richard maintains a naïve innocence concerning the possibility of self-definition in a society based on racist assumptions. Only when arrested on suspicion of a robbery he had nothing to do with does he recognize that his context defines him simply as another "nigger." Unable to reconcile this imposed definition with his drive for social transcendence, he despairs and commits suicide. This act, in turn, destroys Elizabeth's chance for obtaining a greater degree of freedom. She is not, however, simply a victim. Fearing that Richard will be unable to cope with the responsibility of a family, she fails to tell him of her pregnancy. Far from protecting him, this evasion contributes to his destruction by allowing Richard to view his situation as purely personal. Elizabeth's own choice, conditioned by the social refusal to confront reality, combines with the racist legal system to circumscribe her possibilities. Forced to care for her infant son, she marries Gabriel, thus establishing the basic terms for John's subsequent struggle.

Seen in relation to John in "The Seventh Day," Gabriel appears to be one of the most despicable hypocrites in American literature. Seen in relation to his own history in "The Prayers of the Saints," however, he appears victimized by the institutional context of his youth. In turn, he victimizes his family by attempting to force them into narrowly defined roles. The roots of Gabriel's character lie in the "temple-street" dichotomy of his Southern childhood. Encouraged by his religious mother to deny his sensuality, Gabriel undergoes a conversion experience and immerses himself in the role of preacher. As a result, he enters into a loveless asexual marriage with his mother's friend Deborah, herself a victim of the racist psychology—enforced by blacks and whites—which condemns *her* after she has been brutally raped by a group of whites. Eventually, Gabriel's repressed street self breaks out and he fathers a son by the sensual Esther. Again attempting to deny his sensuality, Gabriel refuses to acknowledge this son, Royal. Like John's half-brother Roy, the first Royal immerses himself in the street life which Gabriel denies; he dies in a Chicago barroom brawl. Gabriel fears that Roy will share Royal's fate, but his attempt to crush his second son's street self merely strengthens the resulting rebellion. Faced with the guilt of Royal's death and the sense of impending doom concerning Roy, Gabriel retreats into a solipsism which makes a mockery of his Christian vocation. Far from providing a context for moral responsibility, the Church—both in the South and in the North—simply replaces the original innocence of religious fervor with a cynical vision of religion as a source of the power needed to destroy the innocence of others.

Against this backdrop, John's conversion raises a basic question which will recur in slightly different circumstances in each of Baldwin's novels: Can an individual hope to break the cycle of evasion which has shaped his personal and social context? In John's case, the problem takes on added dimensions, since he remains ignorant of many of the events shaping his life, including those involving his own birth. By framing the prayers with John's conversion, Baldwin stresses the connection between past and present, but the connection can be perceived as either oppressive or liberating. The complex irony of "The Threshing Floor" section allows informed readings of John's conversion as either a surrender to evasion or as a movement toward existential responsibility. Focusing primarily on John's internal experience as he lies transfixed on the church floor, "The Threshing Floor" revolves around a dialogue between an "ironic voice" which challenges John to return to the street and the part of John which seeks traditional salvation. Throughout John's vision, the narrative voice shifts point of view in accord with John's developing perception. As John accepts the perceptions implied by his vision, the ironic voice shifts its attention to yet deeper levels of ambiguity. To the extent that John resolves these ambiguities by embracing the Temple, his experience seems to increase the risk that he will follow Gabriel's destructive example.

Several image patterns, however, indicate that John may be moving nearer to a recognition of his actual complexity. Chief among these are those involving the curse of Ham, the rejection of the father, and the acceptance of apparent opposites. From the beginning of the vision, the ironic voice ridicules John for accepting the curse of Ham, which condemns him both as son and as "nigger." Manipulating John's sense of guilt for having indulged his street self by masturbating, the ironic voice insists that John's very existence "proves" Gabriel's own sexual weakness. If Gabriel condemns John, he condemns himself in the process. As a result, John comes to view himself as the "devil's son" and repudiates his subservience before his "father." Without this essentially negative, and ultimately socially derived, definition of himself, John finds himself in an existential void where "there was no speech or language, and there was no love."

Forced to reconstruct his identity, John progresses from this sense of isolation to a vision of the dispossessed with whom he shares his agony and his humanity. John's vision of the multitude whose collective voice merges with his own suggests suffering as the essential human experience, one obliterating both the safety and the isolation of imposed definitions. Significantly, this vision leads John to Jesus the Son rather than God the Father, marking an implicit rejection of Gabriel's Old Testament vengeance in favor of the New Testament commitment to an all-encompassing love. The son metamorphosizes from symbol of limitation to symbol of liberation. Near the end of his vision, John explicitly rejects the separation of opposites—street and temple, white and black—encouraged by his social context: "The light and the darkness had kissed each other, and were married now, forever, in the life and the vision of John's soul." Returning to his immediate environment from the depths of his mind, John responds not to the call of Gabriel but to that of Elisha, a slightly older member of the congregation with whom he has previously engaged in a sexually suggestive wrestling match reminiscent of that in D. H. Lawrence's *Women in Love* (1920). John's salvation, then, may bring him closer to an acceptance of his own sensuality, to a definition of himself encompassing both temple and street. Baldwin ends the novel with the emergence of the newly "saved" John onto the streets of Harlem. His fate hinges on his ability to move ahead to the higher innocence suggested by his vision of the dispossessed rather than submitting to the experiences which have destroyed and deformed the majority of the saints.

Another Country, Baldwin's greatest popular success, analyzes the effects of this deforming pressure on a wide range of characters, black and white, male and female, homosexual and heterosexual. To accommodate these diverse consciousnesses, Baldwin employs the sprawling form usually associated with political rather than psychological fiction, emphasizing the diverse forms of innocence and experience in American society. The three major sections of *Another Country*, "Easy Rider," "Any Day Now," and "Toward Bethlehem," progress generally from despair to renewed hope, but no single consciousness or plot line provides a frame similar to that of *Go Tell It on the Mountain*. Rather, the novel's structural coherence derives from the moral concerns present in each of the various plots.

Casting a Melvillean shadow over the novel is the black jazz musician Rufus Scott, who is destroyed by an agonizing affair with Leona, a white Southerner recently arrived in New York at the time she meets him. Unable to forge the innocence necessary for love in a context which repudiates the relationship at every turn, Rufus destroys Leona psychologically. After a period of physical and psychological destitution, he kills himself by jumping off a bridge. His sister Ida, an aspiring singer, and his friend Vivaldo Moore, an aspiring white writer, meet during the last days of Rufus' life and fall in love as they console each other over his death. Struggling to overcome the racial and sexual definitions which destroyed Rufus, they seek a higher innocence capable of countering Ida's sense of the world as a "whorehouse." In contrast to Ida and Vivaldo's struggle, the relationship of white actor Eric Jones and his French lover Yves seems Edenic. Although Baldwin portrays Eric's internal struggle for a firm sense of his sexual identity, their shared innocence at times seems to exist almost entirely outside the context of the pressures that destroyed Rufus. The final major characters, Richard and Cass Silenski, represent the cost of the "American dream." After Richard "makes it" as a popular novelist, their personal relationship decays, precipitating Cass's affair with Eric. Their tentative reunion after Richard discovers the affair makes it clear that material success provides no shortcut to moral responsibility.

Baldwin examines each character and relationship in the context of the institutional pressures discouraging individual responsibility. His portrait of Rufus, the major accomplishment of *Another Country*, testifies to a moral insight and a raw artistic power resembling that of Wright and Émile Zola. Forgoing the formal control and emotional restraint of his earlier novels,

Baldwin opens *Another Country* with the image of Rufus who "had fallen so low, that he scarcely had the energy to be angry." Both an exceptional case and a representative figure, Rufus embodies the seething anger and hopeless isolation rendering Baldwin's United States a landscape of nightmare. Seeing his own situation as unbearable, Rufus meditates on the fate of a city tormented by an agony like his own: "He remembered to what excesses, into what traps and nightmares, his loneliness had driven him; and he wondered where such a violent emptiness might drive an entire city." Forcing the reader to recognize the social implications of Rufus' situation, Baldwin emphasizes that his specific situation originates in his own moral failure with Leona. Where Gabriel Grimes remained insulated from his immorality by arrogance and pride, Rufus feels the full extent of his self-enforced damnation. Ironically and belatedly, his destitution clarifies his sense of the extent of his past acceptance of the social definitions which destroy him.

Wandering the streets of Manhattan, Rufus feels himself beyond human contact. Desperately in need of love, he believes his past actions render him unfit for even minimal compassion. His abuse of Leona, who as a white woman represents both the "other" and the source of the most obvious social definitions circumscribing his life as a black male, accounts for his original estrangement from family and friends, who find his viciousness uncharacteristic. All, including Rufus, fail to understand soon enough that his abuse of Leona represents both a rebellion against and an acceptance of the role dictated by racial and sexual definitions. Separated from the psychological source of his art—jazz inevitably rejects the substructure of Euro-American definitions of reality—Rufus falls ever further into a paranoia which receives ample reenforcement from the racist context. Largely by his own choice, he withdraws almost entirely from both his black and white acquaintances. Once on the street following Leona's breakdown, he begins to recognize not only his immediate but also his long-term acceptance of destructive definitions. Thinking back on a brief homosexual affair with Eric to which he submitted out of pity rather than love, Rufus regrets having treated his friend with contempt. Having rejected the other in Eric and Leona, Rufus realizes he has rejected a part of himself. He consigns himself to the ranks of the damned, casting himself beyond human love with his plunge off the bridge.

While not absolving Rufus of responsibility for his actions, Baldwin treats him with profound sympathy, in part because of his honesty and in part because of the enormous power of the social institutions which define him as the other. Throughout *Another Country*, Baldwin emphasizes that white heterosexual males possess the power of definition, although their power destroys them as surely as it does their victims. Television producer Steve Ellis, a moral cripple embodying the basic values of the American economic system, nearly destroys Ida and Vivaldo's relationship by encouraging Ida to accept a cynical definition of herself as a sexual commodity. Vivaldo, too, participates in the cynicism when he visits the Harlem prostitutes, indirectly perpetuating the definitions which reduce blacks to sexual objects, and thus implicating himself in Rufus' death. In fact, every major character with the exception of Eric bears partial responsibility for Rufus' destruction, since each at times accepts the definitions generating the cycle of rejection and denial. The constituting irony, however, stems from the fact that only those most actively struggling for moral integrity recognize their culpability. Vivaldo, who attempts to reach out to Rufus earlier on the night of his suicide, feels more guilt than Richard, who simply dismisses Rufus as a common "nigger" after his mistreatment of Leona.

This unflinching portrayal of moral failure, especially on the part of well-meaning liberals, provides the thematic center of *Another Country*. Baldwin concludes the novel with the image of Yves's reunion with Eric, who is apparently on the verge of professional success with a starring role in a film of a Fyodor Dostoevski novel. This combination of personal and financial success seems more an assertion of naïve hope than a compelling part of the surrounding fictional world. The majority of the narrative lines imply the impossibility of simple dissociation from institutional pressure. Ultimately, the intensity of Rufus' pain and the intricacy of Ida and Vivaldo's struggle overshadow Eric and Yves's questionable innocence. As Ida tells Vivaldo, "Our being together doesn't change the world." The attempt to overcome the cynicism of this perception leads to a recognition that meaningful love demands total acceptance. Ida's later question, "how can you say you loved Rufus when there was so much about him you didn't want to know?" could easily provide the epitaph for the entire society in *Another Country*.

In *Just Above My Head*, Baldwin creates a narrator, Hall Montana, capable of articulating the psychological subtleties of *Go Tell It on the Mountain*, the social insights of *Another Country*, and the political anger of *Tell Me How Long the Train's Been Gone*. Like other observer-participants in American literature, such as Nick Carraway in *The Great Gatsby* (1925) and Jack Burden in *All the King's Men* (1946), Hall tells both his own story and that of a more publically prominent figure, in this case his brother Arthur, a gospel singer who dies two years prior to the start of the novel. Significantly, *Just Above My Head* also reconsiders Baldwin's own artistic history, echoing countless motifs from his earlier writings. Though not precisely a self-reflexive text, *Just Above My Head* takes on added richness when juxtaposed with Baldwin's treatment of religious concerns in *Go Tell It on the Mountain*; the homosexuality theme in *Giovanni's Room*; the relationship between brothers and the musical setting in "Sonny's Blues"; racial politics in *Blues for Mister Charlie* and *Tell Me How Long the Train's Been Gone*; the Nation of Islam in *The Fire Next Time* and *No Name in the Street*; and, most important, the intermingled family love and world politics in *If Beale Street Could Talk*. Baldwin's reconsideration of his own history, which is at once private like Hall's and public like Arthur's, emphasizes the necessity of a continual reexamination of the nature of both self and context in order to reach the higher innocence.

Similarly, Hall's resolve to understand the social and existential meaning of Arthur's experience originates in his desire to answer honestly his children's questions concerning their uncle. Refusing to protect their original innocence—an attempt he knows would fail—Hall seeks both to free himself from the despair of experience and to discover a mature innocence he can pass on to the younger generation. Tracing the roots of Arthur's despair to pressures originating in numerous limiting definitions and failures of courage, Hall summarizes his, and Baldwin's social insight:

> The attempt, more the necessity, to excavate a history, to find out the truth about oneself! is motivated by the need to have the power to force others to recognize your presence, your right to be here. The disputed passage will remain disputed so long as you do not have the authority of the right-of-way. . . . Power clears the passage, swiftly: but the paradox, here, is that power, rooted in history, is also, the mockery and the repudiation of history. The power to define the other seals one's definition of oneself.

Recognizing that the only hope for meaningful moral freedom lies in repudiating the power of definition, Hall concludes: "Our history is each other. That is our only guide. One thing is absolutely certain: one can repudiate, or despise, no one's history without repudiating and despising one's own."

Although Baldwin recognizes the extent to which the definitions and repudiations remain entrenched in institutional structures, his portrayal of Hall's courage and honesty offers at least some hope for moral integrity as a base for social action. If an individual such as Hall can counteract the pressures militating against personal responsibility, he or she may be able to exert a positive influence on relatively small social groups such as families and churches, which in turn may affect the larger social context. Nevertheless, Baldwin refuses to encourage simplistic optimism. Rather than focusing narrowly on Hall's individual process, he emphasizes the aspects of the context which render that success atypical. Although Hall begins with his immediate context, his excavation involves the Korean War, the Civil Rights movement, the rise of Malcolm X, and the role of advertising in American culture. Hall's relation with his family and close friends provides a Jamesian frame for the Dreiserian events of the novel, somewhat as John's conversion frames the historical "Prayers of the Saints" in *Go Tell It on the Mountain. Just Above My Head*, however, leaves no ambiguity concerning the individual's ability to free himself or herself from history. Only a conscious decision to accept the pain and guilt of the past promises any real hope for love, for the higher innocence. Similarly, Baldwin reiterates that, while the desire for safety is understandable, all safety is illusion. Pain inevitably returns, and, while the support of friends and lovers may help, only a self-image based on existential acceptance rather than repudiation makes survival possible.

Arthur's death, occupying a thematic and emotional position similar to Rufus' in *Another Country*, provides the point of departure for Hall's excavation. A gifted gospel singer as a teenager, Arthur rises to stardom as the "emperor of soul." Despite his success, however, he never frees himself from doubts concerning his own identity or feels secure with the experience of love. Even though his parents offer him a firm base of love and acceptance, Arthur feels a deep sense of emotional isolation even as a child, a sense reenforced by his observations of life in Harlem and, later, in the South. Though he accepts his own homosexuality with relatively little anxiety, his society refuses the freedom necessary for the development of a truly satisfying emotional life. The Edenic innocence of Eric and Yves clearly fails to provide a sufficient response to the institutional context of *Just Above My Head*.

Arthur's childhood experiences provide clear warnings against the attempt to maintain innocence through simplistic self-definition. Julia Miller, like John in *Go Tell It on the Mountain*, undergoes a salvation experience and embarks on a career as a child evangelist. Encouraged by her parents, friends of the Montanas who rely on their daughter for economic support, she assumes a sanctimonious attitude which she uses to manipulate her elders. Arthur's parents deplore the indulgence of Julia, unambiguously rejecting that idea that her religious vocation lifts her beyond the "naughty" street side of her personality. Ultimately, and in great pain, Julia confronts this truth. After her mother's death, she discovers that her father Joel views her primarily as an economic and sexual object. His desire to exploit her earning potential even when she says she has lost her vocation reflects his underlying contempt for the spirit. This contempt leads to an incestuous rape which destroys Julia's remaining innocence and drives her to a life as a prostitute in New Orleans. Eventually, Julia recovers from this brutalization, but her example provides a clear warning to Arthur against confusing his vocation as a gospel singer with a trancendence of human fallibility.

The experiences of the members of Arthur's first gospel group, the Trumpets of Zion, reveal how institutions infringe even on those not actively committed to simplifying definitions. At one extreme, the social definitions establish a context which accepts and encourages murder—symbolic and real—of the other. Peanut, a member of the Trumpets and later Arthur's companion on the road, vanishes into the Alabama night following a civil rights rally, presumably murdered by whites seeking to enforce the definition of blacks as niggers. Equally devastating though less direct is the operation of the context on Red, another member of the Trumpets, who turns to drugs in an attempt to relieve the pain of the Harlem streets. Even Hall finds himself an unwilling accomplice to the imposition of social definitions when he is drafted and sent to Korea. Powerless to alter the institutional structure, Hall recognizes, and tells Arthur, that the American military spreads not freedom but repudiation in the third world. Hall's subsequent employment by an advertising agency involves him in another aspect of the same oppressive system. Viewed as an anomaly by his employers, as an atypical high-class nigger, Hall nevertheless participates in the creation of images designed to simplify reality for economic gain which will be used to strengthen the oppressive system. The juxtaposition of Julia's false innocence with the destructive experiences of Peanut, Red, and Hall protects Arthur against the urge to dismiss any aspect of his awareness. A large part of his power as a singer derives from his recognition of the reality of both street and temple, expressed in his ability to communicate sexual pain in gospel songs and spiritual aspiration in the blues.

Arthur, then, appears ideally prepared for the responsible exercise of existential freedom. His failure even to survive underscores the destructive power of the corrupt institutional context. The roots of Arthur's doom lie in his homosexual relationship with Crunch, the final member of the Trumpets. Highly desirable physically, Crunch feels locked into a definition of himself as a sexual object prior to his involvement with Arthur. In its early stages, Arthur and Crunch's love, like that of Yves and Eric in *Another Country*, seems an idyllic retreat, a spot of innocence in the chaos of experience. The retreat, however, proves temporary, in part because Crunch cannot free himself from the urge for self-simplification and in part because of the continuing presence of the outside world. Uneasy with his sexual identity, Crunch becomes involved with Julia when he discovers the extent of her father's abuse. Arthur recognizes that Crunch is not abandoning him by reacting to Julia's pain and accepts the relationship. Granted sufficient time for adjustment, Arthur and Crunch seem capable of confronting their experience and forging a higher innocence as the basis for a lasting love. The time does not exist. Crunch is drafted and sent to Korea. Separated from Arthur's reassurance and tormented by self-doubt, Crunch never fully accepts his sexuality. After his return to Harlem, he and Arthur gradually lose contact.

The repeated losses—of Peanut, Red, Crunch—create a sense of isolation which Arthur never overcomes. The expectation of loss periodically overpowers his determination to communicate, the determination which makes him a great singer. Even during periods of real joy, with his French lover Guy in Paris or with Julia's brother Jimmy, who is both his pianist and his lover, Arthur suffers acute emotional pain. Attempting to survive by rededicating himself to communication, to his artistic excavation of history, Arthur drives himself past the limits of physical and psychological endurance. He dies in the basement bathroom of a London pub after a lover's quarrel, clearly only temporary, with Jimmy. By concluding Arthur's life with an image of isolation, Baldwin emphasizes the power of the limiting definitions to destroy even the most existentially courageous individual.

Arthur's death, however, marks not only a conclusion but also the beginning of Hall's quest for the higher innocence, which he, along with his wife Ruth,

Julia, and Jimmy, can pass on to the younger generation. This higher innocence involves both individual and social elements, ultimately demanding the
mutual support of individuals willing to pursue excavation of their own histories. This support expresses itself in the call and response dynamic, a basic
element of Afro-American oral culture which Arthur employs in his interaction with audiences while singing. As Baldwin re-creates the traditional
form, the interaction begins with the call of a leader who expresses his own
emotional experience through the vehicle of a traditional song which provides
a communal context for the emotion. If the community recognizes and shares
the experience evoked by the call, it responds with another traditional phrase
which provides the sense of understanding and acceptance that enables the
leader to go on. Implicitly the process enables both individual and community
to define themselves in opposition to dominant social forces. If the experience
of isolation is shared, it is no longer the same type of isolation which brought
Rufus to his death. In *Just Above My Head*, the call and response rests on a
rigorous excavation requiring individual silence, courage, and honesty
expressed through social presence, acceptance, and love. Expressed in the
interactions between Arthur and his audiences, between Hall and his children,
between Baldwin and his readers, this call and response provides a realistic
image of the higher innocence possible in opposition to the murderous social
definitions.

As in John's vision in *Go Tell It on the Mountain* and Rufus's self-examination in *Another Country*, the process begins in silence, which throughout
Baldwin's novels offers the potential for either alienation or communication.
The alienating silence coincides thematically with institutional noise—
mechanical, social, political. The majority of Americans, Baldwin insists,
prefer distracting and ultimately meaningless sounds to the silence which
allows self-recognition. Only individuals sharing Arthur's willingness to
remove himself from the noise can hope to hear their own voices and transform
the silence into music. Every moment of true communication in *Just Above
My Head* begins in a moment of silence which effectively rejects the clamor
of imposed definitions. The courage needed for the acceptance of silence
prepares the way for the honest excavation of history which must precede
any meaningful social interaction. The excavation remains a burden, however,
without that interaction. No purely individual effort can alter the overwhelming sense of isolation imposed by social definitions. The individual stage of
the process merely heightens the need for acceptance, presence, and love.
Arthur sounds the call amid the noise; he cannot provide the response. Perhaps, Baldwin indicates, no one, not even Jimmy, can provide a response
capable of soothing the feeling of isolation emanating from early experiences.
Nevertheless, the attempt is vital. Julia recognizes both the necessity and the
limitation of presence when she tells Hall of her relationship with Jimmy: "I
don't know enough to change him, or to save him. But I know enough to be

there. I *must* be there."

If presence—being there—is to provide even momentary relief, it must be accompanied by the honest acceptance underlying love. Refusing to limit his acceptance, Hall answers his son Tony's questions concerning Arthur's sexuality with complete honesty. Understanding fully that his acceptance of Arthur entails an acceptance of the similar complexity in himself and in Tony, Hall surrenders his voice to Jimmy's, imaginatively participating in a love which repudiates social definition, which rises up out of the silence beyond the noise. Implicitly, Hall offers both Tony and his daughter Odessa the assurance of presence, of acceptance, of love. They need not fear rejection if they have the courage to accept their full humanity. The assurance cannot guarantee freedom, or even survival. It can, and does, intimate the form of mature innocence in the world described by the composite voice of Baldwin, Jimmy, and Hall, a world that "doesn't have any morality. Look at the world. What the world calls morality is nothing but the dream of safety. That's how the world gets to be so fucking moral. The only way to know that you are safe is to see somebody else in danger—otherwise you can't be sure you're safe."

Against this vicious safety, a safety which necessitates limiting definitions imposed on others, Baldwin proposes a responsibility based on risk. Only by responding to the call sounding from Arthur, from Jimmy and Hall, from Baldwin, can people find freedom. The call, ultimately, emanates not only from the individual but also from the community to which he or she calls. It provides a focus for repudiation of the crushing definitions. Hall, using Jimmy's voice, describes the call: "The man who tells the story isn't *making up* a story. He's listening to us, and can only give back, to us, what he hears: from us." The responsibility lies with everyone.

Craig Werner

Other major works

SHORT FICTION: *Going to Meet the Man*, 1965

PLAYS: *The Amen Corner*, 1954; *Blues for Mister Charlie*, 1964; *One Day, When I Was Lost: A Scenario Based on the Autobiography of Malcolm X*, 1972.

POETRY: *Jimmy's Blues: Selected Poems*, 1983.

NONFICTION: *Notes of a Native Son*, 1955; *Nobody Knows My Name: More Notes of a Native Son*, 1961; *The Fire Next Time*, 1963; *Nothing Personal*, 1964 (with Richard Avedon); *No Name in the Street*, 1971; *A Rap on Race*, 1971 (with Margaret Mead); *A Dialogue*, 1975 (with Nikki Giovanni); *The Devil Finds Work*, 1976; *The Evidence of Things Not Seen*, 1985; *The Price of the Ticket*, 1985; *Conversations with James Baldwin*, 1989.

CHILDREN'S LITERATURE: *Little Man, Little Man*, 1975.

Bibliography

Kinnamon, Keneth, ed. *James Baldwin*. Englewood Cliffs, N.J.: Prentice-Hall, 1974. A part of the Twentieth Century Views series, this collection contains some important appraisals of Baldwin's work and career by Langston Hughes, Eldridge Cleaver, and Sherley Anne Williams, among others.

Macebuh, Stanley. *James Baldwin: A Critical Study*. New York: Third Press, 1973. A good presentation of the social and historical background of Baldwin's work.

Standley, Fred L., and Nancy V. Burt, eds. *Critical Essays on James Baldwin*. Boston: G. K. Hall, 1988. A collection of contemporary reviews and essays covering Baldwin's entire career.

Sylvander, Carolyn Wedin. *James Baldwin*. New York: Frederick Ungar, 1980. A study which examines in particular the links between Baldwin's works and his life.

Weatherby, W. J. *James Baldwin: Artist on Fire*. New York: Donald I. Fine, 1989. An important biography written by one of Baldwin's friends. Weatherby is, at times, too close to his subject to be objective.

J. G. BALLARD

Born: Shanghai, China; November 15, 1930

Principal long fiction

The Wind from Nowhere, 1962; *The Drowned World*, 1962; *The Drought*, 1964 (later published as *The Burning World*); *The Crystal World*, 1966; *Crash*, 1973; *Concrete Island*, 1974; *High Rise*, 1975; *The Unlimited Dream Company*, 1979; *Hello America*, 1981; *Empire of the Sun*, 1984; *The Day of Creation*, 1987; *Running Wild*, 1988 (novella).

Other literary forms

J. G. Ballard has been a prolific short-story writer; there are more than twenty collections of his stories, though some are recombinations of stories in earlier collections, and the American and British collections constitute two series in which the same stories are combined in different ways. He has written occasional essays on imaginative fiction, and also on surrealist painting—he contributed an introduction to a collection of work by Salvador Dalí. The best of his short fiction is to be found in two retrospective collections: *Chronopolis and Other Stories* (1971) and *The Best Short Stories of J. G. Ballard* (1978).

Achievements

Ballard is one of a handful of writers who, after establishing early reputations as science-fiction writers, subsequently achieved a kind of "transcendence" of their genre origins to be accepted by a wider public. This transcendence was completed by the success of *Empire of the Sun*, which was short-listed for the Booker Prize and won the Guardian Prize before being boosted to best-seller status by a film produced by Steven Spielberg. For a time in the early 1960's, Ballard seemed to constitute a one-man avant-garde in British science fiction, and his influence was considerable enough for him to become established as the leading figure in the movement which came to be associated with the magazine *New Worlds* under the editorship of Michael Moorcock. His interest in science-fiction themes was always of a special kind; he is essentially a literary surrealist who finds the near future a convenient imaginative space. His primary concern is the effect of environment—both "natural" and manmade—upon the psyche, and he has therefore found it appropriate to write about gross environmental changes and about the decay and dereliction of the artificial environment; these interests distance him markedly from other modern science-fiction writers and have helped him to become a writer *sui generis*.

Biography

James Graham Ballard was born and reared in Shanghai, China, where his father—originally an industrial chemist—was involved in the management of the Far East branch of a firm of textile manufacturers. The Sino-Japanese war had begun, and Shanghai was effectively a war zone by the time Ballard was seven years old; all of his early life was affected by the ever-nearness of war. After Japan's entry into World War II and her invasion of Shanghai, Ballard was interned in a prisoner-of-war camp. This was in the summer of 1942, when he was eleven; he was there for more than three years.

Ballard has said that his experience of the internment camp was "not unpleasant"—it was simply a fact of life which, as a child, he accepted. Children were not mistreated by the guards, and the adults made sure that the children were adequately fed even at their own expense. He has observed that his parents must have found the regime extremely harsh. Although his family was among the fortunate few who avoided malaria, his sister nearly died of a form of dysentery.

After his release, Ballard went to England in 1946. His family stayed in the Far East for a while, and his father did not return until 1950, when he was driven out of China by the Communist victory. Ballard has recalled that after spending his early years in "Americanized" Shanghai, England seemed very strange and foreign. He went to Leys' School in Cambridge for a while, then went to King's College, Cambridge, to study medicine. His ultimate aim at this time was to become a psychiatrist. At Cambridge he began writing, initially intending to maintain the activity as a hobby while he was qualifying. In fact, though, he dropped out of his course after two years and subsequently went to London University to read English. The university seems to have found him unsuitable for such a course, and he left after his first year.

He then embarked upon a series of short-term jobs, including working for an advertising agency and selling encyclopedias. Eventually, to end this aimless drifting, he enlisted in the Royal Air Force and was sent for training to Moosejaw, Saskatchewan, Canada. He was not suited to the air force either, but while in Canada he began reading magazine science fiction, and while waiting for his discharge back in England he wrote his first science-fiction story, "Passport to Eternity" (it was not published for some years). Shortly after this, in 1955, he married and worked in public libraries in order to support his family.

In 1956, Ballard began submitting short stories to Ted Carnell, editor of the British magazines *New Worlds* and *Science Fantasy*. Carnell was not only enthusiastic about Ballard's work but also helped him to obtain a new job working on a trade journal. Eventually, Ballard became assistant editor of *Chemistry and Industry*, a job which he held for four years. He moved in 1960 to the small Thames-side town of Shepperton, where he still lives. By this time he had three children and was struggling to find time to devote to his writing. During a two-week annual holiday he managed to write *The Wind from Nowhere*, whose publication in America represented something of a breakthrough for him—the same publisher began to issue a series of short-story collections, and the income from these books allowed him to become a full-time writer. His wife died in 1964, at which time his youngest child was only five years old, and his career as a writer has since been combined with the exacting pressures of being a single parent. In consequence, he has led since 1964 a relatively uneventful life, although his literary career has remained strong. The fame which followed the success of *Empire of the Sun* seems not to have disturbed his life-style at all.

Analysis

J. G. Ballard's first seven novels can be easily sorted into two groups. The first four are novels of worldwide disaster, while the next three are stories of cruelty and alienation set in the concrete wilderness of contemporary urban society. All of his novels are, however, linked by a concern with the disintegration of civilization on a global or local scale.

Ballard's early disaster stories follow a well-established tradition in British imaginative fiction. British science-fiction writers from H. G. Wells to John Wyndham always seem to have been fascinated by the notion of the fragility and vulnerability of man's empire, and have produced many careful and clinical descriptions of its fall. The earlier works in this tradition are didactic tales, insisting on the vanity of human wishes and reveling in the idea that when the crunch comes, only the tough will survive. Ballard, in contrast, is quite unconcerned with drawing morals—his disaster stories are not at all social Darwinist parables. His main concern is with the psychological readjustments which the characters are forced to make when faced with the disintegration of their world: he sees the problem of catastrophic change largely in terms of adaptation.

In *The Wind from Nowhere*, which is considerably inferior to the three other disaster novels, a slowly accelerating wind plucks the man-made world apart. No one can stand firm against this active rebellion of nature—neither the American armed forces nor the immensely rich industrialist Hardoon, who seeks to secrete himself within a gigantic concrete pyramid, which the wind eventually topples into an abyss. *The Wind from Nowhere* has a whole series of protagonists and shows the catastrophe from several viewpoints. This was one of the well-tried methods of retailing disaster stories, but it was unsuited to Ballard's particular ambitions, and in the other novels of this early quartet he employed single protagonists as focal points—almost as measuring devices to analyze in depth the significance of parallel physical and psychological changes.

In *The Drowned World*, Earth's surface temperature has risen and is still gradually rising. Water released by the melting of the ice caps has inundated much of the land, and dense tropical jungle has spread rapidly through what were once the temperate zones, rendering them all but uninhabitable. Ballard suggests that the world is undergoing a kind of retrogression to the environment of the Triassic period. The novel's protagonist is Robert Kerans, a biologist monitoring the changes from a research station in partly submerged London.

The psychological effects of the transfiguration first manifest themselves as dreams in which Kerans sees "himself" (no longer human) wandering a primitive world dominated by a huge, fierce sun. These dreams, he concludes, are a kind of memory retained within the cellular heritage of mankind, now called forth again by the appropriate stimulus. Their promise is that they will free the nervous system from the domination of the recently evolved brain, whose appropriate environment is gone, and restore the harmony of primeval protoconsciousness and archaic environment. Kerans watches other people trying to adapt in their various ways to the circumstances in which they find themselves, but sees the essential meaninglessness of their strategies. He accepts the pull of destiny and treks south, submitting to the psychic metamorphosis that strips away his humanity until he becomes "a second Adam searching for the forgotten paradises of the reborn sun."

The Drowned World was sufficiently original and sophisticated to be incomprehensible to most of the aficionados of genre science fiction, who did not understand what Ballard was about or why. A minority, however, recognized its significance and its import; its reputation is now firmly established as one of the major works of its period.

In *The Drought*, the pattern of physical change is reversed; Earth becomes a vast desert because a pollutant molecular film has formed on the surface of the world's oceans, inhibiting evaporation. The landscape is gradually transformed, the concrete city-deserts becoming surrounded by seas of hot sand instead of arable land, while the seashore retreats to expose new deserts of crystalline salt. The soil dies and civilization shrivels, fires reducing forests and buildings alike to white ash. Ransom, the protagonist, is one of the last stubborn few who are reluctant to join the exodus to the retreating sea. From his houseboat he watches the river dwindle away, draining the dregs of the social and natural order. He lives surrounded by relics of an extinguished past, bereft of purpose and no longer capable of emotional response.

Eventually, Ransom and his surviving neighbors are driven to seek refuge in the "dune limbo" of the new seashore and take their places in a new social order dominated by the need to extract fresh water from the reluctant sea. Here, he finds, people are simply marking time and fighting a hopeless rearguard action. In the final section of the story, he goes inland again to see what has become of the city and its last few inhabitants. They, mad and monstrous, have found a new way of life, hideous but somehow appropriate to the universal aridity—which is an aridity of the soul as well as of the land.

In *The Crystal World*, certain areas of the Earth's surface are subjected to a strange process of crystallization as some mysterious substance is precipitated out of the ether. This is a more localized and less destructive catastrophe than those in *The Drowned World* and *The Drought*, but the implication is that it will continue until the world is consumed. The initially affected area is in Africa, where the novel is set. The central character is Dr. Sanders, the assistant director of a leper colony, who is at first horrified when he finds his mistress and some of his patients joyfully accepting the process of cystallization within the flesh of their own bodies. Eventually, of course, he comes to realize that no other destiny is appropriate to the new circumstances. What is happening is that time and space are somehow being reduced, so that they are supersaturated with matter. Enclaves from which time itself has "evaporated" are therefore being formed—fragments of eternity where living things, though they cannot continue to live, also cannot die, but undergo instead a complete existential transubstantiation. Here, metaphors developed in *The Drought* are literalized with the aid of a wonderfully gaudy invention.

The transformation of the world in *The Crystal World* is a kind of beautification, and it is much easier for the reader to sympathize with Sanders' acceptance of its dictates than with Kerans' capitulation to the demands of his dreams. For this reason, the novel has been more popular within the science-fiction community than either of its predecessors. It is, however, largely a recapitulation of the same theme, which does not really gain from its association with the lush romanticism that occasionally surfaces in Ballard's work—most noticeably in the short stories set in the imaginary American west-coast artists' colony Vermilion Sands, a beach resort populated by decadent eccentrics and the flotsam of bygone star-cults who surround themselves with florid artificial environments.

Seven years elapsed between publication of *The Crystal World* and the appearance of *Crash*. Although Ballard published numerous retrospective collections in the interim, his one major project was a collection of what he called "condensed novels"—a series of verbal collages featuring surreal combinations of images encapsulating what Ballard saw as the contemporary zeitgeist. In the world portrayed in these collages, there is a great deal of violence and perverted sexual arousal. Ubiquitous Ballardian images recur regularly: dead birds, junked space hardware, derelict buildings. Mixed in with these are secular icons: the suicide of Marilyn Monroe, the assassin's victim John F. Kennedy, and other personalities whose fates could be seen as symbolic of the era in decline.

The theme of *Crash* is already well developed in the condensed novels (collected in the United Kingdom under the title *The Atrocity Exhibition* and in the United States under the title *Love and Napalm: Export USA*). Cars, within the novel, are seen as symbols of power, speed and sexualilty—a commonplace psychoanalytic observation, to which Ballard adds the surprising further representation of the car crash as a kind of orgasm. The protagonist of the novel, who is called Ballard, finds his first car crash, despite all the pain and attendant anxiety, to be an initiation into a new way of being, whereby he is forced to reformulate his social relationships and his sense of purpose. Ballard apparently decided to write the book while considering the reactions of members of the public to an exhibition of crashed cars which he held at the New Arts Laboratory in London.

Although it is mundane by comparison with his previous novels—it is certainly not science fiction—*Crash* is by no means a realistic novel. Its subject matter is trauma and the private fantasization of alarming but ordinary events. The hero, at one point, does bear witness to a transformation of the world, but it is a purely subjective one while he is under the influence of a hallucinogen. He sees the landscapes of the city transformed, woven into a new metaphysics by the attribution of a new context of significance derived from his perverted fascination with cars and expressway architecture.

The two novels which followed *Crash* retain and extrapolate many of its themes. *Concrete Island* and *High Rise* are both robinsonades whose characters become Crusoes in the very heart of modern civilization, cast away within sight and earshot of the metropolitan hordes but no less isolated for their proximity. In *Concrete Island*, a man is trapped on a traffic island in the middle of a complex freeway intersection, unable to reach the side of the road because the stream of cars is never-ending. Like Crusoe, he sets out to make the best of his situation, using whatever resources—material and social—he finds at hand. He adapts so well, in the end, that he refuses the opportunity to leave when it finally arrives.

The high-rise apartment block which gives *High Rise* its title is intended to be a haven for the well-to-do middle class, a comfortable microcosm to which they can escape from the stressful outside world of work and anxiety. It is, perhaps, *too* well insulated from the world at large; it becomes a private empire where freedom from stress gives birth to a violent anarchy and a decay into savagery. If *Concrete Island* is spiritually akin to Daniel Defoe's *Robinson Crusoe* (1719), then *High Rise* is akin to William Golding's *Lord of the Flies*, (1954), though it is all the more shocking in translocating the decline into barbarism of Golding's novel from a remote island to suburbia, and in attributing the decline to adults who are well aware of what is happening rather than to children whose innocence provides a ready excuse. As always, Ballard's interest is in the psychological readjustments made by his chief characters, and the way in which the whole process proves to be ultimately cathartic.

A major theme in the condensed novels, which extends into the three novels of the second group, is what Ballard refers to as the "death of affect"— a sterilization of the emotions and attendant moral anesthesia, which he considers to be a significant contemporary trend induced by contemporary life-styles. The greatest positive achievement of the characters in these novels is a special kind of ataraxia—a calm of mind rather different from the one Plato held up as an ideal, which allows one to live alongside all manner of horrors without being unusually moved to fear or pity.

Another gap, though not such a long one, separates *High Rise* from *The Unlimited Dream Company*, a messianic fantasy of the redemption of Shepperton from suburban mundanity. Its protagonist, Blake, crashes a stolen aircraft into the Thames River at Shepperton. Though his dead body remains trapped in the cockpit, he finds himself miraculously preserved on the bank. At first he cannot accept his true state, but several unsuccessful attempts to leave the town and a series of visions combine to convince him that he has a specially privileged role to play: he must teach the people to fly, so that they can transcend their earthly existence to achieve a mystical union with the vegetable and mineral worlds, dissolving themselves into eternity as the chief characters did in *The Crystal World*. Though the name of the central character is significant, the book also appears to be closely allied with the paintings of another artist: the eccentric Stanley Spencer, who lived in another Thames-side town (Cookham) and delighted in locating within its mundane urban scenery images of biblical and transcendental significance.

The kind of redemption featured in *The Unlimited Dream Company* is as ambivalent as the kinds of adaptation featured in earlier novels, and its promise does not carry the same wild optimism that similar motifs are made to carry in most science-fiction and fantasy novels. It is perhaps best to view *The Unlimited Dream Company* as one more novel of adaptation, but one which reverses the pattern of the earlier works. Here, it is not Blake who must adapt to changes in the external world, but Shepperton which must adapt to him—and he, too, must adapt to his own godlike status. Blake is himself the "catastrophe" which visits Shepperton, the absolute at large within it whose immanence cannot be ignored or resisted. If the novel seems to the reader to be upbeat rather than downbeat, that is mainly the consequence of a change of viewpoint—and had the readers who thought *The Drowned World* downbeat been willing to accept such a change, they might have been able to find that novel equally uplifting.

Although *The Unlimited Dream Company* does not represent such a dramatic change of pattern as first appearances suggest, *Hello America* is certainly, for Ballard, a break with his own tradition. There is little in the novel that seems new in thematic terms, although it recalls his short stories much more than previous novels, but there is nevertheless a sense in which it represents a radical departure. The plot concerns the "rediscovery" in the twenty-second century of a largely abandoned America by an oddly assorted expedition from Europe. What they find are the shattered relics of a whole series of American mythologies. The central character, Wayne, dreams of resurrecting America and its dream, restoring the mythology of technological optimism and glamorous consumerism to operational status. He cannot do so, of course, but there is a consistent note of ironic nostalgia in his hopeless ambition. What is remarkable about the book is that it is a confection, an offhand entertainment to be enjoyed but not taken seriously. From Ballard the novelist, this is totally unexpected, though his short fiction has frequently shown him to be a witty writer, and a master of the ironic aside.

This change of direction proved, not unexpectedly, to be a purely temporary matter—a kind of brief holiday from more serious concerns. *Empire of the Sun* recovered all the mesmeric intensity of Ballard's earlier work, adding an extra turn of the screw by relating it to historically momentous events through which the author had actually lived. Although the book's young protagonist is named Jim and is the same age as Ballard was when he was interned by the Japanese, *Empire of the Sun* is—like *Crash* before it—by no means autobiographical in any strict sense. Jim's adventures are as exaggerated as the fictional Ballard's were, but the purpose of the exaggeration is here perfectly clear: what seems from an objective point of view to be a horrible and unmitigated catastrophe is to Jim simply part of the developing pattern of life, to which he must adapt himself, and which he takes aboard more or less innocently. From his point of view, given that the internment camp *is* the world, and not (as it is from the point of view of the adult internees) an intolerable interruption of the world, it is the behavior of the British prisoners which seems unreasonable and hostile, while the Japanese guards are the champions of order. The world does not begin to end for Jim until the war comes toward its close and the orderliness of camp life breaks down; that which others see as a source of hope and a possibility of redemption from their living hell is for Jim something else entirely, to which he reacts in characteristically idiosyncratic fashion. The frightful irony of all this is, as usual, overlaid and disguised by a straight-faced matter-of-factness which forbids the reader to cling to the conventional verities enshrined in an older, inherited attitude toward the war with Japan.

The Day of Creation returns to the Africa of *The Crystal World*, this time disrupted by the seemingly miraculous appearance of a new river whose "discoverer," Dr. Mallory of the World Health Organization, hopes that it may restore edenic life to territory spoiled for millennia by drought and ceaseless petty wars. Mallory's odyssey along the river upon which he bestows his own name might be seen as an inversion of Marlow's journey in Joseph Conrad's *Heart of Darkness* (1902), in which the mysteriously silent girl Noon is the hopeful counterpart of the soul-sick Kurtz; but the redemption promised by the river is a temporary illusion, and Noon herself may only be a figment of Mallory's imagination.

The novella *Running Wild*, thinly disguised as a mass-murder mystery in which the entire adult population of a small town is massacred, is another playfully ironic piece, though rather less gaudy than *Hello, America—*

appropriately, in view of its setting, which is a cosy suburban landscape of the Home Counties; it is a long short story rather than a short novel, but it carries forward the argument of *High Rise* as well as brief black comedies such as "The Intensive Care Unit."

In one of his earliest essays on science fiction—a "guest editorial" which he contributed to *New Worlds* in 1962—Ballard committed the heresy of declaring that H. G. Wells was "a disastrous influence on the subsequent course of science fiction." He suggested that it was time to throw overboard the vocabulary of ideas to which science-fiction writers and readers had become accustomed, and with them its customary narrative forms and conventional plots. It was time, he said, to turn to the exploration of inner space rather than outer space, and to realize that "the only truly alien planet is Earth." He offered his opinion that Salvador Dalí might be the most pertinent source of inspiration for modern writers of science fiction. The rhetorical flourishes which fill this essay caution readers against taking it all *too* seriously, but in the main this is the prospectus which Ballard has been trying to follow. He has practiced what he preached, shaking off the legacy of H. G. Wells, dedicating himself to the exploration of inner space and the development of new metaphysical (particularly metapsychological) systems, and steering well clear of the old plots and narrative formulas. In so doing, he made himself one of the most original writers of his generation; such novels as *Empire of the Sun* and *The Day of Creation* do indeed demonstrate the essential alienness of the planet on which we live.

Brian Stableford

Other major works

SHORT FICTION: *The Voices of Time*, 1962; *Billenium*, 1962; *Passport to Eternity*, 1963; *The Terminal Beach*, 1964; *The Impossible Man*, 1966; *Love and Napalm: Export U.S.A.*, 1969 (originally published as *The Atrocity Exhibition*); *Vermilion Sands*, 1971; *Chronopolis and Other Stories*, 1971; *The Best Short Stories of J. G. Ballard*, 1978; *Myths of the Near Future*, 1982; *Memories of the Space Age*, 1988.

Bibliography

Pringle, David. *Earth Is the Alien Planet: J. G. Ballard's Four-Dimensional Nightmare*. San Bernardino, Calif.: Borgo Press, 1979. A monograph in Borgo's Milford series, featuring a biographical sketch and an excellent analysis of Ballard's work to date, by a critic who has followed the author's career very closely.

_____. *J. G. Ballard: A Primary and Secondary Bibliography*. Boston: G. K. Hall, 1984. A comprehensive bibliography of Ballard's work to date, scrupulously compiled and fully detailed.

Re-Search: J. G. Ballard. San Francisco: Re-Search, 1983. A special issue of a periodical publication devoted to Ballard and his works, including an interview, critical articles, and some unusual items by Ballard; it views Ballard as an *avant-garde* literary figure rather than a science-fiction writer.

Stableford, Brian. "J. G. Ballard." In *Science Fiction Writers*, edited by E. F. Bleiler. New York: Charles Scribner's Sons, 1982. A competent overview of the author's work to date.

JOHN BANVILLE

Born: Wexford, Ireland; December 8, 1945

Principal long fiction

Nightspawn, 1971; *Birchwood*, 1973; *Doctor Copernicus*, 1976; *Kepler*, 1981; *The Newton Letter*, 1982 (novella); *Mefisto*, 1986; *The Book of Evidence*, 1989.

Other literary forms

John Banville's first published book was a collection of short stories, *Long Lankin* (1970, revised 1984), and he has written a small amount of uncollected short fiction. He has also collaborated in writing television adaptations of *The Newton Letter* and *Birchwood*.

Achievements

Banville is the most original and successful Irish novelist of his generation. His work has received numerous awards, including the prestigious James Tait Black Award, the American-Irish Foundation Award, and the GPA Prize. Reviewers have treated each new work of his with increasing respect for its ambition, verbal felicity, and individuality, and for such a comparatively young writer, Banville has inspired a sizable amount of critical commentary. The development of his career coincides with a period of restlessness and experimentation in Irish fiction. Not the least significant of Banville's achievements is that he has availed himself of the artistic example of such postwar masters of fiction as Jorge Luis Borges, Gabriel García Márquez and Italo Calvino. By admitting such influences, as well as those of the great Irish modernists, James Joyce and Samuel Beckett, John Banville's fiction has embodied a new range of options for the Irish novel and has provided an international dimension to an often provincial literary culture.

Biography

John Banville was born in Wexford, the county seat of Ireland's southeasternmost county, on December 8, 1945. He was educated locally, first at the Christian Brothers School and, on the secondary level, at St. Peter's College. After school, he worked for Aer Lingus, the Irish airline. Subsequently, he worked in England for the post office, and briefly, for a London publisher. Returning to Ireland, he worked as a subeditor for *The Irish Press*, a national daily. The recipient of numerous awards, he has also spent a semester in the International Writing Program at the University of Iowa.

Analysis

John Banville's short stories, his novella *The Newton Letter*, and his six novels constitute a remarkably unified and consistent body of work. From the outset of his career, he has shown immense artistic self-possession and an equally assured possession of his themes. Over the years, his style, while not remaining constant, has undergone comparatively little change. It is therefore possible to speak of Banville in terms of a completeness and typicality which most novelists of his age are still in the process of discovering.

The unity and integrity which are the most striking features of Banville's career and oeuvre become more striking still by virtue of being so thematically important in his work. Fascination with the spectacle of the mind in the act of creation is a major concern of this author, and his career may be described in terms of an increasingly deliberate and far-reaching series of attempts to articulate this subject. This preoccupation has given his work a range, ambition, and commitment to large concepts which are extremely rare in modern Irish fiction, and only slightly less rare in contemporary fiction generally.

In addition, the manner in which Banville elaborates his interest in man's creative dimension commands more critical attention than it has received. For example, his fiction is suffused with hints suggesting links between artistic strategies, scientific inquiry, and historical actuality. From these, it is possible to detect a rudimentary, though sustained, critique of traditional epistemological procedures. To complement this critique, the typical Banville protagonist either discovers unsuspected modes of perception or believes that he has no other choice but to set out deliberately to discover them.

Together with the intellectual commitment implicit in such concerns, Banville's work possesses a typically complete and essentially unchanging aesthetic apparatus through which ideas and fiction's critique may be perceived. Since it is central to Banville's artistic vision that fiction's critique of conceptual thinking be considered inevitable and unavoidable, his novels' aesthetic apparatus is largely premised on techniques of doubleness, repetition, echoes, and mirrors. Protagonists often have problematical brothers or missing twins. Personal experience finds its counterpart in historical events. The result is a paradox: The duplicitous character of experience, which renders man's possession of his existence so frail and tentative, impels him, precisely because of that very frailty, to anchor himself in the presumed security of defined abstractions.

Despite the presence of these thematic concerns throughout Banville's output, and despite the fact that his treatment of them has always been marked more by an ironic playfulness than by earnest sermonizing, his first two works of fiction are somewhat callow. In particular, *Nightspawn*, the story of an Irish writer's adventures in Greece on the eve of the Colonel's coup, treats the material with a kind of relentless playfulness which is both tiresome in itself and in questionable taste. Despite the author's admitted—though not uncritical—affection for this novel, and despite its containing in embryonic form the concerns which beset all of his work, *Nightspawn*, as perhaps its title suggests, is an example of a young writer allowing his wonderfully fertile imagination to run to baroque lengths.

It is more appropriate, therefore, to begin a detailed consideration of John Banville's fiction with his second novel, *Birchwood*. Like *Nightspawn*, this novel is written in the first person—arguably Banville's preferred narrative mode. In *Birchwood*, Gabriel Godkin, the protagonist, tells in retrospect the story of his dark heritage and his efforts to escape it. Again, as in *Nightspawn*, much of the material has baroque potential, which the novel's middle section, depicting Gabriel's adventures with the circus of a certain Prospero, accentuates rather than dispels.

The circus escapade shines in the novel like a good deed in an evil world. While Gabriel is within the protected ring of the circus troupe he seems to be essentially immune from the troubles of his past and from the state of famine and unrest which consumes the country through which the circus travels. Thanks to Prospero, he is islanded and becalmed in the surrounding tempest. Yet even under such conditions of childish play, the world is not a safe place. Adult imperfections continually intrude. Crimes are committed in the name of love; futile and obsessive hostilities break out. Innocent Gabriel flees the disintegrating circle—it seems appropriate to think of the circus in etymological terms, since circle and ring possess strong connotations of unity and completeness.

Gabriel forsakes the circus in a state of rather paranoid distress and finds himself, still more distressingly, to have come full circle back to where he started. Now, however, he finds himself compelled to face his origins, which lie in the house of doom which gives this novel its title. The first part of the novel gives the history of the Godkin family. Like the circus sequence, this opening section of *Birchwood* owes more to imagination than it does to actuality. Many readers will be reminded of both Edgar Allan Poe and William Faulkner by Banville's combination of brooding atmosphere and theme of cultural decay upon which this section is premised. Banville's farcical tone, however, without prejudicing young Gabriel's sensitivity, prevents the heavy-handedness and extravagance to which the gothic nature of his material is in danger of giving rise. The seriousness with which the elder Godkins take their insecurities is rendered laughable by the incompetence which ensues from their transparent intensity.

Yet Gabriel, for all of his alienation from his heritage's inadequacies, finds it impossible to do other than to confront them. In a novel which satirically articulates the cultural shibboleth of bad blood, Gabriel feels compelled to carry out an act of blood which will purge his house of the usurper. The usurper in question is Gabriel's twin brother, Michael. The novel ends with Gabriel in sole possession of Birchwood.

This turn of events, however, does not mean that Gabriel is able, or intends, to restore the house to its former glory, a glory in which he never participated. As a writer, his objective seems to be to reclaim the house as it really was, rather than imagine it as something other, something which imaginative treatment would make easier to assimilate. In this objective, students of Irish literature may see a critique of the lofty status often accorded the Big House in the poetry of William Butler Yeats. An appreciation of John Banville's fiction does not require that he be seen as a defacer of the cultural icons of a previous generation. Nevertheless, the status of the Big House in *Birchwood*, coupled with themes of survival, inheritance, and artistic expression, offers a sense of the oblique manner in which this author regards his own cultural heritage, while at the same time situating his regard in the wider, more generic contexts of such concerns as individuality, history, the role of the artist, the nature of the real.

Given the significant, if problematical, status of the Big House in modern Irish literature (Big House being the generic name given to the imposing mansions of the socially dominant, landowning Anglo-Irish class), the degree to which *Birchwood* avoids a specific historical context is noteworthy. There are a sufficient number of clues (the famine and unrest mentioned earlier, the frequent mention of "rebels" in the first part of the novel) to suggest that the locale is Ireland. Yet a larger historical context is obviated by the obsessive, and more psychologically archetypal, quality of Gabriel's sense of his personal history. The result is a novel which is ultimately too reflexive, private, and inward looking to be entirely satisfactory.

It may be that the author himself reached the same conclusion, since in his next two novels, *Doctor Copernicus* and *Kepler*, a specific and detailed sense of history is an important dimension of events. *Doctor Copernicus* inaugurates Banville's most important and ambitious project, and the one on which his international reputation will probably be based. This project consists of four books dealing with the nature of the creative personality, conceived of in terms of the scientific imagination. A subtitle for the series might be, "The Scientist as Artist," meaning that Banville considers that which Copernicus, Kepler, and Isaac Newton (subject of *The Newton Letter*) accomplished in the field of scientific inquiry to be comparable to what an artist might produce. The series concludes with *Mefisto*, which both crystallizes and challenges the assumptions of its predecessors. The most fundamental link between the four books is chronological, *Mefisto* being set in contemporary Ireland. Although there are other more sophisticated connections between each of the four, each may also be read independently.

Doctor Copernicus is a fictionalized biography of the astronomer who revolutionized man's sense of his place in the order of creation. The biography is presented in such a way as to dramatize the crucial tensions between Copernicus and the history of his time. Beginning with the astronomer's unhappy childhood, the novel details the essentially flawed, anticlimactic, unfulfilling (and unfulfillable) nature of human existence as Copernicus experiences it. The protagonist's character is conceived in terms of his inability to give himself fully to the world of men and affairs, whether the affairs are those of state or of the heart.

Sojourning in Italy as a young man, Copernicus has a homosexual affair which temporarily makes him happy. Yet he lacks the self-confidence and will to believe in his happiness and rejects it in an attack of spleen and confusion. Later in his career, he is required to take a political role, negotiating with Lutheran enemies of the Catholic Church, and administering Church properties. Although he discharges his obligations in a responsible manner, it is perfectly clear that, given the choice between being a man of his time or being a student of the stars in their eternal courses, Copernicus prefers the latter isolated, impersonal service. The imperfections of the world—not only in the aggregate, demonstrated by the machinations of history, but also intimately, embodied by the astronomer's syphilitic brother, Andreas—prove emotionally insupportable, philosophically unjustifiable, and morally anesthetizing. Finding no basis for unity and completeness in the sorry state of mortal man, Copernicus takes the not particularly logical, but impressively imaginative, step of considering the heavens.

The astronomer's declared intention in pursuing this line of inquiry is not to bring about the revolution which history commemorates in his name. On the contrary, Copernicus sees his pursuits as conservative, intended to assert a model of order, design, and harmony where it cannot be said for certain one exists. Copernicus' efforts are fueled by his will and spirit, and the intensity of his commitment should not be underestimated because his results are stated in mathematical terms. What his conclusions provide is the fiction of order, a fiction posited on the conceit of mathematics being essentially a rhetoric—a product of mind, not an offspring of matter. Indeed, as Copernicus' career in the world of things and people suggests, his fiction elicits worldlings' assent all the more urgently for being necessarily untrue.

Banville's approach as a biographer in *Doctor Copernicus* is strictly chronological, which gives the novel both scope and a sense of the inevitability of the protagonist's development. Copernicus' integrity, continually challenged, is nourished by the inevitable nature of his spiritual needs and tendencies; in *Kepler*, the approach is fundamentally the same.

Instead of providing a chronology of Kepler's life, however, Banville concentrates on the astronomer's productive years, using flashbacks to illuminate and enlarge aspects of the protagonist's character, as the need arises. This approach shifts the narrative emphasis from the protagonist's temperament, as it was in *Doctor Copernicus*, to the protagonist's working conditions. The effect of this modulation in authorial standpoint is to give historical circumstances greater prominence than previously, and thus provide, from an aesthetic perspective, an image of man in the world which reverses that provided in *Doctor Copernicus*. Kepler is far more life-loving (which Banville communicates as far more capable of love) than his predecessor. He is far more attuned to the eddies and quicksands of the historical forces of his time, consciously aligning himself with one set of forces rather than another, instead of disdainfully and brokenheartedly attempting to rise above them, as Copernicus tries to do.

Kepler's astronomy, therefore, is presented as, in his own eyes, the opposite of Copernicus' model of conservation. Much of Kepler's achievement, in fact, is based on his critique of the predecessor's findings. In addition, Kepler's generally worldly disposition leads him to develop practical applications of astronomical researches. Yet, when most successful in his own eyes, constructing his geometrical model of planetary harmony, he is unwittingly failing. His model is adequate to his own need of it, but is not, by virtue of that adequacy, foolproof. The reader is given a strong sense that Kepler's discoveries, or rather the model which his discoveries serve, introduces as many errors as it corrects in Copernicus' model. In Copernicus' case, the model is the necessary transmutation of sorrow; in Kepler's case, it is the necessary transmutation of joy. Despite fate's cruel blows, Kepler asserts that the world should be considered part of a harmoniously integrated system. Because of fate's cruel blows, Copernicus asserts the same theory.

It would be invidious to conclude that one of these heroic figures suffers more than the others. Banville is at pains, as the dramatic structure of *Kepler* demonstrates, to point out that the astronomer's faith in the world proves to be as destructively alienating as Copernicus' skepticism. The spectacle—which concludes the novel—of this great scientific visionary spending his time and energy attempting to bring his debtors to book is a painfully ludicrous commentary on the all too understandable vanity of human wishes, as well as a cogent expression of Banville's own perspective on his material.

In the novella, *The Newton Letter*, Banville changes his approach, without quite changing his theme. Here the scenario is not biography, but failed biography. The protagonist is not the great scientist, but the apparently less than great modern writer attempting to recapture the scientist's life. This short work, perhaps together with *Doctor Copernicus* the author's most completely successful accomplishment from an artistic standpoint, gives an inverted picture of the procedures which seemed natural in the two earlier works in the series. The presupposition of expository coherence leading to insight and comprehension which was crucial, however unspoken, to the fictionalized biographies has, in *The Newton Letter*, become a subject open to criticism—open, like the procedures of Copernicus and Kepler, to the charge of fiction.

In addition, the fictional biographer (the protagonist of *The Newton Letter*) is failing to complete his work because of Newton's failure to pursue his researches. By this means, the interrelationship between fiction and reality, and the possibility that these terms interchangeably reflect dual perspectives on immutable phenomena, is brought yet more clearly to the forefront of Banville's concerns.

Indeed, as in the case of the earlier novels of the series, life keeps interrupting the Newton biographer. The country house to which he has retreated in order to complete his work, while not possessing the menace and uncertainty of Birchwood, distracts and ultimately ensnares him, so that he is forced to choose between the demands of completeness (his work) and the obligations of incompleteness (his life). The biographer's failed project becomes a synonym for his mortal destiny.

Banville's rejection of the biographical approach to the life of the mind is completed in the final volume of the series, *Mefisto*, in which the protagonist, a mathematician named Gabriel Swan, writes his own story. With this formal development, the procedure of both *Doctor Copernicus* and *Kepler* is completely inverted, and the value of the project both from a biographical and from a scientific point of view is most rigorously challenged. One reason it is possible to make such a claim is that *Mefisto* reaches back beyond its three predecessors to *Birchwood*, to which it bears some strong resemblances.

The most obvious novelty of *Mefisto*, however, is that it does not deal with a historical twentieth century scientist. Most of Banville's readers were not prepared for this development, which is a tribute to Banville's own conception of his project's integrity. It is unlikely, however, that the question of integrity is the only one at issue here. On the one hand, this development is typical of the sly and slapstick humor which pervades Banville's work. On the other hand, the fictitiousness of *Mefisto*'s protagonist is an obvious expression of the status of failure in Banville's oeuvre, the failure from which the artist is obliged to begin, and which his work, by attempting to mask or redeem it, merely makes more obvious. In addition, given that *Mefisto* has a historical context about which it is possible to say much, and that it is a novel which brings to an end a series of works in which historical events were given a prominent and influential place, it must be considered provocative and instructive that *Mefisto* eschews explicit information of a historical nature.

Mefisto is a novel of missing parts. It lacks a sense of specific sense of time and space, though the alert reader will find part 1 of the novel set in a market town in provincial Ireland and part 2 in an Irish city which is presumably Dublin. The hero, Gabriel (a name which, in a novelist as self-conscious as Banville, must be an echo of the protagonist of *Birchwood*, particularly since in part 1 there is a dilapidated, Birchwood-like house) is a mathematician of genius, but it is difficult to deduce what his branch of mathematics is.

It is Gabriel's misfortune to believe that there can be a redemptive function in his symbols and abstractions. He mistakenly believes that, because of the light he finds shining in the purity of math, he can rescue damsels in distress—in genuine distress, like the drug-besotted Adele in part 2. This belief is cultivated by the jauntily cynical and amoral Felix, who fills the role of Mephistopheles, Gabriel's dark angel. There is enough twinning and doubling in the novel to suggest that Felix may also be Gabriel's stillborn twin brother. Events prove both the hopelessness and inevitability of Gabriel's outlook. First, Gabriel is severely burned, the potential fate, no doubt, of all who make Mephistophelian contact. Second, he is brokenhearted by his failure to rescue Adele. Yet the end of the novel finds him rededicating himself to his vision of mathematics, to the rhetoric of perfection and security which it symbolizes.

The combination of failure and rededication on which *Mefisto* ends is an illuminating gloss on one of John Banville's most crucial themes. Echoing a pronouncement of Samuel Beckett's, he believes that the artist necessarily has failure for his theme and that his work articulates that theme's pressing reality. On the other hand, Banville is still romantic enough to conceive of his theme in terms of world-changing, concept-forming figures. Thus, his work is also preoccupied with the meaning of success, which in turn is linked to ideas of progress, clarity, precision, and enlightenment. Failure is relativized by success, and success by failure. The sense of doubleness and unity suggested by such a conclusion is typical of Banville's outlook.

Binary interplay is very much to the fore in Banville's most commercially successful novel, *The Book of Evidence*. This work takes the form of a first-person account, while he is awaiting trial, of a vertiginous fall from grace undertaken by a lapsed mathematician, Freddie Montgomery. In financial straits, Freddy decided to steal a painting, and in order to do so murdered an innocent bystander, a servant. No good comes of these actions, unless it is to reveal to the scapegrace protagonist the necessity that his nature acknowledge limits, and that the limits are those enjoined by the existence of others. As Freddy perceives, his failure to imagine the lives of others leads him into reckless disregard of those lives. His crime is this failure. Through the comprehensiveness and comprehension of his narrative, Freddy arrives at a perspective on his actions which he had previously lacked, having been hitherto driven to act by cupidity, fear, and callowness.

In a reflexive turn typical of Banville, Freddy's book becomes more substantial than his life. For all its narrative discontinuities, the story remains a simple one, reminiscent of a ballad, providing *The Book of Evidence* with an unlikely kinship to *Long Lankin*, whose stories are premised on a ballad. This formal association also suggests *The Book of Evidence*'s indebtedness to two classics of jail literature, both by Oscar Wilde, *De Profundis* (1905; a first-person attempt at vindication) and *The Ballad of Reading Gaol* (1898; with its refrain, "For each man kills the thing he loves," which is clearly the case of Freddy and the stolen painting). Such objective possibilities of order counterpoint Freddy's subjective flaunting of law—not merely the law of the land, which is held at such a distance in *The Book of Evidence* as to seem beside the point, but laws more fundamentally pertaining to the viability of the project of being human, with its obligations to others, obligations which in the distorted form of financial indebtedness to hoodlums motivate Freddy's murderous actions. While conceptually and stylistically *The Book of Evidence* is at least the equal of Banville's earlier attainments, it also articulates much more decisively than does *Mefisto* the author's sense of contemporary social reality, and its uniformly favorable critical reception suggests that it is the work that will earn for Banville the wider readership that his originality, commitment to large questions, and aesthetic poise deserve.

Banville's subject matter and methods of artistic execution are the bases of his reputation for originality. In the context of contemporary fiction, this author is notable for his commitment, for felicity of phrase, and for his relationship to an important fictional genre, the historical novel. He has identified, both by his artistic strategies and his choice of material, with some of the main questions faced by contemporary fiction—identified with them perhaps too conspicuously and with an ease and self-possession uncharacteristic of many contemporary writers. Some readers may find that this author's manner is paradoxically at odds with his central themes. In the context of the modern Irish novel, his voice is precisely the breath of fresh air required to reinvigorate and enlarge an illustrious tradition.

George O'Brien

Other major works
SHORT FICTION: *Long Lankin*, 1970, revised 1984.
SCREENPLAY: *Reflections*, 1984.

Bibliography
Deane, Seamus. "'Be Assured I Am Inventing': The Fiction of John Banville." In *The Irish Novel in Our Time*, edited by Patrick Rafroidi and Maurice Harmon. Lille: Publications de l'Université de Lille, 1975. Excellent discussion of Banville's first three works of fiction by Ireland's leading contemporary critic. Particularly insightful on the reflexive elements in *Long Lankin, Nightspawn*, and *Birchwood*, this article concludes with a challenging critique of the cultural significance of Banville's work.
Imhof, Rudiger. *John Banville: A Critical Introduction*. Dublin: Wolfhound Press, 1989. The first book-length study of Banville's works, up to and including *Mefisto*. Complete with an intellectual guide-map to Banville's fictional preoccupations, as well as a full bibliography.
Irish University Review 11 (Spring, 1981). "A John Banville Special Number." A comprehensive survey of Banville's career, consisting of a number of critical overviews, a bibliography, a wide-ranging interview, and the transcript of a talk given by him at the University of Iowa's Writers'

Workshop—one of Banville's rare formal statements on fiction and authorship.

McMinn, Jo. "An Exalted Naming: The Poetical Fiction of John Banville." *Canadian Journal of Irish Studies* 14 (July, 1988): 17-27. Deals with the various senses in which poetry enters into Banville's fiction, including treatment of his poetic allusions, his attainments as a prose stylist, and the visionary dimension of his work.

O'Brien, George. "John Banville: Portraits of the Artist." In *New Irish Writing*, edited by James D. Brophy and Eamon Grennan. Boston: Twayne, 1989. Concentrating on Banville's science tetralogy, this article appraises the cult of creativity upon which *Doctor Copernicus, Kepler, The Newton Letter,* and *Mefisto* are premised and which they recuperate. The article mainly dwells on Banville's protagonists, but also assesses in passing Banville's preoccupation with the creative act in his earlier works.

"Q. & A. with John Banville." *Irish Literary Supplement.* Spring, 1987, 13. A rare interview with the media-shy author.

JULIAN BARNES

Born: Leicester, England; January 19, 1946

Principal long fiction

Metroland, 1980; *Duffy*, 1980 (as Dan Kavanagh); *Fiddle City*, 1981 (as Dan Kavanagh); *Before She Met Me*, 1982; *Flaubert's Parrot*, 1984; *Putting the Boot In*, 1985 (as Dan Kavanagh); *Staring at the Sun*, 1986; *Going to the Dogs*, 1987 (as Dan Kavanagh); *A History of the World in 10½ Chapters*, 1989.

Other literary forms

Julian Barnes has served as a journalist and columnist for several British newspapers and magazines; he has published numerous essays and book reviews.

Achievements

Barnes is one of a number of younger British writers born after World War II who gravitated toward London and its literary scene. Reacting to the certainties and assumptions of the previous generation, they have often resorted to irony and comedy in viewing the contemporary world. Some have experimented with the form of the traditional novel. Barnes's early novels were narrative and chronological in approach, but his fifth book, *Flaubert's Parrot*, combined fact and fiction, novel and history, biography and literary criticism. For that work he was nominated for Great Britain's most prestigious literary award, the Booker Prize, and was awarded the Geoffrey Faber Memorial Prize. He has also won literary prizes in Italy and France, and he received the E. M. Forster Award from the American Academy of Arts and Letters. In *Staring at the Sun* and *A History of the World in 10½ Chapters*, Barnes continued his exploration of the novel and its form.

Biography

Born in the English Midlands city of Leicester just after World War II to parents who were French teachers, Julian Barnes studied French at Magdalen College, Oxford, from which he was graduated with honors in 1968 with a degree in modern languages. After leaving Oxford, his abiding interest in words and language led him to a position as a lexicographer for the *Oxford English Dictionary Supplement*. In 1972 Barnes became a free-lance writer, preferring that parlous profession to the law. During the 1970's and 1980's, he wrote reviews for *The Times Literary Supplement* and was contributing editor to the *New Review*, assistant literary editor of *New Statesman*, and deputy literary editor of the *Sunday Times* of London. For a decade he served as a television critic, most notably for the London *Observer*, where his comments were witty, irreverent, and provocative.

Influenced by the French writer Gustave Flaubert, particularly his concern for form, style, and objectivity, Barnes's serious novels continued to exhibit his fascination with language and literary experiments, in contrast with the more traditional narrative approach and narrow subject matter of many twentieth century English novelists. Under the pseudonym Dan Kavanagh, Barnes has also published a number of detective novels.

Analysis

Throughout the 1980's Julian Barnes wrote five novels under his own name. Each exhibits wit and irony, wordplay, and an understanding of literary forms.

The first, *Metroland*, is orthodox in technique and approach; divided into three parts, it is a variation on the traditional *Bildungsroman*, or coming-of-age novel. In part 1, the narrator, Christopher Lloyd, and his close friend, Toni, grow up in 1963 in a north London suburb on the Metropolitan rail line (thus the title), pursuing the perennial adolescent dream of rebellion against parents, school, the middle class, and the establishment in general. Convinced of the superiority of French culture and consciously seeking what they believe to be the larger questions of life, they choose to cultivate art, literature, and music in order to astound what they see as the bourgeoisie and its petty concerns.

Part 2, five years later, finds Christopher a student in Paris, the epitome of artistic bohemianism, particularly when compared to Metroland. It is 1968, and French students are demonstrating and rioting in the streets for social and political causes. None of this touches Christopher: he is more concerned about his personal self-discovery than about changing or challenging the wider world.

Nine years later, in part 3, set in 1977, Christopher is back in Metroland, married to Marion, an Englishwoman of his own class, with a child, a mortgaged suburban house, and a nine-to-five job. Toni, still a rebel, chides Christopher for selling out to the enemy. Ironically, however, Christopher is contented with life in Metroland. He consciously examines and questions his present circumstances but accepts their rewards and satisfactions. Questioning and irony are continuing themes in all Barnes's novels, as is the absence of significant character development except for the leading figure. Toni, Christopher's French girlfriend Annick, and Marion, his English wife, are not much more than supporting figures. Relationships are explored through Christopher's narration alone, and Christopher finds himself, his questions, and his life of most concern and interest to him.

Before She Met Me is also a story of an individual's attempt to relate to and understand his personal world. Graham Hendrick, a forty-year-old professor of history, has recently remarried. Now beginning a new life, happy with Ann, his new wife, and outwardly contented, both personally and professionally, Hendrick seems to be an older variation of Christopher and his self-satisfied middle-class existence. As in his first novel, Barnes has included a bohemian writer, Jack Lupton, as a foil for Hendrick's respectable conformity. Before they were married, Ann acted in several minor films, and after viewing one of them, Hendrick, the historian, begins to search out his wife's past. At first his quest seems based on simple curiosity; soon, however, Ann's history begins to take over Hendrick's present life. Losing his professional objectivity as a historian, succumbing to jealousy, compulsively immersing himself in Ann's past, blurring the distinction between the real Ann and her image on the screen, Hendrick becomes completely obsessed. Seeing the present as a world without causes, Hendrick finds his crusade in the past, and that crusade is no longer public but private. Bordering on the melodramatic, *Before She Met Me* is the story of the downward spiral of an individual who can no longer distinguish fantasy from reality. Did the love affairs Ann had on the screen replicate her private life off camera? Were her love affairs in the past continuing in the present?

Barnes poses the question, not only for Hendrick, caught up in his obsession, but also for the reader: what is reality, and can one discover the truth? Like *Metroland*, this novel has many comic and witty moments but ultimately ends tragically. Ann and Lupton had an affair that has since ended, but Hendrick, in his obsessive quest, falsely concludes that it continues; he murders Lupton and then, in Ann's presence, he takes his own life. Although told in the third person, *Before She Met Me* centers on the plight of a single figure questioning his world. Hendrick and his compulsions dominate the novel: his first wife, their child, Ann, and Lupton are figures perceived through his persona.

With his third novel, *Flaubert's Parrot*, Barnes received considerable praise as a significant writer of fiction, less parochial in form and technique than most English novelists of his time. His first book published in the United States, *Flaubert's Parrot* was the recipient of numerous prizes. It too is a novel of questions and obsessions, which unite the past and present. Yet in its collage of literary techniques, it is not a traditional narrative novel, including as it does fiction, biography, history, and literary criticism. As in his earlier works, here Barnes focuses upon a single individual, Geoffrey Braithwaite, an English medical doctor in his sixties, a widower, with a long-standing interest in the French writer Gustave Flaubert. Barnes also has been a student of French and admirer of Flaubert, and early in *Metroland* Christopher reads a work by Flaubert; several critics have examined the possible relationships between the fictional figures—Braithwaite, Christopher, Hendrick—and the author.

Told in the first person, *Flaubert's Parrot* examines Braithwaite's attempt to discover which of two different stuffed parrots on exhibit in competing Flaubert museums is the one that sat on Flaubert's desk when he wrote his short story "Un Cœur simple" ("A Simple Heart"). In the story, an old servant, Félicité, is left after fifty years of service with only a parrot as a companion. When the parrot dies, Félicité has it stuffed. As her health fails, she confuses the parrot with the Holy Ghost, traditionally represented as a dove. On her deathbed she believes that she sees a giant parrot above her head. Braithwaite's quest to determine the real parrot allows him, and Barnes, to pursue with wit and irony numerous aspects of Flaubert's biography; his published works, including *Madame Bovary* (1857); his ideas for works he did not write; his travels; his use of animals in his writings; and his lovers. The novel includes chronologies, a dictionary, and an examination paper.

Yet the work is not concerned only with Braithwaite's interest in Flaubert's past and the two surviving stuffed parrots. As the doctor pursues Flaubert and his parrot, he also begins to reveal his own history. Braithwaite's wife had been frequently unfaithful to him, as Emma Bovary was to her husband Charles, and she had eventually committed suicide. As Braithwaite explores the relationship between Flaubert and his fiction, seeking to know which is the real parrot, he also attempts to understand the realities of his own life and his connection with the fictional Charles Bovary. He becomes obsessive about discovering the truth of the parrots, but he is also obsessive about discovering his own truth. The difficulty, however, is that truth and reality are always elusive, and the discovery of a number of small realities does not result in the illumination of absolute truth. In the course of his discussions, Braithwaite muses upon even the incompetence of specialists in ferreting out the truth; he criticizes a prominent Flaubertian scholar, whom he accuses of pronouncing French badly, of mistakenly identifying a portrait as Flaubert, and of being unable to specify the color of Emma Bovary's eyes.

Flaubert's parrot, too, is seen as a symbol of this dichotomy of fact and fiction. The parrot can utter human sounds, but only by mimicking what it hears; still, there is the appearance of understanding, regardless of whether it exists. Is a writer, such as Flaubert, merely a parrot, writing down human sounds and observing human life without understanding or interpretation? At the end of Braithwaite's search for the real stuffed parrot used by Flaubert while writing his short story, the doctor discovers that dozens of stuffed parrots exist which Flaubert could have borrowed and placed upon his desk. Thus Braithwaite's has been one of many quests with no resolutions, questions without final answers.

Staring at the Sun, Barnes's fourth novel published under his own name, exhibits a stronger narrative line than *Flaubert's Parrot*, but as in the story of Braithwaite, narrative here is not the primary concern of the author; questions remain paramount. The central figure is a lower-middle-class woman, Jean Serjeant, significantly unlike earlier Barnes protagonists because she is naïve and unsophisticated, lacking any intellectual pretensions. The tone of Barnes's portrayal of Jean contrasts sharply with the wit and irony featured throughout *Flaubert's Parrot*. Yet even Jean asks questions, such as what happened to the sandwiches Charles Lindbergh did not eat when he flew over the Atlantic in 1927, and why the mink is so tenacious of life (a statement from a print that hung in her bedroom when she was a child). Those questions have no answers, and Jean muses that questions that do have answers are not real questions.

The novel begins in 1941, with a prologue set during World War II. Sergeant-pilot Prosser is flying back across the Channel to his English base from France, just before dawn. The sun rises from the waves on the eastern horizon, captivating Prosser's attention. Shortly after, he reduces his altitude when he sees the smoke from a steamship far below. As he flies at the lower altitude, the sun comes up again from the sea into his view, and for the second time in a single morning he watches the sun's ascent. He calls this event an ordinary miracle, but he never forgets it. Neither does Jean, after Prosser relates it to her a few months later while temporarily billeted in her parents' home. Prosser soon disappears from Jean's life but not from her memories: he kills himself, she later discovers, by flying directly into the sun. She marries Michael, a policeman who has no time for or interest in questions.

After twenty years of marriage, at the age of forty, Jean becomes pregnant for the first time. She leaves Michael in order to discover what she calls a more difficult, first-rate life; she is more on a quest for self than seeking an escape from her unsatisfactory husband. When her son, Gregory, is old enough to be left alone, Jean begins to travel widely, often by airplane. She pursues her own Seven Wonders of the World. While visiting Arizona's Grand Canyon, she observes an airplane flying below the canyon's rim. At first it seems to her to be against nature, but she concludes instead that it is against reason: nature provides the miracles, such as the Grand Canyon and the double rising of the sun. As the novel proceeds, Jean becomes more like Barnes's other figures and less like her naïve and unsophisticated young self.

Gregory also parallels Barnes's earlier intellectual characters and their questions that can yield no conclusive answers. Afraid of death but contemplating suicide, he meditates upon God and His existence. He posits fourteen possible answers, but no final truth. The last part of the novel is set in the future, a world of intrusive and obtrusive computers. All the world's knowledge has been incorporated into the General Purposes Computer (GPC), open to everyone. Yet it cannot answer why minks are so tenacious of life. A special informational program, TAT (The Absolute Truth), is added to the GPC, but when Gregory asks TAT whether it believes in God, the computer answers that his question is not a real question, and when he asks why it is not a real question, TAT again responds that Greogory's second question is also not a real question. Only "real" questions, it appears, can be answered by computers. In what she believes will be the last incident in her long life, in 2021, Jean, at the age of ninety-nine, accompanied by Gregory, makes a final flight, observing the sun this time as it sets in the west rather than rising in the east, as it had done twice during Prosser's "ordinary miracle" so many years before.

In his last novel of the 1980's, *A History of the World in 10½ Chapters*, Barnes continued his experimentation in form and style. Unlike his earlier novels, this one has no central character. Instead, the reader is presented with a number of chapters or stories, ostensibly historical, which are loosely connected by several common themes. The first tale or fable is a revisionist account of the story of Noah and the ark. Narrated by a woodworm, the story portrays Noah as a drunk, humanity as badly flawed, and God and His plan as leaving much to be desired. Human beings fare equally poorly in the other chapters, and the ark returns in later stories: a nineteenth century Englishwoman searches for the ark on Mount Ararat; a twentieth century American astronaut, also seeking the ark, finds a skeleton that he identifies as Noah's but that is really the bones of the woman explorer; another chapter discusses the ark in the form of the raft Medusa, painted by Théodore Géricault.

In this novel Barnes raises the question of how one turns disaster into art, or how one turns life into art. In a half chapter, or "Parenthesis," he discusses history and love: "History isn't what happened. History is just what historians tell us. . . . The history of the world? Just voices echoing in the dark, images that burn for a few centuries and then fade; stories, old stories that sometimes seem to overlap; strange links, impertinent connections." Barnes connects love to truth, but truth, objective truth, can never be found. Still, Sisyphus-like, one must constantly toil to find it. So it is with love: "We must believe in it, or we're lost." *A History of the World in 10½ Chapters* does not always succeed: the stories do not always successfully relate to one another, and the tone at times fails to achieve the ironic brilliance of *Flaubert's Parrot*.

From *Metroland* to *A History of the World in 10½ Chapters*, Barnes has pursued several ideas that are common in all of his works: Human beings question even though there can be no absolute answers; humanity pursues its obsessions, often resulting in failure. Yet his novels have at the same time evolved in form and approach—the earliest are more traditional and conventional, the latter more experimental. Barnes's wit and irony, his use of history, literary criticism, myth, and fable, his melding of imagination and intellect, and his continuing risk in exploring new forms and methods make him one of the most significant English novelists of his generation.

Eugene S. Larson

Bibliography

Fuentes, Carlos. "The Enchanting Blue Yonder." *The New York Times Book Review*, April 12, 1987, 3, 43. Fuentes, a major Latin American novelist, praises Barnes's *Staring at the Sun* for experimental originality, its sense of enchantment, and its intelligence. He sees Barnes as one of those who are revitalizing the English novel.

Hulbert, Ann. "The Meaning of Meaning." *The New Republic* 196 (May 11, 1987): 37-39. Reviewing *Staring at the Sun*, Hulbert notes Barnes's continuing interest in the relationship between life and art; she comments on the differences in tone and technique between that novel and his earlier works, particularly *Flaubert's Parrot*.

Kermode, Frank. "Obsessed with Obsession." *The New York Review of Books* 32 (April 25, 1985): 15. Kermode, an English literary critic, in his favorable review of *Flaubert's Parrot*, discusses some of the social and literary background of the younger generation of English novelists.

Locke, Richard. "Flood of Forms." *The New Republic* 201 (December 4, 1989): 40-43. Locke, a professor of comparative literature, places Barnes's interest in form and style in the context of modern literature, beginning with Flaubert. He summarizes all the novels, focusing particularly upon *A History of the World in 10½ Chapters*.

Lodge, David. "The Home Front." *The New York Review of Books* 34 (May 7, 1987): 21. Lodge is an English novelist, of the same generation as Barnes but generally less experimental in form. He finds *Staring at the Sun* less successful than *Flaubert's Parrot* and argues that Barnes attempted to incorporate too many elements into the former work.

JOHN BARTH

Born: Cambridge, Maryland; May 27, 1930

Principal long fiction

The Floating Opera, 1956; *The End of the Road*, 1958; *The Sot-Weed Factor*, 1960; *Giles Goat-Boy: Or, The Revised New Syllabus*, 1966; *Chimera*, 1972; *LETTERS*, 1979; *Sabbatical: A Romance*, 1982; *The Tidewater Tales: A Novel*, 1987; *The Last Voyage of Somebody the Sailor*, 1991.

Other literary forms

While John Barth's novels have ensured his eminence among contemporary American writers, his short fictions have been no less influential or controversial. In addition to five novels and one tripartite novel, he has published one collection of shorter works: *Lost in the Funhouse* (1968), the technical involutions of which plumb the nature of narrative itself and disrupt conventional relationships between teller and tale. Barth has also written two essays of particular significance. In "The Literature of Exhaustion," he discusses those writers whose suspicion that certain forms of literature have become obsolete is incorporated both thematically and technically in the fictions they produce. He highlights the successes of Jorge Luis Borges, Vladimir Nabokov and Samuel Beckett in the face of apparent artistic impasse; they acknowledge and push beyond the boundaries staked out by their literary predecessors and employ a potentially stifling sense of "ultimacy" in the creation of new work, so that their forms become metaphors for their aesthetic concerns. "The Literature of Replenishment" seeks to correct any misreading of the former essay as a complaint that contemporary writers have little left to accomplish save the parody of conventions which they arrived upon too late to benefit from themselves. Barth's method is to define and legitimize postmodernism by placing its most interesting practitioners—he singles out Italo Calvino and Gabriel García Márquez for praise—in a direct line of succession which may be traced through the great modernists of the first half of the twentieth century back to Laurence Sterne and Miguel de Cervantes. Both of these essays are collected in *The Friday Book: Essays and Other Nonfiction* (1984).

Achievements

Perhaps Barth's method is a mark of a growing receptivity among readers and critics to formally venturesome fiction; perhaps it is merely a result of the writer's inevitable passage from unexpected new voice to mature artist. Whatever the case, Barth is one avant-gardist who has infiltrated the literary establishment with relative ease, with no perceptible compromise. He remains America's foremost existential novelist, but his approach to the rather somber question of the arbitrariness of moral values and the absence of intrinsic meaning has always been richly overlaid with humor that is at times intricate and esoteric and often expansive and full of delight in its own verbal virtuosity. He has shown a career-long obsession with mythology, with how classical tales may be reconstituted in and provide resonance for contemporary fiction, and with how the novel may continue to respond to the age-old and seemingly insatiable need for the coherent pleasures of narrative.

Barth still has his detractors, whose accusations typically focus on his tendency to overwork his jokes (a condemnation which often attends *Giles Goat-Boy*) or to surrender to vulgar effects (as in his revisionist history of John Smith's encounter with Pocahontas in *The Sot-Weed Factor*). Nevertheless, few would dispute Barth's stature as the most widely appreciated postmodernist, a designation which he embraces despite its connotation of self-absorption and unreadability.

Biography

The quintessential university writer-in-residence, John Barth must take special satisfaction in having witnessed the solid entrenchment of his work in literary anthologies and undergraduate survey courses. He was born John Simmons Barth on May 27, 1930, in Cambridge, Maryland, the contemporary and historical environs of which have provided the setting for much of his writing. He attended Cambridge High School, after which he accommodated his passion for jazz and the drums with a brief stay at the Juilliard School of Music. His unspectacular showing there led him to enroll at The Johns Hopkins University, a move made possible when he won a scholarship he forgot he had applied for. He achieved the highest grade average in the College of Arts and Sciences upon receiving the B.A. in 1951.

To pay off tuition debts and support his wife (Harriet Anne Strickland, whom he had married in 1950), Barth took a job in the Classics Library, where he first became absorbed in the Oriental tale-cycles which would later inform the style and content of his own fiction. During this period came his first publications in student literary magazines, including one story, "Lilith and the Lion," whose appearance in *The Hopkins Review* when Barth was twenty may rightly be considered his first professional work. His master's project was *The Shirt of Nessus*, a novel based on a love triangle including a father and son and populated by rapists, murderers, bootleggers, and lunatics; Barth confesses it a miscarriage, and he says it now rests in the Dorchester marshes on Chesapeake Bay.

Having received his M.A. in the spring of 1952, he began studying for a Ph.D. in the aesthetics of literature while tutoring and teaching freshman composition courses, until the cost of supporting both his family (his third child was born in January, 1954) and his education compelled him to teach full time. He took a position at Pennsylvania State University in 1953; his experience with freshman composition there would eventually find its way into *The End of the Road*. (He did not earn his doctorate until 1969, from the University of Maryland.) While at Penn State, Barth began a series of one hundred stories, in the bawdy manner of Giovanni Boccaccio's *The Decameron* (1348-1353), detailing the history of Dorchester County. He abandoned the project within a year, but fifty of the proposed hundred stories were completed; a handful were published separately and others later were incorporated into *The Sot-Weed Factor*.

Barth advanced from instructor to associate professor at Penn State, where he taught until 1965, and it was during this twelve-year period that he established his reputation. In the fall of 1954, Barth found a photograph of an old showboat; borrowing something of the conversational style of Laurence Sterne's *Tristram Shandy* (1759-1767) and some plot devices from *Don Casmurro* (1900), by the Brazilian novelist Joachim María Machado de Assis, he began *The Floating Opera* in January, 1955. It was completed in three months, but several publishers rejected it, and Appleton-Century-Crofts demanded many revisions before publishing it in 1956. By the fall of 1955, however, Barth was already at work on *The End of the Road*. Like *The Floating Opera*, with which it is often associated as a philosophical companion-piece, it was finished in three months and was ultimately published by Doubleday in 1958.

The Floating Opera was nominated for a National Book Award, which it failed to win; neither the book nor its successor sold well. Barth was denied a Guggenheim grant in 1958, but his school's research fund did manage $250 to send him to Maryland to gather information for his next project. He had expected *The Sot-Weed Factor* to be another three-month venture, but that mammoth refurbishing of the eighteenth century picaresque turned out to be nearly three years in the writing. That novel, too, met with relative public indifference, but it later became his first major critical success when it was released in paperback in 1964.

Giles Goat-Boy was begun in 1960, and it would be six years from inception to publication. In 1965, Barth left Penn State for a full professorship at the State University of New York in Buffalo. *Giles Goat-Boy* introduced Barth to the best-seller lists in 1966, but he was already at work on *Lost in the Funhouse*, a brain-teasing, technically probing collection of multimedia pieces which came out in 1968, for which Barth received his second unsuccessful nomination for a National Book Award.

His next book did earn that elusive honor, however; *Chimera*, Barth's most direct confrontation of ancient narrative in the form of three metafictions, won the National Book Award in 1973. In that same year, Barth changed locale once more, accepting a post at his alma mater, Johns Hopkins. It was not until 1979 that his next book, *LETTERS*, was published. Instead of creating a new form, Barth decided, as he had done in *The Sot-Weed Factor*, to resuscitate a traditional one: in this case, the epistolary novel. *LETTERS* plumbs the author's personal literary history as well, for its principal correspondents are characters from Barth's earlier novels.

Whether the familiar hybrid of writer-teacher nourishes or diminishes creativity will not be decided on the basis of one man's example, but Barth has found the academic atmosphere to be not only hospitable to his talents but also generous as an occasion and setting for his fiction: two of his novels are set specifically in college communities, and the theme of education—be it in a school, under the auspices of a spiritual adviser, or in the shifting, multifarious outside world of affairs—has been repeatedly highlighted in Barth's work. Barth currently lives with his second wife, Shelley Rosenberg (whom he married in 1970), dividing his time between Maryland, where he conducts creative writing seminars, and New York, where he keeps a summer home and does much of his writing.

Analysis

The literary historian and the literary technician meet in the novels and attitudes of John Barth. His eagerness to affirm the artificiality of the art he creates enables him to strip-mine the whole range of narrative that precedes his career for usable personalities and devices; similarly, by beginning with the premise of literature as a self-evident sham, he greatly enlarges the field of possibility within his own fictions, so that outrageous plot contrivances, protean characters (or characters who are essentially banners emblazoned with ruling philosophies), and verbal acrobatics all become acceptable. Barth's general solution for handling the fracture between art and reality is not to heal it, but rather to heighten his readers' awareness of it. This is why, despite his penchant for intellectual confrontation and long interludes of debate in his novels, Barth most often looks to humor—jokes and pranks, parody, and stylistic trickery—to make the philosophy palatable.

Barth meticulously reconstructs the fabric and feel of allegory (*Giles Goat-Boy*) or of the *Künstlerroman* (*The Sot-Weed Factor*), then minimizes the appropriateness of such patterns in the contemporary world by vigorously mocking them. He takes on formidable intellectual questions—the impossibility of knowing external reality, the unavailability of intrinsic values, the fragility of the self in an incurably relativistic universe—but chooses to do so in, to borrow one of his own most durable metaphors, a funhouse atmosphere. In fact, in Barth's fiction, abstract discussion is consistently revealed as a dubious alternative to passionate participation in life. Given the ambiguous state of the self, exposure to the world could be fatal if not for the strategy of fashioning and choosing from among a variety of masks which afford the beleaguered self a sense of definition and a schedule of valid responses to whatever situations the world presents. The willful choosing of masks is Barth's main theme; it suggests that the alternative to despair in the face of universal chaos and indifference is the responsibility to exercise one's freedom, much as an artist exercises his creative faculties in writing and editing tales that satisfy him. In this sense, Barth's heroes are artists of the self, who view the elasticity of character as a challenge to their mythmaking abilities, and who treat their private lives as fictions which are amenable to infinite revision.

"Good heavens," complains Todd Andrews in *The Floating Opera*, "how does one write a novel! I mean, how can anybody stick to the story, if he's at all sensitive to the significance of things?" The doubts and false starts which frustrate the progress of this protagonist's Inquiry—a hodgepodge of papers contained in peach baskets in his hotel room, for which, life being on so tenuous a lease from eternity, he pays rent on a daily basis—reflect those which would potentially stymie Barth himself, were he not to make them part of his subject. Like his narrator/alter ego in *The Floating Opera*, Barth contends with the problem of making art out of nihilism. In Andrews' hands, that problem takes the shape of a book-long (and, he confesses, lifelong) obsession with how, and whether, to live. There is little of traditional suspense to propel the narrative; after all, this is an examination of a decision *not* to commit suicide, so that Andrews' private undertaking of Hamlet's well-known question has led him to accept life, at least provisionally and despite its absence of intrinsic values.

The quality of life is described by the title of the novel and symbolized by the barge show—part vaudeville, part minstrel show—which flashes in and out of view as it moves along the river. No other image in literature so effectively captures the idea of Heraclitean flux: the "performance" is never the same for any two spectators, nor can one resume watching it at the same place in the show as when it last passed by. Furthermore, the nature of this floating phenomenon is operatic: sentimental, bizarre, wildly melodramatic, and often simply laughable. The players are amateurish, and they are best appreciated by an unrefined audience who are not bothered by the gaps in their understanding or by the unevenness of the performance. Andrews entertains the notion of building a showboat that has a perpetual play going on, and the novel itself is the alternative result; like the floating extravaganza, it is "chock-full of curiosities" and considers every possible taste: games, violence, flights of fancy and philosophy, legal and sexual intrigue, war and death, artwork and excrement. The implication here, as emphasized by T. Wallace Whittaker's rendition of William Shakespeare (one of the more delicate turns on the bill, to please the ladies), is that not only are all people players on a stage, but also they are apparently purposeless, scriptless players at that.

There is something of the floating opera in the stylistic range of the novel as well. Todd Andrews is a monologist in the comic, voluble tradition of *Tristram Shandy*. In fact, both men write autobiographical inquiries into the strangeness of the human condition which digress and associate so frequently that they are destined to become life works; both are artists racing to create against death, although Andrews is as likely to be felled by rational suicide as by his heart murmur; and both combine intellectual pursuits with technical "entertainments" (which include, in Barth's novel, repeated paragraphs, a double column of narrative "options," and a reproduction of the handbill announcing the schedule of events in "Adam's Original and Unparalleled Ocean-Going Floating Opera").

Motivation sets these two narrators apart, however, for if Tristram is compelled by life's delights, Andrews is alienated by its absurdity. Andrews is engaged in a search for purpose; his life hangs in the balance. His Inquiry began as an attempt to come to terms with his father's suicide in 1930, an event too complex to chalk up to an escape from debts incurred after the stock-market crash. It then absorbed a letter to his father which, with the obsessive diligence of Franz Kafka in a similar enterprise, Andrews had begun in 1920 and continued to redraft even after his father's death. The Inquiry continued to blossom until, by the time the novel opens in 1954, it is autobiography, journal, and religious/philosophical treatise all in one, and it floats by at the moment of focus on the decision (made on one of two days in June, 1937), after a failed effort, not to commit suicide. (Todd Andrews admonishes the reader not to confuse his name with its meaning of "death" in German; his name, which misspells the German word, is more aptly read as "almost death.")

Given the kinds of experience he relates, his final acceptance of life is rather surprising. His father's suicide is but one of a series of incidents which suggest that life may not be worth the salvaging effort. Sexuality, for example, is represented by his wonder at the ridiculousness of the act when, at age seventeen, he spies himself in a mirror in the midst of intercourse, and later, when his five-year affair with Jane Mack is revealed to have been directed by her husband, Harrison. Andrews' most profound confrontation with his own self, during World War I, reveals him to be "a shocked, drooling animal in a mudhole." When an enemy soldier stumbles upon him, they share their terror, then silent communion and friendship . . . and then Andrews stabs him to death. All actions are equally pointless; all commitments are arbitrary; all attempts to solve human incomprehension are laughable.

From rake to saint to cynic, Andrews endures without much joy as an expert lawyer, although he does admit to a certain detached interest in the law's arbitrary intricacies, epitomized in the search for the legitimate will among the seventeen left to posterity by Harrison Mack, Sr., which, when found, decides the fate of more than one hundred pickle jars brimming with his excrement. Andrews is actually comfortable enough living in the Dorset Hotel among a collection of society's aged castoffs, until a casual reference by his mistress to his clubbed hands initiates a kind of Sartrean nausea at the utter physical fact of himself; his growing detestation of that mortal coil, coupled with an absolute conviction that all value is artificially imposed, leads him to the brink of suicide, in the form of a scheme to blow up the opera boat (which, in the restored 1967 edition of the novel, would include hundreds of spectators, the Macks and Jeannine, their—or possibly Andrews'—daughter among them).

What stays him is the revelation that, if all values are arbitrary, suicide is not less arbitrary; furthermore, even arbitrary values may offer a way to live. This uneasy treaty with a relativistic universe is Andrews' provisional conclusion to the Inquiry, for the suicide does not come off. Some accident—a psychological shudder, an instinct beyond the intellect's dominion, or a spasm of sentimental concern for the little girl who had suffered a sudden convulsion—disrupts the plan, so the novel's philosophical journey concludes in the anticlimax promised by the narrator at the outset. If Barth frustrates some readers by forsaking the questions he has so fastidiously prepared them for, they must understand that the willingness to handle the sublime and the ridiculous alike with a shrug of good humor is part of the point: in the end, even nihilism is shown to be yet one more posture, one more mask.

In his next novel, *The End of the Road*, Barth's speculations on the nature and necessity of masks becomes more formulaic, although with somewhat bleaker results for his hero. Jake Horner—the name is borrowed from William Wycherly's sly seducer in *The Country Wife* (1673)—suffers from "cosmopsis," a disease of hyperconsciousness: the awareness that one choice is no more inherently valid or attractive than another. When a nameless black doctor materializes near a bench at Pennsylvania Station, he discovers Jake as hopelessly rooted to the spot as the statuette Jake keeps of the tortured Laocoön. The doctor recognizes his paralysis and initiates a program of therapy which forces his patient into action. He explains that no matter how arbitrary the system of "choosing" which he advocates may appear, "Choosing is existence: to the extent that you don't choose, you don't exist." All of Jake's subsequent activities—the plot of the novel—represent his execution of the doctor's precepts.

At the outset, Jake's quest is meticulously prescribed *for* him. He is advised to begin with simple, disciplined choices between well-defined alternatives; should he happen to get "stuck" again beyond his mentor's reach, he is to choose artificially according to Sinistrality, Antecedence, and Alphabetical Priority. He is made to worship the hard facts of an almanac and to travel in straight lines to scheduled locations; because it is a monument to fixity, he is to devote himself to teaching of prescriptive grammar at Wicomico State Teachers College. In short, Jake is to undergo Mythotherapy: the regular assignment of roles to the befuddled ego in order to facilitate participation in the world.

Once Jake's quest is complicated by relationships which overextend the narrative "masks" behind which he operates, that neatly contrived therapy proves insufficient. Joe and Rennie Morgan, characters evolved from Harrison and Jane Mack in *The Floating Opera*, confuse his roles: Joe is a strident god whose rational self-control and mechanical theorizing make him his wife's mentor and Jake's intimidator; Rennie's sexuality and mixture of admiration and helplessness toward her husband are provocative, but she involves Jake in a script he cannot handle. His "road" grows tortuous and overwhelming, as his strictly plotted career is diverted into adulterous liaisons and philosophical tournaments, deceit and death. The profundity of his relapse into irresponsibility is much greater this time, however, for he is not the only one victimized by it. By failing to control his roles at critical times, he becomes the instrument of Rennie's death: Rennie will not lie to ensure a safe operation, and Jake's frantic role-playing in order to secure an abortion ends in a grisly death at the hands of Jake's doctor. The reality of Rennie's bleeding on the table is one which, unlike his callous affair with the lonely Peggy Rankin, Jake cannot manipulate or evade; it is the end of the road for him as a free agent in the world. Because he apparently requires further training in order to function successfully, he escapes with the doctor to a new site of the Remobilization Farm.

Of course, Jake's intellectual adversary fares little better under the pressure of real events. Joe Morgan personifies Todd Andrews' supposition that an arbitrary value could be transformed into the "subjective equivalent of an absolute" which might then provide the coherent way of life so crucial to a man who deifies the intellect. Both Jake and Joe begin from the premise of relativism, which explains their mutual attraction, but while Jake tends to succumb to "weatherlessness" (a numbness incurred by the randomness of events and the loss of an essential I), Joe is smug about the rational system he and his wife abide by. That self-assurance sanctions Rennie's being exposed to Jake's influence and provokes Jake to undermine him. When Joe is revealed as something less than pure mind and standards (Jake and Rennie spy him through a window masturbating, grunting, picking his nose), the god loses his authenticity, and the affair merely emphasizes Joe's fall from eminence. Rennie does bring her guilt to Joe, but he returns her to Jake to reenact the betrayal until she can account for it rationally; in the same way, he refuses to face up to the fact of her death, which was indirectly engineered by his experimental obsession, and proves himself to be far more comfortable in handling abstract ideas than in facing up to the welter of uncertainties beyond his field of expertise.

The road's end serves as a final blessing to Jake; the conclusion of the novel is not the completion of a quest but a relief from it. Since the turbulence of the world of affairs has proved unmanageable, he capitulates and numbly offers his "weatherless" self up to the auspices of the doctor, the price for performing Rennie's abortion. Jake retreats into submission after a disastrous initiation into the world.

In his next two novels, Barth grants his philosophical preoccupations the panoramic expansiveness and formal openness of a Henry Fielding or François

Rabelais, as if seeking epic dimension for what might well be considered in his first novels to be merely the idiosyncracies of constipated personalities. *The Sot-Weed Factor* features a riotously inventive plot and a cast of characters including poets and prostitutes, lords and brigands, landowners and Indians, merchants and thieves, but the triumph of the novel is in its authentic language and texture: for some eight hundred pages, Barth's novel impersonates one of those sprawling eighteenth century picaresque English novels, complete with protracted authorial intrusions, outrageous coincidences, dizzying turns of plot, and a relish for lewd humor.

Barth borrows a satirical poem on colonial America by Ebenezer Cooke (1708) for the foundation of his novel and resuscitates Cooke himself to be his hero. Barth's Eben Cooke is a timid, awkward fellow, who, unlike Andrews and Horner, maintains a steadfast virginity—sexual, social, and political—in a world teeming with sin and subterfuge. His steadfast adherence to a chosen mask—that of poet laureate of Maryland—with its requisite responsibilities keeps him on course. Until he happens upon that identity, Eben is overwhelmed by "the beauty of the possible," so much so that he cannot choose among careers; a broad education shared with his twin sister, Anna, at the hands of the ubiquitous Henry Burlingame, serves to increase his wonder rather than to specify a direction, so that the reader discovers him as a young man who haunts the London taverns, somewhat ill at ease among more raucous peers. He cannot muster an identity reliable enough to survive the pressure of alternatives.

What could have become a lifelong "cosmopsic" stagnation is interrupted by an encounter with a whore, Joan Toast; instead of having sex, Eben chooses to defend his innocence, for he sees in it a symbolic manifestation of his ultimate role. He exalts the deliciously earthy Joan into a bodiless goddess of verse; it is this indifference to reality that will enable him to survive, if not to transcend, the subversive and often grotesque facts of the New World, and the astounding contrasts between the poet's rhapsodizing and the world's stubborn brutishness provide much of the novel's ironic humor.

That confrontation with the New World is set into motion by Eben's father, who, when advised of his son's failure to lead a useful life in London, commands him to set off for his tobacco (sot-weed) estate in Maryland. Armed with a sense of his true calling, Eben wins from Lord Baltimore an agreement to write the "Marylandiad," a verse epic glorifying the province he knows nothing about, and is granted the laureateship in writing. The balance of *The Sot-Weed Factor* is a prolonged trial of Eben's confidence: his initiation into political intrigue and worldly corruption lays siege to his high-flown illusions about mankind. The people he meets are rapacious victimizers, ravaged victims, or crass simpletons, and Eben's promised land, his Malden estate, turns out to be an opium den and brothel. One illusion after another is stripped away, until the poet's tribute to Maryland is metamorphosed into the bitter satire on the deformities of America and Americans found in the poem by the historical Cooke.

Eben would not survive the conspiracies and uglinesses of reality were it not for the tutelage and example of Henry Burlingame. Whereas Eben labors to maintain one role—his "true" self—after years of aimlessness, Burlingame accepts and celebrates a series of roles, for he argues that, in a world of "plots, cabals, murthers, and machinations," an elastic personality will prove most useful. Therefore, he ducks in and out of the novel unpredictably, assuming a variety of guises (including that of John Coode, Baltimore's devilish enemy, Lord Baltimore himself, and even Eben Cooke) as the situation demands. Eben's discussions with his mentor, although they do not cause him to forsake his belief in the essential truth of man's perfectibility and of his own career, do instruct him in how to dissemble when necessary, as exemplified during the voyage to America, when an exchange of roles with his servant, Bertram, proves expedient. In a sense, *The Sot-Weed Factor* boils down to the contrast and the tentative accommodations made between the ideal and the real, or between innocence and experience, as represented by the virgin-poet, who is linked to a past (his father) and to a future (his commission), and by the orphaned jack-of-all-trades, who embraces adventures and lovers with equal vivacity.

The Sot-Weed Factor insists on no conclusive resolution between these attitudes; as is Barth's custom throughout his fiction, the struggles between theoretical absolutes must end in compromise. If Eben's first problem is to rouse himself out of languor, his second is to realize the inadequacy of a single, unalterable role. Accordingly, Eben repudiates his sexual abstinence in order to wed the diseased, opium-addicted Joan Toast—his ruined Beatrice, who has followed him secretly to America—and so accepts a contract between the ideal and the actual. Similarly, Burlingame can only win and impregnate his beloved Anna after he completes his search for his family roots, which is to say, after he locates a stable identity. The novel ends in good comic fashion: lovers are finally united; plot confusions are sorted out. Significantly, however, Barth adds twists to these conventions, thereby tempering the comic resolution: Joan dies in childbirth, and Burlingame disappears without trace. Barth replicates the eighteenth century picaresque novel only to parody it; he seduces the reader into traditional expectations only to undermine them.

For many readers, the most satisfying passages in *The Sot-Weed Factor* are not the philosophical or the literary exercises but rather the bawdy set pieces, the comic inventories and the imaginative diaries; nor should any discussion of this novel neglect to mention the war of name-calling between whores, or the "revisionist" rendition of Captain Smith's sexual assault on the otherwise impregnable Pocahontas. Barth has written of his enjoyment of Tobias Smollett's *Roderick Random* (1748) for its "nonsignificant surfaces," and in such glittering surfaces lie the charm of *The Sot-Weed Factor* as well. Fiction invades history and finds in its incongruities and intricacies of plot, character, and motivation a compatible form. Of all the deceptions perpetrated in the novel, perhaps none is so insidious as that of American history itself—the ultimate ruse of civilization, an imperfect concealment of savagery and self-ishness. To remain innocent of the nature of history is irresponsible; Eben Cooke's practiced detachment, as implied by his virginity, is morally unac-ceptable. This lesson enables him to mature both artistically and ethically, and to dedicate himself to the world of which he claims to be poet laureate.

Following immediately upon his satire of the historical past is Barth's satire of the future—a computer narrative. The novel-long analogy ruling *Giles Goat-Boy* transforms the universe into a university; this Newest Testament portrays a world divided (between East and West Campus) and waiting for the Grand Tutor, the Savior of the academic system, to protect Studentdom from the satanic Dean o' Flunks.

Barth provides Giles, an amalgam of multicultural messiah-heroes, as the updated instrument of human destiny. Giles (Grand Tutorial Ideal, Labo-ratory Eugenical Specimen) is the child of the prodigious WESCAC computer and a virgin. Raised as a goat (Billy Bocksfuss) by an apostate scientist-mentor, Max Spielman, he eventually leaves the herd to join humanity as a preacher of the Revised New Syllabus on the West Campus of New Tammany College. The novel traces his attempts to verify and institute his claim to be Grand Tutor. Such a task entails a loss of innocence comparable in kind (although far more extensive in its implications for humanity) to those under-taken by his predecessors in Barth's canon; in *Giles Goat-Boy*, the initiation into complexity assumes a mythical overlay, as the hero passes from his exotic birth to his revelation of purpose in the womb of WESCAC (in whose mechan-ical interior he and Anastasia, a student who serves as Female Principle, come together); to a series of "assignments" through which he must prove his worth; to his role as lawgiver and deposer of the false prophet, Harold Bray; and finally, to his sacrificial death for the sake of mankind.

Giles's career invokes Lord Raglan's systematic program for the stages of the hero's life, and yet the reader is irresistibly drawn to make correlations between the novel's allegorical personalities and events, and counterparts in journalistic reality. East and West Campus are barely fictional versions of Russia and the United States, with the H-bomb, in the form of WESCAC, the source of their power struggle. John F. Kennedy, Nikita Khruschev, Joseph McCarthy, Albert Einstein, and other contemporary world figures populate the novel, as do such ancient luminaries as Moses, Socrates, and Christ Himself (Enos Enoch, accompanied by Twelve Trustees). These tex-tures give *Giles Goat-Boy* the authority of sociopolitical history, but as is the case in *The Sot-Weed Factor*, Barth's penchant for discovering his own artifice casts a thick shadow of unreliability over the proceedings. For example, the reader must share in the doubts over Giles's legitimacy, both filial and messianic: not only do many people fail to accept his Grand Tutorhood (he predicts betrayal by the masses, who will drive him out on a rusty bicycle to his death on Founder's Hill), but also he himself is never completely certain that his words have not been programmed into him by WESCAC. The document itself—the pages before the reader—brought to "J. B." by Giles's son, is framed by disclaimers, editorial commentaries, footnotes, and postscripts, so that, finally, the "true text" is indistinguishable from the apocrypha. Moreover, Barth's liberal infusion of verse, puns, allusions, and stylistic entertainments strains the heroic conventions which he has assembled from a great variety of literary and mythic sources. In short, the quality of revelation as espoused by Gilesianism is consistently affected by the doubt and self-effacement implied in the structure of the narrative.

Despite Barth's typical supply of structural equivocations, *Giles Goat-Boy* is his most ambitious attempt to recognize correspondences between factual and fictional accounts, between politics and mythology, between public and personal history. If the hero's quest leads him into a world of complexity, there is at least, by virtue of these correspondences, the promise of insight. Under Burlingame's direction in *The Sot-Weed Factor*, the reader learns that the human personality, correctly apprehended, is a compendium of various, even contradictory, selves; in *Giles Goat-Boy*, this lesson is applied to the whole history of human learning and progress. Only when Giles accepts the all-encompassing nature of truth—PASS ALL and FAIL ALL are inextricably connected, not separable opposites but parts of a mystical oneness—does he mature into effectiveness. His passage through experience will include failure, but failure will guarantee growth, itself evidence of passage. Giles is a condenser in whom worldly paradoxes and dichotomies—knowledge and instinct, asceticism and responsibility, Spielman and Eirkopf, West and East Campus, and all other mutually resistive characters and systems of thought—manage a kind of synthesis. Keeping in mind that Giles's story originates from a fundamental willingness to accept his humanity over his "goathood," one comes to appreciate that, although the novel is a satirical fantasy, it is inspired by the same receptivity to experience and the same optimistic energy in the face of desperate circumstances that are exalted by the tradition of quest literature.

The image of Giles and Anastasia united in WESCAC is the philosophical center of the novel; at this climactic moment, flesh is integrated with spirit, animal with human, and scientific hardware with "meaty tubes," all in the service of the improvement of the race. The gospel of *Giles Goat-Boy* is that the very impulse to enter the labyrinth is an affirmation, however unlikely the hero's chances against the beasts and devils (such as Stoker, the gloomy custodian of the power station) who reside within. Giles's victory is a transcendence of categories, a faith in the unity of the universe, and that revelation is enough to overcome the lack of appreciation by the undergraduates. No obstacle or imposture of the dozens which antagonize the hero obscures the meeting of goat-boy with computer; the circuitry of myth remains intact, even in this age of broken atoms.

"When my mythoplastic razors were sharply honed, it was unparalleled sport to lay about with them, to have at reality." So proclaimed Jake Horner in *The End of the Road* while praising articulation as his nearest equivalent to a personal absolute. The narrative impulse is the principal source of faith for Barth's array of protagonists, insofar as faith is possible in an undeniably relativistic environment. In *LETTERS*, he allows those characters a fuller opportunity to engage in an authorial perspective. *LETTERS* solidifies Barth's associations with Modernists such as James Joyce and Samuel Beckett; here Barth takes license not only with established literary forms—specifically, the epistolary novel—but also with his private literary past, as he nonchalantly pays visits and respects to old fictional personalities. Because *LETTERS*, by its very form, intensifies one's awareness of the novel as a fabricated document (and, for that matter, of characters as collections of sentences), it is Barth's most transparently metafictional work; as the novel's subtitle unabashedly declares, this is "an old time epistolary novel by seven fictitious drolls and dreamers each of which imagines himself actual." *LETTERS* breaks down into seven parts, one for each letter of the title, and covers seven months of letter-writing. Place the first letter of each of the eighty-eight epistles in *LETTERS* on a calendar so that it corresponds with its date of composition, and the title of the novel will appear; like *Ulysses* (1922), *LETTERS* testifies to the diligence, if not to the overindulgence, of the craftsman.

Among these letter-writers are a group recycled from previous works as well as two figures, Germaine Pitt (Lady Amherst) and the Author, newly created for this book. In spite of Barth's assertions to the contrary, an appreciation of these characters is rather heavily dependent on a familiarity with their pre-*LETTERS* biographies: Todd Andrews emerges from *The Floating Opera* as an elderly lawyer who writes to his dead father and is drawn to incest while enjoying one last cruise on Chesapeake Bay; Jacob Horner remains at the Remobilization Farm to which he had resigned himself at the conclusion of *The End of the Road*, and where his latest Information Therapy demands that he write to himself in an elaborate reconstitution of the past; Ambrose Mensch, the now-mature artist out of "Lost in the Funhouse," directs his correspondences to the anonymous "Yours Truly" whose message he found in a bottle years earlier, and constructs his life, including an affair with Germaine Pitt, in accordance with Lord Raglan's prescription for the hero. The reader also meets descendants of previous creations: Andrew Burlingame Cook VI busily attempts to shape the nation's destiny in a Second American Revolution, and Jerome Bonaparte Bray, a mad rival to Barth himself who may be a gigantic insect, seeks to program a computer-assisted novel, *Numbers*, to compete with the authority of the one that treated him so shabbily.

The third level of writers in *LETTERS* includes the two who have no prior existence in Barth's works: Germaine Pitt, a colorful widow who had been the friend of James Joyce, H. G. Wells, Aldous Huxley, and other literary notables, anxiously campaigns as Acting Provost to ensure the prestige of her college against the administrative dilutions and hucksterism of one John Schott; the Author enters the novel as Pitt's own alternative candidate for an honorary doctorate (which Schott proposes to give to the dubious activist, State Laureate A. B. Cook VI), and he writes to everyone else in the vicinity of *LETTERS*.

The most consistent theme tying the letters and authors together is the conflict between restriction and freedom. The setting is the volatile America of the 1960's, when sexual, moral, political, and even academic norms underwent the most serious reevaluation in American history. Obviously, Barth's creative history is the most evident aspect of this theme, and the repetitions and echoes among his novels and within *LETTERS* seduce the reader into joining his search for pattern in the flux of human affairs. The ambiguous nature of history itself has also been one of his most durable themes—one recalls a chapter in *The Sot-Weed Factor* which examined the question of whether history is "a Progress, a Drama, a Retrogression, a Cycle, an Undulation, a Vortex, a Right- or Left-Handed Spiral, a Mere Continuum, or What Have You"—and the suggestion here is that any sort of orthodoxy can be revealed, especially in times of social crisis, as fictional. Student protests against the Establishment are replicated in the antagonism between characters and an established text; the societal disruptions in the novel disrupt and contaminate the narrative.

In contrast to Samuel Richardson's definitive use of the epistolary form, *LETTERS* is populated by characters who are more than vaguely aware of their unreality, and therefore of the need to bargain with Barth for personal status and support. When the Author intrudes as a character, no convention is above suspicion; although he describes himself as turning away from the "fabulous irreal" toward "a détente with the realistic tradition," if this novel is the result, it is a severely qualified détente, indeed. Perhaps the structural "confusion" of the novel explains the smugness of Reg Prinz, an avant-garde filmmaker who wants to create a version of all of Barth's books in a medium which he feels to be superior and more up-to-date. What had been a playful interest in the relationships between creative media in *Lost in the Funhouse* has escalated in *LETTERS* into a battle for aesthetic dominance between the word-hating Prinz and the word-mongering Barth. (That Prinz is a prisoner of the novel, of course, enables Barth to sway the outcome of this battle, at least temporarily.)

LETTERS, like history itself, concludes in blood and ambiguity; one suspects that Barth means to undergo a catharsis of the books and characters that have obsessed him and that continue to infiltrate his creative consciousness. It is testimony to Barth's ability to elicit admiration for his craft that the reader does not leave *LETTERS*—or, for that matter, most of his fictions—with a sense of defeat. The keynote of his literary career is exuberance; if nihilism and existential gloom have been his thematic preoccupations, their potentially numbing effects are undercut by Barth's cleverness, his stylistic ingenuity, and his campaign for the rewards of narrative.

Barth's *Sabbatical* continues to bend philosophy into escapade. Subtitled "A Romance," *Sabbatical* is rather a postmodernization of romance: all the well-established Barthian formal intrigues, ruminative digressions, plot coincidences (the married pair of main characters, in the same vein as *The Sot-Weed Factor*, are both twins), and other examples of literary self-consciousness complicate the vacation cruise of Fenwick Scott Key Turner, a former CIA agent and a contemporary novelist, and his wife, Susan, herself an established academic and critic. The nine-month sea journey—a frequent theme for Barth—leads to the birth of the novel itself, in whose plot the narrating "parents" seek clues to some conspiratorial Agency "plot" against them. (Fenwick has written an exposé that makes his "life as voyage" a perilous journey indeed—even when on sabbatical.) So the creative couple prepare, nurture, take pride in, and exhaustively analyze their verbal offspring, while the real world blows into their story from the shore in another dizzying mixture of fact and fiction.

Yet, as readers have come to expect from Barth, the imagination is exalted above and beyond its moorings in the "real world," all the while calling attention to its own altitude. As Fenwick declares to his loving coauthor: "I won't have our story be unadulterated realism. Reality is wonderful; reality is dreadful; reality is what it is." The intensity, the scope, and the truth of reality are more appropriately the province of experimental technique.

The Tidewater Tales: A Novel is closely related to *Sabbatical*. Fenwick Scott Key Turner reappears in the guise of Franklin Key Talbott, and Carmen B. Seckler has become the main character Peter Sagamore's mother-in-law, Carla B. Silver. Following the theme of twins in *Sabbatical*, Peter's wife, Katherine, is eight and a half months pregnant with twins. In fact, much of the plot consists of Peter and Katherine sailing around in their sloop *Story* while waiting for Katherine to come to term.

The sloop's name is an obvious reference to both Peter's and Katherine's (and Barth's) profession. Peter is a writer, and Katherine is an oral history expert—a storyteller. The intricate narratives become a line of stories within stories, as Barth concentrates on capturing all of reality within his fictive form.

Barth has consistently affirmed a kind of faith in the saving graces of the fiction whose very tradition he has so vigorously transformed. It is Barth's privilege to be able to objectify and transcend the philosophical predicaments of his characters in those imaginative environments where arbitrariness gives way to intricacy, and frustration to delight.

Arthur M. Saltzman

Other major works
SHORT FICTION: *Lost in the Funhouse*, 1968.
NONFICTION: *The Friday Book: Essays and Other Nonfiction*, 1984.

Bibliography
Harris, Charles B. *Passionate Virtuosity: The Fiction of John Barth*. Urbana: University of Illinois Press, 1983. A study of Barth's first seven books—a deliberate cutoff, as Harris believes that *LETTERS* marked the end of a certain phase in Barth's development as a writer. Included are copious and detailed notes to each chapter as well as a bibliography of works about Barth and an index.

Morrell, David. *John Barth: An Introduction*. University Park: Pennsylvania State University Press, 1976. Morrell provides biographical information in addition to criticism of Barth's work. Although the bibliographical lists are somewhat dated, they are very detailed. Also includes an index.

Schulz, Max F. *The Muses of John Barth: Tradition and Metafiction from "Lost in the Funhouse" to "The Tidewater Tales."* Baltimore: The Johns Hopkins University Press, 1990. Schulz believes that Barth is one of the great modern novelists in the tradition of John Updike. Discusses the place of Barth's canon in Western literature and provides in-depth literary criticism. The annotations for each chapter are helpful in directing the reader for further research. Includes an index.

Waldmeir, Joseph J., ed. *Critical Essays on John Barth*. Boston: G. K. Hall, 1980. This book of essays includes general discussions about Barth's work in addition to pieces on individual novels. Contains an index, as well as references and notes for each essay.

Walkiewicz, E. P. *John Barth*. Boston: Twayne, 1986. Provides biographical information, a chronology of important personal and professional events in Barth's life, and criticism of Barth's work, but only a brief mention of *The Tidewater Tales*. Includes notes, references, primary and secondary bibliographies, and an index.

DONALD BARTHELME

Born: April 7, 1931; Philadelphia, Pennsylvania
Died: July 23, 1989; Houston, Texas

Principal long fiction

Snow White, 1967; *The Dead Father*, 1975; *Paradise*, 1986; *The King*, 1990.

Other literary forms

Donald Barthelme became known first as a short-story writer, perhaps because the third of his long works appeared only three years before his death, and the fourth was posthumous. For some commentators, as a result, Barthelme's name is still primarily associated with short stories—the more so because even his long fiction tends to be composed of the same fragments as his short. Barthelme was also the author of a children's book entitled *The Slightly Irregular Fire Engine: Or, The Hithering Thithering Djinn* (1971).

Achievements

Barthelme was one of the great innovators in fictional techniques of the post-World War II era of American literature. Drawing on the technical discoveries of the Anglo-American modernist authors (including T. S. Eliot, Gertrude Stein, James Joyce, and Samuel Beckett), he developed a type of fiction that was largely structured on principles other than plot and character, the building blocks of nineteenth century "realistic" fiction. His fragmentary, collagelike splicing of historical and literary references expresses a certain world-weariness as well as a sense that history does not advance. Nevertheless, the irony expressed by this style softens a bit in the later works.

In addition to winning the National Book Award for his children's book in 1972, Barthelme was the recipient of a Guggenheim fellowship (1966) and of the PEN/Faulkner Award for Fiction for *Sixty Stories* (1981), one of the two collections of selected stories to appear during his lifetime.

Biography

Donald Barthelme was born in Philadelphia, where his parents were students at the University of Pennsylvania. A few years later, the family moved to Houston, where his father became a professor of architecture at the University of Houston. In high school, Barthelme wrote for both the school newspaper and the school literary magazine. In 1949, he entered the University of Houston, majoring in journalism. During his sophomore year (1950-1951), he was the editor of the college newspaper, the *Cougar*. During this year he also worked as a reporter for the *Houston Post*.

In 1953, Barthelme was drafted into the U.S. Army, arriving in Korea the day the truce was signed, at which point he became the editor of an army newspaper. Upon his return to the United States, he once again became a reporter for the *Houston Post* and returned to the University of Houston, where he worked as a speechwriter for the university president and attended classes in philosophy. Although he attended classes as late as 1957, he ultimately left without taking a degree. When he was thirty, he became the director of Houston's Contemporary Arts Museum.

In 1962, Barthelme moved to New York to become the managing editor of the arts and literature magazine *Location*. His first published story appeared in 1961; his first story for *The New Yorker* appeared in 1963. After that time, most of his works appeared first in this magazine, and eventually Barthelme's name became almost a synonym for an ironic, fragmentary style that characterized its pages in the late 1960's and early 1970's.

Barthelme taught for brief periods at Boston University, the State University of New York at Buffalo, and the College of the City of New York, at the last of which he was Distinguished Visiting Professor of English from 1974 to 1975. He was married twice. His only child was a daughter, Anne Katharine, born in 1964 to his first wife, Birgit. It was for Anne that he wrote *The Slightly Irregular Fire Engine*. At the time of his death from cancer on July 23, 1989, he was survived by his second wife, Marion.

Analysis

For the reader new to Donald Barthelme, the most productive way to approach his works is in terms of what they are not: looking at what they avoid doing, what they refuse to do, and what they suggest is not worth doing. Nineteenth century literature, and indeed most popular ("best-selling") literature of the twentieth century, is principally structured according to the two elements of plot and character. These Barthelme studiously avoids, especially in his earlier works, offering instead a collage of fragments whose coherence is usually only cumulative, rather than progressive. Some readers may find the early works emotionally cold as a result, given that their unity is to be found in the realm of the intellect rather than in that of feeling.

This style has resulted in the frequent classification of Barthelme as a "postmodernist" author, one of a generation of American writers who came to international prominence in the late 1960's and 1970's and who include Thomas Pynchon, John Barth, John Hawkes, William H. Gass, Ishmael Reed, and Kurt Vonnegut, Jr. This label indicates, among other things, that Barthelme's most immediate predecessors are the modernist authors of the early years of the century, such as T. S. Eliot, James Joyce, and Franz Kafka. Yet critics have split regarding whether Barthelme is doing fundamentally the same things as the earlier modernist authors or whether his works represent a significant development of their method.

Barthelme clearly diverges from the modernists in that he seems to lack their belief in the power of art to change the world; his most characteristic stance is ironic, self-deprecating, and anarchistic. Since this ironic posture is productive more of silence than of talk, or at best produces parodic talk, it is not surprising that Barthelme began his career with shorter pieces rather than longer. Nor does it seem coincidental that the novels *Paradise* and *The King* were produced in the last years of his life, by which point his short stories had become slightly less frenetic in pace.

Barthelme's longer works seem to divide naturally into two pairs. The earlier two are dense reworkings of (respectively) a fairy tale and a myth. The second pair are more leisurely, the one involving autobiographical elements, the other making a social point. Barthelme's first longer work, *Snow White*, is reasonably easy to follow, largely by virtue of the clarity with which the author indicates to the reader at all points what it is that he is doing—or rather, what he is avoiding, namely the fairy tale evoked by the work's title. Every reader knows the characters of this fairy tale; in fact, all of them have their equivalents in the characters of Barthelme's version, along with several others unaccounted for in the original. In Barthelme's version of the story, Snow White is twenty-two, lives with seven men with whom she regularly has unsatisfying sex in the shower, and seems to have confused herself with Rapunzel from another fairy story, as she continually sits at her window with her hair hanging out. Her dwarfs have modern names such as Bill (the leader), Clem, Edward, and Dan, and they suffer from a series of ailments, of which the most important seems to be that Bill no longer wishes to be touched. During the day the seven men work in a Chinese baby-food factory.

The closest thing this retelling of the myth has to a prince is a man named Paul, who does not seem to want to fulfill his role of prince. Avoiding Snow White, he spends time in a monastery in Nevada, goes to Spain, and joins the Thelemite order of monks. Ultimately he ends up near Snow White, but only as a Peeping Tom, armed with binoculars, in a bunker before her house. Barthelme's version of the wicked queen is named Jane; she writes poison-pen letters and ultimately makes Snow White a poisoned drink. Paul drinks it instead, and he dies.

The underlying point of the contrast generated by these modernized versions of the fairy-tale characters is clearly that which was the point of Joyce's version of *Ulysses* (1922), namely that there are no more heroes today. This in fact is the crux of the personality problems both of Paul, who does not want to act like a prince though he is one, and Snow White, who is unsure about the nature of her role as Snow White: she continues to long for a prince but at the same time feels it necessary to undertake the writing of a lengthy (pornographic) poem that constitutes her attempt to "find herself."

The Dead Father, Barthelme's second long work, may be seen in formal terms as the author's overt homage to the fictions of the Anglo-American modernists, most notably Stein, Joyce, and Beckett. Certain of its sections appear to be direct appropriations of the formal innovations of Joyce's *Ulysses*. The result is a complex overlayering of techniques that seems as much about literary history as about any more objective subject matter. The text presupposed by this novel is that of the Greek story of Oedipus, and of Sigmund Freud's treatment of it. Freud's version insists on the potentially lethal effects of an overbearing father and suggests that sons must symbolically kill their fathers to attain independence. Without an understanding of the association of father with threat, the plot of this novel can make little sense.

Nineteen men are pulling the Dead Father—who in fact is not really dead until the end, and perhaps not even then—across the countryside by a cable. The Father is huge, like Joyce's Humphrey C. Earwicker from *Finnegans Wake* (1939), covering a great expanse of countryside. There are four children, named Thomas, Edmund, Emma, and Julie, who accompany the Father on his journey to his grave. Along the way his children cut off his leg and his testicles and demand his sword. This does not stop the Dead Father's sexual desires; one of the objectionable aspects of the old man is clearly the fact that he has not ceased to function as a male. An encounter with a tribe known as the Wends, who explain that they have dispensed with fathers entirely, develops the background situation.

The plot is discernible only in flashes through the dense thicket of fragmentary conversations and monologues. The narration of the journey is constantly being interrupted by textual digressions. One of the most developed of these is a thirty-page "Manual for Sons" that the children find and that is reprinted in its entirety in the text. The complexity of this work is undeniable. It differs from *Snow White* in that the underlying mood does not seem to be that of alienation: the power of the Father is too great. Yet it may be that the use of so many modernist techniques splits the technical veneer of the book too deeply from the deeper emotional issues it raises.

Barthelme's third long work, *Paradise*, comes the closest of the four to being a traditional novel. It is set in a recognizable place and time (Philadelphia and New York in the last quarter of the century) and uses the author's standard plot fragmentation to express the state of mind of its protagonist, an architect named Simon, who is going through a sort of midlife crisis. Simon has taken in three women, with whom he sleeps in turn; this arrangement solves none of his problems, which have to do with his previous marriage, his child by that marriage, his other affairs, and the drying up of his architectural inspiration. A number of chapters are set in the form of questions and answers, presumably between Simon and his analyst.

In this work Barthelme draws on his knowledge of the Philadelphia architectural scene (especially the works of Louis Kahn) and seems to be expressing some of his own reactions to aging in the personality of the protagonist. This is certainly the easiest of the four novels for most readers to like.

Barthelme's final long work, *The King*, once again returns to a literary prototype, this time the Arthurian romances. Like the characters in *Snow White*, Barthelme's Arthur, Guinevere, Lancelot, and knights are twentieth century characters; unlike the earlier ones, they are particular public personages, identified with the King and Queen of England during World War II. (At the same time, their language and exploits situate them in the Celtic legends, or at least the Renaissance retelling of these by Sir Thomas Malory.) Barthelme is exploiting his usual anachronistic confusion of times here, yet his purpose in this work seems not to be merely that of comedy. While readers can be distanced from the categories of "friends" and "enemies" that the characters use in their aspect as figures in Arthurian romance, it is more difficult to be this distanced from a conflict still as much a part of contemporary culture as World War II. Barthelme's point seems to be that carnage is carnage and war war, and that from the point of view of a future generation even twentieth century people's moral certainty regarding this more recent conflict will seem as irrelevant and incomprehensible as that of Arthur and his knights.

Though Barthelme never abandons his concern with form over the course of his four novels, it seems clear that the second pair deals with issues that the average educated reader may find more accessible than those treated in the first two. Moving from the textual ironies of the first and second to the more measured plotting of the third and fourth, Barthelme's novels show signs of a gradual emotional warming process for which many readers may be thankful.

Bruce E. Fleming

Other major works

SHORT STORIES: *Come Back, Dr. Caligari*, 1964; *Unspeakable Practices, Unnatural Acts*, 1968; *City Life*, 1970; *Sadness*, 1972; *Amateurs*, 1976; *Great Days*, 1979; *Sixty Stories*, 1981; *Overnight to Many Distant Cities*, 1983; *Forty Stories*, 1987.

NONFICTION: *Guilty Pleasures*, 1974.

CHILDREN'S LITERATURE: *The Slightly Irregular Fire Engine: Or, The Hithering Thithering Djinn*, 1971.

Bibliography

Couturier, Maurice, and Regis Durand. *Donald Barthelme*. London: Methuen, 1982. A brief (80-page) but illuminating consideration of the use of language in Barthelme's fiction, with an eye to situating this use among that of other postmodern authors. Specific works are considered only in fragmentary excerpts.

Gordon, Lois. *Donald Barthelme*. Boston: Twayne, 1981. The most accessible and complete overview of Barthelme's fiction up to 1981. Its 223 pages begin with a biographical sketch and, besides analyses of the first two novels and most of the short-story collections, include a selected bibliography.

Klinkowitz, Jerome. "Donald Barthelme." In *The New Fiction: Interviews with Innovative American Writers*, edited by Joe David Bellamy. Urbana: University of Illinois Press, 1974. One of the most informative, standard sources for biographical information regarding Barthelme's life.

Molesworth, Charles. *Donald Barthelme's Fiction: The Ironist Saved from Drowning*. Columbia: University of Missouri Press, 1982. A pamphlet-length (89-page) book that sets out to offer an evaluative assessment of Barthelme's fiction, including (briefly) the novels, by offering a number of well-founded generalizations about his themes and methods of treatment.

Stengel, Wayne B. *The Shape of Art in the Short Stories of Donald Barthelme*. Baton Rouge: Louisiana State University Press, 1985. This longer (227-page) scholarly work is a readable consideration of Barthelme's short stories, examined under typal rubrics. Despite the lack of overt consideration of the novels, the work is useful in situating the longer works in their larger context.

H. E. BATES

Born: Rushden, England; May 16, 1905
Died: Canterbury, England; January 29, 1974

Principal long fiction

The Two Sisters, 1926; *Catherine Foster*, 1929; *Charlotte's Row*, 1931; *The Fallow Land*, 1932; *The Poacher*, 1935; *A House of Women*, 1936; *Spella Ho*, 1938; *Fair Stood the Wind for France*, 1944; *The Cruise of the Breadwinner*, 1946; *The Purple Plain*, 1947; *Dear Life*, 1949; *The Jacaranda Tree*, 1949; *The Scarlet Sword*, 1950; *Love for Lydia*, 1952; *The Feast of July*, 1954; *The Nature of Love: Three Short Novels*, 1954; *The Sleepless Moon*, 1956; *Death of a Huntsman: Four Short Novels*, 1957; *The Darling Buds of May*, 1958; *A Breath of French Air*, 1959; *An Aspidistra in Babylon: Four Novellas*, 1960; *When the Green Woods Laugh*, 1960; *The Day of the Tortoise*, 1961; *A Crown of Wild Myrtle*, 1962; *The Golden Oriole: Five Novellas*, 1962; *Oh! To Be in England*, 1963; *A Moment in Time*, 1964; *The Distant Horns of Summer*, 1967; *A Little of What You Fancy*, 1970; *The Triple Echo*, 1970.

Other literary forms

H. E. Bates published approximately four hundred short stories in magazines, newspapers, special editions and collections; in fact, he is probably better known as a short-story writer than as a novelist. Many of his more successful efforts were long stories, and so it is natural that he eventually turned to the novella as a favorite medium. Works in this form were published most often in collections, occasionally as independent works, as with *The Cruise of the Breadwinner* (1946) and *The Triple Echo* (1970). His first published work was a one-act play, *The Last Bread* (1926), and throughout his career he aspired to write for the stage, though with little success. *The Day of Glory* had a short run in 1945. A major portion of Bates's nonfiction works consist of essays on nature and country life. In this form, he excelled, bringing to his subject a deep knowledge and understanding based on a lifetime of country living. In addition, he produced three volumes of children's books, a memoir of his mentor Edward Garnett, and a highly regarded though unscholarly study entitled *The Modern Short Story: A Critical Survey* (1941). His autobiography is in three volumes: *The Vanished World* (1969); *The Blossoming World* (1971); and *The World in Ripeness* (1972).

Achievements

From the publication of *The Two Sisters* in 1926 until the outbreak of World War II, Bates was known principally to literati in Britain and America as an accomplished writer of stories and novels about rural England. In spite of good reviews in the highbrow and popular press and the enthusiastic recommendation of such critics and colleagues as David Garnett, Geoffrey West, Richard Church, Edward O'Brien, and Graham Greene, Bates's books sold moderately at best—not more than a few thousand copies each. The one exception to this general neglect came in 1938 with *Spella Ho*, which was well received in England and serialized in condensed form in *The Atlantic*. When war broke out, Bates was recruited for the RAF and given a commission unique in literary and military history: to write short stories about the air war and the men who fought it. The result was two best-sellers, *The Greatest People in the World* (1942) and *How Sleep the Brave* (1943); paperbound copies sold in the hundred of thousands. Following these, and coincident with a change of publishers, Bates produced a string of best-selling novels about the war: *Fair Stood the Wind for France*, *The Purple Plain*, *The Jacaranda Tree*, and *The Scarlet Sword*. To many critics of the time, it appeared that Bates had capitulated to popular taste, but shortly afterward he published his finest novel, *Love for Lydia*. During the 1950's, Bates's reputation assured substantial fees for his magazine stories, but his artistic reputation was more enhanced in this period by the novellas, a number of which recaptured rural life in prewar England. Versatility, however, was his new trademark, as the fiction embraced an ever-widening variety of characters, moods, and settings. In 1958, Bates returned to the ranks of the best-sellers with *The Darling Buds of May*, a farce about the uninhibited Larkin family and modern country life. Four additional Larkin novels followed and were equally successful commercially, but artistically inferior. At the time of his death, Bates had slipped into obscurity once again, yet popular interest remains high, stimulated in part by televised versions of *Love for Lydia*, *Fair Stood the Wind for France*, *A Moment in Time*, and several stories and novellas. Films have been made of *The Purple Plain*, *The Darling Buds of May*, *The Triple Echo*, and "Dulcima." The full measure of Bates's achievement is only beginning to be appreciated.

Biography

Herbert Ernest Bates was born on May 16, 1905, in Rushden, Northamptonshire, England's center of shoe and boot manufacture. His father, employed in the boot factories since boyhood, vowed that his children would never follow the same career; accordingly, H. E., Stanley, and Edna were reared in strict Methodist respectability and educated at local schools. In his early years Bates reacted strongly against the red brick ugliness of his home town, preferring country life with his maternal grandfather, George Lucas. Lucas was by far the most significant influence on Bates's life and fiction, instilling in him a passion for nature and a lifelong interest in rural affairs. A bright student, Bates won a scholarship to nearby Kettering Grammar School, where he performed indifferently until meeting Edmund Kirby, an English master lately returned from World War I. Inspired and encouraged by Kirby, Bates resolved to become a writer, and though he could have attended university, chose not to, electing instead to try newspaper writing and then clerking in a warehouse. There in his spare time he wrote a sprawling novel which Kirby advised him to burn. Undeterred, he tried a second, *The Two Sisters*, which traveled to ten publishers before being read by Jonathan Cape's great discoverer of new talent, Edward Garnett. Garnett recognized, where others had not, the sensitivity, feeling for character, and the gift for nature writing which are the hallmarks of all Bates's fiction.

Having no university connections and never comfortable in London, Bates stayed in Rushden and continued his literary apprenticeship under Garnett and Kirby. Even before this, he had discovered in the Continental masters, especially Anton Chekhov, Ivan Turgenev, Leo Tolstoy, and Guy de Maupassant, the models for his own short fiction. Other influences were Stephen Crane, Ernest Hemingway, Thomas Hardy, and W. H. Hudson. Reading constantly and writing regularly, Bates remained in Rushden until his marriage in 1931. Virtually all the stories and novels of this period are set in and around Rushden and neighboring Higham Ferrers, and much of this work is autobiographical.

In 1931, Bates married Marjorie (Madge) Cox, and the couple made their home in a former barn in Little Chart, Kent, where they remained until Bates's death. Madge has been called "the perfect wife" for Bates: "She made his writing possible by creating an island of stability and calm in which he could work." The move to Kent made no immediate impact on Bates's fiction, as he continued to write stories and novels set in Northamptonshire. By the outbreak of the war, he had exhausted his store of midlands material, but induction into the RAF gave him a whole new set of experiences and widened the scope of his fiction. The stories written for the RAF were first published under the pseudonym "Flying Officer X," but when their authorship became public, Bates's name became a household word. *Fair Stood the Wind for France* was inspired by snippets overheard in barracks and pubs about airmen downed over France. The three war novels which followed in quick succession derived from postings to Burma and India. Royalties from these books made the Bates family (by now grown to six with the birth of two girls and two boys) financially secure for the first time. Of nearly equal importance was an operation in 1947 that relieved Bates of a lifetime of acute intestinal pain.

Financial security and good health may have contributed to a burst of creativity, for *Love for Lydia* and a fine collection of stories, *Colonel Julian*, quickly followed. Inspiration for *Love for Lydia* came from Bates's early Northamptonshire experiences, but the stories show an expanded awareness of contemporary matters. In 1956, however, *The Sleepless Moon* was greeted with such savagery from reviewers that Bates vowed never to write another novel. Unlike Hardy, Bates broke his vow, but with the exception of *The Distant Horns of Summer*, he avoided serious long fiction, concentrating instead on humor (the Larkin novels) and popular materials. For aesthetic outlets, he turned to the short story and the novella. During the last two decades of his life, Bates remained a very private man. Never given to literary cliques nor arty socializing, he lived quietly in Little Chart, traveling extensively to France and Italy, but otherwise indulging his passion for gardening and family life, writing daily from early morning until noon. In 1966, he suffered a severe heart attack, followed by pneumonia, but recovered sufficiently to return to writing. His last works of importance are the three-volume autobiography and *The Triple Echo*, a novella. He died in 1974 in a Canterbury hospital of causes never revealed.

Analysis

H. E. Bates's primary concern as a writer was for the individual and the forces that threaten his or her happiness or fulfillment. He is not, however, a political, social, moral, or philosophical theorist; ideas as such play almost no part in Bates's fiction. Most of his protagonists are "ordinary" people— farmers, laborers, waitresses, housewives, children, pensioners, and young men of no particular education or accomplishments. Curiously, he approaches his material from two very different, almost contradictory, points of view. Many of the stories and a few of the lesser novels are essentially Romantic in outlook, glorifying nature, promoting individual achievement and freedom, assuming the essential goodness of people. On the other hand, many stories, novellas, and virtually all of the most successful novels are naturalistic in their portrayal of individuals at the mercy of forces they cannot understand or control, of nature as indifferent or even hostile, or of life itself as an almost Darwinian struggle. These two viewpoints coexist from the very beginning and contribute to Bates's great versatility. At the same time, the style is always clear and straightforward, uncomplicated by the experimental techniques of modern writing, the story line remaining strong and simple. These features of style and plot, together with the generally rural settings of his fiction, make Bates appear somewhat anachronistic among contemporaries whose themes and techniques are more "modern." Although Bates broke no new ground for fiction, he kept vigorous the historical trends of Continental and American story-writing, while in the novel he continued along lines suggested by Joseph Conrad and Thomas Hardy.

The most ambitious of Bates's early novels, *The Poacher*, is essentially a Bates family history in which the central figure, Luke Bishop, is modeled after Grandfather Lucas, while Bates and his father are seen in Eddie Vine and his father, Walter. Luke Bishop is born about 1860 to a shiftless, poaching, shoemaker father whose ways he follows until the father is killed by a gamekeeper and Luke marries. Like Grandfather Lucas, he takes a small farm on poor soil and wrests from it a living growing produce, grain, pigs, and chickens. Meanwhile, industry moves to Nenweald (Rushden), ending the freewheeling days of the cottage shoemakers, and brings with it the railroad, shops, and a new social tone of middle-class respectability. Bishop's wife, who becomes a school mistress, embodies these new values, while Bishop clings to the old, imparting them to Eddie. At sixty, Luke is convicted of poaching and jailed. After serving his jail sentence, Luke returns to Nenweald only to realize that he no longer belongs there or anywhere; his world has vanished in the steam of factories and railroad engines and in the smoke of World War I.

The Poacher is a powerful and moving personal history which seeks neither glamour nor pity for its central character but takes an unflinching look at the changes in England's farms and small towns between 1880 and 1920. Bates is at his best in the taut, swift scenes of poaching and in re-creating the inner life of his unimaginative, uncouth, and bewildered protagonist. Essentially passive, Bishop is unable to cope with the changes that swirl about him; he is a product of the nineteenth century, ignored by "progress" and changes in mores. Through Bishop, Bates engages the reader's sympathy for those trampled by such progress, but because the novel's point of view is restricted, Bishop's story is not fully integrated into its setting. At times the novel seems claustrophobic, at the edges of the reality it attempts to re-create. As social commentary it is less effective than as personal history; nevertheless, Luke Bishop is a vivid human presence, representing a vigorous but now departed way of life.

In the dramatic opening scene of *Spella Ho*, Bates's most successful prewar novel, Bruno Shadbolt watches his mother die of cold and consumption in an unheated hovel standing in the shadow of Spella Ho, a mansion of fifty-three chimneys. Throughout, the ugly, illiterate, determined, amoral Shadbolt and the aristocratic mansion are the poles between which the action moves. The story traces Shadbolt's slow and uneven rise from carter to wealthy industrialist. Along the way, he is aided by four women who change him in various ways—educating him, teaching him manners, altering his tastes—but who paradoxically leave untouched his essential nature, his monomaniacal drive to overcome poverty and anonymity. In his pursuit of wealth and self-fulfillment, Shadbolt represents nineteenth century industrialists at their worst, but Bates's novel is not a one-sided attack on Victorian greed and materialism. By raising himself, Shadbolt brings prosperity and change to Nenweald (Rushden), providing jobs, goods, housing, transportation, and services to people who eagerly desire them. If Shadbolt's factories exploit workers and despoil the countryside, they also transform the standard of living. In taking this evenhanded approach, Bates is not so much interested in being fair to England's captains of industry as he is in exploring a final crushing irony: that Shadbolt's legacy will be judged in the end as a monstrosity of ugliness and filth, while nothing of his personal triumph or his finer side will remain. Even Spella Ho, which he buys and restores, testifies not to his achievement but to that of refined aristocrats.

In addition to Shadbolt, there is a convincing cast of minor characters, individually rendered in detail. Once again, however, Bates fails to place his characters and action in a convincing context; for a novel concerned with social change, *Spella Ho* is curiously weak in period details. Between its opening in 1873 and its close in 1931, the novel changes little in scenery. The factories, gasworks, bus lines, and houses which Shadbolt builds are said to transform Nenweald utterly, but these changes are merely glimpsed. Once again, therefore, Bates provides a character study of great passion and interest, a fascinating grotesque utterly authentic in personality. In addition, there are vivid and arresting portraits of late Victorian individuals and types, but the characters move through a vague world on which their impact is somehow strangely slight.

For more than a decade after *Spella Ho*, Bates's novels occupied themselves with materials related to World War II. When Bates returned to his older material, therefore, it was with new eyes and understanding, fortified by advances in technique. *Love for Lydia* is unquestionably Bates's finest novel. On one level it parallels F. Scott Fitzgerald's *The Great Gatsby* (1925) as a hymn to the jazz age as lived in the small towns of England. The main characters are young people: Lydia Aspen, heir to a considerable fortune and aristocratic heritage; Richardson, young Bates thinly disguised; Tom and Nancy Holland, son and daughter of solid English farmers; Blackie Johnson, a mechanic and taxi driver; and Alec Sanderson, a small-town playboy of great charm but weak character. Lydia has been reared by her father, unusually sheltered and alone; when he dies, she moves to Evensford (Rushden, once again) to live with her aunts, who encourage her to gain experience of life. She and Richardson fall in love. There is a great deal of essentially innocent dancing and drinking, but Lydia's beauty is fatal: Sanderson, believing that Lydia has rejected him, accidentally drowns while drunk; Tom becomes her new love, only to die by accident or suicide of a shotgun blast. Richardson leaves to work in London, and for two years Lydia stumbles through a cloud of alcohol and dissipation. When Richardson returns, she is recovering in a sanatorium. Eventually they are reconciled.

The self-absorbed 1920's, with its burst of promiscuity and hedonism, is the perfect setting for this exploration of the valuable and permanent qualities desired in human relationships. Love of self, love of life, and romantic love compete, capsizing friendships, shattering values, upsetting traditional social arrangements until some balance can be restored. Self-absorbtion turns Lydia into a kind of Circe, destroying those who love her, and the quiet, uncertain Richardson into a morose, sarcastic loner. Healing comes when these two learn to give of themselves, as when Lydia can accept Blackie's friendship and Richardson finally puts aside his wounded pride to offer Lydia the affection she needs. Unlike the naturalistic novels of the 1930's, *Love for Lydia* is dominated by the interrelationships of its characters. Events are controlled not by unseen forces but by the emotions of the characters, who are responsible for their actions and yet are victims of their own weaknesses and strengths. People in this novel are also fully a part of the world around them: Evensford breathes with its own life of dirty alleys and greasy shops, while, as always in Bates's fiction, the countryside throbs with life. In an unusual reversal, winter is the time of rebirth—the season when Lydia first joins the world and the season in which, three years later, she and Richardson are reunited. Thus, Bates deals not so much with the malaise of the age as with personal choices and the tendency of people to allow the worst in themselves to rule the better.

The Distant Horns of Summer deals with a rather different theme—the nature of "reality." The novel centers on a young girl, Gilly, only seventeen, who has been hired by the parents of five-year-old James to look after the boy for the summer. James, like many children, lives most happily in a make-believe world in which his two friends are Mr. Pimm and Mr. Monday, two elderly men who in James's imagination treat him as a grown-up. Gilly takes the job in part to escape a man with whom she had fallen in love while working in a shop, only to fall in love with a tourist calling himself Ainsworth. He betrays her, of course, and when she tries to locate him, she finds that he, in a sense, does not exist, since she calls him by his assumed name. At the same time, James wanders off and loses himself literally and figuratively in his own world. When Gilly reports him missing, the police concern themselves more with the imaginary Pimm and Monday than with the real boy; a Miss Philpot, slightly dotty and never entirely sober, constructs her own version of events and concludes that Gilly is a nymphomaniac. Even when James is found, the confusions are unresolved.

Bates's exploration of reality has none of the philosophical seriousness of Samuel Beckett's novels; as always, it is with the particular individuals and experiences that he is concerned. Thus, much of the novel is told through the eyes of young James, whose childish confusions about what is "true" and what is not are entirely natural; but James, like children generally, knows quite well what is make-believe and what is not. Thus, he resents Ainsworth's unconvincing attempts to talk about Mr. Pimm and Mr. Monday, just as he is deeply hurt when he discovers that the camera Ainsworth lends him has no film. His pain at this discovery is as real as Gilly's upon learning that Ainsworth is an impostor whose affection for her is merely a pose. "Things are not as they seem" is not an abstract proposition but a concrete issue leading to betrayal and pain. Gilly, James, and Ainsworth are convincingly drawn, and even the minor figures are sharply etched and lifelike. As always, the style is bright and clear, the descriptive passages full of sharp detail, the dialogue natural and idomatic. Like the Kentish summer in which it is set, the novel radiates a mellow ripeness and melancholy which could be mistaken for romantic lassitude were it not that Bates infuses everything with intense vitality.

No discussion of Bates's fiction can afford to ignore his mastery of the short-novel form. With the short-story writer's gift of sketching character swiftly yet fully, and his ability to portray rural settings, Bates creates a number of memorable pieces focusing primarily on character. The earliest of these is *Seven Tales and Alexander* (1929), a romantic, idyllic re-creation of the days when young Bates and Grandfather Lucas would pick fruit to sell at the market. Closer to the novella form per se is *The Cruise of the Breadwinner*, a chilling study of bravery and coming to manhood during World War II. In the 1950's, Bates turned increasingly to this form, publishing two collections. From one of these comes "Dulcima," a curious story of sexual exploitation, centering on Dulcima, a heavy-legged, ungainly woman who attaches herself to a lonely old farmer, cheats him of his money, and taunts him with references to a boyfriend who does not exist. The vain and miserly farmer who thus allows himself to be deluded participates in his own destruction. *An Aspidistra in Babylon*, the title story of a collection published in 1960, reverses the plot of "Dulcima," portraying the seduction of a young girl by a dashing soldier. Told through the girl's eyes, the story centers on trust— hers for the soldier, the soldier's aunt's for her. She is both betrayer and betrayed, stealing from the old woman to finance an elopement with the soldier, who spends the money on another woman. The most unusual of Bates's novellas is among his last—*The Triple Echo*. Set during World War II, it features a young wife whose husband has been captured by the Japanese and a young soldier who eventually goes AWOL. The wife has been turned by farm drudgery into a man, dressing and acting like one. The soldier, to avoid detection by the military police, disguises himself as her sister. Sex roles reverse with the complexity of a Shakespearean comedy, but the story does more than explore androgeny, for beneath it runs an antiwar strain, a suggestion that such unnatural role reversals are part of the ruin of war.

The enduring qualities of Bates's fiction have little to do with the themes he explores, for he is not a modern "problem" writer. Rather, his fiction commands attention because of its style, its treatment of nature, and its explorations of individual character. Bates writes in the purest English, with a sparkling clarity and sure sense of rhythm. Except in the earliest works, his stories and novels are presented vividly, pictorially, directly; there is always an immediacy and sensuousness about his work. He has been compared favorably and accurately with the Impressionist painters, whose works he collected. Most especially, when he writes of nature, whether a bright summer day, a dreary wintry rain, or a brilliant early spring afternoon, his prose quivers with life and brilliant images. Occasionally, he tends toward lushness, but restraint, understatement, and quick, sure strokes are his characteristic virtues. His characters are similarly drawn: They spring from the page whole and solid. Seldom are they sophisticated or intellectual; more often they are inarticulate, emotional, bewildered. Even in the novels, characters seldom develop or reveal complex layers of themselves; rather, they struggle as best they can with what emotional and intellectual equipment they have. Perhaps for this reason, Bates is not an intellectual's writer; his tendency is to look past the beauties of style and the flashes of insight for something that is not there. What is present, however, is fiction of high quality, waiting to receive the attention it deserves.

Dean R. Baldwin

Other major works

SHORT FICTION: *Day's End and Other Stories*, 1928; *Seven Tales and Alexander*, 1929; *The Black Boxer*, 1932; *The Woman Who Had Imagination*, 1934; *Cut and Come Again*, 1935; *Something Short and Sweet*, 1937; *The Flying Goat*, 1939; *My Uncle Silas*, 1939; *The Beauty of the Dead*, 1940; *The Greatest People in the World*, 1942; *How Sleep the Brave*, 1943; *The Bride Comes to Evensford and Other Tales*, 1943; *Colonel Julian*, 1951; *The Daffodil Sky*, 1955; *Sugar for the Horse*, 1957; *The Watercress Girl*, 1959; *Now Sleeps the Crimson Petal*, 1961; *The Fabulous Mrs. V.*, 1964; *The Wedding Party*, 1965; *The Wild Cherry Tree*, 1968; *The Four Beauties*, 1968; *The Yellow Meads of Asphodel*, 1976.

PLAY: *The Last Bread*, 1926; *The Day of Glory*, 1945.

NONFICTION: *Through the Woods*, 1936; *Down the River*, 1937; *The Modern Short Story: A Critical Survey*, 1941; *In the Heart of the Country*, 1942; *Country Life*, 1943; *O More Than Happy Countryman*, 1943; *Edward Garnett*, 1950; *The Country of White Clover*, 1952; *The Face of England*, 1952; *The Vanished World*, 1969; *The Blossoming World*, 1971; *The World in Ripeness*, 1972.

Bibliography

Alderson, Frederick. "Bates Country: A Memoir of H. E. Bates." *London Magazine* 19 (July, 1979): 31-42. A personal account of Alderson's friendship with Bates, including their times together in the RAF during World War II. In his commentary on Bates's writings, Alderson calls Bates's style "impressionistic," using "visual images from the natural world."

Allen, Walter. *The Short Story in English*. Oxford, England: Clarendon Press, 1981. Part of this comprehensive commentary on short-story writers explores the short stories of Bates, whom Allen credits with "consist excellence." Contains extracts from Bates's work to illustrate his range of social types and scenes, with particular emphasis given to *The Cruise of the Breadwinner*.

Baldwin, Dean R. *H. E. Bates: A Literary Life*. Selinsgrove, Pa.: Susquehanna University Press, 1987. This most complete account of Bates's life and work to date defends the quality of Bates's writing, acknowledging that he is largely unknown to Americans. Cites two literary heritages evident in Bates's fiction: the romantic and the naturalistic, which are often in creative tension. A scholarly work that assesses both Bates's writing and biographical details, extended to include contemporary British literary life. Includes a bibliography.

Cavliero, Glen. *The Rural Tradition in the English Novel: 1900-1939.* London: Macmillan, 1977. The chapter entitled "The Enduring Land: H. E. Bates" concerns itself solely with Bates. Examines his craftsmanship and how his work developed according to the contemporary pressures and trends. Accords Bates a high place in his representation of country life. Contains much insight into Bates and his genre.

Vannatta, Dennis. *H. E. Bates.* Boston: Twayne, 1983. A fairly comprehensive study, useful because there is very little book-length scholarship on Bates despite his prolific writing that spanned nearly half a century. Analyzes Bates's fiction, and also includes some biographical information and a look at the literary and social currents that influenced Bates. In "H. E. Bates's Career in Retrospect," Vannatta points out Bates's shortcomings in long fiction. Chapter 8 concerns the later novellas, namely *The Triple Echo*, which Vannatta considers Bates's best. Includes a selected bibliography.

ANN BEATTIE

Born: Washington, D.C.; September 8, 1947

Principal long fiction
Chilly Scenes of Winter, 1976; *Falling in Place*, 1980; *Love Always*, 1985; *Picturing Will*, 1989.

Other literary forms
Beattie has published numerous short stories, including those anthologized in *Distortions* (1976) and a children's book entitled *Goblin Tales* (1975).

Achievements
Hailed by many as the spokesperson for her generation, Beattie has won numerous awards for her novels and short stories of vapid, upper-middle-class characters. Along with several scholastic honors, Beattie has also received a literary award from the American Academy and Institute of Arts and Letters (1980) and a Distinguished Alumnae award from American University (1985). She is a member of the International Association of Poets, Playwrights, Editors, Essayists, and Novelists (PEN).

Biography
The daughter of an administrator in the U.S. Department of Health, Education, and Welfare, James A. Beattie, and Charlotte (née Crosby) Beattie, Ann Beattie was born in Washington, D.C., in 1947 and grew up in its suburbs. As a child, she was encouraged to paint, read, and write. An avid scholar, she enrolled at American University in Washington, D.C., in 1966 and received her B.A. only three years later, in 1969. During this short tenure, she edited the university literary journal and was chosen by *Mademoiselle* magazine to be a guest editor in 1968. After her graduation, Beattie entered the M.A. program at the University of Connecticut as a graduate assistant to study eighteenth century literature. She received her degree in 1970 and began to work toward a doctorate; however, she quickly became frustrated and turned to writing short stories. It was then that—encouraged by her mentor, John O'Hara—she submitted several stories to small-press literary journals. After initial, moderate success with these publications, she finally had "A Platonic Relationship" published by *The New Yorker* in 1974. Later that same year, *The New Yorker* printed two more Beattie short stories, a signal of her arrival in the literary world.

At this, Beattie quit the university to concentrate on her writing. Since then, she has served on the faculties of several universities as a writing instructor. In 1972 she married David Gates, a fellow University of Connecticut student; they were divorced in 1980. She wed artist Lincoln Perry in 1988.

Analysis

Although Beattie's work has often been criticized as pointless and depressing, there is a method to her seeming madness. The stories and novels are not a mix of ennui and untapped angst but rather detailed examinations of the lives of several apparently different—but uniquely similar—people. Not one specific character is repeated in any story, but some, like the Vietnam veteran, appear in different versions and perform different functions, as plot catalysts, for example. At the same time, all Beattie's characters share the same vague feelings of discontent and lack of fulfillment, the knowledge that something is missing in their lives.

Initially, a Beattie character may seem feisty and self-assured, even defensive about his or her lack of enthusiasm. In Beattie's first novel, *Chilly Scenes of Winter*, one player remarks, "[Y]ou could be happy, too, Sam, if you hadn't had your eyes opened in the 60's." The promise of a better life that was given to these characters has been transmogrified into unhappiness and loneliness without relief. Beattie's novels are, accordingly, laced with irony.

Yet it is the acknowledgment of this transgression through the use of irony that provides a saving grace for the stories and novels. The main character of *Chilly Scenes of Winter* is granted all that he wishes; in the end, however, all that he wants is to escape his gratification. Charles, the protagonist, is in love with Laura, a married woman. His desire for her eventually dominates his life, so that he is unable to function without that desire or—as he would believe—without her.

Charles's obsession with Laura colors his relationship with his own family: his mother, Clara; her second husband, Pete; and Charles's sister, Susan. Even though his sister has accepted Pete, Charles refuses to acknowledge him as a replacement for their father, a man whose good qualities are magnified by the virtue of his death. Charles regards Pete as both a loser and a catalyst for Clara's chronic hypochondria. He claims that Pete refuses to accept life as it is and, instead, continues to make excuses for Clara's instability. The irony is that what Charles so clearly perceives as Pete's faults are really his own. Charles cannot—or will not—admit that he, too, fantasizes about the woman he loves and constructs absurd ideas about her that are founded on nothing but his own imagination. Charles will never be able to have a normal life with Laura, just as Pete will never be able to have one with Clara.

There is also the thought, which runs throughout the novel, that marriage itself is not a desirable norm. Sam, Clara's friend, comments, "It's nuts to get married," and indeed none of the relationships in *Chilly Scenes of Winter* seems to bode well for the participants. Pete and Clara's marriage is tainted by her mental illness, Jim and Laura's seems emptied by their lack of interest, and Charles and Laura's relationship is adulterous (and thus unable to be acknowledged).

The lack of sanction for Charles's love is typical of his whole existence. Nothing in his life lives up to his expectations, so he wanders pathetically, searching for both the ideal and the unreal. He is terrified of discovering a truth in his miserable existence, and this fear prevents him from completing his quest for love and a meaningful life. Charles is consumed by the thought that he will develop an "inoperable melanoma," even though there is no indication that he will; it is merely a phrase he has overheard in a hospital room. After Laura leaves Jim, Charles refuses to contact her; he will only drive past her house, hoping for a signal that will never be given.

In contrast to this world where the characters are forced to wander endlessly, searching for a direction, the players in *Falling in Place* are given a very clear signal when a significant event occurs. The story opens with John Knapp, his estranged wife Louise, their children Mary and John Joel, and John's mistress Nina. During the week, John lives with his mother, ostensibly to be close to his job in New York City but really to be far away from Louise and the children and closer to Nina. Naturally, this situation affects his children, and they become bitter and distanced not only from their father but also from their mother. Instead of swimming in a maelstrom of their own emotions, however, the characters in *Falling in Place* actually reach out to others and are influenced by them. John Joel's deviant friend Parker brings the action of the novel to a head: He provides John Joel with a handgun, and the latter proceeds to shoot his sister Mary in the side. When asked why he shot her, John Joel explains to his father, "She was a bitch."

Perhaps this phrase succinctly sums up Beattie's child characters in the story. Instead of behaving like real children, their circumstances force them to become miniature adults, faced with adult problems and desires. John Joel has an eating disorder, his friend Parker smokes a pack of cigarettes a day, and cold Mary dreams of sacrificing her virginity to singer Peter Frampton. They are a sad band of children, imitating the worst habits of their adult counterparts in the worst possible way. John Joel mouths adult words and defines his teenage sister in adult terms.

Finally, John and Louise divorce, freeing themselves and their children to pursue meaningful existences. None however, really believes that he or she will be able to attain this. At one point, John complains to Mary, "Don't you think I might already realize that my existence is a little silly?" Mary replies, "[T]hat's what *Vanity Fair* is like. Things just fall into place." John wonders if his daughter's advocacy of predestination seals her fate or if she simply cannot, or will not, try to imagine a future over which she has any control. Mary is not, however, the only member of her family who refuses to admit to a future. After Nina and John finally unite, Nina begs him to consider her wants: "Acres of land. Children. A big house. Try to *realize* what you love."

John only replies, "You're what I want."

John, then, refuses to real-ize, to make real, his existence with Nina and any sort of happiness they might have. He and his fellow characters are moderately pleased with their ties to the past and present; one boasts of a once-removed acquaintance with Linda Ronstadt. No one, however, will consider the effect of his or her present actions on the future. No one wants to be responsible for shaping a future; all merely accept whatever happens as a logical consequence of an illogical life.

In contrast, the characters in *Love Always* begin by rejoicing that they are "beating the system." Hildon and his ex-student friends run a slick journal named *Country Daze*, the success of which, Hildon maintains, is "proof positive that the whole country is coked-out." Because America, or at least the readership of *Country Daze*, has gone to rack and ruin, Hildon and associates decide that their behavior does not have to measure up to any modern-day standards. Hildon continues his long-standing affair with coworker and advice columnist Lucy, despite his marriage, and Lucy's fourteen-year-old niece, Nicole, is taking a brief vacation with her aunt from her role as a teenage junkie on a popular soap opera.

Nicole is yet another of Beattie's adult children, as are John Joel and Mary in *Falling in Place*. She serves as a foil for the adults in her world who are childishly hiding from the responsibilities and terrors of the outside world in a world of their own devising. Nicole's aunt, Lucy, writes under the name Cindi Coeur. Ironically, she does not wear her heart on her sleeve but rather flees from mature relationships. Lucy is equally unhappy about Nicole's adult behavior, but she does not know what to do about it.

Again, like the characters in *Falling in Place*, the people in *Love Always* identify themselves with rock stars and famous novelists. They seem unwilling or unable to grasp what is necessary for a meaningful adult relationship and, instead, spend much of their time hiding from commitment and bemoaning their circumstances. They never complain of their destiny because it does not really exist for them as a controllable entity. Like children, Beattie's characters are denied—or deny themselves—a voice in their future. As one character complains in *Chilly Scenes of Winter*, "Everybody's so pathetic. What is it? Is it just the end of the 60's?" No. Their pathos is derived from themselves and their unwillingness to take responsibility.

Passivity rather than activity seems to be the hallmark of Beattie's characters. While the world evolves around them they are befuddled and defeated by their inability to do anything. It is only through the actions of other, more noticeable people—celebrities—that Beattie's characters derive a sense of movement, change, and meaningful existence. Numerous prideful references to McDonald's, Janis Joplin, Lucille Ball, and other well-known places, people, and events are the only milestones that the characters use to mark their otherwise undistinguished lives. Perhaps it is because of their paralyzing fear of an unknown doom that the characters seem unable to commit themselves to what could be considered meaningful life-styles. Death and the fear of death pervade their thoughts, so their attraction to the well-known and forever famous can be viewed as their concept of immortality. It is as if frequent mention of a litany of immortals will bestow unending life on the prayer-givers. The question then becomes, is it a life anyone would want to live?

Jennifer L. Wyatt

Other major works

SHORT FICTION: *Distortions*, 1976; *Secrets and Surprises*, 1978; *Jacklighting*, 1981; *The Burning House*, 1982; *Where You'll Find Me*, 1986.

NONFICTION: *Alex Katz*, 1987.

CHILDREN'S LITERATURE: *Goblin Tales*, 1975.

Bibliography

Epstein, Joseph. "Ann Beattie and the Hippoisie." *Commentary* 75 (March, 1983): 54-58. Although Epstein shows no great admiration for Beattie or her work, this article does present a learned overview of her long fiction. Epstein, while reviling the grimness of the novels, points out with clarity Beattie's use of the "anti-plot" and concludes that what she really strives for are "states of feeling" rather than plot or character development.

Iyer, Pico. "The World According to Ann Beattie." *Partisan Review* 50, no. 4 (1983): 548-553. In contrast to some views that Beattie's characters have no depth and merely seem to float through her novels, Iyer argues that they are representations of a new and "peculiarly displaced generation." Iyer is sympathetic to Beattie's tough, frightened people, explaining their lack of commitment through a close examination of their fictive—and Beattie's real—environments, the America of the 1960's.

Murphy, Christina. *Ann Beattie*. Boston: Twayne, 1986. Despite what may be deemed the prematurity of this biography (Beattie is still young and active in her field), this book is very useful for the researcher. In addition to a chronology, notes, a selected bibliography, and an index, the discussion examines Beattie's works from *Distortions* to *Love Always* in a thorough and painstaking manner. The last chapter is devoted to an overview of Beattie's career as a "neorealist," one of a new group of authors.

Shapiro, Barbara. "Ann Beattie and the Culture of Narcissism." *Webster Review* 10 (1985): 86-101. A Freudian interpretation of Beattie's long works, this article closely examines the motivation of her characters as examples of the "culture of narcissism." Shapiro views them as in a stasis of fear over their impending doom and, thus, unable either to take a hand in shaping their destinies or to escape. Shapiro appreciates Beattie's depiction of the generation of the 1970's as a real, troubled generation.

SAMUEL BECKETT

Born: Foxrock, Ireland; April 13, 1906
Died: Paris, France; December 22, 1989

Principal long fiction

Murphy, 1938; *Molloy*, 1951 (English translation, 1955); *Malone meurt*, 1951 (*Malone Dies*, 1956); *L'Innommable*, 1953 (*The Unnamable*, 1958); *Watt*, 1953; *Comment c'est*, 1961 (*How It Is*, 1964); *Mercier et Camier*, 1970 (*Mercier and Camier*, 1974); *Le Dépeupleur*, 1971 (*The Lost Ones*, 1972); *Company*, 1980; *Mal vu mal dit*, 1981 (*Ill Seen Ill Said*, 1981); *Worstward Ho*, 1983.

Other literary forms

Samuel Beckett produced work in every literary genre. His first book, published in 1931, was the critical study *Proust*, and during the next fifteen years, Beckett published a number of essays and book reviews that have yet to be collected in book form. After struggling with an unpublished play entitled Eleuthéria in the late 1940's, he began publication of the series of plays that are as important as his novels to his present literary reputation. These include, notably, *En attendant Godot* (1952; *Waiting for Godot*, 1954), *Fin de partie* (1957; *Endgame*, 1958), *Krapp's Last Tape* (1958), *Happy Days* (1961), and many short pieces for the stage, including mimes. In addition to these works for the stage, he wrote scripts for television, such as *Eh Joe* (1967), scripts for radio, such as *All That Fall* (1957), and one film script, titled *Film* (1967). Most, but not all, of his many short stories are gathered in various collections, including *More Pricks Than Kicks* (1934), *Nouvelles et textes pour rien* (1955; *Stories and Texts for Nothing*, 1967), *No's Knife: Collected Shorter Prose 1947-1966* (1967), *First Love and Other Shorts* (1974), and *Pour finir encore et autres foirades* (1976; *Fizzles*, 1976). Beckett's poetry, most of it written early in his career for periodical publication, has been made available in *Poems in English* (1961) and *Collected Poems in English and French* (1977). Many of the various collections of his short pieces mix works of different literary genres, and Richard Seaver has edited a general sampling of Beckett works of all sorts in an anthology entitled *I Can't Go On, I'll Go On: A Selection from Samuel Beckett's Work* (1976).

Achievements

Beckett did not begin to write his most important works until he was forty years of age, and he had to wait some time beyond that for widespread recognition of his literary achievements. By the time he received the Nobel Prize in Literature in 1969, however, he had established a solid reputation as one of the most important and demanding authors of plays and novels in the twentieth century.

In the 1930's, when he began to write, Beckett seemed destined for the sort of footnote fame that has overtaken most of his English and Irish literary companions in that decade. His work appeared to be highly derivative of the avant-garde coterie associated with *Transition* magazine and especially of the novels of James Joyce, who as an elder Irish expatriate in Paris befriended and encouraged the young Beckett. By the time that he was forty years old and trying to salvage a literary career disrupted by World War II, Beckett's anonymity was such that his own French translation of his first novel *Murphy* had sold exactly six copies by the time he presented the same skeptical Paris publisher with another manuscript.

Nevertheless, it was at that time—the late 1940's—that Beckett blossomed as a writer. He withdrew into a voluntary solitude he himself refers to as "the siege in the room," began to compose his works in French rather than in English, and shed many of the mannerisms of his earlier work. The immediate result was the trilogy of novels that constitutes his most important achievement in prose fiction: *Molloy*, *Malone Dies*, and *The Unnamable*. This period also produced *Waiting for Godot*, and it was this play that first brought Beckett fame. *Waiting for Godot*, considered a formative influence on the Theater of the Absurd, stimulated the first serious critical treatments of Beckett's work. Although Beckett himself attached more importance to his novels than to his plays, it was not until the 1960's that critics went beyond his plays and began to bring his prose works under close scrutiny. Then, as now, most criticism of Beckett's fiction focused on the trilogy and the austere prose fiction in French that followed it.

In the years since then, Beckett's novels have risen in critical estimation from essentially eccentric if interesting experiments to exemplars of self-referential "postmodern" fiction commonly cited by literary theorists. Disagreements about the nature of particular works and skepticism about the bulk of commentary generated by very brief prose fragments have also inevitably accompanied this rather sudden enshrinement of a difficult and extremely idiosyncratic body of work. At present, however, even the most antagonistic analyses of Beckett's novels grant them a position of importance and influence in the development of prose fiction since World War II, and they also accept Samuel Beckett's stature as one of the most important novelists since his friend and Irish compatriot James Joyce.

Biography

Samuel Barclay Beckett was born in Foxrock, a modestly affluent suburb of Dublin, Ireland. He gave Good Friday, April 13, 1906, as his birthdate, but some convincing contrary evidence suggests that this particular day may have been chosen more for its significance than its accuracy. His parents, William and Mary (May) Jones Roe, belonged to the Protestant middle-class known as Anglo-Irish in Ireland. Beckett's childhood, in contrast to the unpleasant imagery of many of his novels, was a relatively cheery one of genteel entertainment at the family home, Cooldrinagh, private education at Portora Royal School in County Fermanagh, and greater success on the cricket green than in the classroom.

Beckett matriculated to Trinity College, Dublin, in 1923, and there he developed his first literary interests. He completed a curriculum in Romance languages at Trinity, and this led to an appointment as lecturer at the École Normale Superieure in Paris after graduation in 1927. In Paris, Beckett began to associate with the bohemian intellectual circles of French, English, and American writers for which the city was then famous. Beckett returned to Dublin for a brief time in 1930 for graduate work and a teaching position at Trinity, but within a few months, he returned to the Continent for travel throughout Germany and France and an extended reunion with his friends in Paris, including James Joyce. His first works of fiction, the stories in *More Pricks Than Kicks* (1934) and the novel *Murphy* (1938), are set in Dublin and its environs, but their intellectual preoccupations and bohemian antagonism toward middle-class complacency derive more from the environment of Paris than that of Ireland.

At the outbreak of World War II, Beckett was a permanent resident of Paris. As an Irish citizen, he could have returned home, but instead, he took refuge from the German occupation of Paris in the French countryside. There, he assisted the Resistance and began to write the novel *Watt* (1953), which marks a movement toward the style of his major fiction in its strangely dislocated senses of time and place. After the war, Beckett was decorated with the Croix de Guerre for his assistance to the French underground, and this award is generally cited as evidence of an essential humanism underlying the frequently misanthropic tenor of his novels. All evidence suggests, however, that the experience of the war increased Beckett's antagonism toward social affiliations and his skepticism about humanistic values.

Beckett returned to Paris after the war, and from 1946 to 1950, he retired into that "siege in the room," his most fertile period in a long literary career. By the time *Waiting for Godot* established his reputation, he had already developed the reclusive life-style which he maintained in his years of fame, despite persistent media attention. He was married to longtime companion Suzanne Deschevaux-Dumesnil in secrecy in London in 1961, and he refused to attend the award ceremony for his Nobel Prize in Literature in 1969. He died in Paris on December 22, 1989.

Analysis

It was a matter of some pleasure to Samuel Beckett that his work resists explication. His most important novels and plays are artfully constructed contemplations on their own form rather than commentaries on the familiar world of causal relationships and social contingencies. His most important novels abandon progressive narrative for the more difficult and subtle suggestiveness of haunting images, deliberate enigmas, and complexly ironic epigrams.

Although Beckett's work resists criticism, the author issued critical statements and congenially submitted to interviews with critics, managing to transform both sorts of critical occasions into intellectual performances as provocative, and occasionally as humorous, as his fiction. Two particular comments by Beckett, out of many stimulating ones, may serve as instructive introductions to the body of his prose works. In his first published book, *Proust*, Beckett wrote that artistic creation is essentially an excavatory process, comparable to an attempt to reach an ideal, impossibly minuscule, core of an onion. Beckett's novels relentlessly pursue this sort of process, stripping away layers of assumptions about the self and the world, peeling away conventional modes of thought to reach a pure essence of existence free of the inevitably distorting effects of intellect, logical structure, and analytical order. This image of the onion is a rich one because it communicates the sense in Beckett's work that this excavatory process is unending, that disposal of each mode of thought reveals yet another, even more resistant habit of mind. Beckett himself often spoke of his novels as a series, and it is this progressive penetration through one form of thought to another that marks the stages in the series.

Thirty years after *Proust*, Beckett submitted to an unusually provocative interview with Tom Driver that was published in Columbia University Forum in the summer of 1961. In this interview, he dwelled specifically on form. After contrasting the orderly form of most art to the intransigently chaotic nature of existence, he said: "The Form and the chaos remain separate. The latter is not reduced to the former. . . . [T]o find a form that accommodates the mess, that is the task of the artist now." Beckett's novels reveal three stages in this attempt to discover a literary form that will accommodate the chaotic nature of existence. In the first stage, represented by *Murphy* and *Watt*, the process is a destructive one of ridiculing literary convention by parody and satire to suggest an as yet undiscovered alternative form of expression. In the second stage, represented by the trilogy, the attempt to give voice to that alternative takes the form of the disordered and at times deliberately incoherent monologues of individual narrators. In the third stage, represented by *How It Is* and the subsequent short prose pieces, the process takes the form of presenting metaphorical worlds that accommodate their own chaos.

This last stage, especially, is marked by the unpleasant emphasis on miserable degradation and the recurring private images that have given Beckett an undeserved reputation for misanthropy and deliberate obscurity. These charges are effectively rebutted by his own stated sense of "the task of the artist now." Beckett's works do not provide relaxing reading experiences. They are designed to disorient, to dislocate, and to thwart intellectual complacency. The formidable difficulties they present to the reader, however, are essential records of the intellectual ambience of advanced mid-twentieth century thought.

Beckett's earliest fiction, the stories in *More Pricks Than Kicks*, described the passive resistance to social conformity and death under anesthesia of a protagonist named Belacqua (an allusion to Dante). Beckett's first novel, *Murphy*, presents the same resistance and senseless death in the story of Murphy, given the most common surname in Ireland. Murphy is the first of numerous Beckett protagonists who seek to relinquish all ties to their environment and their compulsion to make sense of it. The centerpiece of *Murphy* is an analysis of the discrete zones of his mind in the sixth chapter. The third and last of these zones is a darkness of selflessness in which mind itself is obviated. It is this zone beyond consciousness that most Beckett protagonists seek; it is their failure to reach it that creates the tension in most of Beckett's fiction.

Murphy is surrounded by representatives of two frames of reference that prevent his withdrawal from the world. The first is nationality, represented here by character-types such as the drunken Irish poet Austin Ticklepenny and monuments to national ideals such as the statue of Cuchulain in the Dublin General Post Office. The second frame of reference is erudition, represented here by a plethora of arcane references to astronomy, astrology, philosophy, and mathematics. Assaulted by these adjuncts of identity, Murphy remains unable to disengage himself fully from the world, to withdraw completely into the third zone of his mind.

The problem that Beckett confronts in *Murphy* is central to all of his novels: to define consciousness in a novel without the usual novelistic apparatus of recognizable environment, nationality, and psychology. The novel only approaches such a definition in the chapter on Murphy's mind and in the image of an eerily withdrawn character named Mr. Endon. Elsewhere, Beckett is able to suggest an alternative only by destructive means: by heaping scorn on things Irish, by deflating intellectual pretensions, and by parodying novelistic conventions. These forms of ridicule make *Murphy* Beckett's most humorous and accessible novel. The same reliance on ridicule, however, ensures that *Murphy* remains derivative of the very forms of thought and literature it intends to challenge.

Although it was not published until 1953, after *Molloy* and *Malone Dies*, *Watt* was written a decade earlier and properly belongs among Beckett's early novels. It is a transitional work, written in English, in which one can observe intimations of the central concerns of the trilogy of novels written in French.

Like Murphy, Watt is an alienated vagabond seeking succor from the complexities of existence. In the opening and closing sections of this four-part novel, Watt's world is a recognizably Irish one populated with middle-class characters with small social pretensions. In the central two sections, however,

Watt works as a servant on the surreal country estate of a Mr. Knott. *Watt* most resembles Beckett's later fiction in these central sections. In them, Watt ineffectually attempts to master simpler and simpler problems without the benefit of reliable contingencies of cause and effect or even the assurance of a reliable system of language. The structure of the novel is ultimately dislocated by the gradual revelation that the four parts are not in fact presented in chronological order and that they have been narrated by a character named Sam rather than by an omniscient narrator. Sam's account proves unreliable in particulars, thus completing the process by which the novel undermines any illusion of certainty concerning the interaction of the characters Watt ("What?") and Knott ("Not!").

Watt, like *Murphy*, relies on satire of literary precedents and disruption of novelistic conventions. There are allusions in the novel to the work of W. B. Yeats and James Joyce and to the poet Æ (George William Russell), to cite only the Irish precedents. The great disruption of novelistic conventions is effected by "Addenda" of unincorporated material at the end of the text and by pedantic annotations throughout the novel. Nevertheless, *Watt* does look forward to *Molloy* in its central sections, dominated by episodic problems such as the removal of Knott's slops and the attempt of the wretched Lynch family to have the ages of its living members total exactly one thousand. The full emergence of this sort of episodic narrative in Beckett's fiction, however, seems to have required the focus of attention on language itself (rather than on literary conventions) that was one important effect of his decision to begin to compose novels in French rather than English.

Mercier and Camier, although published in 1970, was written in French in 1946, soon after Beckett returned to Paris at the end of the war. Like *Watt*, it is best placed among Beckett's works by date of composition rather than publication. Written at the outset of the "siege in the room" that produced Beckett's major novels, it illuminates the process by which the style of the trilogy emerged from concentration on elements of composition rather than on the social concerns that dominate most conventional novels.

Mercier and Camier is an account of an aimless journey by two decrepit characters out of and back into a city that resembles Dublin. A witness-narrator announces his presence in the opening sentence, but remains otherwise inconspicuous. The descriptions of the two characters' generally enigmatic encounters with others, however, is periodically interrupted by subtly disported tabular synopses that call attention to the arbitrary features of the narrator's accounts. The novel is thus a shrewdly self-conscious narrative performance, with the emphasis falling on the telling rather than on the meaning of the tale.

The belated publication of *Mercier and Camier* was a welcome event because it represents what must have seemed to Beckett an unsatisfactory attempt to open the novel form to accommodate the "mess" he finds dominant in the world. His composition of the novel in French produced a spare prose style and calculated use of language that would prove essential to his later fiction. Like *Watt*, however, the novel retained a peripheral witness-narrator; this may have been one of the sources of Beckett's dissatisfaction with the novel, for immediately after it, he shifted to the monologue essential to the trilogy that followed.

Beckett's major accomplishment in prose fiction is the trilogy of novels begun with *Molloy*, written in French in 1947 and 1948. All three are narrative monologues, all seek to explain origins, and all expose various forms of self-knowledge as delusions. Thus, they approach that ideal core of the onion in their quest for explanations, and they assert the governing "mess" of incoherence, which continues to resist artificial if comforting intellectual fabrications.

In structure, *Molloy*, translated into English by Beckett in collaboration with Patrick Bowles, is the most complex work in the trilogy. The first part of the novel is the narrative of the derelict Molloy, who discovers himself in his mother's room and attempts unsuccessfully to reconstruct his arrival there. The second part is the narrative of the Catholic and bourgeois detective Jacques Moran, who has been commissioned by an authority named Youdi to write a report on Molloy. As Moran's report proceeds, he gradually begins to resemble Molloy. His narrative ends with the composition of the sentence with which it began, now exposed as pure falsehood.

Molloy and Moran are counterparts whose narratives expose the alternative fallacies, respectively, of inward and outward ways of organizing experience. Molloy's self-involved preoccupations, such as his chronic flatulence, function as counterparts of Moran's more social preoccupations, such as Catholic liturgy and his profession. Both are left in unresolved confrontation with the likelihood that the ways they have attempted to make sense of their origins and present circumstances are pure sham. The special brillance of *Molloy* is the manner in which this confrontation is brought about by the terms of each narrator's monologue. The prose style of the novel is dominated by hilarious deflations of momentary pretensions, ironic undercutting of reassuring truisms, and criticism of its own assertions. It is in this manner that *Molloy* manages to admit the "mess" Beckett seeks to accommodate in the novel form: its compelling and humorous narratives effectively expose the limits rather than the fruits of self-knowledge.

Malone Dies is the purest of the narrative performances of Beckett's storytellers. In it, a bedridden man awaits death in his room and tells stories to pass the time. His environment is limited to the room, the view from a window, and a meager inventory of possessions he periodically recounts with inconsistent results. Beyond these, he is limited to the world of his stories about a boy named Sapo, an old man named MacMann, an employee in an insane asylum named Lemuel, and others. All are apparently fictions based on different periods in Malone's own life. At the end of the novel, his narrative simply degenerates and ends inconclusively in brief phrases that may suggest death itself or simply the end of his willingness to pursue the stories further.

It is essential to the novel that Malone criticize his own stories, revise them, abandon them, and rehearse them once again. His predicament is that he knows the stories to be false in many respects, but he has no alternative approach to the truth of his own origins. Like Beckett, Malone is a compulsive composer of fictions who is perpetually dissatisfied with them. As a result, *Malone Dies* is one of the most completely self-critical and self-involved novels in the twentieth century stream of metafictions, or novels about the nature of the novel. It demonstrates, with bitter humor and relentless self-examination, the limits of fiction, the pleasure of fiction, and the lack of an acceptable substitute for fiction.

In *The Unnamable*, Beckett pursues the preoccupations of *Molloy* and *Malone Dies* to an extreme that puts formidable difficulties before even the most devoted reader of the modern novel. In *Molloy*, the focus was on two long narrative accounts; in *Malone Dies*, it narrowed to concentrate on briefer stories; and in *The Unnamable*, it shrinks further to probe the limits of language itself, of words and names. As the title suggests, these smaller units of literary discourse prove to be just as false and unreliable as those longer literary units had in Beckett's previous two novels. In *The Unnamable*, there is no character in the ordinary sense of the term. Instead, there are only bursts of language, at first organized into paragraphs, then only into continuous sentences, and finally into pages of a single sentence broken only by commas.

The premise of the novel is that a paralyzed and apparently androgynous creature suspended in a jar outside a Paris restaurant speaks of himself and versions of himself labeled with temporary names such as Mahood and Worm. As he speaks, however, he is diverted from the content of his speech by disgust with its elements, its words. The names of Murphy, Molloy, and Malone are all evoked with complete disgust at the complacent acceptance of language inherent in the creation of such literary characters. *The Unnamable* thus attempts to challenge assumptions of literary discourse by diverting attention from plot and character to phrase and word. It is tortuous reading because it calls into question the means by which any reading process proceeds.

The preoccupation with speaking in the novel leads naturally to a corollary preoccupation with silence, and *The Unnamable* ends with a paradoxical assertion of the equal impossibility of either ending or continuing. At this point, Beckett had exhausted the means by which he attempted to admit the "mess" into the form of the novels in his trilogy. He managed to proceed, to extend the series of his novels, by exploring the richness of metaphorical and generally horrific environments like that of the unnamable one suspended, weeping, in his jar.

Beckett's critics commonly refer to the series of prose fictions begun with *How It Is* as "post-trilogy prose." The term is useful because it draws a distinction between the methods of Beckett's works as well as their chronology. Even in the midst of the incoherence of *The Unnamable*, there were references to the familiar world, such as the fact that the narrator was located in Paris. In *How It Is* and the works that followed, however, the environment is an entirely metaphorical and distinctly surreal one. Without reference to a familiar world, these works are governed by an interior system of recurrent images and memories. *How It Is* marks the beginning of this final stage in the series of Beckett's works, and so its French title *Comment c'est* is an appropriate phonetic pun meaning both "how it is" and *commencer*, or "to begin."

In *How It Is*, the speaker, named Bom, is a creature crawling in darkness through endless mire, dragging with him a sack of canned provisions, and torturing and being tortured by other creatures with their indispensable can openers. His narrative takes the form of brief, unpunctuated fragments separated by spaces on the page. Each fragment is of a length that can be spoken aloud, as they ideally should be, and the style may be in part a product of Beckett's experience in the production of plays. There is a second character named Pim, against whom the narrator tends to define his own status. The novel, which many prefer to term a prose poem, is thus broken into three parts: before Pim, with Pim, and after Pim.

The Bom and Pim interaction is an excruciating account of misery in a nether world of darkness and slime. It is related entirely in retrospect, however, and the changing relationships of domination and subordination are less important than the manner in which the language of the fragments creates its own system of repetitions and alterations of phrases. *How It Is* dramatizes, in fact, how it *was* for Bom, and in place of clear references to the familiar world, it offers a verbal model for the mechanics of memory. This remains a consistent, if extraordinarily complex, extension of Beckett's attempt to accommodate the "mess" of chaos in the novel form. Its extremely calculated prose creates a sense of the consistent, but inexplicable and ultimately uninformative, impingement of the past on the present.

The Lost Ones is a representative example of Beckett's prose fiction immediately following *How It Is*. He composed many brief prose pieces in this period, abandoned most of them, and resurrected them for publication at the urging of enthusiastic friends. Most are published in collections of his short works. *The Lost Ones*, however, is a more sustained narrative performance (sixty-three pages in the American edition). It was abandoned in an incomplete form in 1966 but retrieved and supplemented with an effective conclusion in 1970. It has also gained greater attention than most of Beckett's works from this period because of an innovative stage adaptation by the Mabou Mines Company in New York City in 1973.

The Lost Ones is unique among Beckett's works because it focuses on a group rather than an individual. In fifteen unnumbered passages of prose, it describes the workings of a huge cylinder populated by male and female figures who maneuver throughout its various areas by means of ladders. The prose style is remarkably understated in comparison to the painful, if metaphorical, imagery of *How It Is*, and the primary action is the continual reorganization of this closed set of persons according to an entropic process of diminishing energies. Mathematical computation, a motif in many of Beckett's novels, is a primary feature in *The Lost Ones*. As language had in so many of Beckett's earlier novels, numerical calculations prove an inadequate means of organizing experience in this work, and the crucial final paragraph added in 1970 is a fatalistic exposure of the worthlessness of these computations as indications of the past, present, or future of this surreal environment. As in many of Beckett's later prose pieces, the metaphorical environment created by the prose is open to many interpretive referents. The text is subtly allusive—the French title, for example, evokes Lamartine—and the viability of literature as an effective indication of past, present, or future is among the possible subjects of this spare and immensely suggestive text.

Excepting *The Lost Ones* and other aborted works, nearly twenty years elapsed between the writing of *How It Is* and the next of Beckett's prose fictions to approach the novel in form if not in length. *Company* ended this relative silence, during which Beckett produced a variety of works in other genres. Like *How It Is* and the intervening works, *Company* presents a generally metaphorical environment and a consistent emphasis on the workings of memory. Unlike Beckett's other late works, however, it was composed in English and apparently generated out of contemplation of distinctly autobiographical images.

Company is a narrative by a figure immobilized on his back in darkness. Despite this surreal premise, it dwells on images of a familiar, suggestively Irish environment marked by features such as Connolly's store and the Ballyogan Road. It thus combines the astringency of Beckett's "post-trilogy prose" with the references to an identifiable world common in the trilogy. It is, however, far from a regression from experimental form or an abandonment of the attempt to accommodate the "mess" in a novel. Instead, it represents the fruit of Beckett's years of careful manipulation of a spare prose style in his second language. Like *How It Is*, *Company* concentrates on the inexplicable workings of memory. Unlike *How It Is*, the novel does so in a passive and restrained mixture of nostalgic and ironic images free of the vulgar and painful hostility of that earlier novel. In less flamboyant ways than Beckett's earlier works, *Company* also manages to underscore its own nature as an artificial, literary construction. Its governing metaphor of "company" manages to encompass both the memories surrounding the narrator and the meeting of author and reader of a literary text.

Company was followed by *Ill Seen Ill Said*, a series of paragraphs consisting primarily of sentence fragments. They describe a woman and her attempt to capture the details of her environment. The devotion to detail is such that vocabulary, rather than image, tends to capture attention, frequently because of intentional neologisms, interior rhymes, and sporadic echoes. It is more an evocation of a mood than a plotted novel, one that reveals the author, having rid himself of complacent use of language in earlier works, as a prose stylist with marked affinities to a poet. *Ill Seen Ill Said*, despite the disparagement of voice in its title, marks the emergence in Beckett's works of a devotion to pure sensation unmodulated by systems of logic or desire. It is in this respect that *Ill Seen Ill Said* is a necessary and inevitable extension of "the task of the artist now" addressed in a long series of novels. Rather than suggesting an alternative literary expression by destructive irony or subverting complacency by incoherent monologue, it attempts to present consciousness free of artificial order in a distinctly lyrical form of prose fiction.

In an early essay on the Irish poet Denis Devlin published in *Transition* in 1938, Beckett offered this dictum: "Art has always been this—pure interrogation, rhetorical question less the rhetoric." Like so many of his statements on other writers, this has a special relevance to Beckett's own literary career. Over a period of a half century, he produced fictions that relentlessly question assumptions of intellectual and literary order. He did so with a single-minded devotion to what he took to be "the task of the artist now" and so compiled an oeuvre that is unique in the twentieth century in its concentration on a central purpose and in its literary expression of the great philosophical preoccupations of its time. Beckett's work has been discussed by critics in reference to other innovative thinkers of the century as disparate as Albert Einstein, Sigmund Freud, and Jean-Paul Sartre. In addition to fueling the literary debates of his time, his work may be said to have created, in part, contemporary literary theories such as structuralism and deconstruction. Despite their formidable difficulties, then, Beckett's novels have an indisputable importance to anyone seriously interested in the intellectual climate of the twentieth century.

John P. Harrington

Other major works

SHORT FICTION: *More Pricks Than Kicks*, 1934; *Nouvelles et textes pour rien*, 1955; (*Stories and Texts for Nothing*, 1967); *No's Knife: Collected Shorter Prose 1947-1966*, 1967; *First Love and Other Shorts*, 1974; *Pour finir encore et autres foirades*, 1976 (*Fizzles*).

PLAYS: *En attendant Godot*, 1952 (*Waiting for Godot*, 1954); *Fin de partie: Suivi de Acte sans paroles*, 1957 (*Endgame: A Play in One Act; followed by Act Without Words: A Mime for One Player*, 1958); *All That Fall*, 1957 (radio play); *Krapp's Last Tape*, 1958; *Embers*, 1959 (radio play); *Act Without*

Words II, 1960 (one-act mime); *Happy Days*, 1961; *Words and Music*, 1962 (radio play); *Cascando*, 1963 (radio play); *Play*, 1963 (English translation, 1964); *Come and Go: Dramaticule*, 1965 (English translation, 1967); *Film*, 1965 (screenplay); *Eh Joe*, 1966 (teleplay; *Dis Joe*, 1967); *Not I*, 1972 (teleplay); *Tryst*, 1976 (teleplay); *That Time*, 1976; *Footfalls*, 1976; *Shades*, 1977 (teleplay); *A Piece of Monologue*, 1979; *Rockaby and Other Short Pieces*, 1981; *Quad*, 1981 (teleplay); *Rockaby*, 1981; *Ohio Impromptu*, 1981; *Catastrophe*, 1982; *Company*, 1983; *What Where*, 1983; *Collected Shorter Plays*, 1984.

POETRY: *Whoroscope*, 1930; *Echo's Bones and Other Precipitates*, 1935; *Poems in English*, 1961; *"Zone"* by Guillaume Apollinaire, 1972 (translation); *Collected Poems in English and French*, 1977.

NONFICTION: *Proust*, 1931.

ANTHOLOGY: *An Anthology of Mexican Poetry*, 1958 (translation).

MISCELLANEOUS: *I Can't Go On, I'll Go On: A Selection from Samuel Beckett's Work*, 1976 (Collection) (Richard Seaver, editor).

Bibliography

Brater, Enoch. *Beyond Minimalism: Beckett's Late Style in the Theater*. New York: Oxford University Press, 1987. Brater examines the style of eight of Beckett's last plays, including *Not I*, *What Where*, *Catastrophe*, and *Ohio Impromptu*. Brater claims that the seeds of these plays can be found in Beckett's first theatrical works, *Waiting for Godot* and *Endgame*. Includes a good bibliography.

Brienza, Susan D. *Samuel Beckett's New Worlds: Style in Metafiction*. Norman: University of Oklahoma Press, 1987. A study of twelve of Beckett's works of fiction written since 1958. Brienza compares the French versions of the works to the English versions to obtain clues to the meaning of Beckett's impenetrable prose. A book for advanced students of Beckett, yet written in a highly readable style.

Davis, Robin J., and Lance S. Butler, eds. *Make Sense Who May: Essays on Samuel Beckett's Later Works*. New York: Barnes & Noble Books, 1988. Contains fifteen essays culled from "Samuel Beckett at Eighty," a conference held in August, 1986, at Stirling University. The essays look at Beckett's work in the 1970's and 1980's in terms of poststructuralism and deconstruction. For advanced students.

Ellman, Richard. *Four Dubliners: Wilde, Yeats, Joyce, and Beckett*. New York: George Braziller, 1988. Examines the Irish roots in Beckett's plays and novels and their subsequent influence on Irish writing. A lively and interesting study of four Irish writers, suitable for all students.

Poutney, Rosemary. *Theatre of Shadows: Samuel Beckett's Drama, 1956-76*. Edited by Anne Skillion. New York: Barnes & Noble Books, 1988. This study of twenty years of Beckett's plays is rich in information. In the first part of the book, Poutney examines the structure of the plays, from *All That Fall* to *Footfalls*. In the second half, she traces the evolution of the works, from manuscript to finished stage play. A valuable book for all Beckett students.

APHRA BEHN

Born: England; July (?), 1640
Died: London, England; April 16, 1689

Principal long fiction

Love Letters Between a Nobleman and His Sister, 1683-1687 (3 volumes); *Agnes de Castro*, 1688; *The Fair Jilt: Or, The History of Prince Tarquin and Miranda*, 1688; *Oroonoko: Or, The History of the Royal Slave*, 1688; *The History of the Nun: Or, The Fair Vow-Breaker*, 1689; *The Lucky Mistake*, 1689; *The Nun: Or, The Perjured Beauty*, 1697; *The Adventure of the Black Lady*, 1698; *The Wandering Beauty*, 1698.

Other literary forms

As a truly professional writer, perhaps the first British female to have written for profit, Aphra Behn moved easily through the various literary genres and forms. Her plays include *The Forced Marriage: Or, The Jealous Bridegroom* (1670); *The Amorous Prince* (1671); *The Dutch Lover* (1673); *The Town Fop* (1676); *Abdelazar* (1676); *The Debauchee* (1677); *The Rover: Or, the Banished Cavalier*, I, II (1677, 1681); *Sir Patient Fancy* (1678); *The Roundheads: Or, The Good Old Cause* (1681); *The False Count* (1681); *The City Heiress: Or, Sir Timothy Treat-All* (1682); *The Lucky Chance* (1686); *The Emperor of the Moon* (1687); *The Widow Ranter* (1689); and *The Younger Brother* (1696).

Although she enjoyed only mild success as a poet, her verse was probably no better or worse than that of a large number of second-rank versifiers of the Restoration. Behn's best poetry can be found in the song "Love in fantastic triumph sate" (1677), from her tragedy of *Abdelazar*, and in a metrical "Paraphrase on Oenone to Paris" for Jacob Tonson's volume of Ovid's *Epistles* (1680). The remainder of her verse includes a long, amorous allegory, *A Voyage to the Isle of Love* (1684); an adaptation of Bernard de Fontenelle's epic which she entitled *A Discovery of New Worlds* (1688); and two occasional pieces: A Pindarick on the Death of Charles II (1685) and "A Congratulatory Poem to Her Most Sacred Majesty" (1688).

Achievements

Behn's achievement as a novelist should be measured principally in terms of the modest gains made by that form in England during the seventeenth century. Prior to *Oroonoko*, the English novel lingered in the shadows of the theater. Thus, the small reading public contented itself with works such as John Lyly's *Euphues, the Anatomy of Wit* (1579), Sir Philip Sidney's *Arcadia* (1590), Thomas Lodge's *Rosalynde* (1590), Thomas Nashe's *The Unfortunate Traveler: Or, The Life of Jack Wilton* (1594), and Thomas Deloney's *Jack of*

Newbury (1597)—all long, episodic stories, sprinkled with overly dramatic characterization and improbable plot structures. In *Oroonoko*, however, Behn advanced the novel to the point where her more skilled successors in the eighteenth century could begin to shape it into an independent, recognizable form.

Behn possessed the natural gifts of the storyteller, and her narrative art can easily stand beside that of her male contemporaries. A frankly commercial writer, she simply had no time, in pursuit of pleasure and the pen, to find a place in her narratives for intellectual substance. Nevertheless, she told a story as few others could, and the force of her own personality contributed both reality and a sense of immediacy to the still inchoate form of seventeenth century British fiction.

Biography

The details of Aphra Behn's birth are not known. The parish register of the Sts. Gregory and Martin Church, Wye, contains an entry stating that Ayfara Amis, daughter of John and Amy Amis, was baptized on July 10, 1640. Apparently, John Johnson, related to Lord Francis Willoughby of Parham, adopted the girl, although no one seems to know exactly when. Ayfara Amis accompanied her stepparents on a journey to Surinam (later Dutch Guiana) in 1658, Willoughby having appointed Johnson to serve as deputy governor of his extensive holdings there. Unfortunately, the new deputy died on the voyage; his widow and children proceeded to Surinam and took up residence at St. John's, one of Lord Willoughby's plantations. Exactly how long they remained is not clear, but certainly the details surrounding the time spent at St. John's form the background for *Oroonoko*.

Recent biographers have established the summer of 1663 as the most probable date of Behn's return to England. At any rate, by 1665 Behn was again in London and married to a wealthy merchant of Dutch extraction, who may well have had connections in, or at least around, the court of Charles II. In 1665 came the Great Plague and the death of Behn's husband; the latter proved the more disastrous for her, specifically because (again for unknown reasons) the Dutch merchant left nothing of substance for her—nothing, that is, except his court connections. Charles II, in the midst of the first of his wars against Holland, hired Aphra Behn as a secret government agent to spy upon the Dutch, for which purpose she proceeded to Antwerp. There she contacted another British agent, William Scott, from whom she obtained various pieces of military information, which she forwarded to London. Although she received little credit for her work, and even less money, Behn did conceive of the pseudonym Astrea, the name under which she published most of her poetry. The entire adventure into espionage proved a dismal failure for her; she even had to borrow money and pawn her valuables to pay her debts and obtain passage back to England. Once home, early in 1667, she found no relief from her desperate financial situation. Her debtors threatened prison, and the government refused any payment for her services. Prison followed, although the time and the exact length of her term remain unknown. Behn's most recent biographers speculate that she was aided in her release by John Hale (d. 1692)—a lawyer of Gray's Inn, wit, intellectual, a known homosexual, the principal subject of and reason for Behn's sonnets, and the man with whom she carried on a long romance. When she did gain her release, she determined to dedicate the rest of her life to writing and to pleasure, to trust to her own devices rather than to rely upon others who could not be trusted.

Behn launched her career as a dramatist in late December, 1670, at the new Duke's Theatre in Little Lincoln's Inn Fields, London. Her tragicomedy *The Forced Marriage* ran for six nights and included in the cast the nineteen-year-old Thomas Otway (1652-1685), the playwright-to-be only recently arrived from Oxford. Because of the length of the run, Behn, as was the practice, received the entire profit from the third performance, which meant that she could begin to function as an independent artist. She followed her first effort in the spring of 1671 with a comedy, *The Amorous Prince*, again at the Duke's; another comedy, *The Dutch Lover*, came to Drury Lane in February, 1673, and by the time of her anonymous comedy *The Rover*, in 1677, her reputation was secure. She mixed easily with the literati of her day, such as Thomas Killigrew, Edward Ravenscroft, the Earl of Rochester, Edmund Waller, and the poet laureate John Dryden, who published her rough translations from Ovid in 1683. With her reputation came offers for witty prologues and epilogues for others' plays, as well as what she wanted more than anything—money. A confrontation with the Earl of Shaftesbury and the newly emerged Whigs during the religious-political controversies of 1678, when she offended Charles II's opponents in a satirical prologue to an anonymous play, *Romulus and Hersilia*, brought her once again to the edge of financial hardship, as she was forced to abandon drama for the next five years.

Fortunately, Behn could fall back upon her abilities as a writer of popular fiction and occasional verse, although those forms were not as profitable as the London stage. Her series *Love Letters Between a Nobleman and His Sister* (1683-1687) and *Poems upon Several Occasions* (1684) were well received, but the meager financial returns from such projects could not keep pace with her personal expenses. When she did return to the state in 1686 with her comedy *The Lucky Chance*, she met with only moderate success and some public abuse. *The Emperor of the Moon*, produced the following season, fared somewhat better, although by then the London audience had lost its stomach for a female playwright—and a Tory, at that. She continued to write fiction and verse, but sickness and the death of her friend Edmund Waller, both in October, 1688, discouraged her. Five days after the coronation of William III and Mary, on April 16, 1689, Behn died. She had risen high enough to merit burial in Westminster Abbey; John Hoyle provided the fitting epitaph: "Here lies proof that wit can never be/Defense enough against mortality."

Analysis

More than a half-century ago, Vita Sackville-West, in trying to estimate Aphra Behn's contribution to English fiction, asked "what has she left behind her that is of any real value?" Sackville-West bemoaned Behn's failure in her fiction to reflect fully London life, London characters, London scenes; attention to exotic themes, settings, and characters merely debased and wasted her narrative gifts. Such a judgment, while plausible, fails to consider Behn's fiction in its historical and biographical context. Her tales abound with German princes, Spanish princesses, Portuguese kings, French counts, West-Indian slaves, and various orders of bishops, priests, and nuns, yet, Behn's *real* world was itself highly artificial, even fantastic: the intrigue of the Stuart court, the ribaldry of the London stage, the gossip of the drawing room, the masquerade, and the card parlor. Behn, in her *real* world, took in the same scenes as did John Dryden, Samuel Pepys, and the Earl of Rochester. Thus, to assert that her fiction neglects her actual experience in favor of fantastic and faraway window dressing may be too hasty a conclusion.

In *Castro*, Behn lets loose various powers of love, with the result that her heroines' passions affect the fortunes of their lovers. Thus, Miranda (*The Fair Jilt*) reflects the raving, hypocritical enchantress whose very beauty drives her lovers mad; Ardelia (*The Nun*) plays the capricious lover, whose passion carries her through a series of men, as well as a nunnery; and Agnes de Castro presents a slight variation from the preceding, in that the titled character is a product of circumstance: she is loved by the husband of her mistress.

Another primary theme in Behn's work is the often discussed noble savage that has traditionally been assigned to *Oroonoko*, as has the subordinate issue of antislavery in that same novel. In 1975, Professor George Guffey suggested a withdrawal from the feminist-biographical positions (those from which the noble savage/antislavery ideals spring) and a movement toward "a hitherto unperceived level of political allusion." Guffey did not label *Oroonoko* a political allegory but did suggest that readers should look more closely at events in England between 1678 and 1688. Guffey maintains that the novelist deplores not the slavery of a black, noble savage but the bondage of a *royal prince*—again a reference to the political climate of the times. The interesting aspect of Guffey's analysis is that his approach lends substance to Behn's principal novel and to her overall reputation as a literary artist, and it parries the complaint that she failed to echo the sound and the sense of her own age.

In 1678, Sir Roger L'Estrange (1616-1704) published *Five Love Letters from a Nun to a Cavalier*, a translation of some fictional correspondence by the minor French writer Guilleraques. Behn used the work as a model for at least three of her prose pieces—*Love Letters Between a Nobleman and His Sister*,

The History of the Nun, and *The Nun*. For the latter two, the novelist took advantage, at least on the surface, of the current religious and political controversies and set forth the usual claims to truth.

There may be some validity to the claim that *The History of the Nun* exists as one of the earliest examinations by a novelist into the psychology of crime and guilt. The events, at the outset, proceed reasonably enough but become less believable, and, by the novel's conclusion, the events appear to be exceedingly unreal. Despite this difficulty, the novel does have some value. Behn demonstrates her ability to develop thoroughly the key aspects of the weaknesses and the resultant sufferings of the heroine, Isabella. Behn immediately exposes the concept that "Mother Church" can take care of a girl's problems, can easily eradicate the desires of the world from her heart and mind, can readily transform a passionate maiden into a true, devoted sister of the faith. In addition, despite her wickedness, Isabella is still very much a human being worthy of the reader's understanding. At every step, the girl pays something for what she does; with each violation against the Church and each crime of passion, she falls deeper into the darkness of her own guilt. What she does, and how, is certainly contrived; how she reacts to her misdeeds reflects accurately the guilty conscience of a believable human being.

The second "Nun" novel, not published until 1697, certainly leads the reader through a more complicated plot entanglement than the 1688 story, but it contains none of the virtue exhibited in the earlier work. The interesting aspect of *The Nun*'s plot is that Behn kills the heroine, Ardelia, first; only afterward do the principal rivals, Don Sebastian and Don Henriques, kill each other in a fight. The interest, however, is only fleeting, for those events do not occur until the end of the novel. All that remains of the bloody situation is Elvira, Don Sebastian's unfaithful sister. After weeping and calling for help, she is seized with a violent fever (in the final paragraph) and dies within twenty-four hours. Certainly, Behn's ingenuity in this piece demands some recognition, if for no other reason than her adeptness, according to James Sutherland, at "moving the pieces around the board."

Because of the relative sanity of its plot, in contrast to the two previous tragedies, *Agnes de Castro* comes close to what Behn's feminist supporters expect of her. In other words, in this piece, pure evil or a series of tragic events cannot be blamed entirely on love or upon reckless female passion. Although Don Pedro genuinely loves his wife's maid-of-honor, Agnes, she, out of loyalty to her mistress, refuses to yield to his passion. Such action encourages the other characters to exhibit equal degrees of virtue. Constantia, Don Pedro's wife, seems to understand that the power of Agnes' charms, although innocent enough, is no match for her husband's frailty of heart over reason. Thus, she resents neither her husband nor her maid; in fact, she is willing to tolerate the presence of Agnes to keep her husband happy.

The novel, however, does not exist as a monument to reason. Something must always arise, either in politics or romance, to disrupt reasonable people's attempts at harmony. In the novel, a vengeful woman lies to Constantia and plants the rumor in her mind that Agnes and Don Pedro are plotting against her. Such a report breaks Constantia's trust in her husband and her maid, and the honest lady dies of a broken heart. The novel, however, remains believable for Behn simply emphasizes the frailty of honor and trust in a world dominated by intrigue and pure hatred. Given the political and religious climates of the decade, the setting and the plot of *Agnes de Castro* are indeed flimsy facades for the court and coffeehouse of seventeenth century London.

Although in *The Fair Jilt*, Behn continued to develop the conflict between love and reason, the novel has attracted critical attention because of its allusions to the writer's own experiences. Again, she lays claim to authenticity by maintaining that she witnessed parts of the events and heard the rest from sources close to the action and the characters. In addition, the events occur in Antwerp, the very city to which the novelist had been assigned for the performance of her spying activities for Charles II's ministers.

From the outset of the novel, Behn establishes the wickedness of Miranda, who uses her beauty to enchant the unsuspecting and even tempts the weak into commiting murder. Obviously, had Behn allowed her major character to succeed in her evil ways, nothing would have been gained from the novel. What results is the triumph of the hero's innate goodness; as weak as he is, he has endured. His loyalty and devotion have outlasted and, to a certain extent, conquered Miranda's wickedness.

Behn's literary reputation today rests almost totally upon a single work, *Oroonoko*. The novel succeeds as her most realistic work principally because she recounts the specifics of Surinam with considerable detail and force. Behn installs her hero amid the splendor of a tropical setting, a Natural Man, a pure savage untouched by the vices of Christian Europe, unaware of the white man's inherent baseness and falsehood.

In lashing out at the weaknesses of her society, Behn does not forget about one of her major concerns—love. Thus, Oroonoko loves the beautiful Imoinda, a child of his own race, but the prince's grandfather demands her for his own harem. Afterward, the monarch sells the girl into slavery, and she finds herself in Surinam—where Oroonoko is brought following his kidnaping. The prince embarks upon a term of virtuous and powerful adventures in the name of freedom for himself and Imoinda, but his captors deceive him. Thereupon, he leads a slave revolt, only to be captured by the white scoundrels and tortured. Rather than see Imoinda suffer dishonor at the hands of the ruthless white planters and government officers, Oroonoko manages to kill her himself. At the end, he calmly smokes his pipe—a habit learned from the Europeans—as his captors dismember his body and toss the pieces into the fire.

The final judgment upon Behn's fiction may still remain to be formulated.

Presently, evaluations of her work tend to extremes. Some critics assert that her novels, even *Oroonoko*, had no significant influence on the development of the English novel, while others argue that her limited attempts at realism may well have influenced Daniel Defoe, Samuel Richardson, Henry Fielding, and others to begin to mold the ostensibly factual narrative into the novel as the twentieth century recognizes it. From Behn came the background against which fictional plots could go forward and fictional characters could function. Her problem, which her successors managed to surmount, was the inability (or refusal) to make her characters and events as real as their fictional environment. That fault (if it was a fault) lay with the tendencies and the demands of the age, not with the writer. Indeed, it is hardly a failure for a dramatist and a novelist to have given to her audience exactly what they wanted. To have done less would have meant an even quicker exit from fame and an even more obscure niche in the literary history of her time.

Samuel J. Rogal

Other major works

PLAYS: *The Forced Marriage: Or, The Jealous Bridegroom*, 1670; *The Amorous Prince*, 1671; *The Dutch Lover*, 1673; *The Town Fop*, 1676; *The Debauchee*, 1677; *The Rover: Or, The Banished Cavalier*, I, II, 1677, 1681; *Abdelazar*, 1676; *Sir Patient Fancy*, 1678; *The Young King*, 1679; *The Round-heads: Or, The Good Old Cause*, 1681; *The False Count*, 1681; *The City Heiress: Or, Sir Timothy Treat-All*, 1682; *The Lucky Chance*, 1686; *The Emperor of the Moon*, 1687; *The Window Ranter*, 1689; *The Younger Brother*, 1696.

POETRY: *Poems upon Several Occasions, with a Voyage to the Island of Love*, 1684; *Miscellany: Being a Collection of Poems by Several Hands*, 1685.

TRANSLATIONS: *Aesop's Fables*, 1687; *Of Trees*, 1689.

MISCELLANEOUS: *La Montre: Or, The Lover's Watch*, 1686 (prose and verse); *The Case for the Watch*, 1686 (prose and verse); *Lycidas: Or, The Lover in Fashion*, 1688 (prose and verse); *The Lady's Looking-Glass, to Dress Herself By: Or, The Art of Charming*, 1697 (prose and verse); *The Works of Aphra Behn*, 1915, 1967 (6 volumes).

Bibliography

Duffy, Maureen. *The Passionate Shepherdess: Aphra Behn, 1640-1689.* London: Jonathan Cape, 1977. A personal, sometimes hard-to-read appraisal of Behn. Based on much research that uncovered new information about this enigmatic figure. Especially good on the historical background of *Oroonoko: Or, The History of the Royal Slave* and her plays; offers interesting ideas on the identity of various people obliquely mentioned in the works.

Goreau, Angeline. *Reconstructing Aphra: A Social Biography of Aphra Behn*. New York: Dial Press, 1980. Draws on Behn's own writings as well as contemporary comments about her, re-creating the life of the first professional woman writer. Like Virginia Woolf, Behn is praised for providing a model for later women who took up the pen. The thirty-seven illustrations contribute to the reconstruction of the age. Little discussion of the fiction and later plays.

Guffey, George. "Aphra Behn's *Oroonoko*: Occasion and Accomplishment." In *Two English Novelists: Aphra Behn and Anthony Trollope: Papers Read at a Clark Library Seminar, May 11, 1974*. Los Angeles: Clark Library, 1975. Argues that *Oroonoko: Or, The History of the Royal Slave* is not an attack on slavery or a celebration of the natural man but rather a defense of James II, who is the model for the hero, as Surinam is made to resemble England.

Link, Frederick M. *Aphra Behn*. New York: Twayne, 1968. After a brief account of Behn's life, this book provides a critical survey of her works, devoting about half to her drama. Concludes with a survey of Behn's reputation since her death and includes a useful annotated bibliography of criticism.

O'Donnell, Mary Ann. *Aphra Behn: An Annotated Bibliography of Primary and Secondary Sources*. New York: Garland, 1986. After a detailed description of more than a hundred primary works, O'Donnell annotates 661 books, articles, essays, and dissertations written about Behn since 1666. These works are listed chronologically. Indexed.

Sackville-West, Vita. *Aphra Behn: The Incomparable Astrea*. New York: Viking Press, 1928. Sackville-West admires the woman more than the writing, though she finds the lyrics praiseworthy. Sympathetic and well written.

Woodcock, George. *The Incomparable Aphra*. London: Boardman, 1948. Behn is not only a good writer but also "a revolutionary influence on the social life and literature of her age," introducing fictional techniques that later writers will develop and arguing against inequality.

SAUL BELLOW

Born: Lachine, Canada; June 10, 1915

Principal long fiction

Dangling Man, 1944; *The Victim*, 1947; *The Adventures of Augie March*, 1953; *Seize the Day*, 1956; *Henderson the Rain King*, 1959; *Herzog*, 1964; *Mr. Sammler's Planet*, 1970; *Humboldt's Gift*, 1975; *The Dean's December*, 1982; *More Die of Heartbreak*, 1987; *A Theft*, 1989; *The Bellarosa Connection*, 1989.

Other literary forms

In addition to his many novels, Saul Bellow has published short stories, plays, and a variety of nonfiction. His stories have appeared in *The New Yorker*, *Commentary*, *Partisan Review*, *Hudson Review*, *Esquire*, and other periodicals, and he has published two collections of short stories, *Mosby's Memoirs and Other Stories* (1968) and *Him with His Foot in His Mouth and Other Stories* (1984; includes short novels). His full-length play *The Last Analysis* was produced for a short run on Broadway in 1964 and published the following year, while three one-act plays, *Orange Soufflé, A Wen*, and *Out from Under*, were staged in 1966 in America and Europe. Another one-act play, *The Wrecker*, was published, though not staged, in 1954. Throughout his career, Bellow has written numerous articles on a variety of topics. In 1976, he published an account of his trip to Israel, *To Jerusalem and Back: A Personal Account*.

Achievements

Often described as America's best living novelist, Bellow has enjoyed enormous critical praise and a wide readership as well. His popularity is, perhaps, surprising, because his novels do not contain the usual ingredients one expects to find in best-selling fiction—suspense, heroic figures, and graphic sex and violence. In fact, his novels are difficult ones that wrestle with perplexing questions, sometimes drawing from esoteric sources such as the anthroposophy of Rudolf Steiner and the psychology of Wilhelm Reich. One of America's most erudite novelists, Bellow often alludes to the work of philosophers, psychologists, poets, anthropologists, and other writers in his fiction. He has stated that the modern movelist should not be afraid to introduce complex ideas into his work. He finds nothing admirable about the anti-intellectualism of many modern writers and believes that most of them have failed to confront the important moral and philosophical problems of the modern age. Opposed to the glib pessimism and the "complaint" of the dominant tradition of modern literature, Bellow has struggled for affirmation at a time when such a possibility is seen by many writers as merely an object of ridicule.

In contrast to many American writers who produced their best work when they were young and then wrote mediocre or poor fiction as they grew older, Bellow has consistently published work of the highest quality. Moreover, his fiction reveals an immense versatility; he has not selected one style and merely repeated it. In his work, one finds highly structured Flaubertian form as well as picaresque narrative, naturalistic realism as well as romance.

Bellow is a master of narrative voice and perspective, a great comic writer (perhaps the best in America since Mark Twain), and a fine craftsman whose remarkable control of the language allows him to move easily from the highly formal to the colloquial. Most important, he writes novels that illuminate the dark areas of the psyche and that possess immense emotional power. Bellow has complained that many contemporary authors and critics are obsessed with symbolism and hidden meanings. A literary work becomes an abstraction for them, and they contrive to evade the emotional power inherent in literature. Bellow's novels do not suffer from abstraction; they deal concretely with passion, death, love, and other fundamental concerns: he is able to evoke the whole range of human emotions in his readers.

Biography

Saul Bellow was born in Lachine, Quebec, Canada, on June 10, 1915, the youngest of four children. Two years before, his parents, Abraham and Liza (Gordon) Bellow, had immigrated to Canada from St. Petersburg, Russia. The family lived in a very poor section of Montreal, where Bellow learned Yiddish, Hebrew, French, and English. When he was nine, the family moved to Chicago.

In 1933, he entered the University of Chicago but two years later transferred to Northwestern University, where he received a bachelor's degree. In 1937, he entered the University of Wisconsin at Madison to study anthropology but left school in December to marry and to become a writer. He was employed briefly with the Works Progress Administration Writers' Project and then led a bohemian life, supporting himself with teaching and odd jobs. During World War II, he served in the merchant marine and published his first novel, *Dangling Man*.

After publishing his second novel, *The Victim*, he was awarded a Guggenheim Fellowship in 1948, which enabled him to travel to Europe and work on *The Adventures of Augie March*. This third novel won the National Book Award for Fiction in 1953 and established Bellow as one of America's most promising novelists.

After his return from Europe in 1950, he spent a large part of the next decade in New York City and Dutchess County, New York, teaching and writing before moving back to Chicago to publish *Herzog*. While *Seize the Day* and *Henderson the Rain King* did not receive the critical attention they deserved, *Herzog* was an enormous critical and financial success, even becoming a best-seller for a period of time.

The next two novels, *Mr. Sammler's Planet* and *Humboldt's Gift*, helped increase his reputation but also created some controversy. *Mr. Sammler's Planet* was critical of the excesses of the late 1960's, and some complained that Bellow had become a reactionary. Although Bellow opposed the Vietnam War, he found it difficult to identify with the "counterculture." *Humboldt's Gift* disturbed some critics, who complained that Bellow's interest in the ideas of Rudolf Steiner indicated that he was becoming an escapist; it was a mistaken assumption. An ardent supporter of Israel, Bellow traveled to that country in 1975 and published an account of his journey, *To Jerusalem and Back*. In 1976 he was awarded the Nobel Prize for Literature.

Bellow has been married four times and has three sons by his first three wives. At present, he lives in Chicago, where he prefers to shun the publicity that other writers cultivate.

Analysis

Saul Bellow's mature fiction can be considered as a conscious challenge to modernism, the dominant literary tradition of the age. For Bellow, modernism is a "victim literature" because it depicts an alienated individual who is conquered by his environment. According to him, this "wasteland" tradition originated in the middle of the nineteenth century with the birth of French realism and culminates in the work of Samuel Beckett and other nihilistic contemporary writers. This victim literature reveals a horror of life and considers humanist values useless in a bleak, irrational world. Modernism assumes that the notion of the individual self which underlies the great tradition of the novel is an outmoded concept, and that modern civilization is doomed.

Bellow has never accepted the idea that mankind has reached its terminal point, but his first two novels owe a large debt to the wasteland modernism that he would explicitly reject in the late 1940's. *Dangling Man* is an existentialist diary that owes much to Fyodor Dostoevski's *Notes from the Underground* (1864). The demoralized protagonist Joseph is left "dangling" as he waits to be drafted during World War II. A moral casualty of war, he has no sense of purpose and feels weary of a life that seems boring, trivial, and cruel. Excessively self-conscious and critical of those around him, he spends most of his time alone, writing in his journal. He can no longer continue his past work, writing biographical essays on philosophers of the Enlightenment. Although he is alienated, he does realize that he should not make a doctrine out of this feeling. The conclusion of the novel reveals Joseph's ultimate failure to transcend his "victimization"; he is drafted and greets his imminent regimentation enthusiastically.

Bellow's next novel, *The Victim*, also depicts a passive protagonist who is unable to overcome his victimization. As Bellow has admitted, the novel is partially modeled on Dostoevski's *The Eternal Husband* (1870) and uses the technique of the *Doppelgänger* as Dostoevski did in *The Double* (1846). Bellow's novel presents the psychological struggle between Asa Leventhal, a Jew, and Kirby Allbee, his Gentile "double." A derelict without a job, Allbee suggests that Leventhal is responsible for his grim fate. Leventhal ponders the problem of his guilt and responsibility and tries to rid himself of his persecuting double. Despite his efforts to assert himself, he is still "dangling" at the end of the book—still a victim of forces that, he believes, are beyond his control.

After his second novel, Bellow became disenchanted with the depressive temperament and the excessive emphasis on form of modernist literature. His first two novels had been written according to "repressive" Flaubertian formal standards; they were melancholy, rigidly structured, restrained in language, and detached and objective in tone. Rebelling against these constricting standards, Bellow threw off the yoke of modernism when he began to write his third novel. The theme, style, and tone of *The Adventures of Augie March* are very different from his earlier novels, for here one finds an open-ended picaresque narrative with flamboyant language and an exuberant hero who seeks to affirm life and the possibility of freedom. While the environment has a profound influence upon Joseph and Asa Leventhal, Augie refuses to allow it to determine his fate. During the course of many adventures, a multitude of Machiavellians seek to impose their versions of reality upon the good-natured Augie, but he escapes from them, refusing to commit himself.

With his third novel, then, Bellow deliberately rejected the modernist outlook and aesthetic. The problem was to find an alternative to modernism without resorting to glib optimism. It seems that he found an alternative in two older literary traditions—in nineteenth century English Romantic humanism and in a comedy that he considers typically Jewish. Unlike the modernists, who denigrate the concept of the individual, Bellow believes in the potential of the self and its powerful imagination that can redeem ordinary existence and affirm the value of freedom, love, joy, and hope.

While comedy in Bellow is a complex matter, its primary function seems to be to undercut the dejection that threatens his heroes. The comic allows Bellow's protagonists to cope with the grim facts of existence; it enables them to avoid despair and gain a balanced view of their problematical situation. Comedy, the spirit of reason, allows them to laugh away their irrational anxieties. Often Bellow seems to encourage his worst anxieties in order to bring them out into the open so that he can dispose of them by comic ridicule.

If *The Adventures of Augie March* presents Bellow's alternative to a "literature of victimization," his subsequent novels can be regarded as probing, exploratory studies in spiritual survival in a hostile environment.

Seize the Day is a much more somber novel than *The Adventures of Augie*

March. Bellow felt that his liberation from Flaubertian formalism had gone too far, and that he must use more restraint in his fourth novel. He realized that Augie was too effusive and too naïve. The protagonist of *Seize the Day* is similar to the protagonists of the first two novels, but while Tommy Wilhelm is a "victim," Bellow's attitude toward him is different from his attitude toward Joseph and Asa Leventhal. In his fourth novel, Bellow sought to show the spiritual rebirth of such a "victim."

The short novel, divided into seven parts, presents the day of reckoning in the life of a forty-four-year-old ex-salesman of children's furniture whose past consists of a series of blunders. Living in the Hotel Gloriana (which is also the residence of his wealthy father, Dr. Adler), Wilhelm feels that he is in a desperate situation. He is unemployed and unable to obtain money from his unsympathetic father. He gives his last seven hundred dollars to be invested for him by the mysterious psychologist Dr. Tamkin, a man who has become not only his surrogate father and financial adviser but also his instructor in spiritual and philosophical matters. Furthermore, Wilhelm's wife, Margaret, from whom he is separated, is harassing him for money. Depressed and confused by the memories of his failures in the past and absorbed by his problems in the present, Wilhelm needs love and compassion. Dr. Adler, Dr. Tamkin, and Margaret all fail him.

Seize the Day is a harsh indictment of a money-obsessed society, where a father is unable to love a son who is unsuccessful. Tamkin's speech on the two souls, no doubt the most important passage in the novel, helps clarify Bellow's social criticism. The psychologist argues that there is a war between man's "pretender soul," his social self, and his "real soul." When the pretender soul parasitically dominates its host, as is common in modern society, one becomes murderous. If one is true to the real soul, however, and casts off the false pretender soul, one can learn to love and "seize the day."

Bellow shows that all of the characters in the novel are products of an exploitative, materialistic society—all are dominated by their pretender souls. Dr. Adler has fought his way up the economic ladder to success. Revered by the residents of the Hotel Gloriana, he is full of self-love. He desires to spend his remaining years in peace and refuses to acknowledge his paternal obligation to his desperate son. Wilhelm's appeals for money are actually pleas for some sign of paternal concern. He provokes his father, trying to disturb the polite barrier of aloofness that the old man has constructed to prevent any kind of real communication between father and son. While Wilhelm is a difficult son for a father to cherish, Dr. Adler is a cold-hearted man who has no real affection for his son, or for anyone else except for himself. When, at the end of the novel, Wilhelm begs him for some kind of sympathy, the hard-boiled Adler brutally rejects him, revealing his hatred for his "soft" son.

Dr. Adler's failure as a father results in Wilhelm's turning to the strange psychologist Dr. Tamkin. Down on his luck, Tamkin is a confidence man hoping to make easy money. He is another one of Bellow's eccentric fast talkers, full of fantastic stories and philosophical and psychological insights. Wilhelm is attracted to him not only because he is a father figure who promises to save him from his dire financial crisis but also because he is one man in a cynical society who speaks of spiritual matters. The direct result of Tamkin's advice is the loss of Wilhelm's money, but while the doctor is a phony whose flamboyant personality enables him to dupe the naïve ex-salesman, he does indirectly allow Wilhelm to obtain a kind of salvation.

Wilhelm is the only character in the novel who is able to forsake his pretender soul. He is a product of society as the other characters are, but he is different from them in his instinctive distaste for the inveterate cynicism at the heart of society. Accepting society's definition of success, he considers himself a failure. He suffers immensely and constantly ponders his life and his errors in the past. Yet while he can at times degenerate into a buffoon indulging in self-pity and hostility, he is also attracted to the idealism that Tamkin occasionally expounds.

A significant moment occurs near the end of the novel when Wilhelm suddenly feels a sense of brotherhood with his fellow travelers in the New York subway. For once he has transcended his self-absorption, though he is immediately skeptical of this intuitive moment. At the very end of the novel, there is another heightened moment in which he does make the breakthrough foreshadowed in the subway scene. Having lost all of his money, he pursues into a funeral home a man who resembles Tamkin. Suddenly he finds himself confronting a corpse, and he begins to weep uncontrollably. His weeping is not merely out of self-pity, as some have suggested, but for mankind. Understanding that death and suffering are an inextricable part of the human condition, he feels humility and is able to overcome his excessive self-absorption. He is finally able to cast off his pretender soul. The work concludes with a powerful affirmation and suggests an alternative to the spiritual death of a materialistic, predatory society.

Bellow's next novel, *Henderson the Rain King* is the first fully realized work of his maturity. It is Bellow's first novel of which one can say that no other writer could have conceived it, much less written it. Although it has some characteristics of the picaresque, the fable, and the realistic novel, *Henderson the Rain King* assumes the most widely used form for longer works during the English romantic era—the quest-romance. The tone of the novel is somewhat different from that typically heard in the quest-romance, however; it is exuberant and comic, and the book is full of wit, parody, farce, and ironic juxtapositions.

The novel might be seen as Bellow's version of Joseph Conrad's *Heart of Darkness* (1902). Like Conrad's Marlow, Eugene Henderson recalls his journey into the heart of Africa and his bizarre adventures there, which culminate in his meeting with a Kurtz-like instructor who has a profound influence upon him. While Kurtz reveals to Marlow man's potential for degradation, Dahfu conveys to Henderson man's promise of nobility. With its allusions to William Wordsworth, Samuel Taylor Coleridge, Percy Bysshe Shelley, and William Blake, the novel affirms the possibility of the individual's regeneration by the power of the human imagination; it is a trenchant rejection of Conrad's pessimism.

The novel can be divided into three basic parts: Chapters 1-4 depict Henderson's alienation; Chapters 5-9 present his journey to the African tribe of the Arnewi; Chapters 10-22 portray his journey to the African tribe of the Wariri and his spiritual regeneration.

The first section presents Henderson's discursive recollections of his life before he set out for Africa, in which he attempts to reveal the reasons for the journey. While these chapters provide a plethora of information about him, he is never able to articulate the reasons for his "quest," as he calls it. Bellow is suggesting in this section that there are no clear-cut reasons for the African journey. Henderson leaves his wife and family for the African wilderness because of his dissatisfaction with his meaningless existence. A millionaire with tremendous energy but no scope for it, Henderson has spent most of his life suffering or making others suffer. Middle-aged, anxious about his mortality, and unable to satisfy the strident inner voice of "I want, I want," he leaves for Africa, hoping to burst "the spirit's sleep," as he phrases it, echoing Shelley's *The Revolt of Islam* (1818).

With his loyal guide Romilayu, he first visits the Arnewi tribe. These people are "children of light" who represent a healthy existence; they are gentle, peaceful, and innocent. Queen Willatale, who rules the tribe, informs Henderson that man wants to live—"grun-tu-molani." It is an important message for Henderson, but he soon demonstrates that he is unable to follow Willatale's wisdom. Desiring to help the tribe, whose water supply has been infested by frogs, he decides to kill the creatures. His bomb is too powerful and destroys the cistern as well as the frogs. Henderson has violated the code of the Arnewi, who abhor violence and have love for all living creatures.

After Henderson leaves the Arnewi, he visits the Wariri, "the children of darkness," who are violent and hostile, reminiscent of the predatory society of Bellow's earlier novels. He does meet one extraordinary individual, however, and establishes a friendship with him. King Dahfu is a noble man who completes Henderson's education begun with the Arnewi. He perceptively observes that Henderson's basic problem is his avoidance of death: he is an "avoider." Dahfu helps him by persuading him to go down into a lion's den to overcome his anxiety over mortality. Dahfu believes, too, that Henderson can absorb the qualities of the lion and slough off his porcine characteristics.

Dahfu is another one of Bellow's eccentric teachers who speaks both wisdom and nonsense. His greatest importance for Henderson is that he embodies the nobility of man, who can by the power of his imagination achieve spiritual regeneration. At the end of the novel, Henderson finally bursts the spirit's sleep and leaves Africa for America. He has a sense of purpose and can love others. He plans to become a physician and will return home to his wife.

Herzog is Bellow's best and most difficult novel to date. It is a retrospective meditation by a middle-aged professor who seeks to understand the reasons for his disastrous past. A complex discursive work, pervaded by sardonic humor, it defies traditional labeling but owes a debt to the novel of ideas, the psychological novel, the epistolary novel, and the romantic meditative lyric. *Herzog* is a meditative work in which the protagonist compulsively remembers and evaluates his past, striving to avoid complete mental break-down. There are reminiscences within reminiscences, and the story of Moses Herzog's life is related in fragments. Bellow's method enables the reader to see how Herzog's imagination recollects and assembles the fragments of the past into a meaningful pattern.

Distraught over his recent divorce from his second wife, Madeleine, Herzog has become obsessed with writing letters to everyone connected with that event as well as to important thinkers, living and dead, who concern him. He associates his domestic crisis with the cultural crisis of Western civilization, and therefore he ponders the ethics of Friedrich Nietzsche as well as those of his psychiatrist Dr. Edvig. His letter-writing is both a symptom of his psychological disintegration and an attempt to meditate upon and make sense of suffering and death.

At his home in the Berkshires, Herzog recalls and meditates upon the events of his recent past; the five-day period of time that he recalls reveals the severity of his psychological deterioration. His mistress Ramona believes that a cure for his nervous state can be found in her Lawrentian sexual passion, but he considers her "ideology" to be mere hedonism; impulsively, he decides to flee from her to Martha's Vineyard, where he has friends. After arriving there, the unstable professor leaves almost immediately and returns to New York. The next evening he has dinner with Ramona and spends the night with her, waking in the middle of the night to write another letter. The following morning he visits a courtroom while waiting for a meeting with his lawyer to discuss a lawsuit against Madeleine. Hearing a brutal child-abuse and murder case causes the distraught professor to associate Madeleine and her lover with the brutal child-murderers; he flies to Chicago to murder them. As he spies upon them, he realizes his assumption is absurd and abandons his plan. The next morning he takes his young daughter Junie for an outing but has a car accident and is arrested by the police for carrying a gun. He confronts an angry Madeleine at the police station and manages to control his own temper. Later, he is released and returns to his run-down home in the Berkshires, and the novel ends where it began.

Interspersed within these recollections of the immediate past are memories of the more distant past. By piecing these together, one learns the sad story of Herzog's domestic life. Feeling a vague dissatisfaction, the successful professor divorced his first wife Daisy, a sensible Midwestern woman, and began affairs with a good-natured Japanese woman, Sono, and the beautiful, bad-tempered Madeleine. After marrying Madeleine, Herzog purchased a house in the Berkshires, where he intended to complete his important book on the Romantics. Soon they returned to Chicago, however, where both saw a psychiatrist, and Madeleine suddenly announced that she wanted a divorce. The shocked Herzog traveled to Europe to recuperate, only to return to Chicago to learn that Madeleine had been having an affair with his best friend and confidant the whole time their marriage had been deteriorating.

Herzog's grim past—his disastrous marriages and the other sad events of his life that he also recalls—becomes emblematic of the pernicious influence of cultural nihilism. Herzog is devoted to basic humanist values but wonders if he must, as the ubiquitous "reality-instructors" insist, become another mass man devoted to a brutal "realism" in the Hobbesian jungle of modern society. His antipathy for the wastelanders' cynicism is strong, but he knows his past idealism has been too naïve. Repeatedly, the "reality instructors" strive to teach ("punish") Herzog with lessons of the "real"—and the "real" is always brutal and cruel. Sandor Himmelstein, Herzog's lawyer and friend, proudly announces that all people are "whores." It is an accurate description not only of Himmelstein but also of his fellow reality instructors. Their cynical view is pervasive in modern society, in which people play roles, sell themselves, and seduce and exploit others for their own selfish ends.

The turning point of the novel is Herzog's revelation in the courtroom episode. Intellectually, he has always known about evil and suffering, but emotionally he has remained innocent. His hearing of the case in which a mother mistreats and murders her son while her lover apathetically watches is too much for him to bear; here is a monstrous evil that cannot be subsumed by any intellectual scheme. In a devastating moment the professor is forced to realize that his idealism is foolish.

At the end of the novel, Herzog has achieved a new consciousness. He recognizes that he has been selfish and excessively absorbed in intellectual abstractions. A prisoner of his private intellectual life, he has cut himself off from ordinary humanity and everyday existence. He sees that his naïve idealism and the wastelanders' cruel "realism" are both escapist and therefore unacceptable attitudes; they allow the individual to evade reality by wearing masks of naïve idealism or self-serving cynicism. The exhausted Herzog decides to abandon his compulsive letter-writing and to stop pondering his past. The threat of madness has passed, and he is on the road to recovery.

Mr. Sammler's Planet is a meditative novel of sardonic humor and caustic wit. The "action" of the novel centers upon the protagonist's recollection of a brief period of time in the recent past, though there are recollections of a more distant past, too. Once again the mental state of the protagonist is

Bellow's main concern. Like Herzog, Artur Sammler has abandoned a scholarly project because he finds rational explanations dissatisfying; they are unable to justify suffering and death. The septuagenarian Sammler is yet another of Bellow's survivors, a lonely humanist in a society populated by brutal "realists."

This seventh novel, however, is not merely a repetition of Bellow's previous works. Sammler is detached and basically unemotional, yet he reveals a mystical bent largely absent in Bellow's other protaganists. He is drawn to the works of Meister Eckhart and other thirteenth century German mystics. While he does not literally believe in their ideas, he finds reading their works soothing. His religious inclination is a recent phenomenon.

Sammler had been reared in a wealthy, secular Jewish family in Krakow. As an adult, he became a haughty, cosmopolitan intellectual, useless to everyone, as he readily admits. On a visit to Poland in 1939, when the Germans suddenly attacked, he, his wife, and others were captured and ordered to dig their own graves as the Nazis waited to murder them. Although his wife was killed in the mass execution, miraculously he escaped by crawling out of his own grave. After the war ended, Sammler and his daughter Shula were rescued from a displaced persons camp by a kind nephew, Dr. Elya Gruner, who became their patron.

The experience of the Holocaust destroyed what little religious inclination Sammler possessed, but in his old age he has become concerned with his spiritual state. Unfortunately, it is difficult to pursue spiritual interests in a materialistic society hostile to them. The basic conflict in the novel is between Sammler's need to ponder the basic questions of existence—a need accentuated by the dying of the noble Gruner—and the distractions of contemporary society. In the primary action of the novel, Sammler's main intention is to visit the dying Gruner, who finds Sammler a source of great comfort. Several "accidents" distract Sammler from his goal, and on the day of his nephew's death, he arrives too late.

The "accidents" which encumber Sammler reveal clearly the "degraded clowning" of contemporary society. Sammler is threatened by a black pickpocket who corners the old man and then exposes himself. In the middle of a lecture he is shouted down by a radical student who says that Sammler is sexually defective. His daughter Shula steals a manuscript from an Indian scholar, and Sammler must waste precious time to recover it. Even Gruner's self-centered children, who have little compassion for their dying father, distract Sammler by their thoughtless actions.

Opposed to Gruner, who is part of the "old system" which esteems the family, the expression of emotion, and the traditional humanist values, is the contemporary generation, a kind of "circus" characterized by role-playing, hedonism, amorality, self-centeredness, and atrophy of feeling. Despite its flaws, Bellow sympathizes with the "old system." The novel concludes after

Sammler, despite the objections of the hospital staff, goes into the post-mortem room and says a prayer for Gruner's soul.

As in Bellow's previous novels, the tension and the humor of *Humboldt's Gift* have their origin in the protagonist's attempt to free himself from the distractions of contemporary society and pursue the needs of his soul. The protagonist Charlie Citrine strives to define for himself the function of the artist in contemporary America. He tries to come to terms with the failure and premature death of his one-time mentor, Von Humboldt Fleisher, who had the potential to be America's greatest modern poet but achieved very little. Charlie wonders if the romantic poet can survive in a materialistic society; he wonders, too, if he can overcome his fear of the grave and exercise his imagination. A writer who has squandered his talent, Charlie has intimations of terror of the grave and intimations of immortality. He spends much time reading the Anthroposophical works of Rudolf Steiner; although he is skeptical of some of Steiner's more esoteric teachings, he is sympathetic to the spiritual world view of anthroposophy, even finding the notion of reincarnation quite persuasive.

The primary nemesis of Charlie's spiritual life is Ronald Cantabile, a small-time criminal. Renata, Charlie's voluptuous mistress, Denise, his ex-wife, and Pierre Thaxter, a confidence man, are also major distractions. When Charlie, on the advice of a friend, refuses to pay Cantabile the money he owes him from a poker game, the criminal harasses him. In fact, the proud, psychopathic Cantabile refuses to leave Charlie alone even after he agrees to pay him the money. He continually humiliates Charlie and even tries to involve him in a plot to murder the troublesome Denise.

Denise, Renata, and Thaxter also distract Charlie from pondering the fate of Humboldt and meditating upon fundamental metaphysical questions. Hoping Charlie will return to her, Denise refuses to settle her support suit and continues to demand more money. When Charlie is forced to put up a two-hundred-thousand-dollar bond, he is financially ruined, and the loss of his money results in the loss of the voluptuous Renata, who decides to marry a wealthy undertaker. A third disillusioning experience involves Thaxter, who has apparently conned Charlie. Charlie had invested a small fortune in a new journal, *The Ark*, which was supposed to restore the authority of art and culture in the United States. Thaxter, the editor of *The Ark*, never puts out the first issue and has, it appears, stolen the money. His confidence game symbolizes America's lack of respect for art and culture, impractical subjects in a practical, technological society.

Charlie does, however, overcome these "distractions." Humboldt's posthumously delivered letter, accompanied by an original film sketch (his "gift") and a scenario that the two had written at Princeton years before, provides the genesis for Charlie's salvation. The original film idea and the scenario of their Princeton years enable Charlie to attain financial security, but more important, Humboldt's letter provides the impetus for Charlie's decision at the end of the novel to repudiate his past empty life and to pursue the life of the imagination. Humboldt's ideas, bolstered by the poetry of Blake, Wordsworth, and John Keats, enable Charlie to avoid the fate of the self-destructive artist. He decides to live in Europe and meditate upon the fundamental questions—in short, to take up a different kind of life.

When, at the end of the novel, Charlie gives Humboldt and the poet's mother a proper burial, Bellow suggests that Charlie's imagination is ready to exert itself and wake him from his self-centered boredom and death-in-life. The final scene of the novel promises Charlie's spiritual regeneration.

Bellow's 1982 novel, *The Dean's December*, is "a tale of two cities," Chicago and Bucharest, in which the protagonist, a dean at an unnamed college in Chicago, ponders private and public problems. Albert Corde experiences at first hand the rigid penitentiary society of the Communist East as well as the anarchic society of the non-Communist West, which seems on the verge of disintegration. The novel is a protest against the dehumanization of the individual. The East has enslaved its population, while the West has "written off" its doomed "Underclass." Like *Humboldt's Gift*, this novel can be seen as a kind of retrospective crisis meditation in which the protagonist attempts to come to terms with an immensely complex and threatening "multiverse," as Augie March calls it.

The complicated plot defies a succinct summary, but one can outline the basic situation. The dean and his wife Minna arrive in Rumania to visit her dying mother. Corde tries to help his despairing wife, who is unable to reconcile herself to the grim reality of her mother's death. He also ponders the controversy that he has provoked in Chicago. The dean has published two articles in *Harper's* in which he comments upon the political and social problems of the city. The articles outrage the powerful members of Chicago society, and the administration of his college disapproves of the controversy that the dean has provoked. Moreover, Corde creates another controversy when he pressures the police to solve the murder of a white graduate student, Rickie Lester. A sensational trial, a media "circus," is the result of the dean's search for justice.

While more than any other novel of Bellow, *The Dean's December* is concerned with contemporary public issues, especially the vile conditions of the inner city, it is also concerned with the spiritual state of the individual. In fact, Bellow suggests that there is a connection between the spiritual malady of the individual and the spiritual anarchy of society. The novel is a protest against not only man's lack of political freedom but also his spiritual enslavement that is the result of his inability to see clearly and to experience reality. Corde implies that this inability to experience reality is largely a product of "seeing" the world with a kind of reductive journalism completely lacking in imagination. Disgusted with contemporary journalism which provides only substitutes for reality, Corde intends to incorporate "poetry" into writing. The novel suggests that in Corde's kind of poetic vision there is hope for the spiritual rebirth of the individual and society.

Three years after the publication of his collection *Him with His Foot in His Mouth and Other Stories*, Bellow published *More Die of Heartbreak*. This comic novel does not have a highly structured plot but might be best described as an elaborate monologue from the overstimulated mind of the bachelor narrator, Kenneth Trachtenberg. Kenneth, an expert in Russian history and culture, is preoccupied with his uncle, Benn Crader, a renowned botanist. The only important "action" in the novel revolves around the attempt of Dr. Layamon, his daughter Matilda, and her fiancé Benn Crader to "extort" money from Benn's relative, Harold Vilitzer, a political racketeer in bad health. Years before, Vilitzer had cheated the Crader family in a real estate deal. The greedy Dr. Layamon sees his daughter's marriage to Benn as a marvelous opportunity to acquire a fortune if Benn will agree to pressure Vilitzer for the money the corrupt politician stole from the Crader family. Although he wants to please his beautiful fiancée and her father, Benn is not enthusiastic about the plan. As the narrator suggests, Benn is a man who should be in search of "higher meanings." At the end of the novel, Benn flees from the Layamons to the North Pole to carry out his research. The implication is that now he will be able to pursue his neglected aesthetic and metaphysical goals.

After being rejected by two periodicals because it was "too long," the short novel *A Theft* was published in 1989 as a paperback original. Like so many of Bellow's works, the plot of this 109-page novel is subordinate to Bellow's interest in character. Just as *Seize the Day* might be considered an intimate psychological exploration of Wilhelm, *A Theft* is a detailed exploration of the soul of the heroine. Clara Velde was brought up on old-time religion but has led a disorganized life, including disappointing love affairs, suicide attempts, and four marriages. Her fourth marriage is not successful, and she is actually in love with "an old flame," Ithiel Regler, a Henry Kissinger-like high-powered adviser to statesmen. For Clara, transcendent love between her and Ithiel is symbolized by an emerald ring that he gave her years ago. When this ring is stolen, Clara finds herself in a troubling search for it and experiences a kind of spiritual quest as well. She feels a special sense of kinship with her self-possessed au pair girl, Gina. In its epiphany-like quality, the conclusion of the novel is reminiscent of *Seize the Day*.

Another paperback original, the short novel *The Bellarosa Connection* is narrated by the wealthy founder of the Mnemosyne Institute in Philadelphia. The institute instructs businesspersons and others in the use of memory. The narrator, a retired widower, focuses his immense powers of recollection on two relatives who haunt him—Harry and Sorella Fonstein. Harry narrowly escaped the Nazi death camps, thanks to the Broadway producer Billy Rose, who made use of his gangster connections in Italy to help Fonstein and others escape to freedom. Billy Rose's generosity is particularly noteworthy, the narrator implies, because the Broadway producer has a sleazy reputation.

In the United States, Harry marries the intelligent, capable Sorella and becomes successful but is frustrated by Rose's repulsing Harry's repeated attempts to meet him and express his gratitude. The central scene of the novel is the dramatic encounter between Sorella and Billy Rose, in which the determined woman attempts to coerce the stubborn producer into meeting her husband by threatening to reveal sordid details of Rose's private life. Despite Sorella's "blackmail," Rose refuses to meet Harry.

As in "The Old System," Bellow in this short novel is pondering how the assimilation of Jews into American life can corrupt not only their values but also their souls. Sorella reflects: "The Jews could survive everything that Europe threw at them. I mean the lucky remnant. But now comes the next test—America." Apparently the United States proves "too much" for at least some of them.

Allan Chavkin

Other major works

SHORT FICTION: *Mosby's Memoirs and Other Stories*, 1968; *Him with His Foot in His Mouth and Other Stories*, 1984.

PLAYS: *The Wrecker*, 1954; *The Last Analysis*, 1964; *A Wen*, 1965; *Under the Weather*, 1966 (also known as *The Bellow Plays:* includes *Out from Under, A Wen*, and *Orange Soufflé*).

NONFICTION: *To Jerusalem and Back: A Personal Account*, 1976.

ANTHOLOGY: *Great Jewish Short Stories*, 1963.

Bibliography

Chavkin, Allan. "The Problem of Suffering in the Fiction of Saul Bellow." *Comparative Literature Studies* 21, no. 2 (1984): 161-174. Called "a major article" in *Saul Bellow: An Annotated Bibliography*, this piece provides an overview of Bellow's work. Chavkin rejects as simplistic the view that suffering in Bellow's fiction reveals "Jewish guilt" and pathological social masochism, as some have argued; instead, Chavkin shows that Bellow's sophisticated attitude toward suffering derives from Dostoyevski's humanism, the nineteenth century English Romantic tradition, Jewish humor, and antimodernism—or, to be exact, from Bellow's interpretations of those four traditions.

Cronin, Gloria L., and Blaine H. Hall. *Saul Bellow: An Annotated Bibliography*. 2d ed. New York: Garland, 1987. The standard bibliography of Bellow's work, this indispensable book includes a list of both primary and secondary sources. Cronin and Hall often annotate articles and reviews with substantive critical analysis. They also indicate the essential critical articles on Bellow's fiction—a feature that will be particularly appreciated by those novice readers who confront for the first time the mass of critical writing on the author.

Cronin, Gloria L., and L. H. Goldman. *Saul Bellow in the 1980's: A Collection of Critical Essays*. East Lansing: Michigan State University Press, 1989. This excellent collection of essays contains both general essays on Bellow's canon and specialized essays on individual works. The general essays consider such topics as Bellow's sense of history, his attitude toward Judaism, women in his novels, his allegiance to the English Romantic tradition, his criticism of the university and American culture, and his interest in character as a subject of his books. The book contains essays on Bellow's later novels, including *The Dean's December* (1982) and *More Die of Heartbreak* (1987). Also includes notes, an index, and an introduction.

Fuchs, Daniel. *Saul Bellow: Vision and Revision*. Durham, N.C.: Duke University Press, 1984. This unique book is the only critical study to make extensive use of Bellow's vast collection of unpublished manuscripts, including his unpublished letters. Fuchs shows the reader how a novel evolves through a number of drafts as Bellow in the process of revision discovers what he wants to say. This book is divided into two parts. In the first part Fuchs analyzes Bellow's literary and cultural milieus, with particular attention to the "modern tradition" and to the "example of Dostoyevski." In the second part, he examines specific works from *The Adventures of Augie March* (1953) to *Humboldt's Gift* (1975). Includes detailed discussions of Bellow's play *The Last Analysis* and some of his short stories, as well as a brief discussion of *The Dean's December* (1982). Fuchs's detailed notes contain much interesting information about Bellow's revisions and other matters. Index.

Goldman, Liela, ed. *Saul Bellow Journal*, 1982 to present. Praised in *American Literary Scholarship: An Annual*, this journal is published twice annually and includes articles on Bellow's work and life, book reviews, and a useful annotated critical bibliography of current work.

Harris, Mark. *Saul Bellow, Drumlin Woodchuck*. Athens: University of Georgia Press, 1980. Although this eccentric book will disappoint those who read it expecting to find a conventional biography, it does contain some interesting (and often comic) anecdotes about Bellow. Harris had hoped to write a biography of Bellow with the writer's cooperation, but the writer refused. Bellow may have felt that a writer must resist efforts to turn him into a monument—or perhaps he did not want Harris as his biographer. Until a conventional biography is published, this book will remain as the most detailed account of Bellow's life available. The absence of an index is unfortunate.

Kiernan, Robert. *Saul Bellow*. New York: Continuum, 1988. This lucidly written book contains chapters on Bellow's fiction, from *Dangling Man* (1944) to *More Die of Heartbreak* (1987). Kiernan also presents an introductory chapter on Bellow's life and career. In addition to providing an insightful analysis of Bellow's fiction, Kiernan intelligently evaluates the individual works in Bellow's canon. Although Kiernan does not discuss Bellow's drama, he does examine the stories and short novels in the writer's two collections. The book includes a chronology, a useful, detailed bibliography of works by and about Bellow, an index, and notes.

ARNOLD BENNETT

Born: Shelton, near Hanley, England; May 27, 1867
Died: London, England; March 27, 1931

Principal long fiction

A Man from the North, 1898; *Anna of the Five Towns*, 1902; *The Grand Babylon Hotel*, 1902; (published in the United States as *T. Racksole and Daughter*); *The Gates of Wrath*, 1903; *Leonora*, 1903; *A Great Man*, 1904; *Teresa of Watling Street*, 1904; *Sacred and Profane Love*, 1905; (published in the United States as *The Book of Carlotta*); *Hugo*, 1906; *Whom God Hath Joined*, 1906; *The Sinews of War*, 1906 (with Eden Phillpotts, published in the United States as *Doubloons*); *The Ghost*, 1907; *The City of Pleasure*, 1907; *The Statue*, 1908 (with Eden Phillpotts); *Buried Alive*, 1908; *The Old Wives' Tale*, 1908; *The Glimpse*, 1909; *Helen with the High Hand*, 1910; *Clayhanger*, 1910; *The Card*, 1911 (published in the United States as *Denry the Audacious*); *Hilda Lessways*, 1911; *The Regent*, 1913 (published in the United States as *The Old Adam*); *The Price of Love*, 1914; *These Twain*, 1915; *The Lion's Share*, 1916; *The Pretty Lady*, 1918; *The Roll-Call*, 1918; *Lilian*, 1922; *Mr. Prohack*, 1922; *Riceyman Steps*, 1923; *Elsie and the Child*, 1924; *Lord Raingo*, 1926; *The Strange Vanguard*, 1928 (published in the United States as *The Vanguard* in 1927); *Accident*, 1928; *Piccadilly*, 1929; *Imperial Palace*, 1930; *Venus Rising from the Sea*, 1931.

Other literary forms

Besides fifteen major novels, Arnold Bennett published thirty-three other novels generally considered potboilers by his critics. Some of them Bennett himself regarded as serious works; others he variously called "fantasias," "frolics," "melodramas," or "adventures." His total published work exceeds eighty volumes, including eight collections of short stories, sixteen plays, six collections of essays, eight volumes of literary criticism, three volumes of letters, six travelogues, and volumes of autobiography, journals, and reviews, as well as miscellaneous short articles, introductions, pamphlets, "pocket philosophies," and a few poems. Much of his journal has never been published. Bennett collaborated in the production of five films and operas, three of which were adapted from his plays and novels. Four of his plays and novels were adapted for film by other screenwriters, and two of his novels were adapted for the stage.

Achievements

Bennett's early novels played an important role in the transition from the Victorian to the modern novel. A somewhat younger contemporary of Thomas Hardy, Henry James, and Joseph Conrad, he helped to displace the "loose, baggy" Victorian novel and to develop the realistic movement in England. With fine detail he portrayed the industrial Five Towns, his fictional version of the six towns of pottery manufacturing in Staffordshire County. His early career was strongly influenced by the aestheticism in form and language found in works by Gustave Flaubert, Guy de Maupassant, and Ivan Turgenev, and he admired the naturalism of Honoré de Balzac, Emile Zola, and the Goncourts. Later, however, he rejected what he called the "crudities and . . . morsels of available misery" of naturalism, and, while retaining an interest in form and beauty, he came to feel that aesthetics alone is an empty literary goal and that the novelist must combine "divine compassion," believability, and the creation of character with the "artistic shapely presentation of truth" and the discovery of "beauty, which is always hidden." With these aims in mind, he chose as the subject of his best works that which is beautiful and remarkable about the lives of unremarkable, middle-class people. Although his novels rarely sold well enough to earn his living, his best novels were highly regarded by critics and fellow authors. He carried on a correspondence of mutual encouragement and criticism with Conrad and H. G. Wells; some of these letters have been published. Conrad, a master of style, wrote: "I am . . . fascinated by your expression, by the ease of your realization, the force and delicacy of your phrases." Despite their acclaim for Bennett's best work, however, even his admirers regretted his propensity to write potboilers for money.

Because of the volume of his work, Bennett is remembered today as a novelist, but in his lifetime his income derived from his equally prodigious output of plays and journalism; his "pocket philosophies" and critical reviews also won him an enormous public prestige. During the 1920's he was virtually the arbiter of literary taste, a reviewer who could make or break a book's sales or a newcomer's career. He was among the first to praise the literary merits of such controversial newcomers as D. H. Lawrence, T. S. Eliot, William Faulkner, Virginia Woolf, and James Joyce. Bennett regarded himself less as a novelist than as a professional writer who should be able to, and did, undertake any genre with competence and craftsmanship. (The exception was poetry; he never wrote poetry to meet his own standards.) His reputation suffered in the latter part of his career for those very qualities, which too often fell short of genius and inspiration. He did reach the level of greatness occasionally, however, and his literary reputation is firmly established with the inclusion of *The Old Wives' Tale* in most lists of the great English novels.

Biography

Enoch Arnold Bennett was born on May 27, 1867, in Shelton, Staffordshire County, England, near the six towns that constitute the Potteries region in cental England, the scene of much of Bennett's early work. His father, Enoch Bennett, was successively a potter, a draper, a pawnbroker, and eventually, through hard work and study, a solicitor. Bennett attended the local schools, where he passed the examination for Cambridge University. He did not attend college, however, because his autocratic father kept him at home as clerk in the solicitor's office.

As a means of escape from the grime and provincialism of the Potteries district, Bennett began writing for the *Staffordshire Sentinel* and studying shorthand. The latter skill enabled him to become a clerk with a London law firm in 1888. In London, he set about seriously to learn to write. He moved to Chelsea in 1891 to live with the Frederick Marriott family, in whose household he was introduced to the larger world of the arts. His first work published in London was a prizewinning parody for a competition in *Tit-Bits* in 1893; this work was followed by a short story in *The Yellow Book* and, in 1898, his first novel, *A Man from the North*. He became the assistant editor and later the editor of the magazine *Woman*, writing reviews pseudonymously as "Barbara," a gossip and advice column as "Marjorie," and short stories as "Sal Volatile." It is generally thought that this experience provided a good background for female characterization. As he became better known as a journalist, Bennett began writing reviews for *The Academy* and giving private lessons in journalism. His journalistic income allowed him in 1900 to establish a home at Trinity Hall Farm, Hockliffe, in Bedfordshire. He brought his family to Hockliffe after his father had been disabled by the softening of the brain which eventually killed him. Bennett wrote prodigiously there, producing not only his admired *Anna of the Five Towns* but also popular potboilers and journalism, including the anonymous "Savoir-Faire Papers" and "Novelist's Log-Book" series for *T. P.'s Weekly*. This production financed some long-desired travel and a move to Paris in 1903.

Bennett lived in France for eight years, some of the busiest and happiest of his life. Shortly after his arrival, he observed a fat, fussy woman who inspired the thought that "she has been young and slim once," a thought that lingered in his mind for five years and inspired his masterwork, *The Old Wives' Tale*. Meanwhile, he continued writing for newspapers and magazines, including the first of his series "Books and Persons," written under the nom de plume "Jacob Tonson" for *The New Age*. Between 1903 and 1907 he also wrote ten novels. In 1907, he married Marguerite Soulié, an aspiring actress who had worked as his part-time secretary. From the beginning of the marriage, it was evident that the two were incompatible, but she did provide him with an atmosphere conducive to his undertaking the novel which had germinated for so long and which he felt beforehand would be a masterpiece. He determined that *The Old Wives' Tale* should "do one better than" Guy de Maupassant's *Une Vie* (1883), and his careful crafting of the book was recognized by critics, who immediately acclaimed it as a modern classic. Before moving back to England in 1913, he wrote six more novels, three of which are among his best: *Clayhanger*, *The Card*, and *Hilda Lessways*. In

1911, he traveled in the United States, where his books were selling well and were highly respected. After the tour, he moved to the country estate Comarques at Thorpe-le-Soken, Essex, where he had access to the harbor for a yacht, his means of gaining what relaxation he could.

The yacht was important to Bennett, because he had suffered since youth from a variety of ailments, mostly resulting from his high-strung temperament. He had a serious stammer or speech paralysis, which exhausted him in speaking; compulsive personal habits; and a liver ailment and chronic enteritis which restricted his diet and caused great discomfort when he ate incautiously. As he grew older, he suffered increasingly from excruciating neuralgia, headaches, and insomnia, almost without relief near the end of his life. Except for the yacht, his recreation was to write; he probably wrote his light works as a relief from the tension of the serious novels, yet he demanded good style from himself even for them. His craftsmanship was conscious and intense, and his drive to produce great quantity while still maintaining quality undoubtedly sapped his strength both physically and psychologically, and contributed to his death at the age of sixty-four.

Bennett's physical maladies were probably exacerbated by World War I and the collapse of his marriage. Although he continued his usual pace of writing during the war—five more novels between 1914 and 1919—much of his energy was spent in patriotic activities ranging from entertaining soldiers to front-line journalism. From May 9, 1918, until the end of the war, he served as volunteer director of British propaganda in France. He refused knighthood for his services. After the war, he tried to restore his depleted finances by writing plays, which had been more remunerative than novels, but the later ones were unsuccessful. In 1921, he and Marguerite separated. He gave her a settlement so generous that for the rest of his life he was under pressure to publish and sell his writing. Contemporary critics believed that these years of low-novel production marked the end of his creativity.

Bennett surprised his critics, however, with *Riceyman Steps*, which was critically acclaimed and was awarded the James Tait Black Novel prize, Bennett's only literary award. This was followed by *Lord Raingo* and *Imperial Palace*, as well as six less distinguished novels and one unfinished at his death. This creative resurgence may have resulted in part from his relationship with Dorothy Cheston, who bore his only child, Virginia, in 1926. His journalistic career had never waned, and in the 1920's he continued his "Books and Persons" series in the *Evening Standard*, with a prestige that influenced the reading public and allowed him to promote the careers of many young authors. Bennett's health was steadily deteriorating, however, and in 1931 he died in his Chiltern Court flat from typhoid fever.

Analysis

As a self-designated professional author, Arnold Bennett not only wrote an extraordinary quantity in a great variety of genres but also created a broad range of themes and characters. A common approach or theme is difficult to detect in a corpus of forty-eight novels which include fantasy, realism, romance, naturalism, satire, symbolism, comedy, tragedy, melodrama, Freudian psychology, allegory, economics, regionalism, cosmopolitanism, politics, medicine, and war. Nevertheless, in spite of this diversity, Bennett is generally esteemed for his realistic novels, which are considered his serious work. In most, if not all, of these fifteen novels, certain related themes recur, rising from his youthful experiences of growing up in Burslem under the domination of his father. His desire to escape the intellectual, aesthetic, and spiritual stultification of his Burslem environment led to a cluster of themes related to escape: rebellion against the ties of the home conflicting with love for one's roots; aspiration versus complacence and philistinism; fear of failure to escape and fear of failure after escape; and the problem of coping with success if it comes. Another cluster of themes relates to his conflict with his father and the shock of his father's debilitating illness and death: the generation gap, emotional repression by dominating parents, the cyclical influence of parents on their children, a soul parent who vies in influence with the natural parent, degeneration and illness, the pathos of decrepitude in old age, awe at the purpose or purposelessness of life.

A Man from the North, Bennett's first novel, includes the themes of aspiration, emotional repression, the soul parent, illness and death, and failure after escape. It is the story of Richard Larch, an aspiring writer from the Potteries, who goes to London to experience the greater intellectual and moral freedom of a cosmopolis. There he meets his soul father, Mr. Aked, a journalist and failed novelist who introduces Larch to the drama—the "tragedy"—of ordinary lives. Aked, however, is an unsuccessful guide; he dies. Larch is also unable to succeed; he eventually marries a woman he does not love and settles down to the sort of life Aked had described. It is the story of what Bennett himself might have been if he had not succeeded after leaving Burslem.

Anna of the Five Towns, on the other hand, is the story of the failure to escape. Anna is repressed by her overbearing and miserly father; under the influence of her soul mother, Mrs. Sutton, she learns to aspire to a few amenities, such as new clothes for her wedding, but these aspirations come too late to change her life significantly. Accepting the values of the community rather than escaping them, she marries Henry Mynors, her more prosperous suitor, rather than Willie Price, the man she loves in her own way. While the themes of these books are similar, they differ in that Anna stays and copes with her environment with some success. She does not escape Bursley (Bennett's fictional name for Burslem), but she escapes her father's control and improves her perceptions of beauty and human relationships to some degree. The books also differ in that *A Man from the North* presents an unrelentingly grim memory of Burslem. Later, however, Bennett read George Moore's *A Mummer's Wife* (1885), and its section on Burslem showed him that "beauty, which is always hidden," could be found in the lives of its people and in art expressing those lives. Thus, Bennett returned to the locale for *Anna of the Five Towns*, and although the portrayal is still grim, Anna's life has tragic beauty. Anna rebels against the ties of home, but she also has some love for her roots there, in the person of Willie Price.

Between *Anna of the Five Towns* and *The Old Wives' Tale*, Bennett wrote eleven minor novels, some of which were serious and some not, but all taught him something that contributed to the greatness of *The Old Wives' Tale*. Several of them were light comedies, and in writing these Bennett developed the assured comic touch which marks even his serious novels. Three of them were Five Towns novels about female characters from various segments of Bursley society; in these he developed those skills in characterizing women which were so admired in his finest novels. These skills were honed in France, where Bennett learned a great deal about the literary presentation of sex. During these years, Bennett said, he learned more about life than he had ever known before.

When Bennett was ready to write his masterpiece, *The Old Wives' Tale*, he had reached full artistic maturity and was at the height of his literary power. He had published one critically acclaimed novel and several others that had allowed him to improve his characterization, especially of women, to temper his realism with humor, and to perfect his themes in various plots. His dislike of Burslem's grime and provincialism had been balanced by compassion for its inhabitants and awareness of what beauty and aspiration could be found there. His personal involvement in the town had been modified by experience in London and Paris, so that he could be objective about the sources of his material. This balance of technique and emotion is reflected in the structure of *The Old Wives' Tale*. The novel counterpoints the lives of two sisters, Constance and Sophia Baines, the first of whom stays in Bursley while the second leaves but later returns. Their stories parallel not only each other but also those of preceding and succeeding generations. In fact, the first section of the book is subtitled "Mrs. Baines" (the mother).

In section one, *The Old Wives' Tale* takes up in mid-career one generation's old wife, with a husband so ill that the wife is running his draper's business and rearing two young daughters. As the girls grow up, Mrs. Baines finds them increasingly hard to handle. During a town festival in which an elephant has to be executed for killing a spectator, Mr. Baines dies. Shortly afterward, Sophia elopes with Gerald Scales, a traveling salesman, and Constance marries Samuel Povey, the former shop assistant, whom Mrs. Baines considers "beneath" her. When Samuel and Constance take over the business, introducing progressive marketing methods. Mrs. Baines retires to live with her elder sister, and dies there. The story of Mrs. Baines, then, is the end of the life of a woman who "was young and slim once," although she is not depicted so and that part of her life is understood only by later comparison with the stories of her daughters.

The cycle of Mrs. Baines continues with Constance, who represents the person who stays in Bursley, held by the roots of the past. As Mrs. Baines's successor, Constance marries a husband whose aspiration is to improve, not to leave, Bursley, and they run the business with a combination of youthful progressiveness and family tradition. Constance and Samuel have a son, Cyril. After a scandal in which Samuel's cousin is executed for murdering his alcoholic wife, Samuel dies. Constance continues the business for a while, unresponsive to further progressive business practices, and spoils her son until he becomes hard for her to manage. She is finally forced to retire from business by changes in the business structure of Bursley, and Cyril escapes from her and Bursley to London to study art. As a result, Constance comes to depend emotionally on Cyril's cousin, Dick.

Sophia, the rebel against Bursley, finds a soul mother in the school teacher, who introduces her to a world of wider intellectual aspiration. In her eagerness to experience more than Bursley offers, however, she elopes with a salesman, who represents sophistication and romance to her. They go to France, where they squander their money and slip into mutual disillusionment and recrimination. After observing the public execution of the murderer of a courtesan, Sophia becomes ill and is abandoned by Gerald. She eventually acquires a boarding house in Paris, where she supports several dependents and survives the siege of Paris through single-minded hoarding and hard work. She becomes a reclusive fixture on her street, much like Constance on her square in Bursley. When she becomes ill and the business becomes hard for her to manage, she sells it and returns to Bursley to grow old and die.

Each daughter's life recapitulates Mrs. Baines's in certain respects. Each marries, loses a husband, succors children or other dependents, runs a business, gradually loses control over her life (the change marked in each case by a symbolic execution), loses health and strength, and retires to die as a burdensome old woman like the one Bennett saw in the Paris restaurant. Further, although they are not women, the two Povey young men, Cyril and his cousin Dick, recapitulate the early years of Sophia and Constance: Cyril, the rebel who leaves Bursley but does not succeed; and Dick, the stay-at-home progressive idealist. At the end, Dick is engaged to marry a slim, young counterpart to Constance, who will no doubt carry on the cycle. The thematic repetitions are not so obvious as they appear here, of course; the variations of individual character allow the reader a sense of more difference than similarity.

The variations also mark a further step in Bennett's use of his themes. Constance and Sophia are not so warped by Bursley as was Anna in *Anna of the Five Towns*; in fact, Sophia, who escapes, is warped more than Constance, who stays. Both have strength derived from their roots, and while neither can be said to escape or to achieve happiness or grace in living, both transcend Bursley more successfully than other townspeople. The theme of their decrepitude in old age is a separate one, also used in other novels, but not related to the escape and success themes. The Baineses are grouped in other Five Towns stories with those who succeed on Bursley's terms. Beginning in 1906 in *Whom God Hath Joined*, in the collection of short stories *The Matador of the Five Towns* (1912), and in *The Old Wives' Tale*, there is a growing emphasis upon those members of Burslem society who have some education, culture, and sophistication. Perhaps Bennett had been reassured by his personal success that his childhood in Burslem could be accepted.

Whether it is true that Bennett had come to accept his past, it is certainly true that his next serious book, *Clayhanger*, was his most nearly autobiographical. After the completion of the trilogy of which *Clayhanger* was the first volume, Bennett turned from the Five Towns to London as the setting for his novels. The Clayhanger trilogy is the story of a man who at first is defeated in his desire to escape Bursley. Having been defeated, however, he learns from his soul father to rise above Bursley's philistinism. Over the years, he breaks one after another of his bonds to Bursley until he has succeeded in escaping intellectually, and eventually, he completely abandons the Five Towns.

Much of this story occurs in the third volume of the trilogy, *These Twain*. *Clayhanger* itself is the story of the generational conflict between Edwin Clayhanger and his father Darius. The conflict is similar to the one between Anna and her father in *Anna of the Five Towns* and between Sophia and Mrs. Baines in *The Old Wives' Tale*, but in *Clayhanger* it is much more intense and more acutely observed. Edwin is sensitively introduced in the first two chapters; he has within him "a flame . . . like an altar-fire," a passion "to exhaust himself in doing his best." He is rebelling against his father, whose highest aspiration for his son is to have him take over his printing business. The advancement of the theme in *Clayhanger* over its treatment in the earlier novels is that the generational conflict is presented sympathetically on both sides. In Chapters Three and Four, Darius is portrayed as sensitively as Edwin has been previously. In an intensely moving chapter, his childhood of promise, stifled at seven years by poverty and abusive child labor, is described. Because Darius as a "man of nine" was unable to "keep the family," they were sent to the poorhouse. They were rescued from this degradation by Darius' Sunday school teacher (his soul father), who had recognized Darius' promise and who got Darius a decent job as a printer's devil. This background of deprivation and emotional sterility prevents Darius from expressing his softer emotions, such as his love for Edwin; his total dedication to the business which he built and by which he supports his family is thoroughly empathetic to the reader. It is no wonder that he can conceive nothing nobler for Edwin than to carry on this decent business. Because Darius can never discuss these traumatic childhood experiences, Edwin never understands him any more than he understands Edwin.

In his desire to hold onto his son and keep him in the family business, Darius simply ignores and overrides Edwin's inchoate talent for architecture. Later, he uses Edwin's financial dependence to squelch his desire to marry Hilda Lessways, whom Edwin has met through the architect Osmond Orgreave. Although Edwin resents his father's domination, he cannot openly rebel; he feels inadequate before his father's dominance, and he looks forward to the day when he will have his vengeance. This day comes when Darius becomes ill with softening of the brain, the same ailment that killed Bennett's own father. The progression of the illness and Edwin's emotions of triumph, irritation, and compassion are exquisitely detailed. Even after Darius' death, however, Edwin is not free from his father's presence, for he becomes increasingly like his father, learning to take pride in the business and to tyrannize over his sisters and Hilda, with whom he is reconciled at the end of the book. *Clayhanger* thus concludes with the apparent defeat of aspiration by the cycle of parental influence.

The hope of eventual success has been raised, however, by the death of Darius, that primary symbol of Bursley repression, and the return of Hilda, the symbol of aspiration. In *Hilda Lessways*, the second book of the trilogy, Bennett picks up her parallel story of generational conflict with her mother and cultural conflict with Turnhill, another of the Five Towns. Hilda's story is far less compelling than Edwin's, though, and adds little to the plot development. More important, its structure repeats what Bennett did successfully in *The Old Wives' Tale*: it contrasts two efforts to cope with Bursley, which provide for a double perspective on the problem, and then brings them together for the denouement made possible by that combined perspective. The double perspective also allows Bennett to maintain his characteristic objectivity and touch of humor. *These Twain* presents the marriage of Edwin and Hilda. Through a series of adjustments and small victories, the two are able to achieve a social success in the Five Towns which allows them to wean themselves emotionally from the Potteries and leave forever. The *Clayhanger* trilogy thus deals with escape and success, rather than some aspect of failure as in the earlier novels.

These Twain was the last Five Towns novel. In changing his fictional settings from Bursley to London or the Continent, Bennett also extended his themes from success or failure in escaping poverty and provincialism to success or failure in handling the accomplished escape. Perhaps that is another reason, besides the ones usually offered, for Bennett's long period of low productivity and substandard potboilers from 1915 to 1922. Between *Anna of the Five Towns* and *The Old Wives' Tale*, one should remember, there had been a similar period of low-quality work during which Bennett perfected skills that made the Five Towns novels great. Similarly, in his postwar characters Audrey Moze, George Cannon, G. J. Hoape, Lilian Share, and Mr. Prohack, Bennett experimented with stories of people who must cope with financial or social responsibilities for which they may have been poorly prepared. Also in these stories he experimented more boldly with varieties of sexual relationships: in *The Lion's Share*, implied lesbianism; in *The Pretty Lady*, prostitution; in *Lilian*, a mistress. Furthermore, although these next qualities do not show up clearly in the low-quality work of this period, the use of symbols and psychological insight must have been developing in Bennett's mind. These qualities emerge rather suddenly and very effectively in the novels beginning with *Riceyman Steps*. They may account for some of the high acclaim which that novel received after the period of reorientation, but the adapted themes were perfected by 1923, as well.

The themes in *Riceyman Steps* are variations on those of the Five Towns novels, not departures which might seem necessary to a metropolitan setting. The decayed and grimy industrial area of Clerkenwell is in many respects Bursley resituated in London. Henry Earlforward, the miser, represents Bursley's industrial materialism. Henry, like Edwin Clayhanger, has succeeded in that environment; he has a well-respected bookstore that offers him financial self-sufficiency. Unlike Edwin, however, Henry's complacent rootedness to Clerkenwell progressively cuts him off from grace, beauty, then love, and finally even life. His wife, Violet, also has financial security, but because she fears the loss of her success, she has become almost as miserly as he. Both are described as sensual; Henry's rich red lips are mentioned several times, and Violet, formerly a widow, wears red flowers in her hat. Money, however, is the chief object of their eroticism. Henry's miserliness is his passion, and he gives Violet her own safe as a wedding gift. Violet becomes "liquid with acquiescence" after seeing the hoarded disorder of his house, and she urges him to bed after he has shown her the gold coins in his private safe. The passion for money soon overrides the related passion of human love. Henry especially, and Violet in acquiescence, lock doors more tightly about themselves to protect their treasures until each is figuratively shut into a private, iron-walled safe. Starving emotionally and intellectually in their isolation, they finally starve themselves physically as well, rather than spend money for adequate food. Here, aspiration gone awry, the fear of failure and the inability to cope with success become literally debilitating diseases. Violet dies of a tumor and malnutrition and Henry of cancer. After death, they are scarcely missed, the ultimate symbols of the stultification which Bennett's characters strive with varying success to escape.

After *Riceyman Steps*, the next few novels—*Lord Raingo*, *Accident*, and *Imperial Palace*—continue the themes of coping with success, and the protagonists are given increasing ability to handle it. Much as Clayhanger finally overcomes the problems of escape, Evelyn Orcham in *Imperial Palace* is the culminating figure in the second cluster of themes. Ironically, Bennett died shortly after he had resolved the problems underlying the themes of his serious novels.

All of Bennett's serious works are firmly rooted in the realistic tradition (although he used more symbolism than has generally been recognized), and he excelled in the presentation of detail that makes his themes and characters credible. In the late years of his career, he was criticized by Virginia Woolf for portraying people's surroundings, rather than the people themselves, and forcing his readers to do his imagining for him, even though he believed that character creating was one of the three most important functions of a novel. Woolf's criticism was sound enough to seriously damage Bennett's standing as a major novelist, and it has been the keystone of critical opinion ever since. Yet, a sense of environmental impact has always been accepted as an important means of characterization in realistic literature. Woolf's criticism says as much about changing styles in literature as it does about the merits of Bennett's fiction. More important, it was a criticism aimed at Bennett's total canon, since his potboilers had not yet died of their natural ailments when Woolf wrote. Sophia and Constance Baines, Edwin and Darius Clayhanger, and Henry Earlforward are finely articulated, memorable characters. It is, after all, for his best work that any artist is remembered. Bennett's sense of place, characters, and universality of themes combine to make his finest novels memorable; *The Old Wives' Tale* is sufficient to secure Bennett's stature as one of the outstanding novelists of his era.

Carol I. Croxton

Other major works

SHORT FICTION: *The Loot of Cities*, 1905; *Tales of the Five Towns*, 1905; *The Grim Smile of the Five Towns*, 1907; *The Matador of the Five Towns*, 1912; *The Woman Who Stole Everything*, 1927; *Selected Tales*, 1928; *The Night Visitor*, 1931.

PLAYS: *Polite Farces*, 1900; *Cupid and Commonsense*, 1908; *What the Public Wants*, 1909; *The Honeymoon: A Comedy in Three Acts*, 1911; *Milestones: A Play in Three Acts*, 1912 (with Edward Knoblock); *The Great Adventure: A Play of Fantasia in Four Sets*, 1913; *The Title*, 1918; *Judith*, 1919; *Sacred and Profane Love*, 1919; *Body and Soul*, 1922; *The Love Match*, 1922; *Don Juan*, 1923; *London Life*, 1924 (with Edward Knoblock); *Flora*, 1927; *Mr. Prohack*, 1927 (with Edward Knoblock); *The Return Journey*, 1928 (produced).

NONFICTION: *Journalism for Women*, 1898; *Fame and Fiction*, 1901; *The Truth About an Author*, 1903; *How to Become an Author*, 1903; *Things That Interested Me*, 1906; *Things Which Have Interested Me*, 1907, 1908; *Books and Persons: Being Comments on a Past Epoch*, 1908-1911; *Literary Taste*,

1909; *Those United States*, 1912 (published in the United States as *Your United States*); *Paris Nights*, 1913; *From the Log of the Velsa*, 1914; *The Author's Craft*, 1914; *Over There*, 1915; *Things That Have Interested Me*, 1921, 1923, 1926; *Selected Essays*, 1926; *Mediterranean Scenes*, 1928; *The Savour of Life*, 1928; *The Journals of Arnold Bennett*, 1929, 1930, 1932-1933.

Bibliography

Batchelor, John. *The Edwardian Novelists*. New York: St. Martin's Press, 1982. After quoting Virginia Woolf's reservations about Bennett's fiction, Batchelor goes on to compare the two novelists, especially in terms of their treatment of women as being socially conditioned. In addition to discussing *Clayhanger, A Man from the North, Anna of the Five Towns*, and *The Old Wives' Tale*, Batchelor examines Bennett's acclaimed short story, "The Death of Simon Fuge."

Drabble, Margaret. *Arnold Bennett*. New York: Alfred A. Knopf, 1974. Drawing from Bennett's *Journals* and letters, this biography focuses on Bennett's background, childhood, and environment, which she ties to his literary works. Profusely illustrated, containing an excellent index (the entry under Bennett provides a capsule summary of his life) and a bibliography of Bennett's work.

Lucas, John. *Arnold Bennett: A Study of His Fiction*. London: Methuen, 1974. After a brief review of Bennett criticism, Lucas examines Bennett's fiction, devoting lengthy treatments to his major novels which are discussed in terms of character and plot. Ardently defends Bennett's realism, which is regarded as equal to that of D. H. Lawrence. This impressionistic study lacks documentation, except for copious quotations from Bennett's work.

Roby, Kinley. *A Writer at War: Arnold Bennett, 1914-1918*. Baton Rouge: Louisiana State University Press, 1972. Although primarily biographical, this book also offers valuable insights into Bennett's work during and after World War I. Defends Bennett's post-1914 work, contending that it was influenced by Bennett's exhaustion of his Five Towns material, by his steadily deteriorating relationship with his wife, Marguerite, and by the war itself. Contains works cited and an excellent index.

Wain, John. "Arnold Bennett." In *Six Modern British Novelists*, edited by George Stade. New York: Columbia University Press, 1974. This well-written essay, more biographical than critical, ties Bennett's life to his work, asserting that *Clayhanger* is Bennett's early life. Focuses on *Clayhanger* and *The Pretty Lady*.

Wright, Walter F. *Arnold Bennett: Romantic Realist*. Lincoln: University of Nebraska Press, 1971. Sees Bennett as vacillating between the two extremes of romanticism and realism and describes his novels as mildly experimental.

THOMAS BERGER

Born: Cincinnati, Ohio; July 20, 1924

Principal long fiction

Crazy in Berlin, 1958; *Reinhart in Love*, 1962; *Little Big Man*, 1964; *Killing Time*, 1967; *Vital Parts*, 1970; *Regiment of Women*, 1973; *Sneaky People*, 1975; *Who Is Teddy Villanova?*, 1977; *Arthur Rex*, 1978; *Neighbors*, 1980; *Reinhart's Women*, 1981; *The Feud*, 1983; *Nowhere*, 1985; *Being Invisible*, 1987; *The Houseguest*, 1988; *Changing the Past*, 1989; *Orrie's Story*, 1990.

Other literary forms

Thomas Berger has published numerous articles, reviews, and short stories in magazines such as the *Saturday Evening Post, Esquire, Harper's*, and *Playboy*. He has written three plays, all unpublished, but one of which, *Other People*, was staged in 1970 at the Berkshire Theatre Festival in Massachusetts.

Achievements

For more than thirty years, Berger has been one of America's most productive, most respected, and most challenging literary figures. His novels, including the highly acclaimed *Little Big Man* and critically and popularly successful works such as *Who Is Teddy Villanova?* and *Neighbors*, seem sure to earn for him a lasting place in American letters. His Reinhart series (four volumes to date) is one of the most unique and significant accomplishments of postwar American literature, forming as it does both a sociological epic and an index to the changing face of the American novel over the last twenty-five years. Acknowledged as a masterful prose stylist, Berger writes novels that are aggressively intelligent without being ostentatiously "difficult," works that are often hilariously funny without losing their serious bite.

In 1970, Richard Schickel correctly identified Berger as "one of the most radical sensibilities now writing in America," and bemoaned the fact that Berger had not received the recognition he deserved. More than a decade later, Thomas R. Edwards intensified this complaint with the charge that the failure to read and discuss Berger's work was no less than "a national disgrace." Edwards, however, was writing on the front page of *The New York Times Book Review* and his praise for *Neighbors* was flanked by an interview with Berger, conducted by Schickel. In short, the recognition and acclaim that so long eluded Berger's writing seem to be catching up with his career, and a growing number of doctoral dissertations and scholarly articles indicates that his work is being studied as well as applauded. Reviewing *Neighbors* for the *Chicago Tribune*, Frederick Busch may have best summed up Berger's stature as a novelist when he said: "This is a novel by Thomas Berger, and everything he writes should be read and considered."

Biography

Thomas Louis Berger was born in Cincinnati, Ohio, on July 20, 1924, and grew up in the nearby suburban community of Lockland. Disenchanted after a short bout with college, Berger enlisted in the Army, serving from 1943 to 1946, his experiences giving him some of the background for his first novel, *Crazy in Berlin*.

After the war, he returned to college, receiving his B.A. at the University of Cincinnati in 1948. He continued his studies as a graduate student in English at Columbia (1950-1951), where he completed course work for an M.A., and he began a thesis on George Orwell, never completing it. Instead, Berger turned his attention to the writers' workshop at the New School for Social Research. In that workshop, under the aegis of Charles Glicksberg, Berger began to write short stories. "I produced one story a week for three months, most of them melancholy in tone, maudlin in spirit, and simple of mind," he recounts, "Hemingway then being my model." Berger dismisses his short fiction, explaining "the marathon is my event, and not the hundred-yard dash." Despite this assessment, Berger's short fiction has appeared in magazines ranging from the *Saturday Evening Post*, to *Harper's*, *Esquire*, *Playboy*, and *North American Review*.

From 1948 through 1951, Berger supported his writing by working as a librarian at the Rand School of Social Science. Between 1951 and 1952, he was a staff member of *The New York Times Index*, and the following year he was a copy editor for *Popular Science Monthly*. Until 1964 and the publication of his third novel, *Little Big Man*, Berger had to supplement the income from his fiction with free-lance editing. From 1971 to 1973, Berger wrote a characteristically idiosyncratic film column for *Esquire*, managing to discuss almost everything *but* major motion pictures of the day.

Since 1950, Berger has been married to Jeanne Redpath, an artist he met at the New School. He has moved about, living among other places in London and on an island in Maine. In 1981-1982, Berger was a visiting lecturer at Yale, and in 1986 he was given an honorary doctor of letters degree by Long Island University. He now lives outside New York City.

Analysis

The dust-jacket blurb written by Thomas Berger for *Who Is Teddy Villanova?* reviews the general scheme of his career, pointing out that each of his novels "celebrates another classic genre of fiction: the western [*Little Big Man*], the childhood memoir [*Sneaky People*], the anatomical romance [*Regiment of Women*], the true-crime documentary [*Killing Time*], and the Reinhart books [*Crazy in Berlin*, *Reinhart in Love*, and *Vital Parts*] together form a sociological epic." *Who Is Teddy Villanova?* extended this pattern to the classic American hard-boiled detective story, *Arthur Rex* extended it to Arthurian romance, *Neighbors* traces its lineage most directly to Franz Kafka, and

Reinhart's Women continues the Reinhart series. In similar fashion, *The Feud* offers Dreiserian slice-of-life naturalism, *Nowhere* celebrates the utopian fantasy, *Being Invisible* acknowledges its precursors in the invisibility narratives of both H. G. Wells and Ralph Ellison, and with *Orrie's Story*, Berger "reinvents" the Greek tragedy of the Oresteia. The mistaken notion that these "celebrations" of classic novel forms are really parodies has dogged Berger's career, but unlike parody, his novels start from rather than aim toward literary traditions; he achieves a testing and broadening of possibilities rather than a burlesquing of limitations. If anything, his celebrations serve as kinds of *deparodisations*, twisting genres already self-conscious to the point of parody in ways that radically defamiliarize them.

Most critics have failed to consider that Berger's manipulations of novel forms are ultimately self-exploring and reflexive literary experiments. He tries to make of each novel an "independent existence," an alternative verbal reality he hopes the reader will approach "without the luggage of received ideas, *a priori* assumptions, sociopolitical axes to grind, or feeble moralities in search of support." This verbal world both owes its existence to a number of traditional and arbitrary literary conventions of representation and seeks to remind the reader that the working of those conventions is of interest and significance in itself—not only as a means to the representation of reality.

Failing to appreciate the independent existence of Berger's fictional worlds, reviewers have misread *Little Big Man* as an indictment of American abuse of Indians, *Regiment of Women* as a polemic for or against the women's movement, *Neighbors* as a critique of suburban life, and so on. Such a topical approach to these novels ignores the possibility that Berger's real theme is language, and that underlying the manically different surfaces of his novels is a constant preoccupation with the ways in which problems of human existence stem from the confusion of language with reality. Again and again, Berger's novels find new ways to suggest that the structures and institutions that order and give meaning to existence are much less important than the ways in which one talks about them, and that the ways one talks about those organizing beliefs inevitably have been designed by someone to influence and/ or manipulate someone else's perception and judgment. His ex-wife spells this out for Reinhart when she chides: "It ought to begin to occur to you that life is just a collection of stories from all points of self-interest."

Accordingly, the lives of Berger's characters are affected more by words than by actions. Victimized by definitions that exclude or threaten them, by rhetoric that makes them lose sight of physical facts, and by language designed more to preclude than to encourage clear thinking, his characters are enslaved by language. For this reason, the plot of a Berger novel typically chronicles the efforts of the protagonist to free himself from someone else's verbal version of reality. In this way, Jack Crabb in *Little Big Man* bounces back and forth not only between white and plains Indian cultures, but also between competing codes of conduct designed to legitimize all manner of cruelty. Berger shows how Jack's greatest problems are actually matters of definition, as he inevitably finds himself defined as white when the situation is controlled by Indians and as Indian when the situation is controlled by whites. All of Berger's novels explore the processes of victimization, as each Berger protagonist struggles, whether consciously or unconsciously, to free himself from the inexorable tendency to think of himself as a victim of outrages and impositions, both humorously small and tragically large.

While Berger refuses to subscribe to any single codified philosophy, whether romantic, existential, or absurd, his characters do live in worlds that seem to operate largely on Nietzschean principles. As Frederick Turner has observed, Berger's moral stance is consistently "beyond sentimentality, beyond classic American liberalism," concerning itself with fundamentals rather than with surfaces. Like Friedrich Nietzsche, Berger assumes that "there are higher problems than the problems of pleasure and pain and sympathy," though few of his characters would subscribe to this view—their pleasure, their pain, and their sympathy being of paramount importance to them.

Those characters are a string of outrageously impossible but compellingly plausible individuals who seem, in Berger's words, to be "persistent liars" and "monsters of one persuasion or another." Berger is uniformly fond of these "monsters," and his characters can never be branded as "good" or "evil," since all are as appealing in their often bizarre excesses as they are sadly humorous in their deficiencies. Most important, all of Berger's characters *do their best*. They may trick, abuse, and betray one another, but in a world where understanding seems full of drawbacks and the irresponsible consistently victimize those who feel obligations, they are finally no more nor less than normal. In the courtroom of his novels, Berger refuses to become either judge or advocate, choosing instead to establish a dialectic of wildly opposing viewpoints. He explains that his job is to maintain these characters in equilibrium, a concern of "art and not politics or sociology."

No analysis of Berger's novels would be complete without mentioning the delights of his prose style. Berger is one of a handful of American writers, contemporary or otherwise, for whom the sentence is an event in itself. His style challenges the reader with precise but often elaborate or serpentine sentences, reflecting his conviction that "the sentence is the cell beyond which the life of the book cannot be traced, a novel being a structure of such cells: most must be vital or the body is dead." What sentence vitality means to Berger can be seen in the way he elaborates the commonplace metaphor of the "ham-fisted" punch in *Who Is Teddy Villanova?*:

> He had struck me on the forehead, that helmet of protective bone, an impractical stroke even for such stout fingers as his, had he not turned his hand on edge and presented to my skull the resilient karate blade that swells out between the base of the smallest digit and the wrist: in his case, the size and consistency of the fleshy side of a loin of pork.

This marvelous punch knocks out Russell Wren, Berger's private-eye narrator, who comes to with the equally meticulous and mannered realization: "My loafers were in a position just ahead of his coal-barge brogans, a yard from where I slumped; meanwhile, my feet, twisted on their edges and crushed under the crease between thigh and buttock, were only stockinged: he had knocked me out of my shoes!" Leonard Michaels described this style as "one of the great pleasures of the book . . . educated, complicated, graceful, silly, destructive in spirit," and his comment applies to all of Berger's novels. Noting that he looks for himself through the English language, Berger states that for him language is "a morality and a politics and a religion."

In Berger's first novel, *Crazy in Berlin*, the twenty-one-year-old Carlo Reinhart, a United States Army medic in occupied Berlin, struggles to reconcile the conflicting claims of Nazism, Judaism, Communism, and Americanism, and his own German heritage—all overshadowed by the more fundamental concepts of friendship, victimization, and survival. This first of the Reinhart novels also features the points of view of a manic series of contradictory characters, including an American intelligence officer who is an idealistic Communist, a Russian officer who wants to become a capitalist, and a cynical ex-Nazi now working as a Russian agent.

In the second Reinhart novel, *Reinhart in Love*, Berger's bumbling protagonist is discharged from the army, in which he had been happy, and returns to civilian life, which he finds singularly disastrous. His comic misadventures are guided by Claude Humbold, a wonderfully devious real-estate agent/con man for whom Reinhart reluctantly works, by the enterprising and calculating Genevieve Raven, whom he is tricked into marrying, and by Splendor Mainwaring, his black friend whose special talent is getting Reinhart into impossible situations.

Had Berger never written anything but *Little Big Man*, he would have earned a respected place in American literary history. This story of Jack Crabb's life in both the Cheyenne and white cultures of the historical as well as the dime-novel Old West has been called variously "the best novel about the West," "a Barthian western," and "a seminal event in what must now seem the most significant cultural and litarary trend of the last decade—the attempt on many fronts to develop structures, styles, ways of thinking that are beyond any version of ethnocentricism." The story has been transcribed ostensibly from the tape-recorded reminiscences of "the late Jack Crabb—frontiersman, Indian scout, gunfighter, buffalo hunter, adopted Cheyenne—in his final days upon this earth." That Jack's final days come 111 years after his first, and that he also claims to have been the sole white survivor of the Battle of the Little Bighorn, raises obvious questions about the truth of his account. Furthermore, Jack's narrative comes to the reader through the patently unreliable editorship of "Ralph Fielding Snell," a fatuous, gullible, self-professed "man of letters" who also happens to mention that he has suffered three or four nervous breakdowns in the past few years. Against these reflexive, metafictional devices, Berger balances the disarming realism of Jack Crabb's narration, its tone resonating with the wondering honesty and credibility of Huck Finn.

Frederick Turner has noted that part of the real power of this narration is derived from Jack's coming "to understand both myth and history as radically human constructs." What Turner means by "radically human constructs" can be understood from the way in which *Little Big Man* combines very different rhetorics or "codes" for talking about the Old West. Indeed, Jack's narrative consists of excerpts from and imitations of actual histories of the West, autobiographies, dime novels, Indian studies, and other codes that are mixed together in unpredictable combinations. This jumbling of codes and vocabularies (for example, Jack may mingle the crassest of frontier expressions with terms such as "colloquy," "circumferentially," "hitherto," or "tumult") exposes the perceptual biases of the "official" codes which have been developed for talking about the Old West—whether by Zane Grey, Francis Parkman, or L. A. Hoebel (an expert on Cheyenne culture). Jack begins to realize that even when his situation seems to be defined by bullets or arrows, the real conflict lies in the clash between the often antithetical ways in which he must think of himself, whether he is to define himself and act according to Cheyenne terms, cavalry terms, capitalist terms, journalistic terms, and so on.

Accordingly, the panorama of Jack's adventures, ranging from his adoption by the Cheyenne to his gunfight with Wild Bill Hickok to his being the only white survivor of Custer's Last Stand, is shadowed by the panorama of his changing narrative styles: not only does Berger pack every classic Western theme into the novel, but he also fills it with subtly varied "codes" that make it—like all of his novels—at least in part an exploration of the workings of language. The genius of this novel is that its metafictional devices are so well woven into the fabric of Jack's fascinating story that they have eluded all but a handful of readers, reviewers, and scholars. By any standards, *Little Big Man* is a masterpiece, one of the most delightful novels ever written.

Killing Time is a kind of reflexive, even self-destructive murder mystery. Based in part on accounts by Frederic Wertham in *The Show of Violence* (1949) and Quentin Reynolds in *Courtroom* (1950) of an actual sensational murder case in 1937, *Killing Time* tells the story of Joseph Detweiler, "an awfully nice guy" who is also a psychopathic murderer. The novel opens with the discovery that someone has murdered three people in an apartment. The plot seems to be developing into a routine murder mystery or police procedural as the investigative machinery goes into action, but the murderer, Joe Detweiler, turns himself in even before police suspicions about him crystallize. The balance of the novel, therefore, focuses on Detweiler's conversations with the police and his lawyer. Berger's book declines, however, to become a courtroom drama and proceeds instead through a variety of conventions from the detective story and the psychological thriller, to the courtroom drama and other well-codified genres.

Although Joe is a multiple murderer and is quite mad, all other personalities in *Killing Time* lack character in comparison. Joe is the criminal, but he alone among the policemen, lawyers, and judges truly believes in law and justice. His philosphy is bizarre, but Joe manages to change the perspectives of all those who know him. What really separates Joe from those around him is his profound mistrust of language. He sees actions as truth, while language is just "talking about talk."

To a significant extent, Berger is "talking about talk" in *Killing Time*, just as he is exploring the nature of language and the nature of fiction, for this is a supremely reflexive novel. The book is full of fictions within its larger fictional frame; all of the characters apart from Joe are cast as conscious and unconscious makers of fiction. For example, Joe's lawyer derives his greatest satisfaction from "a favorable verdict returned by a jury who knew it had been hoaxed," and he explains to Joe that in the courtroom, "reality is what the jury believes." By presenting character after character whose verbal deceptions and artistry are obviously analogous to the techniques of the novelist (one character even becomes a novelist), and by putting his characters in situations analogous to that of the reader of a novel, Berger reminds his reader that the novel is just as much a hoax as any of those created by its characters. As Berger most bluntly states in the front of the book: "A novel is a construction of language and otherwise a lie."

Vital Parts, the third Reinhart novel, picks up the adventures of its protagonist in the 1960's, as the forty-four-year-old Reinhart rapidly adds to the list of windmills with which he has unsuccessfully tilted. Bob Sweet, a flashy boyhood acquaintance, replaces Claude Humbold as his business mentor, luring him into his most dubious venture to date: a cryonics foundation for freezing the dead. His tough-minded wife, Genevieve, and his surly hippie son, Blaine, both despise him, while Winona, his fat, unhappy, sweetly innocent daughter worships him. Caught in a cultural crossfire, Reinhart threatens to succumb to the pressures and perversities of modern life.

Berger's next novel, *Regiment of Women*, managed to offend reviewers and readers on both sides of the women's movement. A dystopian novel set in America in the year 2047, the book presents a society in which traditional male and female roles have been completely reversed. Not only do women control the corporate, artistic, legal, and military machinery of this society, but also they sexually dominate it, strapping dildos over their pants to assault men. In such an inverted society, to be "manly" is to wear dresses and makeup, to hold only powerless jobs, to have silicone breast implants, and to be emotionally incapable of rational thought or significant action. To be "effeminate" is to bind breasts, to wear false beards, to dress in pants and suits, to be rough, physical, aggressive, and to have a reduced life expectancy caused by stress.

Berger's protagonist in this future world is a twenty-nine-year-old insecurity riddled male secretary named Georgie Cornell. An unlikely sequence of events lands him first in prison, arrested for wearing women's clothing (slacks, shirt, tie, and coat) and incorrectly suspected of being a men's liberation agent. Driven to discover accidentally that he is stronger than his female captors, Georgie escapes and is promptly appropriated as an agent/hero by the men's liberation underground. For the rest of the novel, Georgie struggles to discover his "natural" identity, a process which forces him to cast off received idea after received idea, discarding sexual generalizations to forge a particular definition of self. He is joined in this "rebellion" by a woman FBI agent so demented that she wants only to be "masculine"—to wear dresses and makeup, to be gentle and sensitive.

Despite its topical focus, *Regiment of Women* is fundamentally concerned not with sexual roles but with the more basic problem of the hypostatizing power of language. From start to finish, the novel reminds the reader that Georgie's reality has been almost completely gloved by language, and in so doing, also calls attention both to the way language operates in the reader's reality and to the ways in which a novelist manipulates language to create an independent "reality." At the bottom of this concern with language and rhetoric lies Berger's belief that victimization in any realm starts as a linguistic phenomenon in which the generalizations and attendant rhetoric of some self-interest part company with the particulars of immediate experience. Accordingly, *Regiment of Women* is a book much more concerned with the discovery of true individuality and freedom and with the workings of language than with sexual politics.

Berger's seventh novel, *Sneaky People*, is easily his most gentle (although much of its action concerns plans for a murder). *Sneaky People* reveals Berger's ear for the American vernacular as it chronicles the coming of age of a young boy, Ralph Sandifer, in a dreamy small-town world where nothing is as bucolic as it seems. Ralph's father owns a used-car lot and plans to have one of his employees murder Ralph's mother. The drab, mousey-seeming mother secretly writes and sells pornography of the must lurid sort. Indeed, this is a book which seems to say that it is "sneaky" acts which best reveal character, and it is a book that is itself something of a sneaky act, and continues Berger's obsession with the nature of language.

Berger has described *Sneaky People* as "my tribute to the American language of 1939—to be philologically precise, that of the lower-middle class in the eastern Middle West, on which I am an authority as on nothing else." The characters in this novel speak the vital, unleveled, pre-television American vernacular of the 1930's, and the prose style of *Sneaky People* is in a sense the real subject of the book, reflecting Berger's belief that "the possibilities for wit—and thus for life—decline with the homogenization of language."

Berger's mastery of and play with prose style reaches its most exuberant high in *Who Is Teddy Villanova?* which invokes the conventions of the hardboiled detective novel but also defies almost all of the expectations that attend those conventions. *Who Is Teddy Villanova?* gives evidence of Berger's great respect for the masters of this genre—Dashiell Hammett, Raymond Chandler, and Ross Macdonald—but it also adds a number of outlandish twists, most prominent among them being a first-person narrator who introduces himself with "Call me Russell Wren," and who tells his story "in a rococo style reminiscent by turns of Thomas DeQuincey, Thomas Babington Macaulay, and Sir Thomas Malory." Wren is an ex-instructor of English more concerned with finding readers for the play he is writing than with finding out why a series of thugs and policemen brutalize him either in search of or in the name of a mysterious Teddy Villanova, about whom Wren knows absolutely nothing. The novel follows Wren through one misadventure after another as he pursues the elusive Villanova with Ahab's passion and some curiously "fishy" metaphors (a huge thug slips thorugh a doorway "as deftly as a perch fins among subaqueous rocks").

In truth, Wren does confuse his own small-fish situation with that of Herman Melville's great quest, and his confusion is symptomatic of a more profound problem: when faced with experience, Wren always tries to organize it in terms of the fictional worlds of literary and television private eyes. Like Ralph Fielding Snell in *Little Big Man*, another preposterous "man of letters," Wren perpetually falls victim to his own linguistic hypostatizations as he persistently confuses the literary life of fictional detectives with his own situation. A detective who questions him observes: "I suspect you are living the legend of the private eye, which I confess I had always believed mythical." Wren's narrative style is governed by his immersion in the literary myth of the private eye and his prose style is governed by his pseudointellectual background, producing such wonderfully incongruous lines as: "This wench is my ward . . . Toy with her fine foot if you like, but eschew her quivering thigh and the demesnes that there adjacent lie." The result is humorously self-conscious, almost forcing the reader to step back from the action of the novel and consider its implications for the act of reading and for language use itself.

Its dust jacket announces that *Arthur Rex* is "Thomas Berger's salute to the Age of Chivalry from his own enmired situation in the Time of the Cad," and this novel has been prominently praised as "the Arthur story for our times." Berger brings to the Arthur legend both a profound respect for its mythic power and a modern perspective on the nature of its myth, as can be seen in a comment by Sir Gawaine, when, late in his life, he is asked if he does not long for the old days of action. Gawaine answers no, explaining:

I am happy to have had them in my proper time, but of a life of adventure it can be said that there is no abiding satisfaction, for when one adventure is done, a knight liveth in expectation of another, and if the next come not soon enough he falleth in love, in the sort of love that is an adventure, for what he seeketh be the adventure and not the lovingness. And methinks this sequence is finally infantile, and beyond a certain age one can no longer be interested in games.

Berger's version of the Arthur legend in no way diminishes the glory of Arthur's attempt or the measure of his achievement, and it equally honors the stylistic achievement of Sir Thomas Malory's telling of the legend. Berger does devote greater attention to the cause of Arthur's final tragedy, which centers in his account, on the erosion of the innocent belief that life can be governed by the simple principle of opposing good to evil. Complexity finally overwhelms Arthur: to Launcelot, he sadly admits that "evil doing hath got more subtle, perhaps even to the point at which it cannot properly be encountered with the sword." What Arthur does not realize is that strict adherence to a rigid code of conduct may create more problems than it solves, threaten order more than ensure it. Only too late do Arthur and some of his wiser knights begin to understand that the Code of Chivalry, like any inflexible system of abstract principles, comes into conflict with itself if pursued too blindly. In Berger's hands, Arthur's most anguishing discovery is not that he has been betrayed by his queen and his most trusted knight, but that his philosophy has been shallow, because "to the profound vision there is no virtue and no vice, and what is justice to one, is injustice to another."

Arthur recognizes the flaw in his great dream, but Berger makes it clear that Arthur's legend is not to be judged by the success or failure of that dream. The Lady of the Lake assures the dying Arthur that he could not have done better in his life than he did, and the ghost of Sir Gawaine offers to his king the Round Table's poignant epitaph: "We sought no easy victories, nor won any. And perhaps for that we will be remembered."

Earl Keese, Berger's protagonist in *Neighbors*, is a quiet, resonable, forty-nine-year-old suburbanite who tells people that his home sits "at the end of the road," because that phrase sounds less "dispiriting" than "dead end." In fact, his life has long since reached its apparent dead end, and it takes the arrival of mysterious and maddening new neighbors, Harry and Ramona, to confront Keese with a sequence of situations so outrageous that he can no longer maintain the hoax of his previously complacent life. Not only do Harry and Ramona (zany versions of Nietzsche's "free spirits") fail to observe the social amenities, but also they seem committed to deliberate provocation, pushing him to see how far he will go to avoid humiliation.

Their visits increasingly seem like motiveless assaults as their comings and goings produce a series of off-balance events that gradually strip Keese of his easy social assumptions and habitual responses. As his bizarrely embarrassing experiences increasingly blur the line between comedy and nightmare, his relations with all those around him begin to undergo subtle changes. He realizes that his life has grown so stale that Harry's and Ramona's aggravations may actually offer him a salvation of sorts—the chance to take control of and give style to his life. As Keese finally admits to Harry, "Every time I see you as a criminal, by another light you look like a kind of benefactor."

Madcap physical changes punctuate Berger's plot—entrances, exits, fights, a damaged car, a destroyed house—but for all its action, *Neighbors* might best be described as a series of functions of language: puns, platitudes, theories, definitions, excuses, accusations, rationalizations, promises, questions, threats—all acts performed with words. Keese knows better than to trust completely what he sees (he suffers from "outlandish illusions"), but he uncritically does believe his ears, consistently confusing rhetoric with reality, mistaking verbal maps for the territory of experience. In fact, *Neighbors* may offer the most verbal world Berger has created; like *Little Big Man*, it is a book in which language becomes the only operating reality. Vocabularies from law and ethics intertwine throughout the novel, and Berger does not fail to exploit the incongruities of the two lexicons. Terms having to do with guilt, justice, punishment, revenge, motive, confession, blame, crime, and accusation appear on virtually every page, resonating at once with the rhetoric of the courtroom and with that of Franz Kafka's *The Trial* (1925). Keese's "guilt" is not unlike that of Kafka's Joesph K., and the slapstick humor of this book records a deadly serious philosophical trial.

In *Reinhart's Women*, the now fifty-four-year-old Reinhart finally discovers something he can do well: cooking. The novel finds Reinhart ten years after his divorce from Genevieve, living with and supported by his daughter, Winona, now a beautiful and successful fashion model. His son, Blaine, last seen as a surly radical in *Vital Parts*, now is a surly, snobbish, and successful stockbroker, unchanged in his disdain for his father. Having finally admitted that he is hopeless as a businessman, Reinhart has withdrawn from the world and contents himself with managing his daughter's household and with cooking "in a spirit of scientific inquiry." Actually, cooking has become for him an aesthetic philosophy, and for the first time in his life he does not "feel as if he were either charlatan or buffoon." "Food," Reinhart notes, "is kinder than people."

Long completely at the mercy of unmerciful women, particularly his mother and his ex-wife, Reinhart can now even take in stride the news that his daughter is having a lesbian affair with a successful older businesswoman. Age has taught him that "the best defense against any moral outrage is patience: wait a moment and something will change: the outrage, he who committed it, or, most often, oneself."

Winona's lover (a female version of the con men who have always directed Reinhart's forays into business) contrives to lure Reinhart back into the world, first as a supermarket product-demonstrator, then as a guest "chef" for a spot appearance on a local television show, and the novel closes with the strong prospect of his own show: "Chef Carlo Cooks." His apparent successes, however, are not confined to the kitchen, as Reinhart escapes the gentle and loving tyranny of his daughter, emerges unscathed from an encounter with his ex-wife, and begins a promising relationship with a young woman who seems in many ways a female version of himself—intelligent, considerate, awkward. In fact, Reinhart begins to gather around him a small band of kindred souls, hoping to buy and run a quaint small-town café. Once again, the lure of business proves irresistible for Reinhart, and once again the prospect of disaster cannot be discounted, but this time the odds seem more in Reinhart's favor. Jonathan Baumbach has summed up this most recent of the Reinhart books as "Berger's most graceful and modest book, a paean to kindness and artistry, a work of quiet dazzle."

Berger's first novel, *Crazy in Berlin*, started Reinhart, "a stumbling American Odysseus," on what Berger has termed "his long career of indestructibility." The subsequent novels in the series—*Reinhart in Love*, *Vital Parts*, and *Reinhart's Women*—follow Reinhart as he grows older and, ultimately, wiser. Said by one critic to be "a clowning knight errant, pure of heart—that is, a custodian of our conscience and of our incongruities," Reinhart is an incurable idealist who really has no faith in idealism. Complexity, Reinhart's essence, is also his nemesis: he can always see both sides to every argument, feel responsibility for any injustice, and though he realizes that "true freedom is found only by being consistent with oneself," he has a very hard time figuring out how to do this, particularly in the novels before *Reinhart's Women*. Essentially, Reinhart seeks a consistent rationale for his unimpressive, awkward, but indomitable individuality. Combining the features of "a big bland baseball bat" with those of "an avatar of Job the beloved of a sadistic God," Reinhart can never shake the suspicion that he does not fit anywhere, but is nevertheless responsible for the general confusion that surrounds and usually engulfs him.

Reinhart is as ill-suited for despair, however, as he is for success. Although reminded by a successful aquaintance that he is "redundant in the logistics of life," he can never really be disillusioned, even though his dreams steadily fall prey to the practical opportunism of those around him. No match for a mother who can tell him, "if I ever thought you had truck with Filth, I'd slip you strychnine," or a shrewish wife whose advice to him is "if you're going to be an ass-kisser, then you ought to at least kiss the asses of winners," Reinhart can recognize the distinction between his secular search for a Holy Grail and the social meliorism that passes for idealism. Like all of Berger's characters, Reinhart never gives up: an indomitable toughness underlies his numerous weaknesses, and whatever the situation, he always muddles through, scarred but undaunted.

In 1984, Berger almost gained the kind of critical recognition he has so long deserved as literary judges selected *The Feud* for the 1984 Pulitzer Prize—only to have their selection overruled in favor of William Kennedy's *Ironweed* by the Pulitzer administrative committee. What the vagaries and politics of literary prize determination should not obscure is the fact that Berger's twelfth novel (described by Berger as "my most modest work, a little memoir of the place and time of my youth" and "as a kind of Dreiserian slice of life") is a masterpiece of precision the posits its richly textured semblance of small-town life in 1930's America with a perfectly controlled minimum of exposition and a sense of quiet, timeless authority. In its narrowest sense, *The Feud* chronicles the sudden eruption and three-day playing out of an intense feud between two small-town families, the Beelers and the Bullards. Fueled by misunderstanding, misplaced pride, pathological insecurity, small-town xenophobia, self-serving interpretations of events, and the convergence of an incredible sequence of coincidences, this feud is finally remarkable for nothing quite so much as its representation of the way things actually happen in life. The action—both humorous and tragic—of this novel quickly reveals that the dynamics of feuding, quaint though the term may sound, is one of the received structures of human experience, a mold just waiting to be filled—whether by Montagues and Capulets, Hatfields and McCoys, or Beelers and Bullards.

Orrie's Story, Berger's seventeenth novel, re-creates much of the ambience of *The Feud* and *Sneaky People* but sets within that 1930's and 1940's small-town world the classic story of Orestes, son of Agamemnon and Clytemnestra, who, to avenge his father's murder by them, must kill both Clytemnestra and her lover Aegisthus. In the Oresteia of Aeschylus, a tragedy already recast in the Civil War era by Eugene O'Neill's *Mourning Becomes Electra* (1931), Berger has discovered another of the timeless stories of inescapable situations that have always informed and been reinterrogated by his writing. Matching the precision and control of *The Feud* and echoing its mastery of the American idiom, *Orrie's Story* may be Berger's best-written and most starkly powerful novel.

The Feud, *Being Invisible*, *The Houseguest*, and *Orrie's Story* all offer new twists to Berger's fascination with issues of discriminating "kickers" from "kickees," victims from victimizers, the disparate responses of humans confronted by the complexities of responsibility. And while *Nowhere*—which continues the misadventures of Russell Wren, protagonist of *Who Is Teddy Villanova?*, as he finds himself transported to the ironic utopia of a quirky kingdom apparently modeled after American movie musicals—raises issues usually larger than those facing the individual, it continues Berger's unsentimental confrontation with the essential insolubility of human problems. As Berger's protagonist in *Changing the Past* finally discovers after trying on and discarding a number of wishful alternative versions of his own past, "Life is taking your medicine."

Perhaps the one thing on which critics agree is that Thomas Berger's talent is unique. The variety of Berger's novels, a range with no equal in contemporary American literature, underlines the precision of his craft while distracting readers from the steadiness and the seriousness of his purpose. One of America's most original and most gifted novelists, Berger offers what one critic aptly termed a "career of quiet dazzle."

Brooks Landon

Other major work
PLAY: *Other People*, 1970.

Bibliography
Landon, Brooks. *Thomas Berger.* Boston: Twayne, 1989. The first book-length study of Berger, this volume draws from the author's correspondence with Berger to support the thesis that the interpretation of Berger's novels *is* the study of his style. Beginning with a brief overview of Berger's career, Landon analyzes by conceptual grouping Berger's first fifteen novels, examining the considerable influence of Friedrich Nietzsche and affinities with Franz Kafka, Jorge Luis Borges, and Vladimir Nabokov.
Malone, Michael. "Berger, Burlesque, and the Yearning for Comedy." *Studies in American Humor* 2 (Spring, 1983): 20-32. One of the most instructive essays in the two-volume *Studies in American Humor* special issue on Berger, this piece offers a persuasive analysis of Berger's complexity that also considers why his achievements have not been better celebrated. Malone claims that whatever the novel form, Berger writes comedy, as opposed to comic novels, bringing us "to confront our metaphysical (as opposed to our social) bewilderment."
Schickel, Richard. "Bitter Comedy." *Commentary* 50 (July, 1970): 76. This review of *Vital Parts* offers an astute introduction to Berger's writing, positing his theme as "the devastation of the individualist ethic by the spirit of our time" and specifying Berger's basic belief that "as we lose faith in our traditional individualism we seek, at every level of life, compensatory fantasies of power, of escape, of impractical idealism."
Turner, Frederick W. "The Second Decade of *Little Big Man*." *Nation* 205 (August 20, 1977): 149-151. Turner celebrates *Little Big Man* as a "seminal event in what must now seem the most significant cultural and literary trend of the last decade: The attempt on many fronts to develop structures, styles, ways of thinking that are beyond any version of ethnocentrism." A very useful examination of the literary and cultural contexts in which *Little Big Man* achieves its distinction.
Wallace, Jon. "A Murderous Clarity: A Reading of Thomas Berger's *Killing Time*." *Philological Quarterly* 68 (Winter, 1989): 101-114. Superb analysis

of the philosophical implications of Berger's use of sources in *Killing Time*. Wallace is one of the few critics to recognize the interpretive importance of Berger's style.

Wilde, Alan. "Acts of Definition: Or, Who Is Thomas Berger?" *Arizona Quarterly* 39 (Winter, 1983): 314-351. Perhaps the single most instructive essay on Berger's work, offering a phenomenology of Berger that astutely recognizes the inseparability for the author of the concepts of freedom and of self-definition. Wilde finds in Berger's novels, however, a "fear of otherness" that just as easily may be termed "fascination."

ELIZABETH BOWEN

Born: Dublin, Ireland; June 7, 1899
Died: London, England; February 22, 1973

Principal long fiction

The Hotel, 1927; *The Last September*, 1929; *Friends and Relations*, 1931; *To the North*, 1932; *The House in Paris*, 1935; *The Death of the Heart*, 1938; *The Heat of the Day*, 1949; *A World of Love*, 1955; *The Little Girls*, 1964; *Eva Trout*, 1968.

Other literary forms

The first seven of Elizabeth Bowen's novels were republished by Jonathan Cape in Cape Collected Editions between the years 1948 and 1954, when Cape also republished four of her short-story collections: *Joining Charles* (1929), *The Cat Jumps and Other Stories* (1934), *Look at All Those Roses* (1941), and *The Demon Lover* (1945). The other books of short stories are *Encounters* (1923), *Ann Lee's and Other Stories* (1926), *Stories by Elizabeth Bowen* (1959), and *A Day in the Dark and Other Stories* (1965). *The Demon Lover* was published in New York under the title *Ivy Gripped the Steps* (1946) and, as the original title indicates, has supernatural content which scarcely appears in the novels. Bowen's nonfiction consists of *Bowen's Court* (1942), a description of her family residence in Ireland; *Seven Winters* (1942), an autobiography; *English Novelists* (1946), a literary history; *Collected Impressions* (1950), essays; *The Shelbourne* (1951), a work about the hotel in Dublin; *A Time in Rome* (1960), travel essays; and *Afterthought* (1962), broadcasts and reviews. A play, coauthored with John Perry and entitled *Castle Anna* was performed in London in March, 1948, but remains unpublished.

Achievements

Considered a great lady by those who knew her, Bowen draws an appreciative audience from readers who understand English gentility—the calculated gesture and the controlled response. Bowen's support has come from intellectuals who recognize the values of the novel of manners and who liken her work to that of Jane Austen and Henry James. Her contemporaries and colleagues included members of the Bloomsbury Group and of Oxford University, where the classical scholar C. M. Bowra was a close friend. Many readers know Bowen best through her novel *The Death of the Heart* and her short stories, especially "The Demon Lover," "Joining Charles," and "Look at All Those Roses," which are frequently anthologized in college texts. Bowen was made a Commander of the British Empire in 1948, and was awarded the honorary Doctor of Letters degree at Trinity College, Dublin, in 1949, and at Oxford University in 1957. She was made a Companion of Literature in 1965.

Biography

Although born in Ireland, Elizabeth Dorothea Cole Bowen came from a pro-British family who received land in County Cork as an award for fighting with Oliver Cromwell in 1649. The family built Bowen's Court in 1776—what the Irish call a "big house"—as a Protestant stronghold against the mainly Catholic Irish and lived there as part of the Anglo-Irish ascendancy. Bowen was educated in England and spent some summers at Bowen's Court. Not until after the Irish Rising in 1916 did she come to realize the causes of the Irish struggle for independence; and in writing *Bowen's Court*, she admitted that her family "got their position and drew their power from a situation that shows an inherent wrong."

Her barrister father, when he was nineteen, had disobeyed forewarnings and carried home smallpox, which killed his mother and rendered his father mad. Preoccupied with the desire for a son, the attempt to have one nearly killed his wife in 1904, and burdened with the debts of Bowen's Court, he suffered severe mental breakdowns in 1905 and 1906 and again in 1928. He was the cause of Elizabeth's removal to England where, as an Irish outcast, her defense was to become excessively British. Living in a series of locations with her mother, she was kept uninformed of family circumstances; and, as an adult, her novels provided for her an outlet for her sense of guilt, the result of feeling responsible for the unexplained events around her. Her lack of roots was intensified with the death of her mother in 1912.

Bowen studied art, traveled in Europe, and worked as an air-raid warden in London during World War II. In 1923, she married Alan Charles Cameron, who was employed in the school system near Oxford, and they lived there for twelve years. She inherited Bowen's Court in 1928 when her father died; and in 1952, she and her husband returned there to live. Bowen's husband, however, died that year. She sold the home in 1960 and returned to Oxford.

Bowen's career as novelist spanned years of drastic change, 1927 to 1969, and, except for *The Last September*, she wrote about the present; her war experiences are reflected in the short-story collection *The Demon Lover* and in the novel *The Heat of the Day*. After 1935, she also wrote reviews and articles for *The New Statesman* and other publications, the Ministry of Information during World War II, *The Tatler* (in the 1940's), and helped edit the *London Magazine* in the late 1950's. Afflicted with a slight stammer, Bowen lectured infrequently but effectively; two of her B.B.C. broadcasts, "left as they were spoken," may be read in *Afterthought*. After a visit to Ireland in 1973, she died in London, leaving an unfinished autobiographical work, "Pictures and Conversations," which was intended to be published the next year.

Analysis

Elizabeth Bowen had a special talent for writing the conversations of children around the age of nine, as she does in *The House in Paris*. Somewhat corresponding to her personal experience, her novels often present a homeless child, orphaned and shunted from one residence to another, or a child with one parent who dies and leaves the adolescent in the power of outwardly concerned but mainly selfish adults. Frequently, management by others prolongs the protagonist's state of innocence into the twenties, when the woman must begin to assert herself and learn to manage her own affairs. (At age twenty-four, for example, Eva Trout does not know how to boil water for tea.) On the other side of the relationship, the controlling adult is often a perfectly mannered woman of guile, wealthy enough to be idle and to fill the idleness with discreet exercise of power over others. The typical Bowen characters, then, are the child, the unwanted adolescent, the woman in her twenties in a prolonged state of adolescence, and the "terrible woman" of society. Young people, educated haphazardly but expensively, are culturally mature but aimless. Genteel adults, on the other hand, administer their own selfish standards of what constitutes an impertinence in another person; these judgments disguise Bowen's subtle criticism of the correct English.

Typical Bowen themes follow as "loss of innocence," "acceptance of the past," or "expanding consciousness." The pain and helplessness attendant upon these themes and the disguise of plentiful money make them unusual. Although she writes about the privileged class, three of her four common character types do not feel privileged. To handle her themes, Bowen frequently orders time and space by dividing the novels into three parts, with one part set ten years in the past and with a juxtaposition of at least two locations. The ten-year lapse provides a measure of the maturity gained, and the second location, by contrast, jars the consciousness into revaluation of the earlier experience.

The fact that the Bowen women often have nothing to do is very obvious in *The Hotel*, set in Bordighera on the Italian Riviera, but, of greater interest, it is, like Ireland, another place of British occupancy. Guests' activities are confined to walking, talking, taking tea, and playing tennis. Mrs. Kerr is the managing wealthy woman who feeds on the attentions of her protégé, Sydney Warren, and then abandons Sydney when her son arrives. At age twenty-two, Sydney, for lack of better purpose, studies for a doctorate at home in England. Back in Italy, she gets engaged to a clergyman as a means of achieving an identity and popularity; but her better sense forces reconsideration, and she cancels the engagement and asserts her independence.

The Last September, set in 1920 when the hated British soldiers (the Black and Tans) were stationed in Ireland to quell rebellion, shows Sir Richard and Lady Myra Naylor entertaining with tennis parties at their big house. Like Elizabeth Bowen, who wrote in *Afterthought* that this novel was "nearest my heart," Lois Farquar is a summer visitor, aged nineteen, orphaned, and asking herself what she should do. An older woman tells her that her art lacks talent.

Almost engaged to a British soldier, Gerald Lesworth, she might have a career in marriage; but Lady Naylor, in the role of graceful-terrible woman, destroys the engagement in a brilliant heart-to-heart talk, in which she points out that he has no prospects.

As September closes the social season, Gerald Lesworth is killed in ambush; and as Lois—much more aware now and less innocent—prepares to depart for France, her home Danielstown is burned down, which signals her separation from the protected past.

After *Friends and Relations*, Bowen entered the most fruitful part of her career. Her next four novels are generally considered to be her best work. *To the North* has rather obvious symbolism in a protagonist named Emmeline Summers whose lack of feeling makes her "icy." She runs a successful travel agency with the motto "Travel Dangerously" (altering "Live Dangerously" and "Travel Safe"); the motto reflects both her ability to understand intellectually the feelings of others through their experience and her orphan state in homelessness. Emmeline tries to compensate for her weaknesses by imposing dramatic opposites: without a home of her own, she overvalues her home with her widowed sister-in-law, Cecilia Summers; frequently called an angel, she has a fatal attraction to the devil-like character Markie Linkwater. When Cecilia plans to remarry (breaking up the home), when Markie (bored with Emmeline) returns to his former mistress, and when Emmeline's travel business begins to fail rapidly because of her preoccupation with Markie, she smashes her car while driving Markie north; "traveling dangerously" at high speeds, she becomes the angel of death.

The cold of the North suggested by the novel's title also touches other characters. Lady Waters, who offers Emmeline weekends on her estate as a kind of second home, feeds mercilessly on the unhappiness of failed loves and gossip. Lady Waters tells Cecilia to speak to Emmeline about her affair with Markie and thereby initiates the fateful dinner party, which leads to the accident. Pauline, the niece of Cecilia's fiancé, is the orphaned-adolescent character on the verge of becoming aware of and embarrassed by sex. Bowen describes Emmeline as the "stepchild of her uneasy century," a century in which planes and trains have damaged the stability and book knowledge of sexual research (indicated by the reading of Havelock Ellis), thereby freeing relationships but failing to engage the heart. The travel and the lack of warmth make the title a metaphor for the new century's existence. With her tenuous hold on home, love, and career, Emmeline commits suicide.

The House in Paris is set in three locations, which reflect different aspects of the protagonist, Karen Michaelis: England, the land of perfect society; Ireland, the land of awareness; France, the land of passion and the dark past. Parts I and III take place in a single day in Paris; Part II occurs ten years earlier, during four months when Karen was age twenty-three. The evils of the house in Paris become apparent in the flashback and can be appreciated only through recognition of the terrible woman who runs it, Mme. Fisher, and the rootlessness of the foreign students who stay there. Among other students, Mme. Fisher has had in her power Karen and her friend Naomi Fisher (Mme. Fisher's daughter), and the young Max Ebhart, a Jew with no background. Ten years later, when Max wants to break his engagement with Naomi to marry another, Mme. Fisher interferes, and he commits suicide.

The book begins and ends in a train station in Paris. In Part I, Leopold— age nine and the illegitimate child of Karen and Max Ebhart—and Henrietta—age eleven and the granddaughter of a friend of Mme. Fisher—arrive on separate trains: Henrietta from England in the process of being shuttled to another relative, and Leopold from his adoptive parents in Italy to await a first acquaintance with his real mother. Leopold and Henrietta Mountjoy, meeting in the house in Paris, become symbolic of the possibility that, with Mme. Fisher bedridden for ten years (since the suicide) and now dying, the future will be free of the mistakes of the past. Mme. Fisher, in an interview with Leopold, tells him that the possibility of finding himself "like a young tree inside a tomb is to discover the power to crack the tomb and grow up to any height," something Max had failed to do.

Dark, egotistic, self-centered, and passionate like his father, Leopold constructs imaginatively a role for his unknown mother to play and then breaks into uncontrollable weeping when a telegram arrives canceling her visit. The mature and implacable Henrietta, orphaned like Leopold but accustomed to the vicissitudes of adult life, shows him how to crack out of the tomb of childhood. In Part III, quite unexpectedly, Ray Forrestier, who had given up diplomacy and taken up business to marry Karen in spite of her illegitimate child, urges a reunion with Leopold, takes matters into his own hands, and brings Leopold to Karen.

The three part structure of Bowen's novels is most fully realized in *The Death of the Heart*; the parts are labeled "The World," "The Flesh," and "The Devil," which follow the seasons of winter, spring, and summer. The world of Windsor Terrace, the Quaynes' residence in London, is advanced and sterile. Portia enters into this world at age fifteen, an orphan and stepsister to the present Thomas Quayne. Thomas' wife Anna, who has miscarried twice and is childless, secretly reads Portia's diary and is indignant at the construction Portia puts on the household events. Portia sees much "dissimulation" at Windsor Terrace, where doing the "right" thing does not mean making a moral choice. As one of Bowen's radical innocents who has spent her youth in hotels and temporary locations, Portia says no one in this house knows why she was born. She has only one friend in this, her first home: the head-servant Matchett who gives Portia some religious training. Of the three male friends who wait upon Anna—St. Quentin Martin, Eddie, and Major Brutt—Portia fastens on the affections of Eddie.

Spring, in Part II, brings a much-needed vacation for the Quaynes. Thomas and Anna sail for Capri, and Portia goes to stay with Anna's former governess at Seale-on-Sea. At the governess' home, dubbed Waikiki, Portia is nearly drowned in sensuality—the sights, smells, sounds, feelings—of a vulgar and mannerless household. Portia invites Eddie to spend a weekend with her at Seale-on-Sea, which further educates her in the ways of the flesh.

Portia's more open nature, on her return to London in Part III, is immediately apparent to Matchett, who says she had been "too quiet." The Devil's works are represented both obviously and subtly in this section, and they take many identities. St. Quentin, Anna, Eddie, even the unloving atmosphere of Windsor Terrace make up the Devil's advocacy. St. Quentin, a novelist, tells Portia that Anna has been reading her diary, a disloyalty and an invasion of privacy with which, after some contemplation, Portia decides she cannot live. Herein lies the death of her teenage heart, what Bowen calls a betrayal of her innocence, or a "mysterious landscape" that has perished.

Summer at Windsor Terrace brings maturity to Portia, as well as others: Anna must confront her own culpability, even her jealousy of Portia; St. Quentin, his betrayal of Anna's reading of the diary; Thomas, his neglect of his father and his father's memory; and even Matchett takes a terrified ride in the unfamiliar cab, setting out in the night to an unknown location to pick up Portia. They all share in the summer's maturation that Portia has brought to fruition.

William Shakespeare's Portia preferred mercy to justice, paralleling the Portia in this novel. Bowen's Portia observes everything with a "political seriousness." The scaffolding of this novel supports much allusion, metaphor, and drama—all artfully structured. The world, the flesh, and the Devil as medieval threats to saintliness are reinterpreted in this context; they become the locations of the heart that has been thrust outside Eden and comprise a necessary trinity, not of holiness but of wholeness. This novel earns critics' accord as Bowen's best.

Ranked by many critics as a close second to *The Death of the Heart*, in *The Heat of the Day*, Bowen uses the war to purge the wasteland conditions that existed before and during the years from 1940 through 1945. Middle-class Robert Kelway has returned from Dunkirk (1940) with a limp that comes and goes according to the state of his emotions. At the individual level, it reflects the psychological crippling of his youth; at the national level, it is the culmination of the condition expressed by the person who says "Dunkirk was waiting there in us."

Upper-class Stella Rodney has retreated from the privileges of her past into a rented apartment and a war job. Having grown impassive with the century, divorced with a son (Roderick) in the army, she has taken Robert as her lover. She has become so impassive, in fact, that in 1942, a sinister and mysterious government spy named Harrison tells her that Robert has been passing information to the enemy, and she says and does nothing.

Critics have commented frequently on this novel's analogies to *Hamlet* (1600-1601), an obvious example being Holme Dene (Dane home), Robert Kelway's country home. Psychologically weak, Robert is ruled by his destructive mother, who also had stifled his father and planted the seeds of Robert's defection from English ways. While Stella visits Holme Dene and learns to understand Robert, her son visits a cousin who tells him that Stella did not divorce her husband, as was commonly thought, but rather was divorced by him while he was having an affair, although he died soon after the divorce. Roderick, however, has managed to survive Stella's homelessness with a positive and manly outlook and, when he inherits an estate in Ireland, finds that it will give him the foundation for a future.

In *Eva Trout*, the various autobiographical elements of Bowen's work come to life: Bowen's stammer in Eva's reticence, the tragic deaths of both parents, the transience and sporadic education, the delayed adolescence, the settings of hotels and train stations. Eva Trout lives with a former teacher, Iseult Arbles, and her husband Eric while she waits for an inheritance. She turns twenty-four and receives the inheritance, which enables her to leave their home, where the marriage is unstable, to buy a home filled with used furniture. She also escapes the clutches of Constantine, her guardian who had been her father's male lover.

Eva discovers that a woman with money is suddenly pursued by "admirers," and Eric visits her in her new home. Eva subsequently lets Iseult think that Eric has fathered her child, whom she adopts in America. After eight years in American cities, where Eva seeks help for the deaf-mute child Jeremy, Eva and Jeremy return to England. From England, they flee to Paris where a doctor and his wife begin successful training of Jeremy. Back in England, Eva attempts the next phase of reaching security and a normal life. She seeks a husband and persuades the son of Iseult's vicar to stage a wedding departure with her at Victoria Station. All her acquaintances are on hand to see the couple off, but Jeremy—brought from Paris for the occasion—playfully points a gun (he thought a toy) at Eva and shoots her. In the midst of revelry, on the eve of her happiness, Eva drops dead beside the train.

Eva Trout makes a poignant and haunting last heroine for the Bowen sequence and a final bitter statement on the elusiveness of security and happiness.

Grace Eckley

Other major works

SHORT FICTION: *Encounters*, 1923; *Ann Lee's and Other Stories*, 1926; *Joining Charles*, 1929; *The Cat Jumps and Other Stories*, 1934; *Look at All Those Roses*, 1941; *The Demon Lover*, 1945 (published in the United States as *Ivy Gripped the Steps*, 1946); *The Early Stories*, 1951; *Stories by Elizabeth*

Bowen, 1959; *A Day in the Dark and Other Stories*, 1965; *Elizabeth Bowen's Irish Stories*, 1978; *The Collected Stories of Elizabeth Bowen*, 1981.

PLAY: *Castle Anna*, 1948 (with John Perry).

NONFICTION: *Bowen's Court*, 1942; *Seven Winters*, 1942; *English Novelists*, 1946; *Collected Impressions*, 1950; *The Shelbourne: A Center of Dublin Life for More Than a Century*, 1951; *A Time in Rome*, 1960; *Afterthought: Pieces About Writing*, 1962; *Pictures and Conversations*, 1975; *The Mulberry Tree: Writings of Elizabeth Bowen*, 1986.

CHILDREN'S LITERATURE: *The Good Tiger*, 1965.

Bibliography

Austin, Allan. *Elizabeth Bowen*. Rev. ed. Boston: Twayne, 1989. Emphasizes Bowen's ability to depict locale, as in her account of World War II London in *The Heat of the Day*. Her characters worry and react to events more with emotion than with reason. Bowen presents these characters in a distinctive and urbane style. After a survey of Bowen's general traits as an author, Austin follows with a detailed account of the novels and some of the shorter fiction.

Craig, Patricia. *Elizabeth Bowen*. London: Penguin Books, 1986. Most useful for those wishing to read a shorter biography of Bowen than Glendinning's. Written in a vigorous style and included in the Lives of Modern Women series. Like Glendinning, Craig emphasizes Bowen's extensive circle of literary friends. The depiction of events in Bowen's life is good-humored and blunt.

Davenport, Guy. "Elizabeth Bowen and the Big House." *Southern Humanities Review* 8 (1974): 27-34. Brings out the tradition of the big house present in *The Last September*. Houses and their descriptions are key features of Bowen's work; the English house, at which many guests can be present, is the essential background for her portrayal of middle-class life.

Glendinning, Victoria. *Elizabeth Bowen*. New York: Alfred A. Knopf, 1978. The standard biography of Bowen. Portrays Bowen as someone with a dominant personality, charming but at times overwhelming. Gives full coverage to Bowen's Anglo-Irish background and her wide circle of Oxford friends. Her devotion to her husband, which did not preclude extramarital affairs, emerges as a leitmotif of Bowen's rather uneventful life. Gives a detailed account of the genesis of each of the major novels.

Lee, Hermione. *Elizabeth Bowen: An Estimation*. New York: Barnes & Noble Books, 1981. The most detailed critical study of Bowen. Places her in a tradition of Anglo-Irish writers and ranks *The Death of the Heart* as worthy of the highest praise. Considers not only Bowen's novels but her short stories and nonfiction writing as well. Lee ranks a number of the short stories, such as "Summer Night" and "The Cat Jumps," as outstanding.

PAUL BOWLES

Born: New York, New York; December 30, 1910

Principal long fiction
The Sheltering Sky, 1949; *Let It Come Down*, 1952; *The Spider's House*, 1955; *Up Above the World*, 1966; *Points in Time*, 1982.

Other literary forms
Paul Bowles is probably critically appreciated best for his short fiction, even though he is also known for his novels. Famous as a translator especially of Moroccan fiction, he has translated from Arabic, French, and Spanish, and he is a writer of poetry, travel literature, and even music, to which he devoted himself during the 1930's. His autobiography, *Without Stopping*, was well received when it was published in 1972.

Achievements
Bowles has a unique place in American literature. As an exile, he shares with Gertrude Stein, among others, a distanced perspective on his native culture. Through his translations, he has earned an international reputation as an author with a North African sensibility. His fiction reflects a world more often akin to that written about by Jean-Paul Sartre or Albert Camus, and indeed he has been described as America's foremost existentialist writer, a label more likely to restrict him to a time period than to characterize his fiction accurately. Although his nihilism does strike one as a bit recherché, it also has a modern application, reflecting as it does a dark vision of the world as contemporary as the times demand.

For a while, Bowles became a guru of sorts to the Beat generation, although Bowles's attraction for them was as much for his writings about drugs as for his generally pessimistic philosophy. Never an author of wide appeal, he has nevertheless had a loyal following among those interested in experimental and avant-garde writing, and his work has reflected a steady maturation, his 1982 novel, *Points in Time*, receiving praise from, among others, Tobias Wolfe, who wrote that the novel was a completely original performance. Perhaps in the last analysis, Paul Bowles will be best remembered for his originality, his willingness to challenge definitions and the status quo in his fiction. With every work, he has tried to forge new ground.

Biography
Paul Frederic Bowles has spent most of his adult life living abroad, in permanent exile, mostly in Morocco, although for brief periods he has also lived in France, Mexico, and South America. It obviously suits his life, which

has been unconventional by American standards, and it has provided him with congenial environments within which to work both as a writer and as a composer. Admonished as a young man by his disapproving father that he could not expect merely to sit around and loaf as a writer when at home, Paul Bowles found a place where he could sit and invite his soul.

He was born in the Jamaica section of New York City, the only child of a dentist and a mother who was a former schoolteacher. He was a precocious child and began writing at an early age. By the time he was in grade school, he also began composing music, a passion which occupied him more than did writing until after World War I. Immediately after high school, he attended very briefly the School of Design and Liberal Arts before enrolling in the fall of 1928 as a freshman at the University of Virginia, a choice made primarily because it was the school attended by Edgar Allan Poe. In March, he left the university and ran off to Paris, where he was already known as the writer whose poem "Spire Song" had been published in Eugène Jolas' little magazine *transition*. Bowles returned home the next fall and went to work for Dutton's bookstore while trying to write a novel in his spare time. In the spring, he returned to Virginia to complete his freshman year, at which point he ended forever his college career.

By 1929, Bowles had met and been encouraged by Aaron Copland to pursue a career as a composer by returning to Paris to study with Nadia Boulanger, which he did in the spring of 1931. His second Paris sojourn began his literary life when he met and became friends with Gertrude Stein, who took him under her ample wing and tutored him in writing. It was Alice Toklas who suggested that Bowles and Copland, who had joined him abroad, live someplace warm, and she suggested Morocco, to which the two composers moved in the late summer of 1931. It was the beginning of Bowles's exile, his love affair with North Africa, and his life as a writer: It was from Tangier that Bowles sent Stein his first prose efforts and received back from her the encouragement to continue writing, although, as he admitted later, it was not until the 1930's, while watching his wife, Jane, compose her first novel, that he began to work seriously at the writer's trade.

Since the early 1930's, Bowles has lived and worked in, and translated the literature of, Morocco, becoming one of the country's few voices in the West. For a brief time, his experiments with drugs attracted the attention of the Beat writers who visited him in Tangier, as had Tennessee Williams. Bowles has made forays home to write music for the theater and to further various other literary and musical activities.

Analysis
Because of his small output of novels and because of his problematic relationship with American writing, Paul Bowles's reputation has yet to be firmly established. A writer who has always attracted attention, and serious atten-

tion at that, he has not been accorded sufficient critical notice to measure his significance as a writer. To paraphrase Johannes Willem Bertens, one of his most perceptive critics, who has written on the critical response to Bowles's work, Bowles as a novelist can be classified in three categories: romantic, existentialist, and nihilist. As a romantic, Bowles sees modern man in a disjunctive relationship with nature, and that vision has pushed him to depict the march of Western progress in very pessimistic terms, which accounts for one of his most frequently recurring themes, namely, that of a sophisticated Westerner confronting a less civilized and more primitive society in a quest of self-discovery. Such romantic attitudes suggest the reasons for labeling Bowles as an existentialist. The search for an authentic life amid the self-doubts and the fragile, provisional nature of the civilized instincts, as Theodore Solotaroff describes it, places Bowles squarely within the existentialist tradition made more formal and philosophical by such writers as Camus and Sartre. The search for values in a world without God, a world with an ethical vacuum, suggests the third possible interpretation of Bowles's fiction, that of nihilism.

There are those critics, especially Chester E. Eisinger, who understand the novelist's universe as totally without hope, a region devoid of meaning and purpose and thereby representing a nihilistic philosophical position. Again, this position is worked out through the clash between civilizations, or rather through the tension between civilization and the savage. Even Bowles himself has remarked that life is absurd and the whole business of living hopeless, a conviction he shares with most of his central characters, thereby giving credence to any nihilistic interpretation of his fiction. Whichever position one takes, the central details of Bowles's novels remains the same: A Westerner, often an intellectual, searches through an Oriental, less civilized culture for meaning and direction, usually finding neither by the end of the book.

The Sheltering Sky is both Paul Bowles's first novel and his best-known novel. It is a book in which the author set forth those topics or themes which he has pursued throughout the rest of his fiction with almost obsessive tenacity. The story follows an American couple, Port and Kit Moresby, who have traveled to Morocco in search of themselves and to reinvigorate their marriage after years of indifference. The couple appear in Oran shortly after World War II and there experience a series of devastating events which eventually kill Port and destroy the mental stability of his wife, Kit.

Soon after their arrival, Port insists that they travel inland into the desert. Kit is opposed, so Port, accompanied by an Australian photographer and her son, depart, leaving Kit with Tunner, their American friend, who is to escort her on the night train later that day. Bored by the ride, Kit wanders into the fourth-class, or native, section of the train and passes a frightening night among the Arabs, later sleeping with Tunner. Meanwhile, Port has come to the realization that he desires a reconciliation with his wife. The novel follows this hapless pair as they progress farther and farther into the heart of the country, leaving civilization more distantly behind them. Port contracts typhoid and dies, leaving his wife alone to face the rigors of the desert. She is picked up by a passing caravan and made the sexual slave of the leaders of the group. She is both entranced and repulsed by the experience and is soon completely disoriented by her subjugation. Finally, she is rescued by a member of the American embassy only to disappear once again, this time for good, into the Casbah, or native quarter, in Oran.

The Sheltering Sky is considered Bowles's most uncompromisingly existential work and has been read by the critics along this line, with the fragile and provisional nature of civilized instincts being put to the test against the brutality and savagery of the primitive desert. Not only does Port test his febrile psyche against overwhelming powers of the North African terrain, but also he must face the fact that he harbors in himself no reserves, no hope—for it is all too late—of anything better. Unable to commit himself to his wife, or to anything else for that matter, Port is left with a void which, in the end, exacts a heavy price, leaving him utterly alone and unequipped to face the hostile environment. So, too, Kit is stripped of her defenses and forced back on herself, only to discover that she has no inner resolve, either. In the end, these two civilized Americans lack the inner strength to combat the primitive forces, both within and without, which they encounter in their North African adventures.

Although the novel is marred by grave faults, it offers a convincing portrait of the disintegration of a couple of innocents thrust into a cruel environment for which are totally unprepared. The writing in places is luminescent, the locale wonderfully realized—so much so that the novel's shortcomings pale by comparison, leaving a work, if flawed, at least magnificently so, and convincing in its portrait of nihilism in the modern world.

Bowles's second novel, *Let It Come Down*, continues an existentialist quest by following Nelson Dyer, an American bank clerk, who throws over his job to join an old acquaintance who lives in Tangier and who offers Dyer a position in the travel agency he runs there. When he arrives, Dyer finds that his friend Jack Wilcox does not operate a successful agency and in fact seems to possess a mysterious source of income. As the story advances, Dyer's relationship with Wilcox takes on a Kafkaesque tone, as he is obviously not needed at the agency.

Out of money and in desperate need of a job, Dyer accepts an offer to help in a money scheme by transporting cash between a local bank and a shop. Realizing that he is being used for illegal purposes, Dyer takes the money he has been given and flees Tangier, only to discover that he is utterly helpless in a country where he neither speaks the language nor understands the customs. After he has killed his native guide, the novel concludes with Dyer alone and hunted in a foreign country but curiously pleased with his state of affairs as an isolated individual.

Once again, Bowles has thrust an upper-middle-class American into a North African environment and allowed him to become submerged in the native and alien culture. With his loss of identity, Dyer discovers something far more authentic about himself as he is systematically stripped of his civilized supports and is forced to fall back on what little reserves he possesses as an individual human being. This peeling away of the veneer of civilization reveals underneath an emptiness and void which leaves the protagonist, like Port Moresby, totally unprepared for the unfamiliar culture into which he is thrust. Under such pressure, he collapses and must seek refuge in internal strength, of which he possesses precious little. His plunge into an exotic culture, instead of rejuvenating him, debilitates his vigor, leaving him in a weakened if also enlightened condition.

As with other American writers, such as Edgar Allan Poe and Herman Melville, Bowles writes of the exhaustion exacted by primitive cultures on the more civilized. It is a reversal of the romantic notion that cultured man, tired of his culture, can find rejuvenation through an immersion in a more savage environment. Instead, like Joseph Conrad's heroes, Dyer finds only confusion and despair. At least, it may be argued, he discovers the truth, however unpalatable it might be, and the conclusion of the novel leaves him possessed of a dark actuality, if robbed of a comforting illusion.

Bowles's next novel, *The Spider's House*, was set in 1954 against the political upheaval caused by the deposition of Morocco's hereditary ruler, Sultan Mohammed, by the colonial regime of the French. The fiction traces the tension caused by the collapse of the traditional way of life of the native inhabitants of the city of Fez through a fifteen-year-old boy, Amar, who, halfway through the novel, is befriended by John Stenham, an expatriate American writer, who has fallen in love with an American woman tourist named Lee Burroughs. By the conclusion of the novel, John leaves Fez with Lee, abandoning Amar to deal with the destruction of his way of life any way he can.

Although it is not a political novel, *The Spider's House* uses the tensions of the French colonial rule not only to highlight the theme of the disintegration of Moslem culture under the French but also to provide a backdrop against which to play out the drama of the on-again, off-again love affair between Lee and John. Amar is from a devout family but one which is not caught up in the political conflicts between the Istiqlal, the Nationalist party, with their use of terror, and the colonials. Both the French and the Nationalists are bent on stopping the ritual religious festival of *Aid el Kabir*, and Amar, who has been forbidden to leave the Medina where his family resides, gets caught outside the city's walls and is rescued by Lee and John, who have been observing the unfolding cycle of violence that is developing between the French and the Moroccans. John helps Amar return to his family through the city's walls, and Amar offers to take the couple to see the religious celebration in a village outside Fez. The Americans are fascinated by the exotic quality of the Arab life around them and agree to accompany Amar. The festival turns out badly for them, however, when Lee is shocked and repulsed by the rituals of the feast. After a quarrel, Lee and John decide that they are beginning a love affair.

Meanwhile, Amar has received a large sum of money from Lee so that he can join the Nationalists in their fight against the French. Still apolitical, Amar again gets caught up in the action of the revolution and is manipulated by the Istiqlal, barely avoiding capture by the French. At the end of the novel, he wants to rejoin John and Lee but is rebuffed by the novelist, who is set on going off with his new lover. The fiction concludes when Amar is abandoned by his newly won friend into the political turmoil of a struggle he barely understands.

As the critics have pointed out, *The Spider's House* contains a nostalgia for a past which does not belong to either John Stenham or to Bowles, but it is a longing which is nevertheless keenly felt. It has also been described as a deeply religious book, one in which Bowles mourns for a lost religious belief no longer possible in Western civilization, with its emphasis on the rational and the scientific. Certainly, the book focuses on the consequences of destroying a traditional way of life and on a myopic colonialism which blunders along in an attempt to apply Western methods to a totally unsuitable situation. It is the story of all colonial experiences in which a foreign power tries to forge a new life for a people it only partially understands, which accentuates one of the main achievements of the book, the faithful rendering of the North African landscape with its traditions and cultures.

For his fourth novel, Bowles shifted his location to South America and his plot to that of the detective novel. Yet, although seen by many critics as a genre fiction of the whodunit variety, *Up Above the World* is a far cry from a run-of-the-mill thriller. It is, in fact, a deeply psychological study of the disintegration of another couple, Taylor and Day Slade, who, much in the same vein as the Moresbys, undergo a tragic transformation which ultimately destroys them.

The Slades arrive by ship in an unidentified South American country at the port town of Puerto Farol. A woman whom they had befriended on the ship is found dead in her hotel room—murdered, it is discovered later, at the behest of her son by a thug named Thorny. The son, Grover Soto, afraid that the Slades have been a witness to the killing, hunts down the couple, who have by now taken a train to the interior of the country. The Slades are finally subjected to the use of drugs and a variety of brainwashing techniques in order to erase the memory of Mrs. Rainmantle, the murdered woman, from their minds. While recuperating at the ranch of Grover Soto, Day sees some written instructions which were to have been destroyed, and in a moment of panic, Soto drugs and then kills Taylor. As the novel concludes, he is about to do the same with Day.

The novel is a psychological thriller much in the vein of Graham Greene's "entertainments," a lesser work not demanding the exertion either to read or to write that a more serious novel requires. Yet there are certain themes and characters which immediately label the book as one of Bowles's. The wandering Americans confronting themselves amid the exotic background of a less civilized and unknown world, their eventual disintegration as they experience an alien culture, and the search for meaning in what appears to be meaningless lives echo his earlier novels. Even the appearance of chance events, encounters onto which the critics have latched to tie the volume to the thriller genre, are also present in his earlier work. The big difference in *Up Above the World* is the novel's compactness. It is streamlined, and in that sense it provides a faster, perhaps more accessible read, but it is a novel no less interesting for all that.

The critics, especially Bertens, have been particularly hard on this book, largely because of its thriller status, which is unfair, since the novel goes beyond the requirements of mere genre fiction and into a netherworld of the truly black. In many ways, this book is Bowles's most pessimistic and most nihilistic, and, writing in the thriller vein, Bowles has made a contribution to the American fictional form most foreboding and dark, a form, in short, closest to his own hopeless vision.

Bowles's fiction will remain attractive both to the few who truly admire advanced writing and thinking and to a general reading audience. It is unfortunate that Bowles's reputation as a writer's writer has limited the enjoyment of his work by the public, since he not only deserves a wider readership but also has much to offer the general reader. Too easily dismissed as an expatriate writer and therefore of little interest to students of American literature, Bowles's work is nevertheless central to the American literary experience, dealing as it does with the protagonist facing the frontier on the edge of civilization, a position which recalls that of Melville's Ishmael, James Fenimore Cooper's Natty Bumppo, and even Mark Twain's Huck Finn. Finally, critics and the public alike need to read Bowles's fiction for its relevant encounters between modern humankind and an increasingly mechanistic and depersonalized world, a place truly of nihilism and despair. Paul Bowles has written about it all.

Charles L. P. Silet

Other major works

SHORT FICTION: *The Delicate Prey and Other Stories*, 1950; *A Little Stone: Stories*, 1950; *The Hours After Noon*, 1959; *A Hundred Camels in the Courtyard*, 1962; *The Time of Friendship*, 1967; *Pages from Cold Point and Other Stories*, 1968; *Three Tales*, 1975; *Things Gone and Things Still Here*, 1977;

Collected Stories, 1939-1976, 1979; *Midnight Mass*, 1981.

POETRY: *Scenes*, 1968; *The Thicket of Spring: Poems, 1926-1969*, 1972; *Next to Nothing*, 1976; *Next to Nothing: Collected Poems, 1926-1977*, 1981.

NONFICTION: *Yallah*, 1956 (photographs by Peter W. Haeberlin); *Their Heads Are Green and Their Hands Are Blue*, 1963; *Without Stopping*, 1972 (autobiography).

TRANSLATIONS: *No Exit*, 1946 (of Jean-Paul Sartre's play *Huis-clos*); *A Life Full of Holes*, 1964 (of Driss ben Hamed Charhadi's novel); *Love with a Few Hairs*, 1967 (of Mohammed Mrabet's fiction); *The Lemon*, 1969 (of Mrabet's novel); *M'Hashish*, 1969 (of Mrabet's stories); *The Boy Who Set the Fire and Other Stories*, 1974 (of Mrabet's stories); *Hadidan Aharam*, 1975 (of Mrabet's book); *Harmless Poisons, Blameless Sins*, 1976 (of Mrabet's book); *Look and Move On*, 1976 (of Mrabet's book); *The Big Mirror*, 1977 (of Mrabet's book); *Five Eyes*, 1979 (of Abdeslam Boulaich and others' stories); *The Beach Café and The Voice*, 1980 (of Mrabet's stories); *The Chest*, 1983 (of Mrabet's stories); *The Beggar's Knife*, 1985 (of Rodrigo Rey Rosa's stories); *Marriage with Papers*, 1986 (from Mrabet's book).

Bibliography

Patterson, Richard F. *A World Outside: The Fiction of Paul Bowles*. Austin: University of Texas Press, 1987. Instead of a reading guide, Patterson offers a way of reading Bowles. Offers critiques of Bowles's stories with little reference to his personal life. A thorough analysis of his novels and short stories within the context of architectural metaphor and a knowledgeable contribution to criticism on Bowles.

Pounds, Wayne. *Paul Bowles: The Inner Geography*. New York: Peter Lang, 1985. Within the context of the psychology of Sigmund Freud and R. D. Laing, Pounds seeks to define the divided self in Bowles's fiction and examines his relationship to Edgar Allan Poe. This scholarly study shows how Bowles's work diagnoses the ills of Western civilization. Contains a useful bibliography with extensive notes.

Stewart, Lawrence D. *Paul Bowles: The Illumination of North Africa*. Carbondale: Southern Illinois University Press, 1974. A book-length critical study on Bowles, noteworthy for its understanding of his writings. Stewart discusses the three novels and many of the stories that take place in North Africa and chronicles Bowles's travels in that region, providing a wealth of biographical information.

Voelker, Joseph. "Fish Traps and Purloined Letters: The Anthropology of Paul Bowles." *Critique: Studies in Modern Fiction* 17 (Fall, 1985): 25-36. Explores Bowles's travel writing, including his book *Their Heads Are Green and Their Hands Are Blue* and the novels *Let It Come Down* and *The Spider's House*. Voelker applauds Bowles's "supreme artistry" in the creation of his Moslem characters. Contains an interesting analysis of the protagonist in *Up Above the World*, who is both the "adept" and the victim.

Wagner, Linda. "Paul Bowles and the Characterization of Women." *Critique: Studies in Modern Fiction* 27 (Fall, 1985): 15-24. Declares Bowles to be more than a nihilistic existentialist or an imitator of Albert Camus. Examines Bowles's 1982 short montage fiction *Points of Time* for its departure from male-female relations to nature's effect on human beings. Also discusses his first novel, *The Sheltering Sky*, and his collection of stories, *The Delicate Prey and Other Stories*.

KAY BOYLE

Born: St. Paul, Minnesota; February 19, 1903
Died: Mill Valley, California; December 27, 1992

Principal long fiction

Plagued by the Nightingale, 1931; *Year Before Last*, 1932; *Gentlemen, I Address You Privately*, 1933; *My Next Bride*, 1934; *Death of a Man*, 1936; *Monday Night*, 1938; *Primer for Combat*, 1942; *Avalanche*, 1943; *A Frenchman Must Die*, 1946; *1939*, 1948; *His Human Majesty*, 1949; *The Seagull on the Step*, 1955; *Three Short Novels*, 1958; *Generation Without Farewell*, 1960; *The Underground Woman*, 1975.

Other literary forms

Although she has published some fifteen novels, Kay Boyle's principal recognition has been for her shorter works. First published in the small magazines of the 1920's, her stories were collected in *Wedding Day and Other Stories* (1930) and *First Lover and Other Stories* (1933). The 1930's, declared her vintage period by critics, brought an O. Henry Prize for the title story of *The White Horses of Vienna and Other Stories* (1936), followed in 1941 by another for "Defeat," a story on the French collapse which also appeared in *Primer for Combat*. Published widely in *Harper's, The New Yorker, Saturday Evening Post*, and *The Atlantic*, and collected in *Thirty Stories* (1946), Boyle won the praise of contemporaries as the "best story teller now living" and the "economical housewife of the short story technique." Active as an editor and critic on small magazines such as *Contempo* and on progressive political journals, she also translated such European writers as Joseph Delteil, Raymond Radiguet, and Marie-Louise Soupault. Two volumes of short stories, *The Smoking Mountain: Stories of Postwar Germany* (1951) and *Nothing Ever Breaks Except the Heart* (1966), reflect wartime and postwar Europe. Collected recently in *Fifty Stories* (1980), Boyle's short fiction continues to appear in American periodicals.

Her poetry, also first published in small magazines, was collected in *A Glad Day* (1938) and *Collected Poems* (1962). *American Citizen Naturalized in Leadville, Colorado* (1944), based upon the experience of an Austrian refugee in the United States military, is dedicated to Carson McCullers, "whose husband is also overseas," and *Testament for My Students and Other Poems* (1970) concerns "that desperate year, 1968." *This Is Not a Letter and Other Poems* (1985) appeared fifteen years later.

As a European correspondent after World War II, Boyle wrote nonfiction prose of both journalistic and literary distinction, including her reportage of the war crimes trial of Heinrich Babb for *The New Yorker* and her essays on civil rights and the military establishment. Two memoirs, her edition of *The Autobiography of Emanuel Carnevali* (1967) and her chapters in Robert

McAlmon's *Being Geniuses Together, 1920-1930* (1968), capture the literary underground of that period, while a subsequent collection, *The Long Walk at San Francisco State and Other Essays* (1970), reflects the antiwar movement of the 1960's. She has also published three illustrated children's novels, *The Youngest Camel* (1939), and the Pinky novels.

Achievements

Perhaps more consistently and tenaciously than any other twentieth century American writer, Boyle has sought to unite the personal and political, the past and present, the feminine and the masculine. Recognized in both the literary and the popular realms, her rich oeuvre unites the American and the European experience of twentieth century history.

Helpful though it may be as an outline, the conventional division of Boyle's achievement into an aesthetic period before 1939 and a polemical period after may obscure Boyle's constant focus upon the dialectic between subject and object. In the exploration of personal experience, her intense imaginative reconstruction posits the integration of conflicting aspects of the self, the struggle between self-abnegation and self-assertion, and the liberation of the individual from repressive aspects of personal or family relationships. Usually presented as a union of archetypally masculine and feminine characteristics in an individual or in a couple, often a pair of same-sex friends, Boyle's image of the completed self is one of growth beyond confining roles.

In her exploration of the self as a political creature, Boyle asserts the life-affirming potential of the individual and the community against destructive authoritarian or absolutist constructs, whether within the family or in the larger society. In her intense evocation of personal awakening to political morality, Boyle's synthesis reaches beyond the narrowly ideological to affirm the human search for tenderness in a landscape which, although distorted by repression, gives hope for regeneration. Like Thomas Mann, Ignazio Silone, and André Malraux, Boyle seeks to integrate the individual psyche into the larger social milieu, to make the self meaningful in history, exercising that responsibility which Mann called for when he said that had the German intellectual community remained accountable, Nazism would have been prevented.

Using modernist techniques to refute contemporary nihilism, Boyle restores perspective to the confrontation between the individual sensibility and a complex, often hidden, social reality. Her decision to address a broad audience upon political as well as personal themes, sometimes seen as a "betrayal" of her talent, might more fully be understood as a commitment to the exercise of moral responsibility through literature. Exploring the need to unite discordant psychic and political elements and to assert the life-affirming, Boyle provides in her work a model of balanced wholeness in the larger as well as the smaller world.

Biography

The cross between Kay Boyle's Midwestern roots and cosmopolitan experience produced the distinctive flavor of her work. Although born into an upper-class St. Paul family, Boyle spent her early years not in the Midwest but in the eastern United States, France, Austria, and Switzerland, and especially in the mountains, which become a symbol of human transcendence in her work. The active and involved nature of her childhood is expressed in her love of horses, riding, and skiing, and its aesthetic and creative aspect in the family custom of gathering sketches and stories into marbled covers for gift books. Katherine Evans Boyle, the "shining light" to whom Boyle dedicated her first works, provided an image of strength and purpose, introducing her daughter to the most avant-garde of European art and literature, as well as the most progressive of American populist politics. Her grandfather, Jesse Peyton Boyle, a dynamic, charismatic St. Paul businessman whom Boyle later called a "charming reactionary," was a model of the aggressive, compelling patriarch, in contrast to the more vulnerable and intuitive male figure typified by her father, Howard Peyton Boyle.

The next years saw Boyle return to the Midwest and then to the Greenwich Village literary and political circles which would provide her with friends and supporters. A series of financial reversals brought the family to Cincinnati, where Howard Boyle became established in the retail automotive business. After a brief stay at Shipley, Boyle studied violin at the Cincinnati Conservatory and architecture at Ohio Mechanics Institute, later calling hers "no education at all," saying that she had never been "properly through the eighth grade," and had instead pursued writing on her own, a training she advocated later for her students as well. Less than twenty years old, Boyle moved to New York, attended a few classes at Columbia, worked as a secretary, and met Greenwich Village literati of a progressive bent. In the space of her short stay, she worked for *Broom*, a journal of European and American experimentalism, and became acquainted with Harriet Monroe's *Poetry* magazine; with Lola Ridge, whose Gaelic ancestry she shared; and with William Carlos Williams, who became her friend and mentor. Described as a shy, timid ingenue, Boyle appears in Williams' memoirs attending Fourteenth Street parties with John Reed, Louise Bryant, Jean Toomer, Kenneth Burke, and Hart Crane.

The 1920's were another expatriate decade for Boyle. In 1921, she married Richard Brault, a French student whom she had met in Ohio, and she returned with him to his family's provincial seat. Williams recalls meeting a lonely and isolated Boyle in the vicinity of Le Havre, in which atmosphere her first two novels take place. When the marriage deteriorated and ended a few years later, Boyle remained in Paris and the Riviera, playing a central role in the literary underground of American exiles and the European avant-garde. Centered on the publication of small magazines, these groups brought Boyle together with Ernest Walsh, the effervescent poet, critic, and editor of *This Quarter*, the lover and compatriot whose death from lung injuries incurred as a pilot is recounted in *Year Before Last*.

The aesthetic of Boyle's group, represented by *Transition* magazine and Eugene Jolas, was eclectic, drawing on the work of Ernest Hemingway, James Joyce, Gertrude Stein, Ezra Pound, William Carlos Williams, and Carl Sandburg. Experimental, antirational, and antirealist, this loosely knit group ascribed to an informal creed known as Orphism, set down in the 1929 manifesto "the Revolution of the Word," signed by Boyle, Laurence Vail, Hart Crane, and others interested in representing a primarily interior reality in a rhythmic, "hallucinatory" style cognizant of current psychological and anthropological lore and inimical to standard realism and the genteel tradition. It was in this milieu that Boyle developed the lyrical subjectivism reflected in her early poems and stories, a quality she found in D. H. Lawrence and Arthur Rimbaud, Walt Whitman and Edgar Allan Poe, Stein and Joyce.

Following Walsh's death and the birth of her first child, Sharon, Boyle, out of money and dispirited, joined a communal art colony led by Raymond Duncan, Isadora's brother, whose personal charisma and exploitative idealism are reflected in a number of novelistic relationships in which one will is subsumed in another. Rescued from this amalgam of Jean Jacques Rousseau, Leo Tolstoy, and pseudoanarchistic principles by Caresse and Harry Crosby, whose unconventional sun religion and Black Sun Press were underground institutions, Boyle spent her next years in the French and British settings, which are reflected in the novels of the period. In 1931, she married the scholar and poet Laurence Vail, and in the following years bore three more daughters, Apple-Joan, Kathe, and Clover.

Emerging aboveground in the late 1930's with a Simon and Schuster contract, Boyle published a major short-story collection, *The White Horses of Vienna*, which introduced the Lippizanner horses that became an important symbol in later works. Three highly praised short novels and two longer ones followed, including her own favorite, *Monday Night*, and she received a Guggenheim Fellowship to pursue the metaphor of aviation for human history. Before the fall of France in 1939, she wrote about the collapse of Europe's democracies before Fascism. The war novels of that period are usually set in small French villages where an expatriated woman becomes involved in the political choices of various men, usually Austrians made nationless by the Anschluss. As the setting of her fiction moved from the interior to the external world, Boyle's style became more popular, often a journalistic diary, and more suited to the wider audiences of the *Saturday Evening Post* and the *Ladies Home Companion*. This development, decried by some critics, damaged her standing in literary circles in a way that it did not for an author such as Katherine Anne Porter, Boyle's friend, who kept her hackwork clearly separate from her artistic life. The conflict between resistance and collaboration addressed in her novels surfaced in Boyle's private life as well when Vail, whose sentiments are possibly expressed by several characters in *Primer for Combat*, disapproved of her efforts to secure visas for Jewish refugees, citing the "historical necessity" of Fascism. Following their divorce, Boyle married Baron Joseph Von Franckenstein, an Austrian refugee whose experiences are reflected in *American Citizen Naturalized in Leadville, Colorado*, in *His Human Majesty*, and in the general situation of Austrian anti-Fascists in the continental novels of the war period.

After the fall of France, the popular novels *Avalanche* and *A Frenchman Must Die* brought the resistance experience to American audiences. Perhaps because of an establishment bias against best sellers, against explicitly political intent, or, in some cases, against the notion of a woman writing about war and the "masculine side of the male character," as one critic stated, and surely because of their superficial and rather formulaic character, these novels received negative reviews from Diana Trilling, Edmund Wilson, and *The New Yorker*. Despite this criticism, Boyle continued to address the question of individual political choice in short novels such as *Decision*, set in post-Civil War Spain, and in *Sea Gull on the Step*, which points out the growing inappropriateness of American occupation policy. After the war, Boyle's work became even more journalistic in her role as a European correspondent, chiefly in occupied Germany, where Von Franckenstein directed Amerika Dienst, an International Information Agency service, and Boyle reported on the war crimes trial of Heinrich Babb. She also commented upon European moral and political conditions in her short stories of the period, developing as she did so a vision of German and European history that she would use in later novels and in a planned nonfiction project. Like Thomas Mann, Ignazio Silone, and other anti-Fascist intellectuals, Boyle addressed the vulnerabilities which continued to expose Western democracies to the totalitarian threat explored by Erich Fromm, Hannah Arendt, and many others.

Returning in 1953 to an America caught up in the events of McCarthyism, Boyle lost her job with *The New Yorker*, while Von Franckenstein, a war hero captured and tortured in Nazi Germany during his career with the OSS and an able civil servant, was removed from his state department post for his "questionable" loyalty in associating with Boyle, who was deemed a security risk. After frequent testimony by both before Internal Security committees, Von Franckenstein was reinstated in 1957. In 1958, the first American edition of *Three Short Novels*, including *The Crazy Hunter*, *The Bridegroom's Body*, and *Decision*, appeared, followed by *Generation Without Farewell*, Boyle's most ambitious postwar novel.

Following Von Franckenstein's death from cancer in 1963, Boyle continued her political commitment and her writing during the anti-Vietnam War movement, a cause in which her earlier analysis of French colonialism and European Fascism made her especially active. Supporting civil disobedience to military recruitment and induction and to weapons research and manufacture, she organized protest groups and petitions and traveled with one such group to Cambodia, where they brought the war there to media attention. The Christmas Eve of 1967, which Boyle spent in jail for her part in a sit-in at an Oakland induction center, is drawn upon in her novel *The Underground Woman*. As a teacher of creative writing at San Francisco State, she courted dismissal to join the student protest. Having received the San Francisco Art Commission's Award of Honor in 1978, Boyle retired from teaching in 1980, the year in which *Fifty Stories* appeared. In 1982, *Three Short Novels* was reissued with an introduction by the Canadian writer Margaret Atwood.

Analysis

From *Plagued by the Nightingale*, published in the early 1930's, to *The Underground Woman* in the 1970's, Kay Boyle's novels explore a complex dialectic between the personal and the political. Within the individual psyche and the social world as well there is a conflict between the human will to liberation and the authoritarian will to dominance. Not autobiographical in the usual sense, most of Boyle's early novels are imaginative reconsiderations of episodes which, although recognizable in outline in her personal life, are universalized into paradigms of human experience. Her first novel, *Plagued by the Nightingale*, which Hart Crane admired, introduced an expatriate American bride to her husband's family in their decaying French provincial seat. A crippling congenital disease afflicting all the family males, an emblem of general social decay, prevents the young husband, Nicole, from asserting independence, and requires the family to be always on the lookout to perpetuate itself. Bridget, the young wife, and Luc, a family friend whose energy and vivacity have earmarked him for marriage to one of Nicole's three sisters, are alternately drawn into and repelled by the patriarchal family's power to protect and engulf. By making the birth of an heir the condition upon which the young couple's inheritance depends, Nicole's father threatens to bring them entirely within the control of the patriarchal family. Freeing both herself and Nicole from the grasp of this decaying culture, Bridget chooses to bear a child not by Nicole, whose tainted genes would continue the cycle, but by Luc, a vigorous outsider whose health and vitality promise liberation and autonomy. Although ostensibly a narrative of personal life, this first novel becomes political in its exploration of the relationship between the self and the family, the will to immerse oneself in the group or to aspire to self-determination. The decaying and yet compelling power of the patriarchal family becomes a metaphor for Western culture itself in its paralyzing traditionalism and sacrifice of the individual to authority.

Continuing this exploration of personal experience in search of security and selfhood, *Year Before Last* recounts Hannah's final year with her lover Martin, a poet and editor terminally ill with a lung disease. In the conflict between Martin's former lover Eve, who is his partner in the publication of the small magazine that is truly the group's creative life, and Hannah, self-sacrifice and self-assertion in pursuit of love and art are polarized. Eve, "strong and solitary" yet unfulfilled, and Hannah, vulnerable, nurturing, yet unaffirmed, both seek realization through Martin ("What are we but two empty women turning to him and sucking him dry for a taste of life?"), only to find it in themselves as they join in his care. They are complementary aspects of the self united to assert the primacy of love and art. In this resolution of two opposing sets of personal qualities, here presented as a bond between two women in support of a positive male, the self is empowered in the larger world of artistic creation.

This resolving dyad of two women appears in slightly different guise in *My Next Bride*, the final novel of this early self-exploratory group. Victoria, left emotionally and materially destitute, joins an art colony whose tunic-wearing, dancing anarchists are led by a charismatic, idealistic, but ultimately exploitive male, Sorrel, the reverse of the vital, creative male seen in Martin. Searching for security and idealism, Victoria falls instead into complete self-abnegation in a series of underworld trials, including prostitution and abortion, which represent total abandonment of selfhood and self-determination. She finally returns to herself with the support of two friends, one of whom becomes her lesbian lover and symbolizes the union of the submissive and the assertive, the passive and the active that appears in Boyle as an emblem of the healed psyche. Boyle's treatment of homosexual themes, especially her use of the homosexual couple as an image of the completed self, is remarkable for its freedom from negative stereotypes.

In *Gentlemen, I Address You Privately*, Boyle breaks free from the reconstruction of her own experience to enter a totally imaginative landscape with a mythic quality never so markedly present before, a quality which comes to dominate the best of her later work. Here, the dyad is of two men, one a cleric cut off from experience in the contemplative heights of art and religion, the other a sailor plunged entirely into atavistic life at sea. Deserting cell and ship alike, they enter the human world, descending from Mont St. Michel (like all Boyle's mountains, a symbol of the transcendent and the ideal) to the muck of a squatter's hut, where they hide out as farmhands. In the common-law marriage of Quespelle, a brutal peasant who delights chiefly in killing rabbits, and Leonie, a madonnalike yet buddingly fertile female akin to William Faulkner's Lena Grove, the destructive and nurturing forces of the real world appear. This sharply polarized image of the human family, brutal masculinity and submissive femininity, proves too dualistic for reproduction and growth. A more positive figure of the male is posited in Munday, the gentle, intuitive aesthete who acts in defense of the old dog Quespelle intends to shoot, the bedraggled horse, the rabbits, and finally Leonie. Quespelle leaves for the city, Munday is left with Leonie. The two have a "new taste for life," transformed by the love which "binds the two . . . together, hand and foot, and then sends [them] out, away from any other comfort"; Adam and Eve emerge from paradise to establish the human community in this Faulknerian affirmation of the self in opposition to both authoritarian families and absolute ideas.

This liberation is again apparent in the better-known short novels, *Crazy Hunter* and *The Bridegroom's Body*, set in a Lawrentian English countryside where life must break free of repressive families and social structures. In *Crazy Hunter*, Nan must assert herself against the control of her mother, Mrs. Lombe, so she purchases a gelding against her mother's wishes but is disappointed when the horse suddenly goes blind. In condemning the horse to be shot, Mrs. Lombe becomes the authoritarian hunter whose presence is strong in Boyle's novels, her destructive power threatening both her husband Candy and Nan, who must assume her mother's strength without her repressiveness. Nan, in teaching the horse to jump at risk to her life, and Candy, putting his body between the veterinarian's pistol and the horse's flying hooves, establish the father's legitimate power and the daughter's liberation from the mother's control in defense of vital yet vulnerable life. The horse, which becomes for Boyle a symbol of this life-force, retains its conventional identification with passion and strength while taking on more complex qualities of aspiration, idealism, and vulnerable beauty. Usually regarded as a primarily masculine symbol, the horse in Boyle is strongly associated with the gentle, intuitive male, or with the female, and particularly with emerging female sexuality.

In *The Bridegroom's Body*, the repressive domination associated with the mother and confined to the immediate family in *Crazy Hunter* becomes patriarchal in its extension to the entire community in the country estate of the Glouries. A remote, rainy, brooding, and yet potentially fertile land, the estate is dominated by predatory hunters led by Lord Glourie, an insensitive, uncommunicative sportsman, an upper-class Quespelle, whose chief interests are hunting and drinking with other hunters. This predatory patriarchy is mirrored in the natural world by Old Hitches, chief of the swans, whose dominance is threatened by the Bridegroom, a young swan who has set up his nest in defiance of the patriarch and in assertion of a more gentle and intuitive male potency. Lady Glourie, an energetic, forceful woman in her tweeds and sturdy shoes, struggles to maintain life in an atmosphere completely lacking in spiritual and emotional fulfillment by caring for the sick sheep, the swan-master's pregnant wife, and the Bridegroom himself. An isolated figure made illegitimate and ineffective by the hunters, she longs for a female friend, hopes which rise only to be dashed when Miss Cafferty, the nurse called to care for the pregnant woman, proves not a comradely version of Lady Glourie, but rather her total opposite—young, conventionally attractive in her bright green dress, and seemingly vulnerable to male approval.

Miss Cafferty eventually vindicates herself, however, imploring Lady Glourie to "see her own beauty," her strength against the "butchers, murderers—men stalking every corner of the ground by day and night." This plea leaves Lady Glourie with the "chill" which Boyle expresses as the promise of regeneration, of union between the two versions of female strength which have as yet "no record, no sign, no history marked on them."

Recognizing the destructive power of authoritarian personal and political ideologies in a more overtly public way, the psychological detective story *Monday Night* places the search of two American exiles, Wilt and Bernie, against a collapsing moral order in prewar Europe. They pursue the case of Monsieur Sylvestre, a chemist whose testimony holds such sway in the courts that he alone has convicted a series of young men of murder in several mysterious deaths by claiming to find traces of poisonous substances in the victims' "viscera." The Americans learn that Sylvestre himself has been the murderer; this "misanthropy too savage to be repudiated" is motivated by the fact that the young men, like the Bridegroom, affirm some kind of spontaneous and generous emotional life with their families, a life Sylvestre himself has repudiated by rejecting his lover and their young son and follows by expunging himself from his world. Against the backdrop of a brisk arms business carried on with both sides in the Spanish Civil War and instances of French chauvinism and contempt for foreign nationals and their own people in a series of fixed bicycle races, one French spokesman pleads for moral action against destructive totalitarianism ("It is you who could stop it if you, your country really cared"), for "everlasting and violent freedom" against the dead authoritarianism represented by Sylvestre. Expressing the terror of vulnerable humanity, Wilt, awakened to a moral apprehension, questions, "Is it possible that a madman whose passion it has been to toy with human life and with the honor and liberty of countless victims was put in a position of highest authority?"

This individual moral awakening to larger choice underlies all the "war" novels of the 1940's. In an acclaimed short novel, *Decision*, a detached journalist is awakened to the modern hell of Fascist Spain through her chance encounter with two young men, republicans under surveillance, executed for their part in a Madrid prison hunger strike. The human capacity for resistance, expressed by a republican flamenco singer with the phrase "you get up on stage and bellow your heart out," is found in an even more life-affirming form in women, whose "power of the weak," to use Elizabeth Janeway's term, means:

> We, as women, have learned and forgotten more than they have ever set down in books . . . we are sustained in our weakness by something they never even heard a whisper of . . . by a consecration to the very acts of hope, tenderness, love, whatever the name may be, which no man [that is, no fascist] has any share in.

In an awakening not narrowly political but moral in Hannah Arendt's sense, the narrator believes "at that instant . . . in each individual death, and the look of the sky as it must have been to them then, at the last trembling moment of defiance."

This apprehension of personal and political commitment exists in all the longer war novels. Set usually in mountain villages in the Savoy or the Tirol, where the ambiguity of the national identity makes choice necessary, these novels posit some encounter between an American woman exile and one or more men, often Austrian skiers, whose stateless position requires choice of a personal nationality. This interplay occurs in the context of the village and the larger nation, where alternating mendacity and heroism, resistance and collaboration, illustrate the consequences of such choices. In the short novel *1939*, Ferdl Eder's attempts to join the French army, frustrated by chauvinistic discrimination against foreigners, leaves him with no recourse but to accept the hated German passport; he leaves his American lover, who has herself abandoned a secure marriage to assert her choice.

Primer for Combat, the most involved of this group, expresses the need for what Phyl, the American woman, calls "participation . . . in the disaster. In humanity's disaster." Against a tapestry of characters in a French village during the first days of the occupation, in an introspective diary format, Boyle, in a manner reminiscent of Ignazio Silone and André Malraux, posits a complex relationship between Fascism, colonialism, classism, and democracy and self-determination as they are internalized in personal commitment. Phyl is awakened from the moral torpor of her fascination with the Austrian Wolfgang, whose opportunistic collaboration she comes to recognize by contrast with Sepp Von Horneck, another Austrian, who, refusing to exchange liberation for reconstruction, escapes to join the Gaullist forces. Ultimately, Phyl's choice is not between men but between models of human action, acquiescence, or self-assertion. "I have found my own people," she says; "I have found my own side, and I shall not betray them." Fascism is located not within the political but within the personal realm, "not a national indication but an internal one." *Primer for Combat*, the best of the war novels, synthesizes the contradiction between the personal and the political.

In two novels addressing the postwar period of occupation, *Seagull on the Step* and *Generation Without Farewell*, Boyle's vision of the dialectic between the personal and the political becomes more fully a clash between the human and the totalitarian impulses in the heart and in history. In *Generation Without Farewell*, like *His Human Majesty* a study of the human response to authoritarianism, hunters stalk their prey in an occupied German village. Both Germans and Americans, led by the American Colonel Roberts, the universal authoritarian, hunt a wild boar believed hidden in the seemingly primeval forest surrounding the village. An expression of the people's will to survive and affirm the positive aspects of their nationality against the dead hand of their Nazi past, the boar is identified by an American observer, Seth Honer-kamp, with an anti-Fascist spirit and the great composers of the past. Jaeger, an anti-Nazi German searching for his roots in a past not distorted by Fascism, sees in the hunt his people's historic tendency to create an "other" whose extermination becomes an obsession, destroying human liberty and ultimately the very source of the culture. The will to liberty breaks free, however, when Robert's wife Catherine and daughter Milly, both expressions of the repro-ductive and nurturing power contained in the Demeter-Persephone myth so pervasive in Boyle, join Jaeger and Christoph Horn. Horn is Milly's lover, whose identification with the Lippizanner horses in his care connects him with the most fertile and, at the same time, the most transcendent elements of the national spirit they represent. This identification is shared by Milly, whose pregnancy by Horn parallels the mare's pregnancy in a particularly female vision of the survival and continuity of the culture itself. Although the repressive qualities of both German and American authority unite in the hunt for the boar, an attempt to ship the horses to Brooklyn, and an epidemic of polio—the essentially American disease which fatally strikes Horn despite Jaeger and Honerkamp's efforts to secure an iron lung—Catherine joins Milly to protect the coming child, leaving a revitalized Jaeger and Hon-erkamp to continue their pursuit for the life-affirming aspects of both German and American culture.

The myth of the sorrowing mother in search of her daughter appears again in *The Underground Woman*. Against the background of the American anti-war movement, Athena Gregory's psychic restoration is connected to a vision of human transcendence expressed in a community of women. Athena, a university classics teacher, her husband lost to cancer and her daughter to a satanic cult, finds herself jailed during a sit-in at an induction center. Through a process of bonding not only with the other war protesters but also with the black, Hispanic, and poor white women there, she finds personal and political transformation in an intense female friendship with Calliope, an-other older woman whose intuitive, emotional nature balances Athena's own rational analytical one. She also forms a friendship with a young woman musician, who replaces Athena's daughter Melanie, irrevocably lost to a cult serving Pete the Redeemer, an exploitative, charismatic leader who demands complete surrender of the will. Released from jail and from her mourning, Athena asserts her new self in a symbolic defense of all daughters when she successfully resists Pete's attempt to commandeer her home. In this affirma-tive vision of female power, Athena resolves the conflict between her two selves, the respectable, above-ground Athena sprung from Zeus's head and heir to his rationality, and the more emotional, intuitive "underground woman," as she joins Calliope to save the deer from the hunters and the Hispanic prostitute's children from the state. In this late novel, Kay Boyle's vision of personal and political self-affirmation advances the dialectic between subjective experience and objective reality which has marked her work from the beginning.

Janet Polansky

Other major works

SHORT FICTION: *Short Stories*, 1929; *Wedding Day and Other Stories*, 1930; *First Lover and Other Stories*, 1933; *The White Horses of Vienna and Other Stories*, 1936; *The Crazy Hunter and Other Stories*, 1940; *Thirty Stories*, 1946; *The Smoking Mountain: Stories of Postwar Germany*, 1951; *Nothing Ever Breaks Except the Heart*, 1966; *Fifty Stories*, 1980; *Life Being the Best and Other Stories*, 1988.

POETRY: *A Glad Day*, 1938; *American Citizen Naturalized in Leadville, Colorado*, 1944; *Collected Poems*, 1962; *Testament for My Students and Other Poems*, 1970; *This Is Not a Letter and Other Poems*, 1985.

NONFICTION: *365 Days*, 1936 (edited with others); *Breaking the Silence: Why a Mother Tells Her Son About the Nazi Era*, 1962; *The Autobiography of Emanuel Carnevali*, 1967; *Being Geniuses Together, 1920-1930*, 1968 (with Robert McAlmon); *The Long Walk at San Francisco State and Other Essays*, 1970; *Enough of Dying! An Anthology of Peace Writings*, 1972; *Words That Must Somehow Be Said: The Selected Essays of Kay Boyle, 1927-1984*, 1985.

CHILDREN'S LITERATURE: *The Youngest Camel*, 1939, 1959; *Pinky, the Cat Who Liked to Sleep*, 1966; *Pinky in Persia*, 1968.

Bibliography

Carpenter, Richard C. "Kay Boyle: The Figure in the Carpet." *Critique: Studies in Modern Fiction* 7 (Winter, 1964-1965): 65-78. Discusses Boyle's interest in writing about the perennial need for human love, as well as its "frustration and misdirection." Examines short novels such as *The Crazy Hunter*, where, according to Carpenter, the "dazzling style" of Boyle reaches perfection. Also explores Boyle's use of inner monologue in her works.

Ford, Hugh. *Four Lives in Paris*. San Francisco: North Point Press, 1987. Kay Boyle lived in Paris for nearly two decades; she is one of the four "expatriate" artists that Hugh selected for this study. Provides interesting background on Boyle, her beginnings as a writer, her involvement with the magazine *This Quarter*, and her writing "circle" in France.

Howard, Richard. "Poetry Chronicle." Review of *Collected Poems*, by Kay Boyle. *Poetry* 102 (July, 1963): 250-259. Howard is not enthusiastic about this collection and is clearly unimpressed with Boyle's French café image. He does acknowledge, however, that "Miss Boyle has spirit and to spare" and praises her poem *A Winter Fable*, which he calls a "resounding success."

Spanier, Sandra Whipple. *Kay Boyle: Artist and Activist*. Carbondale: Southern Illinois University Press, 1986. A valuable book-length study on Boyle, with emphasis on her commitment to activism, in both her writings and her life. Contains a wealth of biographical information, much of which was supplied by the author herself. The emphasis is on Boyle's life and work in the 1920's and early 1930's. Includes a bibliography.

Yalom, Marilyn. *Women Writers of the West Coast: Speaking of Their Lives and Careers*. Santa Barbara, Calif.: Capra Press, 1983. This volume grew out of a series of public dialogues with a handful of women authors. The entry on Boyle, however, came from an offstage conversation with photographer Margo Davis in March, 1982. Here Boyle recalls her involvement in the antiwar movement in the 1960's, about life in Paris, about being blacklisted in the 1950's, her writing, and the authors whom she admires. A source of valuable background information on Boyle.

T. CORAGHESSAN BOYLE
Thomas John Boyle

Born: Peekskill, New York; 1948

Principal long fiction
Water Music, 1981; *Budding Prospects: A Pastoral*, 1984; *World's End*, 1987; *East Is East*, 1990.

Other literary forms
T. Coraghessan Boyle has published several collections of mostly satirical short stories addressing most of the same themes seen in his longer fiction.

Achievements
Boyle's novels have been praised for their originality, style, and comic energy. At a time when his contemporaries seem obsessed with the mundane details of everyday life—presented in a minimalist style—Boyle approaches fiction as an iconoclastic storyteller who embraces and borrows from the entire history of narrative literature, celebrating the profane, often-absurd complexities of human endeavors. His first collection of stories won the St. Lawrence Award for Short Fiction, *Water Music* received the Aga Khan Award, and the PEN/Faulkner Award for Fiction was given to *World's End*.

Biography
Born into a lower-middle-class family in Peekskill, New York, in 1948, Thomas John Boyle was a rebellious youth who played drums and sang in a rock-and-roll band, drove fast cars, and took recreational drugs. He did not get along with his father, a school-bus driver whose alcoholism killed him at fifty-four in 1972. Boyle's mother, a secretary, was also an alcoholic and died of liver failure. Assuming the name T. Coraghessan Boyle at the State University of New York at Potsdam, Boyle studied saxophone and clarinet until he realized that he lacked the necessary discipline for music and drifted into creative writing. After college, to avoid military service during the Vietnam War, he taught English for two years at Lakeland High School in Shrub Oak, New York, while increasing his use of drugs, including heroin.

In 1972, Boyle entered the creative writing program at the University of Iowa, where he studied under Vance Bourjaily, John Cheever, and John Irving. He also studied nineteenth century English literature and received a Ph.D. in 1977 with a short-story collection, later published as *Descent of Man* (1979), serving as his dissertation. He is head of the writing program at the University of Southern California and lives in Woodland Hills, a suburb of Los Angeles, with his wife, Karen Kvashay (whom he met when they were undergraduates), and their children, Kerrie, Milo, and Spencer.

Analysis

T. Coraghessan Boyle writes colorful, humorous novels about the misconceptions people of different sexes, races, nationalities, and backgrounds have about one another and the misunderstandings—some violent—that result. The clashes between Britons and Africans in *Water Music*, drug entrepreneurs and Northern California rednecks in *Budding Prospects*, Indians and Dutch settlers in New York in *World's End*, and Americans and a half-American Japanese in *East Is East* allow Boyle to satirize the prejudices, eccentricities, and excesses of several cultures.

Boyle populates his ironic fiction with a multitude of diverse characters, each of whom is convinced that his is the only possible way of perceiving and dealing with a complex, changing, often-hostile world. Boyle alternates the viewpoints of these protagonists to present events and issues from all possible sides and increase the irony of the situations. He writes in both a straightforward, economical style and more ornate prose resembling that of such favorite writers as John Barth and Thomas Pynchon. Far from being didactic, Boyle creates serious fiction that entertains through his masterful storytelling ability and through his control of his vivid style.

Water Music alternates between the stories of Scottish explorer Mungo Park and London criminal Ned Rise until their destinies converge in Africa. Park (1771-1806), the first white man to see the Niger River, wrote a best-selling account of his adventures, *Travels in the Interior Districts of Africa* (1797), led a larger expedition into the interior of Africa, and drowned in the rapids of the Niger during an attack by natives. Boyle's fictionalized Park and the low-born Rise are used to contrast the levels of English society and attitudes toward the British Empire.

Park, a public hero, is less than heroic as imagined by Boyle. He thinks that he has had unique experiences because he is unable to recognize the humanity of the Africans he encounters. He selfishly ignores Ailie, his long-suffering fiancée and later devoted wife, thinking nothing of leaving her behind for years while he strives for glory. Park is less concerned with any benefits to humankind resulting from his expeditions than with mere adventure and fame. This need leads him to distort and romanticize his experiences in his writings. The irony of these exploits is that Park would be totally lost without the assistance of such nonwhites as Johnson, born Katunga Oyo. Sold into slavery in America, Johnson learns to read, wins his freedom, becomes a highly respected valet in London, and translates Henry Fielding's *Amelia* (1752) into Mandingo before returning to Africa. His earthy yet sophisticated realism strongly contrasts with Park's muddled idealism. Park's moral blindness suggests some of the causes of the collapse of the Empire.

Ned Rise, on the other hand, is a victim in the tradition of the picaros created by Fielding, Daniel Defoe, and Charles Dickens. (Dickens' mixture of colorful characterizations, humor, and moral outrage, as well as his use of odd names, seems to be a major influence on Boyle.) Rise is stolen from his mother at birth and forced to become a beggar when old enough. He has his right hand mutilated by a cleaver, is nearly drowned, is robbed, is wrongfully imprisoned and hanged—coming to life as he is about to be dissected—loses his true love, Fanny Brunch, is imprisoned again, and is shipped to Africa to become part of Park's fatal expedition. Park's Britain represents culture and privilege; Ned's stands for the poverty and depravity at the extreme other end of the social scale. Yet the ironically named Rise learns to survive.

In the tradition of such classics of the American picaresque novel as John Barth's *The Sot-Weed Factor* (1960) and Thomas Berger's *Little Big Man* (1964), *Water Music* is an enormously entertaining black comedy, a deliberately anachronistic, self-conscious narrative that frequently calls attention to its form and style. Boyle's delight in being a literary show-off, a tendency he has subdued as his career has progressed, led some of the novel's reviewers to dismiss it as a stunt, but *Water Music* quickly developed a cult following and has come to be seen as a clear announcement of the debut of an original, irreverent talent.

Boyle presents another ill-conceived adventure, though on a much smaller scale, in *Budding Prospects: A Pastoral*. Its thirty-one-year-old protagonist, Felix Nasmyth, is a chronic failure given another shot at success by the mysterious Vogelsang, a Vietnam veteran and sociopath. With the assistance of Boyd Dowst, holder of a master's degree in botany from Yale University, Felix is to grow marijuana in rural Northern California. Vogelsang promises the desperate Felix that he will earn a half-million dollars from the enterprise.

Felix and his inept friends Phil and Gesh experience culture shock in isolated Willits, whose aggressively antagonistic citizens consider themselves morally superior to the rest of the decadent world. Obstacles to raising a productive marijuana crop include rain, fire, a hungry bear, a 320-pound alumnus of the state mental hospital's violent ward, and John Jerpbak, a menacing policeman who, like everyone in Willits, knows what Felix is doing. The comedy of *Budding Prospects* results from the dogged perseverance of Felix and friends in this doomed endeavor.

Beside his usual theme of individuals out of their element in a strange environment, Boyle offers a satire of the American free-enterprise system. As he interprets it, the system is motivated primarily by greed, with success coming less through intelligence or hard work than through luck. The dubious morality of Felix's project only adds to the irony. He and his friends want to get rich quickly and are honest only in admitting that they care about nothing but money. That they work harder to fail in an illegal business than they would to earn money honestly is yet another irony in a highly ironic tale. Felix's unreliable narration as he constantly compares himself to the pioneers who settled America adds comic hyperbole. Such humor keeps Boyle's examination of the materialistic side of the American Dream from being preachy.

Boyle returned to a larger canvas with *World's End*, his most ambitious and least comic novel, a consideration of America's self-destructive impulse. The Van Brunts, Dutch settlers in what is now northern Westchester County, New York, in the late seventeenth century, experience conflicts with a hostile nature and the voracious Van Warts, the patroons who own the land they farm. The lives of the Van Brunts become intertwined with those of the Kitchawanks, their Indian neighbors. The greedy machinations of the Van Warts lead to misery for the settlers and Indians and death for several of them.

Boyle alternates chapters about these characters with ones dealing with their twentieth century descendants, including Jeremy Mohonk, the last of the Kitchawanks, whose efforts to regain his birthright (stolen by the Van Warts) earn for him seventeen years in prison. Truman Van Brunt betrays his friends and relatives to save himself, just as one of the original Van Brunts had done. The protagonist of the twentieth century chapters is Walter Van Brunt, reared by Communists after Truman runs away and his mother dies. In the late 1960's, Walter is torn between the countercultural life led by his friends and the wealth and social position of the Van Warts. After losing his wife when she finds him in bed with Mardi Van Wart and losing both his feet in separate motorcycle accidents, Walter tracks down his lost father in Barrow, Alaska, to discover that Truman has spent years researching his family's history to justify his actions. Walter returns home thoroughly disillusioned, and Jeremy Mohonk gains revenge against his enemies by impregnating the wife of the current Van Wart, ironically allowing the despised line to continue.

In *World's End*, Boyle shows how people of different races, sexes, and social and economic backgrounds exploit, betray, and fail one another. The characters either are desperate to control their destinies or consider themselves the victims of fates they are incapable of overcoming. Almost everyone is self-deluding, from the right-wing fanatic Dipe Van Wart in his pathetic attempts to resist change, to Walter, who sees himself as an alienated, existential antihero in the tradition of Meursault in Albert Camus' *L'Étranger* (1942; *The Stranger*, 1946). Walter thinks that his life will fall into place if he can understand his father, yet finding Truman leads only to confusion.

As Boyle rifles English literary traditions as part of his satire in *Water Music*, in *World's End* he draws upon the mythical views of America espoused by such writers as Washington Irving, James Fenimore Cooper, Nathaniel Hawthorne, Herman Melville, and William Faulkner. From the destruction of the virgin wilderness to the exploitation of the Indian to the curses inflicted upon several generations of characters to fatal obsession with the inexplicable, the novel is virtually a catalog of traditional American literary themes.

World's End represents a new maturity in Boyle as an artist. In it he eschews the too-easy irony and too-obvious satire that occasionally weaken his earlier fiction, while he confirms his skill at storytelling. Though *World's End* is a sprawling novel with more than one hundred characters, Boyle exerts masterful control over his complicated, overlapping plots, expecting his readers to share his joy in the manipulation of so many coincidences, parallels, and ironies.

The inability of people of different backgrounds to understand one another is even more at the center of *East Is East* than of Boyle's other novels. Hiro Tanaka, a twenty-year-old cook on a Japanese ship, jumps overboard off the coast of Georgia. Hiro, another Boyle orphan, has never known his father, an American rock musician who loved and left Hiro's mother, an eventual suicide. Ostracized by Japanese society for being half American, Hiro longs to lose himself in the great melting pot but unfortunately washes ashore on isolated Tupelo Island, site of Thanatopsis House, an artists' colony.

After a series of confused encounters with the natives, Hiro finds refuge in the cottage of Ruth Dershowitz. A mediocre writer from California, Ruth is at Thanatopsis thanks to being the lover of Saxby Lights, son of Septima Lights, the colony's founder. Ruth pities the hungry, frightened fugitive from immigration authorities but also longs to incorporate Hiro into a short story with which she is having difficulty. Saxby finds out about Hiro, who is imprisoned, escapes to the Okefenokee Swamp, and is arrested again when near death.

Both the white and the black residents of Tupelo Island are frightened by their Japanese visitor, who is equally bewildered by them. Detlef Abercorn, the immigration official sent to find Hiro, is from Los Angeles and feels totally alienated in the South. An albino, he, like Hiro, has never truly fit in anywhere. Abercorn is assisted by Lewis Turco, a veteran of covert operations in Southeast Asia, who prides himself on being in control in any environment, but he is so paranoid that he creates nothing but chaos. No one in *East Is East* understands or trusts anyone else. The writers, painters, sculptors, and composers at Thanatopsis, who should be able to transcend the cultural differences that handicap the others, are instead so self-absorbed and crippled by petty jealousies that they are totally ineffective as human beings.

Hiro is another Boyle innocent destroyed by his inability to deal with the world's complexities and hostilities and by his own foolishness. Hiro has a system of beliefs—based on Yukio Mishima's theory of the samurai—to help guide him, but Mishima proves tragicomically ineffective in the Georgia swamps. He trusts Ruth, to a degree, because he has no one else, and while she genuinely wants to help, her needs must come first. Ruth, the most fully developed female character in Boyle's novels, ironically finds success through being caught harboring an illegal immigrant, for she then lands a book contract to tell her story. The unscrupulousness of supposedly sensitive artists is as much the target of Boyle's satirical ire as are cultural differences.

The anger in Boyle's novels is tempered by the comedy. Even a relatively somber work such as *World's End* has moments of sublime silliness, as Dipe Van Wart fights middle-age depression by eating dirt from beneath his ancestral home—a fitting comic metaphor for his family's neuroticism and mindless consumption of the land. Boyle's fiction is also notable for the diversity of his style, which changes not only from novel to novel but also from chapter to chapter. He understands well how to play upon the natural rhythms of convoluted sentences and when to resort to the subtler joys of simpler ones, has a vocabulary rivaling Vladimir Nabokov's, and delights in parody. *East Is East* offers the mock Faulkner appropriate to a comic novel set in the South but avoids the overkill occasionally seen in Boyle's short stories and earlier novels. Most important is his ability to create believable, usually sympathetic, characters caught up in absurd quests for truths they are incapable of understanding.

Michael Adams

Other major works

SHORT FICTION: *Descent of Man*, 1979; *Greasy Lake and Other Stories*, 1985; *If the River Was Whiskey*, 1989.

Bibliography

Boyle, T. Coraghessan. Interview by William Brisick. *Publishers Weekly* 232 (October 9, 1987): 71-72. Boyle discusses the influence of growing up in the Hudson River Valley on the creation of *World's End*, his theory about using history in fiction, his difficult relationship with his father, and his dissatisfaction with the way his publishers have handled his books.

_____. "Novel Appeal." Interview by Bruce Weber. *The New York Times Magazine*, March 19, 1989, pt. 2, 57, 70-71. This interview with Boyle in a men's fashion supplement emphasizes his concern with literary, personal, and sartorial style. He discusses his rebellious youth, his taste in clothes, and his delight in giving public readings.

_____. "A Punk's Past Recaptured." Interview by Anthony DeCurtis. *Rolling Stone*, January 14, 1988, 54-57. In his most revealing interview, Boyle talks about his drug use, the importance of understanding history, the influence of Washington Irving on *World's End*, and the autobiographical element in his fiction. He expresses the desire to be like Kurt Vonnegut, Jr., in showing that literature can be both serious and entertaining, and like John Updike in constantly changing his approach to fiction and improving as an artist.

_____. "T. Coraghessan Boyle Plays Twenty Questions with Mark Matousek." *Interview* 18 (January, 1988): 91, 97. Boyle explains his attitudes toward fame, the writing process, drugs, religion, television, the level of intelligence in America, and humor.

RAY BRADBURY

Born: Waukegan, Illinois; August 22, 1920

Principal long fiction

Fahrenheit 451, 1953; *Dandelion Wine*, 1957; *Something Wicked This Way Comes*, 1962; *Death Is a Lonely Business*, 1985; *A Graveyard for Lunatics: Another Tale of Two Cities*, 1990.

Other literary forms

Ray Bradbury's principal literary form has been the short story, and he has published several important collections, including *Dark Carnival* (1947), *The Illustrated Man* (1951), *The Golden Apples of the Sun* (1953), and *I Sing the Body Electric!* (1969). In addition to his short stories and novels, he has published in a wide variety of literary forms, from light verse and poetry to screenplays and dramas. A notable screenplay, which he wrote in collaboration with John Huston, is *Moby Dick* (1956). A representative example of his poetry is *When Elephants Last in the Dooryard Bloomed: Celebrations for Almost Any Day in the Year* (1973) and of his plays is *The Pedestrian* (1966).

Achievements

Although Bradbury became the United States' best-known science-fiction writer, the majority of his work, which ranges from Gothic horror to social criticism, centers on humanistic themes. Aficionados of the genre criticized his science-fiction stories for their scientific and technological inaccuracies, a criticism he shrugs off, stating that his dominating concerns are social, cultural, and intellectual issues, not scientific verisimilitude. His stories, which often explore the dehumanizing pressures of technocracies and the mesmerizing power of the imagination, are widely anthologized and translated into many foreign languages. His ascent from pulp magazines to literary respectability has been intermittently recognized with several awards, including appearances in Martha Foley's annual best American short-story collections, two O. Henry prizes, the Benjamin Franklin Magazine Award, the National Institute of Arts and Letters Award, an Academy Award nomination, and a Golden Eagle Award for his screenplay *Icarus Montgolfier Wright*. His best works are wrenching indictments of the dangers of unrestrained scientific and technological progress, but his work also encourages the hope that humanity will deal creatively with the new worlds it seems driven to construct.

Biography

Ray Bradbury has claimed to have vivid memories of the day he was born, August 22, 1920, and of his birthplace, Waukegan, Illinois, from the time of his birth. His father, Leonard Spaulding Bradbury, whose distant ancestor Mary Bradbury was among those tried for witchcraft in Salem, was a lineman with the Waukegan Bureau of Power and Light; his mother, Esther Marie (née Moberg) Bradbury, emigrated as a child from Sweden. When he was three years old, his mother took him to his first film, *The Hunchback of Notre Dame* (1923), and he was frightened and entranced by Lon Chaney and in his role in *The Phantom of the Opera* (1929). As a child, Bradbury passed through a series of enthusiasms, from monsters to circuses to dinosaurs and eventually to the planet Mars. His development through childhood was aided by an older brother and by an aunt, Neva Bradbury, a costume designer, who introduced him to the theater and to the stories of Edgar Allan Poe.

In 1932, Bradbury's family moved to Arizona, where they had previously spent some time in the mid-1920's, largely because of his father's need to find work. In 1934 the family left behind both Arizona and Waukegan, settling in Los Angeles, which became Bradbury's permanent home. He attended Los Angeles High School and joined the Science Fiction Society (he had earlier begun reading Hugo Gernsback's *Amazing Stories*, which, he said, made him fall in love with the future). After graduation, Bradbury worked for several months in a theater group sponsored by the actress Laraine Day, and for several years he was a newsboy in downtown Los Angeles. He took these jobs to support his writing, an avocation that he hoped would soon become a vocation.

His poor eyesight prevented him from serving in the army during World War II, which left him free to launch his writing career. During the early 1940's he began to publish his stories in such pulp magazines as *Weird Tales* and *Amazing Stories*, but by the late 1940's his work was appearing in such mass-market magazines as *Collier's*, *The Saturday Evening Post*, *The New Yorker*, *Harper's Magazine*, and *Mademoiselle*. Because these magazines paid well, he was able, on September 27, 1947, to marry Marguerite Susan Mc-Clure, a former English teacher at the University of California in Los Angeles. He continued, during the 1950's, to write for the pulp and mass-market magazines, and he routinely collected his stories for publication in books. In the mid-1950's he traveled to Ireland in connection with a screenplay of *Moby Dick* that he wrote with John Huston. Upon his return to the United States, Bradbury composed a large number of television scripts for such shows as *Alfred Hitchcock Presents*, *Suspense*, and *The Twilight Zone*. During the late 1950's and early 1960's, Bradbury's stories and novels focused mostly on his Midwestern childhood—for example, *Dandelion Wine* and *Something Wicked This Way Comes*, the latter his favorite book.

During the 1960's and throughout the 1970's and 1980's, Bradbury's output of fiction decreased, and his ideas found outlets in such forms as plays, poems, and essays. He also became involved in a number of projects, such as "A Journey Through United States History," the exhibit that occupied the upper floor of the United States Pavilion for the New York World's Fair in the mid-1960's. Because of this display's success, the Walt Disney organization hired him to help develop the themes for Spaceship Earth, an important part of Epcot Center at Disney World in Florida. Bradbury also helped design a twenty-first century city near Tokyo. In the 1980's he continued to diversify his activities by collaborating in projects to turn his novel *Fahrenheit 451* into an opera and his novel *Dandelion Wine* into a musical. In 1988 he published his first collection of stories, *The Toynbee Convector*, and in 1990, his first novel, *The Graveyard for Lunatics*, in five years. These stories returned to some of the same subjects and themes that had established his reputation forty years before.

Analysis

Paradoxically, Bradbury's stories look both backward and forward. For him, each story is a way of discovering a self, and the self found in one story is different from the self found in another. He, like all human beings, is made of time, and human beings, like rivers, flow and change, so, adapting Heraclitus' famous statement that no person ever steps twice into the same self. Sometimes Bradbury discovered a self in the past, and sometimes, particularly in his science fiction, he discovered a self in the future. Several critics have pictured him as a frontiersman, ambivalently astride two worlds, who has alternately been attracted to an idealized past, timeless and nostalgic, and to a graphic future, chameleonic and threatening. This creative tension is present both in his own life and in the generation of Americans he liked to depict. It is also intimately connected with the genre—science fiction—with which he became so closely identified.

Bradbury has been called a romantic, and his romanticism often surfaces in the themes he investigates: the conflict between human vitality and spiritless mechanism, between the creative individual and the conforming group, between imagination and reason, between intuition and logic, between the innocence of childhood and the corruptions of adulthood, and between the shadow and light in every human soul. His stories make clear that, in all these conflicts, human beings, not machines, are at the center of his vision. An ambivalence about technology characterizes his life and work. For example, he has never learned to drive, even though he has spent most of his life in Los Angeles, a city that has made the automobile not only an apparent necessity but also an object of worship. He has also refused to use a computer, and he successfully avoided flying in an airplane for the first six decades of his life. Each of these attitudes is rooted in some profoundly emotional experiences; for example, he has never learned to drive because, as a youth, he witnessed the horrible deaths of five people in an automobile accident. Because of his emphasis on basic human values against an uncritical embracing of technical progress, because of his affirmation of the human spirit against modern materialism, and because of his trust in the basic goodness of small-town life against the debilitating indifference of the cities, several critics have accused him of sentimentality and naïveté. Bradbury, who has admitted that he has tried to cultivate a childlike wonder in all that he has done, responds by saying that critics come from the head, whereas he writes from the heart.

The poetic style that he developed was admirably suited to the heartfelt themes that he explored in a cornucopia of highly imaginative stories. He cultivated this style through eclectic imitation and dogged determination. As an adolescent, he vowed to write several hundred words every day, for he believed that quantity would eventually lead to quality. Experience and the example of other writers would teach him what to leave out. According to Bradbury, his style was influenced by such writers as Charles Dickens, Mark Twain, Thomas Wolfe, and Ernest Hemingway. On another occasion, however, he stated that his style came as much from Charlie Chaplin as from Aldous Huxley, from Tom Swift as from George Orwell, from Tom Mix as from Bertrand Russell, and from Edgar Rice Burroughs as from C. S. Lewis. Bradbury has also listed as influences such poets as Alexander Pope, Gerard Manley Hopkins, and Dylan Thomas. Furthermore and surprisingly, he has said that such painters as El Greco and Tintoretto and such composers as Wolfgang Amadeus Mozart and Franz Joseph Haydn showed him how to add color and rhythm to his writing. According to him, all these influences—writers, poets, painters, and musicians—gloried in the joy of creating, and their works overflow with animal vigor and intellectual vitality. Their ardor and delight are contagious, and their honest response to the materials at hand calls forth a similar response in their readers, viewers, and listeners. This enchanting of the audience, similar to casting a magic spell, is what Bradbury tries to do with his kaleidoscopic style—to transform colorful pieces of reality into a glittering picture that will emotionally intensify the lives of his readers.

Bradbury is a profoundly autobiographical writer, and he has often pointed out the childhood, adolescent, and adult experiences that generated many of his stories. Graham Greene once said that there is always one moment in childhood when the door opens and lets the future in. Actually, for Bradbury, there were many such moments. He once said that everything he has ever done—all his activities, loves, and fears—were created by the primitive experiences of monsters and angels he had when he was five years old. He has also said, however, that the most important event in his childhood occurred when he was twelve years old, at a carnival, when the performance of a magician, Mr. Electrico, so energized his imagination that he began to write stories to communicate his fervid visions to others.

Numerous Bradbury stories, including several in his first collection, *Dark Carnival*, have as their provenance specific childhood events. For example, "The Small Assassin," which metamorphoses some of his childhood experi-

ences and fears, tells of a newborn infant, terrified at finding himself thrust
into a hostile world, taking revenge on his parents by first terrorizing, then
murdering them. This story also reveals that Bradbury's view of childhood
innocence is more complex than many critics realize, for, in Bradbury's view,
beneath the façade of innocence lies a cauldron of sin—a dark vision of the
human condition that some critics have called Calvinistic. Another tale, "The
Lake," is based on Bradbury's experience as a seven-year-old, when his
cousin nearly drowned in Lake Michigan. These and other early stories,
which he published in such pulp magazines as *Weird Tales*, *Amazing Stories*,
and *Astounding Science Fiction*, served as his apprenticeship, an opportunity
to perfect his style, deepen his vision, and develop the themes on which he
would play variations in his later, more accomplished short stories, novels,
poems, and dramas.

One of these early themes that also haunted his later fiction is alienation.
Bradbury himself experienced cultural alienation when he traveled to Mexico
in 1945. Americans were then mostly Protestant, individualistic, and preoccupied with getting ahead. Mexicans, on the other hand, were mostly Catholic, communalistic, and preoccupied with death. On his trip to Guanajuato,
northwest of Mexico City, Bradbury was both horrified and fascinated by the
catacombs with their rows of propped-up mummified bodies. A story collected in *Dark Carnival*, "The Next in Line," grew out of this experience. In
this story, a young American wife finds herself, after her traumatic ordeal in
the Guanajuato crypts, alienated both from the strange Mexican society and
from her own body, which she obsessively realizes is a potential mummy.
Bradbury uses the metaphor of death to help the reader comprehend one
reality, life, in terms of another, death. Metaphor thus becomes a medicine, a
way of healing ourselves by envisioning ourselves into new modes of experi-
encing, learning, and surviving.

Although, at first glance, many of Bradbury's early stories seem notable for
their great variety, he did deal, especially in his stories about Mars, with a set
of conflicts that had a common theme, and so, when an editor suggested in
1949 that he compose a continuous narrative, he took advantage of the opportunity, since several of his stories about the colonization of Mars by Earthlings lent themselves to just such a treatment. Using the chronological frame
of 1999 to 2026, Bradbury stitched these stories together with bridge passages that gave the book a semblance of unity (it also presented categorizers
of his works with a problem: some have listed the book as a novel, others as a
short-story collection). Many critics have called *The Martian Chronicles*
Bradbury's masterpiece, a magical and insightful account of the exploitation
of a new frontier, Mars, by Earthlings whose personalities appear to have
been nurtured in small Midwestern American towns. By placing these normal
human beings in an extraordinary setting, Bradbury was able to use the
strange light of an alien world to illuminate the dark regions of human nature.

The apparatus of conventional science fiction makes an appearance, including monsters and supermachines, but Bradbury's basic intent is to explore the conflicts that were troubling postwar America: imperialism, alienation, pollution, racism, and nuclear war. He therefore depicts not a comforting human progress but a disquieting cycle of rises and falls. He also sees the Martian environment, itself transformed by human ingenuity, transforming the settlers. Thus, his ultimate view seems optimistic: humanity will, through creative adaptation, not only survive but thrive. In *The Martian Chronicles* Earthlings metamorphose into Martians, an action that serves as a Bradburian metaphor for the human condition, which is to be always in the process of becoming something else.

Even though scientists criticized *The Martian Chronicles* for its portrayal of Mars as a planet with a breathable atmosphere, water, and canals (known by astronomers in 1950 to be erroneous characteristics), and even though science-fiction devotees found Bradbury's portrayal of Martian colonies implausible, the book was a triumphant success, largely, some have suggested, because of these "weaknesses." Bradbury's Mars mirrored the present and served as the stage upon which his eccentric characters—the misfits, opportunists, and romantics—could remake Mars in their own images (only to find themselves remade by Mars in the process). *The Martian Chronicles* has proved to be enduringly popular. It has passed through several editions, sold millions of copies, and been translated into more than thirty foreign languages.

Another book of interlinked stories, *The Illustrated Man*, followed soon after the publication of *The Martian Chronicles*. In *The Illustrated Man* the device linking the stories together is the tattoos on the skin of one of the characters. Bradbury sets some of his stories on Mars, and a few bear some relation to the cycle of stories in *The Martian Chronicles*. By the early 1950's, Bradbury was a well-established writer, able to place his stories in both pulp and popular magazines and able to profit again when his collections of these stories were published as books. His fourth collection, *The Golden Apples of the Sun*, abandoned the frame narrative that he had been using and instead simply juxtaposed stories from a wide variety of genres—science fiction, fantasy, crime, and comedy.

John Huston, the film director, was impressed by a dinosaur story that Bradbury had written and asked him to come to Ireland to develop a screenplay for his film about another great beast, Moby Dick. Bradbury's experiences in Ireland in 1953 not only led to an excellent screenplay, but it also gave him material for several stories and plays about the Irish. Furthermore, the trip gave him the chance to meet the English philosopher Bertrand Russell and art historian Bernard Berenson, two of his heroes. Berenson had written a fan letter to Bradbury, in which he praised the American's attitude toward writing as "a fascinating adventure."

During this most prolific period in Bradbury's literary life, he also published the book that would generate, along with *The Martian Chronicles*, his greatest success and influence. The story that came to be called *Fahrenheit 451* went through several transformations. In 1947 he had written a short story, "Bright Phoenix," in which the residents of a small town counter government book-burning edicts by memorizing the banned books. In 1951 he expanded this idea into a long story, "The Fireman," which appeared in *Galaxy Science Fiction*. A fire chief informed him that book paper first bursts into flame at 451 degrees Fahrenheit, which gave him the title for his novel-length story set in a future totalitarian state. Some critics interpreted this dystopian novel as an attack against McCarthyism, then at the height of its power, but the book also attacks the tyrannical domination of mass culture, especially in this culture's tendency to eschew complexity of thought and to embrace the simple sentiments of pressure groups. The central irony of the novel concerns firemen whose job is to set fires (burn books) rather than to put them out. Bradbury, a lifelong book lover, used his novel to show how important books are to freedom, morality, and the search for truth. His novel concludes with Montag, a fireman who has rejected his role as book burner, joining a community that strives to preserve books by memorizing them. Some critics have pointed out that this new society, where individuals abandon their identities to "become" the books they have memorized, inculcates a mass behavior as conformist as the one from which they and Montag have escaped, but Bradbury would respond that this new culture allows for a multiplicity of ideas and attitudes and thus provides the opportunity for human creativity to shape a hopeful legacy for the next generation.

From the mid-1950's to the mid-1960's, Bradbury's writings tended to center on his Midwestern childhood, without being camouflaged by a science-fiction or fantasy setting. His novel *Dandelion Wine* is a nostalgic account of a small Illinois town in the summer of 1928. Again, as in so much of his earlier work, his novel was composed of previously published stories, and the superficial unity he imposed on this material was not sufficiently coherent to satisfy several critics. Another similarity to his previous work was his theme of the twin attractions of the past and the future. The twelve-year-old hero finds himself between the secure, uncomplicated world of childhood and the frightening, complex world of adulthood. Despite the loneliness, disease, and death that seem to plague adults, the young man, like the colonists in *The Martian Chronicles*, must transform his past to create his future. Critics accused Bradbury of sentimentality in *Dandelion Wine*, pointing out how depressed and ugly Waukegan, Illinois (the model for Green Town), was at this time. Bradbury answered that he was telling his story from the viewpoint of the child, and factories, trains, pollution, and poverty are not ugly to children. Adults teach children what is ugly, and their judgments about ugliness are not always sound. For a child, as for Bradbury, Green Town was like

William Butler Yeats's Byzantium, a vision of creativity and a dream for action.

Bradbury returned to some of these themes in another novel, *Something Wicked This Way Comes*, in which a father tries to save his son and his son's friend from the evil embodied in a mysterious traveling carnival. The friend, Jim Nightshade (a name indicative of the symbolic burden the characters in this novel must bear), is particularly susceptible to the carnival's temptations, since his shadow side is so powerful. The father ultimately achieves victory by using the power of laughter as his weapon; however, the father also points out that human victories are never final and that each individual must constantly struggle never to permit the good that is in him to become a passive rather than an activating force. The potential for evil exists in every human being (a Christian idea, original sin, that surfaces in many of Bradbury's stories), and unless humans keep their goodness fit through creativity, evil will take over. For Bradbury, love is the best humanizing force that human beings possess.

Something Wicked This Way Comes marked a turning point in Bradbury's career. After this work failed to enhance his status as a significant American novelist, he turned increasingly to plays, poems, and essays. His turn to drama was essentially a return, since he had acted, as a boy, on the stage and on radio, and since he had written several plays when he was young (they were so bad that he vowed never to write plays again until he learned to write competently in other forms). Many of his plays are adaptations of his stories, and most of them have been staged in California, though a few have had productions Off-Broadway in New York. The majority of his plays have been published. His first collection, *The Anthem Sprinters and Other Antics*, appeared in 1963 (the "anthem sprinters" are Irishmen who flee from motion-picture theaters before the national anthem is played). Although his short-story writing diminished during the 1960's, it did not vanish, and in 1969 he published another collection, *I Sing the Body Electric!*, which was a miscellany of science-fiction and fantasy stories. Throughout his life, Bradbury has also been an avid reader of poetry. He often made use of poetic diction in his stories, but, as in the case of his playwriting, he refrained from publishing his poetry until late in his career, because he wanted it to be accomplished and stylistically refined. Heavily indebted to Gerard Manley Hopkins, Dylan Thomas, Walt Whitman, and others, his poetry has not had the success of his stories. Much of the poetry, whimsical in tone, can be categorized as light verse.

During the decade 1980-1990, Bradbury returned to the literary forms that had made him famous. He published a novel, *Death Is a Lonely Business*, his first in twenty-three years, in 1985. This novel and *A Graveyard for Lunatics*, published in 1990, make use of some of the same characters, and both are detective stories with a strong dose of fantasy. Several reviewers found the clash of genres in these novels—detective and fantasy—too disorienting to make the stories effective, but others found Bradbury's re-creation of a bygone era in Southern California history appealing. During the 1980's Bradbury published his first new collection of short stories in nineteen years, *The Toynbee Convector* (a retrospective of a hundred stories, *The Stories of Ray Bradbury*, was published in 1980). As in some of his other collections, the stories of *The Toynbee Convector* contain a number of genres, subjects, and themes. The title story centers on a returned time traveller (the convector is his time machine, named after the historian Arnold Toynbee). He enthralls people with his message that, in the future world he visited, most of the Earth's problems have been solved: the planet's waters had been cleansed; the dolphins and whales had been preserved, and the moon and Mars had been colonized. In the story's concluding twist, however, it turns out that the time traveller had faked his trip to provide twentieth-century humans with hope. Again, the reader encounters one of Bradbury's favorite themes: a lie can create a reality. In this story, a lie was needed to shake the world from its despair. For Bradbury, then, lies are like dreams, in that they are truths waiting to be born.

Several critics have detected a decline in the quality of Bradbury's later work, but the standard he set in the 1950's was very high. Because he has worked in so many different literary forms, and because, within each of these forms, his treatment of a potpourri of subjects had been equally variegated, it is difficult to make neat generalizations about his oeuvre. The public has recognized him as the world's premier science-fiction writer, but only a third of his work has been in this genre. Certainly, his science-fiction stories have revealed that cultivated and craftsmanlike writing is possible in what was seen, before him, as a vulgar genre. Within the science-fiction community, however, a sharp difference of opinion exists about Bradbury's contributions. A sizable segment sees his work as reactionary, antitechnological, and anti-Utopian. As one of these critics put it, Bradbury is a science-fiction writer for people who do not really like science fiction. On the other hand, a large group, which includes a significant segment of the literary community (viewing him as one of their own), sees him as a humanist and a regional writer. This group draws some good arguments from Bradbury's stories: For example, even when he writes about Mars, the planet symbolizes for him the geography—emotional and intellectual—of the American Midwest. In this sense, his regionalism is one of the mind and heart.

Actually, both sides of this debate can find evidence for their views in Bradbury's motley work. He can be both enthusiastic about a future transformed by technology and critical of the dangers posed by technocracies. Ultimately, for him, technology is a *human* creation, and it is therefore subject to the labyrinthine goods and evils of the human heart. Although his best work is deeply humanistic and includes a strong critique of unrestrained technology he is no Luddite. It is true that the technological society has produced many problems—pollution, for example—but human beings love to solve problems; it is a defining characteristic of the species.

Those who see only Bradbury's critique of technology view him as a pessimistic writer. In the proper light, however, his work is really profoundly optimistic. His fiction may rest upon the gloomy foundation of the Fall, but, in traditional theology, the counterpart of the Fall is Redemption, and Bradbury believes that human beings will renew themselves, particularly in space, which he sees as modern man's religious quest. Space, then, is Bradbury's new wilderness, with an infinity of new challenges. In that inexhaustible wilderness, human beings will find themselves and be saved.

Robert J. Paradowski

Other major works

SHORT FICTION: *Dark Carnival*, 1947; *The Martian Chronicles*, 1950; *The Illustrated Man*, 1951; *The Golden Apples of the Sun*, 1953; *The October Country*, 1955; *A Medicine for Melancholy*, 1959; *The Machineries of Joy*, 1964; *I Sing the Body Electric!*, 1969; *The Stories of Ray Bradbury*, 1980; *The Toynbee Convector*, 1988.

PLAYS: *The Anthem Sprinters and Other Antics*, 1963; *The World of Ray Bradbury: Three Fables of the Future*, 1964; *The Day It Rained Forever*, 1966; *The Pedestrian*, 1966; *The Wonderful Ice Cream Suit and Other Plays*, 1972; *Pillar of Fire and Other Plays for Today, Tomorrow, and Beyond Tomorrow*, 1975.

SCREENPLAYS: *It Came from Outer Space*, 1952 (with David Schwartz); *Moby Dick*, 1956 (with John Huston); *Icarus Montgolfier Wright*, 1961 (with George C. Johnson); *The Picasso Summer*, 1967 (with Edwin Boyd).

POETRY: *Old Ahab's Friend, and Friend to Noah, Speaks His Piece: A Celebration*, 1971; *When Elephants Last in the Dooryard Bloomed: Celebrations for Almost Any Day in the Year*, 1973; *Where Robot Mice and Robot Men Run Round in Robot Towns: New Poems, Both Light and Dark*, 1977; *The Haunted Computer and the Android Pope*, 1981.

ANTHOLOGIES: *Timeless Stories for Today and Tomorrow*, 1952; *The Circus of Dr. Lao and Other Improbable Stories*, 1956.

NONFICTION: *Zen in the Art of Writing: Essays on Creativity*, 1989.

Bibliography

Amis, Kingsley. *New Maps of Hell: A Survey of Science Fiction*. New York: Harcourt, Brace, 1960. Known primarily as a novelist, Amis, a British writer, here tackled a genre that had been ignored by serious literary critics. Although the early history of science fiction was as much British as American, Amis discusses science fiction as a characteristically American product, and he praises Bradbury as one of America's most skilled writers, broader in range than any of his colleagues, a writer who has the courage to see life through his strongly held convictions.

Greenberg, Martin Henry, and Joseph D. Olander, eds. *Ray Bradbury.* New York: Taplinger, 1980. Part of the series Writers of the Twenty-first Century, this is an anthology of Bradbury criticism. Some of the articles defend Bradbury against the charge that he is not really a science-fiction writer but an opponent of science and technology; other articles defend him against the charge that he is a sentimentalist. Also includes an extensive Bradbury bibliography compiled by Marshall B. Tymn and an index.

McNelly, Willis E. "Ray Bradbury: Past, Present, and Future." In *Voices for the Future: Essays on Major Science Fiction Writers*, edited by Thomas D. Clareson. Vol. 1. Bowling Green, Ohio: Bowling Green University Popular Press, 1976. McNelly's article argues that Bradbury's themes place him in the mainstream of American life and letters. It should be read in conjunction with the article by A. James Stupple, "The Past, the Future, and Ray Bradbury," which sees Bradbury's work as sensitive to the complexities of the past, which can be simultaneously creative and destructive.

Mogen, David. *Ray Bradbury.* Boston: Twayne, 1986. This scholarly survey of Bradbury's career analyzes the literary influences that formed his style and themes as well as the influences that shaped his reputation. Many references in the notes at the end of the book. Includes a bibliography and an index.

Nolan, William F. *The Ray Bradbury Companion: A Life and Career History, Photolog, and Comprehensive Checklist of Writings with Facsimiles from Ray Bradbury's Unpublished and Uncollected Work in All Media.* Detroit: Gale Research, 1975. The ample title gives a good idea of this book's contents. Since its publication, its information on Bradbury has been updated by Donn Albright, "The Ray Bradbury Index," in several issues of *Xenophile* (May, 1975; September, 1976; November, 1977).

Slusser, George Edgar. *The Bradbury Chronicles.* San Bernardino, Calif.: Borgo Press, 1977. This booklet is part of a series, Popular Writers of Today. Intended for young students and general audiences, this brief work can treat only cursorily some of Bradbury's most important writings. Contains a bibliography.

JOHN BRAINE

Born: Bradford, England; April 13, 1922
Died: London, England; October 28, 1986

Principal long fiction

Room at the Top, 1957; *The Vodi*, 1959 (also known as *From the Hand of the Hunter*, 1960); *Life at the Top*, 1962; *The Jealous God*, 1965; *The Crying Game*, 1968; *Stay with Me till Morning*, 1970 (also known as *The View from Tower Hill*, 1971); *The Queen of a Distant Country*, 1972; *The Pious Agent*, 1975; *Waiting for Sheila*, 1976; *Finger of Fire*, 1977; *One and Last Love*, 1981; *The Two of Us*, 1984; *These Golden Days*, 1985.

Other literary forms

Although John Braine was first and foremost a novelist, he also received recognition for his contributions as a television reporter for *The Spectator*, as a film critic for *The Daily Express*, and as a book reviewer for *The People*. His only stage drama, *The Desert in the Mirror* (1951), was unsuccessful, but he won national awards for two television adaptations of his novels: *Man at the Top* (1970, 1972) and *Waiting for Sheila* (1976). The seriousness of Braine's concern with the general problems facing the novelist is clear in his two most significant nonfiction works: *Writing a Novel* (1974) and *J. B. Priestley* (1978). In the former, he establishes guidelines for the aspiring novelist and shows how a professional writer who cannot afford to make wrong decisions "manufactures books according both to British and American readers." In the latter, Braine celebrates the life and career of a man to whom he has felt closer than "any other living writer."

Achievements

Braine's reputation is that of a frank, serious, tough-minded novelist writing from an Irish-Catholic, lower-middle-class background. His experiences in urban, industrialized Bradford, in the rural area of West Riding, and in the upper-middle-class environment of surburban London also figure prominently in his novels. Through all of his novels runs the theme of the stature of the self. He depicts real characters who have allowed their jobs, social position, material ambitions, class membership, purely physical tendencies, and social and cultural ideals to subvert their essential sensitive and loving selves. His novels belong thematically to a tradition of realistic fiction (associated particularly with England) that tries to find a public significance in personal experience.

Braine's often vitriolic criticism of English society and the frequently harsh reality of his novels have had a marked influence on contemporary British fiction. This influence began in 1957 when his first novel, *Room at the Top*, became an instant success and brought him international recognition. Together with Kingsley Amis, Alan Sillitoe, John Osborne, John Wain, and other contemporaries, Braine ushered in with this novel a new generation of writers whose concerns led commentators to identify them as "Angry Young Men"—an epithet suggesting writers of social protest or critics of man's plight in the modern world. Their works shared a commonality of theme and style: a realistic portrayal of working-class or lower-middle-class life in England, a preference for provincial backgrounds, an anti-hero who directs his protests against the class structure and the welfare state, and an unadorned use of everyday language. Through his hero, Joe Lampton, Braine made a conspicuous contribution to that gallery of "angries": driven by ambition, envy, and greed, Joe possesses no admiration or liking for the class into which he is gate-crashing. He wants its advantages and privileges but not its conventions. Had *Room at the Top* appeared before Amis' *Lucky Jim* (1958) or Osborne's *Look Back in Anger* (1957), Braine's name might be better-known today than those of his contemporaries. Praised for its vitality, honesty, and realism, and criticized for its sentimentality and weak construction, Braine's first novel had the mixture of strengths and weaknesses characteristic of this new generation of writers.

Although *Room at the Top* was one of the most discussed—and probably one of the most praised—novels of 1957, some critics were less than enthusiastic about the promise of this new writer, and they surfaced to review his next two novels. Neither his sequel, *Life at the Top*, nor the intervening novel, *The Vodi*, enjoyed the same popularity and prestige. In considering the former, some critics felt that Braine was merely capitalizing on the success of his first novel; in the words of the reviewer for the *Saturday Review*, *Life at the Top* was "disappointingly close, both in theme and in treatment, to the serials that appear in slick magazines." As for the latter, a number of critics felt that Braine's skillful storytelling and compassionate insights into human suffering failed to compensate for such technical defects as disparity of tone, obscure details, uneven pace, and lack of climactic power. The reviewer for *The Times Literary Supplement* wrote that the book succeeded "not where it [tried] to be new but where it [did again] what was well done in *Room at the Top*."

Admirers of Braine's work were delighted to find that his succeeding novels were not imitations of anything he had written before. Many saw *The Jealous God* as an important turning point in his career. His control of characters, refined style, exploration of a religious theme, and command of point of view and focus dispelled fears that he was a one-novel writer. *The Crying Game*, on the other hand, was praised as an exposé of the decadent urban life but was criticized for weak conflicts and insufficient distance between author and hero. Others found the writing to be hasty and its characters unpleasant. On this disappointing novel with virtually no story, Anthony Burgess commented,

"The hedonism is too often self-conscious, . . . and the narrative style gives off the stale apple smell of old popular magazines."

Braine wrote eight more novels, which met with varying critical success. As an analysis of marital discord, *Stay with Me till Morning* was deemed repetitious and ambiguous, perplexing many critics. Just as unclear, perhaps, was *The Queen of a Distant Country*. Some critics found the conversations about writers and the writer's world to be authentic, while other commentators held that this was an extremely pompous and self-indulgent book about Braine himself. His next two novels—*The Pious Agent* and *Finger of Fire*—were judged to be routinely competent exercises in the spy genre; some felt that they were saved only by Braine's characterization and smooth, sophisticated style. *Waiting for Sheila*, on the other hand, was seen as a working model for Braine's own novelistic methods. It was praised for its plotting, characterization, and celebration of sex, but reviewers regretted that Braine had not allowed himself to be carried away in a longer, in-depth study of decadent London. *One and Last Love* was called by the London *Sunday Times* "a rhapsody" and "deliberately provoking." Reviewers felt that Braine's narrative power and his ability to evoke people and places, past memories and present experience, remain as vivid as ever in this most "autobiographical" novel of all.

Throughout his life, Braine remained capable of surprises. Among postwar British novelists, he is distinguished by his stubborn integrity and by his craftsmanship.

Biography

John Gerard Braine was born April 13, 1922, in the Nonconformist city of Bradford, Yorkshire. His parents, Fred and Katherine, were lower-middle-class Catholics and therefore part of a distinguishable minority. His father was a works superintendent for the Bradford Corporation, his mother a librarian whose Irish-Catholic family had come, along with a colony of Irish, to Yorkshire during the potato famine of the 1840's. With an attitude much like that of the headmaster's wife toward her students in Cyril Connolly's *Enemies of Promise* (1939), Braine's mother expected great things of her son; she "supercharged" him, to use Connolly's word, and he responded both as a student and later as a professional writer.

Braine's formal education, while it lasted, was "very good." From 1927 to 1933 he attented the state-run Thackley Boarding School, where, along with his exposure to Charles Dickens and Thomas Babington Macaulay, he found the predominantly Protestant, working-class atmosphere an asset to an aspiring writer: "One is pitchforked into the only tenable position for a writer; on the outside, looking in." After passing his examinations with honors, he was graduated in 1933 to St. Bede's Grammar School, Heaton, and for the first time was made aware of "a split between the social world of home and school."

At Thackley, Braine had been "a mildly mixed-up little boy"; at St. Bede's, he found himself "wildly at variance with the whole world" as he knew it. In adult life, his recurring nightmare was of being back at St. Bede's and aware of improperly done homework, wasting time, allowing people to get ahead of him, guilt, and above all, physical pain. Although he left school at sixteen without graduating, five years later he received his school certificate by correspondence courses. Braine had no regrets about either school, however, for the experiences gave him what he needed: the essentials of English grammar and lessons about the world in which he lived, "which meant knowing about what had happened in the past."

For the next two years, Braine drifted in typical success-story pattern from one dull job to another—as an assistant in a furniture shop, a secondhand bookshop, and a pharmaceutical laboratory, as well as a "progress chaser" in a piston ring factory. In 1940, he became a librarian at the Bingley (Yorkshire) Public Library and—with time out as a telegrapher in the Royal Navy (1940-1943), a free-lance writer in London (1951-1953), a patient suffering from a recurrence of tuberculosis (between 1952 and 1954), and a student at library school—worked as a librarian until 1957. In that year, the success of *Room at the Top* finally made it possible for him to quit his job and devote all his time to writing. He was then undeniably confirmed in his vocation as a writer.

Although Braine claimed he could not remember ever wanting to be anything but a writer, his struggle toward that goal had little of the heady directness that characterizes Joe Lampton's shortcut to the top. The writer in him first broke loose in 1951, when he left behind the security of a home, job, and family tradition in business to pursue the vocation of a free-lance writer in London. He knew he was a writer, though to prove it he had published only one story and a few poems and articles (the latter in the *Tribune* and *New Statesman*), and had written a play, *The Desert in the Mirror*, which was produced in 1951 in Bingley. Although he was attracted by a desire for independence, the excitement of the "big city," and the illusion of bohemia, the most important reason for his move was the feeling that he had about Bingley in particular and the North in general, "the feeling that there was something to be said." Only by leaving the North could he see it clearly enough to write about it. "It was like stepping away from an oil painting: when one's too near, one can see only a collection of smudges."

The confidence to begin what later became *Room at the Top* (originally entitled *Born Favourite*) came when literary agent David Higham read Braine's profile of his Irish grandmother in *New Statesman*. Paul Scott, then in charge of fiction at Higham's, told Braine he should write a novel, that the novel was his "true medium." In September, Turnstile Press offered him an advance subject to a synopsis and a sample chapter; not until 1953, however—after Turnstile's rejection, his mother's death, treatment for tuberculosis, and four more rejections—was the novel accepted for publication. Looking back on this period in his life, Braine considered that the sacrifices he made were necessary ones: "What gave my novel edge and urgency was my consciousness of what I had sacrificed in order to write it." In the foundations of *Room at the Top* are buried his despair on first arriving in London, his tears after the failure of *The Desert in the Mirror*, and the agony when Turnstile rejected the novel. "There had to be suffering, there had to be failure, there had to be total commitment." Indeed, this commitment continued as Braine went on to write twelve more novels before his death in 1986. In each of the novels, the reader finds a preoccupation with what Braine was most familiar: Northern England, Catholicism, and the relationships between men and women.

Analysis

"What I care about the most," John Braine wrote in the 1960's, "is telling the truth about human beings and the world they live in. . . . And every word I write is a celebration of my love for the created world and everyone and everything within it." In *Room at the Top*, *The Jealous God*, and *Waiting for Sheila*, Braine demonstrates the kind of truth-telling he describes, a truth-telling distinguished by exact observations, honesty of vision, and a clear and workmanlike style. Typically, his heroes are harried by a desire for personal affirmation, a desire they can seldom articulate or suppress. Worldly success, sensual gratification, money especially, are the only ends they know or can name, but none of these slakes their restlessness. Braine's heroes grapple desperately for money, they lacerate themselves climbing to success, yet they remain sullen and bewildered, always hopeful for some unexpected sign by which to release their bitter craving for a state of grace or, at least, illumination. In the midst of humanity's inevitable corruption and consequent need for redemption, Braine implies a vision much like that of J. B. Priestley: "a vision of a just society, a civilized and harmonious whole, a society in which there would be no alienation."

Braine's assault on British life begins with *Room at the Top*, a familiar "rags-to-riches" story about an individual who has glimpses of life beyond the reach of his environment, his struggle to achieve, his success after the sacrifice of his own soul. To this pattern, Braine has added another theme: any society is corrupt which demands the sacrifice of integrity as the price of success. Thus, Joe Lampton, as narrator, represents in the modern British novel a new species: the predatory, northern, working-class hero with long-range ambitions to achieve lusty affluence.

A significant departure for Braine is evident in his fourth novel, *The Jealous God*, in which he draws on his experiences as a Catholic to trace the influence of the Church upon the personal life of a deeply religious yet sensual man. Unlike Joe Lampton, whose ambitions were material, Vincent Dungarvan has spiritual ambitions. Superimposed on this material is a study of an overpowering mother-son relationship; all of this gives new life to what E. M. Forster called "the undeveloped heart."

Waiting for Sheila, on the other hand, looks at an aspect of sex that is a major theme in other Braine novels as well: what it means to be a man. With its tragic implications, vivid class-consciousness, and powerful portrayal of upper-middle-class life in a London suburb, *Waiting for Sheila* typifies the realistic impulse behind all of Braine's writing as he catches the wave of a permissive society.

About *Room at the Top*, Kenneth Allsop quotes Braine as saying: "In the Welfare State the young man on the make has to be a bit tougher and learn how to fiddle more cleverly. My job in writing about Joe Lampton was to look at him clearly." Like all of his novels, this one is rich in class overtones. Braine's working-class hero comes to a large provincial town from a slummy outpost of depression, demanding more than a minimum of material comforts and a chance to sneer at the pretension of the bourgeoisie. Lampton demands the best—"an Aston-Martin, 3-guinea linen shirts, a girl with a Riviera suntan"—and gets it by marrying the rich man's daughter. His triumph over his upbringing and his natural instincts is, however, a sour one; the price of his success is the abandonment of his true love-relationship with an older woman and her subsequent suicide, a catastrophe for which his arrival at the top proves no compensation.

Braine's Yorkshire heritage is a strong presence in the novel. The speech, landscape, and people of his home county reflect a conscious provincialism in much of his work. Here Bradford shows up as the archetypal industrial city which "more than any other in England is dominated by a success ethos." Warley, like Bradford, is a drab, soot-covered city where human life is secondary to trade, where there is little culture, and where there are the very rich and the very poor.

The novel also invites comparisons with the works of Horatio Alger. Like the typical Alger hero, Joe Lampton achieves his ambition not by hard work or even by ruthlessness, but by being lucky enough to attract the attention of a rich man. Whereas the Alger hero does this by saving the rich man's daughter from some menace, Lampton does it by impregnating the rich man's daughter, a girl he does not love. Moreover, whereas Alger leaves the reader with the assurance that his hero is going to live happily ever after, at the end of *Room at the Top*, the reader knows very well that Lampton is bound to lead a miserable life. Powerful in scheme, plot, and, narrative thrust, *Room at the Top* is a moral fable about ambition which very much epitomizes its age.

Essentially a variation on the eternal triangle, Braine's fourth novel, *The Jealous God*, dramatizes the conflict between an unmarried Catholic (Vincent Dungarvan), a divorced Protestant with whom he has an affair (Laura Heycliff), and the teachings of his church. This time, Braine portrays the everyday working-class life of the Irish in a smoke-gray milltown in the north of

England. Unlike *Room at the Top*, *The Jealous God* never visits the modern industrial world of Warley with its struggles for economic and social success. Here, Braine's concerns are spiritual, not material.

Like Joe Lampton, the hero is still an outsider, but this time he is a Catholic history teacher who finds himself torn between his vocation and the novelty of sex. Also unlike Lampton, he is, at thirty, still a virgin, a nonsmoker, and almost a teetotaler. Although his ardently Catholic mother hopes he will go into the Church to make up for his father's failure, Dungarvan is sidetracked by his first affair, with Laura Heycliff, a pretty librarian, and then by his sister-in-law, Maureen, who seduces him. Unlike Lampton, for whom sex was as simple and desirable as money, Dungarvan has a complicated conception of the ideal relationship between the sexes. Unlike Lampton, too, he is not a character type: neither conformist nor rebel, he is himself—confused, full of conflicts, hard to get along with, but himself.

A mixture of romantic novel, egocentric narrative, fantasy, and explicit sexual document, Braine's ninth novel, *Waiting for Sheila*, once again dissects the trappings of success as modern society has come to view it. Jim Seathwaite, a Northerner, is a familiar hero to readers of *Room at the Top*. He moved to a southern Surrey suburb, became successful as general manager of Droylsden's department store, and married Sheila, the chairman's former secretary. The usual Braine touch of price tags places the Seathwaites in the "made it" grade: they own a five-bedroom two-bath home with all of the modern conveniences, including a professionally landscaped garden. Beneath this veneer, however, the reader comes to learn of an inadequate man scarred by a wartime childhood during which his mother was unfaithful to his father, who died the day he discovered her infidelity. Braine's innovative use of the theme of the unfaithful wife (rather than the more common theme of the unfaithful husband) is but one of several departures in this novel.

The novel is deceptively simple in style and structure. For example, throughout the book Braine observes the unities: the reader does not leave Seathwaite's home; the action occurs within a few hours. Braine tells the story in the first person, in a stream-of-consciousness narrative—another departure for him—from the point of view of a thirty-year-old neurotic who has a conscience. He is sitting in solitude and drinking himself stupid while recalling his childhood, his adolescence, and his early manhood in one long, Freudian confession. Almost like a patient on a psychiatrist's couch, he hints, then finally reveals the truth: his wife is also unfaithful, and he feels as helpless as did his father. The reader learns that he finds in the lascivious Sheila the earth-mother and bitch-lover he sensed first, at seven, in his mother—a self-indulgent beauty who drove his working-class father to drink and a muddy grave. Thus, another theme in the work is the nuances and compromises of marriage—a general theme with which Braine is concerned in all of his books.

If he has never been short of detractors, Braine has had his defenders, too.

Over the course of his writing career his reputation grew as a middlebrow writer who mastered the basics of his craft. Few modern writers have had a firmer sense of milieu. His ear for dialogue was accurate, and his grasp of narrative technique impressive. With his talent, his tolerance of human foibles, and his total commitment to writing, Braine has been a significant figure in modern British fiction, an honest and perceptive observer of the social scene.

Dale Salwak

Other major works

NONFICTION: *Writing a Novel*, 1974; *J. B. Priestley*, 1978.

Bibliography

Allsop, Kenneth. "The Neutralists." In *The Angry Decade: A Survey of the Cultural Revolt of the Nineteen-Fifties*. 1958. Reprint. Wendover, England: John Goodchild, 1985. Considers the works of Kingsley Amis and John Wain before examining *Room at the Top*. Also provides biographical information and evaluates Braine's goals as a writer.

Karl, Frederick R. "The Angries." In *A Reader's Guide to the Contemporary English Novel*. Rev. ed. New York: Farrar, Straus & Giroux, 1972. Attacks the writers associated with the Angry Young Men movement, maintaining that their novels are poorly executed, their heroes boring. Karl reserves his harshest judgment for Kingsley Amis' *Lucky Jim* and derides *Room at the Top* and *The Vodi* as trite and formulaic.

Laing, Stuart. "*Room at the Top*: The Morality of Affluence." In *Popular Fiction and Social Change*, edited by Christopher Pauling. New York: St. Martin's Press, 1984. This well-rounded article traces the novel's critical success and analyzes historical, social, and political changes in postwar Britain that are reflected in the novel's themes and the relationships between characters. The title refers to the loss of human values in a society where individuals are driven solely by financial success.

Lee, James W. *John Braine*. New York: Twayne, 1968. The introduction considers Braine in the context of other authors categorized as Angry Young Men. One chapter examines six nonfictional sketches written between 1950 and 1957; another chapter critiques *Room at the Top* and three later novels. Includes a brief selected bibliography.

Salwak, Dale. *Interviews with Britain's Angry Young Men*. San Bernardino, Calif.: Borgo Press, 1984. Braine recalls how he got started as a writer and comments on some of the values in his work, his mother's influence on his success, themes in some of his novels, and a work in progress, the novel *One and Last Love*. He also provides some perspective on his being grouped with the Angry Young Men.

RICHARD BRAUTIGAN

Born: Tacoma, Washington; January 30, 1935
Died: Bolinas, California; September, 1984

Principal long fiction

A Confederate General from Big Sur, 1964; *Trout Fishing in America,* 1967; *In Watermelon Sugar,* 1968; *The Abortion: An Historical Romance,* 1971; *The Hawkline Monster: A Gothic Western,* 1974; *Willard and His Bowling Trophies: A Perverse Mystery,* 1975; *Sombrero Fallout: A Japanese Novel,* 1976; *Dreaming of Babylon: A Private Eye Novel 1942,* 1977; *The Tokyo-Montana Express,* 1980; *So the Wind Won't Blow It All Away,* 1982.

Other literary forms

Richard Brautigan began his literary career as a poet. "I wrote poetry for seven years," he noted, "to learn how to write a sentence." Though a poet for many years, Brautigan maintained that his ambition was to write novels: "I figured I couldn't write a novel until I could write a sentence." Although most of Brautigan's later work was in the novel form, he continued to publish poetry and also produced a collection of short stories (*Revenge of the Lawn: Stories 1962-1970,* 1971).

Achievements

Short-story writer, novelist, and poet, Brautigan created a stream of works which resist simple categories—in fact, defy categorization altogether. Much of his popularity can be attributed to his peculiar style, his unconventional plots, simple language, and marvelous humor which together provide a melancholy vision of American life and the elusive American Dream.

Brautigan's novels are generally characterized by the appearance of a first-person narrator (sometimes identified in the third person as Brautigan himself) who presents an autobiographical, oftentimes whimsical story. Brautigan's work employs simple, direct, short, and usually repetitive sentences. In his best work, he has an uncanny ability to create vibrant and compelling scenes from apparently banal subject matter. It is the voice of the "I," however, that carries the Brautigan novel, a voice that often unifies virtually plotless and quite heterogeneous materials.

Much of Brautigan's work involves the search for simplicity—an expansion of the Emersonian search for pastoral America. Yet, the complacent rural life is no longer available in Brautigan's world: all the trout streams have been sold to the highest bidder, all the campgrounds are already filled, in fact overflowing; yet, the search must go on for new places where the imagination can still roam free—to a pastoral America where the individual can escape the suffocating din of technocracy.

Brautigan's work evolved into a new, unorthodox version of the American novel. His experimentation with language, structure, characterization, plot, and motif broke new ground. Because of this, many critics have been unable to characterize his work with ease. Unable to pinpoint his exact standing, they have dismissed him as a counterculture phenomenon, a faddish nonentity. Although Brautigan's oeuvre is indeed very uneven, his best work is genuinely original and ensures him a lasting place in American literature.

Biography

Richard Brautigan was born and reared in the Pacific Northwest. The son of Bernard F. Brautigan and Lula Mary Keho Brautigan, he spent his early years in Washington and Oregon. His literary career took hold when, in 1958, he moved to San Francisco, California, and began writing poetry in the company of Lawrence Ferlinghetti, Robert Duncan, Philip Whalen, and Michael McClure. The company he kept led to his initial identification as a Beat poet, but Brautigan's unique and now well-known style resisted the classification.

Resisting crass commercialism and the profits linked with corporate America, Brautigan's first books were published primarily for the benefit of his friends and acquaintances. Success finally forced him to allow a New York publication of his work in the 1960's, however, and Grove Press published his *A Confederate General from Big Sur*. Shortly after his change of allegiance from Four Seasons Foundation in San Francisco to Grove Press in New York, Brautigan was invited to become poet-in-residence at Pasadena's California Institute of Technology. Although he had never attended college, he accepted the invitation, and spent the 1967 academic year at the prestigious school.

In 1957, Brautigan married Virginia Diorine Adler. They had one daughter, Ianthe, and later were divorced. In his later years, Brautigan divided his time among three places: Tokyo, San Francisco, and, when in retreat or fishing, a small town in Montana. He died in 1984, an apparent suicide.

Analysis

Richard Brautigan's first published novel, *A Confederate General from Big Sur*, is perhaps his funniest. A burlesque of American society long after the Civil War, the story is told by Jesse, a gentle, shy, withdrawn narrator (not unlike Brautigan himself) who meets Lee Mellon, a rebel, dropout, and activist living in San Francisco. Lee soon moves to Oakland, where he lives, rent-free, at the home of a committed mental patient. The story then moves to Big Sur, where Lee and Jesse live in a cabin, again owned by a mental patient. As Jesse and Lee figure out how to cope with life and no money, they find a fortune of six dollars and some loose change, get rip-roaring drunk in Monterey, and discover Elaine and a great deal of money. Johnston Wade, a crazed insurance man, arrives on the scene, informing everyone that he is fleeing from his wife and daughter (they want to commit him to a mental institution). He leaves as abruptly as he arrived, remembering an important business appointment he must keep. The book ends, as it must, without ending.

In *A Confederate General from Big Sur*, Brautigan is facing the question of how to cope with civilization. The flight from technology toward wilderness holds risks of its own. Brautigan offers no answers. Human life is not unlike that of the bugs sitting on the log Jesse has thrown into the fire. They sit there on the log, staring out at him as the flames leap around them.

The theme of the novel is the ambition to control one's life and destiny. The ownership of the Big Sur log cabin by a mental patient and Johnston Wade's own mental aberrations only serve to illustrate the fleeting control all people have over their lives. Brautigan introduces Wade to burlesque the myth of American destiny. He is a parody, a ridiculous image of American business and technocracy: the self-made man running away from his wife and child who suddenly remembers an important business engagement.

Although not published until 1968, *In Watermelon Sugar* was written in 1964, during Brautigan's evolution from poet to novelist. The book reflects this evolutionary change, for in many ways it is more poetic than novelistic in its form. The story is that of a young man who lives in a small commmunity after an unspecified cataclysm. In the first of the three parts of the book, the shy and gentle narrator tells the reader about himself and his friends. Their peaceful life was not always so, he explains, and he tells about iDEATH, a central gathering place which is more a state of mind than an actual physical location. In the second part of the novel, the narrator has a terrible dream of carnage and self-mutilation. The third part of the book begins with the narrator's awakening, strangely refreshed after the terrible dream. The gentle, leisurely pace of the first part then restores itself.

In Watermelon Sugar is like Aldous Huxley's *Brave New World* (1932): a Utopian novel of the Garden of Eden, springing forth out of the chaos of today's world. It is his vision of the rustic good life in postindustrial society. From watermelons comes the juice that is made into sugar, the stuff of the lives and dreams of the people of iDEATH. By controlling their own lives, by creating their own order, the people of iDEATH recover society from chaos. The sense of order and recurrence is set in the very first line of the book, which both begins and ends "in watermelon sugar." That phrase is also used as the title of the first part of the book, as well as the title of the first chapter. Like a refrain, it sets a pattern and order in a world in which people live in harmony with nature and with their own lives.

Like several of Brautigan's books, *The Abortion: An Historical Romance* spent some time in the library of unpublished books which it describes, where dreams go (and can be found). The world of *The Abortion* is that of a public library in California: not an ordinary library, but one where losers bring their unpublishable books. Again Brautigan's narrator is a shy, introverted recluse—the librarian, unnamed because he is ordinary, like the people who bring their books to the library to have them shelved. Brautigan himself visits the library at one point in the novel, to bring in *Moose*; he is tall and blond, with an anachronistic appearance, looking as if he would be more comfortable in another era. That circumstance is certainly the case with the narrator as well.

There is less action in *The Abortion* than in most of Brautigan's novels; the book plods along slowly, mimicking its central theme, which is that a series of short, tentative steps can lead one out of a personal and social labyrinth and toward the promise of a new life. Before the reader knows it, however, the librarian is out in the rain with a girl; she gets pregnant; and they journey to Tijuana to have an abortion. The girl is called Vida, and she represents life in the twentieth century. The librarian struggles with his inner self, afraid to move from the old ways, afraid to let go of his innocence. Brautigan contrasts him with his partner, Foster, a wild caveman who takes care of the books that have been moved from the library to dead storage in a cave. Foster is loud and outgoing—the opposite of the timid librarian— and he thinks of the library as an asylum.

With Vida, the librarian becomes embroiled in a quest for survival. Vida brings him out of the library into the world of change and conflict. He is frightened by it, but, step by tentative step, he confronts it.

The Abortion is a commentary on American culture. Brautigan draws a loose parallel between the library and American history: the librarian-narrator is the thirty-sixth caretaker of the library; at the time the book was written, there had been thirty-six presidents of the United States. The origins of the mysterious library go back into the American past as well, just as Brautigan himself appears as an anachronism from an earlier, easier time.

While Brautigan laments the times gone by and yearns for the "good old days," the leisurely pace of the library, he also holds out hope for a fresh alternative. American culture has nearly been destroyed—the playboy beauty queen named Vida hates herself, and bombs and industrial technocracy threaten lives and deaden spirits. Strangely enough, by destroying life—by the abortion—one can begin anew, start a new life. The narrator and Vida share this hopefulness, which was widespread in the counterculture when *The Abortion* was published.

With *The Hawkline Monster: A Gothic Western*, Brautigan began a series of novels which adapt the conventions of genre fiction in a quirky, unpredictable manner. Not strictly parodies, these hybrids sometimes achieve wonderful effects—odd, unsettling, comical—and sometimes fall flat. Combining the gothic novel, the Western, and a dash of romance, *The Hawkline Monster* is set in eastern Oregon during 1902 and centers on a magical Victorian house occupied by two equally baffling Victorian maidens with curious habits. The unreality of the situation does not affect the two unruffled Western heroes of the book, however, who methodically go about their task of killing the Hawkline Monster. The problem is not only to find the monster but also to discover what it is; the ice caves under the house complete the unreality of the situation. Brautigan moves lyrically from the mundane to the magical in this fusion of the real and the surreal.

Trout Fishing in America, Brautigan's most famous novel and his best, is a short, visionary inscape on the American nightmare. Brautigan has created a tragic symbol of what has happened to America: the trout streams are all gone, the campgrounds are full; escape to the American pastoral is no longer possible. Yet Brautigan assures his readers that all is not lost—there is still a place where they can find freedom. If all the land is being used and one cannot physically escape the city, then one must escape to the pastoral realm of one's imagination. Trout fishing, Brautigan insists, is thus a way of recapturing the simple while remaining aware of the complex.

Trout Fishing in America, like much of Brautigan's work (including his last novel, *So the Wind Won't Blow It All Away*), is autobiographical. The gentle, withdrawn narrator uses trout fishing as a central metaphor. A victim of the technological world, the narrator creates his own watery realm, complete with its own boundaries—a place where he can find solace from the technological stranglehold. His vision implies that all people have a fundamental right to the abundant richness and good life that America can provide, but that are denied to many because the bankrupt ideas of the past still hold sway. Aware of the complexities of American life, Brautigan seems to be exhorting his readers to recapture the simple life, to escape the confinement of the city for the freedom of the wilderness. If that wilderness in the actual sense is cut off and no longer accessible; if all the trout streams have been developed, dis-assembled, and sold; if the horizon is now not new but old and despoiled; if the parks are already overcrowded; if there is no other way, then one must escape through the imagination.

In *So the Wind Won't Blow It All Away*, Brautigan gives readers a glimpse of what post-Trout-Fishing-in-America life has become. Billed as an "American tragedy," *So the Wind Won't Blow It All Away* instead focuses on the tragedy that America and American life have become: "dust . . . American . . . dust."

Written, as are most of his novels, in the first person, Brautigan's novel is the memoir of an anonymous boy reared in welfare-state poverty somewhere in the Pacific Northwest. Unloved but tolerated by his mother, the boy and his family go from town to town, meeting an odd assortment of minor char-acters. Although undeveloped, these characters serve to carry the novel's theme and serve as victims of the technocracy America has become. There is an old pensioner who lives in a packing-crate shack; adept at carpentry, the old man built a beautiful dock and boat and knows all the best fishing spots on the pond near his home, but he does not use his knowledge or equipment. A gas-station attendant who cares nothing about selling gas but likes to sell worms to fishermen also appears on the scene. There is a thirty-five-year-old alcoholic who traded ambition for beer; charged with the safety of the sawmill, the man dresses in finery (although readers are told that his appearances are not true-to-life), cares nothing about his job, and passes his life by, continually encircled by boys who swoop like vultures to take his empty bottles back to the store for credit. Like America itself, the guard has brittle bones resembling dried-out weeds. Finally, Brautigan introduces a husband and wife who, each night, carry their living-room furniture to the pond, set it up, and fish all night.

Brautigan presents America as having come to the end of its greatness, like the end of a late summer afternoon. The technological success that spurred the country to greatness has resulted in its downfall. The husband and wife have changed all their electrical lamps to kerosene and await the cool evening with its refreshing possibilities, but as they patiently fish in the wrong spot, America goes on, killing its imagination with the technology of mindless television.

So the Wind Won't Blow It All Away ends with the horrible climax of the death of a boy, shot by mistake in an orchard that has been left to die. With that end, however, is the beginning of a new life, for, though the orchard has been left alone to die, new fruit will grow. The novel recalls the message of *The Abortion*: the substitutions of the confinement of the city for the freedom of the wilderness, and of television for imagination are choices people have. With this novel, Brautigan returned to the successful themes of his earliest novels, warning that to go on will result only in dust, American dust.

David Mike Hamilton

Other major works
SHORT FICTION: *Revenge of the Lawn: Stories 1962-1970*, 1971.
POETRY: *The Return of the Rivers*, 1957; *The Galilee Hitch-Hiker*, 1958; *Lay the Marble Tea: Twenty-four Poems*, 1959; *The Octopus Frontier*, 1960; *All Watched Over by Machines of Loving Grace*, 1967; *The Pill Versus the Springhill Mine Disaster*, 1968; *Please Plant This Book*, 1968; *Rommel Drives On Deep into Egypt*, 1970; *Loading Mercury with a Pitchfork*, 1976; *June 30th, June 30th*, 1978.

Bibliography
Abbott, Keith. *Downstream from "Trout Fishing in America": A Memoir of Richard Brautigan*. Santa Barbara, Calif.: Capra Press, 1989. A personal account of Brautigan from a longtime friend. Some of the book is Abbott's own memoirs, but also contains interesting anecdotes and insights into Brautigan's life and work. Chapter 8, "Shadows and Marble," presents

critical commentary on Brautigan's novels, in particular *Trout Fishing in America*.

Bradbury, Malcolm. *The Modern American Novel*. Oxford, England: Oxford University Press, 1983. Chapter 7, "Postmoderns and Others: The 1960s and 1970s," cites Brautigan, placing him in the genre of writers who "celebrated the hippie youth spirit." Bradbury gives succinct but insightful critical commentary on Brautigan's novels. He sees Brautigan as much more than a hippie writer, whose spirit of "imaginative discovery" has spawned a number of literary successors.

Chenetier, Marc. *Richard Brautigan*. London: Methuen, 1983. Assesses Brautigan's writing in the context of the 1960's, and traces the development of his art beyond the confines of a cult figure. An appreciative study that analyzes Brautigan in the light of his poetics.

Hernlund, Patricia. "Author's Intent: *In Watermelon Sugar*." *Critique: Studies in Modern Fiction* 16, no. 1 (1974): 5-17. A sound critical commentary that places *In Watermelon Sugar* beyond its label of a "fad" book. Discusses how the novel describes an entire society and a way of life. Explores the time sequences, the division of the novel into three books, and Brautigan's use of repetition and juxtaposition.

Wanless, James, and Christine Kolodziej. "Richard Brautigan: A Working Checklist." *Critique: Studies in Modern Fiction* 16, no. 1 (1974): 41-52. A compilation of secondary material on Brautigan, complete through 1973. Lists novels (including their serial form), poetry, short stories, and uncollected pieces, as well as reviews and critical commentary on individual works. A valuable resource for the Brautigan scholar.

CHARLOTTE BRONTË

Born: Thornton, England; April 21, 1816
Died: Haworth, England; March 31, 1855

Principal long fiction
Jane Eyre, 1847; *Shirley*, 1849; *Villette*, 1853; *The Professor*, 1857.

Other literary forms
The nineteen poems which Charlotte Brontë selected to print with her sister Anne's work in *Poems by Currer, Ellis, and Acton Bell* (1846) were her only other works published during her lifetime. The juvenilia produced by the four Brontë children—Charlotte, Emily, Anne, and Branwell—between 1824 and 1839 are scattered in libraries and private collections. Some of Charlotte's contributions have been published in *The Twelve Adventurers and Other Stories* (1925), *Legends of Angria* (1933), *The Search After Hapiness* (1969), *Five Novelettes* (1971), and *The Secret and Lily Hart* (1979). A fragment of a novel written during the last year of Brontë's life was published as *Emma* in *Cornhill Magazine* in 1860 and is often reprinted in editions of *The Professor*. *The Complete Poems of Charlotte Brontë* appeared in 1924. Other brief selections, fragments, and ephemera have been printed in *Transactions and Other Publications of the Brontë Society*. The nineteen-volume *Shakespeare Head Brontë* (1931-1938), edited by T. J. Wise and J. A. Symington, contains all of the novels, four volumes of life and letters, two volumes of miscellaneous writings, and two volumes of poems.

Achievements
Brontë brought to English fiction an intensely personal voice. Her books show the moral and emotional growth of a protagonist almost entirely by self-revelation. Her novels focus on individual self-fulfillment; they express the subjective interior world not only in thoughts, dreams, visions, and symbols but also by projecting inner states through external objects, secondary characters, places, events, and weather. Brontë's own experiences and emotions inform the narrative presence. "Perhaps no other writer of her time," wrote Margaret Oliphant in 1855, "has impressed her mark so clearly on contemporary literature, or drawn so many followers into her own peculiar path."

The personal voice, which blurs the distance between novelist, protagonist, and reader, accounts for much of the critical ambivalence toward Brontë's work. Generations of unsophisticated readers have identified with Jane Eyre; thousands of romances and modern gothics have used Brontë's situations and invited readers to step into the fantasy. Brontë's novels, however, are much more than simply the common reader's daydreams. They are rich enough to allow a variety of critical approaches. They have been studied in relation to traditions (Gothic, provincial, realistic, romantic); read for psychological, linguistic, Christian, social, economic, and personal interpretations; analyzed in terms of symbolism, imagery, metaphor, viewpoint, narrative distance, and prose style. Because the novels are so clearly wrought from the materials of their author's life, recent psychoanalytic and feminist criticism has proved rewarding. In Brontë's work, a woman author makes significant statements about issues central to women's lives. Most of her heroines are working women; each feels the pull of individual self-development against the wish for emotional fulfillment, the tension between sexual energies and social realities, the almost unresolvable conflict between love and independence.

Biography

Charlotte Brontë was the third of six children born within seven years to the Reverend Patrick Brontë and his wife Maria Branwell. Patrick Brontë was perpetual curate of Haworth, a bleak manufacturing town in Yorkshire. In 1821, when Charlotte Brontë was five years old, her mother died of cancer. Three years later, the four elder girls were sent to the Clergy Daughter's School at Cowan Bridge—the school which appears as Lowood in *Jane Eyre*. In the summer of 1825, the eldest two daughters, Maria and Elizabeth, died of tuberculosis. Charlotte and Emily were removed from the school and brought home. There were no educated middle-class families in Haworth to supply friends and companions. The Brontë children lived with a noncommunicative aunt, an elderly servant, and a father much preoccupied by his intellectual interests and his own griefs.

In their home and with only one another for company, the children had material for both educational and imaginative development. Patrick Brontë expected his children to read and to carry on adult conversations about politics. He subscribed to *Blackwood's Edinburgh Magazine*, where his children had access to political and economic essays, art criticism, and literary reviews. They had annuals with engravings of fine art; they taught themselves to draw by copying the pictures in minute detail. They were free to do reading that would not have been permitted by any school of the time—by the age of thirteen Charlotte Brontë was fully acquainted not only with John Milton and Sir Walter Scott but also with Robert Southey, William Cowper and (most important) Lord Byron.

In 1826, Branwell was given a set of wooden soldiers which the four children used for characters in creative play. These soldiers gradually took on personal characteristics and acquired countries to rule. The countries needed cities, governments, ruling families, political intrigues, legends, and citizens with private lives, all of which the children happily invented. In 1829, when Charlotte Brontë was thirteen, she and the others began to write down materials from these fantasies, producing a collection of juvenilia that extended ultimately to hundreds of items: magazines, histories, maps, essays, tales, dramas, poems, newspapers, wills, speeches, scrapbooks. This enormous creative production in adolescence gave concrete form to motifs that were later transformed into situations, characters, and concerns of Charlotte Brontë's mature work. It was also a workshop for literary technique; the young author explored prose style, experimented with viewpoint, and discovered how to control narrative voice. A single event, she learned, could be the basis for both a newspaper story and a romance, and the romance could be told by one of the protagonists or by a detached observer.

Because Patrick Brontë had no income beyond his salary, his daughters had to prepare to support themselves. In 1831, when she was almost fifteen, Charlotte Brontë went to Miss Wooler's School at Roe Head. After returning home for a time to tutor her sisters, she went back to Miss Wooler's as a teacher. Over the next several years, all three sisters held positions as governesses in private families. None, however, was happy as a governess; aside from the predictable difficulties caused by burdensome work and undisciplined children, they all suffered when separated from their shared emotional and creative life. A possible solution would have been to open their own school, but they needed some special qualification to attract pupils. Charlotte conceived a plan for going abroad to study languages. In 1842, she and Emily went to Brussels to the Pensionnat Heger. They returned in November because of their aunt's death, but in the following year Charlotte went back to Brussels alone to work as a pupil-teacher. An additional reason for her return to Brussels was that she desired to be near Professor Constantine Heger, but at the end of the year she left in misery after Heger's wife had realized (perhaps more clearly than did Charlotte herself) the romantic nature of the attraction.

In 1844, at the age of twenty-eight, Charlotte Brontë established herself permanently at Haworth. The prospectus for "The Misses Brontë's Establishment" was published, but no pupils applied. Branwell, dismissed in disgrace from his post as tutor, came home to drink, take opium, and disintegrate. Charlotte spent nearly two years in deep depression: her yearning for love was unsatisfied and she had repressed her creative impulse because she was afraid her fantasies were self-indulgent. Then, with the discovery that all three had written poetry, the sisters found a new aim in life. A joint volume of poems was published in May, 1846, though it sold only two copies. Each wrote a short novel; they offered the three together to publishers. Emily Brontë's *Wuthering Heights* (1847) and Anne Brontë's *Agnes Grey* (1847) were accepted. Charlotte Brontë's *The Professor* was refused, but one editor, George Smith, said he would like to see a three-volume novel written by its author. *Jane Eyre* was by that time almost finished; it was sent to Smith on August 24, 1847, and impressed him so much that he had it in print by the middle of October.

Jane Eyre was immediately successful, but there was barely any time for its author to enjoy her fame and accomplishment. Within a single year, her three companions in creation died: Branwell on September 24, 1848; Emily on December 19; Anne on May 28, 1849. When Charlotte Brontë began work on *Shirley*, she met with her sisters in the evenings to exchange ideas, read aloud, and offer criticism. By the time she finished the manuscript she was alone.

Charlotte Brontë's sense that she was plain, "undeveloped," and unlikely to be loved seems to have been partly the product of her own psychological condition. She had refused more than one proposal in her early twenties. In 1852 there was another, from Arthur Bell Nicholls, curate at Haworth. Patrick Brontë objected violently and dismissed his curate. Gradually, however, the objections were worn away. On June 29, 1854, Charlotte Brontë and the Reverend Nicholls were married and, after a brief honeymoon tour, took up residence in Haworth parsonage. After a few months of apparent content— which did not prevent her from beginning work on another novel—Charlotte Brontë died on March 31, 1855, at the age of thirty-eight; a severe cold made her too weak to survive the complications of early pregnancy.

Analysis

The individualism and richness of Charlotte Brontë's work arises from the multiple ways in which her writing is personal: observation and introspection, rational analysis and spontaneous emotion, accurate mimesis and private symbolism. Tension and ambiguity grow from the intersections and conflicts among these levels of writing and, indeed, among the layers of the self.

Few writers of English prose have so successfully communicated the emotional texture of inner life while still constructing fictions with enough verisimilitude to appear realistic. Brontë startled the Victorians because her work was so little influenced by the books of her own era. Its literary forebears were the written corporate daydreams of her childhood and the Romantic poets she read during the period when the fantasies took shape. Certain characters and situations which crystallized the emotional conflicts of early adolescence became necessary components of emotional satisfaction. The source of these fantasies was, to a degree, beyond control, occurring in the region the twentieth century has termed "the unconscious"; by writing them down from childhood on, Brontë learned to preserve and draw on relatively undisguised desires and ego conflicts in a way lost to most adults.

The power and reality of the inner life disturbed Brontë after she had passed through adolescence; she compared her creative urge to the action of opium and was afraid that she might become lost in her "infernal world." When she began to think of publication, she deliberately used material from her own experience and reported scenes and characters in verifiable detail. In this way, she hoped to subdue the exaggerated romanticism—and the overwrought writing—of the fantasy-fictions. "Details, situations which I do not understand and cannot personally inspect," she wrote to her publisher, "I would not for the world meddle with." Her drawing from life was so accurate that the curates and the Yorkes in *Shirley* were recognized at once by people who knew them, and Brontë lost the protection that her pseudonym had provided.

The years of practice in writing fiction that satisfied her own emotional needs gave Brontë the means to produce powerful psychological effects. She uses a variety of resources to make readers share the protagonist's subjective state. The truth of the outside world is only that truth which reflects the narrator's feelings and perceptions. All characters are aspects of the consciousness which creates them: Brontë uses splitting, doubling, and other fairy-tale devices; she replicates key situations; she carefully controls the narrative distance and the amount of information readers have at their disposal.

The unquietness which Brontë's readers often feel grows from the tension between direct emotional satisfactions (often apparently immature) on the one hand, and, on the other, mature and realistic conflicts in motive, reason, and sense of self. Read as a sequence, the four completed novels demonstrate both Brontë's development and the story of woman's relationship to the world. Brontë's heroines find identity outside the enclosed family popularly supposed to circumscribe nineteenth century women. Isolation allows the heroines' self-development, but it impedes their romantic yearning to be lost in love.

At the beginning of *The Professor*, William Crimsworth is working as a clerk in a mill owned by his proud elder brother. He breaks away, goes to Brussels to teach English, survives a brief attraction to a seductive older woman, and then comes to love Frances Henri, an orphaned Anglo-Swiss lace-mender who had been his pupil.

Brontë's narrative devices supply shifting masks that both expose and evade the self. The epistolary opening keeps readers from identifying directly with Crimsworth but draws them into the novel as recipients of his revelations. The masculine persona, which Brontë used frequently in the juvenilia, gives her access to the literary mainstream and creates possibilities for action, attitude, and initiative that did not exist in models for female stories. The juvenile fantasies supply the feud between two brothers; the Belgian scenes and characters come from Brontë's own experiences. Although nominally male, Crimsworth is in an essentially female situation; disinherited, passive, timid. He has, furthermore, an exaggerated awareness and fear of the sexual overtones in human behavior.

Biographical details also go into the making of Frances Henri, the friendless older student working to pay for her lessons in the Belgian school. The poem that Frances writes is one Brontë had created out of her own yearning for Professor Heger. In *The Professor*, the dream can come true; the poem awakens the teacher's response.

Like the central figures on all Brontë novels, both Crimsworth and Frances enact a Cinderella plot. Each begins as an oppressed outcast and ends successful, confident, and satisfactorily placed in society. The details of Crimsworth's story work both symbolically and functionally. The imprisoning situations in the factory and the school reflect his perception of the world. At the same time, these situations are created by his own inner barriers. His bondage as a despised clerk is self-induced; he is an educated adult male who could move on at any time. In Belgium, he plods a treadmill of guilt because of Zoraïde Reuter's sexual manipulativeness—for which he is not responsible. His self-suppression is also seen through Yorke Hunsden, who appears whenever Crimsworth must express strong emotion. Hunsden voices anger and rebellion not permitted to the male/female narrator, and becomes a voyeur alter ego to appreciate Frances and love.

The novel is weakest when it fails to integrate the biography, the emotion, and the ideas. True moral dilemmas are not developed. The heroine, seen through sympathetic male eyes, wins love for her writing, her pride, and her self-possession, and she continues to work even after she has a child. Brontë solves her chronic romantic dilemma (how can a strong woman love if woman's love is defined as willing subordination?) by letting Frances vibrate between two roles: she is the stately directress of the school by day, the little lace-mender by night.

In *Jane Eyre*, Brontë created a story that has the authority of myth. Everything which had deeply affected her was present in the book's emotional content. The traumatic experiences of maternal deprivation, the Clergy Daughters' School, and Maria's death create the events of Jane's early life. The book also taps universal feelings of rejection, victimization, and loneliness, making them permissible by displacement: the hateful children are cousins, not siblings; the bad adult an aunt, not a mother. Rochester's compelling power as a lover derives from neither literal nor literary sources—Rochester is the man Brontë had loved for twenty years, the Duke of Zamorna who dominates the adolescent fantasies, exerting a power on both Jane and the reader that can hardly be explained by reason. Jane defied literary convention because she was poor, plain, and a heroine; she defied social convention by refusing to accept any external authority. Placed repeatedly in situations that exemplify male power, Jane resists and survives. At the end of the narrative, she is transformed from Cinderella to Prince Charming, becoming the heroine who cuts through the brambles to rescue the imprisoned sleeper. Identification is so immediate and so close that readers often fail to notice Brontë's control of distance, in particular the points of detachment when an older Jane comments on her younger self and the direct addresses from Jane to the reader that break the spell when emotions become too strong.

Place controls the book's structure. Events at Gateshead, Lowood, Thornfield, and Moor House determine Jane's development; a brief coda at Fearndean provides the resolution. Each of the four major sections contains a figure representing the sources of male power over women: John Reed (physical force and the patriarchal family), Reverend Brocklehurst (the social structures of class, education, and religion), Rochester (sexual attraction), and St. John Rivers (moral and spiritual authority). Jane protects herself at first by devious and indirect means—fainting, illness, flight—and then ultimately, in rejecting St. John Rivers, by direct confrontation. Compelled by circumstances to fend for herself, she comes—at first instinctively, later rationally—to rely on herself.

The book's emotional power grows from its total absorption in Jane's view of the world and from the images, symbols, and structures that convey multiple interwoven reverberations. The red room—which suggests violence, irrationality, enclosure, rebellion, rebirth, the bloody chamber of emerging womanhood—echoes throughout the book. The Bridewell charade, Jane's paintings, the buildings and terrain, and a multitude of other details have both meaning and function. Characters double and split: Helen Burns (mind) and Bertha Mason (body) are aspects of Jane as well as actors in the plot. Recurring images of ice and fire suggest fatal coldness without and consuming fire within. Rochester's sexuality is the most threatening and ambiguous aspect of masculine power because of Jane's own complicity and her need for love. Her terrors and dreams accumulate as the marriage approaches; there are drowning images, abyss images, loss of consciousness. She refuses to become Rochester's mistress, finally, not because of the practical and moral dangers (which she does recognize) but because she fears her own willingness to make a god of him. She will not become dependent; she escapes to preserve her self.

As Jane takes her life into her own hands, she becomes less needy. After she has achieved independence by discovering a family and inheriting money, she is free to seek out Rochester. At the same time, he has become less omnipotent, perhaps a code for the destruction of patriarchal power. Thus, the marriage not only ends the romance and resolves the moral, emotional, and sexual conflicts, but also supplies a satisfactory woman's fantasy of independence coupled with love.

For the book that would follow *Jane Eyre*, Brontë deliberately sought a new style and subject matter. *Shirley*, set in 1812, concerns two public issues still relevant in 1848—working-class riots and the condition of women. Brontë did historical research in newspaper files. She used a panoramic scene, included a variety of characters observed from life, and added touches of comedy. *Shirley* is told in the third person; the interest is divided between two heroines, neither of whom is a persona. Nevertheless, Brontë is strongly present in the narrative voice, which remains objective only in scenes of action. The authorial commentary, more strongly even than the events themselves, creates a tone of anger, rebellion, suffering, and doubt.

The novel is clearly plotted, although the mechanics are at times apparent.

Brontë shifts focus among characters and uses reported conversations to violate the time sequence so that she can arrange events in the most effective dramatic order. Robert Moore, owner of a cloth mill, arouses the workers' wrath by introducing machinery. Caroline Helstone loves Robert but her affection is not reciprocated. Although Caroline has a comfortable home with her uncle the rector, she is almost fatally depressed by lack of love and occupation. Property-owner Shirley Keeldar discovers that having a man's name, position, and forthrightness gives her some power but fails to make her man's equal; she is simply more valuable as a matrimonial prize. Louis Moore, Shirley's former tutor, loves her silently because he lacks wealth and social position. Eventually Robert, humbled by Shirley's contempt and weakened by a workman's bullet, declares his love for Caroline, who has in the meantime discovered her mother and grown much stronger. Shirley's union with Louis is more ambivalent; she loves him because he is a master she can look up to, but she is seen on her wedding day as a pantheress pining for virgin freedom.

The primary source of women's tribulation is dependency. Caroline Helstone craves occupation to fill her time, make her financially independent, and give her life purpose. Women become psychologically dependent on men because they have so little else to think about. Brontë examines the lives of several old maids; they are individuals, not stereotypes, but they are all lonely. Shirley and Caroline dissect John Milton, search for female roots, and talk cozily about men's inadequacies. They cannot, however, speak honestly to each other about their romantic feelings. Caroline must hold to herself the deep pain of unrequited love.

Although *Shirley* deliberately moves beyond the isolated mythic world of *Jane Eyre* to put women's oppression in the context of a society rent by other power struggles (workers against employers, England against France, Church against Nonconformity), the individualistic ending only partially resolves the divisions. Brontë's narrative tone in the final passage is bleak and bitter. She reminds readers that *Shirley*'s events are history. Fieldhead Hollow is covered by mills and mill housing; magic is gone from the world.

Villette is Brontë's most disciplined novel. Because *The Professor* had not been published, she was able to rework the Brussels experience without masks, as a story of loneliness and female deprivation, deliberately subduing the wish-fulfillment and making her uncompromising self-examination control form as well as feeling. Lucy Snowe is a woman without money, family, friends, or health. She is not, however, a sympathetic friendly narrator like Jane Eyre. Her personality has the unattractiveness that realistically grows from deprivation; she has no social ease, no warmth, no mental quickness. Furthermore, her personality creates her pain, loneliness, and disengagement.

In the book's early sections, Lucy is not even the center of her narrative. She watches and judges instead of taking part; she tells other people's stories instead of her own. She is so self-disciplined that she appears to have neither feelings nor imagination, so restrained that she never reveals the facts about her family or the incidents of her youth that might explain to readers how and why she learned to suppress emotion, hope, and the desire for human contact. Despite—or perhaps because of—her anesthetized feeling and desperate shyness, Lucy Snowe drives herself to actions that might have been inconceivable for a woman more thoroughly socialized. Thrust into the world by the death of the elderly woman whose companion she had been, she goes alone to London, takes a ship for the Continent, gets a job as nursemaid, rises through her own efforts to teach in Madame Beck's school, and begins laying plans to open a school of her own.

The coincidental and melodramatic elements of the story gain authenticity because they grow from Lucy's inner life. When she is left alone in the school during vacation, her repressed need to be heard by someone drives her to enter the confessional of a Catholic church. Once the internal barrier is breached, she immediately meets the Bretton family. Realistically, she must have known they were in Villette; she knew that "Dr. John" was Graham Bretton, but she withheld that information from the reader both because of her habitual secretiveness and also because she did not really "know" the Brettons were accessible to her until she was able to admit her need to reach out for human sympathy. The characterization of Paul Emanuel gains richness and detail in such a manner that readers realize—before Lucy herself dares admit it—that she is interested in him. The phantom nun, at first a night terror of pure emotion, is revealed as a prankish disguise when Lucy is free to express feelings directly.

The novel's ending, however, is deliberately ambiguous, though not in event. (Only the most naïve readers dare accept Brontë's invitation to imagine that Paul Emanuel escapes drowning and to "picture union and a happy succeeding life.") The ambiguity grows from Lucy's earlier statement: "M. Emanuel was away for three years. Reader, they were the three happiest years of my life." In those years, Lucy Snowe prospered, became respected, expanded her school. Her happiness depends not on the presence of her beloved but rather on the knowledge that she is loved. With that knowledge, she becomes whole and independent. No longer telling others' stories, she speaks directly to the reader about her most private concerns. Only when her lover is absent, perhaps, can a woman treasure love and emotional satisfaction while yet retaining the freedom to be her own person.

Sally Mitchell

Other major works

POETRY: *Poems by Currer, Ellis, and Acton Bell*, 1846 (with Emily Brontë and Anne Brontë); *The Complete Poems of Charlotte Brontë*, 1923.

CHILDREN'S LITERATURE: *The Twelve Adventurers and Other Stories*, 1925 (C. K. Shorter and C. W. Hatfield, editors); *Legends of Angria*, 1933 (Fannie E. Ratchford, compiler); *The Search After Hapiness*, 1969; *Five Novelettes*, 1971 (Winifred Gérin, editor); *The Secret and Lily Hart*, 1979 (William Holtz, editor).

MISCELLANEOUS: *The Shakespeare Head Brontë*, 1931-1938 (T. J. Wise and J. A. Symington, editors, 19 volumes).

Bibliography

Fraser, Rebecca. *The Brontës: Charlotte Brontë and Her Family*. New York: Crown, 1988. This thorough and engrossing biography of Charlotte Brontë and the Brontë family is carefully researched and annotated, and offers a vividly written portrait of the Brontës and their world. Makes use of letters, published and unpublished manuscripts, and contemporary news sources to examine this complex literary family. Highly recommended.

Gaskell, Elizabeth C. *The Life of Charlotte Brontë*. 1857. Reprint. London: Penguin Books, 1975. Still an indispensable source for any student of Charlotte Brontë's life, Gaskell's biography offers the insights gained through her long friendship with Brontë. Herself a popular novelist of the time, Gaskell creates a memorable picture of Brontë as both a writer and a woman.

Gerin, Winifred. *Charlotte Brontë: The Evolution of Genius*. Oxford, England: Clarendon Press, 1967. This well-written and exhaustive biography concentrates on Brontë's development as a writer, tracing her emerging style from her early works through her mature, later novels. Gerin, who has also written on Anne and Branwell Brontë, offers a literary biography that successfully interweaves its subject's work with her life.

Lloyd Evans, Barbara, and Gareth Lloyd Evans. *The Scribner Companion to the Brontës*. New York: Charles Scribner's Sons, 1983. Provides an overview of the Brontë family as a whole. Includes the story of the Brontës' tragic history, sections on the young Brontë' juvenilia, discussions of Charlotte, Anne, and Emily's published works, and excerpts from criticisms written about those works at the time they were first published.

McGregor, Ian, ed. *The Brontës: A Collection of Critical Essays*. Englewood Cliffs, N.J.: Prentice-Hall, 1970. This critical perspective on the Brontës' literary careers contains a collection of ten essays by a variety of authors and literary scholars. The essays are valuable in helping to place the Brontës' work within the context of their time and their personal history.

Nestor, Pauline. *Charlotte Brontë*. Savage, Md.: Barnes & Noble Books, 1987. This small but useful book offers a short biography of its subject followed by analyses of her various literary works. Critical reactions of the time and a thorough bibliography make this book an informative source for Brontë researchers.

EMILY BRONTË

Born: Thornton, England; July 30, 1818
Died: Haworth, England; December 19, 1848

Principal long fiction
Wuthering Heights, 1847.

Other literary forms
Poems by Currer, Ellis, and Acton Bell (1846) contains poems by Charlotte, Emily, and Anne Brontë. Juvenalia and early prose works on the imaginary world of Gondal have all been lost.

Achievements
Brontë occupies a unique place in the annals of literature. Her reputation as a major novelist stands on the merits of one relatively short novel which was misunderstood and intensely disliked upon publication, yet no study of British fiction is complete without a discussion of *Wuthering Heights*. The names of its settings and characters, particularly Heathcliff, have become part of the heritage of Western culture familiar even to those who have neither read the novel nor know anything about its author's life and career. Several film versions, the two most popular in 1939 and 1970, have helped perpetuate this familiarity.

The literary achievement of *Wuthering Heights* lies in its realistic portrayal of a specific place and time and in its examination of universal patterns of human behavior. Set in Yorkshire in the closing years of the eighteenth century, the novel delineates the quality of life in the remote moors of northern England, and also reminds the reader of the growing pains of industrialization throughout the nation. In addition, more than any other novel of the period, *Wuthering Heights* presents in clear dialectic form the conflict between two opposing psychic forces, embodied in the settings of the Grange and the Heights and the people who inhabit them. Although modern readers often apply the theories of Sigmund Freud and C. G. Jung to give names to these forces, Brontë illustrated their conflict long before psychologists pigeonholed them. *Wuthering Heights* is so true in its portrayal of human nature that it fits easily into many theoretical and critical molds, from the historical to the psychological. The novel may be most fully appreciated, however, as a study of the nature of human perception and its ultimate failure in understanding human behavior. This underlying theme, presented through the dialectic structure of human perception, unites many of the elements that are sometimes singled out or overemphasized in particular critical approaches to the novel.

Brontë's skill is not confined to representing the world and the human forces at work within her characters, great as that skill is. She has also created a complex narrative structure built upon a series of interlocking memories and perceptions, spanning three generations and moving across several social classes. Told primarily from two often unreliable and sometimes ambiguous first-person points of view, the structure of the novel itself illustrates the limitations of human intelligence and imagination. Faced with choosing between Lockwood or Nelly Dean's interpretation of Heathcliff's life, the reader can only ponder that human perception never allows a full under-standing of another soul.

Biography

Emily Jane Brontë was born at Thornton, in Bradford Parish, Yorkshire, on July 30, 1818, the fifth child of the Reverend Patrick and Maria Brontë. Patrick Brontë had been born in County Down, Ireland, one of ten children, on March 17, 1777. He was a schoolteacher and tutor before obtaining his B.A. from Cambridge in 1806, from where he was ordained to curacies, first in Essex and then in Hartshead, Yorkshire. He married Maria Branwell, of Penzance, in Hartshead on December 19, 1812, and in 1817, they moved to Thornton. The other children at the time of Emily's birth were Maria, Eliz-abeth, Charlotte, and Patrick Branwell; another daughter, Anne, was born two years later. Charlotte and Anne also became writers.

In early 1820, the family moved to Haworth, four miles from the village of Keighley, where the Reverend Brontë was perpetual curate until his death in 1861. Maria Brontë died on September 15, 1821, and about a year later, an elder sister, Elizabeth Branwell, moved in to take care of the children and household. She remained with them until her own death in 1842.

Life at Haworth was spartan but not unpleasant. There was a close and devoted relationship among the children, especially between Charlotte and Emily. Reading was a favorite pastime, and a wide range of books, including the novels of Sir Walter Scott and the poetry of William Wordsworth and Robert Southey, as well as the more predictable classics, were available to the children. Outdoor activities included many hours of wandering through the moors and woods. Their father wanted the children to be hardy and independent, intellectually and physically, indifferent to the passing fashions of the world.

Maria, Elizabeth, and Charlotte had already been sent away to a school for clergymen's daughters, at Cowan's Bridge, when Emily joined them in November, 1824. Emily was not happy in this confined and rigid environment and longed for home. Two of the sisters, Elizabeth and Maria, became ill and were taken home to die during 1825; in June, Charlotte and Emily returned home as well.

From 1825 to 1830, the remaining Brontë children lived at Haworth with their father and Miss Branwell. In June, 1826, their father gave them a set of wooden soldiers, a seemingly insignificant gift that stimulated their imaginative and literary talents. The children devoted endless energy to creating an imaginary world for these soldiers. During these years, Charlotte and [brother] Branwell created in their minds and on paper the land of "Angria," while Emily and Anne were at work on "Gondal." Although all of these early prose works have been lost, some of Emily's poetry contains references to aspects of the Gondal-Angria creations.

In July, 1835, Emily again joined Charlotte, already a teacher, at the Roe Head School. She remained only three months, returning home in October. Three years later, she accepted a position as governess in a school in Halifax for about six months, but returned to Haworth in December; Charlotte joined her there early in the following year. During 1839 and 1840, the sisters were planning to establish their own school at Haworth, but the plan was never carried through.

Charlotte left home again to serve as a governess in 1841, and in February, 1842, she and Emily went to Mme. Héger's school in Brussels to study languages. They returned to Haworth in November because of Miss Branwell's death. Charlotte went back to Brussels to teach in 1843, but Emily never left Yorkshire again.

From August, 1845, the Brontë children were again united at Haworth. They did not have much contact with neighbors, whose educational level and intellectual interests were much inferior to theirs. They kept busy reading and writing, both fiction and poetry. *Wuthering Heights* was probably begun in October, 1845, and completed sometime in 1846, although it was not published until December, 1847, after the success of *Jane Eyre* (1847).

Meanwhile, the sisters published *Poems by Currer, Ellis, and Acton Bell* in May, 1846. Finding a press was very difficult and the pseudonyms were chosen to avoid personal publicity and to create the fiction of male authorship, more readily acceptable to the general public. The reaction was predictable, as Charlotte reports: "Neither we nor our poems were at all wanted." The sisters were not discouraged, however, and they continued to seek publishers for their novels.

The first edition of *Wuthering Heights* was published in 1847 by T. C. Newby, with Anne's *Agnes Grey* as the third volume. It was a sloppy edition and contained many errors. The second edition, published in 1850, after the author's death, was "corrected" by Charlotte. The public reaction to *Wuthering Heights* was decidedly negative; readers were disturbed by the "wickedness" of the characters and the "implausibility" of the action. Until Charlotte herself corrected the misconception, readers assumed that *Wuthering Heights* was an inferior production by the author of *Jane Eyre*.

In October, 1848, Emily became seriously ill with a cough and cold. She suffered quietly and patiently, even refusing to see the doctor who had been called. She died of tuberculosis at Haworth on December 19, 1848. She was buried in the church alongside her mother, her sisters Maria and Elizabeth, and her brother Branwell.

These facts about Emily Brontë's life and death are known, but her character will always remain a mystery. Her early prose works have been lost, only three personal letters survive, and her poems give little insight to her own life. Most information about the Brontë family life and background comes from Mrs. Elizabeth Gaskell's biography of Charlotte and the autobiographical comments on which she based her work. Charlotte comments that Emily was "not a person of demonstrative character" and that she was "stronger than a man, simpler than a child." She had a nature that "stood alone." The person behind this mystery is revealed only in a reading of *Wuthering Heights*.

Analysis

Wuthering Heights is constructed around a series of dialectic motifs which interconnect and unify the elements of setting, character, and plot. An examination of these motifs will give the reader the clearest insight to the central meaning of the novel. Although *Wuthering Heights* is a "classic," as Frank Kermode points out in a recent essay, precisely because it is open to many different critical methods and conducive to many levels of interpretation, the novel grows from a coherent imaginative vision that underlies all the motifs. That vision demonstrates that all human perception is limited and failed. The fullest approach to Emily Brontë's novel is through the basic patterns that support this vision.

Wuthering Heights concerns the interactions of two families, the Earnshaws and Lintons, over three generations. The novel is set in the desolate moors of Yorkshire and covers the years from 1771 to 1803. The Earnshaws and Lintons are in harmony with their environment, but their lives are disrupted by an outsider and catalyst of change, the orphan Heathcliff. Heathcliff is, first of all, an emblem of the social problems of a nation entering the age of industrial expansion and urban growth. Although Brontë sets the action of the novel entirely within the locale familiar to her, she reminds the reader continually of the contrast between that world and the larger world outside.

Besides Heathcliff's background as a child of the streets and the description of urban Liverpool from which he is brought, there are other reminders that Yorkshire, long insulated from change and susceptible only to the forces of nature, is no longer as remote as it once was. The servant Joseph's religious cant, the class distinctions obvious in the treatment of Nelly Dean as well as of Heathcliff, and Lockwood's pseudosophisticated urban values, are all reminders that Wuthering Heights cannot remain as it has been, that religious, social, and economic change is rampant. Brontë clearly signifies in the courtship and marriage of young Cathy and Hareton that progress and enlightenment *will* come and the wilderness *will* be tamed. Heathcliff is both an embodiment of the force of this change and its victim. He brings about a change but cannot change himself. What he leaves behind, as Lockwood attests and the relationship of Cathy and Hareton verifies, is a new society, at peace with itself and its environment.

It is not necessary, however, to examine in depth the Victorian context of *Wuthering Heights* to sense the dialectic contrast of environments. Within the limited setting that the novel itself describes, society is divided between two opposing worlds, Wuthering Heights, ancestral home of the Earnshaws, and Thrushcross Grange, the Linton estate. Wuthering Heights is rustic and wild; it is open to the elements of nature and takes its name from "atmospheric tumult." The house is strong, built with narrow windows and jutting corner-stones, fortified to withstand the battering of external forces. It is identified with the outdoors and nature, and with strong, "masculine" values. Its appearance, both inside and out, is wild, untamed, disordered, and hard. The Grange expresses a more civilized, controlled atmosphere. The house is neat and orderly and there is always an abundance of light—to Brontë's mind, "feminine" values. It is not surprising that Lockwood is more comfortable at the Grange, since he takes pleasure in "feminine" behavior (gossip, vanity of appearance, adherence to social decorum, romantic self-delusion), while Heatchliff, entirely "masculine," is always out of place there.

Indeed, all of the characters reflect, to greater or lesser degrees, the masculine and feminine values of the places they inhabit. Hindley and Catherine Earnshaw are as wild and uncontrollable as the Heights: Catherine claims even to prefer her home to the pleasures of heaven. Edgar and Isabella Linton are as refined and civilized as the Grange. The marriage of Edgar and Catherine (as well as the marriage of Isabella and Heathcliff) is ill-fated from the start, not only because she does not love him, as her answers to Nelly Dean's catechism reveal, but also because each is so strongly associated with the values of his (or her) home that he lacks the opposing and necessary personality components. Catherine is too willful, wild, and strong; she expresses too much of the "masculine" side of her personality (the animus of Jungian psychology), while Edgar is weak and effeminate (the anima). They are unable to interact fully with each other because they are not complete individuals themselves. This lack leads to their failures to perceive each other's true needs.

Even Cathy's passionate cry for Heathcliff, "Nelly, I *am* Heathcliff," is less love for him as an individual than the deepest form of self-love. Cathy cannot exist without him, but a meaningful relationship is not possible, because Cathy sees Heathcliff only as a reflection of her self. Heathcliff, too, has denied an important aspect of his personality. Archetypally masculine, Heathcliff acts out only the aggressive, violent parts of himself.

The settings and the characters are patterned against each other, and explosions are the only possible results. Only Hareton and young Cathy, each of whom embodies the psychological characteristics of both Heights and Grange, can successfully sustain a mutual relationship.

This dialectic structure extends into the roles of the narrators as well. The story is reflected through the words of Nelly Dean—an inmate of both houses, a participant in the events of the narrative, and a confidante of the major characters—and Lockwood, an outsider who witnesses only the results of the characters' interactions. Nelly is a companion and servant in the Earnshaw and Linton households, and she shares many of the values and perceptions of the families. Lockwood, an urban sophisticate on retreat, misunderstands his own character as well as others'. His brief romantic "adventure" in Bath and his awkwardness when he arrives at the Heights (he thinks Cathy will fall in love with him; he mistakes the dead rabbits for puppies) exemplify his obtuseness. His perceptions are always to be questioned. Occasionally, however, even a denizen of the conventional world may gain a glimpse of the forces at work beneath the surface of reality. Lockwood's dream of the dead Cathy, which sets off his curiosity and Heathcliff's final plans, is a reminder that even the placid, normal world may be disrupted by the psychic violence of a willful personality.

The presentation of two family units and parallel brother-sister, husband-wife relationships in each also emphasizes the dialectic. That two such opposing modes of behavior could arise in the same environment prevents the reader from easy condemnation of either pair. The use of flashback for the major part of the narration—it begins *in medias res*—reminds the reader that he or she is seeing events out of their natural order, recounted by two individuals whose reliability must be questioned. The working out of the plot over three generations further suggests that no one group, much less one individual, can perceive the complexity of the human personality.

Taken together, the setting, plot, characters, and structure combine into a whole when they are seen as parts of the dialectic nature of existence. In a world where opposing forces are continually arrayed against each other in the environment, in society, in families, and in relationships, as well as within the individual, there can be no easy route to perception of another human soul. *Wuthering Heights* convincingly demonstrates the complexity of this dialectic and portrays the limitations of human perception.

Lawrence F. Laban

Other major works
POETRY: *Poems by Currer, Ellis, and Acton Bell*, 1846 (with Charlotte Brontë and Anne Brontë); *The Complete Poems of Emily Jane Brontë*, 1941 (C. W. Hatfield, editor).

Bibliography
Benvenuto, Richard. *Emily Brontë*. Boston: G. K. Hall, 1982. This examination of Emily Brontë's life and work offers some biographical material but

concentrates primarily on her writings. Attention is paid not only to *Wuthering Heights* but also to Brontë's poetry, her early essays, and her writings—with her sister Anne—concerning the imaginary land of Gondal, which Benvenuto reconstructs from the poetry and prose fragments still in existence.

Fraser, Rebecca. *The Brontës: Charlotte Brontë and Her Family.* New York: Crown, 1988. Although Fraser's central focus is Brontë's sister, Charlotte, her intelligent and exhaustively researched book offers much valuable material on Emily as well. Its portrait of the Brontës as a family evokes a vivid picture of life in the remote Yorkshire parsonage and its effect in shaping Emily's own work.

Gaskell, Elizabeth C. *The Life of Charlotte Brontë.* 1857. Reprint. London: Penguin Books, 1975. Although the central focus is Charlotte Brontë, this invaluable book is a necessary part of any thorough study of Emily. Gaskell's friendship with Charlotte provides this biography with a unique and informative perspective on the Brontës and their lives.

Hewish, John. *Emily Brontë: A Critical and Biographical Study.* New York: St. Martin's Press, 1969. Part biography and part literary analysis, this study of Brontë places her within the context of her time and society, examining her life and the critical and public reception her work received. Contains an extensive and exceptional bibliography of great use to any Brontë scholar.

Lloyd Evans, Barbara, and Gareth Lloyd Evans. *The Scribner Companion to the Brontës.* New York: Charles Scribner's Sons, 1983. Provides an overview of the Brontë family as a whole. Includes the story of the Brontës' tragic history, sections on the young Brontës' juvenilia, discussions of Charlotte, Anne, and Emily's published works, and excerpts from criticisms written about those works at the time they were first published.

Smith, Anne, ed. *The Art of Emily Brontë.* New York: Barnes & Noble Books, 1976. A collection of critical essays on Brontë's work, covering both her poetry and *Wuthering Heights*. Among the most interesting essays are Keith Sagar's comparison of Brontë and D. H. Lawrence, and Colin Wilson's thought-provoking comments on *Wuthering Heights*, which he views not as a great novel but as a "rough sketch for the masterpiece that should have followed."

Spark, Muriel, and Derek Stanford. *Emily Brontë: Her Life and Work.* New York: Coward, McCann, 1966. Acclaimed novelist Spark provides the biographical section of this study of Brontë, with Stanford supplying the analytical criticism of Brontë's work. Examines the question of how a young, unmarried woman living in isolated circumstances developed a literary style of such power and emotional passion.

ANITA BROOKNER

Born: London, England; July 16, 1938

Principal long fiction

A Start in Life, 1981 (U.S. edition, *The Debut*, 1981); *Providence*, 1982; *Look at Me*, 1983; *Hotel du Lac*, 1984; *Family and Friends*, 1985; *The Misalliance*, 1986; *A Friend from England*, 1987; *Latecomers*, 1988; *Lewis Percy*, 1989; *Brief Lives*, 1990.

Other literary forms

A distinguished historian of eighteenth and nineteenth century French art and culture, Anita Brookner wrote several books of nonfiction before she began to write novels. *Watteau* (1968) is an assessment of the early eighteenth century French artist Antoine Watteau. *The Genius of the Future, Studies in French Art Criticism: Diderot, Stendhal, Baudelaire, Zola, the Brothers Goncourt, Huysmans* (1971) is a collection of six essays on seven French writers; each writer is considered in the context of his time. The greatest space is given to Charles Baudelaire. *Greuze: The Rise and Fall of an Eighteenth-Century Phenomenon* (1972) is a study of the French painter Jean-Baptiste Greuze in a successful attempt to locate the background of a sentimental genre that is distinct from both Rococo and classicism. *Jacques-Louis David* (1980), a biography of the foremost painter of the French revolutionary period, explores the relationship between David's life and work, places that work in the context of contemporary French painting, and details a career that spanned some of the most turbulent years in French history. Brookner's translations include *Utrillo* (1960) and *The Fauves* (1962).

Achievements

Brookner suddenly began to write fiction during her middle years, while still an active teacher and scholar. Although she continued her academic career, she quickly found equal success as a novelist. With the publication of several novels, she gained an international following and widespread critical acclaim. In 1984, Great Britain's prestigious Booker Prize for fiction was awarded to *Hotel du Lac*. Brookner was praised for her elegant and precise prose, her acute sense of irony, and her subtle insights into character and social behavior. Her witty explorations of manners and morals suggest to many a literary kinship to Jane Austen and Barbara Pym. While Brookner's somber, more complex moral vision disallows any sustained comparison to Pym, Austen and Brookner undeniably share a common concern for intelligent, subtle, clever heroines who seek to satisfy both private sensibility and public expectations.

To regard Brookner's novels as simply traditional novels of manners, however, is to misconstrue her art. Brookner's intentions greatly exceed this conventional genre; her achievements, indeed, take her far beyond it. Perhaps it is more useful to note the singularity of her contribution to British letters. Her highly developed pictorial sense; her baroque diction, with its balance of reason and passion; and her allusive, richly textured narratives, haunting in their resonances, reflect at every turn her extensive knowledge of the materials and motifs of eighteenth and nineteenth century paintings and literature.

Her works have been generously admired, but some dissenting voices have been raised. She is occasionally brought to task for fictive worlds too narrow in scope and claustrophobic in their intensity, for overzealous, self-conscious, schematic fiction, and for excessive sentimentality that unfortunately evokes the pulp romance. Brookner's worlds, however, are invariably shaped toward significant moral revelations; technique rarely intrudes to the detriment of story; and her ability to maintain an ironic distance from her characters, one that allows her to reveal sentimentality, to make judgments dispassionately, is one of her greatest strengths as a writer.

Biography

Anita Brookner was born in London, England, on July 16, 1938, to Newsom and Maude Brookner. She was educated at James Allen's Girls' School; King's College, University of London; and received a Ph.D. in art history from the Courtauld Institute of Art in London. From 1959 to 1964, she was visiting lecturer at the University of Reading, Berkshire. In 1968, she was Slade Professor at Cambridge University, the first woman to hold this position. From 1977 to 1987 she taught at the Courtauld Institute of Art, where she lectured on neoclassicism and the Romantic movement. Her fiction career thus far has been crowned by the award of the Booker Prize. Brookner now lives in London.

Analysis

Anita Brookner established her reputation as a novelist with four books published in rapid succession between 1981 and 1984. Written in austerely elegant prose, each of these four novels follows essentially the same course. Each centers on a scholarly, sensitive, morally earnest young woman who leads an attenuated life. None of these heroines has intended a life so circumscribed. As their stories begin, they seek change, liberation from boredom and loneliness. They seek connection to a wider world. While these women are intelligent, endlessly introspective, and possessed of a saving ironic wit, they do not know how to get the things they most desire: the love of, and marriage to, a man of quality. With compassion, rue, and infinite good humor, Brookner makes it abundantly clear that these worthy women, these good daughters, good writers, and good scholars are unknowing adherents to a romantic ideal. Like the shopgirls and "ultra-feminine" women they gaze upon with such wonder and awe, these intellectually and morally superior women accept without question the cultural assumption that marriage is a woman's greatest good. Consistently undervaluing their own considerable talents and professional achievements, these heroines look to love and marriage as a way of joining the cosmic dance of a rational, well-ordered society. Their intense yearning for a transforming love shapes their individual plots; in each case, the conflict between what the romantic imagination wants and what it indeed does get impels these narratives forward. Brookner's concern is to illuminate the worthiness, the loneliness, the longing of these heroines for love and a more splendid life.

Before their stories can end, these women must abandon sentiment and accept their solitary state. Their triumph lies in their ability to confront their fall from romantic innocence and recognize it for what it is. These novels build inexorably toward an ending that is both startling and profoundly moving. While Brookner's heroines must struggle with sentimentality, Brookner herself does not. Her vision is bleak, unsparing. In telling their stories, she raises several other themes: The most notable of these are filial obligation, the "romantic" versus the "realistic" apprehension of life, truth and its relationship to self-knowledge, the determination of proper behavior in society, and the small pleasures that attend the trivia of daily life. Brookner presents her major and minor themes against the background of fictive worlds so powerfully realized that her novels seem to be absorbed as much as read. These are novels of interior reality. Little that is overt happens; dramatic action rests in the consciousness of the heroine, who is always center stage.

Brookner's first novel, *The Debut*, lacks the richness and gradation of tone that marks her later fiction, but is nevertheless well crafted. Set against Honoré de Balzac's *Eugénie Grandet* (1833; English translation, 1859), *The Debut* tells the story of Ruth Weiss, a scrupulous, thoughtful scholar, who finds herself at forty with a life "ruined" by literature. A passionate reader from an early age, now a professor of literature specializing in Balzac, Ruth leads a narrow life alternating between teaching students and caring for an aging father. She blames the tradition of filial duty she found in literature for her mostly cheerless state.

Like Frances Hinton of *Look at Me* and Kitty Maule of *Providence*, Ruth began with expectations. In her youth, she once cast aside the burden of an oppressive heritage, one best symbolized by the deep silence and heavy, dark furniture in the mausoleum of a house she shared with her parents, and had fled England for France. Ostensibly, her goal was to write a dissertation on vice and virtue; in actuality, it was as much to seek air and space and light. Although she at first endured a sense of displacement, exile, a condition that at one time or another afflicts many of Brookner's heroines, over time Ruth's transplant into foreign soil proved successful. Away from her charming, eccentric, but infinitely demanding parents, Ruth flourished. She acquired polish, sophistication, lovers. Yet even as she gloried in her new life, Ruth, like many of Brookner's other heroines, engaged in a constant internal debate over the question of how life is best lived. Does vice or virtue bring victory? She concluded that a life of conventional virtue can spell disaster for one's hopes; regretfully, Balzacian opportunism cannot be discounted. It is better to be a bad winner than a poor loser. Even though she observed that conventional morality tales were wrong, however, Ruth lamented the triumph of vice.

Suddenly called back to England because of what proves to be a final deterioration in her mother's fragile health, Ruth is forced to leave the comfortable, satisfying life she built for herself. Her spirited adventure over, Ruth is unable to extricate herself once more. At forty, the long and beautiful red hair indicative of her youthful potential for rebellion now compressed into a tight chignon, Dr. Ruth Weiss is a felon recaptured. She is tender with her father, gentle with her students, and expects little more from life. She is the first of Brookner's heroines who learns to renounce. Ruth's story is told retrospectively, in a way that recalls the French novel of meditation. The bold configurations of her story suggest the quality of a fable. The narrative also gains a necessary solidity and weight by the many allusions to Balzacian characters and texts. These allusions create a substructure of irony that continues to reverberate long after Ruth's story is complete.

If Ruth is disheartened but finally resigned, Kitty Maule in *Providence*, Brookner's second novel, moves toward outright disillusionment. Kitty is also a professor of literature. Her interests lie in the Romantic movement; this novel, then, like the rest of Brookner's fiction, is filled with ideas, good talk, vigorous intellectual exchanges. Here, both Kitty's private musings and her running seminar on Benjamin Constant's *Adolphe* (1816) provide a context for the exploration of Romantic concerns. Brookner's use of Kitty as a teacher of the Romantic tradition is ultimately highly ironic, for Kitty cannot discern her own romanticism. Curiously, she has moments when she is almost able to see her romanticism for what it is. Yet in the end, she suppresses the would-be insights and retreats into her dreams and passionate longings. What Kitty longs for is love, marriage, and, perhaps, God. Her longing for God goes largely unrecognized; like her fellow Romantics, she requires a sign. Yet her longing for love, the love of one man in particular, is at the perceived center of her life.

The handsome, brilliant, but distant lover of the scholarly, sensitive woman in this novel is Maurice Bishop. Maurice, a professor of medieval history, is noted for his love of cathedrals and God. Wellborn, rich, confident in the manner of those accustomed to deference, Maurice is everything that Kitty wants in life: He is the very cultural ideal of England itself. To be his wife is Kitty's hope of heaven; to capture him, she brings to bear all of her weapons at hand: subtle intelligence, grace of manners, enduring patience, and abiding love. That Kitty's love for Maurice has the fervor of a religious acolyte is suggested by his surname. Maurice may be in love with the idea of a religious absolute, but Kitty's religion is romantic love. All of her repressed romanticism is focused in this elegant, remote man.

Kitty's extreme dependence upon Maurice as the repository of her hopes and dreams stems in large part from her sense of cultural displacement. The child of a French mother and a British father, both dead in their youth, Kitty was born in England and brought up there by her immigrant French grandparents. Despite her British birth, however, Kitty never feels at home in England. In the face of concerted and varied efforts to "belong," she retains a sense of exile. Nor is she truly considered English by her colleagues and acquaintances. The product of her doting French grandparents, Kitty is unaware of her true cultural allegiance; ironically, it is the French heritage that dominates in her English setting. Her manners, clothes, and speech belie her English father. In Maurice, Kitty seeks an attachment that anchors, a place to be. Here and elsewhere in Brookner's fiction, the recurrent theme of the search for a home acquires the force and weight of myth. So powerfully realized is Kitty's intense desire for love, acceptance, and liberation from loneliness that it comes as a shock when Kitty, who is expecting Maurice's proposal of marriage, instead learns of his sudden engagement to a woman who shares his aristocratic background. The novel concludes with Kitty's realization that she had indeed lived in a haze of romantic expectation; the truth is, she has been first, last, and always an outsider.

In addition to the major theme of the passive, excellent, but self-deceived young woman in the service of an illusory ideal, Brookner presents in *Providence* themes which are relevant to all of her works. Maurice's betrayal of Kitty, for example, establishes a motif that recurs in later novels, while Brookner's superbly comic depiction of bored and boring academics, a staple in her fiction, reaches perhaps its finest statement here. If Balzacian allusions underlie *The Debut* and give it additional power, allusions to many French writers, but especially to Constant's *Adolphe* are used to provide ironic commentary on and foreshadowings of Kitty's fate. Most important, however, Kitty Maule herself is arguably the quintessential Brooknerian heroine. Like her fictional sisters, Ruth Weiss of *The Debut*, Frances Hinton of *Look at Me*, Edith Hope of *Hotel du Lac*, and Mimi Dorn of *Family and Friends*, Kitty waits patiently for her life to begin. She is blind to her own worth and discounts her singular achievements; longs for order, a place in a rational world; finds joy in the chores, duties, and routines of everyday life; is sensitive, compassionate, morally deserving. Finally, her final inevitable loss of a man morally her inferior leaves her stripped of all romantic illusions, a convert to reality.

By her own admission a relentless observer, Frances Hinton, the heroine of *Look at Me*, Brookner's third novel, tells her own compelling story. To be sure, all of Brookner's heroines are detached observers, though probably none records and stores information so clinically as does Frances. All of Brookner's heroines suffer, yet perhaps none suffers more intensely than Frances. Like other Brooknerian heroines, Frances is virtuous, sensitive, bright, and in need of a more marvelous life. Like other Brooknerian heroines also, she does not know how to get the things she wants. Frozen into inaction, her intense melancholia is mirrored in the images of death and desolation that surround her. A medical librarian who catalogs prints and engravings of Disease Through the Ages, Frances comments ironically on the scenes of madness, nightmare affliction, and death she must sort and mount. She lives in a tomb of a house where her mother has died; Brookner's use of Frances' house recalls her uses of houses elsewhere: They are symbols of oppressive traditions that constrain and weigh heavily upon those who inhabit them. For Frances, the world is somber, dark. The glittering, stylish couple who offer temporary access to a dazzling social world prove cruelly false. In an act of betrayal so profound that Frances cannot but withdraw from the world she has long sought, the beautiful Nick and Alix Fraser hold Frances up to public ridicule. Her brief liberation from solitariness and the eternal prison of self ends abruptly. Always self-analytic, self-deprecatory, Frances blames her failure to find a place in the world as a failure of egotism or will. She observes that others advance through egotism, but she cannot mimic them. She decides to become a writer. Writing will allow her both to comment on life and to retreat from it.

As is usual in Brookner's works, the dramatic action is largely inner. Hers are novels of the interior; the terrain surveyed is that of the soul. Frances presents a commanding narrative voice as she sorts, gathers, and finally reassembles the fragments of her experience into a unified whole. In fullest voice, she provides useful insights into the processes of the creative, transforming imagination. From the detritus of her daily life she, as writer-at-work, will abstract significant form. If Brookner here provides a mirror of herself busy fashioning art from the materials of the ordinary, the details of eating or dressing or chatting that receive so much attention in her novels, she also repeats the characteristic fusion of the comic and the sad that lends such poignancy to her works. Further, the influence of the pictorial is reflected here as well; characters are often framed in an action, presented with a consciousness of scene or setting. Finally, Frances' long commentary on her experience that is the text of *Look at Me* again evokes the French novel of meditation, a literary form that subtly influences and pervades Brookner's fiction. Notably, as Frances begins to write on the last page of the novel, she is free of self-pity. Solitude may be her lot, but art will vindicate her. Art will represent the triumph of the unvanquished self.

Edith Hope, the heroine of *Hotel du Lac*, Brookner's fourth novel and the winner of the 1984 Booker Prize, is also a writer. Edith writes pulp romances for a living. Yet until she learns better, she believes that romance is only her business, not her frame of mind. Brookner's fiction, however, reveals her tendency sometimes to use names to signal character traits or habits of thought. Such is the case here: Edith is indeed a romantic, although an unknowing one. Edith begins her stay at the Hotel du Lac in ignorance of her true nature; she leaves enlightened as to the deeper, more recessed aspects of her moral being.

It was not Edith's choice to leave England and travel to Switzerland, the setting of *Hotel du Lac*. Edith was sent away because of her severe breach of social decorum: She chose not to appear at her own wedding, thus profoundly humiliating a good man and eminently suitable husband. Her action was shocking to all, including Edith herself. Modest, unassuming, and usually anxious to please, Edith is in many ways a typical Brooknerian heroine. She, too, spends too much time alone, condemned to her own introspection. Her marriage would have broken that isolation. Edith's revolt and subsequent removal to Switzerland provide a context for the discussion of numerous moral and psychological questions. While Edith's story is always foremost, the novel itself alternates between first- and third-person narratives, with philosophical positions being argued, accepted, or dismissed. The central fact that emerges about Edith is her passionate love for a married man whom she only seldom sees. Like his fictional predecessors, Edith's David is exceedingly handsome, elegant, intelligent, and remote. For love of him, Edith jilted her dull but safe fiancé. At the Hotel du Lac, Edith's interactions with the other residents move her to a greater understanding of truth, self-knowledge, and the differences between romance and reality. Numerous other themes are present here as well, including that of "ultrafeminine" as opposed to "feminist" women. Edith understands these women as models of feminine response to feminine experience. In relative isolation at this Swiss hotel, she studies these models and rejects both. The will to power, the utility of egotism as a serviceable instrument in the world, a recurrent Brooknerian theme, also receives much discussion here.

What Edith eventually learns as she evaluates her exchanges and relationships with her fellow guests is accorded significant status by the mythological underpinnings of this novel. Inside the hotel, characters are both particular and types, acting out self-assigned roles in a grand comedy of manners. All the inhabitants exhibit a theatrical sense of themselves; they "present" themselves to this community consciously, deliberately. Such attention to the pictorial, personal presentation is a constant of Brookner's fiction. The details of clothes, manners, and mannerisms convey aspects of self and morality in Brookner's works as they do in the works of Henry James, to whom Brookner alludes in this novel. If inside the hotel the characters are on parade, making their statements with dress, or gesture, once outside the hotel, they are subsumed to the mythicized landscape. Gray mist, conveying a sense of menace and oppression, surrounds everything. Characters make journeys that are important only for their mythic impact. Much movement against this drear landscape takes place as characters are directed toward crucial, definitive moral choices. The landscape helps Edith to perceive her dilemmas; she is finally able to reject a diabolical figure, who offers marriage without love. He forces Edith to recognize her romanticism for what it is. At least in the end, however, when she returns to England and her married lover, Edith knows that she has chosen a cold and solitary path. Her self-determination represents a triumph for her and for this book. Edith is finally transformed by her successful journey to knowledge.

Having laid claim with her first four novels to a sharply defined fictional territory, Brookner has shown in subsequent books a willingness to extend her range. In *Latecomers*, for example, she centers her story for the first time on two male figures—close friends both of whom were refugees brought from Germany to England as children during World War II. *Lewis Percy* features a single protagonist, again a man, in some ways the counterpart of Brookner's earlier heroines.

The book with which Brookner departed most radically from the pattern established in her first four novels was *Family and Friends;* perhaps because it violated readers' expectations, it was sharply criticized by some reviewers. Written in the historical present with virtually no dialogue, *Family and Friends* is an extended meditation on the French tradition. It stems from the ruminations of a narrator who quickly disappears, makes only glancing reappearances, and is curiously never identified. Here, Brookner's concern is not with a particular heroine, but with the Dorn family, rich, most likely German immigrants who fled to England before the start of World War II. The war, when it comes, receives but scant attention; the novel focuses always on the small, interior world of the Dorn family. Little seems to exist outside the family and their immediate interests, sparking again charges of a work too narrow in range.

The lives of the Dorn family and their associates are followed over a period of time. Sofka, the gentle but strong matriarch of the family, is the moral center of the work. Widowed early in life, she rejects the idea of remarriage, directing her loving attentions to her family, instead. Mimi and Betty are her two daughters. While Betty is selfish, willful, theatrical, tricking her family into giving her an independent life quite early, she is nevertheless the child Sofka secretly loves best. Sofka, beautiful and contained, admires her younger daughter's spirit. Mimi is virtuous, dreamy, passive, frozen into inertia in young womanhood when an early feeble attempt to reach out for love was unsuccessful. Mimi languishes for years afterward, until her mother urges her into marriage, and thereby respectability, with a gentle, good man who would normally be her social inferior. Also playing a significant part in the novel are Sofka's two sons: the sensitive, intelligent, responsible Alfred and his handsome, charming brother Frederick. Interestingly, it is Alfred's plight that mirrors the situation of the usual Brooknerian heroine. It is he who is trapped by filial obligation into a life he had not intended; it is he who suffers forever afterward from an unsatisfying search for love and a desire for a larger, more extended world. It is also he who ultimately becomes inured to long-established habits of insularity.

This, then, is the saga of a family whose interior lives and moral relations are acutely realized. Important themes here include familial relations, especially filial obligation; the search for a transcendent love; the need to venture, to dare, if one is to "win" in life. Structured around four wedding pictures, the novel impresses with its unity and intensity of tone; the pervasive, elegant irony; the discerning moral judgments; and the engrossing character portraits. Especially effective also is the novel's lament for the loss of youthful promise, energy, and innocence. The once-vibrant Betty, trapped in middle-aged stasis, is a case in point. Dominating this entire work is a rich narrative voice, stern, compassionate, and often sad. The Dorn family seems to exist in a twilight, dreamlike world outside time. Yet this world, while admittedly narrow, is nevertheless mesmerizing.

Brookner's novels have brought her remarkable success within a very short time. Her taut, spare narratives share distinctive qualities: grace, precision, and elegance of language; ironic commentaries on character and social behavior that both instruct and delight; a tone compounded of the comic and the melancholy; and a moral vision that is both rigorous and compassionate.

Betty H. Jones

Other major works

NONFICTION: *Watteau*, 1968; *The Genius of the Future, Studies in French Art Criticism: Diderot, Stendhal, Baudelaire, Zola, the Brothers Goncourt, Huysmans*, 1971; *Greuze: The Rise and Fall of an Eighteenth-Century Phenomenon*, 1972; *Jacques-Louis David*, 1980.

TRANSLATIONS: *Utrillo*, 1960 (of Waldemar George's biography); *The Fauves*, 1962 (of Jean Paul Crespelle's book).

Bibliography

Haffenden, John. *Novelists in Interview*. London: Methusen, 1985. Includes a lively interview with Anita Brookner (pages 57-75) in which she discusses her novels, the ideas behind her writing, and the existential dilemmas of her characters. A substantial interview that provides a useful background to her works.

Kenyon, Olga. *Women Novelists Today*. New York: St. Martin's Press, 1988.

This current, interesting criticism includes a chapter on Brookner entitled "Anita Brookner and the Women's Novel." Analyzes Brookner's six novellas and how they deal with femininity and romance, as well as the effect of unconscious images of self on conscious behavior. Also looks at the influences of the eighteenth and nineteenth centuries on Brookner's work.

Lasdun, James. "Pre-Modern, Post Modernist." *Encounter* 64 (February, 1985): 42. Lasdun reviews several authors, including Brookner, whom he places in the premodern genre. This is essentially a review of *Hotel du Lac*. While acknowledging Brookner's almost flawless construction and her critical acclaim for this work, Lasdun is not won over by what he terms Brookner's traditional feminine themes, which he believes are out of step with contemporary thought.

Sadler, Lynn Veach. *Anita Brookner*. Boston: Twayne, 1990. The first and only full-length study to date of Brookner's work, which discusses her seven novels. Sadler compares Brookner to Barbara Pym and Margaret Drabble but also shows why Brookner has her own voice in feminist fiction. Analyzes Brookner's heroines and gives insight into the author's use of irony. A fine study on Brookner and an essential resource.

Samarth, Manimi Mayar. "The Internalized Narrative: A Study of Lyricism and Irony in the Novels of Anita Desai and Anita Brookner." *DAI* 49 (September, 1988): 513A. Compares the irony with which Brookner portrays her heroines to the lyricism of Desai's work.

Schlueter, Paul, and June Schlueter, eds. *An Encyclopedia of British Women Writers*. New York: Garland, 1988. A brief but valuable introduction to Brookner's writing, as well as her expertise in art history. Traces Brookner's development as a writer, showing that her mastery of technical elements has increased. Mentions *Family and Friends* as a novel that is "rich and robust, full-bodied and sparkling"—marking a departure for Brookner from the critics' label of autobiographical writer.

CHARLES BROCKDEN BROWN

Born: Philadelphia, Pennsylvania; January 17, 1771
Died: Philadelphia, Pennsylvania; February 22, 1810

Principal long fiction

Wieland: Or, The Transformation, 1798; *Ormond: Or, The Secret Witness*, 1799; *Arthur Mervyn: Or, Memoirs of the Year 1793, Part I*, 1799; *Edgar Huntly: Or, Memoirs of a Sleep-Walker*, 1799; *Arthur Mervyn: Or, Memoirs of the Year 1793, Part II*, 1800; *Clara Howard: In a Series of Letters*, 1801; *Jane Talbot: A Novel*, 1801.

Other literary forms

Charles Brockden Brown published two parts of a dialogue on the rights of women, *Alcuin*, in 1798; the last two sections appeared in William Dunlap's 1815 biography of Brown. Brown's later political and historical essays have not been collected but remain in their original magazine and pamphlet publications. Several fictional fragments appear in *Carwin, the Biloquist, and Other American Tales and Pieces* (1822) and in the Dunlap biography, notably the Carwin story and "Memoirs of Stephen Calvert." Several collected editions of his novels were published in the nineteenth century. Harry Warfel's edition of *The Rhapsodist and Other Uncollected Writings* (1943) completes the publication of most of Brown's literary works. Letters have appeared in scattered books and essays, but they are not yet collected. *Wieland and Memoirs of Carwin*, the first volume in the definitive edition of Brown's fiction underway at Kent State University Press, appeared in 1977.

Achievements

The significant portion of Brown's literary career lasted little more than a year, from 1798 to 1800, during which he published the four novels for which he is best known: *Wieland, Ormond, Arthur Mervyn*, and *Edgar Huntly*. Though his career began with the essays comprising "The Rhapsodist" in 1789 and continued until his death, most of his other fiction, poetry, and prose is thought to be of minor importance.

Brown's literary reputation rests heavily on his historical position as one of the first significant American novelists. An English reviewer, quoted by Bernard Rosenthal in *Critical Essays on Charles Brockden Brown* (1981), wrote in 1824 that Brown "was the first writer of prose fiction of which America could boast." Brown's contemporaries recognized his abilities and he received praise from William Godwin, John Keats, and Percy Bysshe Shelley. Though his American reputation remained unsteady, he was read by nineteenth century novelists such as James Fenimore Cooper, Edgar Allan Poe, and Herman Melville. In the twentieth century, scholars and advanced students of American culture are his most frequent readers; they have rediscovered him in part because his concerns with identity and choice in a disordered world prefigure or initiate some of the major themes of American fiction.

Brown's four best-known novels begin the peculiarly American mutation of the Gothic romance. There are similarities between his novels and the political Gothic of Godwin and the sentimental Gothic of Ann Radcliffe, but Brown's adaptations of Gothic conventions for the exploration of human psychology, the analysis of the mind choosing under stress, and the representation of a truly incomprehensible world suggest that he may be an important bridge between the popular Gothic tradition of eighteenth century England and the American Gothic strain which is traceable through Poe, Melville, and Nathaniel Hawthorne to Henry James, William Faulkner, and such late twentieth century novelists as Joyce Carol Oates.

Biography

Born on January 17, 1771, Charles Brockden Brown was the fifth son of Elijah Brown and Mary Armitt Brown. Named after a relative who was a well-known Philadelphia official, Brown grew up in an intellectual Quaker family where the works of contemporary radicals such as Godwin and Mary Wollstonecraft were read, even though they were unacceptable by society's norms. Brown's health was never good; his parents tended to protect him from an active boy's life and to encourage his reading. When he was eleven, he began his formal education at the Friends' Latin School in Philadelphia under Robert Proud, a renowned teacher and scholar who later wrote *The History of Pennsylvania* (1797). Proud encouraged Brown to strengthen his constitution by taking walks in the country similar to those Edgar Huntly takes with Sarsefield in *Edgar Huntly*. After five or six years in Latin School, Brown began the study of law under Alexander Willcocks (variously spelled), a prominent Philadelphia lawyer. Though he studied law for five or six years until 1792 or 1793, he never practiced. During Brown's years studying law, he taught himself French and increasingly leaned toward literary work. He became a member of the Belles Lettres Club, which met to discuss current literary and intellectual topics. In 1789, he published his first work, "The Rhapsodist," in the *Columbian Magazine*. In 1790, he met and became friends with Elihu Hubbard Smith of Litchfield, Connecticut, a medical student with literary interests. Smith encouraged Brown's literary aspirations, helping to draw him away from law. Brown's acquaintance with Smith brought him to New York City in 1794 where he came to know the members of the Friendly Club, a group of young New York intellectuals, one of whom was to be his first biographer, William Dunlap.

During this period, Brown wrote poetry, and by 1795 he had begun a novel. He began active publishing in 1798 in the Philadelphia *Weekly Magazine*. In the summer of 1798, when he was visiting Smith in New York, he published *Wieland*. Smith died at his work during the yellow fever outbreak of that summer; Brown also became ill, but recovered. In 1799, Brown suddenly became an extremely busy writer. He published two novels and part of a third and also began *The Monthly Magazine and American Review*. In 1800, he published the second half of *Arthur Mervyn*, abandoned his magazine, and joined his brothers in business. After publishing his last two novels in 1801, he turned to political and historical writing. His 1803 pamphlet on the Louisiana Territory was widely read and provoked debate in Congress. In 1803, he began another magazine, *The Literary Magazine and American Register*, which lasted until 1806. His final magazine venture was *The American Register: Or, General Repository of History, Politics, and Science* (1807-1810). He was working on a geography publication when he died on February 22, 1810, of tuberculosis, a disease which had pursued him most of his life.

Brown's personal and intellectual life are known primarily through his writings. He married Elizabeth Linn on November 19, 1804, and his family eventually included three sons and a daughter. There is evidence that Brown entertained the liberal Quaker ideas of his parents, the Deism of Smith, and the ideas of the English radicals at various times. His dialogue on the rights of women, *Alcuin*, advocates sound education and political equality for women and, in the two posthumously published parts, even suggests a utopian state of absolute social equality between the sexes in which there would be no marriage. Though he entertained such radical ideas in his youth, Brown seems to have become more conservative with maturity, affirming in his later works the importance of reason and religion in living a good life.

Analysis

Charles Brockden Brown's aims in writing, aside from attempting to earn a living, are a matter of debate among critics. In his Preface to *Edgar Huntly*, he makes the conventional claim of novelists of the time, that writing is "amusement to the fancy and instruction to the heart," but he also argues the importance as well as the richness of American materials:

> One merit the writer may at least claim:—that of calling forth the passions and engaging the sympathy of the reader by means hitherto unemployed by preceding authors. Puerile superstition and exploded manners, Gothic castles and chimeras, are the material usually employed for this end. The incidents of Indian hostility, the perils of the Western wilderness, are far more suitable; and for a native of America to overlook these would admit of no apology.

This statement suggests several elements of Brown's primary achievement, the development of Gothic conventions for the purposes of exploring the human mind in moments of ethically significant decision. Such an achievement was important for its example to later American novelists.

Brown's novels are like William Godwin's in their use of radical contemporary thought; they are like Ann Radcliffe's in that they continue the tradition of the rationalized Gothic. Brown, however, proves in some ways to be less radical than Godwin, and his fictional worlds differ greatly from Radcliffe's. Brown brings into his novels current intellectual debates about education, psychology and reason, epistemology, ethics and religion. Characters who hold typical attitudes find themselves in situations which thoroughly test their beliefs. The novels do not seem especially didactic; they are rather more like Radcliffe's romances in form. A central character or group undergoes a crisis which tests education and belief. Brown's novels tend to be developmental, but the world he presents is so ambiguous and disorderly that the reader is rarely certain that a character's growth really fits him better for living.

This ambiguity is only one of the differences which makes Brown appear, in retrospect at least, to be an Americanizer of the Gothic. In one sense, his American settings are of little significance, since they are rather simple equivalents of the castle grounds and wildernesses of an Otranto or Udolpho; on the other hand, these settings are recognizable and much more familiar to an American reader. Rather than emphasizing the exoticism of the Gothic, Brown increases the immediacy of his tales by using an American setting. He also increases immediacy and the intensity of his stories by setting them close to his readers in time. Even though his novels are usually told in retrospect by the kinds of first-person narrators who would come to dominate great American fiction, the narratives frequently lapse into the present tense at crises, the narrators becoming transfixed by the renewed contemplation of past terrors. Brown avoids the supernatural; even though his novels are filled with the inexplicable, they do not feature the physical acts of supernatural beings. For example, Clara Wieland dreams prophetic dreams which prove accurate, but the apparently supernatural voices which waking people hear are hallucinatory or are merely the work of Carwin, the ventriloquist. All of these devices for reducing the distance between reader and text contribute to the success of his fast-paced if sometimes over-complicated plots, but they also reveal Brown's movement away from Radcliffe's rationalized Gothic toward the kind of realism that would come to dominate American fiction in the next century.

Perhaps Brown's most significant contribution to the Americanization of the Gothic romance is his representation of the human mind as inadequate to its world. Even the best minds in his works fall victim to internal and external assaults, and people avoid or fall into disaster seemingly by chance. In Radcliffe's fictional world, Providence actively promotes poetic justice; if the hero or heroine persists in rational Christian virtue and holds to his or her faith that the world is ultimately orderly, then weaknesses and error, villains and accidents will be overcome and justice will prevail. In Brown, there are no such guarantees. At the end of *Wieland*, Clara, the narrator, reflects: "If Wieland had framed juster notions of moral duty, and of the divine attributes; or if I had been gifted with ordinary equanimity or foresight, the double-tongued deceiver would have been baffled and repelled." Clara's moralizing is, in fact, useless, even to herself. She was not so "gifted"; therefore, she could never have escaped the catastrophes which befell her. Furthermore, she persists in seeing Carwin, the double-tongued deceiver, as a devil who ruined her brother, even though Carwin is no more than a peculiarly gifted and not very moral human being. Clara is able to moralize in this way only because, for the time being, disasters do not threaten her. Placed once again in the situation in which she completed the first portion of her narrative, she would again reject all human comfort and wish for death. Brown's fictional worlds defy human comprehension and make ethical actions excessively problematic.

This apparent irony in *Wieland* illustrates a final significant development in Brown's adaptation of the Gothic romance. Though it is difficult, given his sometimes clumsy work, to be certain of what he intends, Brown seems to have experimented with point of view in ways which foreshadow later works. *Arthur Mervyn*, written in two parts, seems a deliberate experiment in multiple points of view. Donald Ringe points out that while the first part, told primarily from Mervyn's point of view, emphasizes Mervyn's naïve victimization by a sophisticated villain, the second part, told from a more objective point of view, suggests that Mervyn may unconsciously be a moral chameleon and confidence man. This shifting of point of view to capture complexity or create irony reappears in the works of many major American novelists, notably in Herman Melville's "Benito Cereno" and in William Faulkner.

By focusing on the mind dealing with crises in an ambiguous world, making his stories more immediate, and manipulating point of view for ironic effect, Brown helps to transform popular Gothic conventions into tools for the more deeply psychological American Gothic fiction which would follow.

Clara Wieland, the heroine of *Wieland*, is a bridge between the Gothic heroine of Radcliffe and a line of American Gothic victims stretching from Edgar Allan Poe's narrators in his tales of terror through Henry James's governess in *The Turn of the Screw* (1898) to Faulkner's Temple Drake and beyond. Most of her life is idyllic until she reaches her early twenties, when she encounters a series of catastrophes which, it appears, will greatly alter her benign view of life. When her disasters are three years behind her and she has married the man she loves, Clara returns to her view that the world is reasonably orderly and that careful virtue will pull one through all difficulties.

The novel opens with an account of the Wieland family curse on the father's side. Clara's father, an orphaned child of a German nobleman cast off by his family because of a rebellious marriage, grows up apprenticed to an English merchant. Deprived of family love and feeling an emptiness in his spiritual isolation, he finds meaning when he chances upon a book of a radical Protestant sect. In consequence, he develops an asocial and paranoid personal faith which converts his emptiness into an obligation. He takes upon himself certain duties which will make him worthy of the god he has created. These attitudes dominate his life and lead eventually to his "spontaneous combustion" in his private temple on the estate he has developed in America. The spiritual and psychological causes of this disaster arise in part from his guilt at failing to carry out some command of his personal deity, perhaps the successful conversion of American Indians to Christianity, the project which brought him to America. Clara's uncle presents this "scientific" explanation of her father's death and, much later in the novel, tells a story indicating that such religious madness has also occurred on her mother's side of the family. Religious madness is the familial curse which falls upon Clara's immediate family: Theodore Wieland, her brother; his wife, Catharine; their children and a ward; and Catharine's brother, Pleyel, whom Clara comes to love.

The madness strikes Theodore Wieland; he believes he hears the voice of God commanding him to sacrifice his family if he is to be granted a vision of God. He succeeds in killing all except Pleyel and Clara. The first half of the novel leads up to his crimes and the second half deals primarily with Clara's discoveries about herself and the world as she learns more details about the murders. Clara's ability to deal with this catastrophe is greatly complicated by events that prove to be essentially unrelated to it, but which coincide with it. In these events, the central agent is Carwin.

Carwin is a ventriloquist whose background is explained in a separate short fragment, "Memoirs of Carwin the Biloquist." Because ventriloquism is an art virtually unknown in Clara's world, Carwin seems monstrous to her. As he explains to Clara near the end of the novel, he has been lurking about the Wieland estate and his life has touched on theirs in several ways. He has used his art to avoid being detected in his solitary night explorations of the grounds. The apparently supernatural voices he has created may have contributed to the unsettling of Theodore Wieland, but Wieland's own account during his trial indicates other more powerful causes of his madness. Much more dangerous to Clara has been Carwin's affair with her housekeeper, Judith, for by this means he has come to see Clara as a flower of human virtue and intellect. He is tempted to test her by creating the illusion that murderers are killing Judith in Clara's bedroom closet. This experiment miscarries, leading Clara to think she is the proposed victim. He later uses a "supernatural" voice which accidentally coincides with one of her prophetic dreams; though his purpose is to frighten her away from the place of his meetings with Judith, Carwin confirms Clara's fears and superstitions. He pries into her private diary and concocts an elaborate lie about his intention to rape her when he is caught. Out of envy and spite and because he is able, Carwin deceives

Pleyel into thinking that Clara has surrendered her honor to him.

Throughout these deceptions, Carwin also fosters in Clara the superstition that a supernatural being is watching over and protecting her by warning her of dangers. Carwin's acts are essentially pranks; he never intends as much harm as actually occurs when his actions become threads in a complex net of causality. The worst consequence of his pranks is that Pleyel is convinced that Clara has become depraved just at the moment when she hopes that he will propose marriage, and this consequence occurs because Carwin over-estimates Pleyel's intelligence. Pleyel's accusation of Clara is quite serious for her because it culminates the series of dark events which Clara perceives as engulfing her happy life. Carwin's scattered acts have convinced her that rapists and murderers lurk in every dark corner and that she is the center of some impersonal struggle between forces of good and evil. Pleyel's accusation also immediately precedes her brother's murders. These two crises nearly destroy Clara's reason and deprive her of the will to live.

The attack on Clara's mind is, in fact, the central action of the novel. All the Gothic shocks come to focus on her perception of herself. They strip her of layers of identity until she is reduced to a mere consciousness of her own integrity, a consciousness which is then challenged when she comes to understand the nature of her brother's insanity. When all the props of her identity have been shaken, she wishes for death. Tracing her progress toward the wish for death reveals the central thematic elements of the novel.

The attack on Clara's mind is generated from poles represented by her brother and Pleyel. Wieland crumbles from within and Pleyel is deceived by external appearances. Each falls prey to the weakness to which he is most susceptible. Clara's more stable mind is caught in the midst of these extremes. Theodore Wieland has the family temperament, the tendency to brood in isolation over his spiritual state and over "last things." Pleyel is the gay and optimistic rationalist, skeptical of all religious ideas, especially any belief in modern supernatural agencies. While Wieland trusts his inner voice above all, Pleyel places absolute faith in his senses. Both are certain of their powers to interpret their experience accurately and both are wrong on all counts. Wieland sees what he wants to see and Pleyel's senses are easily deceived, especially by the skillful Carwin. Wieland interprets his visions as divine revelations even though they command murder, and Pleyel believes Clara is polluted even though such a belief is inconsistent with his lifelong knowledge of her.

Clara's sense of identity first suffers when her idyllic world begins to slip away. Her world becomes a place of unseen and unaccountable danger. As her anxiety increases, she finds herself unable to reason about her situation. Brown shows this disintegration in one of his more famous scenes, when Clara comes to believe there is someone in her closet, yet persists in trying to enter it even though she has heard the murderers there and even after her protecting voice has warned her away. Critics take various attitudes toward this scene, which prolongs the reader's wait to learn who is in the closet in order to follow minutely Clara's thoughts and reactions. Brown creates suspense which some critics have judged overwrought, but his main purpose is clearly the close analysis of a strong mind coming apart under great pressure. Even though Pleyel's mistakes emphasize the inadequacy of individual rationality to the complexity of the world, that faculty remains the isolated person's only means of active defense. As Clara's rationality disintegrates, her helplessness increases.

Seeing her world divide into a war between good and evil in which her reason fails to help her, Clara's anxiety develops into paranoia. After Carwin tells how he intended to rape her, she begins to see him as a supernatural agent of Satan. When Pleyel accuses her of self-transforming wickedness with Carwin, Clara loses her social identity. Unable to change Pleyel's mind, she can only see recent events as a devilish plot against her happiness. Just when she thinks she is about to complete her identity in marriage, she is denied the opportunity. When she loses the rest of her family as a result of Wieland's insanity, she loses the last supporting prop of her identity, leaving only her faith in herself, her consciousness of her own innocence, and her belief that the satanic Carwin has caused all of her catastrophes.

Two more events deprive Clara of these remaining certainties. She learns that Wieland rather than Carwin, whom she has suspected, was the murderer, and when she understands Wieland's motives, she loses confidence in her perceptions of herself, for should she be similarly transformed, she would be unable to resist. In fact, she sees herself, prostrate and wishing for death, as already transformed: "Was I not likewise transformed from rational and human into a creature of nameless and fearful attributes?" In this state, she understands her brother's certainty of his own rectitude. She cannot know herself. When she finally meets Carwin and hears how trivial and without malice his acts have been, she is unable to believe him, unable to give up her belief that she is the victim of a supernatural agency. Like Wieland, whom she meets for the last time on the same evening she talks with Carwin, she insists that divinity stands behind her disasters; the paranoid Wielands stand at the head of the line of American monomaniacs of whom Melville's Ahab is the greatest example. Deprived of her ordered world, Clara asserts against it an order which gives her reason, at least, to die. Wieland himself commits suicide when Carwin convinces him he has listened to the wrong voice.

Criticism has been rightly skeptical of the apparent clumsiness of the last chapter, Clara's continuation of the narration three years after Wieland's suicide. That chapter tidies up what had appeared earlier to be a subplot involving the Wielands' ward, Louisa Conway, and it also puts together a conventional happy ending. The recovered Clara marries Pleyel after he resolves several complications, including learning the truth about Clara and losing his first wife. Though it remains difficult to determine what Brown intended, it is unlikely that a writer of Brown's intelligence, deeply interested in the twistings of human thought, could be unaware that Clara's final statement is a manifest tissue of illusion. No attainable human virtue could have saved her or Wieland from the web of events in which they become enmeshed. That she persists in magnifying Carwin's responsibility shows that she fails to appreciate the complexity of human events even as Carwin himself has failed. That the Conway/Stuart family disasters of the last chapter recapitulate her own, emphasizes Clara's failure to appreciate fully the incomprehensibility of her world.

Brown apparently intended in the final chapter to underline the illusory quality of social normality. When life moves as it usually does, it appears to be orderly, and one's ideas of order, because they are not seriously challenged, seem to prevail and become a source of comfort and security. That these ideas of order all break down when seriously challenged, leads Clara to the wisdom of despair: "The most perfect being must owe his exemption from vice to the absence of temptation. No human virtue is secure from degeneracy." Such wisdom is not, however, of much use under normal conditions and is of no use at all in a crisis. Perhaps more useful is Clara's reflection as she looks back from the perspective of three years, her idea that one's perceptions and interpretations, because of their imperfection, must be tested over time and compared with those of other observers. The Wieland family curse and Pleyel's errors might be moderated if each character relied less on his unaided perceptions and interpretations. In the midst of chaos, however, this maxim may be no more helpful than any other; Clara, for example, violently resists the sympathy of friends who might help to restore the order of her mind.

Though not a great novel, *Wieland* is both intrinsically interesting and worthy of study for the degree to which it foreshadows developments of considerable importance in the American novel. By subjecting Clara to a completely disordered world and by taking her through a loss of identity, Brown prepares the way for greater American Gothic protagonists from Captain Ahab to Thomas Sutpen.

Edgar Huntly appears at first to be a clumsily episodic adventure novel, but the more closely one looks at it, the more interesting and troubling it becomes. The protagonist-narrator, Edgar Huntly, writes a long letter to his betrothed, Mary Waldegrave, recounting a series of adventures in which he has participated. This letter is followed by two short ones from Huntly to his benefactor, Sarsefield, and one final short letter from Sarsefield to Huntly. The last letter suggests some of the ways in which the apparent clumsiness becomes troubling. Midway through the novel, Edgar learns that he will probably be unable to marry his fiancée, for her inheritance from her recently murdered brother seems not really to belong to her. Later, it appears that the return of Edgar's recently well-married friend, Sarsefield, once again puts him in a position to marry, but Sarsefield's last letter raises doubts about this event which remain unresolved. The reader never learns whether Edgar and Mary are united. The purpose of Sarsefield's letter is to chastise Edgar.

Edgar's main project in the novel becomes to cure the mad Clithero, who mistakenly believes he has been responsible for the death of Sarsefield's wife, formerly Mrs. Lorimer. By the end of his adventures, Edgar understands the degree to which Clithero is mistaken about events, and believes that when Clithero learns the truth, he will be cured. To Edgar's surprise, when Clithero learns the truth, he apparently sets out to really kill his benefactress, Mrs. Sarsefield. Edgar writes his two letters to Sarsefield to warn of Clithero's impending appearance and sends them directly to Sarsefield, knowing that his wife may well see them first. She does see the second letter, and collapses and miscarries as a result. Sarsefield chastises Edgar for misdirecting the letters, even though Sarsefield knew full well from the first letter that the second was on its way to the same address. While, on the one hand, Edgar's error seems comically trivial, especially in comparison with the misguided benevolence which drives him to meddle with Clithero, on the other hand, the consequences are quite serious, serious enough to make one question why Edgar *and* Sarsefield are so stupid about their handling of the letters. The reader is left wondering what to make of Edgar and Sarsefield; does either of them know what he is doing?

The novel seems intended in part as a demonstration that one is rarely if ever aware of what he or she is doing. Paul Witherington, in *Narrative Techniques in the Novels of Charles Brockden Brown* (1967), notes that the novel takes the form of a quest which never quite succeeds, a story of initiation in which repeated initiations fail to take place. Edgar returns to his home shortly after the murder of his closest friend, Waldegrave, in order to solve the crime and bring the murderer to justice. When he sees Clithero, the mysterious servant of a neighbor, sleepwalking at the murder scene, he suspects Clithero of the murder. When he confronts Clithero, Edgar learns the story of his past. In Ireland, Clithero rose out of obscurity to become the favorite servant of Mrs. Lorimer. His virtue eventually led to Mrs. Lorimer's allowing an engagement between Clithero and her beloved niece. This story of virtue rewarded turned sour when, in self-defense, Clithero killed Mrs. Lorimer's blackguard twin brother. Mrs. Lorimer believed her life to be mysteriously entwined with her brother's and was convinced that she would die when he did. Clithero believed her and was convinced that by killing the father of his bride-to-be he had also killed his benefactress. In a mad refinement of benevolence, he determined to stab her in order to spare her the pain of dying from the news of her brother's death. Failing with the sword, he resorted to the word, telling her what had happened. Upon her collapse, he took flight, ignorant of the actual consequences of his act. Mrs. Lorimer did not die; she married Sarsefield and they went to America. Though Clithero's guilt seems unconnected with the murder of Waldegrave, except that the event has renewed Clithero's anguish over what he believes to be his crime, Edgar still suspects him. Furthermore, Clithero's story has stimulated Edgar's benevolence.

Edgar becomes determined to help Clithero, for even if he is Waldegrave's murderer, he has suffered enough. Clithero retires to the wilderness of Norwalk to die after telling his story to Edgar, but Edgar pursues him there to save him. After three trips filled with wilderness adventures, Edgar receives a series of shocks. He meets the man who is probably the real owner of Mary's inheritance and loses his hope for a speedy marriage. Fatigued from his adventures in the wilderness and frustrated in his efforts to benefit Clithero, perhaps guilty about prying into Clithero's life and certainly guilty about his handling of Waldegrave's letters, he begins to sleepwalk. His sleepwalking mirrors Clithero's in several ways, most notably in that he also hides a treasure, Waldegrave's letters, without being aware of what he is doing. After a second episode of sleepwalking, he finds himself at the bottom of a pit in a cave with no memory of how he arrived there; this is the second apparent diversion from his quest for Waldegrave's murderer.

Edgar takes three days to return to civilization, moving through a fairly clear death and rebirth pattern which parallels the movement from savagery to civilization. His adventures—drinking panther blood, rescuing a maiden, fighting Indians, losing and finding himself in rough terrain, nearly killing his friends, and successfully evading his own rescue while narrowly escaping death several times—are filled with weird mistakes and rather abstract humor. For example, he is amazed at his physical endurance. When he finds himself within a half-day's walk of home, he determines, despite his three days of privation, to make the walk in six hours. Six hours later, he has not yet even gained the necessary road, and, though he knows where he is, he is effectively no closer to home than when he started out. Though he has endured the physical trials, he has not progressed.

Of his earlier explorations of the wilderness, Edgar says, "My rambles were productive of incessant novelty, though they always terminated in the prospects of limits that could not be overleaped." This physical nature of the wilderness is indicative of the moral nature of human life, which proves so complex that while one believes he can see to the next step of his actions, he finds continually that he has seen incorrectly. Edgar repeatedly finds himself doing what he never thought he could do and failing at what he believes he can easily accomplish. The complexities of his wilderness experience are beyond the reach of this brief essay, but they seem to lead toward the deeper consideration of questions Edgar raises after hearing Clithero's story:

If consequences arise that cannot be foreseen, shall we find no refuge in the persuasion of our rectitude and of human frailty? Shall we deem ourselves criminal because we do not enjoy the attributes of Deity? Because our power and our knowledge are confined by impassable boundaries?

In order for Edgar to be initiated and to achieve his quest, he needs to come to a just appreciation of his own limits. Although he can see Clithero's limitations quite clearly, Edgar fails to see his own, even after he learns that he has been sleepwalking, that he has been largely mistaken about the events surrounding the Indian raid, that he has mistaken his friends for enemies, and that he has made many other errors which might have caused his own death. Even after he learns that an Indian killed Waldegrave and that his efforts with Clithero have been largely irrelevant, he persists in his ignorant attempt to cure the madman, only to precipitate new disasters. Edgar does not know himself and cannot measure the consequences of his simplest actions, yet he persists in meddling with another equally complex soul which he understands even less. Before Clithero tells Edgar his story, he says, "You boast of the beneficence of your intentions. You set yourself to do me benefit. What are the effects of your misguided zeal and random efforts? They have brought my life to a miserable close." This statement proves prophetic, for prior to each confrontation with Edgar, Clithero has determined to try to live out his life as best he can; each of Edgar's attempts to help drives Clithero toward the suicide which he finally commits.

Insofar as Edgar's quest is to avenge his friend's murder, he succeeds quite by accident. Insofar as his quest is for ethical maturity, he fails miserably, but no one else in the novel succeeds, either. If a measure of moral maturity is the ability to moderate one's passions to the benefit of others, no one is mature. The virtuous Mrs. Lorimer cannot behave rationally toward her villainous brother, and her suffering derives ultimately from that failure. Clithero will murder out of misguided benevolence. Sarsefield, a physician, will let Clithero die of wounds received from Indians because he believes that to Clithero, "Consciousness itself is the malady, the pest, of which he only is cured who ceases to think." Even though Edgar must assent to this statement, concluding that "Disastrous and humiliating is the state of man! By his own hands is constructed the mass of misery and error in which his steps are forever involved," he still wishes to correct some of Clithero's mistakes. In doing so, he provokes Clithero's suicide. No character understands himself, his limitations, or his actions thoroughly; in the case of each of these characters, benevolence issues in murder, direct or indirect. One of the novel's many ironies is that among Edgar, Sarsefield, and Clithero, only Clithero is never morally responsible for a death other than his own.

In *Edgar Huntly* as in *Wieland*, the stage of human action is beyond human comprehension. In *Wieland*, although there is no sanctuary for the virtuous, virtue remains valuable at least as a source of illusions of order, but in *Edgar Huntly* positive virtue becomes criminal because of inevitable human error.

The phenomenon of sleepwalking and the motif of ignorance of self encourage the reader to consider those darker motives which may be hidden from the consciousness of the characters. Edgar must indeed affirm that men are criminal because they have not the attributes of Deity.

Wieland and *Edgar Huntly* are good examples of Brown's interests and complexity of fiction. His wedding of serious philosophical issues with forms of the popular Gothic novel accounts for his distinctive role in the development of the American novel and his continuing interest for students of American culture.

Terry Heller

Other major works

SHORT FICTION: *Carwin, the Biloquist, and Other American Tales and Pieces*, 1822; *The Rhapsodist and Other Uncollected Writings*, 1943.

NONFICTION: *Alcuin: A Dialogue*, 1798.

Bibliography

Axelrod, Alan. *Charles Brockden Brown: An American Tale*. Austin: University of Texas Press, 1983. This study, a revision of a doctoral dissertation, covers all Brown's novels, with an emphasis on the theme of American identity. The first to contain an early crayon portrait of Brown.

Clark, David L. *Charles Brockden Brown: Pioneer Voice of America*. Durham, N.C.: Duke University Press, 1952. Still the most complete book on Brown, this study combines biography, criticism, and liberal quotations from Brown's papers. Some of Brown's letters were published here for the first time.

Grabo, Norman S. *The Coincidental Art of Charles Brockden Brown*. Chapel Hill: University of North Carolina Press, 1981. A scholarly yet easy-to-read analysis of Brown's major fiction, with a focus on the psychology of the characters and what they reveal about Brown's own mind.

Ringe, Donald A. *Charles Brockden Brown*. New York: Twayne, 1966. Though brief and written to a strict format, this book contains some of the most helpful criticism of Brown's works to be found. The biographical portion is necessarily brief, but each of Brown's novels is discussed in the main portion of the book. Includes a chronology of Brown's life and writings and an annotated bibliography.

Rosenthal, Bernard, ed. *Critical Essays on Charles Brockden Brown*. Boston: G. K. Hall, 1981. A valuable collection of original essays by various scholars, this volume opens with a summary of criticism on Brown up to 1980. The first section contains a good selection 'of early reviews; the second section, containing contemporary articles, includes essays on Brown's lesser-known novels as well as major works.

JOHN BUCHAN

Born: Perth, Scotland; August 26, 1875
Died: Montreal, Canada; February 11, 1940

Principal long fiction

Sir Quixote of the Moors, Being Some Account of an Episode in the Life of the Sieur de Rohaine, 1895; *John Burnet of Barns*, 1898; *A Lost Lady of Old Years*, 1899; *The Half-Hearted*, 1900; *Prester John*, 1910 (published in the United States as *The Great Diamond Pipe*); *Salute to Adventurers*, 1915; *The Thirty-Nine Steps*, 1915; *The Power-House*, 1916; *Greenmantle*, 1916; *Mr. Standfast*, 1919; *Huntingtower*, 1922; *Midwinter: Certain Travellers in Old England*, 1923; *The Three Hostages*, 1924; *John Macnab*, 1925; *The Dancing Floor*, 1926; *Witch Wood*, 1927; *The Courts of the Morning*, 1929; *Castle Gay*, 1930; *The Blanket of the Dark*, 1931; *A Prince of the Captivity*, 1933; *The Free Fishers*, 1934; *The House of the Four Winds*, 1935; *The Island of Sheep*, 1936 (published in the United States as *The Man from the Norlands*); *Sick Heart River*, 1941 (published in the United States as *Mountain Meadow*).

Other literary forms

Although John Buchan is remembered chiefly for his novels, more than half of his published work is in the form of nonfiction prose. He wrote numerous biographies and works of history, and he published speeches and lectures, educational books for children, and countless articles, essays, pamphlets, notes, and reviews. Late in his life, he produced an autobiographical work, and after his death his widow edited and published two collections of selections from his works.

Buchan's fictional works include not only novels, but also a story for children, *The Magic Walking-Stick* (1932), and several collections of short stories. Some of the settings and situations in these stories later appeared in slightly altered form in Buchan's novels, and several of the stories in the later collections make use of characters from the novels, including Richard Hannay, Sandy Arbuthnot, and Sir Edward Leithen. Two of Buchan's volumes of short stories, *The Path of the King* (1921) and *The Gap in the Curtain* (1932), connect independent episodes and are bound together by a narrative frame; as a result, these works are sometimes listed as novels, although the individual episodes are actually quite distinct from one another.

In addition to his prose works, Buchan published a number of poems and edited three volumes of verse. He also edited several works of nonfiction, including Francis Bacon's *Essays and Apothegms of Francis Lord Bacon* (1597, edited in 1894) and Izaak Walton's *The Compleat Angler: Or, The Contemplative Man's Recreation* (1653, edited in 1901).

Achievements

While he was still an undergraduate at Oxford, Buchan received two major prizes for writing: the Stanhope Historical Essay Prize for an essay on Sir Walter Raleigh (1897) and the Newdigate Prize for Poetry for *The Pilgrim Fathers* (1898). He was graduated in 1899 with a first-class honors degree, and shortly thereafter he was appointed private secretary to the High Commissioner for South Africa (1901-1903). This was the first of many prestigious posts that Buchan filled: he was a conservative member of Parliament for the Scottish universities (1927-1935), president of the Scottish History Society (1929-1933), Lord High Commissioner to the general assembly of the Church of Scotland (1933, 1934), chancellor of the University of Edinburgh (1937-1940), and Governor-General of Canada (1935-1940). In 1935, in recognition of his accomplishments and of his new post as governor-general, he was created Baron Tweedsmuir of Elsfield.

In part because of his political prominence and his reputation as a historian, and in part because of his achievements as a novelist, Buchan received honorary doctorates from Oxford, Harvard, Yale, Columbia, McGill, and McMaster Universities, and from the Universities of Glasgow, St. Andrews, Edinburgh, Toronto, Manitoba, and British Columbia. He also became an honorary fellow of Brasenose College, Oxford.

Although Buchan was clearly not a full-time writer of fiction, his achievements as a novelist include some degree of critical success and a great deal of commercial popularity, particularly during the period between World War I and the 1960's. His novels appealed to a wide and varied audience, including schoolboys, laborers, clergymen, academics, members of various professions, and such celebrities as A. J. Balfour, Stanley Baldwin, Clement Atlee, Ezra Pound, C. S. Lewis, J. B. Priestly, King George V, and Czar Nicholas II. Although they have declined in popularity in the United States since the early 1960's, Buchan's novels continue to sell moderately well in Great Britain, and they have been translated into a number of foreign languages, including French, German, Spanish, Dutch, Danish, Czech, Swedish, and Arabic.

Biography

John Buchan was born in Perth, Scotland, on August 26, 1875. He spent his early childhood near the Firth of Forth, an area to which he often returned for holidays and which served as the setting for a great deal of his fiction. His father was a minister of the Free Church of Scotland; his mother was the daughter of a sheep-farmer. From both of his parents, but particularly from his strong-minded mother, Buchan learned to value endurance, hard work, and, above all, perseverance, and he placed such emphasis on these qualities in his novels that many readers have come to regard this emphasis as the hallmark of his work.

When Buchan was thirteen, his father was called to the John Knox Free

Church in Glasgow. There Buchan attended Hutchesons' Grammar School and, later, the University of Glasgow, whose faculty then included such scholars as Lord Kelvin, A. C. Bradley, George Ramsay, and Gilbert Murray; the latter became one of Buchan's closest friends. At the end of his third year at the University of Glasgow, Buchan won a Junior Hulme Scholarship to Oxford University, and in the autumn of 1895, he began his studies at Brasenose College.

Because his scholarship was not sufficient to meet all of his expenses, Buchan earned extra money by reading manuscripts for the publishing firm of John Lane; among the manuscripts that he recommended for publication was Arnold Bennett's first novel, *A Man from the North* (1898). Buchan also became a regular reviewer for several publications and continued to work steadily on his own novels and nonfiction prose. In 1898, he had the distinction of being listed in *Who's Who*: he had at that time six books in print, two in press, and three in progress, and he had published innumerable articles, essays, and reviews. He was also an active member of several prestigious Oxford and London clubs and organizations, notably the Oxford Union, of which he was librarian and later president. In 1899, he sat for his final examinations and earned a first-class honors degree; one year later, having "eaten his dinners" and passed the examination, he was called to the bar.

During the two years following his graduation, Buchan wrote leading articles for *The Spectator*, worked as a barrister, and continued to write both fiction and nonfiction. In 1901, he accepted the post of political private secretary to Lord Milner, who was then High Commissioner for South Africa. During the two years that he spent in that country, Buchan became familiar with the practical administrative aspects of political situations which he had discussed on a more theoretical level in *The Spectator* essays. He also acquired background material for several of his novels, notably *Prester John*.

When he returned to London in 1903, Buchan resumed his legal work at the bar and his literary work on *The Spectator*. In 1906, he became second assistant editor of *The Spectator*, and, in 1907, he accepted the position of chief literary adviser to the publishing firm of Thomas Nelson. He also continued to extend the circle of acquaintances that he had begun to form at Oxford, and he became one of the best-known and most promising young men in London society and politics.

Buchan was greatly attracted to a young lady whom he met at a London dinner party, and on July 15, 1907, he and Susan Grosvenor were married at St. George's, Hanover Square. Their first child, Alice, was born one year later, followed by John (1911), William (1916), and Alastair (1918). Until the outbreak of World War I, the Buchans lived comfortably in London while John Buchan continued to write fiction, legal opinions, and essays and articles for such publications as *The Spectator* and *The Times Literary Supplement*.

Shortly after World War I began, Buchan, who had been asked to write a continuing history of the war for Nelson's and who also acted as correspondent for *The Times*, visited a number of French battlefields as a noncombatant. In 1916, he returned to France as a temporary lieutenant-colonel, acting as press officer and propagandist for the foreign office and working for Field Marshal Lord Douglas Haig as official historian. In February, 1917, he was appointed director of information, in charge of publicity and propaganda. In the midst of all of his war-related activities, between 1914 and 1918, he wrote three of his most popular novels: *The Thirty-Nine Steps*, *Greenmantle*, and *Mr. Standfast*.

When World War I ended, Buchan purchased Elsfield, a country house near Oxford, and settled down to a routine of writing, working at Nelson's, and entertaining his numerous friends, including T. E. Lawrence, Robert Graves, W. P. Ker, Gilbert Murray, and A. L. Rowse. In 1919, he became a director of Reuters news agency, and four years later he became deputy chairman. Buchan's peaceful routine at Elsfield, however, ended in the spring of 1927, when he was elected to parliament as the member for the Scottish Universities, a position he held until 1935. He became as active a member of London society during his term in parliament as he had been as a younger man, and he became increasingly well known and influential in political circles. He was appointed Lord High Commissioner to the general assembly of the Church of Scotland in 1933 and again in 1934, and in 1935 he was appointed to a much more important post: Governor-General of the Dominion of Canada. In recognition of his accomplishments and of his new position, he was created a baron; he chose as his title Lord Tweedsmuir of Elsfield.

Buchan's tenure of office as governor-general (1935-1940) coincided with the growing tension in Europe which eventually led to World War II, and, because his post was largely a ceremonial one, he had to be extremely cautious in his statements and in his behavior. Among the delicate diplomatic situations that he handled well were the visits of President Franklin Delano Roosevelt and of King George VI and Queen Elizabeth to Canada; his greatest error in diplomacy occurred when he made a speech in which he suggested that Canada's defense policy was inadequate. Despite occasional lapses of this type, however, Buchan was a successful governor-general, in part because he made a point of visiting not only such cultural centers as Montreal and Quebec, but also more remote places such as Medicine Hat, Regina, Saskatoon, and Edmonton. In addition to enhancing his popularity as governor-general, these trips provided background material for his last novel, *Sick Heart River*.

As the end of his five-year term of office approached, Buchan was asked to allow himself to be nominated for another term. He refused because of his steadily declining health and he had planned to leave Canada at the end of 1940. On February 6, 1940, however, he suffered a cerebral hemorrhage and, falling, struck his head; five days later he died. He left an autobiographical work, a novel, a children's history of Canada, a volume of essays, and a volume of lectures, all of which were published posthumously, as well as an unfinished novel and two chapters of a nonfiction work; these chapters appear at the end of the autobiography.

Analysis

Despite his manifold activities, John Buchan is remembered primarily as a writer of implausible but exciting adventure fiction with overtones of the nineteenth century romance. Most of his novels fall into the general category of thrillers, but a few, such as *Salute to Adventurers*, *Midwinter*, *Witch Wood*, and *The Blanket of the Dark*, are more accurately classified as historical romances. Despite some variations in form and emphasis, however, all of Buchan's novels share certain features which contribute to the characteristic flavor of his fiction; these include melodramatic sequences, unusually effective descriptions of landscape and atmosphere, frequent references to such qualities as endurance and perseverance, and exciting but comparatively nonviolent action.

The melodramatic quality of Buchan's fiction arises from a number of sources, including his admiration for the highly melodramatic thrillers of E. Phillips Oppenheim and his own overdeveloped sense of the theatrical. Although Buchan was seldom original in his choice of melodramatic elements, he made good use of them in enhancing the suspense and excitement of his novels. For example, *Prester John*, *Greenmantle*, *The Three Hostages*, *The Dancing Floor*, and *Witch Wood* owe a great deal of their atmosphere and effect to indistinctly defined and therefore singularly mysterious antique rituals and ceremonies, including pagan sacrifice and devil worship. Other novels, including *Huntingtower*, *Midwinter*, and *The House of the Four Winds*, feature royalty in distress and simple but noble-hearted adventurers who risk their lives for "the cause." Buchan also made frequent use of such staple elements of melodramatic fiction as secret societies, talismans and tokens, fairylike heroines (milky-skinned and graceful), exotic villainesses (brunette and slinky), and characters who bear a Burden of Secret Sorrow.

As these examples suggest, Buchan did not hesitate to employ many of the clichés of the thriller and romance genres. Moreover, his work is not only derivative, but also repetitive, containing numerous examples of devices which he found successful and therefore used repeatedly. For example, in addition to the novels that make use of some form of magic and those that deal with royalty and adventurers, he wrote five novels in which foiling the villain depends upon decoding a cipher, six in which one of the villains tries to mesmerize the protagonist, and eleven in which one of the villains passes for a time as an irreproachable member of society. In addition to reusing successful plot devices, Buchan had the irritating habit of repeating certain favorite words, including "eldritch," "dislimn," "totem," and "frowst."

Buchan's tendency to repeat himself is not surprising in view of the speed with which he wrote. In the period between 1915 and 1936, he produced twenty-one volumes of fiction and almost thirty volumes of nonfiction. Despite his hasty writing, his repetitiveness, and his overuse of clichés, however, Buchan was by no means a mere hack. He wrote disciplined, polished, occasionally elegant prose, seldom stooping to sensationalism and describing even the most exciting or dramatic scenes in a clear and narrative style that was seldom equaled in the thriller fiction of that period. More important, like Sir Walter Scott and Robert Louis Stevenson, whose work Buchan greatly admired, he was not only acutely sensitive to local color and atmosphere but also gifted in expressing that sensitivity in his fiction. He was particularly adept at making use of settings with which he was familiar: many of his novels, including *The Thirty-Nine Steps*, *John Macnab*, and *Witch Wood*, are set in the Scottish countryside where Buchan grew up and to which he often returned; *Prester John* is set in South Africa, where Buchan served as Lord Milner's secretary; several novels, including *The Power House* and *The Three Hostages*, contain scenes in the parts of London that he frequented during the years before World War I and during his term in parliament; and most of the action in *Sick Heart River* takes place in the far north of Canada, which he visited during his term as governor-general.

Buchan's depiction of these familiar settings and of the atmospheres associated with them is both denotative and connotative, and this combination, which is responsible for a great deal of the power and charm of his books, does much to raise his work above the level of run-of-the-mill adventure fiction. The denotative quality of Buchan's descriptions stems from his talent in selecting the salient features of a landscape and producing vividly lifelike verbal pictures of them in disciplined and concise prose. The connotative quality results from his ability to imbue the landscape with an atmosphere that is so vivid that it might almost be called a personality, and to derive from the landscape a mood or even a moral valence that complements the action of the novel. In *Witch Wood*, for example, the open and innocent Scottish countryside is marred by a black wood, which is not only an appropriate setting for the devilish rites that take place in it, but also, the novel implies the cause of them in some obscure manner.

In a number of Buchan's novels, the complementary relationship between the setting and the action reaches the level of allegory when the protagonist and, in some cases, other characters, undertake a long and arduous journey through a landscape that includes steep hills, swamps or difficult waters, natural pitfalls, and traps designed by enemies who often pose as friends. The difficulties that arise in the course of this journey provide opportunities for the exciting chase scenes and the suspenseful action that are essential to adventure literature, but they also do more: as a character overcomes each of the obstacles presented by the landscape through which he moves, he acquires or displays appropriate qualities of soul that redeem him or confirm him in his moral character and status. This allegorical use of landscape, which is clearly based on one of Buchan's favorite books, John Bunyan's *The Pilgrim's Progress* (1678), serves as the central plot device in almost all of his best-known novels, including *The Thirty-Nine Steps*, *The Power-House*, *Greenmantle*, *Mr. Standfast*, *Midwinter*, and *Sick Heart River*.

The most important effect of Buchan's repeated use of landscape as an allegory is the stress that this technique enables him to place upon the redeeming quality of certain types of behavior. In order to overcome the obstacles that beset them, the characters in his novels must display courage, endurance, and, above all, perseverance in hard work despite fatigue, setbacks, and apparently hopeless delays. These qualities are so central to his novels that all of his major characters are defined and evaluated in terms of them. Some characters already possess these attributes before the action begins and are finally triumphant because they successfully apply to a particular set of circumstances the qualities they had already developed and, in some cases, displayed in earlier adventures; other characters develop these attributes as the action progresses.

The protagonist with predeveloped virtues is a character type common to almost all adventure literature, and, in most cases, Buchan's treatment of it is not particularly memorable. In the novels that center around Sir Edward Leithen, however, Buchan handles the theme quite effectively, showing that even someone who spends a great deal of time at a desk can possess the courage, endurance, and perseverance of a true hero. Further, in addition to these basic qualities, Buchan endows Leithen with a degree of sensitivity that allows him to absorb and to respond to the influences of various landscapes, thus deriving from his adventures not only the satisfaction of accomplishing his external objective, but also increased insight, depth of soul, and spiritual regeneration. This theme is consistent and progressive in the Leithen novels, so that in the last one, *Sick Heart River*, Leithen's renewal of soul, resulting from his responsiveness to the influences of the environment, is carried almost to the point of apotheosis.

In addition to characters such as Leithen, who clearly possess the qualities necessary for success, Buchan's novels include a number of lesser characters who, as the action progresses, display or attain unexpected greatness of soul through unaccustomed exertion and suffering. Buchan was generally successful in dealing with such characters, in part because of the surprising liberality of his attitude toward character types who would, in most of the other adventure literature of that period, have no redeeming—or even redeemable—qualities whatsoever. Because his initial description of these characters is unusually balanced, their conversion in the course of participating in the adventure is far more convincing than it otherwise would have been.

One such character, found in Buchan's thriller, *Mr. Standfast*, is a World War I conscientious objector named Launcelot Wake who first appears as a hot-eyed, sallow young man ridiculing everything that is held sacred by the protagonist, Brigadier-General Richard Hannay. Nevertheless, Hannay, and through him the reader, finds it impossible to dislike Wake, who is strong-willed, intelligent, and sincere in his beliefs. As he willingly accompanies Hannay on a difficult and dangerous climb through an Alpine pass, voluntarily exposing himself to enemy fire on the front lines, and finally receiving his death wound, Wake gradually achieves dignity, self-respect, and spiritual regeneration—yet he remains, to the end of the novel, a staunch pacifist who resolutely refuses to take up arms. No other major thriller-writer of Buchan's generation would have had the tolerance or the breadth of mind to make a demi-hero of a recusant conscientious objector, particularly in a novel written in the middle of World War I while its author was on active service as a lieutenant-colonel in the British army.

As Buchan's sympathetic depiction of Launcelot Wake suggests, his overall point of view was far from the bellicose and sometimes Fascist attitude associated with writers such as "Sapper," Edgar Wallace, and Gerard Fairlie, whose protagonists unhesitatingly inflict physical injury and even death upon villains whom they encounter. Buchan's protagonists seldom administer any form of punishment, and if the villains die at all it is usually the result of an accident or, more rarely, at the hands of a minor character in the story. In *Greenmantle*, for example, the exotically beautiful villainess is accidentally killed by artillery fire; in *Mr. Standfast*, a German spy is killed by German fire in the trenches; in *The Three Hostages*, the arch-villain falls to his death despite Hannay's efforts to save him; in *Midwinter*, one traitor is placed on parole in consideration of his wife's feelings and another is sent into exile; in *Witch Wood*, the principal warlock is beset by his own demons and dies in his madness. Buchan never dwelt upon or glorified any form of bloodshed, and some of his novels involve no violence at all, stressing instead imaginative if occasionally melodramatic situations, suspenseful action, and seemingly insurmountable challenges to the strength and determination of the characters.

Although all of his novels share certain common features, in some cases Buchan made use of one of his three major series protagonists, each of whom imbues the novels in which he appears with his distinctive flavor. By far the most popular of these is Richard Hannay, who is the central figure in *The Thirty-Nine Steps*, *Greenmantle*, *Mr. Standfast*, and *The Three Hostages*, and appears in *The Courts of the Morning* and *The Island of Sheep*. Hannay is by far the most typical thriller hero whom Buchan created: physically strong and morally intrepid, he is always ready for a bracing climb in the Scottish hills or a brisk run across the moors, usually dodging at least two sets of pursuers and an occasional dog. Becomingly modest regarding his own accomplishments and courage, Hannay generously admires the greatness—albeit perverted greatness—of his foes. Although several villains, including the old man with the hooded eyes in *The Thirty-Nine Steps*, Hilda von Einem in *Green-*

mantle, and most notably, Dominic Medina in *The Three Hostages*, try to hypnotize Hannay, he is protected by his solid common sense and by a strong will fortified by frequent cold baths. He is also more sportsmanlike than practical; for example, when he finally gets a clear shot at the highly elusive and dangerous villain of *Mr. Standfast*, he allows him to escape yet again because firing at him under those conditions seems "like potting at a sitting rabbit." On the other hand, Hannay is far from being one of the mindless anti-intellectuals who infest early twentieth century thriller literature. In *Mr. Standfast*, for example, he willingly undertakes a course of reading in the English classics, and throughout the series most of his attitudes and reflections are, if not profound, at least reasonably intelligent.

Although Hannay is by no means a mere beefy dolt, many of the opinions expressed in the course of his first-person narration reflect the prejudices common to his generation and social class, and these include racial and ethnic attitudes which many readers find offensive. Since most of the slighting references to blacks, Germans, Italians, Russians, and Jews that appear in Buchan's work are concentrated in the Hannay stories, it is possible to argue, as several of Buchan's supporters have done, that Hannay's attitudes and language arise from his characterization rather than from the kind of prejudice on Buchan's part that is associated with such writers as "Sapper," Gerald Fairlie, and Dornford Yates. Buchan's partisans also point out that there are comparatively few such references even in the Hannay books, and that these are not nearly so virulent as similar references in the works of many of Buchan's contemporaries. Further, Buchan is known to have supported a number of Jewish causes; for example, in 1932 he succeeded Josiah Wedgwood as chairman of a pro-Zionist parliamentary committee, and in 1934 he spoke at a demonstration organized by the Jewish National Fund.

Buchan's detractors, on the other hand, point to passages in his personal correspondence that are critical of various ethnic groups. They also maintain that his attitude toward blacks, formed in part during his experience in South Africa, was paternalistic and patronizing, and it is certainly true that even when he meant to express admiration for members of the black race, as he did in *Prester John*, his attitude and his choice of language were often unconsciously—and therefore all the more offensively—condescending. Perhaps the fairest conclusion that can be drawn from this controversy is that, although some of Buchan's racial and ethnic prejudices would be considered offensive today, the prejudices that he attributed to the fictional character of Richard Hannay are probably more extreme than his own. Further, by the standards of his age and class he was commendably moderate in his use of racial and ethnic stereotypes.

Buchan's second series protagonist was Dickson McCunn. The three McCunn novels are the most overtly, yet humorously, romantic of Buchan's thrillers: *Huntingtower* features an exiled Russian princess who is loved by a left-wing poet and rescued with the help of a group of Glasgow street urchins, and *Castle Gay* and *The House of the Four Winds* deal with the restoration of the rightful Prince of Evallonia with the help of the same urchins (now grown), a reluctant newspaper magnate, and a circus elephant. McCunn himself is a middle-aged, recently retired grocer who looks forward to "Seeing Life" and "Doing Noble Deeds." He dreams of becoming involved in pure Sir Walter Scott adventures, and, because of his dreams, he tends to view real-life people and situations through a rosy, romantic haze; for example, he reverences the rather weak and worldly Prince of Evallonia as the embodiment of all the qualities associated with the Bonnie Prince Charlie of legend. Nevertheless, McCunn is saved from being ridiculous by his solid common sense and essential decency and by Buchan's implication that, if what McCunn sees is not precisely what *is*, it is at least what *should be*.

The dramatic, in some respects melodramatic, quality of the McCunn novels is blessedly undercut by the verbal and situational humor that is their hallmark. In *Huntingtower*, for example, Wee Jaikie, the street boy who later bcomes the true protagonist of *Castle Gay* and *The House of the Four Winds*, helps to rescue a Romanov princess while singing garbled versions of Bolshevik hymns that he learned at a socialist Sunday School. Similarly, at one point in *The House of the Four Winds*, a friend of Jaikie who assists him in a series of swashbuckling episodes appears outside his second-story window mounted on an elephant named Aurunculeia and asks in German for a match. Through his handling of these humorously improbable situations, Buchan gently ridiculed the more preposterous aspects of an excessively romantic view of life, while retaining and even enhancing those qualities which he never ceased to admire, such as constancy, devotion, and faith.

Buchan's last series protagonist, Sir Edward Leithen, is featured in four novels: *The Power-House*, *John Macnab*, *The Dancing Floor*, and *Sick Heart River*. These are somewhat atypical adventure stories, largely because they are "about" not only a series of suspenseful activities, but also a group of central themes, including the thinness of civilization and the ethic of success. These themes are expressed through the first-person narration of Leithen, who is a far more sophisticated and reflective character than Richard Hannay, Buchan's other first-person series narrator.

In view of the legal and political background with which Buchan endowed Leithen, it is not surprising that he demonstrates an intense awareness of the thinness of the shell of civilization within which he and his contemporaries desire to believe themselves safe. This concept is explored from a number of perspectives within the series: for example, in *The Power-House*, which is the earliest Leithen novel and the closest to the traditional thriller mode, the expression of this theme centers around the imminence of violence and the vulnerability of ordinary individuals, while in the more recondite novel *The Dancing Floor*, the thinness of civilization is associated with the terrifying attractiveness of obscurely fearsome pre-Christian religious rites to whose power Leithen himself, in many respects the quintessential civilized man, nearly succumbs.

Buchan provided a balance for the sensibility that Leithen displays in his reflections upon the thinness of civilization by attributing to him not only a shrewd and practical legal mind, but also a respect for worldly success which is so marked that it borders upon careerism. Although this emphasis upon competitive success is by no means confined to the Leithen novels, it is most evident in them. Leithen himself is greatly in demand as a solicitor, is elected to parliament, and eventually becomes solicitor-general, and more important, the novels which he narrates contain numerous approving references to persons who are not merely successful but unsurpassed in their fields. Nevertheless, a close reading of the Leithen novels shows that although worldly success is spoken of with respect, it is treated not as an end in itself, but as a testimony to the stamina, hard work, and perseverance of the individual who has attained it. If the Leithen novels abound in references to success, they also abound in references to exhaustion, and both types of references apply to the same individuals. Success in competition with others in one's field is, in the Leithen's novels, simply an extension of the Bunyanesque ethic of hard work and perseverance which, in all of Buchan's fiction, leads to success in competition with villains and with natural forces. Further, in all of Buchan's novels worldly success is second in importance to more basic values, such as courage, honor, and compassion. To Leithen and to Buchan's other major characters, success is admirable but it is emphatically not enough.

As the preceding discussion indicates, Buchan's novels are written in polished prose and include sensitive descriptions of settings which are incorporated into both the plots of the novels and the development of the characters. Further, his liberal attitudes not only redeem his work from jingoism, egregious racism, and gratuitous violence, but also contribute to the development of less stereotyped, more varied, and more complex characters than are usually found in adventure fiction. Buchan was not, however, a serious literary figure and never claimed to be. He wrote his novels quickly and in the midst of numerous distractions, seldom revised, and often made use of clichéd situations and of devices which he himself had used, in many cases repeatedly, in earlier stories. Further, although he did create some unusually good characters, he also created a large number of cardboard ones. His villains, in particular, are with few exceptions unsubstantial figures whose machinations are overshadowed to the point of eclipse by the journey and chase scenes that dominate and, in this respect, upset the balance of several of his novels. The structure of the novels is further weakened by the fact that, although the emphasis which Buchan places upon the moral order seldom becomes overtly didactic, it does provide an excuse for the use of a profusion of providential occurrences which are virtually indistinguishable from mere blatant coincidences. Despite their flaws, however, Buchan's novels are well-written and sensitive tales of adventure whose *raison d'être* is to provide salutary entertainment; that they usually succeed in doing so is no minor accomplishment.

Joan DelFattore

Other major works

SHORT FICTION: *Grey Weather: Moorland Tales of My Own People*, 1899; *The Watcher by the Threshold and Other Tales*, 1902; *The Moon Endureth: Tales and Fancies*, 1912; *The Path of the King*, 1921; *The Runagates Club*, 1928; *The Gap in the Curtain*, 1932.

POETRY: *The Pilgrim Fathers, 1898*, 1898; *Ordeal by Marriage: An Eclogue*, 1915; *Poems, Scots and English, 1917*, revised 1936; *The Poetry of Neil Munro*, 1931.

NONFICTION: *Scholar Gipsies*, 1896; *Sir Walter Raleigh, 1897*, 1897; *Brasenose College*, 1898; *The African Colony: Studies in the Reconstruction*, 1903; *The Law Relating to the Taxation of Foreign Income*, 1905; *A Lodge in the Wilderness*, 1906; *Some Eighteenth Century Byways and Other Essays*, 1908; *What the Home Bill Means*, 1912; *The Marquis of Montrose*, 1913; *Andrew Jameson, Lord Ardwall*, 1913; *Britain's War by Land*, 1915; *The Achievements of France*, 1915; *Nelson's History of the War*, 1915-1919 (24 volumes); *The Battle of Jutland*, 1916; *The Battle of Somme, First Phase*, 1916; *The Future of the War*, 1916; *The Purpose of the War*, 1916; *The Battle of Somme, Second Phase*, 1917; *The Battle-Honours of Scotland 1914-1918*, 1919; *The Island of Sheep*, 1919 (with Susan Buchan); *The History of South African Forces in France*, 1920; *Francis and Riversdale Grenfell: A Memoir*, 1920; *Miscellanies, Literary and Historical*, 1921 (2 volumes); *A Book of Escapes and Hurried Journeys*, 1922; *The Last Secrets: The Final Mysteries of Exploration*, 1923; *The Memory of Sir Walter Scott*, 1923; *Days to Remember: The British Empire in the Great War*, 1923 (with Henry Newbolt); *Lord Minto: A Memoir*, 1924; *Some Notes on Sir Walter Scott*, 1924; *The History of the Royal Scots Fusiliers, 1678-1918*, 1925; *The Man and the Book: Sir Walter Scott*, 1925; *Two Ordeals of Democracy*, 1925; *Homilies and Recreations*, 1926; *The Fifteenth Scottish Division, 1914-1919*, 1926 (with John Stewart); *To the Electors of the Scottish Universities*, 1927; *Montrose*, 1928; *The Cause and the Causal in History*, 1929; *What the Union of the Churches Means to Scotland*, 1929; *Montrose and Leadership*, 1930; *The Revision of Dogmas*, 1930; *The Kirk in Scotland, 1560-1929*, 1930 (with George Adam Smith); *Lord Rosebery, 1847-1930*, 1930; *The Novel and the Fairy Tale*, 1931; *Sir Walter Scott*, 1932; *Julius Caesar*, 1932; *Andrew Lang and the Border*, 1933; *The Margins of Life*, 1933; *The Massacre of Glencoe*, 1933; *Gordon at Khartoum*, 1934; *Oliver Cromwell*, 1934; *The Principles of Social Service*, 1934; *The Scottish Church and the Empire*, 1934; *The University, the*

Library, and the Common Weal, 1934; *The King's Grace, 1910-1935*, 1935 (published in the United States as *The People's King: George V*); *The Western Mind, An Address*, 1935; *A University's Bequest to Youth, An Address*, 1936; *Augustus*, 1937; *The Interpreter's House*, 1938; *Presbyterianism: Yesterday, Today, and Tomorrow*, 1938; *Canadian Occasions: Addresses by Lord Tweedsmuir*, 1940; *Comments and Characters*, 1940 (W. Forbes Gray, editor); *Memory Hold-the-Door*, 1940 (published in the United States as *Pilgrim's Way: An Essay in Recollection*); *The Clearing House: A Survey of One Man's Mind*, 1946 (Lady Tweedsmuir, editor).

CHILDREN'S LITERATURE: *Sir Walter Raleigh*, 1911; *The Magic Walking-Stick*, 1932; *The Long Traverse*, 1941 (published in the United States as *Lake of Gold*).

EDITED TEXTS: *Essays and Apothegms of Francis Lord Bacon*, 1894; *Musa Piscatrix*, 1896; *The Compleat Angler: Or, The Contemplative Man's Recreation*, 1901; *Great Hours in Sport*, 1921; *A History of English Literature*, 1923; *The Nations of Today: A New History of the World*, 1923-1924; *Modern Short Stories*, 1926; *The Teaching of History*, 1928-1930 (11 volumes).

ANTHOLOGY: *The Northern Muse*, 1924.

Bibliography

Buchan, Anna. *Unforgettable, Unforgotten*. London: Hodder & Stoughton, 1945. A personal look at Buchan's life by one of his sisters. Indexed and illustrated, it is especially good for his early life.

Buchan, William. *John Buchan: A Memoir*. Toronto: Griffen House, 1982. Written by his son, this very readable biography humanizes Buchan by concentrating on his personal, rather than public, life. Based on William's childhood memories, as well as his own expertise as a novelist, poet, and literary critic. Well indexed and contains a good bibliography.

Cawelti, John G., and Bruce A. Rosenberg. *The Spy Story*. Chicago: University of Chicago Press, 1987. Cawelti's essay, "The Joys of Buchaneering," argues that Buchan's Richard Hannay stories are the crucial link between the spy adventures and the espionage novels of the twentieth century. Buchan developed a formula that was adopted and given various twists by successive authors. Includes an excellent bibliography and appendices.

Daniell, David. *The Interpreter's House: A Critical Assessment of John Buchan*. London: Nelson, 1975. Concentrates on the tension between Calvinism and Platonism in Buchan's life, identified as the key to appreciating and understanding Buchan and his works. Scholarly and very thorough, the book refutes many of the common myths about Buchan.

Himmelfarb, Gertrude. "John Buchan: An Untimely Appreciation." *Encounter* 15 (September, 1960): 46-53. A very good, brief introduction to the various themes and characters that run through his novels. Dispenses with some of the more obvious popular misconceptions about Buchan as a writer—for example, that he was an anti-Semite. Also deals with Buchan's attitude towards race, class, and imperialism.

Smith, Janet Adam. *John Buchan and His World*. New York: Charles Scribner's Sons, 1979. Only 128 pages, this is an updated version of an earlier biography. Makes use of new materials provided by Buchan's family and publisher. Illustrated and well written, the biography concentrates on Buchan's life as both a writer and a public servant.

PEARL S. BUCK

Born: Hillsboro, West Virginia; June 26, 1892
Died: Danby, Vermont; March 6, 1973

Principal long fiction

East Wind: West Wind, 1930; *The Good Earth*, 1931; *Sons*, 1932; *The Mother*, 1934; *A House Divided*, 1935; *House of Earth*, 1935; *This Proud Heart*, 1938; *The Patriot*, 1939; *Other Gods: An American Legend*, 1940; *Dragon Seed*, 1942; *China Sky*, 1942; *The Promise*, 1943; *China Flight*, 1945; *Portrait of a Marriage*, 1945; *The Townsman*, 1945 (as John Sedges); *Pavilion of Women*, 1946; *The Angry Wife*, 1947 (as John Sedges); *Peony*, 1948; *Kinfolk*, 1949; *The Long Love*, 1949 (as John Sedges); *God's Men*, 1951; *The Hidden Flower*, 1952; *Bright Procession*, 1952 (as John Sedges); *Come, My Beloved*, 1953; *Voices in the House*, 1953 (as John Sedges); *Imperial Woman*, 1956; *Letter from Peking*, 1957; *Command the Morning*, 1959; *Satan Never Sleeps*, 1962; *The Living Reed*, 1963; *Death in the Castle*, 1965; *The Time Is Noon*, 1967; *The New Year*, 1968; *The Three Daughters of Madame Liang*, 1969; *Mandala*, 1970; *The Goddess Abides*, 1972; *All Under Heaven*, 1973; *The Rainbow*, 1974.

Other literary forms

An overwhelmingly prolific writer, Pearl S. Buck wrote short stories; juvenile fiction and nonfiction; pamphlets; magazine articles; literary history; biographies; plays (including a musical); educational works; an Oriental cookbook; and a variety of books on America, democracy, Hitler and Germany, Japan, China, Russia, the mentally retarded, the sexes, and the Kennedy women. In addition, she translated *Shui Hu Chuan* (1933, *All Men Are Brothers*) and edited a book of Oriental fairy tales, several Christmas books, and a book of Chinese woodcuts. Besides *The Good Earth*, her finest works are her biographies of her parents, *The Exile* (1936) and *Fighting Angel: Portrait of a Soul* (1936). *The Exile* portrays the unhappy and frustrating life of her mother, a missionary wife. *Fighting Angel*, a better biography because of its greater objectivity, shows the ruthless missionary zeal of Buck's father. Of her early articles, "Is There a Case for Foreign Missions?," printed in *Christian Century* in 1933, created a furor in its charges that missionaries, and churches themselves, lacked sympathy for the people, worrying more about the numbers of converts than the needs of the flock. Buck also delivered several important addresses which reveal much about her own literary philosophy, including her Nobel Prize lecture on the Chinese novel. *Of Men and Women* (first issued in 1941; reissued in 1971 with a new epilogue) is one of Buck's most important nonfictional works because it gives her views of Chinese and American family life and her warnings about "gunpowder" American women who are educated for work yet lead idle and meaningless lives at home.

During World War II, Buck delivered many speeches and published articles, letters, and pamphlets on the Asian view of the war, particularly on colonial rule and imperialism. Her most famous war essay is probably "Tinder for Tomorrow." Buck's canon further includes personal works, such as the auto-biographical *My Several Worlds: A Personal Record* (1954) and *A Bridge for Passing* (1962). Several of her plays were produced off Broadway or in summer stock.

Achievements

Buck has been enormously successful with popular audiences, more so than with the literati. She is the most widely translated author in all of American literary history. In Denmark, for example, her popularity exceeded that of Ernest Hemingway and John Steinbeck in the 1930's, and in Sweden, ten of her books were translated between 1932 and 1940, more than those of any other American author. *The Good Earth*, her most famous work, has been translated into more than thirty languages (seven different translations into Chinese alone) and made into a play and a motion picture.

Buck's early novels received much acclaim. *The Good Earth* was awarded the Pulitzer Prize; in 1935, she was awarded the William Dean Howells medal by the American Academy of Arts and Letters for the finest work in American fiction from 1930 to 1935, and in 1936, she was elected to membership in the National Institute of Arts and Letters. In 1938, she was awarded the Nobel Prize, the third American to receive it and the first woman, for her "rich and generous epic description of Chinese peasant life and masterpieces of biography." *The Good Earth*, a staple of high school and undergraduate reading, is undoubtedly a masterpiece; and her missionary biographies, *The Exile* and *Fighting Angel*, though currently neglected, have merit in the depth of their analysis. Three other books of the 1930's—*Sons*, *The Mother*, and *The Patriot*—have effective passages. In all her works, Buck evinces a deep humanity, and she did much to further American understanding of Asian culture.

Buck has not fared so well with the literary establishment. Critics of the 1930's disdained her work because she was a woman, because her subjects were not "American," and because they thought she did not deserve the Nobel Prize. Her success in writing best-seller after best-seller and her opti-mistic faith in progress and humanity have irked later critics. She did, however, achieve success by her own standards. Her books have reached and touched middle-class American women, an enormous body of readers largely ignored by serious writers. Her innate storytelling ability does "please," "amuse," and "entertain" (her three criteria for good writing) but even the kindest of her admirers wish that she had written less, spending more time exploring the minds of her characters and polishing her work.

Biography

Pearl S. Buck was born Pearl Comfort Sydenstricker on June 26, 1892, in the family home at Hillsboro, West Virginia, to Absalom and Caroline (Stulting) Sydenstricker. Her parents were missionaries in China, home on a furlough. After five months she was taken to China. Her parents' marriage was not a particularly happy one because of their disparate natures. Her mother, fun-loving and witty, was torn by her devotion to God; her father, single-minded and zealous, had success with his mission but not with his family. Buck grew up in Chinkiang, an inland city on the Yangtze River. In 1900, during the Boxer Rebellion, her family was forced to flee and she experienced the horrors of racism. Her education included one year at boarding school in Shanghai and four years at Randolph-Macon Women's College in Virginia.

In 1917, she married John Lossing Buck, an agricultural specialist. They lived in Nanhsuchon in Anhwei province (the setting of *The Good Earth*). Buck learned much about farming from her husband and from her own observations. After five years, they moved southward to Nanking, where her husband taught agriculture and she taught English at the university. She published her first article in *The Atlantic* (January, 1923); "In China, Too" described the growing Western influence in China.

Tragedy struck Buck's life with the birth of Carol, her only natural child, who was mentally retarded (she later adopted eight children). She took Carol to the United States for medical treatment in 1925. When her husband took a year's leave of absence, Buck studied English at Cornell University and received her master's degree. Her first published novel, *East Wind: West Wind*, combined two short stories, one of which was originally published in 1925 in *Asia* magazine. She had written a novel before *East Wind: West Wind*, but the novel was destroyed by soldiers entering her home in the 1926-1927 Nationalist Communist uprising. (During the takeover of Nanking, Buck and her family barely escaped, hiding in a mud hut until relief came.) On March 2, 1931, *The Good Earth* appeared, creating a literary sensation.

Buck's early literary influences included her parents and her old Chinese nurse. Her parents, of course, encouraged her to read the Bible and told her tales of their American homeland, while her nurse told her fantastic Buddhist and Taoist legends of warriors, devils, fairies, and dragons. She learned to speak Chinese before English, but she learned to read and write in English sooner than in Chinese. She read incessantly, Charles Dickens as a child and later Theodore Dreiser. Émile Zola and Sinclair Lewis were also important in her adult life. She paid particular tribute to Dickens: "He opened my eyes to people, he taught me to love all sorts of people." Even as a child, she decided to write: "One longs to make what one loves, and above all I loved to hear stories about people. I was a nuisance of a child, I fear, always curious to know about people and why they were as I found them." Her first writing appeared in the children's section of the Shanghai *Mercury*; in college, she contributed stories to the campus monthly and helped write the class play.

The Bucks were divorced in 1932, and that same year Pearl married her publisher, Richard J. Walsh, president of John Day and editor of *Asia* magazine. Their marriage lasted until his death in 1960. Buck loved both the United States and China throughout her life, serving as an intermediary between the two. In her last years, she was bitterly disappointed when the Chinese Communists would not grant her a visa, despite the *rapprochement* between the United States and China.

Buck's parents instilled into their daughter principles of charity and tolerance. Her love for the needy was also awakened by Miss Jewell, the mistress of her boarding school. Jewell took Buck along as an interpreter on errands of mercy—to visit institutions for slave girls who had fled from their masters and institutions where prostitutes went for help. Buck's own humanitarian efforts began in 1941 with the founding of the East and West Association, which endeavored to increase understanding between diverse cultures. During World War II, Buck actively spoke against racism, against the internment of Japanese-Americans, and against the yielding of democratic privileges during wartime.

Her sympathy extended to all, but especially to children and the helpless. In 1949, she and her husband founded Welcome House, an adoption agency for Amerasian children. In 1954, her letter of protest to *The New York Times* led to the changing of a policy which put immigrants in federal prisons with criminals. In 1964, she founded the Pearl S. Buck Foundation to care for Amerasian children who remain overseas. She also worked for the Training School, a school for the retarded in Vineland, New Jersey. For her many humanitarian efforts, she received the Brotherhood Award of the National Conference of Christians and Jews, the Wesley Award for Distinguished Service to Humanity and more than a dozen honorary degrees from American colleges and universities.

Along with her extensive humanitarian activities, Buck continued to write. Because her American novels *This Proud Heart* and *Other Gods* were not well received, Buck assumed the pen name "John Sedges" to write with freedom on American subjects. Between 1945 and 1953, five novels were published under this name while she wrote Asian stories under her own name. Unfortunately, as Buck's humanitarian efforts increased, the quality of her fiction declined. Its strident and moralistic tone reflected her growing concern with social issues rather than artistic technique. She continued writing, however, and by the time of her death in 1973 had written more than eighty novels and novellas.

Analysis

Pearl S. Buck's reputation for excellence as a writer of fiction rests solely on *The Good Earth* and segments of a few of her other novels of the 1930's.

The appeal of *The Good Earth* is undeniable and easy to explain: its universal themes are cloaked in the garments of an unfamiliar and fascinating Chinese culture. Echoing many elements of life, the book speaks of animosity between town and country, love of land, decadent rich and honest poor, marital conflicts, interfering relatives, misunderstandings between generations, the joys of birth and sorrows of old age and death, and the strong bonds of friendship. Added to these universal themes is the cyclical movement of the growth and decay of the crops, the decline of the House of Hwand and the ascent of the House of Wang, the changes of the years, and the birth and death of the people.

Buck fittingly chose to tell her story in language reminiscent of the Bible with its families and peoples who rise and fall. Her style also owes something to that of the Chinese storytellers, to whom she paid tribute in her Nobel Prize lecture, a style which flows along in short words "with no other technique than occasional bits of description, only enough to give vividness to place or person, and never enough to delay the story." Most of Buck's sentences are long and serpentine, relying on balance, parallelism, and repetition for strength. While the sentences are long, the diction is simple and concrete. She chooses her details carefully: her descriptions grow out of close observation and are always concise. The simplicity of the diction and the steady, determined flow of the prose fit the sagalike plot. In Chinese folk literature, the self-effacing author, like a clear vessel, transmits but does not color with his personality the life which "flows through him." So, also, Buck presents her story objectively. Her authorial presence never intrudes, though her warm feeling for the characters and her own ethical beliefs are always evident.

The strength of the novel also lies in its characterization, particularly that of the two main characters, O-lan and her husband Wang Lung. Whereas characters in Buck's later novels too easily divide into good and bad, the characters of *The Good Earth*, like real people, mix elements of both. Ching, Wang Lung's faithful, doglike friend and later overseer, early in the novel joins a starving mob who ransack Wang Lung's home for food; Ching takes Wang Lung's last handful of beans. The eldest son is a pompous wastrel, but he does make the House of Hwang beautiful with flowering trees and fish ponds and he does settle into the traditional married life his father has planned for him. Even O-lan, the almost saintly earth mother, seethes with jealousy when Wang Lung takes a second wife, and she feels contempt and bitterness for the House of Hwang in which she was a slave. Her major flaw is her ugliness. Wang Lung delights the reader with his simple wonder at the world and with his perseverance to care for his family and his land, but he, too, has failings. In middle age, he lusts for Lotus, neglecting the much-deserving O-lan, and in old age, he steals Pear Blossom from his youngest son. Rather than confusing the morality of the novel, the intermingling of good and bad increase its reality. Buck acknowledged literary indebtedness to Émile Zola, and the influence of naturalism is evident in *The Good Earth* in its objective, documentary presentation and its emphasis on the influence of environment and heredity. Unlike the naturalists, however, Buck also credits the force of free will.

The Good Earth aroused much fury in some Chinese scholars, who insisted that the novel portrays a China that never was. Younghill Kang criticized the character of Wang Lung. Professor Kiang Kang-Hu said that Buck's details and her knowledge of Chinese history were inaccurate. Buck defended herself by granting that customs differed in the many regions of China. In later novels, she retaliated by harshly portraying Chinese scholars such as Kang and Kiang, who, she believed, distorted the picture of the real China either because of their ignorance of peasant life or because of their desire to aid propagandistic efforts of the Chinese government. Other native Chinese, including Phio Lin Yutang, sprang to Buck's defense, insisting on the accuracy of her portrayal.

Like *The Good Earth*, *The Mother* follows the cyclical flow of time: the protagonist, who begins the novel in vigorous work, caring for an elderly parent, ends the novel as an elderly parent himself, cared for by the new generation. *The Mother* is also written in the simple, concrete, and sometimes poetic style of *The Good Earth*. The old mother-in-law, for example, in her early morning hunger, "belched up the evil winds from her inner emptiness." *The Mother*, however, portrays a different side of Chinese peasant life from that seen in *The Good Earth*—a more brutal one. The main character, named only "the mother," is carefully drawn; the other characters are flat and undeveloped, serving only as objects for her attention.

Deserted by her irresponsible, gambling husband, the mother lies about her spouse's absence to protect her family and cover her shame. She proves easy prey for her landlord's agent, by whom she becomes pregnant, later aborting the baby by taking medicine. Her eldest son eventually supports her, but his unfeeling wife will not tolerate having his blind sister underfoot. A husband is found for the blind girl, but when the mother travels to visit her daughter after a year, she discovers that the husband is witless and her daughter, after much mistreatment, has died. Even more sorrow darkens the mother's life. Her younger and most beloved son joins the Communists, is used as their dupe, and finally is arrested and beheaded.

This is not the honest-work-brings-rewards world of Wang Lung, but a world of victims, deformity, hatred, and cruelty. It is a portrait of the life of a woman in China, where girl babies routinely were killed and young girls of poor families were sold as slaves. Only new life—the excitement of birth and spring—balances the misery of the mother's life.

In *The Good Earth* and *The Mother*, Buck provides compelling visions of old age. Her children are mostly silent and inconsequential, her adolescents merely lusty and willful, but her elderly are individuals. The old father in *The*

Good Earth cackles with life, drawing strength from his grandchildren-bed-fellows. Wang Lung drowses off into a peaceful dream with his Pear Blossom. The mother-in-law basks in the sun and prides herself on wearing out her burial shrouds. The elderly mother in *The Mother* is frustrated because she no longer has the strength to work the land but remains as active as possible, trying to save her blind daughter and her Communist son, finally turning her affections to a new grandchild.

The main flaw in *The Mother* is that the mother seems too distant, too self-contained, for the reader to identify with her, to accept her as the universal mother that Buck intends her to be. The mother's story is interesting, but the reader does not feel her shame or her misery as he does O-lan's, nor does he feel her delight or her pride as he does Wang Lung's. Also, Buck's feelings about Communism are blatantly evident in the simplistic and oft-repeated phrase that the Communists are a "new kind of robber."

As Buck became more interested in social and political issues and in the media—magazines, film, and radio—her fiction began to deteriorate. She claimed, "The truth is I never write with a sense of mission or to accomplish any purpose whatever except the revelation of human character through a life situation." Her fiction, however, did not demonstrate this belief: more and more it became a forum for her own social and political ideas rather than an exploration of human character and life. Further, Hollywood and women's magazines began to influence her stories: they became drippingly romantic.

Dragon Seed is one of Buck's most popular post-1930's works, with the first half of the novel containing many of the strengths of her earlier work. Her characters are not as fully realized as the mother or Wang Lung, but the story is intriguing. A peasant farming family work the land, much as their ancestors have done for centuries, until the coming of war—flying airships and enemy troops—thrusts them into a world of violence and deprivation. As long as Buck keeps her eye sharp for details, describing the atrocities the people must endure and their struggles to understand what is happening to them, the novel remains interesting.

In the second half of the novel, however, Buck's purposes split. Rather than concentrating on the war story—the people and their experiences—she uses the novel to argue that the Western world is blind and uncaring about the troubles of the Chinese in World War II. In contrast to this didacticism are the Hollywood-style love-stories of Lao-Er and Jade and Lao San and Mayli. The dialogue between the happily married Lao-Er and Jade seems straight from a "B"-movie, and the overly coincidental coming together of Lao San and Mayli is a women's magazine romance of the self-made man and the rich, beautiful woman. Buck tries to portray the strong new woman of China (and the Western world) in Jade and Mayli, but they are *too* strong, *too* clever, almost always posturing with a defiant chin against the sunset. At one point in the novel, Buck even writes that Jade is so skillful in disguising herself that she should have been a film actress. O-lan, in her stoic silence—grudging, jealous, yet loving—is a believable woman; Jade and Mayli are creatures of fantasy.

Buck's power as a novelist derived from her intelligence, her humanity, her interesting stories, and her ability to make Chinese culture real to readers from all over the world. Her weaknesses as a novelist include didacticism, sentimentalism, and an inability to control her energy long enough to explore deeply, revise, and improve. In her later novels, she lost control of her point of view, her language, and her characterization. Her legacy is an enduring masterpiece, *The Good Earth*, and an inestimable contribution to cultural exchange between China and the West.

Ann Willardson Engar

Other major works

SHORT FICTION: *The First Wife and Other Stories*, 1933; *Today and Forever*, 1941; *Twenty-Seven Stories*, 1943; *Far and Near, Stories of Japan, China and America*, 1947; *American Triptych*, 1958; *Hearts Come Home and Other Stories*, 1962; *The Good Deed and Other Stories*, 1969; *Once Upon a Christmas*, 1972; *East and West*, 1975; *Secrets of the Heart*, 1976; *The Lovers and Other Stories*, 1977; *The Woman Who Was Changed and Other Stories*, 1979.

NONFICTION: *East and West and the Novel*, 1932; *The Exile*, 1936; *Fighting Angel: Portrait of a Soul*, 1936; *The Chinese Novel*, 1939; *Of Men and Women, 1941*, 1971; *American Unity and Asia*, 1942; *What America Means to Me*, 1943; *China in Black and White*, 1945; *Talk About Russia: With Masha Scott*, 1945; *Tell the People: Talks with James Yen About the Mass Education Movement*, 1945; *How It Happens: Talk About the German People, 1914-1933, with Erna von Pustau*, 1947; *American Argument: With Eslanda Goods*, 1949; *The Child Who Never Grew*, 1950; *My Several Worlds: A Personal Record*, 1954; *Friend to Friend: A Candid Exchange Between Pearl Buck and Carlos F. Romulo*, 1958; *A Bridge for Passing*, 1962; *The Joy of Children*, 1964; *Children for Adoption*, 1965; *The Gifts They Bring: Our Debt to the Mentally Retarded*, 1965; *The People of Japan*, 1966; *To My Daughters with Love*, 1967; *China As I See It*, 1970; *The Kennedy Women: A Personal Appraisal*, 1970; *The Story Bible*, 1971; *Pearl S. Buck's America*, 1971; *China Past and Present*, 1972.

CHILDREN'S LITERATURE: *The Young Revolutionist*, 1932; *Stories for Little Children*, 1940; *One Bright Day and Other Stories for Children*, 1952; *Johnny Jack and His Beginnings*, 1954; *The Man Who Changed China: The Story of Sun Yat-Sen*, 1953; *Fourteen Stories*, 1961; *The Chinese Story Teller*, 1971.

TRANSLATION: *All Men Are Brothers*, 1933.

Bibliography

Cavasco, G. A. "Pearl Buck and the Chinese Novel." *Asian Studies* 5 (1967): 437-450. A laudatory analysis of Buck's Chinese fiction, the study divides her work into three categories. Argues forcefully that these novels, including the Pulitzer Prize-winning *The Good Earth*, remain her best work and will always be popular because they adhere to the structure of Chinese fiction.

Doyle, Paul A. *Pearl S. Buck*. Rev. ed. Boston: Twayne, 1980. Excellent and balanced introduction to Buck the woman and the writer. Neither adulates nor derides Buck but examines her work carefully and concludes that she was an important writer.

Harris, Theodore F. *Pearl S. Buck: A Biography*. 2 vols. New York: John Day, 1969. Harris' work, written in very close collaboration with Buck, is an uncritical examination of her life. The second volume, made up entirely of personal correspondence, reveals Buck's general philosophy.

Spencer, Cornelia. *Revealing the Human Heart: Pearl S. Buck*. Chicago: Encyclopaedia Britannica, 1964. Biographical study by Buck's sister for juvenile readers. Contains some useful facts, no literary criticism, and eulogizes the writer.

Thompson, Dody Weston. "Pearl Buck." In *American Winners of the Nobel Prize*, edited by Warren G. French and Walter E. Kidd. Norman: University of Oklahoma Press, 1968. Surveys some of Buck's work, reveals its strengths and limitations, and suggests that her appeal is limited to students, idealists, and the unsophisticated.

FREDERICK BUECHNER

Born: New York, New York; July 11, 1926

Principal long fiction

A Long Day's Dying, 1950; *The Season's Difference*, 1952; *The Return of Ansel Gibbs*, 1958; *The Final Beast*, 1965; *The Entrance to Porlock*, 1970; *Lion Country*, 1971; *Open Heart*, 1972; *Love Feast*, 1974; *Treasure Hunt*, 1977; *The Book of Bebb*, 1979; *Godric*, 1980; *Brendan*, 1987; *The Wizard's Tide*, 1990.

Other literary forms

Frederick Buechner has published an autobiography in two slim volumes: *The Sacred Journey* (1982) and *Now and Then* (1983). He has also published a number of theological and homiletical volumes—idiosyncratic and often humorous works which illuminate his fiction and his novelistic techniques: *The Magnificent Defeat* (1966); *The Hungering Dark* (1969); *The Alphabet of Grace* (1970); *Wishful Thinking: A Theological ABC* (1973); *Telling the Truth* (1977); *Peculiar Treasures* (1979); *A Room Called Remember* (1984); and *Whistling in the Dark: A Theologized ABC* (1988). Finally, Buechner contributed commentary for the art book, *The Faces of Jesus* (1974).

Achievements

Buechner's major achievement as a novelist is his ability to "sanctify the profane," to depict in his novels the essentially religious nature of all human endeavor, to communicate the meaning of Christian faith in a time in which the Christian vocabulary and world view are considered defunct and impotent. An ordained Presbyterian minister, Buechner demonstrates in his post-conversion works a Christian theological viewpoint and an essential optimism about the human condition in an earthy, disarmingly comic narrative style.

While several of his volumes of nonfiction have achieved a very wide circulation, Buechner's readership as a novelist has been relatively small since his appearance on the literary scene with his 1950 novel, *A Long Day's Dying*, a book conceived and substantially written while he was an undergraduate student at Princeton. This first work was highly praised by leading critics, who noted its labored, "Jamesian" narrative voice—a fact which amuses and bewilders Buechner, who claimed to have read little of James at the time of its writing. His following two novels, *The Season's Difference* and *The Return of Ansel Gibbs*, were much less successful, and between 1958 and 1965, Buechner's narrative style and his subject matter radically changed. *The Final Beast* in 1965 signaled Buechner's evolution from a "modernist storyteller" into a comic novelist possessing a keen sense of life's ambiguities and con-traditions—all tempered by his Christian vision. *The Final Beast*, the four "Bebb" novels, and his fictionalized "lives of the saints," represented in *Godric* and *Brendan*, constitute a unique canon of works that infuse his narrative proclamation of the Christian faith with a unique vitality and style neither preachy nor romantic. Buechner's prose reveals new metaphors by which faith can be experienced and communicated, a transformation of the secular into the sacred—demonstrating the presence of the Divine in all living things. By his own account, Buechner is an apologist to "the cultured despisers" of religion:

> My novels are not Sunday School stories with detachable morals at the end. They are my attempt to describe the world as richly and truly as perhaps only fiction can describe it, together with the truth that God is mysteriously with us in the world. That is in essence what I am saying to Christians and to anybody else who will listen. ("Interview," in *Christianity and Literature*, XXXII, Fall, 1982.)

Biography

Carl Frederick Buechner was born in New York City on July 11, 1926, one of two sons of Carl Frederick and Katherine Buechner. The family, like many challenged by the Great Depression, moved a great deal during his childhood, a childhood prematurely ended by the suicide of his father when Buechner was ten. This event more than any other helps to explain the substance of Buechner's early literary preoccupations before his conversion to Christianity. After he was graduated from the Lawrenceville School in New Jersey in 1943, Buechner attended Princeton University. He completed his B.A. in English in 1948, after serving in the military from 1944 to 1946. It was during his later undergraduate years at Princeton that he conceived and wrote his first novel, *A Long Day's Dying*, "a study of the relationships of a small, sophisticated and highly articulate group of people" including a college student, his widowed mother and grandmother, and his mother's several lovers—characters and situations emblematic of Buechner's early baroque style and content. "Maroo," the grandmother in *A Long Day's Dying*, is clearly based on Buechner's grandmother, Naya, whom he lovingly commemorates as a witty and worldly-wise influence and inspiration for his fiction in his memoir *The Sacred Journey*. Buechner returned to his alma mater, the Lawrenceville School, in 1948 to teach English; during that time, he also conducted summer creative writing sessions at New York University.

Buechner's second book, *The Season's Difference*, appeared in 1952; it is a prophetic work in that, though it still bears the mannered style of his first novel, it deals with a strongly religious theme: the effect of a religious experience upon the lives of a sophisticated coterie of people in an academic setting. Two years later, Buechner himself would undergo a religious conversion which would lead him to Union Theological Seminary in New York. During his seminary training, he conducted an employment clinic in an East

Harlem Protestant parish. Paul Tillich, one of his professors at Union Theological Seminary, had a profound influence on his view of culture and theology; Tillich taught Buechner that the presence of the Divine permeates human society, and thereby sparked a dramatic change in Buechner's narrative strategies. Buechner was ordained a Presbyterian minister in 1958, just after his third novel, *The Return of Ansel Gibbs*, was published. This novel marked a transition from his two earlier works in its transcendence of his earlier baroque style and its topical subject matter.

From 1958 to 1967, Buechner served as school minister and chair of the Department of Religion at Phillips Exeter Academy, and during this time completed his fourth novel, *The Final Beast*, and two homiletical volumes, *The Magnificent Defeat* and *The Hungering Dark*. Since 1967, Buechner has become a full-time writer and lecturer, living with his wife, Judith, and his family in Vermont. During the 1970's, Buechner completed five novels: *The Entrance to Porlock* and the celebrated Bebb tetralogy, *Lion Country*, *Open Heart*, *Love Feast*, and *Treasure Hunt*.

For a time it appeared that Buechner's literary reputation would rest upon this raucous quartet of novels, but with the increasing appreciation for his abilities as a historical novelist evident in his *Godric* (1980) and *Brendan* (1987), Buechner has established himself as a versatile and unpredictable artist. These two "lives of the saints" narratives set, respectively, in the twelfth and sixth centuries A.D., are departures in time and place from Buechner's more typical settings but nevertheless are framed in the same orthodox Christian yet comic terms characteristic of the Bebb tetralogy. In *The Wizard's Tide*, published in 1990, Buechner returned to the overtly autobiographical stance he had employed in his early fiction, treating his father's suicide directly and therapeutically in the form of a children's story. Buechner's papers have been collected at Wheaton (Illinois) College, and his work remains of great interest both to Christian believers and to critics weary of the minimalism and secularism of much modern fiction.

Analysis

In a 1971 issue of *Publishers Weekly*, Frederick Buechner revealed to an interviewer the secret of what has been a prolific career:

> Writing *is* a kind of ministry. I do not feel I am doing much different in my preaching and in my writing. . . . The process of telling a story is something like religion if only in the sense of having a plot leading to a conclusion that makes some kind of sense.

Buechner's view of narrative, exemplified in his novels after *The Season's Difference*, is that storytelling reveals the form of human life, its direction and its meaning. Each human life contains a hidden agenda, a pattern of events that bears close attention and a listening ear; since most people are deaf and blind to this agenda, it is up to the storyteller, the writer of novels, the creator of metaphors, to reveal that agenda. When he or she is successful, the novelist not only lays bare the meaning of human events but also reveals—sometimes in spite of himself—the presence of the Divine in human affairs. Since Buechner believes God works "behind the scenes" and almost never explicitly in history (the grand exception being the "magnificent defeat," the crucified Christ and his resurrection), he finds the novel an appropriate medium for conveying theological truth.

Given his view of narrative, one is not surprised to find Buechner's novels populated by characters whose lives contain a central ambiguity, a tension between faith and doubt, which Buechner the storyteller does not attempt to resolve. His task is to present the ambivalence of human life as faithfully as possible in the hope that, as the reader sees his own ironies and incongruities, he will be led to a consideration of their source and their potential resolution. While some of Buechner's characters come to a faith with which they can face life, others reject supernatural notions out of hand. Others fall in between, reflecting Buechner's own sentiments that he himself is only a "part-time Christian" because, as he writes in *The Alphabet of Grace*, "part of the time seems to be the most I can live out my faith."

All of Buechner's fictional works are deeply introspective, even contemplative in texture, despite his sometimes comic stance; as such, they form a rich complement to Buechner's memoirs and meditations. Buechner's oeuvre is thus strikingly symmetrical and consistent, with the chief demarcations reflected in the evolution of his narrative technique. Consequently, Buechner's fiction is best studied chronologically, since his work falls into four fairly distinct periods and modes. The early Buechner novels, *A Long Day's Dying* and *The Season's Difference*, form one unit for analysis, reflecting his early penchant for a psychological interrogation of his characters; two transitional novels, *The Return of Ansel Gibbs* and *The Final Beast*, prepare the reader for Buechner's newfound prowess for explicit exploration of religious themes; a third period contains his enigmatic *The Entrance to Porlock* and the four ribald and boisterous novels which form the celebrated Bebb tetralogy; a fourth slot includes Buechner's *Godric* and *Brendan*, and *The Wizard's Tide*, representing the mature, even nostalgic Buechner, a writer whose narrative powers are fully developed and whose themes are fully consistent with his settled world view.

A Long Day's Dying and *The Season's Difference* form a novelistic couplet of rarefied and intellectualized treatments of modern life, its tensions and its ethical malaise. Their style, referred to by critics of the time as "mandarin" and intentionally "mythic," overshadows characterization and plot; one critic asserted that *A Long Day's Dying* in particular was an example of "writing for a teacher"—reflecting the dominance at that time of the New Criticism, which emphasized and prized such features as "ambiguity" and "ambivalence." The estrangement of the modern age from its genteel and cultured roots is a primary theme in both works: *A Long Day's Dying* documents the fragility of relationships in postwar America and the absence of a moral center; *The Season's Difference* confronts the same scenario while exploring in particular the callousness of its characters toward the mystical and the supernatural. While neither of these novels is as explicitly "religious" as Buechner's later works, their thematic concerns foreshadow dilemmas voiced in *The Final Beast* and the Bebb novels, whose resolutions are intertwined with faith and acceptance of Divine providence.

Modern life as depicted in these two novels has no place for innocence. Paul Steitler, the cynical English professor in *A Long Day's Dying*, says that his mission is to corrupt young innocents who, in their naïveté, fail to realize that "they're never going to have it so good again." "In a few years," he laments, "they're going to break their legs and need the crutches I'm offering now, but they don't believe it . . . at moments like these, I really don't myself." The "crutches" he can offer them—a stoical resignation and a weak antidote for their felt loss of religious convictions—recall Matthew Arnold's prophecy that poetry would replace religion in the future's brave new world. Steitler, Buechner's prototypal "clear-eyed realist," is a foil for the more trusting, priest-like character of Tristram Bone. Bone, nevertheless, is a failed "priest"; he is no mediator of the Divine, no consoler of the downtrodden. Empty of spiritual substance, he can recognize "sin" but can offer no redemption, either for himself or for his beloved Elizabeth and her son, Leander. The one potential center of moral conviction and action in the novel is Maroo, Leander's grandmother. Her death signals the spiritual demise of those whom she might have influenced and reflects the fate of all those who confront the secular world with merely secular weapons. The novel's title comes from Book 10 of John Milton's *Paradise Lost* (1667), an ironic counterpoint that juxtaposes the eventual reconciliation of Adam and Eve with the painful alienation of the novel's characters from one another.

The Season's Difference continues several of the themes Buechner articulated in *A Long Day's Dying* while emphasizing more strongly the skepticism of the modern age toward the experience of the supernatural. Though Buechner treats this theme with great earnestness and includes several passages of crisp, refreshingly direct prose, the merits of this work are blunted by its extraordinarily verbose and philosophical mode of narration. Despite these weaknesses, however, Buechner's second novel clearly anticipates the apologetics of later works, his defense of God's ways to secularized man.

The Return of Ansel Gibbs and *The Final Beast*, Buechner's first two postseminary novels, reflect a dramatic shift in narrative technique; his emerging understanding of theology-as-story seems to have transformed his novelistic sensibilities. Gone for the most part are "drawing-room" characters and situations; in their place are social issues, direct, unpretentious dialogue, and, for the first time, a sense of humor. It is in *The Return of Ansel Gibbs* that

Buechner first broaches explicitly the possibility of Christian faith as a viable option in the modern world, something placed in the mouth of Dr. Kuykendall. Kuykendall is loosely based on one of Buechner's seminary professors, and it is he who serves as Gibbs's mentor and counselor as Gibbs vacillates about accepting a cabinet post. Buechner has Kuykendall address a seminary audience, articulating both the risk of faith and its problematic nature:

> If you tell me Christian commitment is a thing that has happened once and for all like some kind of spiritual plastic surgery . . . you're either pulling the wool over your own eyes or trying to pull it over mine. Every morning you should wake up in your beds and ask yourself: "Can I believe it all again today?"

The exigencies of modern life make faith—along with hope, love, courage, commitment—a daily affirmation, not a once-and-for-all declaration, not the faith in "cheap grace" which Dietrich Bonhoeffer railed against. The "return" of Ansel Gibbs is a rediscovery of life's center, its core; fearful that he is aloof and detached, Gibbs fights his way out of his own ambivalence to confront a world made not of words but of people and relationships. Still, Gibbs cannot quite embrace a "holy cause," one which is reflected in Kuykendall's implicit call for prophetic responsibility on Gibbs's part; this is Buechner's way of presenting the tension of faith, of making room for the agnostic who can bring himself only to say that "you can cross your fingers and hold your tongue and do what you can in the time that's left."

Buechner's transition from a mannered stylist into a colloquial and whimsical storyteller was complete in *The Final Beast*, his fourth novel. Appearing seven years after *The Return of Ansel Gibbs*, *The Final Beast* reflects Buechner's years of preaching and pastoral work, which tempered and softened his narrative technique. In his most autobiographical work of fiction, Buechner is at ease, conversational and delightfully humorous. While *The Final Beast* takes up themes introduced earlier in Buechner's writing, there is a discernible boldness and joyousness in this novel previously submerged or excluded in his work. Its protagonist, Theodore Nicolet, is a recently widowed young minister whose religious experience is analogous to Buechner's own. Searching for a sign of God's presence, Nicolet retreats to the countryside, composing a Sunday sermon on the grass near his father's barn. Here there is no dramatic "Damascus road" encounter; instead, in this tranquil, pastoral setting, Nicolet hears the "click-clack" of two apple branches brushing against each other. In *The Alphabet of Grace*, Buechner explains Nicolet's experience and, implicitly, his own as "the occasional, obscure glimmering through of grace. The muffled presence of the holy. The images, always broken, partial, ambiguous of Christ." Man can ultimately only bear "the click-clack"; any more of the Divine presence would be overwhelming, devastating. God must not intrude; He must imply. Despite these glimmers of grace, the novel is not all sweetness and light; the "beast" of the novel's title refers, evidently, to the "mark of the beast" discussed in the Book of Revelation; it is the undeniable presence of evil in a world created by a gracious God. Nicolet's joyful affirmation of life and of God's care is counterbalanced by the character of Irma Reinwasser, a German native and concentration-camp victim who has suffered much. Irma cannot bring herself to put confidence in "Harold," the name by which Nicolet's children refer to God (a garbling of the Lord's Prayer: "Harold be thy name"). Though she cannot express faith, her vicarious sacrifice on behalf of Nicolet after the young minister's integrity is compromised demonstrates her implicit understanding of redemptive love. While some critics complained that *The Final Beast* was the predictable effort of a "minister-novelist," the novel in fact inaugurated a revitalization of religious fiction and represented an achievement matched among contemporary writers only by such figures as Reynolds Price and Walter Percy.

Buechner's next novel, *The Entrance to Porlock* was in some ways an experiment: a whimsical treatment of serious themes in which he used L. Frank Baum's Oz stories for mythical resonance. This was a 180-degree turn from *A Long Day's Dying*, in which Buechner employed an elaborate—and somewhat stultifying—Greek mythology to convey his thematic concerns. *The Entrance to Porlock* is the story of Peter Ringkoping and his family, a household of dreamers, each on a quest to discover self and therefore to come to grips with the reality of his life. Along the way, Peter, looking for a "heart," discovers it in his recognition that he loves the land of which he is about to divest himself; Tip is a Dorothy-like character, seeking a home, which he finds toward the end of the novel; Tommy, eventually facing himself as he is, is the scarecrow finding a brain; Nels is a lion seeking courage, which is mustered up in confronting a problematic situation with a student; finally, Hans Strasser plays the Wizard's role, inspiring each of the Ringkopings to introspection and a renewal of self.

The Entrance to Porlock, whose title is derived from Samuel Taylor Coleridge's famous account of the composition of "Kubla Khan," was in Buechner's estimation the most difficult book he has ever attempted to write. Written in the aftermath of the political assassinations of the late 1960's, *The Entrance to Porlock* is a dreamy, lyrical book that exhorts the reader to press on in the face of ugliness and brutality, an affirmation of the human spirit's resiliency. Despite its highly symbolic texture, the book is eminently readable and, in its own way, exuberant. A reader could not have been prepared, however, for the rollicking and ribald novels that would follow it and that, some critics say, would represent Buechner's greatest creation.

In the 1970's, Buechner published four novels centered around his most animated and most fully realized character, Leo Bebb: *Lion Country*, *Open Heart*, *Love Feast*, and *Treasure Hunt*. These four novels form a tetralogy which was reissued as one volume entitled *The Book of Bebb* in 1979 (it is upon this 1979 format that the following analysis will be based). Buechner took advantage of the reissuing of the four novels to make some slight revisions, none of which materially altered the structure, characterization, or tone of his raucously comic creations. The Bebb novels well illustrate the wry comment of one critic who suggested that Buechner's art is too religious for the secular reader and too secular for the religious reader. Buechner creates Leo Bebb as the supreme example of grace operating through the least likely channel; Bebb is profane, earthy, sometimes blasphemous in the way he chooses to "preach the gospel." Nevertheless, he is but one more reminder that all men have feet of clay, that God loves his creatures in spite of their shortcomings, and that the evidence of grace is all around for people to see; what people lack, Buechner intimates, are "eyes to see and ears to hear." In Leo Bebb, Buechner is—in Flannery O'Connor's terms—"shouting to the hard of hearing and drawing large figures for the almost blind." Bebb is perhaps the most memorable fictional character of the 1970's; his stories take their place alongside John Updike's Rabbit series, and Bebb is sacred counterpart to Updike's Rabbit Angstrom. In *The Book of Bebb*, one sees most clearly the fruition of Buechner's narrative strategies and the fulfillment of his writing "ministry" in the sanctification of the profane.

Leo Bebb is a "rogue preacher," founder of Church of Holy Love, and later, the Church of the Open Heart. His story is told by his son-in-law, Antonio Parr—who originally intends to expose Bebb as a charlatan, an operator of a shameless religious diploma mill. While Bebb is the fulcrum upon which the tetralogy balances—even after his death in the third novel, *Love Feast*, one is not quite done with Bebb, since he is "reincarnated" as Jimmy Bob in *Treasure Hunt*—in many ways the tetralogy is the private journey of Antonio Parr, a tracing of one man's "sacred journey." Parr's narration is the best witness to Buechner's dictum, advanced in his memoir *The Sacred Journey*, that God "speaks to us not just through the sounds we hear . . . but through events in all their complexity and variety, through the harmonies and disharmonies and counterpoint of all that happens." While faith is Leo Bebb's "business," Parr is not so easily won; his encounter with Bebb and the trail of sorrows, joys, paradoxes, and incongruities that follow it serve to illustrate the winding path a man's life takes. Faith, as Buechner wants to underscore, is difficult: "Hard as hell," in Bebb's words.

Reading *The Book of Bebb*, one has the sense of following a single continuous narrative—a remarkable achievement, given the fact that the four novels were written over a six-year period without an initial design for a tetralogy. Buechner accounts for the unity of the four works by reference to the ease with which the characters and situations came to him; whereas he regards *The Entrance to Porlock* as the first "Caesarian birth" of his writing career, the Bebb novels flowed freely from his imagination. Speaking of *Lion Country*, Buechner declares "I could hardly wait to get to it in the morning, and I hated to leave it when I had to go home in the afternoon . . . the whole thing was finished in about six to eight weeks." In regard to its expansion into a tetralogy, Buechner explains that when he wrote the last sentence of *Lion Country*, "I thought I had finished with them all for good but soon found that they were not finished with me."

The Book of Bebb is Buechner's "loveletter" to that "beloved stranger," his reader, who might for a moment entertain the reality of the author's characters. Bebb and Parr, their intermingled families, the colorful cast of characters surrounding them—the profane Indian chief who wants to restore his sexual potency, the "octogenarian dottiness" of a UFO museum director— all of these richly crafted creations awaken the reader to the oddness of life, which is incarnated in its very ordinariness, in the mundane world through which life's meaning is mediated and God's presence is confirmed.

Leafing through a dictionary of saints, Buechner happened upon the story of the twelfth century churchman Godric, which immediately captured the novelist's imagination and provoked another fictional experiment. Using a narrative style that might be characterized as "colloquial Anglo-Saxon," *Godric* emerges as a narrative trek into the past to discover an earlier incarnation of Leo Bebb. Godric is no rogue preacher, but neither is he a conventional saint. From the first sentence of the novel, "Five friends had I and two of them snakes," the reader is taken on a lively journey into a historical epoch strangely like the present one. Here, one discovers that the Middle Ages were no less troubled than the twentieth century; more important, one discovers that the faith of medieval Christians was achieved no more easily than it is among modern man. Mirrored in the experience of Godric—a man desperately trying to avoid celebrity and sainthood—are the same ambiguities and tensions that confront contemporary believers and agnostics. Turning the clock back is no guarantee of simplicity or of easy answers. The earthiness of Godric's time is reassuring, however—Buechner's way of saying that the human condition is unaltered by time and space. Men and women, in Buechner's view, have always had the same needs, hopes, dreams, and sorrows they have today.

Godric is a chronicle whose narrator is Godric himself. Here, Buechner has created a credible voice, flavored with archaic cadences and intonations, which evokes the past and the present simultaneously, thus engaging the reader on two levels. The novel ends with a tremendous irony; Reginald, Godric's faithful companion and servant, is left to write the epilogue to Godric's eloquent autobiography. In so doing—filling his prose with Latinate locutions and fatuous exaggerations—he unwittingly provides a dramatic counterpoint to Godric's spiritual pilgrimage. Reginald's elegy presents faith, Godric's in particular, in an idealized manner, conveying the opposite of his master's actual experience. Godric's life was characterized not by constant victory and miracle but by daily struggle. By making Godric "larger than life," Reginald condemns him to being less than a man, merely a cartoon.

Encouraged by the acclaim accorded *Godric*, Buechner once again selected an obscure saint around which he could build another narrative; in *Brendan*, Buechner chose the Irish churchman born in A.D. 484 and who is believed by some to have traveled to the New World on his missionary voyages. Unlike *Godric*, *Brendan* presents someone other than the title character as the narrator. Finn, Brendan's unbelieving but sympathetic traveling companion, is brilliantly realized as an authentically distant, prudently skeptical Irish voice who chronicles the adventures of the itinerant Brendan with a power and a profundity that depict the fragility and resiliency of faith. Once again, Buechner displays his prodigious gift for anachronistic speech that is at once ancient and contemporary; as one critic suggested, *Brendan* begs to be read aloud.

In many ways, *Godric* and *Brendan* encompass the best features of Buechner's work: a wry, sometimes bawdy humor; a willingness to focus the profound spiritual dimensions of existence through the filter of a single, human life; and a principled reliance on the power of symbolic narrative to intimate the transcendent directly to the soul. Such qualities are equally present in *The Wizard's Tide*, a book which brings Buechner full circle to the painful autobiographical reflection he first explored in *The Final Beast*. In the guise of a book for children, *The Wizard's Tide* explores the Great Depression through the eyes of a young boy whose father commits suicide. Filled with period detail, the novel evokes a wistful nostalgia in the reader for a time of simpler ethics and for clearer answers to life's conundrums. The book's title refers to "the Wizard of Oz tide," the "tide that brings you home," even when one is adrift at sea without hope of seeing the shore again: Buechner's confirming and comforting metaphor for the promise of restoration and resurrection found in the Christian gospel.

Buechner is a literary jack-of-all-trades, impressive in his control of diverse fictional and nonfictional modes of discourse. He is at once a leading Christian apologist, a writer of meditations, a homiletician, a novelist, and an autobiographer. The common strain through all of these roles is Buechner's conviction that life is, in the end, a story: a story to be celebrated, a story to be endured, but above all, a story to be told. No one who has read a bit of Buechner's prose can come away from it knowing less of himself; his readers are, finally, the parish of this novelist-turned-minister-turned-storyteller.

Bruce L. Edwards

Other major works

NONFICTION: *The Magnificent Defeat*, 1966; *The Hungering Dark*, 1969; *The Alphabet of Grace*, 1970; *Wishful Thinking: A Theological ABC*, 1973; *The Faces of Jesus*, 1974; *Telling the Truth*, 1977; *Peculiar Treasures*, 1979; *The Sacred Journey*, 1982; *Now and Then*, 1983; *A Room Called Remember*, 1984; *Whistling in the Dark: A Theologized ABC*, 1988.

Bibliography

Aldridge, John W. *After the Lost Generation*. New York: McGraw-Hill, 1951. An early and thus dated consideration of Buechner's fiction in the context of several other mid-century writers, which nevertheless provides a historical perspective on Buechner's emerging place in American letters.

Davies, Marie-Helene. *Laughter in a Genevan Gown: The Novels of Frederick Buechner, 1970-1980*. Grand Rapids, Mich.: W. B. Eerdmans, 1983. A basically theological inquiry into the Christian premises of Buechner's fiction, ordered chronologically but handicapped somewhat by its sometimes unimaginative, stilted use of the novelist's theological works to aid the explication of his fiction.

Gibble, Kenneth. "Listening to My Life: An Interview with Frederick Buechner." *Christian Century* 100 (November 16, 1983): 1042-1045. A very informative interview with Buechner in which he candidly discusses the relationship between his own biography, his fictional subject matter, and his narrative technique.

McCoy, Marjorie Casebier. *Frederick Buechner: Novelist/Theologian of the Lost and Found*. San Francisco: Harper & Row, 1989. The best full-length treatment of Buechner's oeuvre, from his early modernist novels to his postconversion fiction and theological works; a very personal exposition written with unadorned sympathy for Buechner's Christian viewpoint. The subtitle refers to Buechner's thematic interest in depicting lost souls stumbling their way toward a benevolent destiny.

Nelson, Rudolph. "The Doors of Perception: Mystical Experience in Frederick Buechner's Fiction." *Southwest Review* 68 (Summer, 1983): 266-275. A succinct examination of the principal themes of Buechner's fiction, with insight into how his fiction confronts and makes sensible "the direct experience of the divine as real and near."

Woelfel, James. "Frederick Buechner: The Novelist as Theologian." *Theology Today* 40 (October, 1983): 273-291. A perceptive overview of Buechner's life and career as theologian and preacher, and as novelist; a good place to start for a condensed summary of Buechner's primary themes and preoccupations that will key the reader to interpreting his later works.

JOHN BUNYAN

Born: Elstow, England; November, 1628
Died: London, England; August 31, 1688

Principal long fiction

Grace Abounding to the Chief of Sinners, 1666; *The Pilgrim's Progress from This World to That Which Is to Come*, Part I, 1678; *The Life and Death of Mr. Badman*, 1680; *The Holy War*, 1682; *The Pilgrim's Progress from This World to That Which Is to Come the Second Part*, 1684.

Other literary forms

Between 1656 and 1688, John Bunyan published forty-four separate works, including prose narratives and tracts, sermons, and verse; ten posthumous publications appeared in a folio edition of 1692, which the author himself had prepared for the press. A nearly complete edition, in two volumes, was printed between 1736 and 1737, another in 1767 by George Whitefield, and a six-volume Edinburgh edition in 1784. The best of Bunyan's verse can be found in a small collection (c. 1664) containing "The Four Last Things," "Ebal and Gerizim," and "Prison Meditations." In addition, he wrote *A Caution to Stir Up to Watch Against Sin* (1664), a half-sheet broadside poem in sixteen stanzas; *A Book for Boys and Girls: Or, Country Rhymes for Children* (1686); *Discourse of the Building, Nature, Excellency, and Government of the House of God* (1688), a poem in twelve parts.

Achievements

The spirit of seventeenth century Protestant dissent burst into flame within the heart and mind of Bunyan. He attended only grammar school, served in the parliamentary army at age sixteen, and returned to Bedfordshire to undergo religious crisis and conversion. Imprisoned after the Restoration of Charles II for refusing to obey the laws against religious dissent, he turned to his pen as the only available means of performing his divinely ordained stewardship. He wrote his most significant work, the vision of *The Pilgrim's Progress*, while in jail, and the piece became a companion to the Scriptures among lower-class English Dissenters. His limited education came from two sources: the *Actes and Monuments* (1563) of John Foxe, containing the accounts of the martyrdom of sixteenth century English Protestants; and the Authorized Version of the Bible, the content and style of which he skillfully applied to his own prose.

Bunyan's art grew out of his natural abilities of observation and analysis. He was a Puritan and a product of the Puritan movement yet, as can be seen clearly from the autobiographical *Grace Abounding to the Chief of Sinners*, he was chiefly interested in actual human experience, not in religious doctrine for its own sake. His allegorical characters—Mr. Timorous, Mr. Talkative,

Mrs. Diffidence, Mr. By-ends, Lord Turn-about, Mr. Smooth-man, Mr. Facing-bothways—originated in everyday life. Similarly, the Valley of Humiliation, the Slough of Despond, Vanity Fair, and Fair-speech can be found by all people everywhere, no matter what their culture or religion. In *The Pilgrim's Progress*, Bunyan universalized his Puritanism, depicting every earnest Christian's search for salvation, every upright person's attempt to achieve some degree of faith. He wrote to awaken conscience, to strenghten faith, and to win souls—the last being the true object of his evangelical mission. At the same time, he managed to write tracts and narratives worthy of recognition as *literature*—even, in certain instances, as masterpieces.

Biography

John Bunyan was born at the village of Elstow, in Bedfordshire (one mile south of Bedford) in November, 1628. The parish register of Elstow records his baptism on November 30. His father, Thomas Bunyan, a native of Elstow, married three times between January, 1623, and August, 1644; John Bunyan was the first child of his father's second marriage—on May 23, 1627, to Margaret Bentley, also of Elstow. The boy's father was a "whitesmith," a maker and mender of pots and kettles, although by the time the son adopted the same vocation, the job reference had changed to "tinker." Young Bunyan attended a nearby grammar school (either the one at Bedford or another at Elstow), where he learned to read and write—but little else. In fact, what he did learn he promptly forgot after his father removed him from school to help in the family forge and workshop. When, in 1644, his mother died and the elder Bunyan promptly remarried, Bunyan lost all interest in his family; he entered the parliamentary army in November, at age sixteen, and remained until the disbanding of that force in 1646. He then returned to Elstow and the family trade.

At the end of 1648 or the beginning of 1649, Bunyan married a pious but otherwise unidentified woman who bore him four children—one of whom, Mary, was born blind. He spent some four years wrestling with his finances and his soul, and in 1653 joined a dissenting sect that met at St. John's Church, Bedford. Shortly after his removal to that city in 1655, his wife died, and two years later he was called upon to preach by the Baptist sect whose church he had joined. In 1659, he married again, to a woman named Elizabeth, who spent considerable time rearing his children, bearing him two more, and trying to secure her husband's release from a series of prison terms.

Bunyan's career as a writer cannot be separated from his difficulties immediately preceding and during the Restoration of Charles II. The period of Cromwell's Commonwealth produced a number of dissenting preachers, both male and female, who achieved their offices through inspiration rather than ordination; they professed to be filled with inner light and the gifts of the Holy Spirit rather than with learning. Charles II had promised to tolerate these preachers, but the established Church, in November, 1660, set about to persecute and to silence them. Thus, Bunyan, who chose imprisonment rather than silence, spent all but a few weeks of the next eleven years in jail in Bedford, where he preached to his fellow prisoners, made tagged laces, and wrote religious books—the most noteworthy being his spiritual autobiography, *Grace Abounding to the Chief of Sinners.* He was freed in September, 1672, when Charles II, through his Declaration of Indulgence, suspended all penal statutes against Nonconformists and papists.

Upon his release from prison, Bunyan returned to his ministerial duties at St. John's Church in Bedford, this time with a license (given to him by royal authority) to preach. By 1675, however, he was again imprisoned in Bedford, the result of refusing to declare formal allegiance to Charles II (against whom he had no real objection) and the Church of England. While serving this particular sentence, Bunyan produced his most significant piece of prose, *The Pilgrim's Progress.* Bunyan's major prose works were written within the last ten years of his life, the period during which he both suffered from intolerance and received honors from the intolerant. In the last year of his life, he served as the unofficial chaplain to Sir John Shorter, the Lord Mayor of London. Indeed, Bunyan endured the entire tide of religious and political trauma of the middle and late seventeenth century: parliamentary acts, ministerial changes, popish plots, the rebellious factions. His work bears testimony to that endurance, to the patience of a nonpolitical yet deeply pious man who lost much of his freedom to the impatience of a supposedly pious but terribly political religious establishment.

Bunyan died on August 31, 1688, at the London house of his friend, John Strudwick, a grocer and chandler. Supposedly, in order to settle a dispute between a father and his son, he rode through heavy rain and caught a severe cold that led to his death. He was buried in Bunhill Fields, the burial ground of London Dissenters.

Analysis

John Bunyan viewed his life as a commitment to Christian stewardship, to be carried on by gospel preaching and instructive writing. Although practically everything that he wrote reflects that commitment, he possessed the ability to create interesting variations on similar themes, keeping in mind the needs of his lower-class audience. Thus, *The Pilgrim's Progress* is an allegory of human life and universal religious experience. In *The Life and Death of Mr. Badman,* Bunyan abandoned allegory and developed a dialogue betweeen Mr. Wiseman and Mr. Attentive through which he publicized the aims and methods of the late seventeenth century bourgeois scoundrel, whose lack of principle and honesty was well known among Bunyan's readers (the victims of Mr. Badman). Finally, his first major work, *Grace Abounding to the Chief of Sinners,* is a "spiritual autobiography" which presents adventures and experiences not unlike those undergone by any human being at any moment in history who must wrestle with the fundamental questions of life. The function of Bunyan's prose in every case was to spread the Word of God and to establish a holy community of mankind in which that Word could be practiced. Once the Word took hold, Bunyan believed, the world would become a veritable garden of peace and order.

Published in 1666, *Grace Abounding to the Chief of Sinners* remains one of the most significant spiritual autobiographies by an English writer. Bunyan's style is perhaps more formal in this piece than in *The Pilgrim's Progress*, although he did well to balance the heavy phrasing of Scripture (as it appeared in the Authorized Version) with picturesque, colloquial English. A richly emotional work in which such highly charged experiences as the Last Judgment and the tortures of Hell become as clear as the mundane experiences of daily existence, Bunyan's autobiography is a narrative of spiritual adventure set against the backdrop of a real village in Britain. Although he omitted specific names and dates, obviously to universalize the piece, he did not forget to describe what he had seen after his return from the army: the popular game of "cat," with its participants and spectators; the bellringers at the parish church; the poor women sitting, in sunlight, before the door of a village house; the puddles in the road. Woven into this fabric of reality are the experiences of the dreamer; the people of Bedford appear as though in a vision on the sunny side of a high mountain, as the dreamer, shut out by an encompassing wall, shivers in the cold storm. Such interweaving of reality and fantasy was to take place again, with greater force and allegorical complexity, in the first part of *The Pilgrim's Progress*.

Bunyan's intention in *Grace Abounding to the Chief of Sinners* was to point the way by which average Christians, convinced of their own sins, can be led by God's grace to endure the pain of spiritual crisis. He determined to record how, as an obscure Bedfordshire tinker, he had changed his course from sloth and sin to become an eloquent and fearless man of God. Of course, when he wrote the work, he had been in prison for ten years, and (as stated in the Preface) he set about to enlighten and assist those from whom he had, for so long a period, been separated.

From the confinement of his prison cell, Bunyan felt the desire to survey his entire life—to grasp his soul in his hands and take account of himself. Thus, *Grace Abounding to the Chief of Sinners* emerged from the heart and the spirit of a man isolated from mankind to become not merely one more testimonial for the instruction of the faithful, but a serious, psychological self-study—one so truthful and so sincere (and also so spontaneous) that it may be the first work of its kind. Bunyan's language is simple and direct, and his constant references to Scripture emphasize the typicality of his experiences as a struggling Christian. His fears, doubts, and moments of comfort are filtered through the encounter between David and Goliath and God's deliverance of the young shepherd, while his lively imagination gathers images from the Psalms and the Proverbs and reshapes them to fit the context of his spiritual experiences.

Bunyan's ability to universalize his experience is supremely evident in *The Pilgrim's Progress*, perhaps the most successful allegory in British literature. *The Pilgrim's Progress* has as its basic metaphor the familiar idea of life as a journey. Bunyan confronts his pilgrim, Christian, with homely and commonplace sights: a quagmire, the bypaths and shortcuts through pleasant country meadows, the inn, the steep hill, the town fair on market day, the river to be forded. Such places belong to the everyday experience of every man, woman, and child; on another level, they recall the holy but homely parables of Christ's earthly ministry, and thus assume spiritual significance. Those familiar details serve as an effective background for Bunyan's narrative, a story of adventure intended to hold the reader in suspense. Bunyan grew up among the very people who constituted his audience, and he knew how to balance the romantic and the strange with the familiar. Thus, Christian travels the King's Highway at the same time that he traverses a perilous path to encounter giants, wild beasts, hobgoblins, and the terrible Apollyon, the angel of the bottomless pit with whom the central character must fight. Other travelers are worthy of humorous characterization as they represent a variety of intellectual and moral attitudes, while Christian himself runs the gamut of universal experience, from the moment he learns of his sins until the account of his meeting with Hopeful in the river.

As always, Bunyan molds his style from the Authorized Version of the Bible. By relying upon concrete, common language, he enables even the simplest of his readers to share experiences with the characters of *The Pilgrim's Progress*. Even the conversations relating to complex and tedious theological issues do not detract from the human and dramatic aspects of the allegory: Evangelist pointing the way; Christian running from his home with his fingers stuck in his ears; the starkness of the place of the Cross in contrast to the activity of Vanity Fair: the humorous but terribly circumstantial trial. It is this homely but vivid realism which accounts for the timeless appeal of Bunyan's allegory. *The Pilgrim's Progress* reveals the truth about mankind—its weakness, its imperfection, its baseness, but also its search for goodness and order.

The Life and Death of Mr. Badman represents Bunyan's major attempt at a dialogue, a confrontation between the Christian and the atheist, between the road to Paradise and the route to Hell. Mr. Wiseman, a Christian, tells the story of Mr. Badman to Mr. Attentive, who in turn comments upon it. Badman is an example of the reprobate, one whose sins become evident during childhood. In fact, he is so addicted to lying that his parents cannot distinguish when he is speaking the truth. Bunyan does not place much blame upon the parents, for they indeed bear the burden of their son's actions; they even attempt to counsel him and to redirect his ways. The situation becomes worse, however, as Badman's lying turns to pilfering and then to outright stealing. All of this, naturally, leads to a hatred of Sunday, to the Puritan demands of that day: reading Scripture, attending conferences, repeating sermons, praying to God. Wiseman, the defender of the Puritan Sabbath, maintains that little boys, as a matter of course, must learn to appreciate the Sabbath; those who do not are victims of their own wickedness. Hatred of the Sabbath leads to swearing and cursing, which become as natural to young Badman as eating, drinking, and sleeping.

Badman's adult life is painstakingly drawn out through realistic descriptions, anecdotes, and dialogue. He cheats and steals his way through the world of debauchery and commerce and creates misery for his wife and seven children. Growing in importance, he forms a league with the devil and becomes a wealthy man by taking advantage of others' misfortunes. When the time comes for his end, he cannot be saved—nor does Bunyan try to fabricate an excuse for his redemption and salvation. As Mr. Wiseman states, "As his life was full of sin, so his death was without repentance." Throughout a long sickness, Badman fails to acknowledge his sins, remaining firm in his self-satisfaction. He dies without struggle, "like a chrisom child, quietly and without fear."

The strength of *The Life and Death of Mr. Badman* derives in large part from Bunyan's ability to depict common English life of the mid- and late seventeenth century. The details are so accurate, so minute, that the reader can gain as much history from the piece as morality or practical theology. Bunyan places no demands upon the reader's credulity by providential interpositions, nor does he alter his wicked character's ways for the sake of a happy ending. In portraying Badman's ways, Bunyan concedes nothing, nor does he exaggerate. Badman succeeds, gains wealth and power, and dies at peace with himself. Bunyan creates a monstrous product of sin and places him squarely in the center of English provincial life. The one consolation, the principal lesson, is that Badman travels the direct route to everlasting hell-fire. On his way, he partakes of life's pleasures, is gratified by them as only an unrepentant sinner could be. For Bunyan, the harsh specificity of Badman's life is a sufficient lesson through which to promote his version of positive Christianity.

Beneath the veil of seventeenth century British Puritanism, for all its seeming narrowness and sectarian strife, there was something for all persons of all eras—the struggle to know God, to do His will, to find peace. If Bunyan's first major prose work was a spiritual autobiography, then it is fair to state that the principal efforts that followed—*The Pilgrim's Progress* and *The Life and Death of Mr. Badman*—constituted one of the earliest spiritual histories of all mankind.

Samuel J. Rogal

Other major works

POETRY: *A Caution to Stir Up to Watch Against Sin*, 1664; *A Book for Boys and Girls: Or, Country Rhymes for Children*, 1686; *Discourse of the Building, Nature, Excellency, and Government of the House of God*, 1688.

RELIGIOUS WRITINGS: *Some Gospel Truths Opened*, 1656; *A Vindication . . . of Some Gospel Truths Opened*, 1657; *A Few Signs from Hell*, 1658; *The Doctrine of the Law and Grace Unfolded*, 1659; *Profitable Meditations Fitted to Man's Different Condition*, 1661; *I Will Pray with the Spirit*, 1663; *A Mapp Shewing the Order and Causes of Salvation and Damnation*, 1664; *One Thing Is Needful*, 1665; *The Holy City: Or, The New Jerusalem*, 1665; *A Confession of My Faith and a Reason for My Practice*, 1671; *A New and Useful Concordance to the Holy Bible*, 1672; *A Defence of the Doctrine of Justification By Faith*, 1672; *The Strait Gate: Or, The Great Difficulty of Going to Heaven*, 1676; *Saved by Grace*, 1676; *A Treatise of the Fear of God*, 1679; *A Holy Life, the Beauty of Christianity*, 1684; *Solomon's Temple Spiritualized: Or, Gospel Light Fecht Out of the Temple at Jerusalem*, 1688; *The Jerusalem Sinner Saved*, 1688.

Bibliography

Battestin, Martin C. ed. *British Novelists, 1660-1800*. Vol. 39 in *Dictionary of Literary Biography*. Detroit: Gale Research, 1985. Presents biographical details of interest, remarking on Bunyan's religious conversion, a central theme in his life and work. Discusses at length *The Pilgrim's Progress*, and also mentions in passing *The Holy War* and *The Life and Death of Mr. Badman*. Notes that Bunyan's fiction arises from a "particular religious faith in a particular historical setting."

Collmer, Robert G. *Bunyan in Our Time*. Kent, Ohio: Kent State University Press, 1989. A collection of distinguished literary criticism and appraisals of Bunyan. Includes essays on his use of language, satire and its biblical sources, and *The Pilgrim's Progress* as allegory. Of particular interest are the esssays on Marxist perspectives on Bunyan and a comparison between Bunyan's quest and C. S. Lewis' quest in *The Pilgrim's Regress* (1933).

Harrison, G. B. *John Bunyan: A Study in Personality*. New York: Archon Books, 1967. A short study that traces the mind and personality of Bunyan as shown in his writings. Discusses his conversion, his imprisonment, and his roles as pastor and writer. The close analysis of minor works makes this an important critical source.

Kelman, John. *The Road: A Study of John Bunyan's "Pilgrim's Progress."* 2 vols. Port Washington, N.Y.: Kennikat Press, 1912. These volumes are intended as a commentary or textbook, to be read point by point with *The Pilgrim's Progress*. An evangelical approach to Bunyan, filled with praise for his work. Gives close analysis to the text from a strongly Christian point of view.

Newey, Vincent. *"The Pilgrim's Progress": Critical and Historical Views*. Liverpool, England: Liverpool University Press, 1980. Brings together critical essays on *The Pilgrim's Progress* to provide fresh, detailed, and varied approaches to this work. Discusses the tension between allegory and naturalism and Bunyan's handling of the language and values of the people. Indispensable to the serious scholar of this work.

Sadler, Lynn Veach. *John Bunyan*. Boston: Twayne, 1979. A useful introduction to beginning readers of Bunyan. Discusses his life, his religious milieu, and his works. Places *Grace Abounding to the Chief of Sinners* in the genre of "spiritual autobiography." Most of the literary criticism goes to *The Pilgrim's Progress*, but there is also discussion of *The Life and Death of Mr. Badman* and *The Holy War*. Also includes a selected bibliography.

ANTHONY BURGESS
John Anthony Burgess Wilson

Born: Manchester, England; February 25, 1917

Principal long fiction

Time for a Tiger, 1956; *The Enemy in the Blanket*, 1958; *Beds in the East*, 1959; *The Doctor Is Sick*, 1960; *The Right to an Answer*, 1960; *Devil of a State*, 1961; *One Hand Clapping*, 1961 (as Joseph Kell); *The Worm and the Ring*, 1961; *A Clockwork Orange*, 1962; *The Wanting Seed*, 1962; *Honey for the Bears*, 1963; *Inside Mr. Enderby*, 1963 (as Joseph Kell); *The Eve of Saint Venus*, 1964; *Nothing Like the Sun: A Story of Shakespeare's Love-Life*, 1964; *The Long Day Wanes*, 1965 (includes *Time for a Tiger*, *The Enemy in the Blanket*, *Beds in the East*); *A Vision of Battlements*, 1965; *Tremor of Intent*, 1966; *Enderby*, 1968 (includes *Mr. Enderby*, *Enderby Outside*); *Enderby Outside*, 1968; *MF*, 1971; *The Clockwork Testament: Or, Enderby's End*, 1974; *Napoleon Symphony*, 1974; *Beard's Roman Woman*, 1976; *Moses: A Narrative*, 1976; *Abba, Abba*, 1977; *1985*, 1978; *Man of Nazareth*, 1979; *Earthly Powers*, 1980; *The End of the World News*, 1983; *Enderby's Dark Lady*, 1984; *The Kingdom of the Wicked*, 1985; *The Pianoplayers*, 1986; *Any Old Iron*, 1989.

Other literary forms

In addition to his novels, Anthony Burgess has published eight works of literary criticism. He has paid tribute to his self-confessed literary mentor, James Joyce, in such works as *Re Joyce* (1965) and *Joysprick* (1973). His book reviews and essays have been collected in *The Novel Now* (1967), *Urgent Copy* (1968), and *But Do Blondes Prefer Gentlemen? Homage to Qwert Yuiop and Other Writings* (1986). His fascination with language and with the lives of writers has led to such works as *Language Made Plain* (1964), *Here Comes Everybody* (1965), *Shakespeare* (1970), and *Flame into Being: The Life and Work of D. H. Lawrence* (1985). An autobiographical work, *Little Wilson and Big God*, was published in 1987, and a collection of short fiction, *The Devil's Mode*, in 1989.

Achievements

In his novels, Burgess has extended the boundaries of English fiction. His inventive use of language, his use of symphonic forms and motifs, his rewriting of myths and legends, his examination of cultural clashes between the Third World and the West, and his pursuit of various ways to tell a story have established him as one of the chief exemplars of postmodernism. His novels are studied in contemporary fiction courses, and he has also achieved popular success with such works as *A Clockwork Orange* and *Earthly Powers*. Stanley Kubrick's controversial film *A Clockwork Orange* (1971) further established Burgess' popular reputation.

Biography

John Anthony Burgess Wilson was born in Manchester, England, on February 25, 1917. His mother and sister died in the influenza epidemic of 1918. Of Irish background, his mother had performed in the music halls of the period and was known as "the Beautiful Belle Burgess." His father performed as a silent-film pianist and when he remarried, played piano in a pub called "The Golden Eagle," owned by his new wife; Burgess himself began to compose music when he was fourteen. Burgess was graduated from the Bishop Bilsborrow School and from Xaverian College in Manchester; in 1940, he wrote his senior honors thesis on Christopher Marlowe, while Nazi bombs fell overhead.

In October, 1940, Burgess joined the army and was placed in the Army Medical Corps. He was later shifted to the Army Educational Corps—a prophetic move, since he became a teacher for nearly twenty years afterwards. In 1942, Burgess married Llewela Isherwood Jones, a Welsh fellow student. He spent three years, from 1943 to 1946, with the British Army on Gibraltar, during which time he wrote his first novel, *A Vision of Battlements* (which was not published until 1965).

Burgess left the army as a sergeant major and as a training college lecturer in speech and drama in 1946 to become a member of the Central Advisory Council for Adult Education in the armed forces. He lectured at Birmingham University until 1948, when he served as a lecturer in phonetics for the Ministry of Education in Preston, Lancashire. From 1950 until 1954, he taught English literature, phonetics, Spanish, and music at the Banbury grammar school in Oxfordshire.

Throughout these years, Burgess was painfully aware of his Irish heritage and Catholic religion. Though he had renounced Catholicism early, the Irish-Catholic stigma remained with him in rigorously Protestant England. His decision to apply for the job of education officer for the Colonial Service may have had something to do with his desire to leave England and his need to exile himself physically from a homeland that had already exiled him in spirit. From 1954 to 1957, he was the Senior Lecturer in English at the Malayan Teachers Training College in Kahta Baru, Malaya. There, he had more leisure time to write, and he published his first novel, *Time for a Tiger*, in 1956 under his middle names, "Anthony Burgess." Members of the Colonial Service were not allowed to publish fiction under their own names.

Burgess continued working for the Colonial Service as an English language specialist in Brunei, Borneo, from 1957 to 1959 and published two more novels, which, with his first, eventually constituted his Malayan trilogy, *The*

Long Day Wanes. The clash between the manners and morals of East and West became the major focus of his early novels.

Apparent tragedy struck in 1959, when Burgess fainted in the classroom and was rushed to a neurological institute in London. There, he was given a year to live, after excruciating medical tests; the diagnosis was a possible brain tumor. Unable to teach, virtually penniless, Burgess set himself to writing as much as he could in order to provide for his wife. Not only had she already shown signs of the cirrhosis of the liver that was eventually to kill her, but also she had attempted suicide. In the next three years, Burgess wrote and published nine novels, including *A Clockwork Orange* and *Inside Mr. Enderby*.

On the first day of spring, March 20, 1968, Llewela Burgess finally died. That October, Burgess married Liliana Macellari, a member of the linguistics department at Cambridge; they had had a son, Andrew, in 1964. The personal guilt involved with his first wife's death always haunted Burgess and provided one of the major underlying themes of his fiction. "Guilt's a good thing," Burgess once said, "because the morals are just ticking away very nicely." In fact, persistent guilt shadows all of his characters and consistently threatens to overwhelm them completely.

Burgess, Liliana, and Andrew left England in October, 1968; they moved to Malta, to Bracciano in Italy, and eventually settled in Monaco. Burgess remained a prolific writer. In 1980, he published *Earthly Powers*, a long and ambitious novel on which he had been working for more than ten years. He continued to compose symphonies, write film scripts and television scripts, and review at great length in major newspapers and periodicals. Throughout the 1980's, the pace of his production did not slacken.

Analysis

Anthony Burgess shares with many postmodernist writers an almost obsessive awareness of his great modernist predecessors—particularly James Joyce. The vision which Burgess inherited from modernism is informed by the anguish of a sensitive soul lost in a fragmented, shattered world. Each of Burgess' novels reveals one central character virtually "at sea" in a landscape of battered, broken figures and events. Burgess conveys this fragmented worldview by means of many of the literary devices of his modernist predecessors. Often he employs a stream-of-consciousness narration, in which his main character tells his own story; he also has used what T. S. Eliot, reviewing Joyce's *Ulysses* (1922), called the "mythic method," in which contemporary chaos is compared with and contrasted to heroic myths, legends, religious ceremonies, and rituals of the past. As Eliot remarked, the mythic method "is simply a way of controlling, of ordering, of giving a shape and significance to the intense panorama of futility and anarchy which is contemporary history."

Like many postmodernists, convinced that most literary forms are serious games devised to stave off approaching chaos and collapse, Burgess delights in the play of language for its own sake. Here again, Joyce is a prime source of inspiration: surprising images, poetic revelations, linguistic twists and turns, and strange evocative words nearly overwhelm the narrative shape of *Ulysses* and certainly overwhelm it in *Finnegans Wake* (1939). Burgess' best novels are those in which language for its own sake plays an important role, as in *Enderby*, *Nothing Like the Sun*, *A Clockwork Orange*, and *Napoleon Symphony*.

At the heart of his vision of the world lies Burgess' Manichaean sensibility, his belief that there is "a duality that is fixed almost from the beginning of the world and the outcome is in doubt." God and the Devil reign over a supremely divided universe; they are equal in power, and they will battle to the end of the world. In the Manichaean tradition—most notably, that of the Gnostics—Burgess sees the world as a materialistic trap, a prison of the spirit and a place devised by the Devil to incarcerate man until his death. Only art can break through the battlelines; only art can save him. The recasting of a religious commitment in aesthetic terms also belongs to the legacy of modernism. Burgess' Manichaean vision produces such clashes of opposites as that between East and West, between the self and the state, and between a single character and an alien social environment. These recurring polarities structure Burgess' fiction.

This principle of polarity or opposition is evident in the early novel *The Right to an Answer*, in which J. W. Denham, businessman and exile, returns to his father's house in the suburban British Midlands and finds a provincial, self-satisfied community engaged in wife-swapping, television-viewing, and pub-crawling. He remains a detached observer, longing for a kind of communion he cannot find, and in his telling his own tale, he reveals himself as friendless, disillusioned, and homeless.

The wife-swapping quartet at the Black Swan pub is disturbed by the entrance of Mr. Raj, a Ceylonese gentleman, interested in English sociology and in satisfying his lust for white women. He plays by no rules but his own and espouses a kind of deadly Eastern realism that threatens the suburban sport. Moving in with Denham's father, he unfortunately kills the old man by "currying" him to death with his hot dishes. The upshot of this clash of cultural and social values is that Raj kills Winterbottom, the most innocent member of the *ménage à quatre*, and then kills himself.

Throughout the novel, Burgess explores both Denham's point of view and Raj's within the seedy suburban landscape. Their viewpoints reflect the irreconcilable differences between East and West, between black and white, between sex and love, and between true religion and dead ritual. Denham's stream-of-consciousness narration eventually reveals his own spirit of exile, which he cannot overcome. He remains disconnected from both worlds, from

England and the East, and epitomizes the state of lovelessness and isolation that has permeated modern culture. This early novel clearly explores Burgess' main themes and narrative forms.

In the guise of a thriller *à la* James Bond, *Tremor of Intent* explores a world of "God" and "Not-God," a profoundly Manichaean universe. Soviet spies battle English spies, while the real villains of the novel, the "neutralists," play one camp off against the other purely for personal gain. Burgess derides the whole notion of the spy's realm, but he insists that taking sides is essential in such a world, whether ultimate good or evil is ever really confronted.

Denis Hillier, aging technician and spy, writes his confessional memoirs in the light of his possible redemption. His Catholic sense of original sin never falters for an instant, and he is constantly in need of some higher truth, some ultimate communion and revelation. In the course of the novel, he fights every Manichaean division, drinks "Old Mortality," sees himself as a "fallen Adam," and works his way toward some vision of hope. Finally, he abandons the spy game and becomes a priest, exiling himself to Ireland. From this new perspective, he believes that he can approach the real mysteries of good and evil, of free will and predestination, beyond the limiting and limited categories of the Cold War.

Hillier's opposite in the novel is Edwin Roper, a rationalist who has jettisoned any religious belief and who hungers for an ultimately unified universe based on scientific truth and explanation. Such rationalism leads him to the Marxist logic of Soviet ideology, and he defects to the Russian side. Hillier has been set to rescue him. One section of the novel consists of Roper's autobiographical explanation of his actions; its flat, logical prose reflects his methodical and disbelieving mind, in contrast to Hillier's more religious sensibility.

Within the complicated plot of the novel, self-serving scoundrels such as Mr. Theodorescu and Richard Wriste set out to destroy both Hillier and Roper and gather information to sell to the highest bidder. They fail, owing largely to the actions of Alan and Clara Walters, two children on board the ship that is taking Hillier to meet Roper. The children become initiated into the world of double agents and sexual intrigue, and Theodorescu and Wriste are assassinated.

Burgess displays his love of language for its own sake in exotic descriptions of sex, food, and life aboard a cruise ship. Such language intensifies the Manichaean divisions in the book, the constant battle between the things of this world and the imagined horrors of the next. The very language that Hillier and Roper use to tell their own stories reveals their own distinctly different personalities and visions.

Tremor of Intent insists on the mystery of human will. To choose is to be human; that is good. Thus, to choose evil is both a good and a bad thing, a Manichaean complication that Burgess leaves with the reader. In allegorical terms the novel presents the problems of free will and its consequences which underlie all of Burgess' fiction.

Nothing Like the Sun, Burgess' fanciful novel based on the life of Shakespeare, showcases every facet of his vision and technique as a novelist. Shakespeare finds himself caught between his love for a golden man and a black woman. Sex feeds the fires of love and possession, and from these fires grows his art, the passion of language. From these fires also comes syphilis, the dread disease that eventually kills him, the source of the dark vision that surfaces in his apocalyptic tragedies. Shakespeare as a writer and Shakespeare as man battle it out, and from that dualistic confrontation emerges the perilous equilibrium of his greatest plays.

In part, Burgess' fiction is based on the theories about Shakespeare's life which Stephen Dedalus expounds in *Ulysses*. Dedalus suggests that Shakespeare was cuckolded by his brother Richard, that Shakespeare's vision of a treacherous and tragic world was based on his own intimate experience. To this conjecture, Burgess adds the notion that the Dark Lady of the sonnets was a non-Caucasian and that Shakespeare himself was a victim of syphilis. All of these "myths" concerning Shakespeare serve Burgess' Manichaean vision: sex and disease, art and personality are ultimately at war with one another and can only be resolved in the actual plays that Shakespeare wrote.

Nothing Like the Sun is written in an exuberant, bawdy, pseudo-Elizabethan style. It is clear that Burgess relished the creation of lists of epithets, curses, and prophecies, filled as they are with puns and his own outrageous coinings. Burgess audaciously attempts to mime the development of Shakespeare's art as he slowly awakens to the possibilities of poetry, trying different styles, moving from the sweet rhymes of "Venus and Adonis" to the "sharp knives and brutal hammers" of the later tragedies.

The book is constructed in the form of a lecture by Burgess himself to his Malayan students. He drinks as he talks and explains his paradoxical theories as he goes along. His passing out from too much drink at the novel's end parallels Shakespeare's death. He puns also with his real last name, Wilson, regarding himself as in fact "Will's son," a poet and author in his own right.

Earthly Powers, Burgess's longest novel, features perhaps his most arresting first sentence: "It was the afternoon of my 81st birthday, and I was in bed with my catamite when Ali announced that the archbishop had come to see me." Thus begin the memoirs of Kenneth Toomey, cynical agnostic and homosexual writer, a character based loosely on Somerset Maugham.

Toomey's memoirs span the twentieth century—its literary intrigues, cultural fashions, and political horrors. Toomey is seduced on June 16, 1904, that Dublin day immortalized by Joyce in *Ulysses*, revels in the Paris of the 1920's, the Hollywood of the 1930's, and the stylish New York of the 1940's and 1950's; his old age is spent in exotic exile in Tangiers and Malta in the 1970's. During his long life he writes plays and movie scenarios, carries on with a host of male secretary-lovers, and experiences the traumas of Nazism and Communism. He abhors the state-controlled collective soul which he sees as the ultimate product of the twentieth century.

Burgess' huge, sprawling novel displays a plot crowded with coincidence and bursting with stylistic parodies and re-creations. A priest on his way to becoming pope saves a dying child, only to see him grow up to be the leader of a fanatical religious cult akin to that of Jim Jones in Guyana. An American anthropologist and his wife are butchered during a Catholic mass in Africa: the natives there take the commands of the ceremony all too literally and swallow their visitors.

Toomey believes that evil lies firmly within man and that his experiences of this century prove that the world is a murderous place. His Manichaean opposite in faith is his brother-in-law, Carlo Campanati, the gambler-gourmet priest who becomes Pope Gregory XVII. Evil remains external to man, the Pope maintains; man is essentially good. In Burgess' jaundiced view of things, such misconceived idealism produces only further evils. Any similarities between Gregory and John XXIII are strictly intentional.

The world of *Earthly Powers* is Toomey's world, a bright place with clipped, swift glimpses of fads and fashion. Librettos, snippets of plays, even a re-creation of the Garden of Eden story from a homosexual point of view appear in this modernist memoir. The style itself reflects Burgess' conception of the "brittle yet excruciatingly precise" manner of the homosexual.

Earthly Powers wobbles. More than six hundred pages of bright wit can cloy. Verbal surfaces congeal and trail off into trivial documentation. The Pope's spiritual observations impede the novel's progress, encased as they are in lectures, sermons, and tracts. Indeed, Gregory's is as thin a character as Toomey's is an interesting one.

The book proves that Toomey is right: things are rotten. No amount of linguistic fun, modernist maneuverings, or Manichaean machinations can change the fact that this is the worst of all possible worlds. Chunks of smart conversation cannot hide that fact; they become stupefying and evasive in the end. The nature of man's free will, however, and its legacy of unquestionable evil in the twentieth century pervade Burgess' fat book and linger on to undermine any "safe" position the reader may hope to find.

Burgess' Manichaean nightmare in *A Clockwork Orange* occupies the center of his most accomplished book. The language of *nadsat* in its harsh, Russian-accented diction, the ongoing battle between the State and Alex the *droog*, the vision of an urban landscape wracked with violence and decay, the mysterious interpenetration of Beethoven and lust, and the unresolved issues of good and evil reflect and parallel one another so completely that the novel emerges as Burgess' masterpiece.

The issue raised is an increasingly timely one: can the state program the individual to be good? Can it eradicate the individual's right to freedom of choice, especially if in choosing, he chooses to commit violent and evil acts? Burgess replies in the negative. No matter how awful Alex's actions become, he should be allowed to choose them.

Since the novel is written from Alex's point of view, the reader sympathizes with him, despite his acts of rape and mayhem. Alex loves Beethoven; he "shines artistic"; he is brighter than his ghoulish friends; he is rejected by his parents. He is in all ways superior to the foul futuristic landscape that surrounds him. When the state brainwashes him, the reader experiences his pain in a personal, forthright manner. The violence in the rest of the book falls upon outsiders and remains distanced by the very language Alex uses to describe his actions.

Burgess' slang creates a strange and distant world. The reader approaches the novel as an outsider to that world and must try diligently to decode it to understand it. Never has Burgess used language so effectively to create the very atmosphere of his fiction. The Russian-influenced slang of the novel is a *tour de force* of the highest order and yet functions perfectly as a reflection of Alex's state of mind and of the society of which he is a rebellious member.

The world of *A Clockwork Orange* recognizes only power and political force. All talk of free will dissolves before such a harrowing place of behaviorist psychologists and social controllers. Individual freedom in such a world remains a myth, not a reality, a matter of faith, not an ultimate truth. Everyone is in some sense a clockwork orange, a victim of his or her society, compelled to act in a social order that celebrates only power, manipulation, and control.

Even the cyclical form of *A Clockwork Orange* reveals a world trapped within its own inevitable patterns. At first, Alex victimizes those around him. He in turn is victimized by the state. In the third and final part of the novel, he returns to victimize other people once again: "I was cured all right." Victimization remains the only reality here. There are no loopholes, no escape hatches from the vicious pattern. The frightening cityscape at night, the harsh language, the paradoxical personality of Alex, the collaborationist or revolutionary tactics of Alex's "friends," and the very shape of the novel reinforce this recognition of utter entrapment and human decay. "Oh, my brothers," Alex addresses his readers, as Eliot in *The Waste Land* (1922) quoted Charles Baudelaire: "*Hypocrite lecteur, mon semblable, mon frère.*"

Despite Burgess' pessimistic vision of contemporary life and the creative soul's place in it, the best of his novels still reveal a commitment to literature as a serious ceremony, as a game which the reader and the writer must continue to play, if only to transcend momentarily the horrors of Western civilization in the twentieth century.

Samuel Coale

Other major works
SHORT FICTION: *The Devil's Mode*, 1989.

NONFICTION: *English Literature: A Survey for Students*, 1958 (as John Burgess Wilson); *The Novel Today*, 1963; *Language Made Plain*, 1964; *Here Comes Everybody: An Introduction to James Joyce for the Ordinary Reader*, 1965 (published in the United States as *Re Joyce*, 1965); *The Novel Now*, 1967, rev. ed., 1971; *Urgent Copy: Literary Studies*, 1968; *Shakespeare*, 1970; *Joysprick: An Introduction to the Language of James Joyce*, 1972; *Ernest Hemingway and His World*, 1978; *On Going to Bed*, 1982; *This Man and Music*, 1983; *Flame into Being: The Life and Work of D. H. Lawrence*, 1985; *But Do Blondes Prefer Gentlemen? Homage to Qwert Yuiop and Other Writings*, 1986 (also known as *Homage to Qwert Yuiop*, 1985); *Little Wilson and Big God*, 1987.

CHILDREN'S LITERATURE: *A Long Trip to Teatime*, 1976.

TRANSLATION: *Oedipus the King*, 1972.

Bibliography

Aggeler, Geoffrey, ed. *Critical Essays on Anthony Burgess*. Boston: G. K. Hall, 1986. A collection of well-regarded criticism on Burgess, with particular attention given to his "linguistic pyrotechnics." Aggeler's introduction presents an overview of Burgess' work and discussion of his novels, followed by a *Paris Review* interview with Burgess.

Bergonzi, Bernard. "Anthony Burgess." In *Contemporary Novelists*, edited by James Vinson. London: St. James Press, 1976. Mentions Burgess' early interest in music, which he later brought into his novels, and his emergence as a novelist after World War II. Although acknowledging Burgess' ingenuity and inventiveness, Bergonzi cites flaws in his work and notes a lack of recent development.

Bloom, Harold, ed. *Modern Critical Views: Anthony Burgess*. New York: Chelsea House, 1987. A compilation of fine critical essays, including an essay by the eminent critic of James Joyce, Robert Martin Adams, who considers Joyce's influence on Burgess. In the introduction, Bloom presents his views on Burgess' writing, citing *Inside Mr. Enderby* as one of the most underrated English novels of this era.

Boytinck, Paul W. *Anthony Burgess: An Annotated Bibliography and Reference Guide*. New York: Garland, 1985. A checklist of Burgess' works up to 1984, including bibliographical background on Burgess and extracts from reviews, essays, and articles on his work. An excellent and informative resource for both the beginning reader and scholar of Burgess.

Critique: Studies in Modern Fiction 27 (Fall, 1981). This special issue gathers together seven critical essays on Burgess, some of which are appreciative— "Burgess is clearly in command of his material" in reference to *Earthly Powers*—and others which are less favorable—"Burgess' plots have a tendency to twitch and gyrate."

Mathews, Richard. *The Clockwork Orange Universe of Anthony Burgess*. San

Bernardino, Calif.: Borgo Press, 1978. This admiring monograph traces the thematic and temporal concerns that led Burgess to write his futuristic novels, including *A Clockwork Orange*. Mathews discusses ten novels that fit the metaphor of "clockwork universe."

FANNY BURNEY

Born: King's Lynn, England; June 13, 1752
Died: London, England; January 6, 1840

Principal long fiction

Evelina: Or, The History of a Young Lady's Entrance into the World, 1778; *Cecilia: Or, Memoirs of an Heiress*, 1782; *Camilla: Or, A Picture of Youth*, 1796; *The Wanderer: Or, Female Difficulties*, 1814.

Other literary forms

In addition to editing the memoirs of her father—the noted organist, composer, and music historian, Dr. Charles Burney (1726-1814)—Fanny Burney wrote an *Early Diary, 1768-1778* (1889) and then a later *Diary and Letters, 1778-1840* (1842-1846). The first work, not published until 1889, contains pleasant sketches of Samuel Johnson, James Boswell, David Garrick, and Richard Brinsley Sheridan. Notable figures from government and the arts march across the pages of the early diary, which scholars have claimed surpasses her fiction in literary quality. The latter diary and correspondence appeared between 1842 and 1846; the seven volumes are notable for the record of the writer's meeting in her garden with the insane George III of England, the account of her glimpse of Napoleon I, and the recollections of her chat with the weary Louis XVIII of France.

Of her eight dramatic productions, three are worthy of mention: *The Witlings* (never published); *Edwy and Elgiva; A Tragedy*, written in 1790, performed at Drury Lane on March 21, 1795, and withdrawn after the first night; and *Love and Fashion*, written in 1800, accepted by the manager at Covent Garden, but never performed. Finally, Burney published, in 1793, a political essay entitled *Brief Reflections Relative to the French Clergy*, an address to the women of Great Britain in behalf of the French emigrant priests.

Achievements

Most critics tend to place the reputation of Burney within the shadow of her most immediate successor, Jane Austen. Reasons for this assessment are not immediately clear, especially in the light of responses to the novels from contemporary readers. Burney's problem during the past two centuries, however, has not concerned popularity, subject matter, or even literary style; rather, certain personal circumstances under which she wrote seriously reduced her artistic effectiveness and considerably dulled her reputation. Essentially, Burney produced fiction at a time in history when a lady of means and social standing could not easily write fiction and still be considered a lady. Adding to that inhibition was the aura of her noted and influential father and his circle of even more influential friends: Samuel Johnson, Mrs. Hester Lynch Thrale Piozzi, Oliver Goldsmith, and Sir Joshua Reynolds. Both her father and his friends held literary standards not always easy for a self-educated young woman to attain. She burned her early manuscript efforts, wrote secretly at night, and published anonymously; she labored under the artistic domination of her father and the advice of his friends; she remained cautious, intimidated by and dependent on elderly people who served as guardians of her intellect.

Nevertheless, Burney succeeded as a novelist and achieved significance as a contributor to the history and development of the English novel. She brought to that genre an ability to observe the natural activities and reactions of those about her and to weave those observations through narrative structures and character delineations similar to those employed by her predecessors: Samuel Johnson, Henry Fielding, Samuel Richardson, Tobias Smollett, Aphra Behn, Mary De La Riviere Manley, Eliza Heywood, and Clara Reeve. In her Preface to *Evelina*, she set forth the criteria that, throughout her fiction, she would develop and maintain. For Burney, the novel would be the means by which to portray realistic persons and to represent the times in which they functioned. In her own concept of the form, those characters had to be real but not necessarily true; they had to be drawn "from nature, though not from life." Further, those same fictional characters had to confront and, hopefully, solve complex human problems—problems that they might avoid for a time but eventually would be forced to encounter.

Although Burney's four novels were published anonymously, the sophisticated readers of the day recognized the woman's point of view and immediately set the works apart from those of their contemporaries. The female readership, especially, both appreciated and praised the woman's view of the contemporary world; on the other hand, the young dandies of the late-eighteenth century and the pre-Victorian age scoffed at the novels' heroines as comic sentimentalists, products of blatant amateurism, and characteristic examples of a sex that would continue to be dominated by men.

The real basis on which to place Burney's popularity, however, rests with the ability of the novelist to develop fully the effects of female intelligence upon and within a society dominated by men and to convince her audience that coexistence between the sexes was far more beneficial than the dominance of one over the other. The essential differences between Fanny Burney and her female predecessors (Aphra Behn is the most obvious example) is the extent to which the issue of feminism was developed and then thrust forward as a major consideration.

As a woman writing about women, Burney could not cling too long to the models that the past century had provided for her. Despite the mild increase in the numbers of female novelists during the last quarter of the eighteenth century, Burney had little guidance in developing the woman's point of view.

She had, essentially, to find her own way within the confines of a limited world and even more limited experience. Thus, she determined early to purge her fictional environment of masculine influence. In its place, she would establish the importance of her titled characters as working parts in the machinery of eighteenth century British society. Burney's heroines do not convey appearances of being rebels, radicals, or social freaks; rather, their creator has drawn each one of them with a fine and firm hand. As a group, they are indeed meant to be carbon copies of one another; individually, each portrays a young lady in pursuit of traditional goals: marriage, money, and the discovery of the self.

Biography

Fanny (Frances) Burney, later Madame D'Arblay, the third of six children of Charles Burney and Esther Sleepe Burney, was born on June 13, 1752, at King's Lynn, Norfolk, where her father served as church organist while recuperating from consumption. In 1760, his health completely restored, Burney moved his family to London, where he resumed his professional involvements in teaching, composition, and music history. Upon the death of Esther Burney on September 28, 1761, two of the children (Esther and Susannah) went to school in Paris, while Frances remained at home. Apparently, Dr. Burney feared that his middle daughter's devotion to her grandmother (then living in France) would bring about the child's conversion to Catholicism. He seemed prepared to change that point of view and send Frances to join her sisters, when, in 1766, he married Mrs. Stephen Allen: thus, the fourteen-year-old girl remained at home in London, left to her own educational aims and directions, since her father had no time to supervise her learning. She had, at about age ten, begun to write drama, poetry, and fiction; on her fifteenth birthday, she supposedly burned her manuscripts because she felt guilty about wasting her time with such trifles.

Still, she could not purge her imagination, and the story of Evelina and her adventures did not die in the flames of her fireplace. Her brother, Charles, offered the first two volumes of *Evelina* to James Dodsley, who declined to consider an anonymous work for publication; Thomas Lowndes, however, asked to see the completed manuscript. After finishing *Evelina* and then securing her father's permission, Burney gave the work to the London publisher, who issued it in January, 1778, and paid the writer thirty pounds and ten bound copies. Its success and popularity owed some debt to Dr. Burney, who passed the novel on to Mrs. Thrale, a prominent figure in London's literary society. From there, it made its way to the select seat of London's intellectual empire, presided over by Dr. Johnson, Joshua Reynolds, and Edmund Burke. Shortly afterward, Fanny Burney met Mrs. Thrale, who took the new novelist into her home at Streatham (south of London) and introduced her to Johnson, Reynolds, Sheridan, and Arthur Murphy—all of whom pressed her to write drama. The result took the form of *The Whitlings*, a dramatic piece that, principally because of her father's displeasure over the quality of the work, she never published.

Returning to the form that produced her initial success, Burney published *Cecilia* in the summer of 1782, further advancing her literary reputation and social standing. She met Mary Delany, an intimate of the royal family, who helped secure for her an appointment in July, 1786, as second keeper of the Queen's robes, a position worth two hundred pounds per year. Her tenure at court proved to be more of a confinement than a social or political advantage because of the menial tasks, the rigid schedule, and the stiffness of the Queen and her attendants.

The activities and events at court, however, did contribute to the value of Burney's diaries, though her health suffered from the extreme physical demands of her labors. She continued in service until July, 1791, at which time she sought and gained permission to retire on a pension of one hundred pounds per annum. Then followed a period of domestic travel aimed at improving her health, followed by her marriage, on July 31, 1793, to General Alexandre D'Arblay, a comrade of the Marquis de Lafayette and a member of the small French community living at Juniper Hall, near Mickleham (north of Dorking, in Surrey). The couple's entire income rested with Madame D'Arblay's pension, and thus she sought to increase the family's fortunes through her writing. A tragedy, *Edwy and Elgiva*, lasted but a single night at Drury Lane, but a third novel, *Camilla*, generated more than three thousand pounds from subscriptions and additional sales, although the piece failed to achieve the literary merit of *Evelina* or *Cecilia*.

In 1801, General D'Arblay returned to France to seek employment but managed only a pension of fifteen hundred francs. His wife and son, Alexander, joined him the next year, and the family spent the succeeding ten years at Passy, in a state of quasi-exile that lasted throughout the Napoleonic wars. Madame D'Arblay and her son returned to England in 1812, and there, the novelist attended her aged father until his death in April, 1814. Her last novel, begun in France in 1802 and entitled *The Wanderer*, appeared early in 1814. Again, the financial returns far exceeded the literary quality of the piece; there were considerable buyers and subscribers but extremely few readers. After Napoleon's exile, the novelist returned to her husband in Paris; she then went to Brussels after the Emperor's return from Elba. General D'Arblay, meanwhile, had been seriously injured by the kick of a horse, which brought about an immediate end to his military career. The family returned to England to spend the remainder of their years: General D'Arblay died on May 3, 1818, and Alexander died on January 19, 1837—less than a year after having been nominated minister of Ely chapel. In November, 1839, Madame D'Arblay suffered a severe illness and died on January 6, 1840, in her eighty-seventh year.

Analysis

Despite the relative brevity of her canon, Fanny Burney's fiction cannot be dismissed with the usual generalizations from literary history: specifically that the author shared the interests of her youthful heroines in good manners. She possessed a quick sense for the comic in character and situation, and those talents distinctly advanced the art of the English novel in the direction of Jane Austen. From one viewpoint, she indeed exists as an important transitional figure between the satiric allegories of the earlier eighteenth century and the instruments that portrayed middle-class manners in full flourish during the first quarter of the nineteenth century.

Burney's contemporaries understood both her method and her purpose. Samuel Johnson thought her a "real wonder," one worth being singled out for her honest sense of modesty and her ability to apply it to fiction; while Edmund Burke seemed amazed by her knowledge of human nature. Three years after her death, Thomas Babington Macaulay proclaimed that the author of *Evelina* and *Cecilia* had done for the English novel what Jeremy Collier, at the end of the seventeenth century, did for the drama: maintain rigid morality and virgin delicacy. Macaulay proclaimed that Fanny Burney had indeed vindicated the right of woman "to an equal share in a fair and noble promise of letters" and had accomplished her task in clear, natural, and lively "woman's English."

Nevertheless, Fanny Burney contributed more to the English novel than simply the advancement of her sex's cause. Her heroines are mentally tormented and yet emerge as wiser and stronger human beings. The fictional contexts into which she placed her principal characters are those that readers of every time and place could recognize: situations in which the proponents of negative values seem to prosper and the defenders of virtue cling tenaciously to their ground. Burney's women must learn the ways of a difficult world, a society composed of countless snares and endless rules; they must quickly don the accoutrements for survival: modesty, reserve, submission, and (above all else) manners. What makes Burney's depiction of women in society particularly poignant is the knowledge that the author herself had to endure trials of survival. An awareness of the author's accounts of actual struggles for social survival, then, becomes a necessity for understanding and appreciating the problems confronted by her fictional characters.

In Burney's first novel, *Evelina*, the titled character brings with her to London and Bristol two qualities most difficult for a young provincial girl to defend: her sense of propriety and her pure innocence—the latter quality not to be confused with ignorance. In London, Evelina stumbles into false, insecure situations because she does not comprehend the rules of the social game. During the course of eighty-five epistles, however, she learns. The learning process is of utmost importance to Burney, for it serves as both plot for her fiction and instruction for her largely female readership. Once in London, life unfolds new meanings for Evelina Anville, as she samples the wares of urbanity: assemblies, amusements, parks and gardens, drawing rooms, operas, and theaters. Accompanying the activities is a corps of sophisticates by whose rules Evelina must play: Lord Orville, the well-bred young man and the jealous lover; Sir Clement Willoughby, the obnoxious admirer of Evelina who tries (through forged letters) to breach the relationship between Orville and Evelina; Macartney, the young poet whom Evelina saves from suicide and against whom Orville exercises his jealous streak; Captain Mirvan, the practical joker who smiles only at the expense of others; Mrs. Beaumont, who would have the heroine believe that good qualities originate from pride rather than from principles; Lady Louisa Larpent, the sullen and distraught (but always arrogant) sister of Lord Orville who tries to separate her brother from Evelina; Mr. Lovel, a demeaning fop who constantly refers to Evelina's simple background; the Watkins sisters, who chide Evelina because they envy her attractiveness to young men.

Despite these obstacles of situation and character, however, Evelina does not lack some protection. The Reverend Arthur Villars, her devoted guardian since the death of her mother, guides and counsels the seventeen-year-old girl from his home in Dorsetshire. Villars receives the major portion of Evelina's letters; in fact, he initally advises her to be wary of Lord Orville, but then relents when he learns of his ward's extreme happiness. Since Evelina cannot count on immediate assistance from Villars, she does rely on several people in London. Mrs. Mirvan, the amiable and well-bred wife of the captain, introduces Evelina to a variety of social affairs, while their daughter, Maria, becomes the heroine's only real confidante, sharing mutual happiness and disappointment. Finally, there is the Reverend Villars' neighbor, Mrs. Selwyn, who accompanies Evelina on a visit to Bristol Hot Wells. Unfortunately, the one person closest to Evelina during her London tenure, her maternal grandmother, Madame Duval, proves of little use and even less assistance. A blunt, indelicate, and severe woman, she is bothered by her granddaughter's display of independence and vows that the young lady will not share in her inheritance.

Villars emerges as the supporting character with the most depth, principally because he is ever present in the letters. From the novel's beginning, the heroine reaches out to him for guidance and support, scarcely prepared "to form a wish that has not [his] sanction." The local clergyman, Villars serves as parent for a motherless and socially fatherless young lady who, for the first time, is about to see something of the world. Thus, Villars' caution and anxiety appear natural, for he knows the bitter effects of socially unequal marriages, as in the cases of Evelina's own parents and grandparents. He naturally mistrusts Lord Orville and fears the weakness of the young girl's imagination. Everyone knows that as long as Evelina remains obedient to Villars' will, no union between her and Orville can occur. Once the girl's father, Sir John Belmont, repents for his many years of unkindness to his daughter and then bequeaths her thirty thousand pounds, however, the guardian cleric no longer remains the dominant influence. Lord Orville proceeds to put his own moral house in order and supplants his rivals; the reserve felt by Evelina because of the Reverend Villars' fears and anxieties gradually disintegrates, and the romance proceeds towards its inevitable conclusion.

The process may be inevitable, but it is sufficiently hampered by a series of struggles and conflicts, as is typical of the late eighteenth century novel of manners. Both her grandmother and Mrs. Mirvan provide Evelina with fairly easy access to fashionable society, but the socialites in that society involve the girl in a number of uncomfortable and burdensome situations. For example, Biddy and Polly Branghton and Madam Duval use Evelina's name in requesting the use of Lord Orville's coach. Evelina realizes the impropriety of the request and knows that Orville's benevolence would never permit him to refuse it. Furthermore, Tom Branghton, an admirer of Evelina, solicits business from Orville also by relying on Evelina's name; he does so after damaging the borrowed vehicle. Evelina's innocence forces her to bear the responsibility for her relatives' actions and schemes, although she opposes all that they attempt. Fortunately, the fierce determination with which she advances her innocence and honesty enables her to endure such problems until rescued, in this case, by Lord Orville and Mrs. Selwyn. Vulgarity (Madam Duval), ill breeding (the Branghtons), and impertinence (Sir Clement Willoughby) eventually fall before the steadfastness and the force of Evelina's emerging wisdom and strength. Burney here demonstrates the specific means by which an eighteenth century woman could surmount the perplexities of that era.

If Evelina Anville must defend her innocence and honesty against the social vultures of London and Bristol, Cecilia Beverley, the heroine of *Cecilia*, carries the added burden of retaining a fortune left to her by an eccentric uncle. She must withstand assaults upon her coffers from a variety of attackers. One of her guardians, Mr. Harrel, draws heavily upon Cecilia's funds to repay the moneylenders who underwrite his fashionable existence. At the other extreme, Mr. Briggs, the third legally appointed guardian, manages Cecilia's money during her minority. Although wealthy in his own right, Briggs evidences obvious eccentricity and uncouthness; he is a miser who wants the heroine to live with him to conserve money. In the middle stands another guardian, Compton Delvile, who has priorities other than money; however, he can hardly be recommended as an asset to the development of his ward. Simply, Delvile cares only to preserve the family name, and beneath his pride lie hard layers of meanness. Against such onslaughts upon her morality and her fortune, Cecilia must rebel; she is both angry and bewildered at what Burney terms as "acts so detrimental to her own interest."

Unlike Evelina, who has many opportunities to address and receive concerns from a surrogate parent, Cecilia has few people and even less guidance upon which to rely. *Cecilia* revealed to the world not only a trio of impotent guardians, but also a number of irritating male characters who devote considerable time to tormenting her. Obviously bent upon revealing the grotesqueness and instability of London life, Burney created a variety of grotesque and unstable supporting players: Harrel, Dr. Lyster, Mrs. Wyers, and Mrs. Hill are some examples. Clearly, Burney's characters in *Cecilia* were total strangers to the mainstream of the late-eighteenth century fictional world, even though they truly belonged to reality. While at times creating humorous scenes and incidents, these ugly characters nevertheless produced a disturbing effect upon the novelist's reading audience. Unfortunately, from a social or historical perspective, that audience was not yet ready for significant action to affect social change, which meant that much of the novel's force was lost amid the apathy of its audience.

The publication of *Camilla*, eighteen years after *Evelina* and fourteen following *Cecilia*, marked the reappearance of a young lady entering society and enduring shameful experiences. Like her immediate predecessor, Cecilia Beverley, Camilla Tyrold has money problems, only hers involve involuntary indebtedness. Also like Cecilia, the novel contains several grotesque minor characters, whose manners and actions play psychological havoc with Camilla's attempts to overcome her distress. Particularly vulgar are Mr. Dubster and the mercenary Mrs. Mittin, aided by the over-scholarly Dr. Orkborne and the foppish Sir Sedley Clarendel. A major problem, however, is that these characters are pulled from the earlier novels. On the surface, *Camilla* gives evidence that Burney has matured as a writer and as a commentator on the affairs of women, but that maturity did not broaden her literary experience. If anything, there are signs of regression, for Camilla definitely lacks Evelina's common sense and her instinct toward feminine resourcefulness.

Camilla further suffers from its length; Burney barely holds the plot together through countless episodes, intrigues, misunderstandings, all in front of a backdrop of drollery and absurdity. Stripped of its comic elements, the novel is no more than an overstrained romance. Burney's motive, however, was to draw the exact conditions that brought about Camilla's collection of debts and thus contributed to her highly anxious state of mind. Burney rises to her usual level of excellence in detailing the plight of a woman distracted and deprived by misfortune not of her own doing. For late-eighteenth century woman, especially, such misfortune carried with it an underlying sense of shame. Thus, Burney gave to English prose fiction a sense of psychological depth not always apparent in the works of her female counterparts or in those fictional efforts written by men but concerned with women.

Burney's last novel, *The Wanderer*, appeared in 1814 and became lost in the new sensibility of Jane Austen and Maria Edgeworth. The work, however, reveals Burney's determination that the nineteenth century should not forget its women. Her heroine—known variously as L. S. (or Ellis), Incognita, Miss

Ellis, and Juliet—determines that the cause of her suffering points directly
to the fact that she was born a woman, which automatically places her on
the lowest rung of the social order. The woman's lot contains little beyond
the usual taboos, disqualifications, discomforts, and inconveniences; and the
novelist, through the various predicaments of Juliet Granville, rarely allows
her readers to forget the degree to which her heroine must suffer because of
society's insensitivity and stupidity. *The Wanderer*, as in Burney's previous
novels, has a number of supporting characters; some of those, while they do
not always understand Juliet's plight, at least try to help her through her
difficulties. Others, such as Mrs. Ireton and Miss Arbe, represent the tyranny,
frivolity, and insensitivity of the times and thus merely compound Juliet's
problems.

The strength of *The Wanderer*, however, lies in its thematic relationship to
the three earlier novels. Although Burney tends to repeat herself, particularly
through her minor characters—and again the plot hardly deserves the length
of the narrative—her ability to depict the misgivings of those who are driven
by external circumstances to earn a livelihood through unaccustomed means
is powerful. In coming to grips with an obvious and serious problem of her
time she demonstrated how her major fictional characters and herself, as a
character from the real world, could indeed rely successfully upon the
resources endowed upon all individuals, female as well as male. If nothing
else, the novelist showed her society and the generations that followed not
only how well women could function in the real world, but also how much
they could contribute and take advantage of opportunities offered them. In
a sense, Burney's compositions belong to social history as much as to literature, and they serve as some of the earliest examples of a struggle that has
yet to be won.

Samuel J. Rogal

Other major works
PLAYS: *Edwy and Elgiva*, 1790; *Love and Fashion*, 1800.
NONFICTION: *Brief Reflections Relative to the French Emigrant Clergy*, 1793;
Memoirs of Dr. Charles Burney, 1832 (edited); *The Early Diary of Frances
Burney, 1768-1778*, 1889; *Diary and Letters, 1778-1840*, 1842-1846 (7 vol-
umes).

Bibliography
Bloom, Harold, ed. *Fanny Burney's "Evelina": Modern Critical Interpretations*. New York: Chelsea House, 1988. This group of essays, written
between 1967 and 1988, focuses on Burney's first novel. Included are
essays by Ronald Paulson, Susan Staves, Patricia Meyer Spacks, Judith
Lowder Newton, Mary Poovey, Jennifer A. Wagner, and Julia L. Epstein.

Bloom's introduction disparages the feminist tendency of recent Burney criticism, even though this volume includes primarily feminist approaches to Burney's work. This collection of focused essays provides an illuminating look at current critical opinion of *Evelina*.

Doody, Margaret Anne. *Frances Burney*. New Brunswick, N.J.: Rutgers University Press, 1988. Emphasizes Burney's life as an author as a source for her novels. This psychological approach can be useful, but can, at times, but conjectural. Doody spends less time on the details of Burney's life than most biographers, focusing instead on her writing, both on its own and in relation to Burney's life. Also devotes equal space to Burney's plays. Includes illustrations of the Burney family, a family tree, and a good index. No bibliography is provided, but the notes are a good source of other material relating to Burney.

Epstein, Julia L. *The Iron Pen: Frances Burney and the Politics of Women's Writing*. Madison: University of Wisconsin Press, 1989. Takes a feminist approach, focusing primarily on the violence, hostility, and danger in Burney's work. Finds these parts of her novels to be generally controlled, but occasionally bursting forth into rage. This study meshes moments of physical and emotional danger and pain from Burney's life with similar images in her novels. Epstein's interest lies in Burney's construction of a self-image that plays down danger and violence but that she is frequently unable to control. The bibliography and index are excellent and quite helpful.

Simons, Judy. *Fanny Burney*. Totowa, N.J.: Barnes & Noble Books, 1987. Contains a condensed look at Burney's life. The introductory biographical essay places Burney in a tradition of other women writers, such as Elizabeth Inchbald, Mary Wollstonecraft Godwin, and Eliza Haywood, and discusses these women's views on their roles in society. Includes a chapter on the heroines of Burney's novels; a chapter on each of her four best-known works, *Evelina, Cecelia, Camilla*, and *The Wanderer*; and one on her journals and plays. The bibliography is short but helpful, especially since it includes a section on works about women's history in the eighteenth century.

Straub, Kristina. *Divided Fictions: Fanny Burney and Feminine Strategy*. Lexington: University Press of Kentucky, 1987. Examines the "ambiguous social definition of the woman novelist at mid-century," specifically as it related to Burney. A feminist approach grounded in eighteenth century cultural history. Devotes three chapters to *Evelina*, one to *Cecelia*, and one to both *Camilla* and *The Wanderer*. Straub's introductory chapter, "Critical Methods and Historic Contexts," is excellent and useful, as well as the chapter "The Receptive Reader and Other Necessary Fictions," which makes intriguing points about Burney's reaction to the publicity of being a novelist and part of the literary circles of her day.

WILLIAM S. BURROUGHS

Born: St. Louis, Missouri; February 5, 1914

Principal long fiction

Junkie, 1953; *The Naked Lunch*, 1959 (republished as *Naked Lunch*, 1962); *The Soft Machine*, 1961; *The Ticket That Exploded*, 1962; *Dead Fingers Talk*, 1963; *Nova Express*, 1964; *The Wild Boys: A Book of the Dead*, 1971; *Cities of the Red Night*, 1981; *The Place of Dead Roads*, 1983; *The Burroughs File*, 1984; *Queer*, 1985; *The Western Lands*, 1987.

Other literary forms

Because of their experimental techniques, William Burroughs' works are especially difficult to classify within established literary forms. *Exterminator!* (1973), for example, although published as a "novel," is actually a collection of previously published poems, short stories, and essays. Other unclassifiable works are book-length experiments, often written in collaboration and in the "cut-up, fold-in" technique pioneered by Burroughs, which might be considered novels by some. Examples of such works are *Minutes to Go* (1960), written in collaboration with Sinclair Beiles, Gregory Corso, and Brion Gysin; *The Exterminator* (1960), written with Gysin; *Time* (1965), which contains drawings by Gysin; and *Oeuvre Croisee* (1976), written in collaboration with Gysin and reissued as *The Third Mind* in 1978. *White Subway* (1965), *Apomorphine* (1969), and *The Job: Interviews with William S. Burroughs* (1970), written in collaboration with Daniel Odier, are additional short-story and essay collections. *The Dead Star* (1969) is a journalistic essay that contains photocollage inserts; *APO-33 Bulletin: A Metabolic Regulator* (1966) is a pamphlet; and *Electronic Revolution 1970-71* (1971) is an essay that fantasizes bizarre political and business uses for the cut-up, fold-in technique. Burroughs has also published scores of essays, stories, and articles in numerous journals, periodicals, and short-lived magazines. One of Burroughs' most revealing publications, *The Yage Letters* (1963), collects his correspondence with Allen Ginsberg concerning Burroughs' 1952 expedition to South America in search of yage, a legendary hallucinogen. In these letters, Burroughs is Govinda, the master, to Ginsberg's Siddhartha, the disciple.

Achievements

Although his novel, *Naked Lunch*, was made notorious by American censorship attempts and consequently became a best-seller, Burroughs writes primarily for a cult audience. He is essentially a fantasist and satirist, is often misread, and in these respects has accurately been compared to Jonathan Swift. Both writers focus on the faults and evils of man and society, employ fantastic satire to ridicule these shortcomings, and hope through this vehicle to effect some positive change in the human condition. Burroughs' works are exceptionally vicious satires, however, "necessarily brutal, obscene and disgusting"—his own description of them—because they must mime the situations from which their recurring images and metaphors (of drug addiction, aberrant sexual practices, and senseless violence) are drawn.

Superficially, Burroughs' satiric attacks are aimed at mankind's "addictions" to pleasure or power in any of the many forms either craving might take. Men who, obeying the dictates of "the algebra of need," will stop at nothing to fulfill their desires have, in the terms of the moral allegory Burroughs creates, "lost their human citizenship" and become nonhuman parasites feeding on the life essences of others. They shamelessly lie, cheat, and manipulate to attain what Burroughs' associative imagery repeatedly equates with perversion, excrement, and death. Burroughs' satire, however, cuts deeper than this. It attacks not only man and his addictions, but also the structures of the cultures that enable these addictions to flourish and proliferate. It attacks the myths and linguistic formulas that imprison man, the stone walls of patriotism and religion. It demands that men first free themselves from these "word and image addictions" before they kick their more obvious habits and regain their humanity, and thus calls for nothing less than a revolution of consciousness.

The Grove Press edition of *Naked Lunch* became a national best-seller and was cleared of obscenity charges in Los Angeles in 1965 and in Massachusetts in 1966. Ginsberg and Norman Mailer, who asserted that Burroughs is "the only American novelist living today who may conceivably be possessed by genius," were among those who testified in the book's defense. While it does detail with exceptional brutality the ugly, revolting, and perverse, *Naked Lunch* is at bottom a strikingly moral but darkly comic work that employs irony and allegory, as well as more unconventional techniques, to satirize much that is false and defective in modern American life in particular and human nature in general. Especially effective as a subliminal argument against heroin abuse, the book's successful publication in America elevated its heretofore practically unknown author to membership in the literary elite.

Many reviewers, however, some seemingly oblivious to the irony of Burroughs' works, have not been responsive or sympathetic to his themes and techniques, and none of his novels since *Naked Lunch*, with the exception of *The Wild Boys: A Book of the Dead*, has received comparable critical acclaim. While *Naked Lunch* was lauded by Terry Southern, Mary McCarthy, Karl Shapiro, and Marshall McLuhan, as well as by Ginsberg and Mailer, the less successfully realized subsequent novels were considered by some critics, not totally inaccurately, as "language without content" and "the world's greatest put-on." Burroughs himself admits that "*Naked Lunch* demands silence from the reader. Otherwise he is taking his own pulse." He warns that his novels do not present their "content" in the manner the reader ordinarily anticipates. One of the triumphs of Burroughs' unique style is that he has created a low-content form, a narrative near vacuum, upon which the unwary reader is tempted to project his own psyche, personal myths, or forgotten dreams. While they do have their own message to convey, his works also encourage the reader to develop or invent his private fictions and to append them to the skeletal narrative structure provided by the author. The reader is thus invited to create the work as he reads it. In place of relying on the easily perceived, clearly coherent story the reader might have expected, Burroughs's best work keeps one reading through the hypnotic fascination of the author's flow of images and incantatory prose.

Biography

William Seward Burroughs was born on February 5, 1914, in St. Louis, Missouri, to Perry Mortimer Burroughs, son of the industrialist who invented the cylinder that made the modern adding machine possible, and Laura Lee, a direct descendant of Robert E. Lee, Civil War general and commander in chief of the Confederate army. Dominated by his mother's obsessive Victorian prudery and haunted by vivid nightmares and hallucinations, Burroughs led a restless childhood. He was educated in private schools in St. Louis and Los Alamos, New Mexico, where he developed seemingly disparate fascinations with literature and crime, and later studied ethnology and archaeology at Harvard University, where he encountered a set of wealthy homosexuals. He was graduated with an A.B. in 1936.

Subsequently, Burroughs traveled to Europe, briefly studied medicine at the University of Vienna, and returned to the United States and Harvard to resume his anthropological studies, which he soon abandoned because of his conviction that academic life is little more than a series of intrigues broken by teas. Although he attempted to use family connections to obtain a position with the Office of Strategic Services, Burroughs was rejected after he deliberately cut off the first joint of one finger in a Vincent van Gogh-like attempt to impress a friend. Moving to New York City, he worked as a bartender and in an advertising agency for a year and underwent psychoanalysis. Burroughs entered the army in 1942 as a glider pilot trainee, engineered his discharge for psychological reasons six months later, and then moved to Chicago, where he easily found work as an exterminator and a private detective, among other odd jobs.

In 1943, Burroughs returned to New York City and met Joan Vollmer, a student at Columbia University whom he married on January 17, 1945. She introduced Burroughs to Jack Kerouac, who in turn introduced him to Ginsberg. The Beat generation was born in Burroughs' 115th Street apartment after Burroughs acquainted Kerouac and Ginsberg with the writings of William Blake, Arthur Rimbaud, and others; the three friends soon emerged as leaders of the movement. Late in 1944, Herbert Huncke, a Times Square hustler involved in criminal activity to support his drug habit, introduced

Burroughs to the use of morphine and its derivatives. Burroughs was for most of the next thirteen years a heroin addict who frequently altered his place of residence to evade the police.

He moved to Waverly, Texas, where he tried farming, in 1946; had a son, William, Jr., in 1947; and voluntarily entered a drug rehabilitation center at Lexington, Kentucky, in 1948. Returning to Waverly and already back on drugs, Burroughs was hounded by the police until he moved to Algiers, Louisiana, later that same year. To avoid prosecution for illegal possession of drugs and firearms after a 1949 raid on his Algiers farm, Burroughs relocated to Mexico City in 1950, where he began writing *Junkie*. He continued his archaeological studies at Mexico City University, pursuing an interest in the Mayan codices. On September 7, 1951, Burroughs accidentally killed his wife while allegedly attempting to shoot a champagne glass off her head while playing "William Tell." Although Mexican authorities let the matter drop, Burroughs soon left Mexico for the jungles of Colombia.

He returned again to New York City in 1953, the year *Junkie* was published, lived for a while with Ginsberg, and then settled in Tangier, Morocco, where from 1955 to 1958 he was frequently visited by other Beat writers and worked on the manuscript that would develop into his quartet of science-fiction-like novels: *Naked Lunch*, *The Soft Machine*, *Nova Express*, and *The Ticket That Exploded*. In 1957, Burroughs again sought treatment for his heroin addiction. This time he placed himself in the care of John Yerby Dent, an English physician who treated drug addicts with apomorphine—a crystalline alkaloid derivative of morphine—a drug Burroughs praises and mythologizes in his writings. The following year, cured of his addiction, Burroughs moved to Paris, where *The Naked Lunch* was published in 1959.

In 1960, Gysin, who had helped Burroughs select the Paris edition of *The Naked Lunch* from a suitcase full of manuscript pages, introduced his experimental "cut-up" technique to Burroughs and collaborated with him on *The Exterminator* and *Minutes to Go*. Burroughs' literary reputation was firmly established with the American publication of *Naked Lunch* in 1962, and by the mid-1960's Burroughs had settled in London. He returned to St. Louis for a visit in 1965, covered the Democratic National Convention for *Esquire* in 1968, and moved again to New York to teach writing at City College of New York in 1974. In 1975, he embarked on a reading tour of the United States and conducted a writers' workshop in Denver, Colorado. After returning to London briefly, Burroughs settled in New York. In 1983, he was inducted into the American Academy and Institute of Arts and Letters.

Analysis

William Burroughs did not begin writing seriously until 1950, although he had unsuccessfully submitted a story entitled "Twilight's Last Gleaming" to *Esquire* in 1938. His first novelistic effort, *Queer*, which deals with homosexuality, also remains unpublished. Allen Ginsberg finally persuaded Ace Books to publish Burroughs' first novel, *Junkie*, which originally appeared with pseudonym William Lee, as half of an Ace double paperback. It was bound with Maurice Helbront's *Narcotic Agent*. While strictly conventional in style, *Junkie* is a luridly hyperbolic, quasi-autobiographical first-person account of the horrors of drug addiction. Of little literary merit in itself, this first novel is interesting in that it introduces not only the main character, Lee, but also several of the major motifs that appear in Burroughs' subsequent works: the central metaphor of drug addiction, the related image of man reduced to a subhuman (usually an insectlike creature) by his drug and other lusts, and the suggestion of concomitant and pervasive sexual aberration.

In *Naked Lunch* and its three less celebrated sequels, *The Soft Machine*, *Nova Express*, and *The Ticket That Exploded*, Burroughs weaves an intricate and horrible allegory of human greed, corruption, and debasement. Like Aldous Huxley's *Brave New World* (1932) and George Orwell's *Nineteen Eighty-Four* (1949), these four works seize on the evils or tendencies toward a certain type of evil—that the author sees as particularly malignant in the contemporary world—and project them into a dystopian future, where, magnified, they grow monstrous and take on an exaggerated and fantastic shape. While progressively clarifying and developing Burrough's thought, these novels share themes, metaphorical images, characters, and stylistic mannerisms. In them, Burroughs utilizes the "cut-up, fold-in" technique which has its closest analog in the cinematic technique of montage. He juxtaposes one scene with another without regard to plot, character, or, in the short view, theme to promote an association of the reader's negative emotional reaction to the content of certain scenes (sexual perversion, drug abuse, senseless violence) with the implied allegorical content of others (examples of "addictions" to drugs, money, sex, power). The theory is that if such juxtapositions recur often enough, the feeling of revulsion strategically created by the first set of images will form the reader's negative attitude toward the second set of examples.

In these novels, Burroughs develops a science-fiction-like, paranoid fantasy wherein, on a literal level, the Earth and its human inhabitants have been taken over by the Nova Mob, an assortment of extraterrestrial, non-three-dimensional entities who live parasitically on the reality of other organisms. Exploitation of the Earth has reached such proportions that the intergalactic Nova Police have been alerted. The Nova Police are attempting to thwart the Nova Mob without so alarming them that they will detonate the planet in an attempt to destroy the evidence (and thus escape prosecution in the biologic courts) while trying to make what escape they can. The most direct form of Nova control, control that enables the Nova Mob to carry on its viruslike metaphysical vampirism with impunity, is thought control of the human population through control of the mass communication media. Nova Mob concepts and perspectives attach themselves to and are replicated by the terrestrial host media much as a virus invades and reproduces through a host organism, a thought-control process analogous to the "cut-up, fold-in" technique itself. By the middle of *Nova Express*, the reader is caught up in a war of images in which the weapons are cameras and tape recorders. The Nova Police and the inhabitants of Earth have discovered how to combat the Nova Mob with their own techniques (of which these novels are examples) and are engaged in a guerrilla war with the Nova Criminals, who are desperately trying to cut and run. The ending of *The Ticket That Exploded* is optimistic for Earth but inconclusive, leaving the reader to wonder if the Earth will be rid of the Nova Mob or destroyed by it.

A vividly and relentlessly tasteless fantasy-satire that portrays man's innate greed and lack of compassion in general and contemporary American institutions and values in particular, *Naked Lunch* immerses the reader in the impressions and sensations of William Lee (Burroughs' pseudonym in *Junkie*). Lee is an agent of the Nova Police who has assumed the cover of a homosexual heroin addict because with such a cover he is most likely to encounter Nova Criminals, who are all addicts of one sort or another and thus prefer to operate through human addict collaborators. Nothing of importance seems to occur in the novel, and little of what does happen is explained. Only toward the conclusion does the reader even suspect that Lee is some sort of agent "clawing at a not-yet of Telepathic Bureaucracies, Time Monopolies, Control Drugs, Heavy Fluid Addicts." The "naked lunch" of the title is that reality seen by Lee, that "frozen moment when everyone sees what is on the end of every fork." The random scenes of mutilation and depravity, bleak homosexual encounters, and desperate scrambles for drug connections into which the book plunges yield its two key concepts: the idea of addiction, the central conceit that men become hooked on power, pleasure, illusions, and so on much as a junkie does on heroin, and that of "the algebra of need," which states simply that when an addict is faced with absolute need (as a junkie is) he will do anything to satisfy it.

The Nova Criminals are nonhuman personifications of various addictions. The Uranians, addicted to Heavy Metal Fluid, are types of drug addicts. Dr. Benway, Mr. Bradley Mr. Martin (a single character), and the insect people of Minraud—all control addicts—are types of the human addiction to power. The green boy-girls of Venus, addicted to Venusian sexual practices, are types of the human addiction to sensual pleasure. The Death Dwarf, addicted to concentrated words and images, is the analog of the human addiction to various cultural myths and beliefs; he is perhaps the most pathetic of these depraved creatures. Burroughs explains that "Junk yields a basic formula of 'evil' virus: the face of evil is always the face of total need. A dope fiend is a man in total need of dope. Beyond a certain frequency need knows absolutely no limit or control." As John Ciardi noted,

Only after the first shock does one realize that what Burroughs is writing about is not only the destruction of depraved men by their drug lust, but the destruction of all men by their consuming addictions, whether the addiction be drugs or over-righteous propriety or sixteen-year-old-girls.

Burroughs sees *The Soft Machine* as "a sequel to *Naked Lunch*, a mathematical extension of the Algebra of Need beyond the Junk virus." Here, the consuming addiction, displayed again in juxtaposition with scenes of drug abuse and sexual perversion, and through a number of shifting narrators, is the addiction to power over others. The central episode is the destruction by a time-traveling agent of the control apparatus of the ancient Mayan theocracy (Burroughs' primary archaeological interest), which exercises its control through the manipulation of myths; this is a clear analog of the present-day struggle between the Nova Police and the Nova Mob that breaks into the open in the subsequent two novels.

The time traveler uses the same technique to prepare himself for time travel as Burroughs does in writing his novels, a type of "cut-up, fold-in" montage: "I started my trip in the morgue with old newspapers, folding in today with yesterday and typing out composites." Since words tie men to time, the time traveler character is given apomorphine (used to cure Burroughs of his heroin addiction) to break this connection.

The "soft machine" is both the "wounded galaxy," the Milky Way seen as a biological organism diseased by the viruslike Nova Mob, and the human body, riddled with parasites and addictions and programmed with the "ticket," obsolete myths and dreams, written on the "soft typewriter" of culture and civilization. Burroughs contends that any addiction dehumanizes its victims. The Mayan priests, for example, tend to become half-men, half-crab creatures who eventually metamorphosize into giant centipedes and exude an erogenous green slime. Such hideous transformations also strike Lee, a heroin addict, and other homosexuals. Bradley the Buyer, who reappears as Mr. Bradley Mr. Martin, Mr. and Mrs. D., and the Ugly Spirit, has a farcical habit of turning into a bloblike creature who is addicted to and absorbs drug addicts.

Instances of metamorphosis are almost innumerable in *Nova Express* and *The Ticket That Exploded*. These novels most clearly reveal the quartet's plot and explore the Nova Mob's exploitation of media. Here addiction to language is investigated. As Stephen Koch argues, here

Burroughs's ideology . . . is based on an image of consciousness in bondage to the organism: better, of consciousness as an organism, gripped by the tropisms of need. Consciousness is addicted—it is here the drug metaphor enters—to what sustains it and gives it definition: in particular, it is addicted to the word, the structures of language that define meaning and thus reality itself.

Thus, while in *The Soft Machine* the time traveler is sent to Trak News Agency (whose motto is "We don't report the news—we write it") to learn how to defeat the Mayan theocracy by first learning "how this writing the news before it happens is done," in *The Ticket That Exploded* it is axiomatic that "you can run a government without police if your conditioning program is tight enough but you can't run a government without bullshit."

Contemporary existence is seen ultimately as a film that is rerun again and again, trapping the human soul like an insect imprisoned in amber, negating any possibility of choice or freedom. In these last two novels, Burroughs issues a call for revolt against man's imprisoning addiction to language. In *Nova Express*, he notes that "their garden of delights is a terminal sewer" and demands that everyone heed the last words of Hassan I Sabbah (cribbed out of context from Fyodor Dostoevski's Ivan Karamazov): "Nothing is True—Everything is Permitted." In *The Ticket That Exploded*, he rages, "Better than the 'real thing'?—There is no real thing—Maya—Maya—It's all show business."

Burroughs' other notably science-fiction-like novel, *The Wild Boys*, is also composed of scenes linked more by associated images than by any clearly linear narrative framework. Here, the author posits a bizarre alternative to the problematical apocalypse-in-progress depicted in his earlier quartet. In a world wrecked by famine and controlled by police, the wild boys, a homosexual tribe of hashish smokers, have withdrawn themselves from space and time through indifference and have developed into a counterculture complete with its own language, rituals, and economy. The existence of this counterculture, of course, poses a threat to those who create the false images upon which the larger, repressive, external society is based; but the wild boys cannot be tamed because their cold indifference to the mass culture entails a savagery that refuses to submit to control. Although Burroughs' thinking clearly becomes more political in *The Wild Boys* and in the book that followed it, *Exterminator!*, a collection of short stories and poems that revolve around the common theme of death through sinister forces, his primary concern for freedom from the controllers and manipulators—chemical, political, sexual, or cultural—has remained constant from the beginning of his literary career.

Continuing the utopian vision of *The Wild Boys*, but encompassing it into a larger, more anthropological context, Burroughs' next three works form a trilogy to expand his vision of society and its place in the natural order. The first book in the series, *Cities of the Red Night*, continues the twin themes of freedom from control and the power of mythmaking, but does so on a much larger scale. One of Burroughs' longest works, *Cities of the Red Night* is unique in that in it he sustains a rather conventional narrative voice, utilizing conventional popular genre, to achieve a re-creation of history through fantasy and myth.

The novel begins with three distinct plots, which seem at first to be only tenuously related. One plot concerns a retroactive utopia founded by eigh-

teenth century pirates, which Burroughs uses as a foundation for social criticism. A second plot, from which the title comes, depicts mythical "cities
of the red night," which existed in prehistoric time and function as a dysto-
pia through which the reader views present culture. A third plot involves a
present-day investigator who traces the mystery of a deadly virus known as
B-23 to its historical origins in the "cities of the red night." Each plot
employs conventions from one popular genre or another: The story of the
utopian pirates' colony reads very much like a boys' adventure story; the
story of the advanced prehistoric cities takes its structure from science fiction; and the story of the investigation of the virus lends itself to the conventions of the hard-boiled detective story.

In the second book of the trilogy, *The Place of Dead Roads*, Burroughs
continues the process of mythmaking. His protagonist is Kim Carsons, a late
nineteenth century gunslinger who utilizes a sort of "hole in time," a phenomenon introduced in *Cities of the Red Night*. Through this hole, Carsons
becomes a time-traveler, moving precariously across time and space, encountering different cultures and time periods in an effort to forge some sense of
the whole, some sense of control over his own destiny. He seeks fulfillment in
disparate, almost lonely, homosexual encounters, in drugs, and in the sense
of power he feels by manipulating others.

The story begins with a clipping from a Boulder newspaper which tells the
reader that William Seward Hall, who writes Western novels under the pen
name Kim Carsons, was shot in a gunfight in the year 1899. The story then
introduces the character Carsons and, after a disjointed series of adventures
and misadventures, returns the reader to that same date when Carsons loses
his life, as if to say that destiny will not be averted in the end. The similarity
of Carsons' true name to Burroughs' is striking here because, like Hall,
Burroughs tends to fictionalize himself as author, as though an author can
reach his true potential only through the life of his character—perhaps another way of understanding Burroughs' fascination with somehow circum-
venting destiny through manipulation.

In the third book of the trilogy, *The Western Lands*, the reader learns that
Carsons was not shot by his opponent, Mike Chase, but by a killer from the
Land of the Dead named Joe, described as a NO (Natural Outlaw), whose job
it is to break natural laws. The Western land itself is a mythical place, a
utopian vision of a place beyond our images of earth and heaven—a land
where natural law, religious law, and human law have no meaning. It is a
paradise, but a paradise difficult to reach.

The intent of Burroughs' trilogy is first to create a science-fiction myth
which explains all of human history; then to reveal the power of fantasy and
myth to offer alternative histories; and finally, by realizing these alternative
histories, to explore alternative anthropological patterns by which to organize
society. The three separate plots interrelate and merge at various points

throughout the trilogy, but eventually each is abandoned before completion—a technique that, Burroughs claims, allows the reader to create his or her own stories, to engage his or her own sense of mythmaking. The reader is encouraged to play a kind of "what if" game along with Burroughs: What if the Spanish had not defeated the new world into submission? What if the true foundations of liberty and individual freedom had taken hold in the Third World? What if all of our assumptions, whether religious, historical or psychological, are wrong? This process of mythmaking in Burroughs is not a means to an end, but rather the object of the struggle—the great creative process of defining and redefining ourselves, which is our ultimate defense against those who would manipulate us.

Donald Palumbo

Other major works

NONFICTION: *The Yage Letters*, 1963 (with Allen Ginsberg); *APO-33 Bulletin: A Metabolic Regulator*, 1966; *The Job: Interviews with William S. Burroughs*, 1970 (with Daniel Odier); *Electronic Revolution 1970-71*, 1971; *Letters to Allen Ginsberg: 1953-1957*, 1983; *The Adding Machine: Collected Essays*, 1985.

MISCELLANEOUS: *The Exterminator*, 1960 (with Brion Gysin); *Minutes to Go*, 1960 (with Sinclair Beiles, Gregory Corso, and Brion Gysin); *Time*, 1965; *White Subway*, 1965; *The Dead Star*, 1969; *Apomorphine*, 1969; *The Last Words of Dutch Schultz*, 1970; *Exterminator!*, 1973; *The Book of Breeething*, 1974; *Oeuvre Croisee*, 1976 (with Brion Gysin, also known as *The Third Man*, 1978); *Blade Runner: A Movie*, 1979; *Interzone*, 1989.

Bibliography

Cook, Bruce. *The Beat Generation*. New York: Charles Scribner's Sons, 1971. Cook's survey of the Beat generation emphasizes their social impact rather than their literary importance. He devotes a chapter to Burroughs' work, notably *Naked Lunch*, describing it as primarily self-revelation. He includes a biography of Burroughs and an interview that takes place in London.

Goodman, Michael Barry. *Contemporary Literary Censorship: The Case History of Burroughs' "Naked Lunch."* Metuchen, N.J.: Scarecrow Press, 1981. Michael Goodman offers a narrative history of the writing, publication, critical reception, and subsequent censorship of *Naked Lunch* in the United States, a work he describes as one of the last works to receive such treatment in such a universal way. Provides much previously unpublished Burroughs material.

Lee, Robert A. "William Burroughs and the Sexuality of Power." *Twentieth Century Studies* 2 (November, 1969): 74-88. Lee analyzes the structure and imagery in several of Burroughs' novels, including *Junkie, Naked Lunch, The Soft Machine, The Ticket That Exploded*, and *Nova Express*. Lee argues that Burroughs' theme of the sexuality of power forms a basis for his mythology. He praises Burroughs as a moralist and serious social critic.

Mottram, Eric. *William Burroughs: The Algebra of Need*. London: Marion Boyars, 1977. Mottram sees Burroughs' works as a radical critique of Western power structures and the myths that support them, classifying the writer as an anarchic individualist. Mottram's comparisons of Burroughs with other radical thinkers is insightful and unique.

Skerl, Jennie. *William S. Burroughs*. Boston: Twayne, 1985. Skerl attempts to provide an overview of contemporary thought on Burroughs' art and life for the general reader and literary historian. She also argues, in a rather concise analysis section, that Burroughs' art comes from a worldview that revolves around the "hipsterism" ideas of Norman Mailer.

Tanner, Tony. *City of Words, American Fiction 1950-1970*. New York: Harper & Row, 1971. Tanner's influential survey of the contemporary American novel includes a lengthy chapter on Burroughs. His discussion centers on *Junkie, The Yage Letters, Naked Lunch, The Ticket That Exploded*, and *Nova Express*. Tanner sees Burroughs as giving major emphasis to a central theme in contemporary American literature—namely, the conflict between the dream of freedom and the dread of control.